QA 76.9 D343 M8S 2007 c.3

D0787039

Multimedia Data Mining and Knowledge Discovery

Valery A. Petrushin and Latifur Khan (Eds)

Multimedia Data Mining and Knowledge Discovery

 Springer

Valery A. Petrushin, MS, PhD
Accenture Technology Labs
Accenture Ltd
161 N. Clark St.
Chicago, IL 60601, USA

Latifur Khan, BS, MS, PhD
EC 31
2601 N. Floyd Rd.
Richardson, TX 75080-1407, USA

British Library Cataloguing in Publication Data
A catalogue record for this book is available from the British Library

Library of Congress Control Number: 2006924373

ISBN-10: 1-84628-436-8   Printed on acid-free paper
ISBN-13: 978-1-84628-436-6

© Springer-Verlag London Limited 2007

Apart from any fair dealing for the purposes of research or private study, or criticism or review, as permitted under the Copyright, Designs and Patents Act 1988, this publication may only be reproduced, stored or transmitted, in any form or by any means, with the prior permission in writing of the publishers, or in the case of reprographic reproduction in accordance with the terms of licences issued by the Copyright Licensing Agency. Enquiries concerning reproduction outside those terms should be sent to the publishers.

The use of registered names, trademarks, etc. in this publication does not imply, even in the absence of a specific statement, that such names are exempt from the relevant laws and regulations and therefore free for general use.

The publisher makes no representation, express or implied, with regard to the accuracy of the information contained in this book and cannot accept any legal responsibility or liability for any errors or omissions that may be made.

Whilst we have made considerable efforts to contact all holders of copyright material contained in this book, we may have failed to locate some of them. Should holders wish to contact the Publisher, we will be happy to come to some arrangement with them.

9 8 7 6 5 4 3 2 1

Springer Science+Business Media
springer.com

Contents

Part III. Multimedia Data Indexing and Retrieval

Part IV. Multimedia Data Modeling and Evaluation

11. Cognitively Motivated Novelty Detection in Video
Data Streams **209**
James M. Kang, Muhammad Aurangzeb Ahmad, Ankur Teredesai,
and Roger Gaborski

Part V.   Applications and Case Studies

Preface

In recent years we witnessed the real revolution in media recordings and storage. Because of advances in electronics, computing engineering, storage manufacturing, and networking, the market is flooded with cheap computers, mass memory, camera phones, and electronic devices for digitizing and producing visual and audio information. Ten years ago only a professional studio could create an audio CD or a DVD, but today everybody can do it, using a home computer. Under threat of the digital expansion, the entertainment, show, and education industries started changing their business models. Tomorrow nobody will be surprised to find that a personal computer has a terabyte hard disk and four gigabyte RAM. This phenomenon has made corporate, public, and personal multimedia repositories widespread and fast growing. Currently, there are some commercial tools for managing and searching multimedia audio and image collections, but the need for tools to extract hidden useful knowledge embedded within multimedia collections is becoming pressing and central for many decision-making applications. The tools needed today are tools for discovering relationships between objects or segments within images, classifying images on the basis of their content, extracting patterns in sound, categorizing speech and music, recognizing and tracking objects in video streams, etc.

Today data mining efforts are going beyond the databases to focusing on data collected in fields like art, design, hypermedia, and digital media production, medical multimedia data analysis and computational modeling of creativity, including evolutionary computation. These fields use variety of data sources and structures, interrelated by the nature of the phenomenon. As a result there is an increasing interest in new techniques and tools that can detect and discover patterns that can lead to a new knowledge in the problem domain, where the data have been collected. There is also an increasing interest in the analysis of multimedia data generated by different distributed applications, like collaborative virtual environments, virtual communities, and multiagent systems. The data collected from such environments include record of the actions in them, audio and video recordings of meetings and collaborative sessions, variety of documents that are part of the business process, asynchronous threaded discussions, transcripts from synchronous communications, and other data records. These heterogeneous multimedia data records require sophisticated preprocessing, synchronization, and other transformation procedures before even getting to the analysis stage.

On the other hand, researchers in multimedia information systems, in the search for techniques for improving the indexing and retrieval of multimedia information are looking into new methods for discovering indexing information. Variety of techniques from machine learning, statistics, databases, knowledge acquisition, data visualization, image analysis, high performance computing, and knowledge-based systems, have been used mainly as a research handcraft activity. The development of ontologies and vocabularies for multimedia data fosters the adoption and merging with the Semantic Web technology. The emerging international standards for multimedia content description (MPEG-7) and multimedia resources delivery and usage (MPEG-21) promise to expedite the progress in the field giving a uniform data representation and the open multimedia framework.

This book is based mostly on extended and updated papers that have been presented at the two Multimedia Data Mining Workshops—MDM KDD 2003 and MDM KDD 2004 that held in conjunction with the ACM SIGKDD Conference in Washington, DC, August 2003 and the ACM SIGKDD Conference in Seattle, WA, August 2004, respectively. The book also includes several invited surveys and papers. The book chapters give a snapshot of research and applied activities in the multimedia data mining.

The editors are grateful to the founders and active supporters of the Multimedia Data Mining Workshop Series Simeon Simoff, Osmar Zaiane, and Chabane Djeraba. We also thank the reviewers of book papers for their well-done job and organizers of ACM SIGKDD Conferences for their support.

We thank the Springer-Verlag's employees Wayne Wheeler, who initiated the book project, Catherine Brett, and Frank Ganz for their help in coordinating the publication and editorial assistance.

Chicago, IL   *Valery A. Petrushin*
Dallas, TX   *Latifur Khan*
January 2006

List of Contributors

Nitin Agarwal
Department of Computer Science and
Engineering
Arizona State University
Tempe, AZ 82857
USA
nitin.agarwal@asu.edu

Muhammad A. Ahmad
Rochester Institute
  of Technology
102 Lomb Memorial Drive
Rochester, NY 14623-5608
USA
maa2454@cs.rit.edu

Sergio A. Alvarez
Computer Science Department
Boston College
Chestnut Hill, MA 02467
USA
alvarez@cs.bc.edu

Marie-Aude Aufaure
Computer Science Department
SUPELEC
Plateau du Moulon
3, rue Joliot Curie
F-91 192 Gif-sur-Yvette Cedex
France
Marie-Aude.Aufaure@supelec.fr

Robert P. Biuk-Aghai
Faculty of Science and Technology
University of Macau
Avenida Padre Tomás Pereira, S.J.
Taipa
Macau S.A.R.
China
robertb@umac.mo

Fatma Bouali
LIFL UMR CNRS 8022
France
Fatma.Bouali@univ-lille2.fr

Marinette Bouet
LIMOS – UMR 6158 CNRS
Blaise Pascal University of
Clermont-Ferrand II
Campus des Cézeaux 24, avenue des
Landais
F-63173 Aubiere Cedex
France
Marinette.Bouet@cust.univ-
bpclermont.fr

Stefan Brecheisen
Institute for Computer Science
University of Munich
Oettingenstr. 67, 80538 Munich,
Germany
brecheis@dbs.ifi.lmu.de

K. Selcuk Candan
Department of Computer Science and
Engineering
Arizona State University, Tempe, AZ
82857
USA
candan@asu.edu

Min Chen
Distributed Multimedia Information
System Laboratory
School of Computing & Information
Sciences
Florida International University
Miami, FL 33199
USA
mchen005@cs.fiu.edu

Shu-Ching Chen
Distributed Multimedia Information
System Laboratory
School of Computing & Information
Sciences
Florida International University
Miami, FL 33199
USA
chens@cs.fiu.edu

Charles Daniel
Pennsylvania State University –
Harrisburg
Middletown, PA 17057
USA

Marten J. den Uyl
VicarVision b.v.
Singel 160, 1015 AH
Amsterdam
The Netherlands
denuyl@vicarvision.nl

Qin Ding
Pennsylvania State University –
Harrisburg
Middletown, PA 17057

USA
qding@psu.edu

Chabane Djeraba
LIFL – UMR USTL CNRS 8022
Universite de Lille1, Bât. M3
59655 Villeneuve d'Ascq Cedex
France
djeraba@lifl.fr

Jianping Fan
Dept of Computer Science
University of North Carolina – Charlotte
Charlotte, NC 28223
USA
jfan@uncc.edu

Farshad Fotouhi
Department of Computer Science
Wayne State University
Detroit, MI 48202
USA
fotouhi@wayne.edu

Roger Gaborski
Rochester Institute of Technology
102 Lomb Memorial Drive
Rochester, NY 14623-5608
USA
rsg@cs.rit.edu

Yuli Gao
Dept of Computer Science
University of North Carolina – Charlotte
Charlotte, NC 28223
USA
ygao@uncc.edu

Anatole V. Gershman
Accenture Technology Labs
Accenture Ltd.
161 N. Clark St.
Chicago, IL 60601
USA
anatole.v.gershman@accenture.com

William Grosky
Department of Computer and
Information Science
University of Michigan – Dearborn
Dearborn, MI 48128
USA
wgrosky@umich.edu

Dimitrios Gunopulos
Computer Science & Engineering
Department
University of California, Riverside
Riverside, CA 92521
USA
dg@cs.ucr.edu

Amaury Hazan
Music Technology Group
Pompeu Fabra University
Ocata 1, 08003 Barcelona
Spain
ahazan@iua.upf.es

Koichi Ideno
Graduate School of Science and
Technology
Kobe University,
Nada, Kobe, 657-8501
Japan
ideno@ai.cs.scitec.kobe-u.ac.jp

Menno Israël
ParaBot Services b.v.
Singel 160, 1015 AH Amsterdam
The Netherlands
m.israel@parabots.nl

James M. Kang
Department of Computer Science and
Engineering
University of Minnesota
Minneapolis, MN 55455
USA
jkang@cs.umn.edu

Takeshi Kawato
Computer Science Department
Worcester Polytechnic Institute
Worcester, MA 01609
USA
takeshi@wpi.edu

Eamonn Keogh
Computer Science & Engineering
Department
University of California, Riverside
Riverside, CA 92521
USA
eamonn@cs.ucr.edu

Latifur Khan
Department of Computer Science
University of Texas at Dallas
75083 Richardson, Texas
USA
lkhan@utdallas.edu

Jong Wook Kim
Department of Computer Science and
Engineering
Arizona State University
Tempe, AZ 82857
USA
jong@asu.edu

Hans-Peter Kriegel
Institute for Computer Science
University of Munich
Oettingenstr. 67,
80538 Munich
Germany
kriegel@dbs.ifi.lmu.de

Peer Kröger
Institute for Computer Science
University of Munich
Oettingenstr. 67, 80538 Munich,
Germany
kroegerp@dbs.ifi.lmu.de

Chuanjun Li
Department of Computer Science
The University of Texas at Dallas
Richardson, Texas 75083
USA
chuanjun@utdallas.edu

Xin Li
Department of Computer Science
Oklahoma City University
Oklahoma City
OK 73106
USA
xinli@okcu.edu

Jessica Lin
Department of Information and Software
Engineering,
George Mason University
Fairfax, VA 22030
USA
jessica@ise.gmu.edu

Huan Liu
Department of Computer Science and
Engineering
Arizona State University
Tempe, AZ 82857
USA
huan.liu@asu.edu

Hangzai Luo
Dept of Computer Science
University of North Carolina – Charlotte
Charlotte, NC 28223
USA
hluo@uncc.edu

Libor Machala
Department of Experimental Physics
Palacky University
Svobody 26
779 00 Olomouc
Czech Republic
machala@sloup.upol.cz

Esteban Maestre
Music Technology Group
Pompeu Fabra University
Ocata 1, 08003 Barcelona, Spain
emaestre@iua.upf.es

Sylvain Mongy
LIFL – UMR USTL CNRS 8022
Universite de Lille1, Bât. M3
59655 Villeneuve d'Ascq Cedex
France
mongy@lifl.fr

Clark F. Olson
Computing and Software Systems
University of Washington, Bothell
18115 Campus Way NE
Campus Box 358534
Bothell, WA 98011-8246
USA
cfolson@u.washington.edu

Nilesh Patel
Department of Computer and
Information Science
University of Michigan – Dearborn
Dearborn, MI 48128
USA
patelnv@umich.edu

Valery A. Petrushin
Accenture Technology Labs
Accenture Ltd.
161 N. Clark St.
Chicago, IL 60601
USA
valery.a.petrushin@accenture.com

Martin Pfeifle
Institute for Computer Science
University of Munich
Oettingenstr. 67
80538 Munich
Germany
pfeifle@dbs.ifi.lmu.de

Balakrishnan Prabhakaran
Department of Computer Science
University of Texas at Dallas,
75083 Richardson, Texas
USA
praba@utdallas.edu

Pavel Praks
Department of Mathematics and
Descriptive Geometry
Department of Applied Mathematics
VSB – Technical University of
Ostrava
17 Listopadu 15, 708 33 Ostrava,
Czech Republic
pavel.praks@vsb.cz

Daniela Stan Raicu
Intelligent Multimedia Processing
Laboratory
School of Computer Science,
Telecommunications, and
Information Systems (CTI)
DePaul University
Chicago, Illinois
USA
draicu@cs.depaul.edu

Rafael Ramirez
Music Technology Group
Pompeu Fabra University
Ocata 1
08003 Barcelona
Spain
rafael@iua.upf.es

Carolina Ruiz
Computer Science Department
Worcester Polytechnic Institute
Worcester, MA 01609
USA
ruiz@cs.wpi.edu

Matthias Schubert
Institute for Computer Science

University of Munich
Oettingenstr. 67,
80538 Munich
Germany
schubert@dbs.ifi.lmu.de

Xavier Serra
Music Technology Group
Pompeu Fabra University
Ocata 1, 08003 Barcelona
Spain
xserra@iua.upf.es

Ishwar K. Sethi
Department of Computer Science and
Engineering
Oakland University
Rochester, MI 48309
USA
isethi@oakland.edu

Kimiaki Shirahama
Graduate School of Science and
Technology
Kobe University
Nada, Kobe 657-8501
Japan
kimi@ai.cs.scitec.kobe-u.ac.jp

Mei-Ling Shyu
Department of Electrical and Computer
Engineering
University of Miami
Coral Gables, FL 33124
USA
shyu@miami.edu

Simeon J. Simoff
Faculty of Information Technology
University of Technology,
Sydney
P.O. Box 123
Broadway NSW 2007
Australia
simeon@it.uts.edu.au

Vaclav Snasel
Department of Computer Science
VSB - Technical University of
Ostrava
17 Listopadu 15, 708 33 Ostrava
Czech Republic
vaclav.snasel@vsb.cz

Reshma Suvarna
Department of Computer Science and
Engineering
Arizona State University
Tempe, AZ 82857, USA
reshma.suvarna@asu.edu

Ankur Teredesai
Rochester Institute of Technology
102 Lomb Memorial Drive
Rochester, NY 14623-5608, USA
amt@cs.rit.edu

Kuniaki Uehara
Graduate School of Science and
Technology
Kobe University
Nada, Kobe 657-8501
Japan
uehara@ai.cs.scitec.kobe-u.ac.jp

Egon L. van den Broek
Center for Telematics and Information
Technology (CTIT) and
Institute for Behavioral Research (IBR)
University Twente
P.O. box 217, 7500 AE Enschede,
The Netherlands
e.l.vandenbroek@utwente.nl

Peter van der Putten
LIACS
University of Leiden
P.O. Box 9512
2300 RA Leiden
The Netherlands
putten@liacs.nl

Michail Vlachos
IBM T. J. Watson Research
Center
Hawthorne, NY 10532
USA
vlachos@ibm.com

Lei Wang
Department of Computer Science
University of Texas at Dallas,
75083 Richardson, Texas
USA
leiwang@utdallas.edu

Gang Wei
Accenture Technology Labs
Accenture Ltd.
161 N. Clark St.
Chicago, IL 60601
USA
gang.wei@accenture.com

Chengcui Zhang
Department of Computer & Information
Science
University of Alabama at Birmingham
Birmingham, AL 35294-1170
USA
zhang@cis.uab.edu

Ruofei Zhang
Computer Science Department
Watson School
SUNY Binghamton
Binghamton, NY, 13902-6000
USA
rzhang@cs.binghamton.edu

Zhongfei (Mark) Zhang
Computer Science Department
Watson School,
SUNY Binghamton
Binghamton, NY 13902-6000
USA
zhongfei@cs.binghamton.edu

Arthur Zimek
Institute for Computer Science
University of Munich

Oettingenstr. 67, 80538 Munich
Germany
zimek@dbs.ifi.lmu.de

Part I

Introduction

1. Introduction into Multimedia Data Mining and Knowledge Discovery

Valery A. Petrushin

Summary. This chapter briefly describes the purpose and scope of multimedia data mining and knowledge discovery. It identifies industries that are major users or potential users of this technology, outlines the current state of the art and directions to go, and overviews the chapters collected in this book.

1.1 What Is Multimedia Data Mining?

The traditional definition of data mining is that it "is the process of automating information discovery" [1], which improves decision making and gives a company advantages on the market. Another definition is that it "is the exploration and analysis, by automatic or semiautomatic means, of large quantities of data in order to discover meaningful patterns and rules" [2]. It is also assumed that the discovered patterns and rules are meaningful for business. Indeed, data mining is an applied discipline, which grew out of the statistical pattern recognition, machine learning, and artificial intelligence and coupled with business decision making to optimize and enhance it. Initially, data mining techniques have been applied to structured data from databases. The term "knowledge discovery in databases," which is currently obsolete, reflects this period. However, knowledge is interpretation of data meanings and knowledge discovery goes beyond finding simple patterns and correlations in data to identifying concepts and finding relationships. Knowledge-based modeling creates a consistent logical picture of the world. In recent years the term "predictive analytics" has been widely adopted in the business world [3].

On one hand growing computer power made data mining techniques affordable by small companies, but on the other, emergence of cheap massive memory and digital recording electronic devices, such as scanners, microphones, cameras, and camcorders, allowed digitizing all kind of corporate, governmental, and private documents. Many companies consider these electronic documents as valuable assets and other sources of data for data mining. For example, e-mail messages from customers and recordings of telephonic conversations between customers and operators could serve as valuable sources of knowledge about both customers' needs and the quality of service. Unprecedented growing information on the World Wide Web made it an indispensable source of data for business intelligence. However, processing new sources of semistructured (Web pages, XML documents) and unstructured (text, images, audio, and video recordings) information required new data mining methods and tools.

Recently, two branches of data mining, text data mining and Web data mining, have emerged [4, 5]. They have their own research agenda, communities of researchers, and supporting companies that develop technologies and tools. Unfortunately, today multimedia data mining is still in an embryonic state. It could be explained by immature technology, high cost of storing and processing media data, and the absence of successful stories that show the benefits and the high rate of return on investments into multimedia data mining.

For understanding multimedia data mining in depth, let us consider its purpose and scope. First, let us describe what kinds of data belong to the multimedia data. According to MPEG-7 Standard [6], there are four types of multimedia data: audio data, which includes sounds, speech, and music; image data (black-and-white and color images); video data, which include time-aligned sequences of images; and electronic or digital ink, which is sequences of time aligned 2D or 3D coordinates of a stylus, a light pen, data glove sensors, or a similar device. All this data is generated by specific kind of *sensors*.

Second, let us take a closer look at the term *multimedia data mining*. The word *multimedia* assumes that several data sources of different modalities are processing at the same time. It could be or could not be the case. A data mining project can deal with only one modality of data, for example, customers' audio recordings or surveillance video. It would be better to use the term *media data mining* instead, but the word *media* usually connotes by mass media such as radio and television, which could be or could not be the data source for the data mining project. The term *sensor data mining* extends the scope too far covering such sensors as radars, speedometers, accelerometers, echo locators, thermometers, etc. This book is devoted to discussing the first three media types mentioned above and we shall use the term *multimedia data mining* and the acronym MDM keeping in mind the above discussion.

The MDM's primary purpose is to process media data alone or in a combination with other data for finding patterns useful for business. For example, analyze customer traffic in a retail store using video recordings to find optimal location for a new product display. Besides explicit data mining projects, the MDM techniques can be used as a part of complex operational or manufacturing processes. For example, using images for finding defective products or indexing a video database of company's meetings.

The MDM is a part of multimedia technology, which covers the following areas [7, 8]:

- Media compression and storage.
- Delivering streaming media over networks with required quality of service.
- Media restoration, transformation, and editing.
- Media indexing, summarization, search, and retrieval.
- Creating interactive multimedia systems for learning/training and creative art production.
- Creating multimodal user interfaces.

The major challenge that the MDM shares with the multimedia retrieval is the so-called semantic gap, which is the difficulty of deriving a high-level concept such as "mountain landscape" or "abnormal customer behavior" from low-level features such as color histogram, homogeneous texture, contour-based shape, motion trajectory, etc., that are extracted from media data. A solution of this problem requires creating an ontology that covers different aspects of the concept and a hierarchy of recognizers that deduce the probability of the concept from the probabilities of its components and relationships among them.

1.2 Who Does Need Multimedia Data Mining?

To answer the above question, we consider the application areas of MDM and related industries and companies who are (potential) users of technology. The following are the five major application areas of MDM:

Customer Insight—Customer insight includes collecting and summarizing information about customers' opinions about products or services, customers' complains, customers' preferences, and the level of customers' satisfaction of products or services. All product manufacturers and service providers are interested in customer insight. Many companies have help desks or call centers that accept telephone calls from the customers. These calls are recorded and stored. If an operator is not available a customer may leave an audio message. Some organizations, such as banks, insurance companies, and communication companies, have offices where customers meet company's representatives. The conversations between customers and sales representatives can be recorded and stored. The audio data serve as an input for data mining to pursue the following goals:

- Topic detection—The speech from recordings is separated into turns, i.e., speech segments spoken by only one speaker. Then the turns are transcribed into text and keywords are extracted. The keywords are used for detecting topics and estimating how much time was spent on each topic. This information aggregated by day, week, and month gives the overview of hot topics and allows the management to plan the future training taking into account the emerging hot topics.
- Resource assignment—Call centers have a high turn around rate and only small percentage of experienced operators, who are a valuable resource. In case when the call center collects messages, the problem is how to assign an operator who will call back. To solve the problem, the system transcribes the speech and detects the topic. Then it estimates the emotional state of the caller. If the caller is agitated, angry, or sad, it gives the message a higher priority to be responded by an experienced operator. Based on the topic, emotional state of the caller, and operators' availability the system assigns a proper operator to call back [9].
- Evaluation of quality of service—At a call center with thousands of calls per day, the evaluation of quality of service is a laborious task. It is done by people who listen to selected recordings and subjectively estimate the quality of service. Speech recognition in combination with emotion recognition can be used for automating the evaluation and making it more objective. Without going into

deep understanding of the conversation meaning, the system assigns a score to the conversation based on the emotional states of speakers and keywords. The average score over conversations serves as a measure of quality of service for each operator.

Currently, there are several small companies that provide tools and solutions for customer management for call centers. Some tools include procedures that are based on MDM techniques. The extension of this market is expected in the future.

Surveillance—Surveillance consists of collecting, analyzing, and summarizing audio, video, or audiovisual information about a particular area, such as battlefields, forests, agricultural areas, highways, parking lots, buildings, workshops, malls, retail stores, offices, homes, etc. [10]. Surveillance often is associated with intelligence, security, and law enforcement, and the major uses of this technology are military, police, and private companies that provide security services. The U.S. Government is supporting long-term research and development activities in this field by conducting the Video Analysis and Content Extraction (VACE) program, which is oriented on development technology for military and intelligence purposes. The National Institute of Standards and Technology is conducting the annual evaluation of content-based retrieval in video (TRECVID) since 2000 [11]. However, many civilian companies use security services for protecting their assets and monitoring their employees, customers, and manufacturing processes. They can get valuable insight from mining their surveillance data. There are several goals of surveillance data mining:

- Object or event detection/recognition—The goal is to find an object in an image or in a sequence of images or in soundtrack that belongs to a certain class of objects or represents a particular instance. For example, detect a military vehicle in a satellite photo, detect a face in sequence of frames taken by a camera that is watching an office, recognize the person whose face is detected, or recognize whether sound represents music or speech. Another variant of the goal is to identify the state or attributes of the object. For example, classify an X-ray image of lungs as normal or abnormal or identify the gender of a speaker. Finally, the goal can be rather complex for detecting or identifying an event, which is a sequence of objects and relationships among objects. For example, detect a goal event in a soccer game; detect violence on the street, or detect a traffic accident. This goal is often a part of the high-level goals that are described below.

- Summarization—The goal is to aggregate data by summarizing activities in space and/or time. It covers summarizing activities of a particular object (for example, drawing a trajectory of a vehicle or indicating periods of time when a speaker was talking) or creating a "big picture" of activities that happened during some period of time. For example, assuming that a bank has a surveillance system that includes multiple cameras that watch tellers and ATM machines indoors and outdoors, the goal is to summarize the activities that happened in the bank during 24 h. To meet the goal, unsupervised learning and visualization techniques are used. Summarization also serves as a prerequisite step to achieve another goal—*find frequent and rare events.*

- Monitoring—The goal is to detect events and generate response in real time. The major challenges are real-time processing and generating minimum false alarms. Examples are monitoring areas with restricted access, monitoring a public place for threat detection, or monitoring elderly or disabled people at home.

Today we witness a real boom in video processing and video mining research and development [12–14]. However, only a few companies provide tools that have elements of data mining.

Media Production and Broadcasting—Proliferation of radio stations and TV channels makes broadcasting companies to search for more efficient approaches for creating programs and monitoring their content. The MDM techniques are used to achieve the following goals:

- Indexing archives and creating new programs—A TV program maker uses raw footage called *rushes* and clips from commercial libraries called *stockshot libraries* to create a new program. A typical "shoot-to-show" ratio for a TV program is in the range from 20 to 40. It means that 20–40 hours of rushes go into one hour of a TV show. Many broadcasting companies have thousands of hours of rushes, which are poorly indexed and contain redundant, static, and low-value episodes. Using rushes for TV programs is inefficient. However managers believe that rushes could be valuable if the MDM technology could help program makers to extract some "generic" episodes with high potential for reuse.
- Program monitoring and plagiarism detection—A company that pays for broadcasting its commercials is interested to know how many times the commercial has been really aired. Some companies are also interested how many times their logo has been viewed on TV during a sporting event. The broadcasting companies or independent third-party companies can provide such service. The other goals are detecting plagiarism in and unlicensed broadcasting of music or video clips. This requires using MDM techniques for audio/video clip recognition [15] and robust object recognition [16].

Intelligent Content Service—According to Forrester Research, Inc, (Cambridge, MA) the Intelligent Content Service (ICS) is "a semantically smart content-centric set of software services that enhance the relationship between information workers and computing systems by making sense of content, recognizing context, and understanding the end user's requests for information" [17]. Currently, in spite of many Web service providers' efforts to extend their search services beyond basic keyword search to ICS, it is not available for multimedia data yet. This area will be the major battlefield among the Web search and service providers in next 5 years. The MDM techniques can help to achieve the following goals:

- Indexing Web media and using advanced media search—It includes creating indexes of images and audio and video clips posted on the Web using audio and visual features; creating ontologies for concepts and events; implementing advance search techniques, such as search images or video clips by example or by sketch and search music by humming; using Semantic Web techniques to infer the context and improve search [18]; and using context and user feedback to better understand the user's intent.
- Advanced Web-based services—Taking into account exponential growth of information on the Web such services promise to be an indispensable part of

everybody's everyday life. The services include summarization of events according to the user's personal preferences, for example, summarizing a game of the user's favorite football or basketball team; generating a preview of a music album or a movie; or finding relevant video clip for a news article [19].

Knowledge Management—Many companies consider their archives of documents as a valuable asset. They spend a lot of money to maintain and provide access to their archives to employees. Besides text documents, these archives can contain drawings of designs, photos and other images, audio and video recording of meetings, multimedia data for training, etc. The MDM approaches can provide the ICS for supporting knowledge management of companies.

1.3 What Shall We See in the Future?

As to the future development in the multimedia data mining field, I believe that we shall see the essential progress during the next 5 years. The major driven force behind it is creating techniques for advanced Web search to provide intelligent content services to companies for supporting their knowledge management and business intelligence. It will require creating general and industry-specific ontologies, develop recognizers for entities of these ontologies, merging probabilistic and logical inferences, and usage of metadata and reasoning represented in different vocabularies and languages, such as MPEG-7 [6], MPEG-21 [20, 21], Dublin Core [22], RDF [23], SKOS [24], TGM [25], OWL [26], etc.

Another force, which is driven by funding from mostly governmental agencies, is video surveillance and mass media analysis for improving intelligence, military, and law enforcement decision making.

Mining audio and video recordings for customer insight and using MDM for improving broadcasting companies' production will also be growing and elaborating in the future.

From the viewpoint of types of media, most advances in video processing are exected in research and development for surveillance and broadcasting applications, audio processing will get benefits from research for customer insight and creating advanced search engines, and image processing will benefit from developing advanced search engines As to electronic ink, I believe this type of multimedia data will be accumulated and used in data mining in the future, for example, for estimating the skills level of a user of an interactive tool or summarizing the contribution to a project of each participant of a collaborative tool.

1.4 What Can You Find in This Book?

As any collection of creative material the chapters of the book are different in style, topics, mathematical rigidity, level of generality, and readiness for deployment. But altogether they build a mosaic of ongoing research in the fast changing dynamic field of research that is the multimedia data mining.

The book consists of five parts: The first part, which includes two chapters, gives an introduction into multimedia data mining. Chapter 1, which you are reading now, overviews the multimedia data mining as an industry. Chapter 2 presents an overview of MDM techniques. It describes a typical architecture of MDM systems and covers approaches to supervised and unsupervised concept mining and event discovery.

The second part includes five chapters. It is devoted to multimedia data exploration and visualization. Chapter 3 deals with exploring images. It presents a clustering method based on unsupervised neural nets and self-organizing maps, which is called the dynamic growing self-organizing tree algorithm (DGSOT). The chapter shows that the suggested algorithm outperforms the traditional hierarchical agglomerative clustering algorithm.

Chapter 4 presents a multiresolution clustering of time series. It uses the Haar wavelet transform for representing time series at different resolutions and applies k-means clustering sequentially on each level starting from the coarsest representation. The algorithm stops when two sequential membership assignments are equal or when it reaches the finest representation. The advantages of the algorithm are that it works faster and produces better clustering. The algorithm has been applied to clustering images, using color and texture features.

Chapter 5 describes a method for unsupervised classification of events in multicamera indoors surveillance video. The self-organizing map approach has been applied to event data for clustering and visualization. The chapter presents a tool for browsing clustering results, which allows exploring units of the self-organizing maps at different levels of hierarchy, clusters of units, and distances between units in 3D space for searching for rare events.

Chapter 6 presents the density-based data analysis and similarity search. It introduces a visualization technique called the reachability plot, which allows visually exploring a data set in multiple representations and comparing multiple similarity models. The chapter also presents a new method for automatically extracting cluster hierarchies from a given reachability plot and describes a system prototype, which serves for both the visual data analysis and a new way of object retrieval called navigational similarity search.

Chapter 7 presents an approach to the exploration of variable length multiattribute motion data captured by data glove sensors and 3-D human motion cameras. It suggests using the singular value decomposition technique to regularize multiattribute motion data of different lengths and classify them applying support vector machine classifiers. Classification motion data using support vector machine classifiers is compared with classification by related similarity measures in terms of accuracy and CPU time.

The third part is devoted to multimedia data indexing and retrieval. It consists of three chapters. Chapter 8 focuses on developing an image retrieval methodology, which includes a new indexing method based on fuzzy logic, a hierarchical indexing structure, and the corresponding hierarchical elimination-based A^* retrieval algorithm with logarithmic search complexity in the average case. It also deals with user relevance feedbacks to tailor the semantic retrieval to each user's individualized query preferences.

Chapter 9 presents a methodology that uses both clustering and characterization rules to reduce the search space and produce a summarized view of an annotated image database. These data mining techniques are performed separately on visual descriptors and textual information such as annotations, keywords, etc. A visual ontology is derived from the textual part and enriched with representative images associated to each concept of the ontology. The ontology-based navigation is used as a user-friendly tool for retrieving relevant images.

Chapter 10 describes a methodology and a tool for end user that allows creating classifiers for images. The process consists of two stages: First, small image fragments called patches are classified. Second, frequency vectors of these patch classifications are fed into a second-level classier for global scene classification (e.g., city, portrait, or countryside). The first-stage classifiers can be seen as a set of highly specialized feature detectors that define a domain-specific visual alphabet. The end user builds the second-level classifiers interactively by simply indicating positive examples of a scene. The scene classifier approach has been successfully applied to several problem domains, such as content-based video retrieval in television archives, automated sewer inspection, and pornography filtering.

The fourth part is a collection of eight chapters that describe approaches to multimedia data modeling and evaluation. Chapter 11 presents an approach to automatic novelty detection in video stream and compares it experimentally to human performance. The evaluation of human versus machine-based novelty detection is quantified by metrics based on location of novel events, number of novel events, etc.

Chapter 12 presents an effective approach for event detection using both audio and visual features with its application in the automatic extraction of goal events in soccer videos. The extracted goal events can be used for high-level indexing and selective browsing of soccer videos. The approach uses the nearest neighbor classifier with generalization scheme. The proposed approach has been tested using soccer videos of different styles that have been produced by different broadcasters.

Chapter 13 describes an approach for mining and automatically discovering mappings in hierarchical media data, metadata, and ontologies, using the structural information inherent in hierarchical data. It uses structure-based mining of relationships, which provides high degrees of precision. The approach works even when the mappings are imperfect, fuzzy, and many-to-many.

Chapter 14 proposes a new approach to high-level concept recognition in images using the salient objects as the semantic building blocks. The novel approach uses support vector machine techniques to achieve automatic detection of the salient objects, which serve as a basic visual vocabulary. Then a high-level concept is modeling using the Gaussian mixture model of weighted dominant components, i.e., salient objects. The chapter proves the efficiency of the modeling approach, using the results of broad experiments obtained on images of nature.

Chapter 15 is devoted to a fundamental problem—image segmentation. It introduces a new MPEG-7 friendly system that integrates a user's feedback with image segmentation and region recognition, supporting the user in the extraction of image region semantics in highly dynamic environments. The results obtained for aerial photos are provided and discussed.

Chapter 16 describes techniques for query by example in an image database, when the exemplar image can have different position and scale in the target image and/or be captured by different sensor. The approach matches images against the exemplar by comparing the local entropies in the images at corresponding positions. It employs a search strategy that combines sampling in the space of exemplar positions, the Fast Fourier Transform for efficiently evaluating object translations, and iterative optimization for pose refinement. The techniques are applied to matching exemplars with real images such as aerial and ground reconnaissance photos. Strategies for scaling this approach to multimedia databases are also described.

Chapter 17 presents a neural experts architecture that enables faster neural networks training for datasets that can be decomposed into loosely interacting sets of attributes. It describes the expressiveness of this architecture in terms of functional composition. The experimental results show that the proposed neural experts architecture can achieve classification performance that is statistically identical to that of a fully connected feedforward neural networks, while significantly improving training efficiency.

Chapter 18 describes a methodology that allows building models of expressive music performance. The methodology consists of three stages. First, acoustic features are extracted from recordings of both expressive and neutral musical performances. Then, using data mining techniques a set of transformation rules is derived from performance data. Finally, the rules are applied to description of inexpressive melody to synthesize an expressive monophonic melody in MIDI or audio format. The chapter describes, explores, and compares different data mining techniques for creating expressive transformation models.

Finally, the fifth part unites seven chapters that describe case studies and applications. Chapter 19 presents a new approach for supporting design and redesign of virtual collaborative workspaces, based on combining integrated data mining techniques for refining the lower level models with a reverse engineering cycle to create upper-level models. The methodology is based on the combination of a new model of vertical information integration related to virtual collaboration that is called the information pyramid of virtual collaboration.

Chapter 20 presents a time-constrained sequential pattern mining method for extracting patterns associated with semantic events in produced videos. The video is separated into shots and 13 streams of metadata are extracted for each shot. The metadata not only cover such shot's attributes as duration, low-level color, texture, shape and motion features, and sound volume, but also advanced attributes such as the presence of weapons in the shot and sound type, i.e., silence, speech, or music. All metadata are represented as quantized values forming finite alphabets for each stream. Data mining techniques are applied to stream of metadata to derive patterns that represent semantic events.

Chapter 21 describes an approach for people localization and tracking in an office environment using a sensor network that consists of video cameras, infrared tag readers, a fingerprint reader, and a pan-tilt-zoom camera. The approach is based on a Bayesian framework that uses noisy, but redundant data from multiple sensor streams and incorporates it with the contextual and domain knowledge. The experimental results are presented and discussed.

Chapter 22 presents an approach that allows estimating a potential attractiveness of a banner image based on its attributes. A banner image is an advertisement that is designed to attract Web users to view and eventually to buy the advertised product or service. The approach uses a Bayesian classifier to predict the level of the click-thru rates based on the features extracted from the banner image GIF file, such as image dimensions, color features, number of frames in an animated file, and frames' dynamic and chromatic features. The experimental results are discussed.

Chapter 23 presents an approach that allows deriving users' profiles from their performance data when they are working with a video search engine. The approach suggests a two-level model. The goal of the first level is modeling and clustering user's behavior on a single video sequence (an intravideo behavior). The goal of the second level is modeling and clustering a user's behavior on a set of video sequences (an intervideo behavior). The two-phase clustering algorithm is presented and experimental results are discussed.

Chapter 24 presents a method for an automatic identification of a person by iris recognition. The method uses arrays of pixels extracted from a raster image of a human iris and searches for similar patterns using the latent semantic indexing approach. The comparison process is expedited by replacing the time consuming singular value decomposition algorithm with the partial symmetric eigenproblem. The results of experiments using a real biometric data collection are discussed.

Chapter 25 deals with data mining of medical images. It presents the research results obtained for texture extraction, classification, segmentation, and retrieval of normal soft tissues in computer tomography images of the chest and abdomen. The chapter describes various data mining techniques, which allow identifying different tissues in images, segmenting and indexing images, and exploring different similarity measures for image retrieval. Experimental results for tissue segmentation, classification and retrieval are presented.

References

1. Groth R. *Data Mining. A Hands-On Approach for Business Professionals*. Prentice Hall, Upper Saddle River, NJ, 1998.
2. Berry MJA, Linoff G. *Data Mining Techniques for Marketing, Sales, and Customer Support*. Wiley Computer Publishing, New York, 1997.
3. Agosta L. The future of data mining—Predictive analytics. IT View Report, Forrester Research October 17, 2003. Available at: http://www.forrester.com/Research/LegacyIT/0,7208,32896,00.html.
4. Berry MW (Ed.). *Survey of Text Mining: Clustering, Classification, and Retrieval*. Springer-Verlag, New York, 2004, 244 p.
5. Zhong N, Liu J, Yao Y (Eds.). *Web Intelligence*. Springer, New York, 2005; 440 p.
6. Manjunath BS, Salembier Ph, Sikora T (Eds.). *Introduction to MPEG-7. Multimedia Content Description Interface*. Wiley, New York, 2002, 371 p.
7. Maybury MT. *Intelligent Multimedia Information Retrieval*. AAAI Press/MIT Press, Cambridge, MA, 1997, 478 p.

8. Furht B (Ed.). *Handbook of Multimedia Computing*. CRC Press, Boca Raton, FL, 1999, 971 p.
9. Petrushin V. Creating emotion recognition agents for speech signal. In Dauntenhahn K, Bond AH, Canamero L and Edmonds B. (Eds.), *Socially Intelligent Agents. Creating Relationships with Computers and Robots*. Kluwer, Boston, 2002, pp. 77–84.
10. Remagnino P, Jones GA, Paragios N, Regazzoni CS. *Video-based Surveillance Systems. Computer Vision and Distributed Processing*. Kluwer, Boston, 2002, 279 p.
11. TRECVID Workshop website. http://www-nlpir.nist.gov/projects/trecvid/.
12. Furht B, Marques O. (Eds.). *Handbook of Video Databases. Design and Applications*. CRC Press, Boca Raton, FL, 2004, 1211 p.
13. Rosenfeld A, Doermann D, DeMenthon D. *Video Mining*. Kluwer, Boston, 2003, 340 p.
14. Zaiane OR, Simoff SJ, Djeraba Ch. *Mining Multimedia and Complex Data. Lecture Notes in Artificial Intelligence*, Vol. 2797. Springer, New York, 2003; 280 p.
15. Kulesh V, Petrushin VA, Sethi IK. Video clip recognition using joint audio-visual processing model. In *Proceedings of 16th International Conference on Pattern Recognition* (ICPR'02), 2002, Vol. 1, pp. 1051–1054.
16. Helmer S, Lowe DG. Object recognition with many local features. In *Workshop on Generative Model Based Vision*, Washington, DC, 2004.
17. Brown M, Ramos L. Searching For A Better Search, IT View Tech Choices. Forrester Research, August 29, 2005. Available at: http://www.forrester.com/Research/Document/0,7211,37615,00.html
18. Stamou G, Kollias S. *Multimedia Content and the Semantic Web*. Wiley, New York, 2005, 392 p.
19. Kulesh V, Petrushin VA, Sethi IK. PERSEUS: Personalized multimedia news portal. In Proceedings of IASTED Intl Conf. on Artificial Intelligence and Applications, September 4–7, 2001, Marbella, Spain, pp. 307–312.
20. Kosch H. *Distributed Multimedia Database Technologies Supported by MPEG-7 and MPEG-21*. CRC Press, Boca Raton, FL, 2004, 258 p.
21. Bormans J, Hill K. MPEG-21 Multimedia framework. Overview. Available at: http://www.chiariglione.org/mpeg/standards/mpeg-21/mpeg-21.htm.
22. The Dublin Core Metadata Initiative website. http://dublincore.org/ .
23. Resource Description Framework (RDF). http://www.w3.org/RDF/.
24. Simple Knowledge Organisation System (SKOS): http://www.w3.org/2004/02/skos/.
25. Thesaurus for Graphic Materials (TGM): http://www.loc.gov/rr/print/tgm1/.
26. OWL. Web Ontology Language Overview. http://www.w3.org/TR/owl-features/.

2. Multimedia Data Mining: An Overview

Nilesh Patel and Ishwar Sethi

Summary. Data mining has been traditionally applied to well-structured data. With the explosion of multimedia data methods—videos, audios, images, and Web pages, many researchers have felt the need for data mining methods to deal with unstructured data in recent years. This chapter provides an overview of data mining efforts aimed at multimedia data. We identify examples of pattern discovery models that have been addressed by different researchers and provide an overview of such methods.

2.1 Introduction

Data mining refers to the process of finding interesting patterns in data that are not ordinarily accessible by rudimentary queries and associated results with the objective of using discovered patterns to improve decision making. Traditionally, data mining has been applied to well-structured data, the kind of data that resides in large relational databases. Such data have well-defined, nonambiguous fields that lead easily to mining. In recent years, however, multimedia data—pictures, graphics, animations, audio, videos, and other multimodal sensory streams—have grown at a phenomenal rate and are almost ubiquitous. As a result, not only the methods and tools to organize, manage, and search such data have gained widespread attention but the methods and tools to mine such data have become extremely important too because such tools can facilitate decision making in many situations. For example, the mining of movement patterns of customers from the video routinely collected at shopping malls can be used to improve the layout of merchandize in stores or the layout of shops in the mall.

The mining of multimedia data is more involved than that of traditional business data because multimedia data are *unstructured* by nature. There are no well-defined fields of data with precise and nonambiguous meaning, and the data must be processed to arrive at fields that can provide content information about it. Such processing often leads to nonunique results with several possible interpretations. In fact, multimedia data are often subject to varied interpretations even by human beings. For example, it is not uncommon to have different interpretation of an image by different experts, for example radiologists. Another difficulty in mining of multimedia data are its heterogeneous nature. The data are often the result of outputs from various kinds of sensor modalities with each modality needing its own way of processing. Yet another distinguishing aspect of multimedia data is its sheer volume. All these characteristics of multimedia data make mining it challenging and interesting.

The goal of this chapter is to survey the existing multimedia data mining methods and their applications. The organization of the chapter is as follows. In Section 2.2, we describe the basic data mining architecture for multimedia data and discuss aspects of data mining that are specific to multimedia data. Section 2.3 provides an overview of representative features used in multimedia data mining. It also discusses the issues of feature fusion. Section 2.4 describes multimedia data mining efforts for concept mining through supervised techniques. Methods for concept mining through clustering are discussed in Section 2.5. Section 2.6 discusses concept mining through the exploitation of contextual information. Event and feature discovery research is addressed in Section 2.7. Finally, a summary of chapter is provided in Section 2.8.

2.2 Multimedia Data Mining Architecture

The typical data mining process consists of several stages and the overall process is inherently interactive and iterative. The main stages of the data mining process are (1) domain understanding; (2) data selection; (3) cleaning and preprocessing; (4) discovering patterns; (5) interpretation; and (6) reporting and using discovered knowledge [1]. The domain understanding stage requires learning how the results of data-mining will be used so as to gather all relevant prior knowledge before mining. Blind application of data-mining techniques without the requisite domain knowledge often leads to the discovery of irrelevant or meaningless patterns. For example, while mining sports video for a particular sport, for example, cricket, it is important to have a good knowledge and understanding of the game to detect interesting strokes used by batsmen.

The data selection stage requires the user to target a database or select a subset of fields or data records to be used for data mining. A proper domain understanding at this stage helps in the identification of useful data. This is the most time consuming stage of the entire data-mining process for business applications; data are never clean and in the form suitable for data mining. For multimedia data mining, this stage is generally not an issue because the data are not in relational form and there are no subsets of fields to choose from.

The next stage in a typical data-mining process is the preprocessing step that involves integrating data from different sources and making choices about representing or coding certain data fields that serve as inputs to the pattern discovery stage. Such representation choices are needed because certain fields may contain data at levels of details not considered suitable for the pattern discovery stage. The preprocessing stage is of considerable importance in multimedia data mining, given the unstructured nature of multimedia data.

The pattern-discovery stage is the heart of the entire data mining process. It is the stage where the hidden patterns and trends in the data are actually uncovered. There are several approaches to the pattern discovery stage. These include association, classification, clustering, regression, time-series analysis, and visualization. Each of these approaches can be implemented through one of several competing methodologies, such as statistical data analysis, machine learning, neural networks, and pattern recognition. It is because of the use of methodologies from several disciplines that data mining is often viewed as a multidisciplinary field.

The interpretation stage of the data mining process is used to evaluate the quality of discovery and its value to determine whether previous stages should be revisited or not. Proper domain understanding is crucial at this stage to put a value on discovered patterns. The final stage of the data mining process consists of reporting and putting to use the discovered knowledge to generate new actions or products and services or marketing strategies as the case may be. An example of reporting for multimedia data mining is the scout system from IBM [2] in which the mined results are used by coaches to design new moves.

The architecture, shown in Figure 2.1, captures the above stages of data mining in the context of multimedia data. The broken arrows on the left in Figure 2.1 indicate that the process is iterative. The arrows emanating from the domain knowledge block on the right indicate domain knowledge guides in certain stages of the mining process.

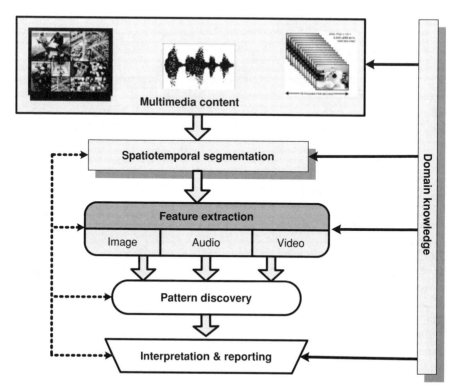

Fig. 2.1. Multimedia data mining architecture.

The spatiotemporal segmentation step in the architecture of Figure 2.1 is necessitated by the unstructured nature of multimedia data. This step breaks multimedia data into parts that can be characterized in terms of certain attributes or features. Thus, in conjunction with the feature extraction step, this step serves the function similar to that of the preprocessing stage in a typical data mining process. In image data mining, the spatiotemporal step simply involves image segmentation. Both region- and edge-based image segmentation methods have been used at this stage in different applications. Although many researchers tend to treat image segmentation for data mining identical to image segmentation needed for computer vision systems, there is an important difference between the requirements for the two segmentations. The image segmentation for a computer vision system should be such that it can operate without any manual intervention and it should be quantitatively accurate so as to allow the vision system to interact with its environment. On the other hand, image segmentation for most data mining applications has no requirement of interacting with its environment. Thus, it can incorporate manual intervention and can be approximate so as to yield features that can reasonably capture the image content. In many image mining applications, therefore, the segmentation step often involves simple blob extraction or image partitioning into fixed size rectangular blocks. With video data, the spatiotemporal step involves breaking the video into coherent collections of frames that can be processed for feature extraction as a single unit. This is typically done via a shot detection algorithm wherein the successive video frames are compared to determine discontinuity along the time axis. A number of shot detection algorithms have been developed in the last 15 years, mostly as a way to organize video data indexing and retrieval [3–8].

Many video mining applications deal with raw or unedited video data, for example, in surveillance and traffic monitoring, as opposed to edited video data typical of entertainment and broadcast video. In such situations, no shot detection type of operation is needed and the unedited video is directly processed to locate events of interests. With audio data, the spatiotemporal step is essentially a temporal step wherein the audio data are segmented either at the phoneme or word level or the data are broken into windows of fixed size.

The pattern discovery step in the multimedia data mining architecture of Figure 2.1 is not much different from mining of traditional and scientific data. Depending on the goal of the discovery stage, the methods for association, classification, clustering, regression, time-series analysis, and visualization are used at this stage. While traditional methods such as decision tree classifier, k-nearest neighbor classifier, k-means clustering, self-organizing feature map (SOFM) continue to be used for pattern discovery in multimedia data, support vector machines (SVMs) have been used widely in recent data mining applications [9, 10]. The SVM is primarily a classifier method that supports both regression and classification tasks and can handle multiple continuous and categorical variables. The SVM finds a solution by mapping the original data to a high-dimensional space where a hyperplane to separate two classes of data can be found. The solution hyperplane is obtained by maximizing the margin of separation between two classes of data in the mapped space. In the standard SVM formulation, the optimal hyperplane is found by solving a quadratic optimization problem. Since

SVM optimization problem grows dramatically with increasing number of training examples, several variations toward using SVMs have been suggested. One such variation is known as *chunking* in which the SVM is trained iteratively with chunks of training cases selected through some scheme. One popular scheme for selecting new training cases is based on *active learning* [11] in which the new training examples are selected through a query function. Such methods have been shown to reduce the overall training time and training set size without sacrificing predictive accuracy.

Examples of pattern discovery models addressed widely in the multimedia data mining community are mining concepts or automatic annotation of multimedia data and discovering events and features. Most multimedia data mining efforts to date have been devoted to the concept mining problem. The reason for such a multitude of efforts lies in the *semantic gap* that users of content-based multimedia information retrieval experience while searching for information through queries such as "find images containing multistory buildings" or "find me a picture of Tajmahal."[1] Dealing with such queries requires providing a retrieval system external knowledge either through manual annotation or through automatic discovering of concepts with or without external supervision. Although manual annotation can be more accurate, it is not practical with ever-increasing multimedia data. Thus, the preferred approach for bridging the semantic gap is to automatically mine concepts or key word associations.

2.3 Representative Features for Mining

Color, edges, shape, and texture are the common image attributes that are used to extract features for mining. Feature extraction based on these attributes may be performed at the global or local level. For example, color histogram of an image may be obtained at a global level or several localized histograms may be used as features to characterize the spatial distribution of color in an image. Similarly, the shape of a segmented region may be represented as a feature vector of Fourier descriptors to capture global shape property of the segmented region or a shape could be described in terms of salient points or segments to provide localized descriptions. There are obvious trade-offs between global and local descriptors. Global descriptors are generally easy to compute, provide a compact representation, and are less prone to segmentation errors. However, such descriptors may fail to uncover subtle patterns or changes in shape because global descriptors tend to integrate the underlying information. Local descriptors, on the other hand, tend to generate more elaborate representation and can yield useful results even when part of the underlying attribute, for example, the shape of a region is occluded, is missing. In the case of video, additional attributes resulting from object and camera motion are used.

In the case of audio, both the temporal and the spectral domain features have been employed. Examples of some of the features used include short-time energy, pause rate, zero-crossing rate, normalized harmonicity, fundamental frequency,

---

[1] Tajmahal is a famous 15th-century monument in Agra, Uttar Pradesh, India.

frequency spectrum, bandwidth, spectral centroid, spectral roll-off frequency, and band energy ratio. Many researchers have found the cepstral-based features, mel-frequency cepstral coefficients (MFCC), and linear predictive coefficients (LPC), very useful, especially in mining tasks involving speech recognition. While many researchers in this field place considerable emphasis on later processing, Scheirer and Slaney [12] conclude that the topology of the feature space is rather simple, and thus, there is very little difference between the performances of different classifiers. In many cases, the selection of features is actually more critical to the classification performance. In [13], a total of 143 classification features for the problem of general audio data classification are examined to show that cepstral-based features such as the MFCC and LPC provide better classification accuracy than temporal and spectral features.

The MPEG-7 standard provides a good representative set of features for multimedia data. The features are referred as *descriptors* in MPEG-7. The MPEG-7 Visual description tools describe visual data such as images and videos while the Audio description tools account for audio data. A brief description of audiovisual features in the MPEG-7 standard is given here; more details can be found in [14]. The MPEG-7 visual description defines the following main features for color attributes: Color Layout Descriptor, Color Structure Descriptor, Dominant Color Descriptor, and Scalable Color Descriptor. The Color Layout Descriptor is a compact and resolution invariant descriptor that is defined in YCbCr color space to capture the spatial distribution of color over major image regions. The Color Structure Descriptor captures both color content and information about its spatial arrangement using a structuring element that is moved over the image. The Dominant Color Descriptor characterizes an image or an arbitrarily shaped region by a small number of representative colors. The Scalable Color Descriptor is a color histogram in the HSV Color Space encoded by Haar transform to yield a scalable representation. While the above features are defined with respect to an image or its part, the feature Group of Frames-Group of Pictures Color (GoFGoPColor) describes the color histogram aggregated over multiple frames of a video.

The texture descriptors in MPEG-7 are the Edge Histogram Descriptor, Homogenous Texture Descriptor, and Texture Browsing Descriptor. The Edge Histogram Descriptor captures the spatial distribution of edges by dividing the image in 16 nonoverlapping regions. Four directions of edges (0, 45, 90, 135) are detected in addition to nondirectional ones leading to an 80-dimensional vector. The Homogeneous Texture Descriptor captures texture information in a 30-dimensional vector that denotes the energy of 30 spatial-frequency channels computed using Gabor filters. The channels are defined by partitioning the frequency space in angular direction at 30 and by octave division in the radial direction. The Texture Browsing Descriptor is a very compact descriptor that characterizes texture in terms of regularity, coarseness, and directionality.

MPEG-7 provides for two main shape descriptors; others are based on these and additional semantic information. The Region Shape Descriptor describes the shape of a region using Angular Radial Transform (ART). The description is provided in terms of 40 coefficients and is suitable for complex objects consisting of multiple disconnected regions and for simple objects with or without holes. The Contour Shape Descriptor describes the shape of an object based on its outline. The descriptor uses the curvature scale space representation of the contour.

The motion descriptors in MPEG-7 are defined to cover a broad range of applications. The Motion Activity Descriptor captures the intuitive notion of intensity or pace of action in a video clip. The descriptor provides information for intensity, direction, and spatial and temporal distribution of activity in a video segment. The spatial distribution of activity indicates whether the activity is spatially limited or not. Similarly, the temporal distribution of activity indicates how the level of activity varies over the entire segment. The Camera Motion Descriptor specifies the camera motion types and their quantitative characterization over the entire video segment. The Motion Trajectory Descriptor describes motion trajectory of a moving object based on spatiotemporal localization of trajectory points. The description provided is at a fairly high level as each moving object is indicated by one representative point at any time instant. The Parametric Motion Descriptor describes motion, global and object motion, in a video segment by describing the evolution of arbitrarily shaped regions over time using a two-dimensional geometric transform.

The MPEG-7 Audio standard defines two sets of audio descriptors. The first set is of low-level features, which are meant for a wide range of applications. The descriptors in this set include Silence, Power, Spectrum, and Harmonicity. The Silence Descriptor simply indicates that there is no significant sound in the audio segment. The Power Descriptor measures temporally smoothed instantaneous signal power. The Spectrum Descriptor captures properties such as the audio spectrum envelope, spectrum centroid, spectrum spread, spectrum flatness, and fundamental frequency. The second set of audio descriptors is of high-level features, which are meant for specific applications. The features in this set include Audio Signature, Timbre, and Melody. The Signature Descriptor is designed to generate a unique identifier for identifying audio content. The Timbre Descriptor captures perceptual features of instrument sound. The Melody Descriptor captures monophonic melodic information and is useful for matching of melodies. In addition, the high-level descriptors in MPEG-7 Audio include descriptors for automatic speech recognition, sound classification, and indexing.

A number of studies have been reported in recent literature concerning the performance of MPEG-7 descriptors for a variety of applications. For example, the MPEG-7 shape features have been used to recognize human body posture [15], the defect types in defect images [16], and Zhang and Lu [17] report a comparative study of MPEG-7 shape descriptors and conclude that while both the contour-based curvature scale-space descriptor (CSSD) and the region-based Zernike-moments descriptors perform well for image retrieval, the Fourier descriptors outperform CSSD. In another study, Eidenberger [18] has shown that most MPEG-7 descriptors are highly redundant and sensitive to color shades. Overall, the studies demonstrate that MPEG-7 descriptors are outperformed in several applications by other features. This is not surprising because these descriptors were established to optimize the browsing and retrieval applications of multimedia.

2.3.1 Feature Fusion

An important issue with features extracted from multimedia data is how the features should be integrated for mining and other applications. Most multimedia analysis is usually performed separately on each modality, and the results are brought together at a later stage to arrive at final decision about the input data. This approach is called *late fusion* or *decision-level fusion*. Although this is a simpler approach, we lose valuable information about the multimedia events or objects present in the data because, by processing separately, we discard the inherent associations between different modalities. A series of psychological experiments has shown the importance of synergistic integration of multiple modalities in the human perception system. A typical example of such experiments is the well-known McGurk effect [19]. The other approach for combining features is to represent features from all modalities together as components of a high-dimensional vector for further processing. This approach is known as *early fusion*. The data mining through this approach is known as *cross-modal analysis* because such an approach allows the discovery of semantic associations between different modalities [20].

2.4 Supervised Concept Mining

The concept mining in multimedia is also referred to as automatic annotation or annotation mining. There appears to be three main pattern discovery approaches that have been used for automatic annotation in multimedia data mining. These approaches primarily differ in terms of how external knowledge is provided to mine concepts. In the first approach, an annotator who assigns single or multiple concepts or key words to each multimedia document or its parts provides the external knowledge. This can be viewed as a supervised learning approach. The second approach for automatic annotation is through unsupervised learning or clustering. In this approach, multimedia documents are clustered first and then the resulting clusters are assigned key words by an annotator. Through cluster profiling, rules are next extracted for annotating future documents. The third approach does not rely on manual annotator at all; instead, it tries to mine concepts by looking at the contextual information, for example, the text surrounding an image or the closed caption text of a video. The supervised approach is discussed here; the other two approaches are discussed in the following sections.

Within the supervised framework of automatic annotation, three data mining methods have been used. These are annotation by classification; annotation by association; and annotation by statistical modeling.

2.4.1 Annotation by Classification

Annotation by classification has attracted the most attention, especially for annotating images. The methods for image classification for assigning key words generally differ from traditional object recognition methods in that these methods tend to perform recognition and classification with little or no segmentation chiefly relying on low-level image features to perform the task. An early example of this is the work of Yu and Wolf [21], who used one-dimensional Hidden-Markov Model (HMM) for classifying images and videos as indoor–outdoor scenes. Some other examples of image classification methods for assigning key words include the works by Vailaya et al. [22], Sethi et al. [23], and Blume and Ballard [24]. Vailaya et al. use a Bayesian framework for classification of outdoor images wherein the images are first divided into the categories of *city* and *landscape* images with landscape images being further subdivided into *sunset, forests*, and *mountain* classes. Their method relies on features derived from color and edge orientation histograms. Sethi, Coman, and Stan [23] use a decision-tree learning scheme to generate classification rules that link the spatial arrangement of colors to predict associated key words. The spatial layout of color in each image is represented by dividing each image into 64 blocks and by calculating the dominant color for each block. The color space used by them is the HSV color space. Their approach generates rules like *If image blocks in the upper half have more than 50% pixels with hue values between 0 and 25, have less than 14% of pixels with hue values between 25 and 41, and have more than 26% of pixels with saturation values between 80 and 100, then the image is considered a sunset image with an estimated accuracy of 90%.*

Several researchers have relied on vector quantization to perform annotation by classification. Blume and Ballard, for example, use a learning vector quantization-based classifier to classify each and every pixel after using Haar wavelet transform to generate a feature vector for every image pixel to capture information about the local brightness, color, and texture. The classified pixels are then grouped into anno-tated image regions. Blume and Ballard have demonstrated their method to annotate regions with key words such as *sky, forest*, and *water*. Another example of vector-quantization-based classification to predict classification categories is the work done by Mustafa and Sethi [25]. In their approach, a concept-specific codebook is built for each concept using images representing that concept. For example, images rep-resenting the concept fire are used to build a codebook for fire. Similarly, images representing *water* are used to build a water-specific codebook. The codebooks are built by using subimages of a certain size. In order to use the codebooks thus built for identifying different concepts in unseen images, every codeword is associated with its own dissimilarity measure that defines whether a particular codeword from a particular concept codebook is sufficiently similar to a block of image pixels in an image being annotated. If a number of codewords from a specific codebook are found similar to image blocks for a given image, then that image is assigned the concept associated with the codebook providing the majority of similar codewords. The approach has been applied to annotate images with three different kinds of *fires, sky, water*, and *grass*, demonstrating that the codebook-based approach is suitable for images whose category can be identified through low-level features such as color. Such features are primary identifiers of what Biederman [26] calls as *mass noun en-tities* such as *grass, water*, and *snow*. These entities do not have definite boundaries as opposed to count noun entities, for example *airplanes,* with concrete boundaries.

Images with count noun entities cannot be categorized without using shape-based features.

2.4.2 Annotation by Association

Annotation by association methodology is a direct extension of the traditional association rule mining that was developed to mine patterns of associations in transaction databases. Each transaction involves certain items from a set of possible items. Given N transaction and d as the size of the set of possible items, the collection of transactions can be represented as a size $N \times d$ matrix. Since each transaction involves only very few items, the transaction matrix is very sparse. Association mining tries to discover frequent itemsets, that is, the items that appear together frequently in the transaction matrix, in the form of rules wherein the presence of a particular item in a transaction predicts the likely presence of some other items. A typical rule has the form $X \Rightarrow Y$ with support s and confidence c, implying that s% of the transactions contain both X and Y and c% of the transactions that support X also support Y.

Different methods for annotation by association mining differ in terms of how items and transactions are defined to take advantage of existing association rule mining algorithms, for example the well-known Apriori algorithm [27]. An early example of applying association rule mining for image annotation is provided by the work of Ordonez and Omiecinski [28], who consider segmented images to compute the co-occurrences of regions that are deemed similar. The regions are treated as items, and each image constitutes an equivalent of a transaction to extract association rules of the form, "The presence of regions X and Y imply the presence of region Z with support s and confidence c." Ding et al. [29] follow a different strategy to define items and transactions in their work with mining remotely sensed imagery. They divide spectral bands into several small windows, and each window is considered an item. The pixels in their equivalency constitute transactions. Their rule extraction also considers auxiliary information, such as crop yield, at each pixel location to produce rules of the form, "A window in band 1 at $[a_1, b_1]$ and a window in band 2 at $[a_2, b_2]$ results in crop yield y with support s and confidence c." The problem with pixel-level association rules is that pixel-level information is susceptible to noise and furthermore pixels are highly correlated in spatial directions and thus the transactions cannot be considered independent. Tesic et al. [30] present a similar approach to derive the equivalent of the transaction matrix for images. First, the images are partitioned into fixed size rectangular regions. By operating at block level, their method is better at dealing with noise and transaction independence. MPEG-7 textual descriptors are then extracted for each region. A previously constructed learning vector quantizer-based codebook, serving as a visual thesaurus, then provides labels for image regions. The labeled regions are then treated as analogous to items in a transaction database and their first- and second-order spatial co-occurrences are tabulated next. An adaptation of the Apriori algorithm is then used to extract association rules. The method has been used to mine aerial video-graphic images with good success. Another example of annotation by association is the work of Teredesai et al. [31], who use multirelational rule mining to allow for multiple descriptions for each image arising from multiple sources of labeling.

2.4.3 Annotation by Statistical Modeling

In this approach, a collection of annotated images is used to build models for joint distribution of probabilities that link image features and key words. An early example of this approach is the work of Mori et al. [32], who used a simple co-occurrence model to establish links between words and partitioned image regions. Recently, this approach has started receiving more attention. In the linguistic indexing approach of Li and Wang [33], the two-dimensional multiresolution hidden Markov model (2DMHMM) is used to build a stochastic model for each image category. The 2D MHMM captures statistical properties of feature vectors and their spatial dependence at different levels. The model assumes a first-order Markov chain across the resolutions to define statistical dependencies at different resolutions. The model further assumes that given a block's state, that is, image category label, at any resolution, the corresponding feature vector of the block is conditionally independent of any other states and blocks. This allows the chain rule to be used to compute associated probabilities from training images. Feature extraction is done by partitioning each image into blocks of suitable size, and a six-dimensional feature vector is extracted for each block. The feature vector consists of three components that carry color information of the block and three components that carry texture information. The process of feature extraction is performed at multiple levels for each image giving rise to feature vectors of the same dimensionality that capture information at different levels of details. Li and Wang report modeling of 600 concepts, using an annotated database of 60,000 images. The capability to model such a large number of concepts is one of the strengths of this approach.

Barnard et al. [34] have studied two classes of stochastic models to link images with words. Their approach requires images to be segmented into regions unlike Li and Wang's approach of fixed partitioning. The eight largest regions from each image are selected and a 40-dimensional feature vector, capturing size, shape, color, and texture information, is computed for each region. Figure 2.2 shows one of the models studied by Barnard et al. In this hierarchical model, each node captures relationships between regions and concepts. Higher level nodes capture relationships for key words that are present in many images while nodes at progressively lower levels capture key words that are specific to fewer images. A Gaussian distribution for regions and a multinomial distribution for key words model the joint distribution for probabilities at each node. The results shown by Barnard et al. demonstrate that the models, such as the hierarchical model of Figure 2.2, are able to generate annotation for unseen images; however, the performance depends heavily on the quality of segmentation and manual labeling during training.

Another recent work in this area is due to Jeon et al. [35], who use the relevance-based language models [36, 37] to perform automatic annotation. They assume that every image can be described using a small vocabulary of blobs. The joint distribution of words and blobs is learned using a training set of annotated images to form a model

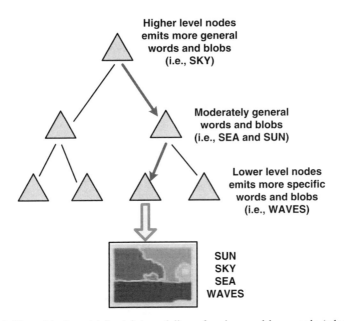

Fig. 2.2. A hierarchical model for joint modeling of regions and key words (adopted from Barnard et al. [34]).

that they call as the cross-media relevance model (CMRM) for images. The CMRM is then used to generate word probabilities for each blob in the test set, which are then combined to build a vector of word probabilities for each image. By keeping the top few probabilities, their approach is then able to generate a few key words for each unseen image.

2.5 Concept Mining Through Clustering

Clustering is another popular data mining methodology that several researchers have used to uncover relationships between key words and images. Clustering-based annotation has been performed at the image level, at the subimage level, and at the region-level after segmentation.

An example of annotation through clustering at the image level is the work of Stan and Sethi [38]. The interesting aspect of this work is cluster profiling in a lower dimensional feature space or in a subspace of the original feature space. Figure 2.3 shows the conceptual architecture of their system to discover relationships between low-level features and key words. Low-level image features such as dominant image colors and their spatial layout are first computed for annotated images. The resulting vectors are next clustered using a hierarchical clustering scheme that allows an easier control over the number of resulting clusters as well as the use of an arbitrary similarity measure. Each of the resulting clusters is analyzed to find the components of the feature

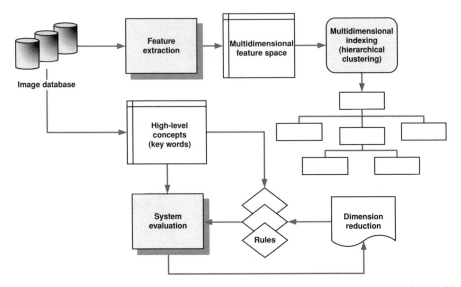

Fig. 2.3. Conceptual architecture for concept mining through clustering (taken from Stan and Sethi [23]).

space that are important for that particular cluster, that is, its own subspace. This is done by ranking features for each cluster in terms of their variance. Features showing variance less than a certain cutoff value are considered important for the corresponding cluster and are retained to specify the subspace for the corresponding cluster. It is this subspace wherein the cluster prototype description is generated. Such a description consists of mean feature values for each subspace feature and the corresponding variances that determine the region of influence for the cluster. Assuming the existence of associated key words for images clustered, key words associated with images in each cluster are next counted and ranked. Only the most frequent key words are then retained to generate mining rules in IF-THEN form. The approach has been applied to generate rules for concepts such as *sunset, landscape*, and *arid*, using color features only. Stan and Sethi [39], in a related work, present another approach for discovering the relationships. In this approach, clusters are visualized through multidimensional scaling in two dimensions. Through visualization, thumbnails of images in a cluster or cluster prototypes are displayed to an annotator who can select a cluster or images close to the cluster prototype for annotation and assign key words as shown in Figure 2.4. Being interactive, the approach offers a compromise between the two extremes of annotation, manual and fully automatic.

While the above examples of work dealt with annotation at image level, doing clustering at subimage level provides better flexibility for annotation because different subimages may represent different concepts. An approach for clustering-based annotation at the subimage level is presented by Mori et al. [32]. In their approach, subimages are clustered through vector quantization to generate codewords. Each image is allowed to be associated with multiple concepts, for example an outdoor image

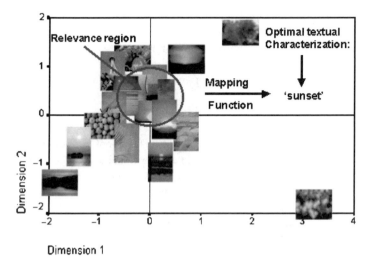

Fig. 2.4. Interactive annotation through multidimensional scaling of cluster centers (taken from Stan and Sethi [39]).

may have *mountains, sky,* and *lake* associated with it. All subimages inherit multiple concepts associated with the parent image. Once the codebook is constructed, inherited concepts for each codeword are used to set up voting probabilities for different concepts given an image. The experimental results presented in [32] indicate that the method is suitable for linking pictures and words; however, the performance could be improved by restricting the domain of pictures and concepts. This is not surprising given that human beings use a great deal of external knowledge in describing the content of an image.

2.6 Concept Mining Using Contextual Information

The text associated with images, for example, in the form of an image caption or the text accompanying an image on a Web page, forms a rich source of external knowledge that can be used to derive semantic links for image features. In a video, the analysis of accompanying audio or closed caption text can yield invaluable information to link visual or audio features with semantic concepts. In all of the examples cited here, contextual information thus available minimizes or rather eliminates the need for an external annotator.

Srihari describes one of the early examples of how text associated with pictures can be used to facilitate image retrieval [40]. Although the work is limited to associating names with faces, it provides an effective example of using external knowledge sources to do annotation. Many methods seeking to link external knowledge sources with images or their features rely on latent semantic indexing (LSI), a popular and powerful technique for text retrieval that has shown to be capable of learning "hidden associations" between the terms of text documents in the vector model of information retrieval [41, 42]. The LSI approach is based on the singular value decomposition (SVD) method of statistical analysis and is similar to principal component analysis (PCA). The major difference between the two is that the SVD method is applicable when we have a single set of observations and the PCA method applies when we have multiple sets of observations.

The use of LSI for text retrieval involves first forming a term-document matrix. Such a matrix is obtained by first doing preprocessing of the documents to filter out the stop words and convert the remaining words to their root form through stemming. After that, the term weighs for each document are calculated to obtain a vector representation for each document. These vectors then define the term-document matrix, where rows represent the terms and each column represents a document. The singular value decomposition of the term-document matrix then is used to determine a new representation. In the new vector space, each axis corresponds to a "concept" which is related with the terms. It is this relationship that shows similarities between different terms. The previous work [43] in this area has exploited these similarities by applying LSI methodology to bilingual documents, for example in French and English, to determine the associations between French and English words.

There are a few different ways in which LSI has been used to mine concepts in images. In one of the early works involving LSI and image retrieval [44], LSI is used only on text accompanying images to find several concepts that might relate to an image. Although the approach is able to improve retrieval accuracy, no explicit associations between image features and key words are discovered. Consequently, the approach has a limited use. Zhao and Grosky [45] suggest a better approach to exploit LSI. In their approach, the text surrounding an image is processed first to generate a vector representation for the surrounding text. Next, the associated image is processed to extract its low-level features to generate a feature vector representation for the image. A composite vector consisting of appended text and image vectors is then used to represent each image and its surrounding text. These composite vectors then form the columns of the term-document matrix of the LSI approach and the image features and key words of the surrounding text form the terms. The results presented by Zhao and Grosky using 43 different concepts taken from news headlines show that LSI is able to capture relationships between key words and image features.

Instead of using LSI for mining concepts that link key words with visual features, Stan and Sethi [46] have used it to mine associations between different features themselves. Using the bins of a global color histogram as terms, they form the term-document matrix for a collection of images where the global color histogram of each image constitutes its vector representation. By experimenting with 2000 images and a quantized histogram of 192 bins, they have shown that LSI can uncover patterns of color that tend to occur together. These color patterns then can be assigned semantic meanings through supervision.

The other approach to generate concepts for association with images is to perform analysis of the audio and closed captions associated with video. For example, a number of methods for audio classification have been developed that assign audio segments one of the predetermined labels [47–49]. In the case of audio only, the automatic speech recognition can be performed on segments classified as speech. By analyzing closed captions where available, it is also possible to generate a list of key words that can be associated with a video clip. The key words thus generated from either audio classification or closed captions or both can be used to perform the function of contextual knowledge with LSI to mine concepts for automatic annotation. Kulesh et al. present an approach [50] along these lines in their PERSEUS project where the contextual information from different sources is exploited to track news stories on the Internet for the creation of a personal news portal.

While most work on association mining in multimedia has typically focused on linking multimedia features with key words or captions, recently several researchers have been studying the mining of cues to semantically link different modalities. An example of such a cross-modal association is provided by the work of Li et al. [51] in which three different approaches for cross-modal association are implemented and compared. The three approaches are latent semantic indexing (LSI), cross-modal factor analysis (CFA), and cross-modal canonical correlation analysis (CCA). In the LSI model of cross-modal association discovery, a composite feature vector carrying information from two or more modalities is formed and subjected to singular-value-decomposition to obtain associations. A drawback of this approach as noted by Li et al. is that LSI does not distinguish features from different modalities in the joint space. The set of linear transformations from LSI provide an optimal fit of the over-all distribution of different features. However, the optimal solution based on overall distribution may not best represent semantic relationships between features of different modalities, since distribution patterns among features from the same modality will also greatly impact LSI's results. A solution to the above problem is possible by treating features from different modalities as two subsets and focus only on semantic patterns between these two subsets. Under the linear correlation model, the problem becomes one of finding the optimal transformations that can best identify the coupled patterns or the semantic structure between features of two different subsets. Two such transformations are possible through the multivariate statistical analysis methods of factor analysis and canonical correlation analysis. The experimental results presented by Li et al. show that CFA yields the best cross-modal association results. Although CCA follows the same approach of treating different modalities as two subsets, its performance is impacted because associations are more susceptible to noise or small variations in features.

2.7 Events and Feature Discovery

An event in multimedia literature implies an occurrence of an interesting action, for example a car chase. While it is common to characterize an event as an interesting temporal composition of objects, a better characterization of an event is an interesting spatiotemporal instance. This allows us to include spatial combinations of objects, for example the presence of a face in front of a map in an image, as events too. Detection of events has received considerable interest in multimedia literature. For example, there is a large amount of literature related to the detection of events in sports videos. Methods have been developed to detect and highlight events for basketball [52, 53], baseball [54], soccer [55, 56], and tennis [57]. With the increasing use of cameras for monitoring and surveillance, many researchers have developed methods to detect events in such videos [58, 59]. The primary motivation for large interest in event detection has been that events provide an excellent framework for indexing and summarizing multimedia data.

Event detection implies knowledge of known patterns forming the event; this, in turn, means that specific detectors for different events can be built. The existing literature on event detection exemplifies this where the detectors look for predefined combinations of objects through heuristics, rule-based, or classification methods. Event discovery, on the other hand, implies no prior knowledge of the event characteristics. In fact, the only supposition for event discovery is that the event is something out of the ordinary; that is, an event is an interesting outlier combination of objects. With this viewpoint, the literature on event discovery is sparse and only recently researchers have begun to look for event discovery in multimedia data mining [58, 59].

An example of recent work on event discovery is the work of Divakaran and his group [60, 61] with raw audio and video, which they term as *unscripted media*. Their framework for event discovery is shown in Figure 2.5. In this framework, the multimedia data are windowed and processed to extract features. These features are viewed as time series data, which are converted to a time series of discrete labels through classification and clustering. For example, audio data from a sport broadcast can be classified into a series of distinct labels such as Applause, Cheering, Music, Speech, and Speech with Music. Unusual subsequences in the discrete time series of labels are next detected as outliers by eigenvector analysis of the affinity matrix constructed from estimated statistical models of subsequences of the time series. The length of the subsequences used for statistical model building determines the context in which the events are discovered. The overlap between the subsequences determines the resolution at which the events are discovered. The detected outliers are then ranked on the basis of how well they deviate from background sequences. The interestingness of the ranked outliers is next determined by bringing in the domain knowledge to discover interesting events in the data. Divakaran and his group have successfully applied this methodology to discover events in audio broadcasts of sports and audio captured at traffic intersections. For example, they have shown that their approach was able to discover "ambulance crossing" event in audio data.

Another example of event discovery is the work of Zhong et al. [62], where an unsupervised technique is presented for detecting unusual activity in a large video set. In their method, the video is divided into small segments of equal lengths and each segment is classified into one of the many prototypes using color, texture, and motion features. The detection of unusual events is done by performing a co-occurrence analysis of feature prototypes and video segments. The method has been applied to surveillance video and shown to discover events such as cars making U-turns and backing-off. Another recent example of event discovery work is the semisupervised adapted hidden Markov Model (HMM) framework [17] in which the usual or background event models are first learned from the training data. These models are then used to compute the likelihood of short subsequences of the test data to locate outliers

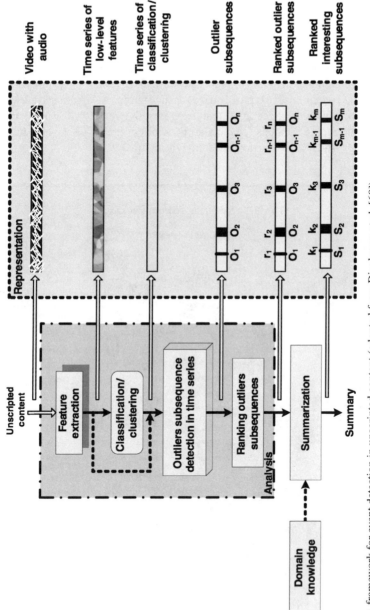

Fig. 2.5. A framework for event detection in unscripted content (adopted from Divakaran et al. [60]).

that show up with small likelihood values. The outliers are then used to adapt the background models to create models for unusual events and locate new unusual event types by iterating the process. The method has been applied to audio and audio-visual data to automatically discover events, such as discovery of interruptions in a multimedia presentation because of questions from audience and laughter from audience.

A related problem to event discovery is the feature discovery problem. A large body of multimedia processing research has dealt with the extraction of features and their use in building indices for content browsing and retrieval. The features described earlier or their variations are typically used for such purposes. While such an approach of using predefined or handcrafted features generally works well, it is tempting to employ data mining methods for the automatic discovery of low-level features that might be best suitable for a given collection of multimedia.

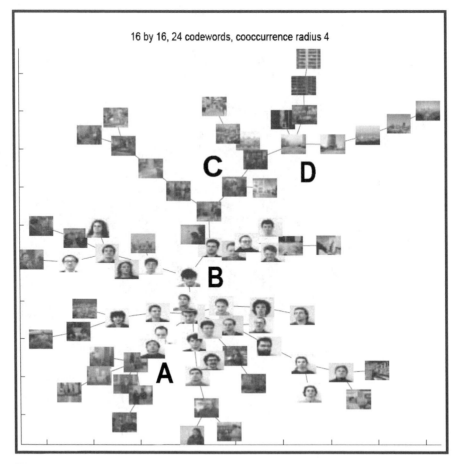

Fig. 2.6. Minimal spanning graph representation of three categories of images using discovered features (taken from Ma et al. [63]).

An example of a feature discovery approach is provided by the work of Mukhopadhyay et al. [63], who have used it to build features for the retrieval and browsing of a collection of images of faces, people, and buildings. Their feature discovery approach is designed for shape features that are extracted from edges of objects in images. After edge extraction, each edge image is partitioned into subimages of a certain size, for example, 16×16. These subimages are then used to construct a codebook whose entries are the low-level features discovered. The salient point of this work is that the codebook is built using the Hausdorff metric [64], which is able to take into account perceptual similarity of edge fragments, an important requirement for retrieval. By looking at the co-occurrences of the discovered features, Mukhopadhyay, Ma, and Sethi have shown that images of different characteristics tend to get clustered in different groups and that there exists a gradual change in clusters as one moves from one cluster to another neighboring cluster as shown in the minimal spanning graph of Figure 2.6.

Lam and Ciesielski [65] describe another example of feature discovery for discovering texture features through genetic programming [66]. In this work, the input is the gray-level histograms of 16×16 subimages. Through genetic programming, various combinations of inputs are searched and evaluated through a fitness function based on how well different texture subimages are separated. The results seem to indicate that discovered texture features are able to yield classification accuracies close to some well-known texture features. Thus, it is a promising approach for building features.

2.8 Conclusion

The multimedia data mining is an active and growing area of research. While the majority of the work has been devoted to the development of data mining methodologies to deal with the specific issues of multimedia data, the origin of the multimedia data mining lies in the pioneering work of Fayyad and his coworkers [67–69] at NASA in the early nineties when they developed several applications including the cataloging of astronomical objects and identification of volcanoes. Since then, several applications of multimedia data mining have been investigated [70–74]. Many of the recent multimedia data mining applications are focused on traffic monitoring and video surveillance, possibly due to increased attention to homeland security. In the coming years, we expect the multimedia data mining applications to grow especially in areas of entertainment and medicine. Almost all of the multimedia data mining efforts to date have been with the centralized data mining algorithms; however, this is expected to change as more and more multimedia content is searched and accessed through peers.

References

1. Sethi I. *Data Mining in Design and Manufacturing*. Kluwer Academic Publishers; 2001.
2. Dimitrova N, Jasinschi R, Agnihotri L, Zimmerman J, McGee T, Li D. *The Video Scout System: Content-Based Analysis and Retrieval for Personal Video Recorders*. CRC Press; 2003.

3. Patel N, Sethi I. Statistical approach to scene change detection. In *Proceedings IS&T/SPIE Conference on Storage and Retrieval for Media Databases*, 1995;2420:329–338.
4. Patel N, Sethi I. *Compressed Video Processing for Cut Detection.* VISP 1996, Vol. 143, pp. 315–323.
5. Lupatini G, Saraceno C, Leonardi R. Scene break detection: A comparison. Research Issues in Data Engineering. In *Workshop on Continuos Media Databases and Applications*, 1998, pp. 34–41.
6. Gargi U, Kasturi R, Strayer S. Performance characterization of video-shot-change detection methods. *IEEE Transaction on Circuits and Systems for Video Technology* 2000;10(1).
7. Lienhart R. Reliable transition detection in videos: A survey and practitioner's guide. *International Journal of Image and Graphics* 2001;1(3):469, 486.
8. Hampapur A, Jain R, Weymouth T. Production model based digital video segmentation. *Multimedia Tools and Applications* 1995;1:9, 45.
9. Joachims T. *Kernel Methods—Support Vector Learning.* MIT Press, 1999.
10. Burges C. A tutorial on support Vector Machines for Pattern Recognition. *Data Mining and Knowledge Discovery* 1998;2(2):121, 167.
11. Li M, Sethi I. SVM-based classifier design with controlled confidence. In: *Proceedings of 17th International Conference on Pattern Recognition* (ICPR 2004). Cambridge, UK, 2004, pp. 164–167.
12. Scheirer E, Slaney M. Construction and evaluation of a robust multifeature speech/music discriminator. In: *Proceedings of IEEE International Conference on Acoustics, Speech, Signal Processing*, April 1997, pp. 1331–1334.
13. Li D, Sethi I, Dimitrova N, McGee T. Classification of general audio data for content-based retrieval. *Pattern Recognition Letters* 2001;22:533–544.
14. MPEG-7: The generic multimedia content description standard, Part 1. *IEEE MultiMedia* 2002;9(2):78–87.
15. Goldmann L, Karaman M, Sikora T. Human body posture recognition using MPEG-7 descriptors. In: *IS&TSPIE's Electronic Imaging 2004*. San Jose, CA, 2004, pp. 18–22.
16. Pakkanen J, Ilvesmki A, Iivarinen J. Defect image classification and retrieval with MPEG-7 descriptors. In: *Proceedings of the 13th Scandinavian Conference on Image Analysis*, Göteborg, Sweden, 2003, pp. 349–355.
17. Zhang D, Lu G. Evaluation of MPEG-7 shape descriptors against other shape descriptors. *Multimedia System* 2003;9(1):15–30.
18. Eidenberger H. Statistical analysis of MPEG-7 image descriptions. *ACM Multimedia Systems Journal*, 2004;10(2):84–97.
19. McGurk H, MacDonald J. Hearing lips and seeing voices. *Nature* 1976;264:746–748.
20. Li D, Dimitrova N, Li M, Sethi I. Multimedia content processing through cross-modal association. In *MULTIMEDIA '03: Proceedings of the eleventh ACM international conference on Multimedia*. New York: ACM Press, 2003, pp. 604–611.
21. Yu H, Wolf W. Scenic classification methods for image and video databases. In *In SPIE International Conference on Digital Image Storage and Archiving Systems*, Vol. 2606, 1995, pp. 363–371.
22. Vailaya A, Jain A, Zhang H. On image classification: City vs. landscape. *Pattern Recognition* 1998;31:1921–1936.
23. Sethi I, Coman I, Stan D. Mining association rules between low-level image features and high-level semantic concepts. In: *Proceedings SPIE Conference on Data Mining and Knowledge Discovery*, April 2001.

24. Blume M, Ballard D. Image annotation based on learning vector quantization and localized Haar wavelet transform features; 1997. Available from: citeseer.ist.psu.edu/blume97image.html
25. Mustafa A, Sethi I. Creating agents for locating images of specific categories. In: *IS&T Electronic Imaging 2004*, San Jose, CA, 2004.
26. Biederman I. Recognition by components: A theory of human understanding. *Psychological Review* 1987;94:115–147.
27. Agrawal R. *Fast Discovery of Association Rules*. Advances in Knowledge Discovery and Data Mining, AAAI Press/The MIT Press 1996, pp. 307–328.
28. Ordonez C, Omiecinski E. Discovering association rules based on image content. In: *ADL '99: Proceedings of the IEEE Forum on Research and Technology Advances in Digital Libraries*. Washington, DC: IEEE Computer Society; 1999, p. 38.
29. Ding Q, Ding Q, Perrizo W. Association rule mining on remotely sensed images using p-trees. In: *In Proceedings of PAKDD*, 2002.
30. Tesic J, Newsam S, Manjunath B. Mining image datasets using perceptual association rules. In: *SIAM International Conference on Data Mining*, Workshop on Mining Scientific and Engineering Datasets. San Francisco, CA; 2003, pp. 71–77.
31. Teredesai A, Ahmad M, Kanodia J, Gaborski R. CoMMA: A framework for integrated multimedia mining using multi-relational associations. *Knowledge and Information Systems: An International Journal*, in press.
32. Mori Y, Takahashi H, Oka R. Image-to-word transformation based on dividing and vector quantizing images with words. In: *MISRM'99 First International Workshop on Multimedia Intelligent Storage and Retrieval Management*, 1999.
33. Li J, Wang J. Automatic linguistic indexing of pictures by a statistical modeling approach. *IEEE Transactions on Pattern Analysis and Machine Intelligence* 2003;25(9):1075–1088.
34. Barnard K, Duygulu P, Forsyth D. Trends and advances in content-based image and video retrieval. In Press.
35. Jeon J, Lavrenko V, Manmatha R. Automatic image annotation and retrieval using cross-media relevance models. In: *In Proceedings of the 26th international ACM SIGIR Conference*, 2003, pp. 119–126.
36. Lavrenko V, Choquette M, Croft W. Cross-lingual relevance models. In: *Proceedings of the 25th Annual International ACM SIGIR Conference*, 2002, pp. 175–182.
37. Lavrenko V, Croft W. Relevance-based language models. In: *In Proceedings of the 24th International ACM SIGIR Conference*, 2001, pp. 120–127.
38. Stan D, Sethi I. Mapping low-level image features to semantic concepts. In: *Proceedings IS&T/SPIE Conference on Storage and Retrieval for Media Databases*, San Jose, CA, 2001.
39. Stan D, Sethi I. eID: A system for exploration of image databases. *Information Processing and Management* 2003;39:335–361.
40. Srihari R. Automatic indexing and content-based retrieval of captioned images. In: *IEEE Computer*, Vol. 28, 1995, pp. 49–56.
41. Berry M, Dumais S, OfBrien G. Using linear algebra for intelligent information retrieval. *SIAM Review* 1995;37:573–595.
42. Deerwester S, Dumai S, Furnas G, Landauer T, Harshman R. Indexing by latent semantic analysis. Journal of American Society for Information Science 1990;41:391–407.
43. Dumais S, Landauer T, Littman M. Automatic Cross-Linguistic Information Retrieval using Latent Semantic Indexing. In: *Proceedings SIGIR*, pp. 16–23.

44. Cascia M, Sethi S, Sclaroff S. Combining textual and visual cues for content-based image retrieval on the world wide web. In: *Proceedings of IEEE Workshop on Content-Based Access of Image and Video Libraries*, Santa Barbara, CA, 1998, pp. 24–28.
45. Zhao R, Grosky W. *Distributed Multimedia Databases: Techniques and Applications.* Hershey, PA: Idea Group Publishing.
46. Stan D, Sethi I. Color patterns for pictorial content description. In: *Proceedings of the 17th ACM Symposium on Applied Computing*, 2002, pp. 693–698.
47. Wijesekera D, Barbara D. Mining cinematic knowledge: Work in progress. In: *Proceedings of International Workshop on Multimedia Data Mining (MDM/KDD'2000)*, Boston, MA, 2000, pp. 98–103.
48. Snoek C, Worring M. Multimodal video indexing: A review of the state-of-the-art. *Multimedia Tools and Applications* 2005;25(1):5–35.
49. Lau R, Seneff S. Providing sublexical constraints for word spotting within the ANGIE framework. In: *Proc. Eurospeech '97*, Rhodes, Greece, 1997, pp. 263–266.
50. Kulesh V, Petrushin V, Sethi I. Video Clip Recognition Using Joint Audio-Visual Processing Model. In: *ICPR (2002)*, 2002, pp. 500–503.
51. Li D, Li M, Nevenka D, Sethi I. Multimedia content processing through Cross-Modality Association. In: *Proceedings of the 11th ACM Int'l Conf. Multimedia*, Berkeley, CA, 2003, pp. 604–611.
52. Zhou W, Vellaikal A, Jay-Kuo C. Rule-based video classification system for basketball video indexing. In: *ACM Multimedia Workshops*, 2000, pp. 213–216.
53. Nepal S, Srinivasan U, Reynolds G. Automatic detection of "Goal" segments in basketball videos. In: *MULTIMEDIA '01: Proceedings of the Ninth ACM International Conference on Multimedia*. New York: ACM Press, 2001, pp. 261–269.
54. Rui Y, Gupta A, Acero A. Automatically extracting highlights for TV baseball programs. In: *MULTIMEDIA '00: Proceedings of the Eighth ACM International Conference on Multimedia*. New York: ACM Press, 2000, pp. 105–115.
55. Gong Y, Sin L, Chuan C, Zhang H, Sakauchi M. Automatic parsing of TV soccer programs. In: *IEEE Conference on Multimedia Computing and Systems*, 1995.
56. Tovinkere V, Qian R. Detecting semantic events in soccer games: Towards a complete solution. In: *Proceedings of ICME 2001*, Tokyo, Japan, 2001.
57. Wang J, Parameswaran N. Analyzing tennis tactics from broadcasting tennis video clips. In: *11th International Multimedia Modelling Conference (MMM'05)*, pp. 102–106.
58. Tucakov V, Ng R. Identifying unusual spatiotemporal trajectories from surveillance videos. In: *In Proceedings of 1998 SIGMOD Workshop on Research Issues on Data Mining and Knowledge Discovery (DMKD'98)*, Seattle, WA, 1998.
59. Oh J, Lee J, Kote S, Bandi B. Multimedia data mining framework for raw video sequences. In: Zaiane SJSimoff, Djeraba Ch, editors. Mining multimedia and complex data, Lecture Notes in Artificial Intelligence, Vol. 2797, Springer, 2003, pp. 18–35.
60. Divakaran A, Miyaraha K, Peker K, Radhakrishnan R, Xion Z. Video mining using combinations of unsupervised and supervised learning techniques. In: *SPIE Conference on Storage and Retrieval for Multimedia Databases*, Vol. 5307, 2004, pp. 235–243.
61. Goh S, Miyahara K, Radhakrishan R, Xiong Z, Divakaran A. Audio-visual event detection based on mining of semantic audio-visual labels. In: *SPIE Conference on Storage and Retrieval for Multimedia Databases*, Vol. 5307, 2004, pp. 292–299.
62. Zhong H, Shi J, Visontai M. Detecting unusual activity in video. In: *Proc. CVPR*, 2004.
63. Mukhopadhyay R, Ma A, Sethi I. Pathfinder networks for content based image retrieval based on automated shape feature discovery. In: *Sixth IEEE International Symposium on Multimedia Software Engineering (ISMSE 2004)*, FL, 2004.

64. Ma A, Mukhopadhyay R, Sethi I. Hausdorff metric based vector auantization of binary images. In: *Proceedings Intíl Conference on Information and Knowledge Engineering*, Las Vegas, Nevada, 2003, pp. 315–320.
65. Lam B, Ciesielski V. Discovery of human-competitive image texture feature extraction programs using genetic programming. *GECCO* 2004;2:1114–1125.
66. John K. *Genetic Programming: On the Programming of Computers by Means of Natural Selection*. Cambridge, MA: The MIT Press, 1992.
67. Smyth P, Burl M, Fayyad U, Perona P. Knowledge discovery in large image databases: Dealing with uncertainties in ground truth. In: *In Proc. of AAAI-94 Workshop on KDD*, Seattle, WA, 1994, pp. 109–120.
68. Fayyad U, Weir N, Djorgovski S. Automated analysis of a large-scale sky survey: The SKICAT System. In: *In Proceedings 1993 Knowledge Discovery in Databases Workshop*, Washington, DC, 1993, pp. 1–13.
69. Fayyad U, Smyth P. Image database exploration: Progress and challenges. In: *In Proceedings 1993 Knowledge Discovery in Databases Workshop*, Washington, DC, 1993, pp. 14–27.
70. Zhu X, Wu X, Elmagarmid A, Feng Z, Wu L. Video data mining: Semantic Indexing and event detection from the association perspective. *IEEE Transactions on Knowledge and Data Engineering* 2005;17(5):665–677.
71. Yoneyama A, Yeh C, Jay-Kuo C. Robust vehicle and traffic information extraction for highway surveillance. *EURASIP Journal on Applied Signal Processing*. 2005;14:2305–2321.
72. Yoneyama A, Yeh C, Jay-Kuo C. Robust traffic event extraction via content understanding for high way surveillance system. *IEEE International Conference on Multimedia and Expo*, 2004.
73. Za O, Han J, Li Z, Hou J. Mining multimedia data. In: *CASCON '98: Proceedings of the 1998 Conference of the Centre for Advanced Studies on Collaborative Research*. IBM Press, 1998.
74. Oh J, Lee J, Kote S. Real Time Video Data Mining for Surveillance Video Streams. In: *Proceedings of the Seventh Pacific-Asia Conference on Knowledge Discovery and Data Mining*, Seoul, Korea, 2003, pp. 222–233.

Part II

Multimedia Data Exploration and Visualization

3. A New Hierarchical Approach for Image Clustering

Lei Wang and Latifur Khan

Summary. The key problem in achieving efficient and user-friendly retrieval in the domain of image is the development of a search mechanism to guarantee delivery of minimal irrelevant information (high precision) while ensuring that relevant information is not overlooked (high recall). The unstructured format of images tends to resist the deployment of standard search mechanism and classification techniques. As a method to provide better organization of images, clustering is an important aspect for effective image retrieval. In this chapter, we introduce a clustering method based on unsupervised neural nets and self-organizing maps. In dynamic growing self-organizing tree algorithm (DGSOT), a hierarchy is constructed from top to bottom. We observe that DGSOT outperforms the traditional Hierarchical Agglomerative Clustering (HAC) algorithm in terms of E-measure.

3.1 Introduction

The development of technology in the field of digital media generates huge amounts of nontextual information, such as audio, video, and images, as well as more familiar textual information. The potential for the exchange and retrieval of information is vast, and at times daunting. In general, users can be easily overwhelmed by the amount of information available via electronic means. The need for user-customized information selection is clear. The transfer of irrelevant information in the form of documents (e.g., text, audio, and video) retrieved by an information retrieval system which are of no use to the user wastes network bandwidth and frustrates users. This condition is a result of inaccurate representations of the documents in the database, as well as confusion and imprecision in user queries, since users are frequently unable to express their needs efficiently and accurately. These factors contribute to the loss of information and to the provision of irrelevant information. Therefore, the key problem to be addressed in information selection in the domain of image is the development of a search mechanism that will guarantee the delivery of a minimum of irrelevant information (high precision), as well as ensuring that relevant information is not overlooked (high recall).

The unstructured format of images tends to resist the deployment of standard search mechanism and classification techniques. As a method to provide better organization of images, clustering is important for effective image retrieval. A good image database system should provide users different kind of access modes that include searching, browsing, and navigating. The database should be organized properly to support all these modes of access. Indexing techniques can support searching. Browsing is supported by abstraction techniques that summarize images in a good manner. Image navigation need to use methods that group related images together. Obviously, a good clustering method is highly required for all these. The ability of the system to retrieve relevant documents based on search criteria could be greatly increased if they were able to provide an accurate clustering method.

Most of information retrieval methods are based on features [15, 38]. These features can be key words or phrases in a text-based information retrieval system. And, the counterparts for images are color, texture and shape etc. As compared to text-based information retrieval, image has opaque relationship with computes and feature extraction is more difficult. Images consist of various objects, each of which may be used to effectively classify the image [6, 7, 22]. Dynamic growing self-organizing tree (DGSOT) [21, 22] discussed in this chapter constructs a hierarchy using a self-organizing tree that constructs a hierarchy from top to bottom. Similarity of images is based on similarity of objects that appear in images. In addition, object similarity takes into account three image features: color, shape, and texture. The idea here is that features will reflect the content of images in some degree. Different features will reflect different aspects of images. After detecting objects in images, we extract color, shape, and texture information and express those using vectors. Then considering these three features, we calculate the similarity between objects applying vector space model. Before image clustering, we cluster objects according to similarities between objects and assign a weight for each object cluster. Next, we construct a vector for each image on the basis of weights of object clusters and calculate similarities between images using vector space model. Finally, on the basis of image similarities, we cluster images and build hierarchy, using clustering algorithms.

We have observed that our DGSOT outperforms hierarchical agglomerative clustering in terms of precision, recall, and E-measure. The main contributions of this work will be as follows.

We propose a new mechanism that can be used to generate hierarchy automatically, and to make our approach scalable. For this, we propose various clustering algorithms for the construction of top to bottom hierarchies based on unsupervised learning and a self-organizing map. In this regard, a new DGSOT algorithm is presented. We demonstrate that DGSOT outperforms most widely used agglomerative hierarchical clustering algorithms in terms of precision, recall, and E-measure.

Section 3.2 discusses related works. Section 3.3 presents our approach in detail. Section 3.4 presents result. Section 3.5 contains our conclusion and possible areas of future work.

3.2 Related Works

Several systems exist today that attempt to classify images based on their content. Successful classification of an image and its contents relates directly to how well relevant images may be retrieved when a search is preformed. Most image storing systems such as QBIC and VisualSEEK limit classification mechanism to describing an image based on metadata such as color histograms, texture, or shape features [3, 12, 13, 30, 31, 34, 36, 37]. These systems have high success in performing searches in which the users specify images containing a sample object, or a sample texture pattern. Should a user ask for an image depicting a basketball game, the results become less accurate. This is due to the fact that although an image may contain a basketball, it does not depict a basketball game. Systems that contain only metadata regarding the objects contained in an image cannot provide an accurate classification of the entire image.

In our system, we have a hierarchy where similar images are grouped together. This similarity is based not only on features directly but also on all features along with finer granularity (individual object) rather than coarser grain (i.e., entire image). For example, a football game image may contain green field, goalposts, and football objects. An image containing only a football would be classified as a football game based on color similarity analysis. On the other hand, shape or texture similarity may also misclassify image. On the basis of purely shape similarity, we may identify a basketball as a football. Therefore, neither color-based nor shape-based similarity is adequate to classify images. We need to combine these two similarities together to understand semantic meaning of images. Therefore, to classify images effectively, we need a hierarchy where images based on color, shape, and texture features are grouped together.

Other systems attempt to provide images with more precise descriptions by analyzing other elements surrounding images, such as captions [33, 35], or HTML tags on Web pages [14]. These systems use this information to assist image classification and generate meaningful description for images. This approach, tied together with metadata on images such as histograms, texture, and color sampling, has the potential to yield high-precision results in image classification. Examining the textual descriptions associated with an image provides additional information that may be used to classify the image more accurately [24, 45]. Unfortunately, this approach does not take into account the connections among individual objects presented in a sample image. Such connections provide useful information in the form of relationships among objects presented in the image, which could be used to classify the image's content.

3.3 Hierarchy Construction and Similarity Measurement

An efficient clustering method is desired for images. In this section we present our approach in detail.

First of all, we segment all input images into objects (see [44] for more details) and calculate similarities between each two objects on the basis of color, texture and shape features. Second, we cluster similar objects into various groups based on object similarity (see Section 3.3.1 for more details). On the basis of object groups, we deduct weight by calculating term frequency and inverse document frequency (see Section 3.3.2 for more details). Third, we construct a vector for each image and calculate similarities between each two images, using vector model. Image vectors are decided

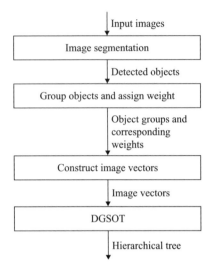

Fig. 3.1. Major steps of our approach.

by the objects contained in each image, and the vector length will be the number of object groups (see Section 3.3.2 also). Finally, use some clustering algorithm to cluster images based on image similarity. For this, several existing techniques are available such as hierarchical agglomerative clustering algorithm (HAC) [10, 32, 42], self-organizing map (SOM) [17, 19, 23], and self-organizing tree (SOTA) [1, 11]. In this chapter, we use our algorithm named dynamic growing self-organizing tree (DGSOT) (see Section 3.3.3). Note that object similarity is determined by the combination of color similarity, texture similarity and shape similarity. The major steps are shown in flow chart in Figure 3.1.

Basically, image segmentat process has three steps [44]. First, we need to extract color edges from areas of different color. Second, on the basis of the color edges we discovered in step one, we divide the image into several subregions by using region-growing techniques. In the final step, adjacent regions having similar colors are merged together. Here we recognize the object boundary, and later we will try to group similar objects together. Since we avoid object identification or classification by exploiting clustering (i.e., unsupervised), we firmly believe we will get better result (see Section 3.4).

3.3.1 Object Clustering

After segmenting images into objects, some of objects have semantic meanings and some do not have. Let us assume that we have N images in database. After segmentation, we have total M detected objects, and then we cluster these M objects into t different groups $C_1, C_2, \ldots C_t$ according to similarities between objects. Basically, if visual features of objects such as color, shape, or texture are similar, it would be very possible that the objects have similar semantic meanings. Hence, we calculate object similarities, using color, shape, and texture features. Consequently, these object similarities exhibit semantic similarities between objects. So, before knowing object similarity, we need to calculate color, shape, and texture similarity first.

3.3.1.1 Color Similarity Measure

Color similarity measurement is important in computer vision research. Many methods have been proposed [9, 29, 39, 43]. To compute color similarity, we extract color information from object i pixel by pixel and construct a color vector $Vi(v_{1,i}, v_{2,i}, \ldots v_{p,i}, \ldots v_{k,i})$ to express the color histogram. Each item in this vector represents the percentage of pixels whose hue value locates in specific interval. For example, $v_{p,i}$ is the percentage of pixels whose hue values are between $2^*\pi^*p/k$ and $2^*\pi^* (p+1)/k$ in object i, because the range of hue value in HSI color space is from 0 to $2^*\pi$. For each object, there is a unique V, so we could evaluate the degree of color similarity between object i and object j. That is,

$$sim_c(i, j) = \frac{\vec{i_c} \bullet \vec{j_c}}{\left|\vec{i_c}\right| \times \left|\vec{j_c}\right|} = \frac{\sum_{p=1}^{k} v_{p,i} \times v_{p,j}}{\sqrt{\sum_{p=1}^{k} v_{p,i}^2} \times \sqrt{\sum_{p=1}^{k} v_{p,j}^2}} \tag{3.1}$$

The value of k affects the accuracy of color similarity. Along with increasing of k, accuracy will increase also. In our case, we choose $k = 12$.

3.3.1.2 Shape Similarity Measure

The computation of shape similarity is a little bit more complicated [4, 26, 41]. To support similarity queries, Lu and Sajjanhar [27] introduced fixed resolution (FR) representation method. We accept the idea of this method basically, but made some changes during implementation. First, we need to find major axis for each object that is the longest line joining two points on the boundary. Rotate an angle θ around mass centroid of an object to make its major axis to be parallel to x-axis and keep the centroid above the major axis. The reason to do that is to normalize the object to make it invariant to rotation [8]. The coordinates of the centroid are as below. $\sigma(x, y)$ is surface density function.

$$\bar{x} = \frac{\iint x\sigma(x, y)dA}{M} \qquad \bar{y} = \frac{\iint y\sigma(x, y)dA}{M} \tag{3.2}$$

After doing normalization, we create a $q * q$ grid, which is just big enough to cover the entire object, and overlaid on the object. The size of each cell is same. Define a shape vector $U_i(u_{1,i}, u_{2,i}, \ldots u_{p,i}, \ldots u_{q2,i})$ sized q_2 which corresponds to q_2 cells. Each item in the vector stands for the percentage of pixels in corresponding cell. The higher the q value is, the higher the accuracy. Of course, raise the calculation cost as result. If images are simple, it is not necessary to choose a high q. In our case, q is 4, which is good enough for small simple images. We could calculate the degree of shape similarity between two shape vectors. Formula is similar to Equation (3.1).

$$sim_s(i, j) = \frac{\vec{i}_s \bullet \vec{j}_s}{\left|\vec{i}_s\right| \times \left|\vec{j}_s\right|} = \frac{\sum_{p=1}^{q^2} u_{p,i} \times u_{p,j}}{\sqrt{\sum_{p=1}^{q^2} u_{p,i}^2} \times \sqrt{\sum_{p=1}^{q^2} u_{p,j}^2}} \quad (3.3)$$

3.3.1.3 Texture Similarity Measure

The texture retrieval is harder than color and shape, because there is no clear definition of "texture." The texture of an image region is decided by gray level distribution. Basically, there are three kinds of approaches to extract texture features: spectral approach, structural (or syntactic) approach, and statistical approach. For statistical approach, according to the order of the utilized statistical function, we have two categories of descriptors: First-Order Texture Features and Second-Order Texture Features [16]. The difference is that the first-order statistics do not provide information about the relative positions of different gray levels. In our method, intensity value in a region is homogeneous, so the positions of different gray levels are not very important here. To reduce calculation complexity, we choose to use first-order texture features to generate texture feature vector.

We define I be the variable representing the gray level of regions, P(I) be the fraction of pixels with gray level I, and N_g be the number of possible gray levels.

So, the moments are

$$m_i = E\left[I^i\right] = \sum_{I=0}^{N_g-1} I^i P(I) \qquad i = 1, 2, \ldots \quad (3.4)$$

Central moments are

$$\mu_i = E[(I - E[I])^i] = \sum_{I=0}^{N_g-1} (I - m_1)^i P(I) \quad (3.5)$$

For any given I, we can have most frequently used central moments μ_2, μ_3, μ_4. Generate texture vector using central moments. Similarity between two texture vectors is still similar to Equation (3.1).

3.3.1.4 Combined Similarity

Finally, using linear similarity combination, we can simply assign 1/3 for the weights of all three features here. We could change weights to adjust object-clustering result. We define a threshold T_{obj}. If and only if the similarity between two objects is larger than T_{obj}, the two objects can be in same group. The object similarity between each pair of objects in same group must be higher than T_{obj}. It is possible that one object appears in more than one group.

In addition to the above method, we plan to try another method for objects clustering, using Dempster–Shafer evidence combination. In that case, we will consider three sources of evidence: color, shape, and texture. Obviously, all these evidences are independent from each other. Assume that we have n object clusters $(C_1, C_2, \ldots C_n)$ currently, and each cluster has an eigen-object $(obj_1, obj_2, \ldots obj_n)$. For an input object, calculate the orthogonal sum of three belief functions ($m_{C,S,T}$) using Dempster combination formula for each cluster. Finally, the cluster having highest $m_{C,S,T}$ will own the new object. We define another threshold T_b. If the $m_{C,S,T}$ for all existed clusters are less than T_b, we need to create a new object cluster.

3.3.2 Vector Model for Images

Image clustering is based on image similarity. To calculate image similarity, we construct an image vector $W_l(w_{1,l}, w_{2,l} \ldots w_{i,l}, \ldots w_{t,l})$ rather than compare images directly. The size of vector W is same as the total number of object clusters. Each item in the image vector is the weight for corresponding object cluster in the image l. For example, $w_{i,l}$ is the weight of object cluster C_i in the image l.

To get image vector, we borrow the idea of the vector model for text information [2]. Images correspond to documents and object clusters correspond to terms. Let N be the total number of images and n_i be the number of images in which the objects in cluster C_i ever appears. Define the normalized frequency $f_{i,j}$ as below.

$$f_{i,l} = \frac{\text{freq}_{i,l}}{\max_h \text{freq}_{h,l}} \tag{3.6}$$

$\text{freq}_{i,l}$ is the number of times the cluster C_i appears in the image l. The maximum is calculated over all clusters which ever appeared in the image l. Such frequency is normally referred to as the *tf factor*, which indicates how well the cluster i describes the image l. But if the objects from one cluster appear in most of images, the cluster is not very useful for distinguishing a relevant image from a nonrelevant one. So, we need to define an inverse document frequency idf_i for C_i as following.

$$\text{idf}_i = \log \frac{N}{n_i} \tag{3.7}$$

Balancing above two factors, we have the weight of cluster.

$$w_{i,l} = f_{i,l} \times \text{idf}_i = f_{i,l} \times \log \frac{N}{n_i} \tag{3.8}$$

After computing image vectors, we could get similarity between any two images by calculating the degree of similarity between two image vectors.

$$\text{sim}_{\text{img}}(i, j) = \frac{\vec{i} \bullet \vec{j}}{|\vec{i}| \times |\vec{j}|} = \frac{\sum_{h=1}^{t} w_{h,i} \times w_{h,j}}{\sqrt{\sum_{h=1}^{t} w_{h,i}^2} \times \sqrt{\sum_{h=1}^{t} w_{h,j}^2}} \tag{3.9}$$

3.3.3 Dynamic Growing Self-Organizing Tree (DGSOT) Algorithm

The DGSOT is a tree structure self-organizing neural network. It is designed to discover the correct hierarchical structure of the underlying data set. The DGSOT grows in two directions: vertical and horizontal. First, in the direction of vertical growth, the DGSOT adds children, and in the direction of horizontal growth, the DGSOT adds more siblings. In vertical growth of a node, only two children are added to the node. In horizontal growth we strive to determine suitable number of children to represent data that are associated with the node. Thus, the DGSOT chooses the right number of subclusters at each hierarchical level during the tree construction process. During the tree growth, a learning process similar to the self-organizing tree algorithm (SOTA) is adopted.

The pseudo code of DGSOT is shown below:

Step 1: [Initialization] initially the tree has only one root node. The reference vector of this root node is initialized with the centroid of the entire collection, and all data will be associated with the root. The time parameter t is initialized to 1.

Step 2: [Vertical Growing] the leaves whose heterogeneity is greater than a threshold will change itself to a node x and create two descendent leaves. The reference vector of a new leaf is initialized with the node's reference vector.

Step 3: [Learning] for each input data associated with node, x, the winner is found (using KLD see Sections 3.3.3.1 and 3.3.3.4), and then the reference vectors of the winner and its neighborhood are updated. If the relative error of the entire tree is larger than a threshold, called error threshold (T_E), t is increased by 1, i.e., $t = t + 1$, and then Step 3 is repeated.

Step 4: [Horizontal Growing] for each lowest node (not leaf), if the horizontal growing stop rule is unsatisfied, a child leaf is added to this node; if it is satisfied, a child leaf is deleted from this node, and the horizontal growth is terminated.

Step 5: [Learning] for each input data, the winner is found (using KLD, see Section 3.3.3.4), and then the reference vectors of the winner and its neighborhood are updated. If the relative error of the entire tree is larger than a threshold, called error threshold (T_E), t is increased by 1, i.e., $t = t + 1$, and then Step 5 is repeated.

Step 6: [Expansion] if there are more levels necessary in the hierarchy (i.e., vertical growing stop rule is reached), then return to Step 2; otherwise, stop.

Step 7: [Pruning] the leaf node with node data associated with it is deleted.

Let d be the branch factor of the DGSOT, then the height of the DGSOT will be lgd$N$, where N is the number of data. Let K be the average number of learning iterations to expand the tree one more level. Because in each learning iteration all data need to be distributed, the time complexity to build a full DGSOT will be O ($K^* N^*$ lgd$N$).

3.3.3.1 Learning Process

In DGSOT, the learning process consists of a series of procedure to distribute all the data to leaves and update of the reference vectors. Each procedure is called a *cycle*. Each *cycle* contains a series of *epochs*. Each *epoch* consists of a presentation of all input data and each presentation has two steps: finding the best math node and updating the reference vector. Similar to SOTA, the input data is compared only to the leaf nodes to find the best match node, which is known as the *winner*. The leaf node c, which has the minimum distance to the input data x, is the best match node/winner.

$$c : \quad ||x - n_c|| = \min_i \{||x - n_i||\} \tag{3.10}$$

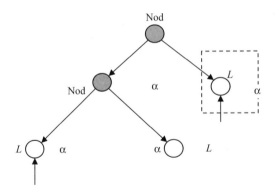

Fig. 3.2. Different neighborhoods of winner (indicated by arrow) in DGSOT.

After a *winner c* is found, the reference vectors of the winner and its neighborhood will be updated using the following function:

$$\Delta w_i = \varphi(t) \times (x - w_i) \tag{3.11}$$

Where $\varphi(t)$ is the learning function:

$$\varphi(t) = \alpha \times \eta(t) \tag{3.12}$$

$\eta(t)$ is the learning rate function, α is the learning constant, and t is the time parameter. The convergence of the algorithm depends on a proper choice of α and $\eta(t)$. During the beginning of the learning function $\eta(t)$ should be chosen close to 1, thereafter, it decreases monotonically. One choice can be $\eta(t) = 1/t$.

Since neighborhood will be updated, there are two types of neighborhoods of a winning cell: If the sibling of the *winner* is a leaf node, then the neighborhood includes the winner, the parent node, and the sibling nodes. On the other hand, if the sibling of the winning cell is not a leaf node, the neighborhood includes only the *winner* and its parent node (see Figure 3.2). The updating of the reference vector of siblings is important so that data similar to each other are brought into same subtree. The α the winner, the parent node and the sibling nodes will have different values. Parameters α_w, α_m, and α_s are used for the winner, the parent node, and the sibling node, respectively. Note that the parameter values are not equal. The order of the parameters is set as $\alpha_w > \alpha_s > \alpha_m$. This is different from the SOTA setting, which is $\alpha_w > \alpha_m > \alpha_s$. In SOTA, an inorder traversal strategy is used to determine the topological relationship in the neighborhood. And in DGSOT, a postorder traversal strategy is used to determine the topological relationship in the neighborhood. In our opinion, only the nonequal α_w and α_s are critical to partitioning the input data set into different leaf nodes. The goal of updating the parent node's reference vector is to make it more precise to represent all the data associated with its children (see KLD, Section 3.3.3.4).

The *Error* of the tree, which is defined as the summation of the distance of each input data to the corresponding *winner*, is used to monitor the convergence of the learning process. A learning process has converged when the relative increase of

Error of the tree falls below a given threshold.

$$\left| \frac{\text{Error}_{t+1} - \text{Error}_t}{\text{Error}_t} \right| < \text{ErrorThreshold} \tag{3.13}$$

It is easier to avoid over training the tree in the early stages by controlling the value of *Error* of the tree during training.

3.3.3.2 Vertical Growing

In DGSOT, a nongreedy vertical growing is used. During vertical growing the leaves whose heterogeneity is greater than a threshold will change itself to a node and create two descendent leaves. The reference vectors of these leaves will be initialized by their parents.

There are several ways to determine the heterogeneity of a leaf. One simple way is to use the number of data associated with a leaf as its heterogeneity. This simple approach controls the number of elements that appear in each leaf node. The other way is to use the average error e of a leaf as its heterogeneity. This approach does not depend on the number of data associated with a leaf node. The average error e of a leaf is defined as the average distance between the leaf node and the input data associated with the leaf:

$$e_i = \sum_{j=1}^{D} \frac{d(x_j, n_i)}{|D|} \tag{3.14}$$

where D is the total number of input data assigned to the leaf node i. $d(x_j, n_i)$ is the distance between data j and leaf node i. n_i is the reference vector of the leaf node i.

For the first approach, the data will be evenly distributed among the leaves. But the average error of the leaves may be different. For the second approach, the average error of each leaf will be similar to the average error of the other leaves. But the number of data associated with the leaves may vary substantially. In both approaches, the DGSOT can easily stop at higher hierarchical levels, which will save the computational cost.

3.3.3.3 Horizontal Growing

In each vertical growing, only two leaves are created for a growing node. In each horizontal growing, the DGSOT tries to find an optimal number of leaf nodes (subcluster) of a node to represent the clusters in each node's expansion phase. Therefore, DGSOT adopts a dynamically growing scheme in each horizontal growing stage. For a lowest nonleaf node (heterogeneous one), a new child (subcluster) is added to the existing children. This process continues until a certain stop rule is reached. Once the stop rule is reached, the number of children nodes is optimized. For example, in a tree a nonleaf node has three children. If the horizontal growing criterion does not match the stop rule, a new child is added. Similarly, if the addition of a new child satisfies the stop rule, the child is deleted and the horizontal growing is stopped. After each addition/deletion of a node, a learning process is performed (see Sections 3.3.3.1 and 3.3.3.4).

Determining the true number of clusters, known as the cluster validation problem, is a fundamental problem in cluster analysis. It will be served as a stop rule. Several kinds of indexes have been used to validate the clustering [46]: one index based on external and internal criteria. This approach is based on statistical tests along with high computational cost. Since the DGSOT algorithm tries to optimize the number of clusters for a node in each expansion phase, the cluster validation is used heavily. Therefore, the validation algorithms used in DGSOT must have a light computational cost and can be easily evaluated. Here we suggest average distortion (AD) measure.

AD is used to minimize intracluster distance. The average distortion of a subtree is defined as

$$AD = \frac{1}{N} \sum_{i=1}^{N} |d(x_i, w)|^2 \qquad (3.15)$$

where N is the total number of input data assigned in the subtree, and w is the reference vector of the winner of input data x_i. The AD is the average distance between input data and its winner. During DGSOT learning, the total distortion is already calculated and the AD measure is easily computed after the learning process is finished. If the AD versus the number of clusters is plotted, the curve is monotonically decreasing. There will be much smaller drop after the number of clusters is greater than the "true" number of the clusters, because crossing this point we add more clusters simply to partitions within, rather between, "true" clusters. After a certain point the curve becomes flat. This point indicates the optimal number of the clusters in the original data set. Then the AD can be used as a criterion to choose the optimal number of clusters. In horizontal growing phase, if the relative value of AD after adding a new sibling is less than a threshold ε (Equation 3.16), then the new sibling will be deleted and the horizontal growing will stop.

$$\frac{|AD_{K+1} - AD_K|}{AD_K} < \varepsilon \qquad (3.16)$$

where K is the number of siblings in a subtree and ε is a small value, generally it is less than 0.1.

3.3.3.4 *K*-Level up Distribution (KLD)

Clustering in a self-organizing neural network is a distortion-based competitive learning. The nearest neighbor rule is used to make the clustering decision. In SOTA, data associated with then parent node will be distributed only between its children. If data are incorrectly clustered in the early stage, these errors cannot be corrected in the later learning process.

To improve the cluster result, we propose a new distribution approach called K-level up distribution (KLD). Data associated with a parent node will be distributed not only to its children leaves but also to its neighboring leaves. The following is the KLD strategy:

- For a selected node, its K level ancestor node is determined.
- The subtree rooted by the ancestor node is determined.
- Data assigned to the selected node will be distributed among all leaves of the subtree.

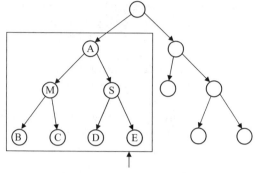

One level up redistribution scope

Fig. 3.3. One level up distribution ($K = 1$).

For example, Figure 3.3 shows the scope of $K = 1$. Now, the data associated with node M needs to be distributed to the new created leaves. For $K = 1$, the immediate ancestor of M will be determined, which is A. The data associated with node M will be distributed to leaves B, C, D, and E of the subtree rooted by A. For each data, the winning leaf will be determined among B, C, D, and E using Equation (3.10). Note that if $K = 0$, data of M will be distributed between leaf B and C. This latter approach is identical to the conventional approach.

3.4 Experiment Results

As of today we are developing a system for image segmentation and clustering. A user can input an image for segmentation, the system will output detected boundary and all segmented regions in thumbnail format (see Figure 3.4). Users can double click thumbnails to view result with bigger size (as shown in Figure 3.4). Then from these segmented images, similar objects will be grouped together, and weigh will be assigned for each group (see Section 3.3.1). Thus, an image will be represented by a vector with a set of objects along with weights (see Section 3.3.2). Next, we have built a hierarchy using DGSOT by exploiting these vectors (see Section 3.3.3). Figure 3.5 has shown a hierarchical tree to display the clustering result.

One of the purposes of this experiment is to demonstrate how accurate the clustering is. The image data set contains a set of images, which are belonged to six different categories such as basketball, baseball, bats, football, goggle, and playground. After segmentation using our algorithms [44], the total number of objects is around 1500. In this experiment, we use 80% of these images as training data to generate the hierarchical tree and use the rest 20% of these images as testing data to evaluate the result. The clustering accuracy is evaluated by using common E-measure [40]. The definition of E is shown in Equation (3.17). After each round, we reshuffle the data set and do it again with different training and testing data set. The percentages for training and testing data are still 80 and 20, respectively. We have repeated these for

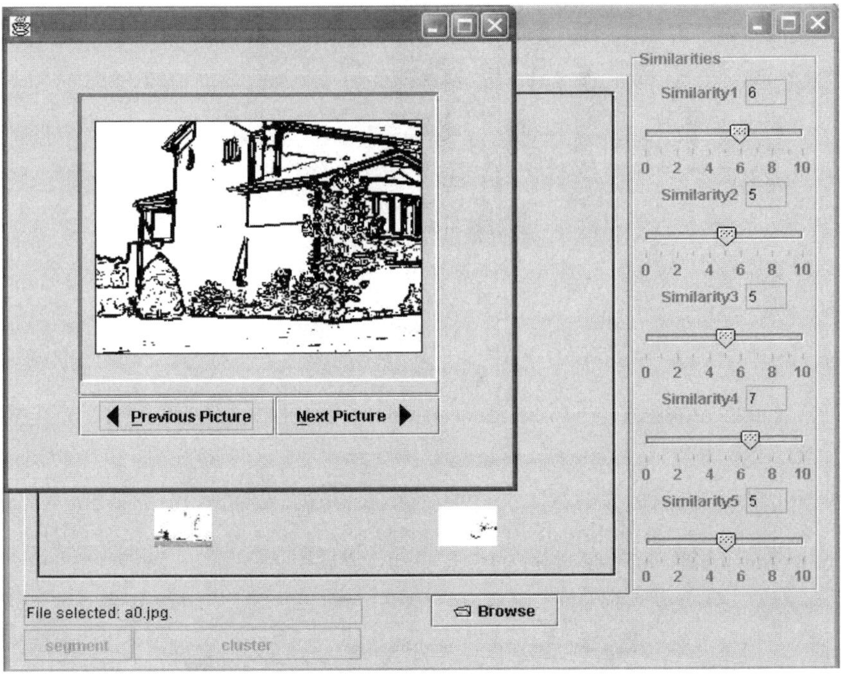

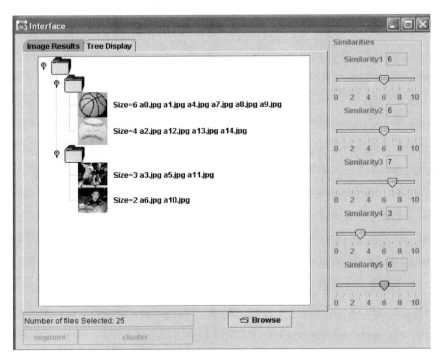

Fig. 3.4. Segmentation result for an image.

Fig. 3.5. Hierarchical tree for clustering result.

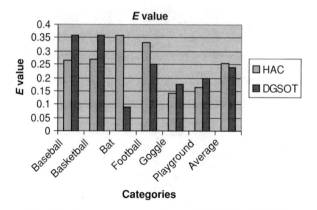

Fig. 3.6. *E*-measure comparisons of DGSOT and HAC.

five rounds. The final *E*-measure is the average of *E*-measures that we got in each round above. The error threshold in Equation (3.13) for DGSOT is set to 0.01 and sibling threshold ε in Equation (3.16) is set to 0.02.

$$E(p, r) = 1 - \frac{2}{1/p + 1/r} \qquad (3.17)$$

where p and r are standard precision and recall of the cluster with respect to the set of images. E varies between 0 and 1. E is equal to 0 when p and r are all 1, and 1 when both p and r are 0. We average p and r, using formula (3.17) to calculate the E value for clustering. We tested cluster accuracy when query images are from different categories. Figure 3.6 shows the results of *E*-measure for above categories and average using two cluster algorithms, DGSOT and the most widely used, hierarchical agglomerative clustering (HAC) respectively. In Figures 3.6, x-axis represents different categories and y-axis is *E*-measure.

The average precision of DGSOT and HAC is 0.84 and 0.80 respectively. The average *recall* of all these clusters of DGSOT and HAC is 0.73 and 0.75 respectively. Figure 3.6 shows the comparative *E*-measures for these two algorithms. Results show that DGSOT (average $E = 23.8\%$) outperforms HAC algorithm (average $E = 25.6\%$).

3.5 Conclusion and Future Works

In this chapter we have proposed new automatic image clustering methods. To develop a hierarchy, we developed a dynamic growing self-organizing tree algorithm (DGSOT) that constructs a hierarchy from top to bottom and compared it to traditional Hierarchical Agglomerative Clustering (HAC) algorithm.

We would like to extend this work in the following directions. First, we would like to do more experiments for different data set. Second, we would like to experiment with other knowledge base (like CYC). Third, we would implement some image-searching algorithm based on hierarchical tree we got in this chapter. Finally, we will develop algorithms to integrate newly coming images into the existing hierarchy structure.

References

1. Albers S, Westbrook J. Self-organizing data structures. In: *Online Algorithms: The State of the Art*, Springer, Fiat-Woeginger, 1998.
2. Baeza-Yates R, Ribeiro-Neto B. Modern Information Retrieval, ISBN 0-201-39829-X, 1999.
3. Barber R, Equitz W, Faloutsos C, Fickner M, Niblack W, Petkovic D, Yanker P. Query by content for large on-line image collections. *IEEE Journal*, 1995.
4. Belongie S, Malik J, Puzicha J. Matching shapes. Computer Vision, 2001. ICCV 2001. In: *Proceedings of Eighth IEEE International Conference*, Vol. 1, 2001.
5. Bodner R, Song F. Knowledge-based approaches to query expansion in information retrieval. In: *Proceedings of Advances in Artificial Intelligence*, Springer, New York, pp. 146–158.
6. Breen C, Khan L, Ponnusamy A, Wang L. Ontology-based image classification using neural networks. In: *Proceedings of SPIE Internet Multimedia Management Systems III*, Boston, MA, July, 2002, pp. 198–208.
7. Breen C, Khan L, Ponnusamy A. Image classification using neural networks and ontologies. In: *Proceedings of International Workshop on Web Semantics*, Aix-en-Provence, France, 2002, pp. 98–102.
8. Chakrabarti K, Ortega-Binderberger M, Porkaew K, Mehrotra S. Similar shape retrieval in MARS. In: *Proceedings of IEEE International Conference on Multimedia and Expo*, 2000.
9. Chitkara V. *Color-Based Image Retrieval Using Compact Binary Signatures*. Master's thesis, Dept. of Computing Science, University of Alberta, 2001.
10. Downs GM, Willett P, Fisanick W. Similarity searching and clustering of chemical structure databases using molecular property data. *J. Chem. Inf. Comput. Sci.* 1994;34(5):1094–1102.
11. Dopazo J, Carazo JM. Phylogenetic reconstruction using an unsupervised growing neural network that adopts the topology of a phylogenetic tree. *Journal of Molecular Evolution* Vol 44, 226–233, 1997.
12. Equitz W and Niblack W. Retrieving images from a database using texture—algorithms from the QBIC system. Technical Report RJ 9805, Computer Science, IBM Research Report, May 1994.
13. Flickner M, Sawhney H, et al. Query by image and video content: The QBIC system. *IEEE Comput. Mag.*, 28(9):23–32, September 1995.
14. Frankel C, Swain MJ, Athitsos V. *WebSeer: An Image Search Engine for the World Wide Web*, University of Chicago Technical Report TR-96-14, July 31, 1996.
15. Hampton C, Persons T, Wyatt C, Zhang YCh. Survey of Image Segmentation, 1998.
16. Haralick RM, Shanmugam K, Dinstein I. Textural features for image classification, *IEEE Transactions on Systems, Man and Cybernetics*, 3:610–621, 1973
17. Honkela T, Kaski S, Lagus K, Kohonen T. Websom: Self-organizing maps of document collections. In: *Proceedings of Workshop on Self-Organizing Maps 1997 (WSOM'97)*, Espoo, Finland, June 1997.

18. Hotho A, Mädche A, Staab AS. Ontology-based Text Clustering, Workshop Text Learning: Beyond Supervision, 2001.
19. Kaski S, Nikkila J, and Kohonen T. Methods for interpreting a self-organized map in data analysis. In: *Proc. 6th European Symposium on Artificial Neural Networks (ESANN98)*, D-Facto, Brugfes, Belgium, 1998.
20. Khan L, Luo F. Automatic Ontology Derivation from Documents. IEEE Transactions on Knowledge and Data Engineering (TKDE), August 2002.
21. Khan L, Luo F. Ontology construction for information selection. In: *14th IEEE International Conference on Tools with Artificial Intelligence*, Washington DC, November 2002.
22. Khan L, Wang L. Automatic ontology derivation using clustering for image classification. In: *Eighth International Workshop on Multimedia Information Systems*, Tempe, Arizona, November 2002.
23. Kohonen T. *Self-Organizing Maps*, Second Edition, Springer 1997.
24. Konak ES. *A Content-Based Image Retrieval System for Texture and Color Queries*, M.Sc. Thesis, Department of Computer Engineering, Bilkent University, Ankara, Turkey, August 2002.
25. Lance GN and Williams WT. A General Theory of Classificatory Sorting Strategies: 1. Hierarchical Systems. *Computer Journal*, 9, 373–380, 1966
26. Loncaric S. A survey of shape analysis techniques. *Pattern Recognition*, 1998;31(8):983–1001.
27. Lu G and Sajjanhar A. Region-based shape representation and similarity measure suitable for content-based image retrieval. Springer Verlag Multimedia Systems, 1999.
28. Murtagh, F. Complexities of Hierarchic Clustering Algorithm: State of Art, Computational Statistics Quarterly, 1984;1:101–113.
29. Sebe N, Lew MS, Loupias E, Tian Q and Huang TS. Color Indexing Using Wavelet-based Salient Points. Submitted to IEEE Workshop on Content-based Access of Image and Video Libraries (CBAIVL-2000), June 2000.
30. Niblack W, Barber R et. al. The QBIC project: Querying images by content using color, texture and shape. In *Proc. SPIE Storage and Retrieval for Image and Video Databases*, Feb 1994.
31. Pentland A, Picard RW, Sclaroff S. Photobook: Tools for Content-based manipulation of image databases. In *Proc. of Storage and Retrieval for Image and Video Databases II*, Vol. 2185, pp. 34–47, Bellingham, WA, 1994.
32. Rasmussen EM, Willett P. Efficiency of hierarchical agglomerative clustering using the icl distributed array oricessor. *Journal of Documentation*, 1989;45(1).
33. Row N, Frew B. Automatic classification of objects in captioned depictive photographs for retrieval, intelligent multimedia information retrieval, Chapter 7, M. Maybury, AAAI Press, 1997.
34. Scassellati B, Alexopoulos S, Flickner M. Retrieving images by 2D shape: A comparison of computation methods with human perceptual judgments. In: *Proc. SPIE Storage and Retrieval for Image and Video Databases*, 1994.
35. Smeaton AF, Quigley A. Experiments on using semantic distances between words in image caption retrieval. In: *Proc. of the Nineteenth Annual International ACM SIGIR Conference on Research and Development in Information Retrieval*, 1995.
36. Smith JR, Chang S. Intelligent multimedia information retrieval, edited by Mark T. Maybury. In: *Querying by Color Regions Using the VisualSEEk Content-Based Visual Query System*, 1996.
37. Smith JR and Chang S. Visualseek: A fully automated content-based image query system. In: *Proc. ACM Multimedia 96*, 1996.

38. Smith JR, Chang S. Multi-stage classification of images from features and related text. In: *4th Europe EDLOS Workshop*, San Miniato, Italy, Aug 1997.
39. Stricker MA, Orengo M. Similarity of color images. In: SPIE Proceedings, Vol. 2420, 1995.
40. Van Rijsbergen CJ. *Information Retrieval*. Butterworths, London, 1979.
41. Veltkamp RC. Shape matching: Similarity measures and algorithms. In: *Shape Modelling International*, pp. 188–197, May 2001.
42. Ellen M. Voorhees. Implementing Agglomerative hierarchic clustering algorithms for use in document retrieval. *Information Processing & Management*, 1986;22(6):465–476.
43. Cheetham W, Graf J. Case based reasoning in color matching, case-based reasoning research and development. In: *Proceedings of the Second International Conference on Case Based Reasoning*, Springer-Verlag, Providence, RI, 1997.
44. Wang L, Khan L, Breen C. Object boundary detection for ontology-based image classification. In: Third International Workshop on Multimedia Data Mining, Edmonton, Alberta, Canada, July 2002.
45. Zöller T, Hermes L, Buhmann JM. Combined color and texture segmentation by parametric distributional clustering. In: R. Kastouri, D. Laurendeau, C. Suen (Eds.), *Proc. of the International Conference on Pattern Recognition*, Vol. 2, pp. 627–630, IEEE Computer Society, 2002.
46. Halkidi M, Batistakis Y, Vazirgiannis M. On clustering validation techniques. *JIIS*, 2001;17:107–145.

4. Multiresolution Clustering of Time Series and Application to Images

Jessica Lin, Michail Vlachos, Eamonn Keogh, and Dimitrios Gunopulos

Summary. Clustering is vital in the process of condensing and outlining information, since it can provide a synopsis of the stored data. However, the high dimensionality of multimedia data today presents an insurmountable challenge for clustering algorithms. Based on the well-known fact that time series and image histograms can both be represented accurately in a lower resolution using orthonormal decompositions, we present an anytime version of the *k-means* algorithm. The algorithm works by leveraging off the multiresolution property of wavelets. The dilemma of choosing the initial centers for *k-means* is mitigated by assigning the final centers at each approximation level as the initial centers for the subsequent, finer approximation. In addition to casting *k-means* as an anytime algorithm, our approach has two other very desirable properties. We observe that even by working at coarser approximations, the achieved quality is better than the batch algorithm, and that even if the algorithm is run to completion, the running time is significantly reduced. We show how this algorithm can be suitably extended to chromatic and textural features extracted from images. Finally, we demonstrate the applicability of this approach on the online image search engine scenario.

4.1 Introduction

The vast growth of disk technology in the past decade has enabled us to store large multimedia databases, such as audio, video, images, time series, etc. While storage is no longer an impediment, it has become increasingly clear that an interactive process is needed for humans to efficiently browse through the enormous amount of data. Clustering has proven to be an invaluable tool for distinguishing homogeneous object groups and for producing representatives of the discovered clusters. For example, image clustering is essential for many applications, such as geospatial applications (aerial and satellite photographs), medicine (distinction of tumor images), robot vision (object recognition), online searching (annotation of images), etc. In addition to the high dimensionality of such data, one has to be careful in extracting features that are coherent with the human perceptual system. Such features include, but are not limited to, color, texture, shape, and location. Essentially, the objective is to select content descriptors that are tailored to a specific application and will lead to discovery of homochromous or homomorphic objects.

Although numerous clustering algorithms have been proposed, the majority of them work in a batch fashion, thus hindering interaction with the end users. Here we address the clustering problem by introducing a novel anytime version of the popular *k-means* clustering algorithm [9, 18] based on the wavelet decomposition. Anytime algorithms are valuable for large databases, since results are produced progressively and are refined over time [11]. Their utility for data mining has been documented at length elsewhere [2, 20]. While *k-means* algorithm and wavelet decompositions have both been studied extensively in the past, the major novelty of our approach is that it mitigates the problem associated with the choice of initial centers, in addition to providing the functionality of user interaction.

The algorithm works by leveraging off the multiresolution property of wavelets [6]. In particular, an initial clustering is performed with a very coarse representation of the data. The results obtained from this "quick and dirty" clustering are used to initialize a clustering at a finer level of approximation. This process is repeated until the "approximation" is the original "raw" data or until the clustering results stabilize. Furthermore, our approach allows the user to interrupt and terminate the process at any level. In addition to casting the *k-means* algorithm as an anytime algorithm, our approach has two other very unintuitive properties. The quality of the clustering is often better than the batch algorithm, and even if the algorithm is run to completion, the time taken is typically much less than the time taken by the batch algorithm. We first formulate it as a generic time series problem, since the histograms we extract from images can be well treated as time series. In particular, the high dimensionality and high feature correlation suggest that a time-series algorithm can be suitably applied to image histograms. In this setting, we illustrate the speedup and scalability of the algorithm, in addition to its improved accuracy. Then we show how this novel algorithm can be applied on histograms extracted from image colors and texture. In addition, we demonstrate how a clustering postfiltering step can enhance the interpretability of the results from online image search engines.

The rest of this paper is organized as follows. In Section 4.2, we review related work, and introduce the necessary background on the wavelet transform and *k-means* clustering. In Section 4.3, we introduce our algorithm. Section 4.4 contains a comprehensive comparison of our algorithm to classic *k-means* on real data sets. In Section 4.5, we apply the algorithm on image data. Section 4.6 summarizes our findings and offers suggestions for future work.

4.2 Background and Related Work

Since our work draws on the confluence of clustering, wavelets, and anytime algorithms, we provide the necessary background on these areas in this section.

4.2.1 Background on Clustering

One of the most widely used clustering approaches is hierarchical clustering, due to the great visualization power it offers [14]. Hierarchical clustering produces a nested

Table 4.1. An outline of the *k-means* algorithm

Algorithm *k-means*
1. Decide on a value for k.
2. Initialize the k cluster centers (randomly, if necessary).
3. Decide the class memberships of the N objects by assigning them to the nearest cluster center.
4. Reestimate the k cluster centers, by assuming that the memberships found above are correct.
5. If none of the N objects changed membership in the last iteration, exit. Otherwise go to 3.

hierarchy of similar groups of objects, according to a pairwise distance matrix of the objects. One of the advantages of this method is its generality, since the user does not need to provide any parameters such as the number of clusters. However, its application is limited to only small data sets, due to its quadratic (or higher order) computational complexity.

A faster method to perform clustering is *k-means* [2, 18]. The basic intuition behind *k-means* (and a more general class of clustering algorithms known as iterative refinement algorithms) is shown in Table 4.1.

The *k-means* algorithm for N objects has time complexity of $O(kNrD)$ [18], with k the number of clusters specified by the user, r the number of iterations until convergence, and D the dimensionality of the points. The shortcomings of the algorithm are its tendency to favor spherical clusters, and the fact that the knowledge on the number of clusters, k, is required in advance. The latter limitation can be mitigated by placing the algorithm in a loop, and attempting all values of k within a large range. Various statistical tests can then be used to determine which value of k is most parsimonious. Since *k-means* is essentiality a hill-climbing algorithm, it is guaranteed to converge on a local but not necessarily global optimum. In other words, the choices of the initial centers are critical to the quality of results. Nevertheless, in spite of these undesirable properties, for clustering large data sets of time-series, *k-means* is preferable due to its faster running time.

In order to scale the various clustering methods to massive data sets, one can either reduce the number of objects, N, by sampling [2], or reduce the dimensionality of the objects [1, 3, 8, 14, 15, 17, 19, 24, 25]. In the case of time series, the objective is to find a representation at a lower dimensionality that preserves the original information and describes the original shape of the time-series data as closely as possible. Many approaches have been suggested in the literature, including the Discrete Fourier Transform (DFT) [1, 8], Singular Value Decomposition [17], Adaptive Piecewise Constant Approximation [15], Piecewise Aggregate Approximation (PAA) [4, 25], Piecewise Linear Approximation [14], and the Discrete Wavelet Transform (DWT) [3, 19]. While all these approaches have shared the ability to produce a high-quality reduced-dimensionality approximation of time series, wavelets are unique in that their representation of data is intrinsically multiresolution. This property is critical to our proposed algorithm and will be discussed in detail in the next section.

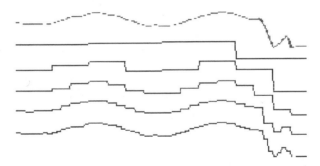

Fig. 4.1. The Haar Wavelet can represent data at different levels of resolution. Above we see a raw time series, with increasing faithful wavelet approximations below

Although we choose the Haar wavelet for this work, the algorithm can generally utilize any wavelet basis. The preference for the Haar wavelet is mainly based on its simplicity and its wide usage in the data mining community.

4.2.2 Background on Wavelets

Wavelets are mathematical functions that represent data or other functions in terms of the averages and differences of a prototype function, called the analyzing or mother wavelet [6]. In this sense, they are similar to the Fourier transform. One fundamental difference is that wavelets are localized in time. In other words, some of the wavelet coefficients represent small, local subsections of the data being studied, as opposed to Fourier coefficients, which always represent global contributions to the data. This property is very useful for multiresolution analysis of data. The first few coefficients contain an overall, coarse approximation of the data; additional coefficients can be perceived as "zooming-in" to areas of high detail. Figure 4.1 illustrates this idea.

The Haar Wavelet decomposition works by averaging two adjacent values on the time series function at a given resolution to form a smoothed, lower dimensional signal, and the resulting coefficients are simply the differences between the values and their averages [3]. The coefficients can also be computed by averaging the differences between each pair of adjacent values. The coefficients are crucial for reconstructing the original sequence, as they store the detailed information lost in the smoothed signal. For example, suppose that we have a time series data T =<2 8 1 5 9 7 2 6>. Table 4.2 shows the decomposition at different resolutions. As a result, the Haar wavelet decomposition is the collection of the coefficients at all resolutions, with the

Table 4.2. Haar wavelet decomposition on time series <2 8 1 5 9 7 2 6>

Resolution	Averages	Differences (coefficients)
8	<2 8 1 5 9 7 2 6>	
4	<5 3 8 4>	< −3 −2 1 −2>
2	<4 6>	<1 2>
1	5	−1

overall average being its first component: $<5 \; -1 \; 1 \; 2 \; -3 \; -2 \; 1 \; -2>$. It is clear to see that the decomposition is completely reversible and the original sequence can be reconstructed from the coefficients. For example, to get the signal of the second level, simply compute $5 \pm (-1) = <4, 6>$.

Recently there has been an explosion of interest in using wavelets for time series data mining. Researchers have introduced several non-Euclidean, wavelet-based distance measures [13, 22]. Chan and Fu [3] have demonstrated that Euclidean distance indexing with wavelets is competitive to Fourier-based techniques [8].

4.2.3 Background on Anytime Algorithms

Anytime algorithms are algorithms that trade execution time for quality of results [11]. In particular, an anytime algorithm always has a best-so-far answer available, and the quality of the answer improves with execution time. The user may examine this answer at any time, and choose to terminate the algorithm, temporarily suspend the algorithm, or allow the algorithm to run to completion.

The usefulness of anytime algorithms for data mining has been extensively documented [2, 20]. Suppose a batch version of an algorithm takes a week to run (not an implausible scenario in data mining massive data sets). It would be highly desirable to implement the algorithm as an anytime algorithm. This would allow a user to examine the best current answer after an hour or so as a "sanity check" of all assumptions and parameters. As a simple example, suppose that the user had accidentally set the value of k to 50 instead of the desired value of 5. Using a batch algorithm, the mistake would not be noted for a week, whereas using an anytime algorithm the mistake could be noted early on and the algorithm restarted with little cost.

The motivating example above could have been eliminated by user diligence! More generally, however, data mining algorithms do require the user to make choices of several parameters, and an anytime implementation of k-means would allow the user to interact with the entire data mining process in a more efficient way.

4.2.4 Related Work

Bradley et al. [2] suggest a generic technique for scaling the k-means clustering algorithms to large databases by attempting to identify regions of the data that are compressible, that must be retained in main memory, and regions that may be discarded. However, the generality of the method contrasts with our algorithm's explicit exploitation of the structure of the data type of interest.

Our work is more similar in spirit to the dynamic time warping similarity search technique introduced by Chu et al. [4]. The authors speed up linear search by examining the time series at increasingly finer levels of approximation.

4.3 Our Approach—the *ik-means* Algorithm

As noted in Section 4.2.1, the complexity of the k-means algorithm is $O(kNrD)$, where D is the dimensionality of data points (or the length of a sequence, as in the case of time series). For a data set consisting of long time-series, the D factor can burden the clustering task significantly. This overhead can be alleviated by reducing the data dimensionality.

Another major drawback of the *k-means* algorithm derives from the fact that the clustering quality is greatly dependant on the choice of initial centers (i.e., line 2 of Table 4.1). As mentioned earlier, the *k-means* algorithm guarantees local, but not necessarily global optimization. Poor choices of the initial centers can degrade the quality of clustering solution and result in longer execution time (See [9] for an excellent discussion of this issue). Our algorithm addresses these two problems associated with *k-means*, in addition to offering the capability of an anytime algorithm, which allows the user to interrupt and terminate the program at any stage.

We propose using the wavelet decomposition to perform clustering at increasingly finer levels of the decomposition, while displaying the gradually refined clustering results periodically to the user. We compute the Haar Wavelet decomposition for all time-series data in the database. The complexity of this transformation is linear to the dimensionality of each object; therefore, the running time is reasonable even for large databases. The process of decomposition can be performed offline, and the time-series data can be stored in the Haar decomposition format, which takes the same amount of space as the original sequence. One important property of the decomposition is that it is a lossless transformation, since the original sequence can always be reconstructed from the decomposition.

Once we compute the Haar decomposition, we perform the *k-means* clustering algorithm, starting at the second level (each object at level i has $2^{(i-1)}$ dimensions) and gradually progress to finer levels. Since the Haar decomposition is completely reversible, we can reconstruct the approximate data from the coefficients at any level and perform clustering on these data. We call the new clustering algorithm i*k-means*, where i stands for "incremental." Figure 4.2 illustrates this idea.

The intuition behind this algorithm originates from the observation that the general shape of a time series sequence can often be approximately captured at a lower resolution. As shown in Figure 4.1, the shape of the time series is well preserved, even at very coarse approximations. Because of this desirable property of wavelets, clustering results typically stabilize at a low resolution.

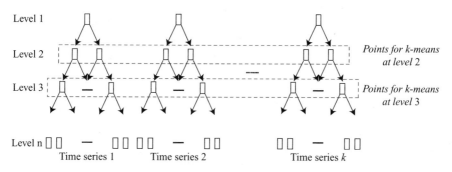

Fig. 4.2. *k-means* is performed on each level on the reconstructed data from the Haar wavelet decomposition, starting with the second level.

Table 4.3. An outline of the i*k-means* algorithm

Algorithm i*k-means*
1. Decide on a value for k.
2. Initialize the k cluster centers (randomly, if necessary).
3. Run the *k-means* algorithm on the level$_i$ representation of the data
4. Use final centers from level$_i$ as initial centers for level$_{i+1}$. This is achieved by projecting the k centers returned by *k-means* algorithm for the 2^i space in the 2^{i+1} space.
5. If none of the N objects changed membership in the last iteration, exit. Otherwise go to 3.

At the end of each level, we obtain clustering results on the approximation data used at the given level. We can therefore use that information to seed the clustering on the subsequent level. In fact, for every level except the starting level (i.e., level 2), which uses random initial centers, the initial centers are selected on the basis of the final centers from the previous level. More specifically, the final centers computed at the end of level i will be used as the initial centers on level $i + 1$. Since the length of the data reconstructed from the Haar decomposition doubles as we progress to the next level, we project the centers computed at the end of level i onto level $i + 1$ by doubling each coordinate of the centers. This way, they match the dimensionality of the points on level $i + 1$. For example, if one of the final centers at the end of level 2 is <0.5, 1.2>, then the initial center used for this cluster on level 3 is <0.5, 0.5, 1.2, 1.2>. This approach mitigates the dilemma associated with the choice of initial centers, which is crucial to the quality of clustering results [9]. It also contributes to the fact that our algorithm often produces better clustering results than the *k-means* algorithm. The pseudocode of the algorithm is provided in Table 4.3.

The algorithm achieves the speedup by doing the vast majority of reassignments (Line 3 in Table 5.1), at the lower resolutions, where the costs of distance calculations are considerably lower. As we gradually progress to finer resolutions, we already start with good initial centers. Therefore, the number of iterations r until convergence will typically be much lower.

The i*k-means* algorithm allows the user to monitor the quality of clustering results as the program executes. The user can interrupt the program at any level, or wait until the execution terminates once it stabilizes. Typically we can consider the process stabilized if the clustering results do not improve for more than two stages. One surprising and highly desirable finding from the experimental results (as shown in the next section) is that even if the program is run to completion (i.e., until the last level, with full resolution), the total execution time is generally less than that of clustering on the raw data.

4.3.1 Experimental Evaluation on Time Series

To show that our approach is superior to the *k-means* algorithm for clustering time series, we performed a series of experiments on publicly available real data sets. For completeness, we ran the i*k-means* algorithm for all levels of approximation, and recorded the cumulative execution time and clustering accuracy at each level. In reality, however, the algorithm stabilizes in early stages and can be terminated much sooner. We compare the results with that of *k-means* on the original data. Since both algorithms start with random initial centers, we execute each algorithm 100 times with different centers. However, for consistency we ensure that for each execution, both algorithms are seeded with the same set of initial centers. After each execution, we compute the error (more details will be provided in Section 4.4.2) and the execution time on the clustering results. We compute and report the averages at the end of each experiment. By taking the average, we achieve better objectiveness than taking the best (minimum), since in reality, we would not have the knowledge of the correct clustering results, or the "oracle," to compare against our results (as in the case with one of our test data sets).

4.3.2 Data Sets and Methodology

We tested on two publicly available, real data sets. The data set cardinalities range from 1,000 to 8,000. The length of each time series has been set to 512 on one data set, and 1024 on the other. Each time series is *z*-normalized to have mean value of 0 and standard deviation of 1.

- **JPL**: This data set consists of readings from various inertial sensors from Space Shuttle mission STS-57. The data are particularly appropriate for our experiments since the use of redundant backup sensors means that some of the data are very highly correlated. In addition, even sensors that measure orthogonal features (i.e., the *X*- and *Y*-axis) may become temporarily correlated during a particular maneuver; for example, a "roll reversal" [7]. Thus, the data have an interesting mixture of dense and sparse clusters. To generate data sets of increasingly larger cardinalities, we extracted time series of length 512, at random starting points of each sequence from the original data pool.
- **Heterogeneous**: This data set is generated from a mixture of 10 real-time series data from the UCR Time Series Data Mining Archive [16]. Figure 4.3 shows the 10 time-series we use as seeds. We produced variations of the original patterns by adding small time warping (2–3% of the series length), and interpolated Gaussian noise. Gaussian noisy peaks are interpolated using splines to create smooth random variations. Figure 4.4 shows how data are generated.

In the Heterogeneous data set, we know that the number of clusters (k) is 10. However, for the JPL data set, we lack this information. Finding k is an open problem for the *k-means* algorithm and is out of scope of this chapter. To determine the optimal k for *k-means*, we attempt different values of k, ranging from 2 to 8. Nonetheless, our algorithm outperforms the *k-means* algorithm regardless of k. In this chapter we show only the results with k equals to 5. Figure 4.5 shows that our algorithm produces the same results as does the hierarchical clustering algorithm, which is generally more costly.

4.3.3 Error of Clustering Results

In this section we compare the clustering quality for the i*k-means* and the classic *k-means* algorithm.

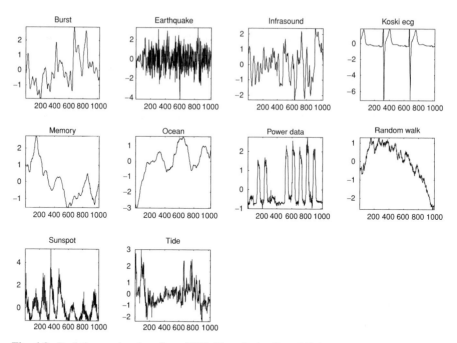

Fig. 4.3. Real-time series data from UCR Time Series Data Mining Archive. We use these time series as seeds to create our heterogeneous data set.

Since we generated the heterogeneous data sets from a set of given time series data, we have the knowledge of correct clustering results in advance. In this case, we can simply compute the clustering accuracy by summing up the number of correctly classified objects for each cluster c and then dividing by the data set cardinality. This is done by the use of a confusion matrix. Note the accuracy computed here is equivalent to "recall," and the error rate is simply $\varepsilon = 1 -$ accuracy.

The error is computed at the end of each level. However, it is worth mentioning that in reality, the correct clustering information would not be available in advance. The incorporation of such known results in our error calculation merely serves the purpose of demonstrating the quality of both algorithms.

For the JPL data set, we do not have prior knowledge of correct clustering information (which conforms more closely to real-life cases). Lacking this information, we cannot use the same evaluation to determine the error.

Since the *k-means* algorithm seeks to optimize the objective function by minimizing the sum of squared intracluster errors, we can evaluate the quality of clustering by using the objective functions. However, since the *ik-means* algorithm involves data with smaller dimensionality except for the last level, we have to compute the objective functions on the raw data, in order to compare with the *k-means* algorithm. We show that the objective functions obtained from the *ik-means* algorithm are better than those from the *k-means* algorithm. The results are consistent with the work of [5], in which the authors show that dimensionality reduction reduces the chances of

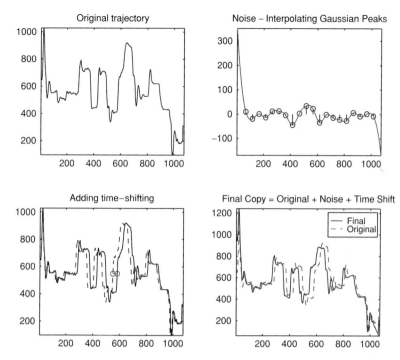

Fig. 4.4. Generation of variations on the heterogeneous data. We produced variation of the original patterns by adding small time shifting (2–3% of the series length), and interpolated Gaussian noise. Gaussian noisy peaks are interpolated using splines to create smooth random variations.

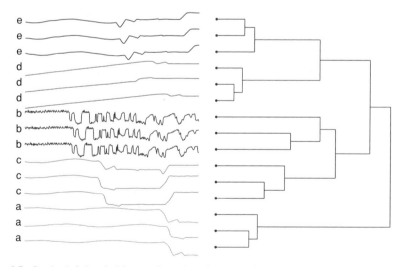

Fig. 4.5. On the left-hand side, we show three instances from each cluster discovered by the *ik-means* algorithm. We can visually verify that our algorithm produces intuitive results. On the right-hand side, we show that hierarchical clustering (using average linkage) discovers the exact same clusters. However, hierarchical clustering is more costly than our algorithm.

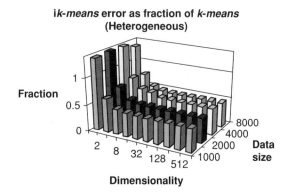

Fig. 4.6. Error of i*k-means* algorithm on the heterogeneous data set, presented as fraction of the error from the *k-means* algorithm. Our algorithm results in smaller error than the *k-means* after the second stage (i.e., four dimensions), and stabilizes typically after the third stage (i.e., eight dimensions).

the algorithm being trapped in a local minimum. Furthermore, even with the additional step of computing the objective functions from the original data, the i*k-means* algorithm still takes less time to execute than the *k-means* algorithm.

In Figures 4.6 and 4.7, we show the errors/objective functions from the i*k-means* algorithm as a fraction of those obtained from the *k-means* algorithm. As we can see from the plots, our algorithm stabilizes at early stages and consistently results in smaller error than the classic *k-means* algorithm.

4.3.4 Running Time

In Figures 4.8 and 4.9, we present the cumulative running time for each level on the i*k-means* algorithm as a fraction to the *k-means* algorithm. The cumulative running

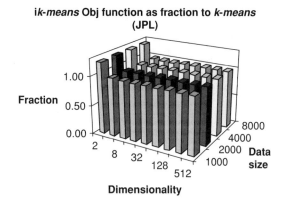

Fig. 4.7. Objective functions of i*k-means* algorithm on the JPL data set, presented as fraction of error from the *k-means* algorithm. Again, our algorithm results in smaller objective functions (i.e., better clustering results) than the *k-means*, and stabilizes typically after the second stage (i.e., four dimensions).

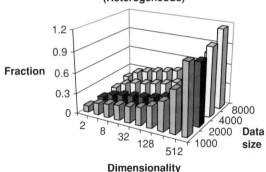

ik-means cumulative time as fraction of k-means (Heterogeneous)

Fig. 4.8. Cumulative running time for the heterogeneous data set. Our algorithm typically cuts the running time by half as it does not need to run through all levels to retrieve the best results.

time for any level i is the total running time from the starting level (level 2) to level i. In most cases, even if the ik-means algorithm is run to completion, the total running time is still less than that of the k-means algorithm. We attribute this improvement to the good choices of initial centers for successive levels after the starting level, since they result in very few iterations until convergence. Nevertheless, we have already shown in the previous section that the ik-means algorithm finds the best result in relatively early stage and does not need to run through all levels.

4.4 ik-means Algorithm vs. k-means Algorithm

In this section (Figs. 4.10 and 4.11), rather than showing the error/objective function on each level, as in Section 4.4.2, we present only the error/objective function returned by the ik-means algorithm when it stabilizes or, in the case of JPL data set, outperforms

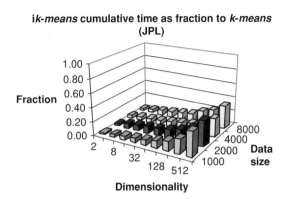

ik-means cumulative time as fraction to k-means (JPL)

Fig. 4.9. Cumulative running time for the JPL data set. Our algorithm typically takes only 30% of time.

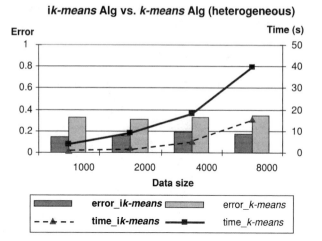

Fig. 4.10. The i*k-means* algorithm is highly competitive with the *k-means* algorithm. The errors and execution time are significantly smaller.

the *k-means* algorithm in terms of the objective function. We also present the time taken for the i*k-means* algorithm to stabilize. We compare the results with those of the *k-means* algorithm. From the figures we can observe that our algorithm achieves better clustering accuracy at significantly faster response time.

Figure 4.12 shows the average level where the i*k-means* algorithm stabilizes or, in the case of JPL, outperforms the *k-means* algorithm in terms of objective function. Since the length of the time series data is 1024 in the heterogeneous data set, there are 11 levels. Note that the JPL data set has only 10 levels since the length of the time series data is only 512. We skip level 1, in which the data have only one dimension

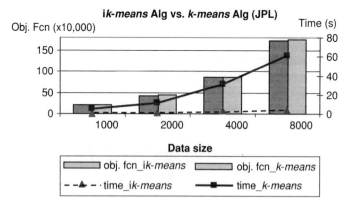

Fig. 4.11. i*k-means* vs. *k-means* algorithms in terms of objective function and running time for JPL data set. Our algorithm outperforms the *k-means* algorithm. The running time remains small for all data sizes because the algorithm terminates at very early stages.

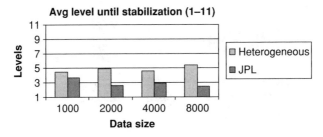

Fig. 4.12. Average level until stabilization. The algorithm generally stabilizes between level 3 and level 6 for heterogeneous data set, and between level 2 and 4 for the JPL data set.

(the average of the time series) and is the same for all sequences, since the data have been normalized (zero mean). Each level i has $2^{(i-1)}$ dimensions. From the plot we can see that our algorithm generally stabilizes at levels 3–6 for the heterogeneous data set and at levels 2–4 for the JPL data set. In other words, the *ik-means* algorithm operates on data with a maximum dimensionality of 32 and 8, respectively, rather than 1024 and 512.

4.5 Application to Images

In this section we provide preliminary results regarding the applicability of our approach for images.

Image data can be represented as "time" series by combining different descriptors into a long series. Although the notion of "time" does not exist here, a series formed by the descriptors has similar characteristics as time series, namely, high dimensionality and strong autocorrelation.

The simplest and perhaps the most intuitive descriptor for images is the color. For each image, a color histogram of length 256 can be extracted from each of the RGB components. These color histograms are then concatenated to form a series of length 786. This series serves as a "signature" of the image and summarizes the image in chromatic space. To demonstrate that this representation of images is indeed appropriate, we performed a simple test run on a small data set. The data set consists of three categories of images from the Corel image database: diving, fireworks, and tigers. Each category contains 20 images. The clustering results are shown in Figure 4.13.

As it shows, most images were clustered correctly regardless of the variety presented within each category, except for 2: the last two images in the Fireworks cluster belong to the Tigers cluster. A closer look at the images explains why this happens. These two misclustered Tiger images have relatively dark background compared to the rest of images in the same category, and since we used color histograms, it is understandable that these two images were mistaken as members of the Fireworks cluster.

The clustering results show that representing images using merely the color histogram is generally very effective, as it is invariant to rotation and the exact contents

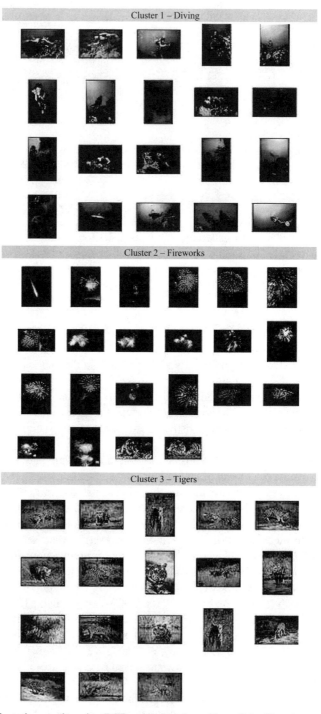

Fig. 4.13. Clustering results using RGB color descriptor. Two of the Tiger images were mis-clustered in the fireworks cluster due to similar color decomposition.

of the images. However, the misclustering also implies that the color descriptor alone might not be good enough to capture all the essential characteristics of an image and could be limited for images with similar color decomposition.

To mitigate this shortcoming, more descriptors such as texture can be used in addition to the color descriptor. In general, the RGB components are highly correlated and do not necessarily coincide with the human visual system. We validate this observation empirically, since our experiments show that a different chromatic model, HSV, generally results in clusters of better quality.

For texture, we apply Gabor-wavelet filters [23] at various scales and orientations, which results in an additional vector of size 256. The color and texture information are concatenated and the final vector of size 1024 is treated as a time series. Therefore, the method that we proposed in the previous sections can be applied unaltered to images. Notice that this representation can very easily facilitate a weighted scheme, where according to the desired matching criteria we may favor the color or the texture component.

Figure 4.14 shows how the time series is formed from an image. A well-known observation in the image retrieval community is that the use of large histograms suffers from the "curse of dimensionality" [10]. Our method is therefore particularly applicable in this scenario, since the wavelet (or any other) decomposition can help reduce the dimensionality effectively. It should also be noted that the manipulation of

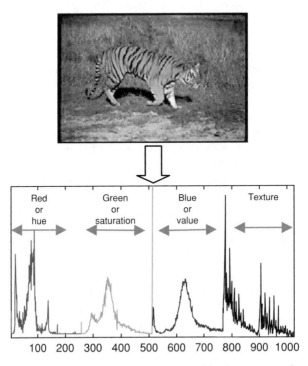

Fig. 4.14. An example of the image vector that is extracted for the purposes of our experiments.

Table 4.4. Clustering error and running time averaged over 100 runs. Our method is even more accurate than hierarchical clustering, which requires almost an order of magnitude more time.

	Error			Time (s)		
	Hier.	*k-means*	*ik-means*	Hier.	*k-means*	*ik-means*
RGB	**0.31**	0.37	0.37	50.7	11.18	4.94
HSV	0.36	**0.26**	**0.26**	49.8	11.12	**6.82**
HSV+ TEXTR	0.24	0.25	**0.19**	55.5	11.33	3.14
HSV+ TEXTR+ good centers	N/A	0.22	**0.17**	N/A	8.26	**2.89**

the image features as time series is perfectly valid. The characteristics of "smoothness" and autocorrelation of the time series are evident here, since adjacent bins in the histograms have very similar values.

We demonstrate the usefulness of our approach on two scenarios.

4.5.1 Clustering Corel Image Data sets

First, we perform clustering on a subset of images taken from the Corel database. The data set consists of six clusters, each containing 100 images. The clusters represent diverse topics: diving, fireworks, tigers, architecture, snow, and stained glass, some of which have been used in the test-run experiment. This is by no means a large data set; however, it can very well serve as an indicator of the speed and the accuracy of the *ik-means* algorithm. In our case studies, we utilize two descriptors, color and texture, and compare two color representations: RGB and HSV. We compare the algorithm with *k-means*, and with hierarchical clustering using Ward's linkage method. Our approach achieves the highest recall rate and is also the fastest method. Since the performance of *k-means* greatly depends on the initial choice of centers, we also provided "good" initial centers by picking one image randomly from each cluster. Even in this scenario our algorithm was significantly faster and more accurate. The results, shown in Table 4.4, are generated using the L1 distance metric. Although we also tested on the Euclidean distance, using L1 metric generally results in better accuracy for our test cases.

The advantages of our algorithm are more evident with large, disk-based data sets. To demonstrate, we generate a larger data set from the one we used in Table 4.4, using the same methodology as described in Figure 4.4. For each image in the data set, we generate 99 copies with slight variations, resulting in a total of 60,000 images (including the original images in the data set). Each image is represented as a time series of length 1024; therefore, it would require almost 500 MB of memory to store the entire data set. Clustering on large data sets is resource-demanding for *k-means*, and one single run of *k-means* could take more than 100 iterations to converge. In addition, although it is common for computers today to be equipped with 1 GB or more memory, we cannot count on every user to have the sufficient amount of memory installed. We also need to take into consideration other memory usage required by the intermediate steps of *k-means*. Therefore, we will simulate the disk-based clustering environment by assuming a memory buffer of a fixed size that is smaller than the size of our data set.

Running *k-means* on disk-based data sets, however, would require multiple disk scans, which is undesirable. With i*k-means*, such concerns are mitigated. We know from the previous experimental results that i*k-means* stabilizes on early stages; therefore, in most cases we do not need to operate on the fine resolutions. In other words, we will read in the data at the highest resolution allowed, given the amount of memory available, and if the algorithm stabilizes on these partial-Haar coefficients, then we can stop without having to retrieve the remaining data from the disk.

For simplicity, we limit our buffer size to 150 MB, which allows us to read in as much as 256 coefficients (a 4:1 reduction for time series length of 1024). With limited memory resources, we would need to use the disk-based *k-means* algorithm. However, to make it simple for *k-means*, we run *k-means* on the smoothed data with a reduction ratio of 4:1 (i.e., equivalent to the reconstructed time series at the finest resolution of the partial-Haar). Although performing data smoothing prior to *k-means* aligns more closely to the underlying philosophy of i*k-means* and is a logical thing to do, it lacks the flexibility of i*k-means* in terms of data reduction. Overall, i*k-means* still offers the advantages associated with being multi-resolutional.

In fact, our experiment shows that i*k-means* stabilizes before running on the finest resolution of the partial-Haar coefficients. Since the data set was generated from six clusters, intuitively, we could assume that an image has the same cluster label as the "seed" image that generated it, and that we could evaluate clustering accuracy by comparing the class labels to the correct labels. However, it is also possible that in the data generation process, too much noise is introduced such that the generated image should not belong in the same cluster as the seed image. Though unlikely, as we control the amount of noise to be added such as limiting time shifting to 2–3% of the length of time series data, to avoid any bias, we arbitrarily increase the number of clusters to 10. In this scenario, we compare the projected objective functions instead, as this is the most intuitive way to evaluate *k-means* clustering. In both scenarios, i*k-means* achieves higher accuracy than *k-means*. With $k = 6$, i*k-means* outperforms *k-means* starting at the third level, using only four coefficients which, naturally, also results in shorter running time. With $k = 10$, however, i*k-means* outperforms *k-means* at a later level (level 6), thus resulting in longer running time.

4.5.2 Clustering Google Images

For the second paradigm we used a real-world example from the image search feature of Google. All online image search engines gather information based only on key words. Therefore, the image query results can be from very diverse disciplines and have very different content. For example, if one searches for "bass," the result would be

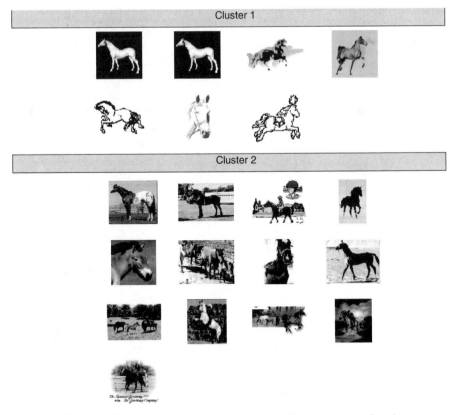

Fig. 4.15. Clustering results on the image query "horse" posed at Google

a mixture of images about "fish" and "musical instruments." Although in some cases we might be able to avoid the ambiguity by supplying more descriptive key words, it is not always trivial to find the right key words that describe exactly the images we have in mind. In this specific case, a postfiltering of the matches using texture features can create separate clusters of images, and as a consequence, lead to a more intuitive presentation of the results. In order for such a postfiltering step to become a reality, it is obvious that one must utilize an extremely lightweight algorithm. We posed several queries on Google and we grouped the results into clusters. Here we present representative results for the word "horse." The first 20 images are retrieved. The images are passed on to our algorithm and clustered into two groups. Figure 4.15 presents the results. We can see that there is an obvious separation between the hand-drawn pictures and the photographic images. These experiments suggest that online image search could be augmented by a clustering step, in the spirit of the well-known "Scatter/Gather" framework [12].

The results could be improved by using relevance feedback. In addition, compact histogram representations, as well as the use of more robust distance functions such as the dLog distance proposed in [21], could further boost the performance for the proposed algorithm.

4.6 Conclusions and Future Work

We have presented an approach to perform incremental clustering at various resolutions, using the Haar wavelet transform. Using *k-means* as our clustering algorithm, we reuse the final centers at the end of each resolution as the initial centers for the next level of approximation. This approach mitigates the dilemma associated with the choices of initial centers for *k-means* and significantly improves the execution time and clustering quality. Our experimental results indicate that this approach yields faster execution time than the traditional *k-means* approach, in addition to improving the clustering quality of the algorithm. The anytime algorithm stabilizes at very early stages, eliminating the needs to operate on high dimensionality. In addition, the anytime algorithm allows the user to terminate the program at any stage.

Since image histograms extracted from colors and textures can be suitably treated as time series, we further demonstrate the efficacy of our algorithm on the image data. In future work, we plan to examine the possibility of reusing the results (i.e., objective functions that determine the quality of clustering results) from the previous stages to eliminate the need to recompute all the distances.

Acknowledgments

We thank B. S. Manjunath and Shawn Newsam for providing the Gabor filter code.

References

1. Agrawal R, Faloutsos C, Swami A. Efficient similarity search in sequence databases. In: *Proceedings of the 4th Int'l Conference on Foundations of Data Organization and Algorithms*; 1993 Oct 13–15; Chicago, IL; pp. 69–84.
2. Bradley P, Fayyad U, Reina C. Scaling clustering algorithms to large databases. In: *Proceedings of the 4th Int'l Conference on Knowledge Discovery and Data Mining*; 1998 Aug 27–31; New York, NY, pp. 9–15.
3. Chan K, Fu AW. Efficient time series matching by wavelets. In: *Proceedings of the 15th IEEE Int'l Conference on Data Engineering*; 1999 Mar 23–26; Sydney, Australia; pp. 126–133.
4. Chu S, Keogh E, Hart D, Pazzani M. Iterative deepening dynamic time warping for time series. In: *Proceedings of the 2nd SIAM International Conference on Data Mining*; 2002 Apr 11–13; Arlington, VA.
5. Ding C, He X, Zha H, Simon H. Adaptive dimension reduction for clustering high dimensional data. In: *Proceedings of the 2nd IEEE International Conference on Data Mining*; 2002 Dec 9–12; Maebashi, Japan, pp. 147–154.

6. Daubechies I. Ten Lectures on Wavelets. Number 61 in CBMS-NSF regional conference series in applied mathematics, Society for Industrial and Applied Mathematics; 1992; Philadelphia.

7. Dumoulin J. NSTS 1988 News Reference Manual. http://www.fas.org/spp/civil/sts/

8. Faloutsos C, Ranganathan M, Manolopoulos Y. Fast subsequence matching in time-series databases. In: *Proceedings of the ACM SIGMOD Int'l Conference on Management of Data*; 1994 May 25–27; Minneapolis, pp. 419–429.

9. Fayyad U, Reina C, Bradley P. Initialization of iterative refinement clustering algorithms. In: *Proceedings of the 4th International Conference on Knowledge Discovery and Data Mining*; 1998 Aug 27–31; New York, NY; pp. 194–198.

10. Gibson S, Harvey R. Analyzing and simplifying histograms using scale-trees. In: *Proceedings of the 11th Int'l Conference on Image Analysis and Processing*; 2001 Sept 26–28; Palermo, Italy.

11. Grass J, Zilberstein S. Anytime algorithm development tools. *Sigart Artificial Intelligence* 1996;7:2.

12. Hearst MA, Pedersen JO. Reexamining the cluster hypothesis: Scatter/gatter on retrieval results. In: *Proceedings of the 19th Annual International ACM SIGIR Conference on Research and Development in Information Retrieval*; 1996 Aug 18–22; Zurich, Switzerland.

13. Huhtala Y, Kärkkäinen J, Toivonen H. Mining for similarities in aligned time series using wavelets. Data Mining and Knowledge Discovery: Theory, Tools, and Technology. *SPIE Proceedings Series* 1999; 3695:150–160. Orlando, FL.

14. Keogh E, Pazzani M. An enhanced representation of time series which allows fast and accurate classification, clustering and relevance feedback. In: *Proceedings of the 4th Int'l Conference on Knowledge Discovery and Data Mining*; 1998 Aug 27–31; New York, NY; pp. 239–241.

15. Keogh E, Chakrabarti K, Pazzani M, Mehrotra S. Locally adaptive dimensionality reduction for indexing large time series databases. In: *Proceedings of ACM SIGMOD Conference on Management of Data*. 2001 May 21–24; Santa Barbara, CA; pp. 151–162.

16. Keogh E, Folias T. The UCR Time Series Data Mining Archive (http://www.cs.ucr.edu/~eamonn/TSDMA/index.html). 2002.

17. Korn F, Jagadish H, Faloutsos C. Efficiently supporting ad hoc queries in large datasets of time sequences. In: *Proceedings of the ACM SIGMOD Int'l Conference on Management of Data*; 1997 May 13–15; Tucson, AZ, pp. 289–300.

18. McQueen J. Some methods for classification and analysis of multivariate observation. In: Le Cam L, Neyman J, eds. *5th Berkeley Symp. Math. Stat. Prob.* 1967; 281–297.

19. Popivanov I, Miller RJ. Similarity search over time series data using wavelets. In: *Proceedings of the 18th Int'l Conference on Data Engineering*; 2002 Feb 26-Mar 1; San Jose, CA, pp. 212–221.

20. Smyth P, Wolpert D. Anytime exploratory data analysis for massive data sets. In: *Proceedings of the 3rd Int'l Conference on Knowledge Discovery and Data Mining*; 1997 Aug 14–17; Newport Beach, CA, pp. 54–60.

21. Stehling RO, Nascimento MA, Falcão AX. A compact and efficient image retrieval approach based on border/interior pixel classification. In: *Proceedings of the ACM Intl. Conf. on Information and Knowledge Management*; 2002 Nov 4–9; McLean, VA.

22. Struzik Z, Siebes A. The Haar wavelet transform in the time series similarity paradigm. In: *Proceedings of Principles of Data Mining and Knowledge Discovery*, 3rd European Conference; 1999 Sept 15–18; Prague, Czech Republic; pp. 12–22.

23. Wu P, Manjunath BS, Newsam S, Shin HD. A texture descriptor for browsing and similarity retrieval. *Journal of Signal Processing: Image Communication* 2000;16:1–2;33–43.
24. Wu Y, Agrawal D, El Abbadi A. A comparison of DFT and DWT based similarity search in time-series databases. In: *Proceedings of the 9th ACM CIKM Int'l Conference on Information and Knowledge Management*. 2000 Nov 6–11; McLean, VA; pp. 488–495.
25. Yi B, Faloutsos C. Fast time sequence indexing for arbitrary lp norms. In: *Proceedings of the 26th Int'l Conference on Very Large Databases*; 2000 Sept 10–14; Cairo, Egypt; pp. 385–394.

5. Mining Rare and Frequent Events in Multi-camera Surveillance Video

Valery A. Petrushin

Summary. This chapter describes a method for unsupervised classification of events in multicamera indoors surveillance video. This research is a part of the Multiple Sensor Indoor Surveillance (MSIS) project, which uses 32 webcams that observe an office environment. The research was inspired by the following practical problem: how automatically classify and visualize a 24-h long video captured by 32 cameras? The self-organizing map (SOM) approach is applied to event data for clustering and visualization. One-level and two-level SOM clustering are used. A tool for browsing results allows exploring units of the SOM maps at different levels of hierarchy, clusters of units, and distances between units in 3D space. A special technique has been developed to visualize rare events.

5.1 Introduction

The rapidly increasing number of video cameras in public places and business facilities, such as airports, streets, highways, parking lots, shopping malls, hospitals, hotels, and governmental buildings can create many opportunities for public safety and business applications. Such applications range from surveillance for threat detection in airports, schools and shopping malls, monitoring highways, parking lots and streets, to customer tracking in a bank or in a store for improving product displays and preventing thefts, to detecting unusual events in a hospital, and monitoring elderly people at home, etc. These applications require the ability automatically detecting and classifying events by analyzing video or imagery data.

In spite of that video surveillance has been in use for decades, the development of systems that can automatically detect and classify events is an active research area. Many papers have been published in recent years. In most of them specific classifiers are developed that allow recognizing objects such as people and vehicles and tracking them [1–3] or recognizing relationships between objects (e.g., a person standing at an ATM machine) and actions (e.g., a person picks up a cup) [4]. The others propose general approaches for event identification using clustering. In [5] the authors segment raw surveillance video into sequences of frames that have motion, count the proportion of foreground pixels for segments of various lengths, and use a multilevel hierarchical clustering to group the segments. The authors also propose a measure of abnormality for a segment that is a relative difference between average distance for elements of the cluster and average distance from the sequence to its nearest neighbors. The weaknesses of the approach are as follows.

- Segments of higher motion often are subsequences of segments of lower average motion and when they are clustered the subsequences of the same event belong to different clusters.
- Location and direction of movement of the objects are not taken into account.
- The other features, such as color, texture, and shape, which could be useful for distinguishing events, are not taken into account.

The authors of [6] describe an approach that uses a 2D foreground pixels' histogram and color histogram as features for each frame. The features are mapped into 500 feature prototypes using the vector quantization technique. A surveillance video is represented by a number of short (4 s) overlapping video segments. The relationship among video segments and their features and among features themselves is represented by a graph in which edges connect the segments to features and features to features. The weights on the edges reflect how many times each feature occurred in each video segment, and similarity among features. To visualize the graph, it is embedded in a 3D space using the spectral graph method. To categorize the video segments, the authors use the k-means clustering on the video segments' projections. The larger clusters are defined as usual events, but small and more isolated clusters as unusual events. A new video segment can be classified by embedding it into common space and applying k-nearest neighbor classifier. The advantages of this approach are the following:

- Taking into account similarity among features.
- Attractive visualization of results.

But the disadvantages are

- High computational complexity of the graph embedding method.
- Dependence of the results on the length of video segments.

Developing techniques for visualization of large amount of data always attracted attention of data mining researchers. Visualization is an indispensable part of the data exploration process. Finding efficient algorithms for event detection and summarization, skimming and browsing large video and audio databases are the major topics of multimedia data mining [7, 8]. Many visualization techniques have been developed in traditional data mining. They use clustering that follows by a mapping into 2D or 3D space. For example, using the principal component analysis the data mapped into principal component space and then visualized using two or three first components. Another well-known and widely used approach is Self-Organizing Maps (SOM) or Kohonen Neural Networks [9]. This approach has been applied for analysis and visualization of variety of economical, financial, scientific, and manufacturing data sets [10]. From the viewpoint of our research the most interesting application is the PicSOM, which is a content-based interactive image retrieval system [11]. It clusters images using separately color, texture, and shape features. A user chooses what kind of features he would like to use and picks up a set of images that are similar to his query. The system uses SOM maps to select new images and presents them back to the user. The feature SOM maps highlight the areas on the map that correspond to the features of the set of currently selected images. The interaction continues until the user reaches his goal.

Our research described below is devoted to creating a method for unsupervised classification of events in multicamera indoors surveillance video and visualization of results. It is a part of the Multiple Sensor Indoor Surveillance project that is described in the next section. Then we describe sequentially our data collection and preprocessing procedure, one- and two-level clustering using SOM, techniques for detecting rare events, an approach to classification of new events using Gaussian mixture models (GMM) that are derived from SOM map, and a tool for visualization and browsing results. Finally, we summarize the results and speculate on the future work.

5.2 Multiple Sensor Indoor Surveillance Project

This research is a part of the Multiple Sensor Indoor Surveillance (MSIS) project. The backbone of the project consists of 32 AXIS-2100 webcams, a PTZ camera with infrared mode, a fingerprint reader, and an infrared badge ID system that has 91 readers attached to the ceiling. All this equipment is sensing an office floor for Accenture Technology Labs. The webcams and infrared badge system cover two entrances, seven laboratories and demonstration rooms, two meeting rooms, four major hallways, four open-space cube areas, two discussion areas, and an elevator waiting hall. Some areas overlap with up to four cameras. The total area covered is about 18,000 ft^2 (1,670 m^2). The fingerprint reader is installed at the entrance and allows matching an employee with his or her visual representation. The backbone architecture also includes several computers, with each computer receiving signals from 3–4 webcams, detecting "events" and recording the images for that event in JPEG format. The event is defined as any movement in the camera's field of view. The signal sampling frequency is not stable and on average is about 3 frames per second. The computer also creates an event record in an SQL database. Events detected by the infrared badge ID system and the results of face recognition using PTZ cameras go to the other database. The event databases serve as a common repository for both people who are doing manual search of events and automatic analysis.

The objectives of the MSIS project are to

- Create a realistic multisensor indoor surveillance environment;
- Create an around-the-clock working surveillance system that accumulates data in a database for three consecutive days and has a GUI for search and browsing; and
- Use this surveillance system as a base for developing more advanced event analysis algorithms, such as people recognition and tracking, using collaborating agents, and domain knowledge.

The following analyses and prototypes have been developed or are planned to be developed in the nearest future:

- Searching and browsing of the Event Repository database using a Web browser.
- Creating an event classification and clustering system.
- Counting how many people are on the floor.
- Creating a people localization system that is based on evidence from multiple sensors and domain knowledge (see Chapter 21 in this book for details).
- Creating an awareness map that shows a person's location and what he or she is doing at any given moment.
- Creating a real-time people tracking system that gives an optimal view of a person based on prediction of the person's behavior.
- Creating a system that recognizes people at a particular location and interacts with them via voice messaging.

The below-described research was inspired by the following practical problem: how automatically classify and visualize a 24-h video captured by 32 cameras?

First we implemented a Web-based tool that allows users searching and browsing the Event Repository by specifying the time interval and a set of cameras of interest. The tool's output consists of a sequence of events sorted by time or by camera and time. Each event is represented by a key frame and has links to the event's sequence of frames. Using the tool, a user can quickly sort out events for a time interval that is as short as 1–2 h, but can be overloaded with a large number of events that occurred during 24 h, which counts from 300 to 800 events per camera. The tool does not give the user a "big picture" and is useless for searching for rare events. These reasons motivated our research for unsupervised classification of events.

5.3 Data Collection and Preprocessing

Our raw data are JPEG images of size 640 by 480 pixels that are captured by AXIS-2100 webcams at the rate 2–6 Hz. Each image has a time stamp in seconds passed from the midnight of the day under consideration. To synchronize images' time stamps taken by different computers, we used an atomic clock program to set up time on each computer. The background subtraction algorithm is applied to each image to extract foreground pixels. We use two approaches for background modeling—an adaptive single frame selection and estimating median value for each pixel using a pool of recent images. After subtracting the background, morphological operations are applied to remove noise. Then the following features are extracted from the image:

- Motion features that characterize the foreground pixels' distribution (64 values). The foreground pixels' distribution is calculated on an 8-by-8 grid, and the value for each cell of the grid is the number of foreground pixels in the cell divided by the cell's area.
- Color histogram (8 bins) of the foreground pixels in the RGB color space ($3 * 8 = 24$ values).

Then the above data are integrated by tick and by event. The *tick* is a time interval which it is set up to 1 s in our case. The notion of tick and its value is important

Fig. 5.1. Summary frame for an event.

because we deal with multiple nonsynchronized cameras with overlapping fields of view. Ticks allow loosely—up to the tick—synchronizing cameras' data. They also allow regularizing frame time series taken with varying sampling rates. The data integration by tick and event consists of averaging motion and color data. For visual representation of a tick or an event, a "summary" frame is created. It accumulates all foreground pixels of all images from the tick/event into one image. The summary frames serve as key frames for representing ticks/events. Figure 5.1 gives an example of a summary frame of an event.

Before presenting details of our approach for estimating an event boundaries, let us consider what kind of events we can expect to find in an indoor office environment. A camera can watch a hallway, a meeting room, a working space such as cubicles or laboratories, a recreational area such as a coffee room, or a multipurpose area that is used differently at different time of the day.

Let us assume that we are using a percentage of foreground pixels F in the image as an integral measure of motion. If the camera watches a hallway, then most events present people walking along the hallway, getting in and out of offices, or standing and talking to each other. Most events last for seconds and some for several minutes. In this case the plot of F over time looks as number of peaks that represent short events and some trapezoidal "bumps" that correspond to longer events (Figure 5.2a). In Figures 5.2 and 5.3 the x-axis presents time in seconds and y-axis presents the average percentage of foreground pixels (F-measure) during a tick. Some bumps can have peaks that correspond to combinations of transient and long-term events. If a camera watches a meeting room, then we have long periods of time when the room is empty ($F = 0$) that interchange with periods when a meeting is in process. The latter has a trapezoidal F-plot with a long base and some volatility that corresponds to

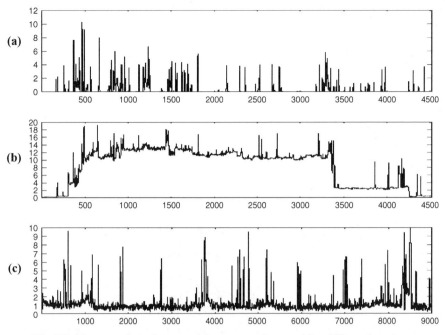

Fig. 5.2. Foreground pixels patterns for cameras that watching different locations.

people movement during the meeting and some small peaks that correspond to events when participants arriving and leaving the room (Figure 5.2b). In case of a recreational area camera, the events are typically longer than for a hallway but much shorter than for a meeting room camera. They correspond to events when people getting into the area for drinking coffee, having lunch, reading, talking on their mobile phones, or talking to each other.

If a camera watches a busy working area such as cubicles or laboratories, then we have such events as people arriving at and leaving their working places, sitting down and standing up, moving and communicating with each other. The F-plot for such camera never goes to zero at working hours and looks like a long volatile meeting (Figure 5.2c).

Having watched F-plots for several cameras, we came to the conclusion that, first, F-measure can be used for event boundaries estimation, and, second, the notion of event is a relative one. For example, on the one hand, the whole meeting can be considered as an event, but, on the other hand, it may be considered as a sequence of events, such as, people arriving for the meeting, participating in the meeting, and leaving the room. Each of these events can be divided into shorter events down to a noticeable movement. These observations encouraged us to use the wavelet decomposition of F-signal to detect events at different levels. We used the wavelet decomposition of levels from 2 to 5 with Haar wavelet for calculating approximation and details. Then we applied a threshold to approximation signal that slightly exceeds the noise level to find the boundaries of major events such as meetings (mega-events),

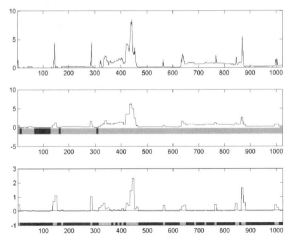

Fig. 5.3. Event boundaries detection using Haar wavelets.

and another threshold to the absolute value of highest detail signal to find internal events (micro-events). Figure 5.3 presents the results of event detection for a signal of length 1024 s using wavelet decomposition of level 3. The top plot presents the original F-signal; the middle plot is its level 3 approximation, and the bottom plot presents its level 3 details. The boundaries of macro- and micro-events presented in the lower parts of the middle and bottom plots correspondingly. The comparison of automatic extraction of micro-events boundaries with manual extraction gives a high agreement coefficient (75–90%) but people tend to detect less events, but the events are more meaningful. The boundaries of micro events are used for data integration.

After integrating data by tick and by event, we have two sets of data for each camera. The tick-level data set record consists of the following elements: tick value from the beginning of the day, names of the first and last frames of the tick, and integrated motion and color data. The event-level data set record consists of a unique event identification number, first and last tick values, names of the first and last frames of the event, and integrated motion and color data. We used both of these data sets for unsupervised classification and visualization presented below.

5.4 Unsupervised Learning Using Self-Organizing Maps

We applied the self-organizing map approach to tick/event data for clustering and visualization. We use 2D rectangular maps with hexagonal elements and Gaussian neighborhood kernels.

5.4.1 One-Level Clustering Using SOM

In one-level clustering approach we use both motion and color data to build the map. For creating maps we used the SOM Toolbox for MATLAB developed at the Helsinki

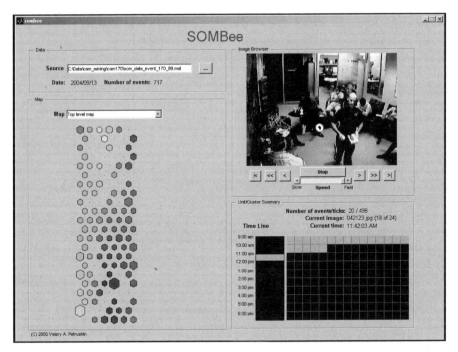

Fig. 5.4. Visualization tool displays a self-organizing map for event data.

University of Technology [12]. The toolbox allows displaying maps in many ways varying the units' sizes and colors. In our experiments we found that the size of maps for tick data can reach 1400 units (70 by 20) and for event data—about 250 units (25 by 10). Figure 5.4 presents the map for event data of a camera that observes a multipurpose area. It presents 717 events on 22-by-6 lattice (132 units). The unit's size reflects the number of events attracted by this unit (the number of hits). The unit's size is calculated using the formula (5.1).

$$s(u) = 0.5 \cdot (1 + \frac{hits(u)}{\max_u hits(u)}) \qquad (5.1)$$

where $s(u)$ is the size of unit u, and $hits(u)$ is the number of data points attracted by the unit u. It means that if a unit has at least one hit then its size is not less than 0.5, and the size of the unit is proportional to the number of hits. The units with zero hits are not displayed. The units' colors show the topological similarity of the prototype vectors.

A visualization tool that is described below allows exploring the contents of each unit. However, the number of units can be large that makes unit browsing very laborious. Next step is to apply the k-means algorithm for clustering map units (prototype vectors) [13]. As the number of units is about one order smaller than the number of raw data, we can run the k-means algorithm with different number of intended clusters, sort the results according to their Davies–Bouldin indexes [14], and allow users browsing clusters of units. The Davies–Bouldin index of a partitioning $P = (C_1, C_2, \ldots, C_L)$ is specified by the formula (5.2),

$$DBI(P) = \frac{1}{L} \sum_{i=1}^{L} \max_{i \neq j} \left\{ \frac{S(C_i) + S(C_j)}{D(C_i, C_j)} \right\}$$ (5.2)

where $C_i, i = \overline{1, L}$ are clusters, $S(C) = \dfrac{\sum_{k=1}^{N} \|x_k - c\|}{N}$ is the within-cluster distance of the cluster C, which has elements $x_k, k = \overline{1, N}$ and the centroid $c = \frac{1}{N} \sum_{k=1}^{N} x_k$, and $D(C_i, C_j) = \|c_i - c_j\|$ is the distance between clusters' centroids (between-cluster distance).

We do k-means clustering of units for the number of clusters from 2 to 15 for event data and from 2 to 20 for tick data. Then the visualization tool allows the user to pick up a clustering from a menu where each clustering is shown with its Davies–Bouldin index. Figure 5.5 presents the clustered map for the event data of the same camera and a legend that shows the number of events in each cluster. The centroid unit of each cluster is presented in complementary color. When the number of clusters is large, some clusters may consists of several transitional units that have no raw data (events or ticks) associated with them. The visualization tool allows browsing events or ticks by cluster.

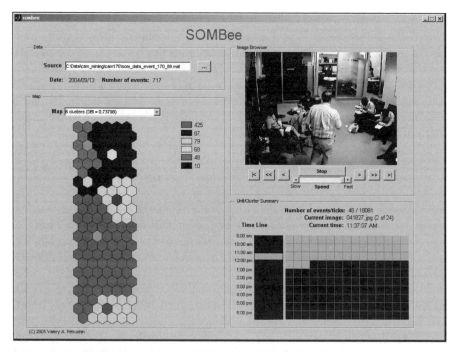

Fig. 5.5. Visualization tool displays the results of clustering of SOM units for event data.

5.4.2 Two-Level Clustering Using SOM

Our raw data have two kinds of features: motion and color features. In two-level clustering we explore these features consequentially. On the top level, only motion features are used to create the main map. Then we use k-means clustering for the map units as we described above. After this, for each obtained cluster we build a SOM map using color features. Such separation of features allows differentiating more precisely spatial events and easier detecting unusual events. In indoor environment, where most of moving objects are people, who change their clothes every day, the variance of color features is higher than the variance of motion features. Separating motion features allows collecting them over longer periods and creating more robust classifiers. To create a classifier, we accumulated motion data during a week, built an SOM map, and applied k-means clustering to its units. The whole SOM map M can be considered as a Gaussian Mixture Model (GMM) [15] with the probability density function represented by (5.3).

$$f(x|M) = \sum_{i=1}^{N} w_i \cdot f_i(x \mid \lambda_i) \text{ and } \sum_{i=1}^{N} w_i = 1 \qquad (5.3)$$

where $f(\cdot \mid \lambda_k)$ is the probability density function for model λ_k, $\lambda_k = \mathcal{N}(\mu_k, \Sigma_k)$ is a Gaussian model for k-th unit with mean μ_k and covariance matrix Σ_k, N is the number of units in the map. It is often assumed that the covariance matrix is diagonal.

Each unit of the map has a Gaussian kernel associated with it and a weight w_i, which is proportional to the number of data points attracted by the unit (the number of hits for this unit). The log-likelihood of a data point x to belongs to the map is estimated using Equation (5.4).

$$\log L(x \mid M) = \log \left(\sum_{i=1}^{N} w_i \cdot f(x \mid \lambda_i) \right) \qquad (5.4)$$

On the other hand, for a partitioning $P = (C_1, C_2, \ldots, C_L)$ each cluster can be viewed as a GMM with the log-likelihood function represented by (5.5).

$$\log L(x \mid C_k) = \log \left(\sum_{i \in C_k} w_i \cdot f(x|\lambda_i) \right) \qquad (5.5)$$

A new piece of data can be classified by calculating likelihood using GMM associated with each cluster and assigning the new data to the cluster with maximal likelihood (5.6). The same procedure can be applied to color features. Combining motion-based classifiers on top level with color-based classifiers on the second level, we obtain a hierarchical classifier.

$$C_{k^*} = \arg\max_{C_k} \{\log L(x|C_k)\} \qquad (5.6)$$

5.4.3 Finding Unusual Events

In some cases, finding unusual events is of special interest. But what we should count as an unusual event is often uncertain and requires additional consideration. An event can be unusual because it happened at unusual time or at unusual place or had unusual appearance. For example, finding a person working in his office at midnight is an unusual event, but the same event happened at noon is not. A person standing on a table would be considered as an unusual event in most office environments. Many people wearing clothes of the same color would be considered as an unusual event unless everybody is wearing a uniform. Everybody agrees that an unusual event is a rare event at given time and space point. But a rare event may not be an unusual one. For example, a person sitting in his office on weekend could be a rare but not surprising event.

After thoughtful deliberation, we decided to use computers for finding rare and frequent events leaving humans to decide how unusual or usual they are. In our research we distinguish between *local* rare/frequent events—these are events that happened during one day—and *global* rare/frequent events—those that happened during longer period of time and the surveillance system accumulated data about these events. We also distinguish between events that happened during regular working hours and out of them.

For finding local rare events, we are using an automatic procedure that indicates areas of the SOM map that contain potential rare events. This procedure assigns 1 of 13 labels for each unit of SOM map based on the number of hits attracted by the unit and the distances from the unit to its neighbors using Equation (5.7),

$$R_{nm} = \{u : hits(u) \leq H_n \cap \min_{v \in Nb(u)} \{D(u, v)\} \geq D_m\} \tag{5.7}$$

where $H_n = \{5, 10, 20, 40, {}^*\}$is the list of hit levels (* stands for "any"), $D_m = \{0.9, 0.75, 0.5\} \cdot \max_{u,v \in M} (u, v)$ is list of distance levels, $Nb(u)$ is a set of neighbors of the unit u, and $hits(u)$ is the number of hits of unit u.

For visualizing local rare events, we use two approaches. The first is to display the SOM map with a particular color assigned to each R_{nm} class. The color spans over different shades of red–orange–yellow, depending on the n–m combination. The map allows the user identify and explore areas that have high potential to have rare events. The second approach is a 3D surface that shows distances between units of the SOM map and indicates how many data points (hits) belong to each unit using markers with sizes that are proportional to the number of hits. Figure 5.6 shows the 3D visualization for event data. A user can rotate the axes searching manually for "highlanders"—small unit markers that are located on the top of peaks or for "isolated villages" which are sets of small unit markers that are located in closed "mountain valleys". Using the combination of (semi-)automatic and manual approaches allows the user finding promptly local rare events.

For detecting global rare events, the following procedure is proposed. First, the GMM classifier is applied to a new event/tick motion data. If it gives a high probability for a small cluster, then the system declares that a rare event of particular type is found.

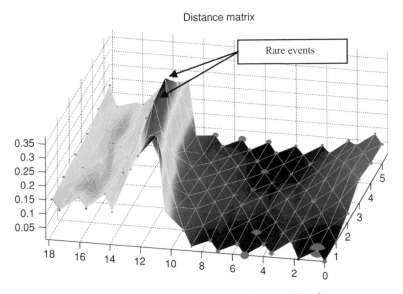

Fig. 5.6. Visualization of distances between units for searching for rare events.

If the classifier gets low probabilities for all clusters then the system indicates that it is a new (and rare) spatial event. Such events are accumulated and can be used for building a new version of GMM classifier. In case when the event belongs to a moderate or frequent event cluster, the system applies the corresponding color-based GMM classifier to detect rare or new events regarding their color features.

5.5 Visualization Tool

The above-described techniques have been integrated into an event visualization tool. Figures 5.4 and 5.5 show snapshots of the tool. The tool's GUI consists of four panels—Data, Map, Image Browsers, and Unit/Cluster Summary. Using the Data panel, the user selects and loads data. Currently each camera has a separate file for its tick and event data. The file contains preprocessed raw data and SOM data for chosen SOM architecture—one- or two-level SOM map. The user selects the desired map from a menu. The map is displayed in the Map panel or in a separate window.

The Map panel displays the current SOM map, which could be the top-level map that shows color coded units with unit sizes reflecting the number of hits, a cluster map of different number of clusters with color-coded units, or a map for indicating potential rare events. The 3D surface that presents distances between units and the number of hits in each unit is displayed in a separate window (see Figure 5.6). The user can rotate the 3D surface for hunting for local rare events.

When the user clicks on a unit or a cluster of units on the SOM map, the contents of the unit or cluster is displayed in the Unit/Cluster Summary panel. This panel presents information about the current item (unit or cluster). It shows the number of events and/or ticks in the current item, the name of image displayed in the Image Browser panel and its time. It also has two plots. The left bar plot shows the distribution of event or tick data in time. The right plot shows all data (ticks or events) that are related to the current item. A small square corresponds to each piece of data. The color of the square indicates the time interval that the piece of data belongs to. When the user clicks on a square, the corresponding summary frame is displayed in the Image Browser panel.

The Image Browser panel displays the visual information related to the current selected tick or event in the Unit/Cluster Summary panel. Using the browser's control buttons, the user can watch the first or last frame of the tick/event, go through the tick/event frame by frame forward and backward, and watch a slide show going in both directions. The speed of the slide show is controlled by the speed slider. Clicking on the image brings the current frame in full size into a separate window allowing the user to see details. This feature proved to be very useful for exploring busy summary images.

5.6 Summary

We described an approach to unsupervised classification and visualization of surveillance data captured by multiple cameras. The approach is based on self-organizing maps and enables us to efficiently search for rare and frequent events. It also allows us creating robust classifiers to identify incoming events in real time. A pilot experiment with several volunteers who used the visualization tool for browsing events and searching for rare events showed both its high efficiency and positive feedback about its GUI.

Although we applied this approach for indoor surveillance in office environment, we believe that it is applicable in the larger context of creating robust and scalable systems that can classify and visualize data for any surveillance environment. The real bottleneck of the approach is not creating SOM maps (it takes just several minutes to create a map for 24-h tick data with 86400 records), but feature extraction and data aggregation.

In the future we plan to extend our approach to visualize data of a set of cameras with overlapping fields of view, embed the GMM-based classifier into visualization tool for detecting global rare events, and improve the graphical user interface.

References

1. Kanade T, Collins RT, Lipton AJ. Advances in Cooperative Multi-Sensor Video Surveillance. In: *Proc. DARPA Image Understanding Workshop*, Morgan Kaufmann, November 1998; pp. 3–24.
2. Siebel NT, Maybank S. Fusion of Multiple Tracking Algorithms for Robust People Tracking. In: *Proc. 7th European Conference on Computer Vision (ECCV 2002)*, Copenhagen, Denmark, May 2002; Vol. IV, pp. 373–387.

3. Krumm J, Harris S, Meyers B, Brumitt B, Hale M, Shafer S. Multi-camera Multi-person Tracking for EasyLiving. In: *Proc. 3rd IEEE International Workshop on Visual Surveillance*, Dublin, Ireland, July 1, 2000.
4. Ayers D, Shah M. Monitoring Human Behavior from Video taken in an Office Environment. Image and Vision Computing, October 1, 2001;19(12):833–846.
5. Oh J-H, Lee J-K, Kote S, Bandi B. Multimedia Data Mining Framework for Raw Video Sequences. In: Zaiane OR, Simoff SJ, Djeraba Ch. (Eds.) *Mining Multimedia and Complex Data*. Lecture Notes in Artificial Intelligence. Springer, 2003, Vol. 2797, pp. 18–35.
6. Zhong H, Shi J. Finding (un)usual events in video. *Tech. Report* CMU-RI-TR-03-05, 2003.
7. Amir, A., Srinivasan, S., and Ponceleon, D. Efficient video browsing using multiple synchronized views. In: A. Rosenfeld, D. Doermann, and D. DeMenthon (Eds.) *Video Mining*, Kluwer Academic Publishers, 2003, Vol. 1–30.
8. Gong Y. Audio and visual content summarization of a video program. In: Furht B, Marques O. (Eds.) *Handbook of Video Databases*. Design and Applications, CRC Press, 2004; 245–277.
9. Kohonen T. *Self-Organizing Maps*. Springer-Verlag, 1997.
10. Oja E, Kaski S. (Eds.) *Kohonen Maps*. Elsevier, 1999.
11. Laaksonen JT, Koskela JM, Laakso SP, Oja E. PicSOM—content-based image retrieval with self-organizing maps. *Pattern Recognition Letters*, 2000;21(13/14):1199–1207.
12. Vesanto J, Himberg J, Alhoniemi E, Parhankangas J. *SOM Toolbox for Matlab 5*, Helsinki University of Technology, Report A57, 2000.
13. Vesanto J, Alhoniemi I. Clustering of self-organizing maps. *IEEE Trans. on Neural Network*, 2000;11(3):586–600.
14. Davies DL, Bouldin DW. A cluster separation measure. *IEEE Trans. on Pattern Analysis and Machine Intelligence*, 1979; PAMI-1:224–227.
15. McLachlan G, Peel D. *Finite Mixture Models*, Wiley, 2000.

6. Density-Based Data Analysis and Similarity Search

Stefan Brecheisen, Hans-Peter Kriegel, Peer Kröger, Martin Pfeifle, Matthias Schubert, and Arthur Zimek

Summary. Similarity search in database systems is becoming an increasingly important task in modern application domains such as multimedia, molecular biology, medical imaging, computer-aided engineering, marketing and purchasing assistance as well as many others. Furthermore, the feature transformations and distance measures used in similarity search build the foundation of sophisticated data analysis and mining techniques. In this chapter, we show how visualizing cluster hierarchies describing a database of objects can aid the user in the time-consuming task to find similar objects and discover interesting patterns. We present related work and explain its shortcomings that led to the development of our new methods. On the basis of reachability plots, we introduce methods for visually exploring a data set in multiple representations and comparing multiple similarity models. Furthermore, we present a new method for automatically extracting cluster hierarchies from a given reachability plot that allows a user to browse the database for similarity search. We integrated our new method in a prototype that serves two purposes, namely visual data analysis and a new way of object retrieval called navigational similarity search.

6.1 Introduction

In recent years, an increasing number of database applications have emerged for which efficient and effective similarity search and data analysis is substantial. Important application areas are multimedia, medical imaging, molecular biology, computer-aided engineering, marketing and purchasing assistance, etc. [1–8]. In these applications, there usually exist various feature representations and similarity models that can be used to retrieve similar data objects or derive interesting patterns from a given database. Hierarchical clustering was shown to be effective for evaluating similarity models [9,10]. Especially, the reachability plot generated by *OPTICS* [11] is suitable for assessing the quality of similarity models and compare the meaning of different representations to each other. To further extract patterns and allow new methods of similarity search, cluster extraction algorithms can extract cluster hierarchies representing a concrete categorization of all data objects.

In this chapter, we present methods that employ hierarchical clustering and visual data mining techniques to fulfill various tasks for comparing and evaluating distance models and feature extractions methods. Furthermore, we introduce an algorithm for automatically detecting hierarchical clusters and use this hierarchy for navigational similarity search. In ordinary similarity search systems, a user is usually obliged to provide an example query object to which the retrieved database objects should be similar. In contrast, navigational similarity search allows a user to browse the database using the extracted cluster hierarchy to navigate between groups of similar objects. In order to evaluate our ideas, we developed a research prototype. Its basic functionality is to display the cluster structure of a given data set and to allow navigational similarity search. Furthermore, we integrated two components called VICO and CLUSS. *VICO* (*VI*sually *C*onnected *O*bject Orderings) is a tool for evaluating and comparing feature representations and similarity models. The idea of VICO is to compare multiple reachabilty plots of one and the same data set. *CLUSS* (*CLU*ster Hierarchies for *S*imilarity *S*earch) is an alternative hierarchical clustering algorithm that was especially developed to generate cluster hierarchies being well suited for navigational similarity search.

To sum up, the main topics of this chapter are as follows:

- We describe methods for evaluating data representations and similarity models. Furthermore, we sketch possibilities to visually compare these representations and models.
- We present an alternative approach to the retrieval of similar objects, called navigational similarity search. Unlike conventional similarity queries, the user does not need to provide a query object but can interactively browse the data set.
- We introduce a new cluster recognition algorithm for the reachability plots generated by OPTICS. This algorithm generalizes all the other known cluster recognition algorithms for reachability plots. Although our new algorithm does not need a sophisticated and extensive parameter setting, it outperforms the other cluster recognition algorithms w.r.t. quality and number of recognized clusters and subclusters. The derived cluster hierarchy enables us to employ OPTICS for navigational similarity search.
- We introduce an alternative method for generating cluster hierarchies that provides a more intuitive access to the database for navigational similarity search. The advantage of this method is that each of the derived clusters is described by a set of well-selected representative objects giving the user a better impression of the objects contained in the cluster.

The remainder of the chapter is organized as follows: We briefly introduce the clustering algorithm OPTICS in Section 6.2. In Section 6.3, we present the main application areas of our new methods for data analysis and navigational similarity search. Section 6.4 introduces a novel algorithm for extracting cluster hierarchies, together with an experimental evaluation. An alternative way to derive cluster hierarchies for navigational similarity search is presented in Section 6.5. The chapter concludes in Section 6.6 with a short summary.

6.2 Hierarchical Clustering

In the following, we will briefly review the hierarchical density-based clustering algorithm OPTICS, which is the foundation of the majority of the methods described in this chapter.

The key idea of density-based clustering is that for each object o of a cluster the neighborhood $\mathcal{N}_\varepsilon(o)$ of a given radius ε has to contain at least a minimum number *MinPts* of objects. Using the density-based hierarchical clustering algorithm OPTICS yields several advantages due to the following reasons:

- OPTICS is—in contrast to most other algorithms—relatively insensitive to its two input parameters, ε and *MinPts*. The authors in [11] state that the input parameters just have to be large enough to produce good results.
- OPTICS is a hierarchical clustering method which yields more information about the cluster structure than a method that computes a flat partitioning of the data (e.g., k-means [12]).
- There exists a very efficient variant of the OPTICS algorithm, which is based on a sophisticated data compression technique called "Data Bubbles" [13], where we have to trade only very little quality of the clustering result for a great increase in performance.
- There exists an efficient incremental version [14] of the OPTICS algorithm.

OPTICS emerges from the algorithm DBSCAN [15], which computes a flat partitioning of the data. The clustering notion underlying DBSCAN is that of density-connected sets (cf. [15] for more details). It is assumed that there is a metric distance function on the objects in the database (e.g., one of the L_p-norms for a database of feature vectors).

In contrast to DBSCAN, OPTICS does not assign cluster memberships but computes an *ordering* in which the objects are processed and additionally generates the information, which would be used by an extended DBSCAN algorithm to assign cluster memberships. This information consists of only two values for each object, the *core distance* and the *reachability distance*.

Definition 1 (core distance). *Let $o \in DB$, MinPts $\in \mathbb{N}$, $\varepsilon \in \mathbb{R}$, and MinPts-dist(o) be the distance from o to its MinPts-nearest neighbor. The* core distance *of o w.r.t. ε and MinPts is defined as follows:*

$$Core\text{-}Dist(o) := \begin{cases} \infty & \text{if } |\mathcal{N}_\varepsilon(o)| < MinPts \\ MinPts\text{-}dist(o) & \text{otherwise.} \end{cases}$$

Definition 2 (reachability distance). *Let $o \in DB$, MinPts $\in \mathbb{N}$ and $\varepsilon \in \mathbb{R}$. The* reachability distance *of o w.r.t. ε and MinPts from an object $p \in DB$ is defined as follows:*

$$Reach\text{-}Dist(p, o) := \max\left(Core\text{-}Dist(p), distance(p, o)\right).$$

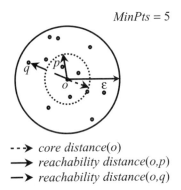

Fig. 6.1. Illustration of core level and reachability distance.

Figure 6.1 illustrates both concepts: The reachability distance of p from o equals to the core distance of o and the reachability distance of q from o equals to the distance between q and o.

The original output of OPTICS is an ordering of the objects, a so called *cluster ordering*:

Definition 3 (cluster ordering). *Let $MinPts \in \mathbb{N}$, $\varepsilon \in \mathbb{R}$, and CO be a totally ordered permutation of the database objects. Each $o \in D$ has additional attributes $o.P$, $o.C$ and $o.R$, where $o.P \in \{1, \ldots, |CO|\}$ symbolizes the position of o in CO. We call CO a cluster ordering w.r.t. ε and MinPts if the following three conditions hold:*

(1) $\forall p \in CO : p.C = Core\text{-}Dist(p)$
(2) $\forall o, x, y \in CO :$
    $o.P < x.P \wedge x.P < y.P \Rightarrow Reach\text{-}Dist(o, x) \leq Reach\text{-}Dist(o, y)$
(3) $\forall p, o \in CO : R(p) = \min\{Reach\text{-}Dist(o, p) \mid o.P < p.P\}$, *where* $\min \emptyset = \infty$.

Intuitively, Condition (2) states that the order is built on selecting at each position i in CO that object o having the minimum reachability to any object before i. $o.C$ symbolizes the core distance of an object o in CO whereas $o.R$ is the reachability distance assigned to object o during the generation of CO. We call $o.R$ the *reachablity* of object o throughout the chapter. Note that $o.R$ is only well-defined in the context of a cluster ordering.

The cluster structure can be visualized through so-called reachability plots, which are 2D plots generated as follows: the clustered objects are ordered along the x-axis according to the cluster ordering computed by OPTICS and the reachabilities assigned to each object are plotted along the abscissa. An example reachability plot is depicted in Figure 6.2. Valleys in this plot indicate clusters: objects having a small reachability value are closer and thus more similar to their predecessor objects than objects having a higher reachability value.

The reachability plot generated by OPTICS can be cut at any level ε_{cut} parallel to the abscissa. It represents the density-based clusters according to the density threshold ε_{cut}: A consecutive subsequence of objects having a smaller reachability value than

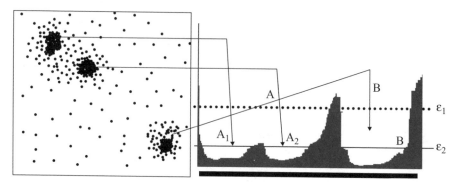

Fig. 6.2. Reachability plot (right) computed by OPTICS for a sample 2-D data set (left).

ε_{cut} belongs to the same cluster. An example is presented in Figure 6.2: For a cut at the level ε_1 we find two clusters denoted as A and B. Compared to this clustering, a cut at level ε_2 would yield three clusters. The cluster A is split into two smaller clusters denoted by A_1 and A_2 and cluster B decreased its size. Usually, for evaluation purposes, a good value for ε_{cut} would yield as many clusters as possible.

6.3 Application Ranges

The introduced methods combine techniques from hierarchical clustering and data visualization for two main purposes, data analysis and similarity search. In the following, we will propose several applications in both areas for which our introduced methods are very useful.

6.3.1 Data Analysis

The data analysis part of our prototype is called VICO. It allows a user to cluster data objects in varying representations and using varying similarity models. The main purpose of VICO is to compare different feature spaces that describe the same set of data. For this comparison, VICO relies on the interactive visual exploration of reachability plots. Therefore, VICO displays any available view on a set of data objects as adjacent reachability plots and allows comparisons between the local neighborhoods of each object. Figure 6.3 displays the main window of VICO. The left side of the window contains a so-called tree control that contains a subtree for each view of the data set. In each subtree, the keys are ordered w.r.t. the cluster order of the corresponding view. The tree control allows a user to directly search for individual data objects. In addition to the object keys displayed in the tree control, VICO displays the reachability plot of each view of the data set.

Since valleys in the reachability plot represent clusters in the underlying representation, the user gets an instant impression of the richness of the cluster structure in each representation. However, to explore the relationships between the representations, we

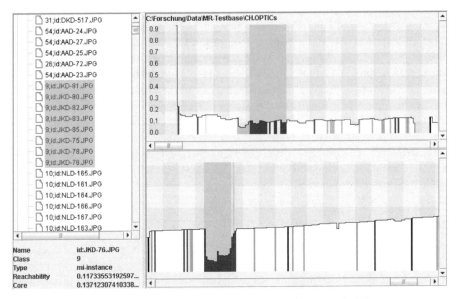

Fig. 6.3. VICO displaying OPTICS plots of multirepresented data.

need to find out whether objects that are clustered in one representation are also similar in the other representation. To achieve this type of comparison, VICO allows the user to select any data object in any reachability plot or the tree control. By selecting a set of objects in one view, the objects are highlighted in any other view as well. For example, if the user looks at the reachability plot in one representation and selects a cluster within this plot, the corresponding object keys are highlighted in the tree control and identify the objects that are contained in the cluster. Let us note that it is possible to visualize the selected objects as well, as long as there is a viewable object representation. In addition to the information about which objects are clustered together, the set of objects is highlighted in the reachability plots of the other representations as well. Thus, we can easily decide whether the objects in one representation are placed within a cluster in another representation as well or if they are spread among different clusters or are part of the noise. If there exist contradicting reachability plots for the same set of data objects, it is interesting to know which of these representations is closer to the desired notion of similarity. Thus, VICO allows the user to label data objects w.r.t. predefined class values. The different class values for the objects are displayed by different colors in the reachability plot. Thus, a reachability plot of a data space that matches the user's notion of similarity should display clusters containing objects of the same color. Figure 6.3 displays a comparison of two feature spaces for an image data set. Each image is labelled w.r.t. the displayed motive.

Another feature of VICO is the ability to handle multiinstance objects. In a multiinstance representation, one data object is given by a set of separated feature objects. An example are CAD parts that can be decomposed to a set of spatial primitives, which can be represented by a single feature vector. This way, the complete CAD part is represented by a set of feature vectors, which can be compared by a variety of distance functions. To find out which instances are responsible for clusters of multiinstance objects, VICO allows us to cluster the instances without considering the multiinstance object they belong to. Comparing this instance plot with the plot derived on the complete multiinstance objects allows us to analyze which instance clusters are typical for the clusters on the complete multiinstance object. Thus, for multiinstance settings, VICO highlights all instances belonging to some selected multiinstance object. To conclude, VICO allows even nonexpert users to evaluate similarity models, directly compares different similarity models to each other, and helps exploring the connection between multiinstance distance functions and the underlying distance metrics in the feature space of instances.

6.3.2 Navigational Similarity Search

For similarity search, the idea of our system is to provide navigational access to a database. This way, it is possible to browse a database of objects in an explorer-like application, instead of posing separated similarity queries. A main problem of these similarity queries is that a user always has to provide a query object to which the retrieved objects should be as similar as possible. However, in many application scenarios finding a query object is not easy. For example, an engineer querying a CAD database would have to specify the 3D shape of a CAD part before finding similar parts. Sketching more complicated parts might cause a considerable effort. Thus, similarity queries are often quite time-consuming. The alternative idea of navigational similarity search offers an easier way to retrieve the desired objects. The idea is to use an extracted hierarchy of clusters as a navigation tree. The root represents the complete data set. Each node in the tree represents a subcluster consisting of a subset of data objects for which the elements are more similar to each other than in the father cluster. The more specialized a cluster is the more similar its members are to each other. To describe the members of a cluster, one or more representative objects are displayed. Browsing starts at a general level. Afterward, the user follows the path in the cluster hierarchy for which the displayed representatives resemble the image in the user's mind in a best possible way. The browsing terminates when the user reaches a cluster for which the contained objects match the user's expectation. Another advantage of this approach is that the cluster usually contains the complete set of similar objects. For similarity queries, the number of retrieved results either can be specified in the case of kNN queries or is implicitly controlled by a specified query range. However, both methods usually do not retrieve all objects that could be considered as similar.

6.4 Cluster Recognition for OPTICS

In this section, we address the task of automatically extracting clusters from a reachability plot. Enhancing the resulting cluster hierarchy with representative objects for each extracted cluster allows us to use the result of OPTICS for navigational similarity search. After a brief discussion of recent work in that area, we propose a new approach for hierarchical cluster recognition based on reachability plots called *Gradient Clustering*.

6.4.1 Recent Work

To the best of our knowledge, there are only two methods for automatic cluster extraction from hierarchical representations such as reachability plots or dendrograms—both are also based on reachability plots. Since clusters are represented as valleys (or dents) in the reachability plot, the task of automatic cluster extraction is to identify significant valleys.

The first approach proposed in [11] called ξ-clustering is based on the steepness of the valleys in the reachability plot. The steepness is defined by means of an input parameter ξ. The method suffers from the fact that this parameter is difficult to understand and hard to determine. Rather small variations of the value ξ often lead to drastic changes of the resulting clustering hierarchy. As a consequence, this method is unsuitable for the purpose of automatic cluster extraction.

The second approach was proposed by Sander et al. [16]. The authors describe an algorithm called Tree Clustering that automatically extracts a hierarchical clustering from a reachability plot and computes a cluster tree. It is based on the idea that *significant* local maxima in the reachability plot separate clusters. Two parameters are introduced to decide whether a local maximum is significant: The first parameter specifies the minimum cluster size; that is, how many objects must be located between two significant local maxima. The second parameter specifies the ratio between the reachability of a significant local maximum m and the average reachabilities of the regions to the left and to the right of m. The authors in [16] propose to set the minimum cluster size to 0.5% of the data set size and the second parameter to 0.75. They empirically show that this default setting approximately represents the requirements of a typical user.

Although the second method is rather suitable for automatic cluster extraction from reachability plots, it has one major drawback. Many real-world data sets consist of narrowing clusters that is, clusters each consisting of exactly one smaller subcluster (cf. Fig. 6.4).

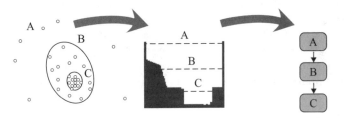

Fig. 6.4. Sample narrowing clusters: data space (left); reachability plot (middle); cluster hierarchy (right).

Since the Tree Clustering algorithm runs through a list of all local maxima (sorted in descending order of reachability) and decides at each local maximum m, whether m is significant to split the objects to the left of m and to the right of m into two clusters, the algorithm cannot detect such narrowing clusters. These clusters cannot be split by a significant maximum. Figure 6.4 illustrates this fact. The narrowing cluster A consists of one cluster B, which is itself narrowing consisting of one cluster C (the clusters are indicated by dashed lines). The Tree Clustering algorithm will find only cluster A since there are no local maxima to split clusters B and C. The ξ-clustering will detect only one of the clusters A, B, or C depending on the parameter ξ but also fails to detect the cluster hierarchy.

A new cluster recognition algorithm should meet the following requirements:

- It should detect all kinds of subclusters, including narrowing subclusters.
- It should create a clustering structure which is close to the one which an experienced user would manually extract from a given reachability plot.
- It should allow an easy integration into the OPTICS algorithm. We do not want to apply an additional cluster recognition step after the OPTICS run is completed. In contrast, the hierarchical clustering structure should be created on-the-fly during the OPTICS run without causing any noteworthy additional cost.
- It should be integrable into the incremental version of OPTICS [14], as most of the discussed application ranges benefit from such an incremental version.

6.4.2 Gradient Clustering

In this section, we introduce our new *Gradient Clustering* algorithm that fulfills all of the above-mentioned requirements. The idea behind the new cluster extraction algorithm is based on the concept of *inflexion points*. During the OPTICS run, we decide for each point added to the result set, that is, the reachability plot, whether it is an inflexion point or not. If it is an inflexion point we might be at the start or at the end of a new subcluster. We store the possible starting points of the subclusters in a list, called *startPts*. This stack consists of pairs $(o.P, o.R)$. The Gradient Clustering algorithm can easily be intergrated into OPTICS and is described in full detail, after we have formally introduced the new concept of inflexion points.

In the following, we assume that CO is a cluster ordering as defined in Definition 3. We call two objects $o_1, o_2 \in CO$ adjacent in CO if $o_2.P = o_1.P + 1$. Let us recall that $o.R$ is the reachability of $o \in CO$ assigned by OPTICS while generating CO. For any two objects $o_1, o_2 \in CO$ adjacent in the cluster ordering, we can determine the gradient of the reachability values $o_1.R$ and $o_2.R$. The gradient can easily be modelled as a 2D vector where the y-axis measures the reachability values ($o_1.R$ and $o_2.R$) in the ordering, and the x-axis represent the ordering of the objects. If we assume that each object in the ordering is separated by width w, the gradient of o_1 and o_2 is the vector

$$\vec{g}(o_1, o_2) = \begin{pmatrix} w \\ o_2.R - o_1.R \end{pmatrix}.$$

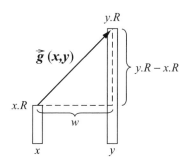

Fig. 6.5. Gradient vector $\vec{g}(x, y)$ of two objects x and y adjacent in the cluster ordering.

An example for a gradient vector of two objects x and y adjacent in a cluster ordering is depicted in Figure 6.5.

Intuitively, an inflexion point should be an object in the cluster ordering where the gradient of the reachabilities changes significantly. This significant change indicates a starting or an end point of a cluster.

Let $x, y, z \in CO$ be adjacent, that is,

$$x.P + 1 = y.P = z.P - 1.$$

We can now measure the difference between the gradient vectors $\vec{g}(x, y)$ and $\vec{g}(y, z)$ by computing the cosine of the angle between the vectors $\vec{g}(x, y)$ and $\vec{g}(z, y)$ ($= -\vec{g}(y, z)$). The cosine of this angle is equal to -1 if the angle is $180°$; that is, the vectors have the same direction. On the other hand, if the gradient vectors differ a lot, the angle between them will be clearly smaller than $180°$ and thus the cosine will be significantly greater than -1. This observation motivates the concepts of inflexion index and inflexion points:

Definition 4 (inflexion index). *Let CO be a cluster ordering and $x, y, z \in CO$ be objects adjacent in CO. The* inflexion index *of y, denoted by $II(y)$, is defined as the cosine of the angle between the gradient vector of x, y ($\vec{g}(x, y)$) and the gradient vector of z, y ($\vec{g}(z, y)$), formally:*

$$II(y) = \cos \varphi_{(\vec{g}(x,y),\vec{g}(z,y))} = \frac{-w^2 + (y.R - x.R)(y.R - z.R)}{\|\vec{g}(x, y)\| \, \|\vec{g}(z, y)\|},$$

where $\|\vec{v}\| := \sqrt{v_1^2 + v_2^2}$ is the length of the vector $\vec{v}$.

Definition 5 (inflexion point). *Let CO be a cluster ordering and $x, y, z \in CO$ be objects adjacent in CO and let $t \in \mathbb{R}$. Object y is an* inflexion point *iff*

$$II(y) > t.$$

The concept of inflexion points is suitable to detect objects in CO which are interesting for extracting clusters.

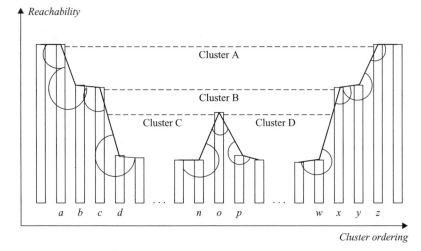

Fig. 6.6. Illustration of inflexion points measuring the angle between the gradient vectors of objects adjacent in the ordering.

Definition 6 (gradient determinant). *Let CO be a cluster ordering and $x, y, z \in CO$ be objects adjacent in CO. The* gradient determinant *of the gradients $\vec{g}(x, y)$ and $\vec{g}(y, z)$ is defined as*

$$gd(\vec{g}(x, y), \vec{g}(z, y)) := \begin{vmatrix} w & -w \\ x.R - y.R & z.R - y.R \end{vmatrix}$$

If x, y, z are clear from the context, we use the short form $gd(y)$ for the gradient determinant $gd(\vec{g}(x, y), \vec{g}(y, z))$.

The sign of $gd(y)$ indicates whether $y \in CO$ is a starting point or an end point of a cluster. In fact, we can distinguish the following two cases, which are visualized in Figure 6.6:

- $II(y) > t$ and $gd(y) > 0$:
  Object y is either a starting point of a cluster (e.g., object a in Fig. 6.6) or the first object outside of a cluster (e.g., object z in Fig. 6.6).
- $II(y) > t$ and $gd(y) < 0$:
  Object y is either an end point of a cluster (e.g., object n in Fig. 6.6) or the second object inside a cluster (e.g., object b in Fig. 6.6).

Let us note that a local maximum $m \in CO$ which is the cluster separation point in [16] is a special form of the first case (i.e., $II(m) > t$ and $gd(m) > 0$).

The threshold t is independent from the absolut reachability values of the objects in CO. The influence of t is also very comprehensible because if we know which values for the angles between gradients are interesting, we can easily compute t. For example, if we are interested in angles $<120°$ and $>240°$ we set $t = \cos 120° = -0.5$.

```
algorithm gradient_clustering(ClusterOrdering CO, Integer MinPts, Real t)
  startPts := emptyStack;
  setOfClusters := emptySet;
  currCluster := emptySet;
  o := CO.getFirst();                          // first object is a starting point
  startPts.push(o);

  WHILE o.hasNext() DO                          // for all remaining objects
    o := o.next;
    IF o.hasNext() THEN
      IF II(o) > t THEN                         // inflexion point
        IF gd(o) > 0 THEN
          IF currCluster.size() >= MinPts THEN
            setOfClusters.add(currCluster);
          ENDIF
          currCluster := emptySet;
          IF startPts.top().R <= o.R THEN
            startPts.pop();
          ENDIF
          WHILE startPts.top().R < o.R DO
            setOfClusters.add(set of objects from startPts.top() to last end point);
            startPts.pop();
          ENDDO
          setOfClusters.add(set of objects from startPts.top() to last end point);
          IF o.next.R < o.R THEN               // o is a starting point
            startPts.push(o);
          ENDIF
        ELSE
          IF o.next.R > o.R THEN               // o is an end point
            currCluster := set of objects from startPts.top() to o;
          ENDIF
        ENDIF
      ENDIF
    ELSE                                        // add clusters at end of plot
      WHILE NOT startPts.isEmpty() DO
        currCluster := set of objects from startPts.top() to o;
        IF (startPts.top().R > o.R) AND (currCluster.size() >= MinPts) THEN
          setOfClusters.add(currCluster);
        ENDIF
        startPts.pop();
      ENDDO
    ENDIF
  ENDDO

  RETURN setOfClusters;
END. // gradient_clustering
```

Fig. 6.7. Pseudo code of the Gradient Clustering algorithm.

Obviously, the Gradient Clustering algorithm is able to extract narrowing clusters. Experimental comparisons with the methods in [16] and [11] are presented in Section 6.4.3.

The pseudo code of the Gradient Clustering algorithm is depicted in Figure 6.7, which works like this. Initially, the first object of the cluster ordering *CO* is pushed to the stack of starting points *startPts*. Whenever a new starting point is found, it is pushed to the stack. If the current object is an end point, a new cluster is created containing all objects between the starting point on top of the stack and the current end point. Starting points are removed from the stack if their reachablity is lower than the reachability of the current object. Clusters are created as described above for all removed starting points as well as for the starting point which remains in the stack. The input parameter *MinPts* determines the minimum cluster size, and the parameter *t* was discussed above. Finally the parameter *w* influences the gradient vectors and proportionally depends on the reachability values of the objects in *CO*.

After extracting a meaningful hierarchy of clusters from the reachability plot of a given data set, we still need to enhance the found clustering with suitable representations. For this purpose, we can display the medoid of each cluster, that is, the object having the minimal average distance to all the other objects in the cluster.

6.4.3 Evaluation

Automatic cluster recognition is very desirable when analyzing large sets of data. In the following, we will first evaluate the quality and then the efficiency of the three cluster recognition algorithms using two real-world test data sets. The first data set contains approximately 200 CAD objects from a German car manufacturer, and the second one is a sample of the Protein Databank [17] containing approximately 5000 protein structures. We tested on a workstation featuring a 1.7 GHz CPU and 2 GB RAM.

6.4.3.1 Effectivity

Both the car and the protein data set exhibit the commonly seen quality of unpronounced but nevertheless to the observer clearly visible clusters. The corresponding reachability plots of the two data sets are depicted in Figure 6.8.

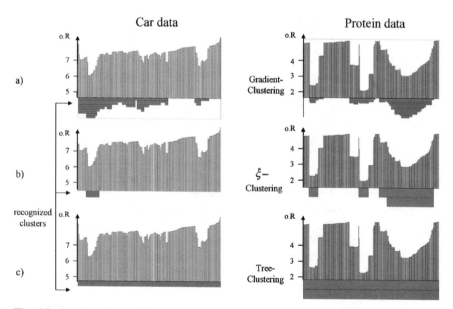

Fig. 6.8. Sample cluster of car parts. (a) Gradient Clustering, (b) ξ-Clustering, (c) Tree Clustering.

Figure 6.8c shows that the Tree Clustering algorithm does not find any clusters at all in the car data set, with the suggested default ratio parameter of 75% [16]. In order to detect clusters in the car data set, we had to adjust the ratio parameter to 95%. In this case Tree Clustering detected some clusters but missed some other important clusters and did not detect any cluster hierarchies at all. If we have rather high reachability values, for example, values between 5 and 7 as in Figure 6.8 for the car data set, the ratio parameter for the Tree Clustering algorithm should be set higher than for smaller values. In the case of the protein data set we detected three clusters with the default parameter setting, but again missed out on some important clusters. Generally, in cases where a reachability graph consists of rather high reachability values or does not present spikes at all, but clusters are formed by smooth troughs in the waveform, this cluster recognition algorithm is unsuitable. Furthermore, it is inherently unable to detect narrowing clusters where a cluster has one subcluster of increased density (cf. Fig. 6.4).

On the other hand, the ξ-clustering approach successfully recognizes some clusters while also missing out on significant subclusters (cf. Fig. 6.8b). This algorithm has some trouble recognizing cluster structures with a significant differential of "steepness." For instance, in Figure 6.4 it does not detect the narrowing cluster B inside of cluster A because it tries to create steep down-areas containing as many points as possible. Thus, it will merge the two steep edges if their steepness exceeds the threshold ξ. On the other hand, it is able to detect cluster C within cluster A.

Finally, we look at our new Gradient Clustering algorithm. Figure 6.8a shows that the recognized cluster structure is close to the intuitive one, which an experienced user would manually derive. Clusters which are clearly distinguishable and contain more than *MinPts* elements are detected by this algorithm. Not only does it detect a lot of clusters, but it also detects a lot of meaningful cluster hierarchies, consisting of narrowing subclusters.

To sum up, in all our tests the Gradient Clustering algorithm detected much more clusters than the other two approaches, without producing any redundant and unnecessary cluster information.

6.4.3.2 Efficiency

In all tests, we first created the reachability plots and then applied the algorithms for cluster recognition and representation. Let us note that we could also have integrated the Gradient Clustering into the OPTICS run without causing any noteworthy overhead.

The overall runtimes for the three different cluster recognition algorithms are depicted in Table 6.1 Our new Gradient Clustering algorithm does not only produce

Table 6.1. CPU time for cluster recognition.

	Car data (200 parts)	Protein data (5000 molecules)
ξ-clustering	0.221 s	5.057 s
Tree Clustering	0.060 s	1.932 s
Gradient Clustering	0.310 s	3.565 s

the most meaningful results, but also in sufficiently short time. This is due to its runtime complexity of $O(n)$.

It theoretically and empirically turned out that the Gradient Clustering algorithm seems to be more practical than recent work for automatic cluster extraction from hierarchical cluster representations.

6.5 Extracting Cluster Hierarchies for Similarity Search

6.5.1 Motivation

So far, our prototype works fine by computing, extracting, and visualizing the hierarchical density-based cluster structure of a data set. The density-based cluster model has been chosen because of several criteria. One very important aspect among these criteria is its effectivity in finding clusters of different size and shape. However, this clustering notion needs not to be the best cluster model for navigational similarity search. For this application, the use of OPTICS may have two limitations. In this section, we will discuss these limitations and a possible solution for them.

The first limitation of using the density-based clustering notion is that OPTICS may place two objects that are rather similar, that is, near in the feature space, into two separate clusters. As a consequence, these two objects may be displayed in completely different subtrees of the cluster hierarchy; that is, the relationship between these two points in the cluster hierarchy is rather weak. This problem is visualized in Figure 6.9: object A is obviously much more similar to object B than to object C. However, since A and C belong to the same cluster, both objects will be considered as similar by OPTICS. A and C will be placed in a similar subtree of the cluster hierarchy, whereas B may end up in a completely different subtree. This is against the intuitive notion of similarity that would expect A and B having a closer relationship in the cluster hierarchy than A and C.

The second limitation is that a cluster of complex shape and huge size can usually not be represented by one representative object. However, the idea of navigational similarity search depends on the suitability of the object that is displayed to represent the objects in a cluster.

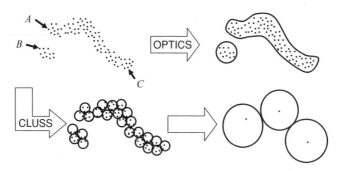

Fig. 6.9. A new cluster model for navigational similarity search.

In order to solve these limitations, we propose a novel way of computing the cluster hierarchy and suitable representations. The general idea is that we are interested in small spherically shaped clusters rather than in clusters of arbitrary size and shape. Intuitively, we can select a given number of representative objects that represent their spherical neighborhood in a best possible way. These representatives can build the lowest level of a cluster hierarchy tree. The next level of the tree (above a given level) can then be built by choosing again the most representative objects from the representatives in the level below until we do not have enough representatives and, thus, have reached the root of the hierarchy. The most important aspect in this strategy is the definition of the representative power of an object. We will discuss this issue and outline a novel procedure to generate the cluster hierarchy in the following.

The idea of this new approach is sketched in Figure 6.9: a data set with two clusters of different size and shape is clustered. Using OPTICS, both clusters are well separated and we can observe both of the mentioned problems: objects that are member of the larger cluster but are quite near (i.e., similar) to the objects in the smaller cluster will have a significantly poor relationship in the cluster hierarchy to the objects in the smaller cluster. On the other hand, objects that are much less similar but are members of the same (larger) cluster will have a strong relationship to each other in the hierarchy. In addition, it is not clear how to represent the larger cluster with its complex shape by a meaningful representative. Our new approach generates representatives for small convex clusters step by step. As it can be seen from Figure 6.9, this results in a hierarchy that is much more suitable for interactive similarity search. For example, the objects of the smaller cluster will be represented by the same object in the root node of the hierarchy as the objects that belong to the large cluster but are located at the border of that cluster near the smaller cluster. This reflects the intuitive notion of similarity more accurately.

6.5.2 Basic Definitions

The basic idea is to extract a sufficient amount of dedicated objects that represents the other objects in a best possible way. Such objects are called *representatives* and should be associated with a set of non representatives, called the *border shadow* of a representative.

Definition 7 (border shadow). *Let REP be a set of representative objects and $\varepsilon \in \mathbb{R}$. The* border shadow *of a representative $r \in REP$ is defined by*

$$r.bordershadow := \{o \in REP \mid dist(o, r) \leq \varepsilon\}.$$

The border shadow of r contains the set of objects in the (hyper-) sphere around r with radius ε. Obviously, a global value for the size of the representative area for each representative is not appropriate, since it does not reflect the local data distribution. Thus, we define an additional, adaptive set of representative objects, the so-called *core shadow* of a representative.

Definition 8 (core distance). *Let REP be a set of representative objects, $k \in \mathbb{N}$ and $r \in REP$. The* core distance *of r is defined by:*

$$r.coredist := \begin{cases} 0 & if \ |\mathcal{N}_\varepsilon(r)| < k \\ k\text{-}nn\text{-}dist(r) & else. \end{cases}$$

Definition 9 (core shadow). *Let REP be a set of representative objects and $r \in REP$. The* core shadow *of r is defined by:*

$$r.coreshadow := \{o \in REP \mid dist(o, r) \leq r.coredist\}.$$

The core shadow of r contains the set of objects in the (hyper-) sphere around r with radius $k\text{-}nn\text{-}dist(r)$. Obviously, this radius adapts to the local density of objects around r.

Both the border shadow and the core shadow can be used to define the quality of a representative.

Definition 10 (quality of a representative). *Let REP be a set of representative objects and $r \in REP$. The* quality *of r is defined by*

$$r.quality := \begin{cases} 0 & if \ |\mathcal{N}_\varepsilon(r)| < k \\ \dfrac{\mathcal{N}_\varepsilon(r)}{1+k\text{-}nn\text{-}dist(r)} & else. \end{cases}$$

The key idea of our hierarchical clustering approach is to find on each level of the hierarchy an optimal (w.r.t. quality) set of representatives such that the representatives have nonoverlapping core shadows (overlapping border shadows are allowed).

6.5.3 Algorithm

The general idea of the algorithm is to start with the whole database as the initial set of representatives. In the i-th iteration, we take the set of current representatives REP_i and compute the new set of representatives REP_{i+1}. To ensure that we get the best representatives, we sort REP_i by descending quality values (cf. Definition 10). Theoretically, we can recursively select the representative r having the highest quality from the sorted REP_i list, add r with its border shadow to REP_{i+1}, and remove all further objects from REP_i that are in the core shadow of r.

However, we have to take care that core shadows of representatives in REP_{i+1} do not overlap. For that purpose, we test for each not yet selected representative $r \in REP_i$ whether its core shadow overlaps the core shadow of any object in REP_{i+1}. To support this intersection query efficiently, we can organize the objects in REP_{i+1} in a spatial index structure (data structure *send*). If there is no such overlap, we add r and its border shadow to REP_{i+1} (and *send*) and remove all objects in the core shadow of r from REP_i. If the core shadow of r intersects the core shadow of any already selected representatives in REP_{i+1}, we have to distinguish two cases. (1) If r is within the border shadow of any representative in REP_{i+1} we can remove r because it is represented by at least one representative. (2) If r is not within the border shadow of any representative in REP_{i+1} we cannot remove r since it is not yet represented. We will have to test for r at a later time, whether it is in the border

```
algorithm cluster_representatives(SetOfObjects DB, Integer k)
  REP_0 := emptySet;
  REP_1 := DB;
  i := 1;

  WHILE REP_i != REP_i-1 DO
    compute new epsilon;
    send = emptySpatialIndex;
    wait = emptySpatialIndex;
    sort REP_i in descending order w.r.t. quality values;
    r := REP_i.removeFirst();

    WHILE r.quality == 0 AND REP_i.size > 0 DO
      IF r.coreshadow does not intersect the core shadow of any object in send THEN
        send.add(r);
        FOR EACH s IN wait DO
          IF s is in r.bordershadow DO
            wait.remove(s);
          ENDIF
        ENDDO
      ELSE
        IF r is not in border shadow of any object in send DO
          wait.add(r);
        ENDIF
      ENDIF
      r := REP_i.removeFirst();
    ENDDO

    REP_i+1 := REP_i;
    REP_i+1.addAll(send);
    REP_i+1.addAll(wait);
    i++;
  ENDDO
END. // cluster_representatives
```

Fig. 6.10. Pseudo code of the cluster representatives algorithm.

shadow of a representative chosen later. For that purpose, we add those points to an additional data structure called *wait*. Thus, when adding a new representative r to REP_{i+1}, we have to test whether there are objects in *wait* which are in the border shadow of r. If so, we delete those objects from *wait*. The algorithm terminates if we gain no more new representatives after an iteration, that is, $REP_{i+1} = REP_i$.

In summary, in each iteration, we do the following (cf. the pseudo code in Figure 6.10):

1. Sort REP_i by descending quality values.
2. As long as there are representatives in REP_i having a quality greater than 0, take and remove the first object r from the sorted REP_i list:
   If $r.coreshadow$ does not intersect the core shadow of any object in REP_{i+1} (cf. object c in Fig. 6.11):
   - add r along with $r.coreshadow$ and $r.bordershadow$ to REP_{i+1},
   - add r to *send*,
   - remove all objects in *wait* which are in the border shadow of r (range-query against *wait*).
   Else (i.e., $r.coreshadow$ intersects the core shadow of at least one object in REP_{i+1}):

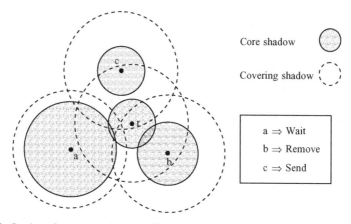

Fig. 6.11. Sorting of representatives acording to intersections of their core shadows and border shadows.

- If r is not in the border shadow of any object in REP_{i+1}, add r to $wait$ (cf. object a in Fig. 6.11).
- If r is in the border shadow of any object in REP_{i+1}, do nothing (r is already removed from REP_i; cf. object b in Fig. 6.11).
3. Add all remaining objects in REP_i and $wait$ to REP_{i+1}.

6.5.4 Choice of ε in the i-th Iteration

The quality of a representative r depends not only on the parameter k (specifying the number of neighbors of r which are taken into account for quality computation) but also on the radius ε of the local area around r. A global value for ε is not appropriate since the dataspace is getting sparser in each iteration. A dynamically adapting value for ε is deemed more appropriate.

If we assume that DB is a set of n feature vectors of dimensionality d (i.e., $DB \subseteq \mathbb{R}^d$) and each attribute value of all $o \in DB$ is normalized (i.e., falls into the range $[0, MAX]$ for a specified, fixed MAX) the volume of the data space can be computed by

$$Vol(DB) = MAX^d.$$

If the n objects of DB are uniformly distributed in $Vol(DB)$, we expect one object in the volume $Vol(DB)/n$ and k objects in the volume $k \cdot Vol(DB)/n$. Thus, the expected k-nearest neighbor distance of any object $o \in DB$ is equal to the radius r of a hypersphere having this volume $k \cdot Vol(DB)/n$. Since the volume of a hypersphere with radius r can be computed by

$$V_{\text{Sphere}}(r) = \frac{\sqrt{\pi^d}}{\Gamma(d/2 + 1)} \cdot r^d,$$

where Γ denotes the well-known Gamma function, we can compute the expected k-nn-distance $\hat{r}$ of the objects in DB by solving the following equation:

$$\frac{\sqrt{\pi^d}}{\Gamma(d/2+1)} \cdot \hat{r}^d = k \cdot \frac{MAX^d}{n}.$$

Simple algebraic transformations yield:

$$\hat{r} = MAX \cdot \sqrt[d]{\frac{k \cdot \Gamma(d/2+1)}{n \cdot \sqrt{\pi^d}}}.$$

For simplicity reasons, we can also compute:

$$\hat{r} = MAX \cdot \sqrt[d]{\frac{k}{n}}.$$

Let us note that this is the correct value of the expected k-nn-distance if we use the L_∞-norm instead of the L_2-norm.

In the i-th iteration, an appropriated choice for ε as the expected k-nn-distance of the objects in REP_i:

$$\varepsilon = MAX \cdot \sqrt[d]{\frac{k}{|REP_i|}}.$$

If we further assume $MAX = 1$ (i.e., all attributes have normalized values in $[0, 1]$), we have

$$\varepsilon = \sqrt[d]{\frac{k}{|REP_i|}}.$$

6.5.5 The Extended Prototype CLUSS

We have implemented the proposed ideas in Java and integrated a GUI to visualize the cluster hierarchy and cluster representatives. The resulting prototype is called CLUSS, which uses the newly proposed method for generating the cluster hierarchy and suitable cluster representatives. A sample sceenshot of CLUSS is depicted in Fig. 6.12. The hierarchy is now visualized by means of a tree (upper right frame in Fig. 6.12). For clearness, the subtrees of each node of the tree is not visualized per default but can be expanded for browsing by clicking on the according node. The hierarchy tree is also visualized in the frame on the left-hand side of the GUI. The frame on the lower right side in Figure 6.12 displays the representatives at the nodes that are currently selected.

We performed some sample visual similarity search queries, using CLUSS, and compared it to the cluster hierarchy created by OPTICS and Gradient Clustering. In fact, it turned out that using CLUSS allows a more accurate interactive similarity search. The hierarchy generated by CLUSS differs from that generated by its comparison partner and is more meaningful. So CLUSS provided better results for navigational similarity search, for applications of visual data mining, employing

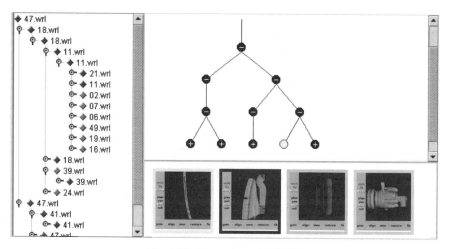

Fig. 6.12. Screenshot of CLUSS.

OPTICS is more appropriate, especially, if the application calls for clustering solutions that detect clusters of different sizes and shapes.

6.6 Conclusions

In this chapter, we combined hierarchical clustering and data visualization techniques to allow data analysis, comparison of data models and navigational similarity search. The idea of comparing data spaces using hierarchical density-based clustering is to display connected reachability plots and compare these to reference class models using color coding. Navigational similarity search describes a novel approach to retrieve similar data objects. Instead of posing similarity queries, our new approach extracts a cluster hierarchy from a given set of data objects and uses the resulting cluster tree to navigate between sets of similar objects. To extract a cluster hierarchy from a reachability plot generated by the density-based hierarchical clustering algorithm OPTICS, we introduced a new method for cluster extraction called Gradient Clustering. OPTICS produces a meaningful picture of the density distribution of a given data set and is thus well suited for data analysis. However, in many applications the cluster hierarchy derived from the reachability plot might not provide intuitive access for navigational similarity search. Therefore, we described an alternative hierarchical clustering approach called CLUSS that facilitates the interactive similarity search in large collections of data.

References

1. Jagadish HV. A retrieval technique for similar shapes. In: *Proc. ACM SIGMOD Int. Conf. on Management of Data (SIGMOD'91)*, Denver, CO; 1991, pp. 208–217.

2. Agrawal R, Faloutsos C, Swami A. Efficient similarity search in sequence databases. In: *Proc. 4th. Int. Conf. on Foundations of Data Organization and Algorithms (FODO'93)*, Evanston, IL. vol. 730 of Lecture Notes in Computer Science (LNCS). Springer; 1993, pp. 69–84.

3. Faloutsos C, Barber R, Flickner M, Hafner J, et al. Efficient and effective querying by image content. *Journal of Intelligent Information Systems* 1994;3:231–262.

4. Faloutsos C, Ranganathan M, Manolopoulos Y. Fast subsequence matching in time-series databases. In: *Proc. ACM SIGMOD Int. Conf. on Management of Data (SIGMOD'94)*, Minneapolis, MN; 1994, pp. 419–429.

5. Agrawal R, Lin KI, Sawhney HS, Shim K. Fast similarity search in the presence of noise, scaling, and translation in time-series databases. In: *Proc. 21th Int. Conf. on Very Large Databases (VLDB'95)*; 1995, pp. 490–501.

6. Berchtold S, Keim DA, Kriegel HP. Using extended feature objects for partial similarity retrieval, *VLDB Journal* 1997;6(4):333–348.

7. Berchtold S, Kriegel HP. S3: Similarity search in CAD database systems. In: *Proc. ACM SIGMOD Int. Conf. on Management of Data (SIGMOD'97)*, Tucson, AZ; 1997, pp. 564–567.

8. Keim DA. Efficient geometry-based similarity search of 3D spatial databases. In: *Proc. ACM SIGMOD Int. Conf. on Management of Data (SIGMOD'99)*, Philadelphia, PA; 1999, pp. 419–430.

9. Kriegel HP, Kröger P, Mashael Z, Pfeifle M, Pötke M, Seidl T. Effective Similarity Search on Voxelized CAD Objects. In: *Proc. 8th Int. Conf. on Database Systems for Advanced Applications (DASFAA'03)*, Kyoto, Japan; 2003, pp. 27–36.

10. Kriegel HP, Brecheisen S, Kröger P, Pfeifle M, Schubert M. Using sets of feature vectors for similarity search on voxelized CAD objects. In: *Proc. ACM SIGMOD Int. Conf. on Management of Data (SIGMOD'03)*, San Diego, CA; 2003, pp. 587–598.

11. Ankerst M, Breunig MM, Kriegel HP, Sander J. OPTICS: Ordering points to identify the clustering structure. In: *Proc. ACM SIGMOD Int. Conf. on Management of Data (SIGMOD'99)*, Philadelphia, PA; 1999, pp. 49–60.

12. McQueen J. Some methods for classification and analysis of multivariate observations. In: *5th Berkeley Symp. Math. Statist. Prob.*, Vol. 1; 1967, pp. 281–297.

13. Breunig MM, Kriegel HP, Kröger P, Sander J. Data bubbles: Quality preserving performance boosting for hierarchical clustering. In: *Proc. ACM SIGMOD Int. Conf. on Management of Data (SIGMOD'01)*, Santa Barbara, CA; 2001, pp. 79–90.

14. Achtert E, Böhm C, Kriegel HP, Kröger P. Online hierarchical clustering in a data warehouse environment. In: *Proc. 5th IEEE Int. Conf. on Data Mining (ICDM'05)*, Houston, TX; 2005, pp. 10–17.

15. Ester M, Kriegel HP, Sander J, Xu X. A density-based algorithm for discovering clusters in large spatial databases with noise. In: *Proc. 2nd Int. Conf. on Knowledge Discovery and Data Mining (KDD'96)*, Portland, OR. AAAI Press; 1996, pp. 291–316.

16. Sander J, Qin X, Lu Z, Niu N, Kovarsky A. Automatic extraction of clusters from hierarchical clustering representations. In: *Proc. 7th Pacific-Asia Conference on Knowledge Discovery and Data Mining (PAKDD 2003)*, Seoul, Korea; 2003. pp. 75–87.

17. Berman HM, Westbrook J, Feng Z, Gilliland G, Bhat TN, Weissig H, et al. The Protein Data Bank. *Nucleic Acids Research* 2000;28:235–242.

7. Feature Selection for Classification of Variable Length Multiattribute Motions*

Chuanjun Li, Latifur Khan, and Balakrishnan Prabhakaran

Summary. As a relatively new type of multimedia, captured motion has its specific properties. The data of motions has multiple attributes to capture movements of multiple joints of a subject, and has different lengths for even similar motions. There are no row-to-row correspondences between data matrices of two motions. To be classified and recognized, multiattribute motion data of different lengths are reduced to feature vectors by using the properties of Singular Value Decomposition (SVD) of motion data in this chapter. Different feature selection approaches are explored, and by applying Support Vector Machines (SVM) to the feature vectors, we can efficiently classify and recognize real-world multiattribute motion data. With our data sets of hundreds of 3D motions with different lengths and variations, classification by SVM is compared with classification by related similarity measures, in terms of accuracy and CPU time.

7.1 Introduction

Captured motion stream is a relatively new type of multimedia and can have a variety of applications: gait analysis (physical medicine and rehabilitation), virtual reality, as well as in entertainment fields such as animations and video gaming industry. The motions recorded by gesture sensing devices (such as the data glove CyberGlove) and 3D human motion capture cameras (such as the Vicon cameras) have multiple attributes and multiple dimensions. For instance, a gesture sensing device such as CyberGlove has multiple sensors that transmit values to indicate motions of a hand, and a motion capture system generates multiple degrees of freedom (DOF) data for human motions. As a result, a multiattribute motion yields a matrix over the motion duration, rather than a multidimensional vector as for a time series sequence.

Motion classification identifies a motion class to which an unknown motion most likely belongs, and poses several challenges:

- Each of the motion data set has dozens of attributes rather than one attribute as for a time series sequence. Motion data of multiple attributes are aggregate data, and should be considered together to make the motions meaningful.

---

* This chapter is extended from our previous work [1].

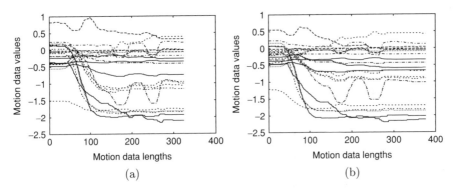

Fig. 7.1. Data for two similar motions. Similar motions can have different lengths, and different corresponding attribute pairs can have different variations at different time, hence there are no row-to-row correspondences between data of similar motions.

- The matrices of motion data can be of variable lengths, even for similar motions. Motions are carried out with different speeds at different time. They can have different durations, and motion sampling rates may also be different. There are no continuous row-to-row correspondences between data of similar motions as shown in Figure 7.1.

High accuracy classification makes the effective applications of new motions possible, and requires the extraction of highly representative feature vectors of motions. Instead of considering motion data rows/frames for motion identification, we consider the geometric structures of motion matrices in a high-dimensional space. If a motion frame has dimension n, then a motion sequence of length m can be taken to be m vectors in an nD space. The distributions of the nD vectors are explored for feature extraction in this chapter. We obtain feature vectors for motion patterns, using the Singular Vector Decomposition (SVD) properties of the motion matrices, since SVD optimally exposes the geometric structure of a matrix. Different approaches to extracting feature vectors are explored on the basis of how information is to be extracted from SVD. We then classify the vectors for all the motions. The learning machines can be trained for classification by using a training set of vectors each of which has a unique class label. After training, the machines can determine the class label of a new motion and thus classify the new motion during a testing phase.

There are many classification techniques for different applications. Classification by Support Vector Machines (SVM) has been proven to be computationally efficient especially when dealing with relatively large data sets [2] and has been successfully applied to solve many real-world problems [3–5]. This chapter explores the feasibility of SVM in motion classification and experiments with different criteria for class decision. Experiments with hand gestures and human motions achieve 95–100% classification accuracy.

In comparison with classification by using SVM, we also computed the similarities of motion data in the testing data sets with motion data in the training data sets.

The similarity measures used are the weighted-sum SVD [6], Eros [7], MAS [8], and kWAS [9], similarity measures proposed recently for capturing similarities of variable-length multiattribute motion patterns.

This chapter extends our previous work in [1] in the following ways:

- Different feature vectors are explored. The new feature vectors try to consider more information from SVD.
- SVM with probability estimate is explored. This option provides the possibility of segmenting streams by SVM for further work.
- Various human motions captured by infrared cameras are experimented in addition to hand gestures.
- Comparison with new similarity measures is made.

The rest of the chapter is organized as follows. Section 7.2 gives a brief review of related work. Section 7.3 contains the background knowledge of SVM, SVD, and dynamic time warping (DTW). Section 7.5 proposes a new approach to classifying multiattribute motion data, using SVD and SVM, and the classification is further verified by using DTW for motion directions. Section 7.6 experimentally evaluates the accuracy and CPU time of our proposed approach, followed by Section 7.7, which concludes this chapter.

7.2 Related Work

Recognition of multiattribute sequences has obtained increasing attentions in recent years. Mostly distance measures are defined for multiattribute data to reflect the similarities of multiattribute data. In [10], multiattribute sequences of equal lengths are considered. Scaling and shifting transformations are considered when defining sequence distances and an index structure is proposed for shift and scale transformations. Similarity search of multiattribute sequences with different lengths cannot be solved by the distance definitions and the index as proposed in [10].

Multiattribute sequences are partitioned into subsequences in [11]. Each of the partitioned subsequences is contained in a Minimum Bounding Rectangle (MBR). Every MBR is indexed and stored into a database by using an R-tree or any of its variants. Estimated MBR distances are used to speed up the searching of similar motions. If two sequences are of different lengths, the shorter sequence is compared with the other by sliding from the beginning to the end of the longer sequence. When two similar sequences with different durations or with local accelerations and decelerations are considered, other approaches would be needed.

Dynamic time warping (DTW) and longest common subsequence (LCSS) are extended for similarity measures of multiattribute data in [12]. Before the exact LCSS or DTW is performed, sequences are segmented into MBRs to be stored in an R-tree. On the basis of the MBR intersections, similarity estimates are computed to prune irrelevant sequences. Both DTW and LCSS have a computational complexity of $O(wd(m+n))$, where w is a matching window size, d is the number of attributes, and m, n are the lengths of two data sequences. When w is a significant portion of m

or n, the computation can be even quadratic in the length of the sequences, making it nonscalable to large databases with long multiattribute sequences. It has been shown in [12] that the index performance significantly degrades when the warping length increases. Even for a small number of 20 MBRs per long sequence, the index space requirements can be about a quarter of the data set size.

Hidden Markov models (HMMs) have been used to address speech and handwriting recognition [13, 14] as well as American Sign Language (ASL) recognition problems [15]. Different states should be specified for each sign or motion unit when HMMs are involved, the number of words in a sentence is required to be known beforehand, and grammar constraints should also be known beforehand for using HMMs. When the specified states are not followed, or motion variations are relatively large, recognition accuracy would decrease dramatically. This is true even when legitimate or meaningful motions are generated for HMM-based recognitions. This chapter addresses the classification of individual motions, no states or grammar constraints are involved for individual motions. Thus HMMs are not suitable for our classification purpose.

Shahabi et al. [16] applied learning techniques such as Decision Trees, Bayesian classifiers and Neural Networks to recognize static signs for a 10-sign vocabulary, and achieved 84.66% accuracy. In [6], a weighted-sum SVD is defined for measuring the similarity of two multiattribute motion sequences. The similarity definition takes the minimum of two weighted sums of the inner products of right singular vectors. Eros as proposed in [7] computes the similarity of two motion patterns by using angular similarities of right singular vectors. The angular similarities are weighted by a different weight obtained from singular values of all available motion patterns in the database. The singular value weight vector is the same for similarity computation of all motion patterns.

Li et al. define a similarity measure for multiattribute motion data in [8] as follows.

$$\Psi(Q, P) = |u_1 \cdot v_1| \times (\vec{\sigma} \cdot \vec{\lambda} - \eta)/(1 - \eta)$$

where u_1 and v_1 are the first singular vectors of Q and P, respectively, $\vec{\sigma} = \sigma/|\sigma|$, $\vec{\lambda} = \lambda/|\lambda|$, and σ and λ are the vectors of the singular values of $Q^T Q$ and $P^T P$, respectively. Weight parameter η is to ensure that the normalized singular value vectors $\vec{\sigma}$ and $\vec{\lambda}$ and the first right singular vectors u_1 and v_1 have similar contributions to the similarity measure and is determined by experiments. η can be set to 0.9 for the multiattribute motion data. This similarity measure captures the most important information revealed by the first right singular vectors and the singular values, and can be applied to prune most of the irrelevant motion data, and inner products of equal-length reinterpolated first left singular vectors have been used as the first attempt to consider motions with different directions or with repetitions.

We refer to the similarity measure as defined in [8], which captures the main angular similarity of two motions as MAS hereafter. Furthermore, kWAS as proposed in [9] considers the angular similarities of the first k right singular pairs weighted by the associated singular values.

In contrast, this chapter addresses motion classification by utilizing SVD, SVM, and DTW. Different feature extraction approaches are explored, and different class

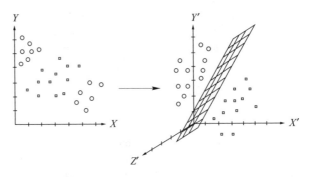

Fig. 7.2. Optimal hyperplane illustration.

decision criteria are experimented with motion data generated for both hand gestures and human motions.

7.3 Background

This section gives some background knowledge of singular value decomposition and support vector machines for feature extraction and motion classification.

7.3.1 Support Vector Machines

Support vector machines are a class of learning machines that aim at finding optimal hyperplanes, the boundaries with the maximal margin of separation between every two classes, among different classes of input data or training data in a high-dimensional feature space $\mathcal{F}$, and new test data can be classified using the separating hyperplanes. The optimal hyperplanes, obtained during a *training* phase, make the smallest number of training errors. Figure 7.2 illustrates an optimal hyperplane for two classes of training data.

Let $\{x_i, y_i\}, i = 1, 2, \ldots, L$ be L training data vectors x_i with class labels y_i, and $y_i \in \{-1, +1\}$ for binary classification. Given an input vector x, an SVM constructs a classifier of the form

$$g(x) = sign(\sum_{i=1}^{L} \alpha_i y_i K(x_i, x) + b)$$

where $\{\alpha_i\}$ are nonnegative Lagrange multipliers each of which corresponds to an example from the training data, b is a bias constant, and $K(\cdot, \cdot)$ is a kernel satisfying the conditions of Mercer's theorem [4]. Frequently used kernel functions are the polynomial kernel $K(x_i, x_j) = (x_i \cdot x_j + 1)^d$ and Gaussian Radial Basis Function (RBF) $K(x_i, x_j) = e^{-|x_i - x_j|^2 / 2\sigma^2}$.

The above decision function does not produce a probability. In many applications, a posterior probability, rather than an uncalibrated decision value, is needed for capturing the classification uncertainty. Efforts of mapping SVM outputs to posterior probabilities have been made in [4,17]. Platt [17] uses a sigmoid function to estimate the binary class probability which is monotonic in g:

$$p(y = +1|g) = \frac{1}{1 + \exp(Ag + B)}$$

The parameters A and B can be fitted by using maximum likelihood estimation.

For multiclass classification, class probabilities can be estimated from binary class probabilities by pairwise coupling. Wu et al. [18] propose a multiclass probability approach which is more stable than other popular existing methods by using the following optimization:

Optimization:

$$\min_{p} \sum_{i=1}^{k} \sum_{j:j \neq i} (r_{ij}p_j - r_{ji}p_i)^2$$

under the constraints:

$$\sum_{i=1}^{k} p_i = 1, \, p_i \geq 0, \forall i$$

where r_{ij} are the binary class probability estimates of $\mu_{ij} \equiv P(y = i|y = i \text{ or } j, x)$ as obtained in [17].

The above optimization problem can be solved using Gaussian elimination after some algebra as shown in [18]. The vectors for which $\alpha_i > 0$ after optimization are called *support vectors*. Support vectors lie closest to the optimal hyperplane. After training, only the support vectors of the training data are used to represent the classifiers, and other training vectors have no influences.

For multiclass classification, two commonly used methods are one-versus-rest and one-versus-one approaches. The one-versus-rest method constructs k classifiers for k classes, each of which separates that class from the rest of the data, and a test data point will be classified in the class with the highest probability estimate. The one-versus-one method constructs a classifier for each pair of classes. The probability of a test data vector belonging to one class is estimated from binary class probabilities, and the class with the largest posterior is the winning class for the test vector: $\arg\max_i[p_i]$. The one-versus-one method will be used for this work because of its simplicity and high classification accuracy [19].

SVM basically applies to classification of vectors, or uniattribute time series data. To classify multiattribute data, which are matrices rather than vectors, we need to transform or reduce multiattribute matrices into vectors. We propose to use SVD to reduce multiattribute motion data to feature vectors. Before showing how to extracting feature vectors, we present a brief introduction of SVD in the following subsection.

7.3.2 Singular Value Decomposition

As proven in [20], for any real $m \times n$ matrix A, there exist orthogonal matrices

$$U = [u_1, u_2, \ldots, u_m] \in R^{m \times m}, \, V = [v_1, v_2, \ldots, v_n] \in R^{n \times n}$$

$$A = \begin{bmatrix} 1.1 & 2.2 & 3.3 & 4.4 & 5.5 \\ 1.5 & 2.6 & 3.7 & 4.8 & 5.9 \\ 2.3 & 3.4 & 4.5 & 5.6 & 6.7 \\ 3.6 & 4.7 & 5.8 & 6.9 & 7.1 \\ 4.5 & 5.7 & 6.9 & 7.2 & 8.3 \\ 5.8 & 7.3 & 9.2 & 11.6 & 13.8 \end{bmatrix}$$

$$= \begin{bmatrix} -0.2388 & -0.5360 & -0.3535 & 0.1605 & -0.4683 & -0.5345 \\ -0.2642 & -0.4301 & -0.2866 & 0.1400 & -0.0238 & 0.8018 \\ -0.3151 & -0.2184 & -0.1529 & 0.0990 & 0.8651 & -0.2673 \\ -0.3817 & 0.3366 & -0.4920 & -0.7038 & -0.0604 & 0.0000 \\ -0.4386 & 0.5938 & -0.1623 & 0.6450 & -0.1124 & 0.0000 \\ -0.6602 & -0.1188 & 0.7079 & -0.1830 & -0.1244 & 0.0000 \end{bmatrix} \begin{bmatrix} 33.7448 & 0 & 0 & 0 & 0 \\ 0 & 2.3277 & 0 & 0 & 0 \\ 0 & 0 & 0.6587 & 0 & 0 \\ 0 & 0 & 0 & 0.4985 & 0 \\ 0 & 0 & 0 & 0 & 0.0207 \\ 0 & 0 & 0 & 0 & 0 \end{bmatrix} \begin{bmatrix} -0.2537 & 0.6262 & 0.6581 & -0.1571 & -0.2928 \\ -0.3377 & 0.4551 & -0.1716 & 0.1735 & 0.7869 \\ -0.4296 & 0.2635 & -0.5715 & 0.3573 & -0.5402 \\ -0.5196 & -0.1832 & -0.2122 & -0.8070 & 0.0146 \\ -0.6058 & -0.5457 & 0.4073 & 0.4078 & 0.0545 \end{bmatrix}^T$$

Fig. 7.3. SVD of a 6×5 example matrix A.

such that

$$A = U \Sigma V^T$$

where $\Sigma = \mathrm{diag}(\sigma_1, \sigma_2, \ldots, \sigma_{\min(m,n)}) \in R^{m \times n}$, $\sigma_1 \geq \sigma_2 \geq \ldots \geq \sigma_{\min(m,n)} \geq 0$. The σ_i is the ith singular value of A in the nonincreasing order and the vectors u_i and v_i are the ith left and right singular vectors of A for $i = \min(m, n)$, respectively. The singular values of a matrix A are unique, and the singular vectors corresponding to distinct singular values are uniquely determined up to the sign [21]. Figure 7.3 shows an SVD example for a 6×4 matrix A.

The ith largest singular value σ_i of A is actually the 2-norm or Euclidean length of the ith largest projected vector Ax, which is orthogonal to all the $i - 1$ larger orthogonal vectors as shown by

$$\sigma_i = \max_U \min_{x \in U, \|x\|_2 = 1} \| Ax \|_2$$

where the maximum is taken over all i-dimensional subspaces $U \subseteq \Re^n$ [20]. Note that σ_1 is the largest 2-norm of A projections onto any x directions:

$$\sigma_1 = \max_{\|x\|_2 = 1} \| Ax \|_2$$

Hence the right singular vectors are the corresponding projection directions of the associated singular values, and the singular values account for the Euclidean lengths of different vectors projected by the row vectors in A onto different right singular vectors.

When A is subtracted by the its respective column means as for the covariance matrix used for principal component analysis (PCA), the first right singular vector v_1 gives the direction along which the multi-dimensional row vectors or points contained in A have the largest variance, and the second right singular vector v_2 is the direction with the second largest variance, and so on. The singular value σ_i reflects the variance along the corresponding ith singular vector. Figure 7.4 shows the data in an 18×2 matrix and its first singular vector v_1 and second singular vector v_2. Along the first singular vector v_1, data points have the largest variance as shown in Figure 7.4. If A has nonzero means, column means contribute to both singular values and right singular vectors.

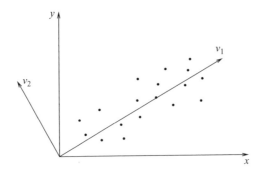

Fig. 7.4. Geometric structure of a matrix exposed by its SVD.

The right singular vectors of a matrix A can be proven to be actually the corresponding singular vectors of $M = A^T A$, and the singular values of A are the square roots of the corresponding singular values of M. Hence the computations of right singular vectors and singular values can be done by computing the singular vectors and singular values of the symmetric matrix $M = A^T A$. For symbolic convenience, we will use u_1 and σ to represent the respective first singular vector and singular value vector of $M = A^T A$, and use v_1 and λ to represent those of another motion B with corresponding $M' = B^T B$.

7.4 Feature Vector Extraction Based on SVD

7.4.1 SVD Properties of Motion Data

When two motions are similar, the row vectors in the motion matrices should cover similar trajectories in the n-dimensional space; hence, the geometric structures of the motion data matrices are similar. Identically, for two similar motions, all corresponding singular vectors should be close to each other, and the corresponding singular values should also be proportional to each other. For realistic motions with variations, singular vectors associated with different singular values have different sensitivities to the motion variations. If a singular value is large and well separated from its neighbors, the associated singular vector would be relatively insensitive to small motion variations. On the other hand, if a singular value is among a poorly separated cluster, its associated singular vector would be highly sensitive to motion variations.

Figure 7.5 shows the accumulative singular values for hand gestures captured by a data glove CyberGlove and human body motions captured by multiple digital cameras as described in Section 7.6. It shows that the first two singular values account for more than 95% of the sum of singular values, while the others might be very small. If the column means are small, the variance along the first singular vector would be the largest and the first singular value accounts for most of the variances. The first singular vectors of similar motions would be close to each other as shown in Figure 7.6 whereas others might not be close to each other as shown in Figure 7.7. If the column means

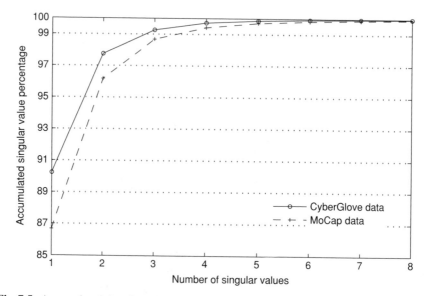

Fig. 7.5. Accumulated singular value percentages in singular value sums for two data sources: CyberGlove data and captured human body motion data. There are 22 singular values for one CyberGlove motion, and 54 singular values for one captured motion.

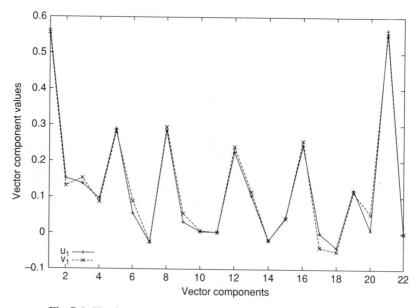

Fig. 7.6. The first singular vectors u_1 and v_1 for two similar motions.

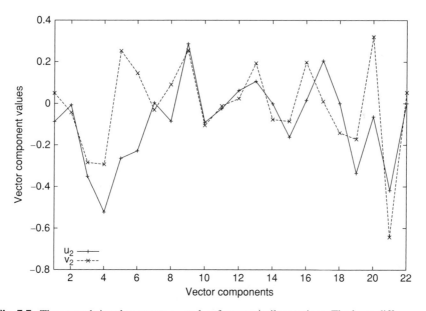

Fig. 7.7. The second singular vectors u_2 and v_2 for two similar motions. The large differences in the second singular vectors show that the second singular vectors might not be close to each other because of the variations in the similar motions.

are large, the first singular value would mainly account for column means and the associated variance might not be the largest. In this case, the first singular vector would be close to the column mean vector if the direction of the largest variance is different from the direction of the large column mean vector, and the second singular vector would be close to the direction with the largest variance as illustrated in Figure 7.8.

7.4.2 Feature Vector Extraction

We can extract the feature vectors from the singular vectors and singular values according to how they can capture the similarity of motions. The first singular vectors are the most dominating factors contributing to the similarity of two motions due to their associated large singular values. Other singular vectors are less reliable in capturing the similarities due to their associated singular values that might be small and approach zero. Hence we can use singular values as weights to reflect the reliability of the associated singular vectors. On the other hand, since the singular values are the Euclidean lengths or 2-norms of projections of the motion matrices A on their associated singular vectors, they reflect the shapes of the hyper-ellipsoids Ax with x being a unit 2-norm vector. The hyper-ellipsoid shapes should be similar for similar motions; hence, the normalized singular values should be proportional. In other words, if the normalized singular value vectors $\vec{\sigma} = \sigma/|\sigma|$ is for one motion and $\vec{\lambda} = \lambda/|\lambda|$ is for another, then $\vec{\sigma}$ should be close to $\vec{\lambda}$ if the two motions are similar to each

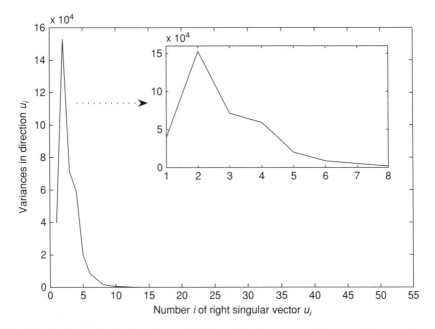

Fig. 7.8. Variances in the directions of different singular vectors. Because of large column means, variance in the direction of the first singular vector might not be the largest.

other. Two different feature vectors can thus be extracted as follows by using only dominating information from singular vectors and singular values.

1. The first singular vector u_1 concatenated by the normalized singular value vector $\vec{\sigma}$ or
2. The weighted first singular vector $w_1 u_1$ followed by the weighted second singular vector $w_2 u_2$, with $w_i = \sigma_i / \sum_{i=1}^{n} \sigma_i$.

Since the right singular vector u_1 can have opposite signs, the following steps can be taken to obtain consistent signs for u_1 of similar patterns.

1. Generate a matrix S with rows being the first right singular vectors u_1 of all known patterns.
2. Subtract the elements of S by their corresponding column means, and update S to be the resulting matrix with zero column means.
3. Compute the SVD of S and let its first right singular vector be s_1.
4. Project the first right singular vector u_1 of patterns (or pattern candidates) onto s_1 by computing $u_1 \cdot s_1$.
5. Negate all components of any u_1 if the corresponding the inner product $u_1 \cdot s_1 < 0$, and let u_1 be the negated vector.

As $|u_1| = 1$ and $|s_1| = 1$, the inner product $u_1 \cdot s_1 = |u_1||s_1| \cos(\alpha)$ ranges over $[-1, 1]$, where α is the angle between the two vectors. Since the projections of u_1 onto

s_1 have the largest variances among projections on any unit vectors, we can expect that $u_1 \cdot s_1$ will not cluster around zero. Our experiments with hundreds of patterns of different sources show that no pattern has $|u_1 \cdot s_1| < 0.3$. Because similar patterns should have close projections $|u_1 \cdot s_1|$, reasonable variations in similar patterns would not result in $u_1 \cdot s_1$ projections of opposite signs if their u_1 signs are the same. That is, only if the u_1 signs of similar motions are opposite can their $u_1 \cdot s_1$ projections have different signs. Hence, u_1 of similar motions would have the same sign by requesting $u_1 \cdot s_1 > 0$.

Similarly, the above steps can be repeated for u_2 with all u_1 replaced by u_2, resulting in consistent signs for the second singular vectors of similar motions. We refer to any of the above extracted feature vectors as f if not stated otherwise.

7.5 Classification of Feature Vectors Using SVM

After a feature vector is extracted from SVD of a motion matrix, it can be classified by SVM classifiers. Before classification, the SVM classifiers need to be trained in order to have support vectors and optimal hyperplanes. All the feature vectors of training motion data sets are used as inputs to SVM classifiers for training. This training phase can be done offline (see the top portion of Figure 7.9). Similarly, we generate testing data sets and these testing data can be classified by the SVMs that have already been trained offline with training data sets.

Classification by SVM classifiers with decision values and by SVM classifiers with probability estimates in the SVM software package [19] are done for accuracy comparison, and the RBF kernel function is used for training. The type of kernel utilized by the SVM is inconsequential as long as the capacity is appropriate for the amount of training data and complexity of the classification boundary [4]. Both the training vectors and the testing vectors have the following format:

$$c\ 1 : f_1\ 2 : f_{k2} \dots 2n : f_{2n}$$

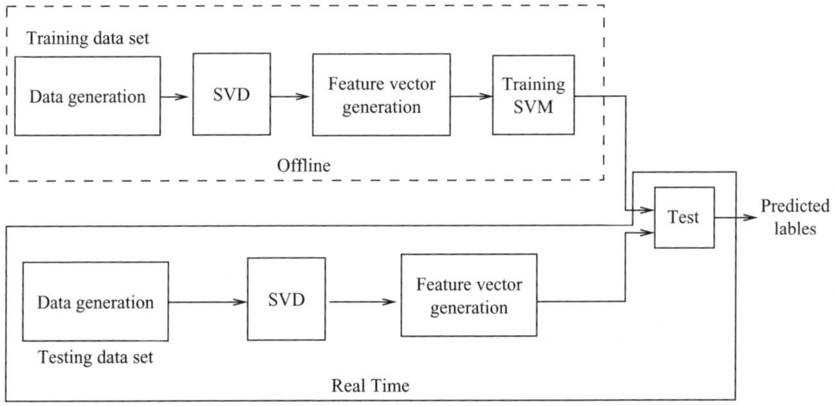

Fig. 7.9. Multiattribute motion data classification flowchart.

where c is an integer label identifying the class of the training vector f, and f_i is the ith component of f.

Feature vectors for similar motions are given the same class label c, and one-versus-one multiclass SVM is employed for classification. The class label c in the testing data is used just for the purpose of obtaining classification accuracy.

For motions following similar trajectories but in different directions, it can be proved that the extracted feature vectors would be similar [1]. Further recognition of motions in different directions can be done by applying dynamic time warping distance to motion data projections on the associated first right singular vectors as shown in [1].

7.6 Performance Evaluation

This section evaluates the extracted feature vectors by classifying them with SVM classifiers with both decision values and probability estimates. Hand gestures and various dances were generated for classification. Classification accuracy and CPU time are compared with those obtained by similarity computation using the weighted-sum SVD similarity measure [6], Eros [7], the MAS [8], and kWAS [9].

7.6.1 Hand Gesture Data Generation

We generated motion data for different hand motions, using a data glove called CyberGlove. Motions of a hand are captured by 22 sensors located at different positions of the glove, and one sensor generates one angular value at about 120 times/second. One hundred ten different motions were carried out, and three similar motions were generated for each of them. Each motion has a different duration from all the others, and all the resultant motion data matrices have different lengths ranging from about 200 to about 1500 rows. The data matrix of one motion can have more than two times the length of the data matrix of a similar motion. Each data matrix of different motions is given a unique class label, and similar motions have the same class label.

7.6.2 Motion Capture Data Generation

The motion capture data come from various human motions captured collectively by using 16 Vicon cameras and the Vicon iQ Workstation software. A dancer wears a suit of nonreflective material, and 44 markers are attached to the body suit. After system calibration and subject calibration, global coordinates and rotation angles of 19 joints/segments can be obtained at about 120 frames per second for any motion. Patterns with global 3D positional data can be disguised by different locations, orientations, or different paths of motion execution as illustrated in Figure 7.10(a). Since two patterns are similar to each other because of similar relative positions of corresponding body segments at corresponding time, and the relative positions of different segments are independent of locations or orientations of the body, we can transform the global position data into local position data.

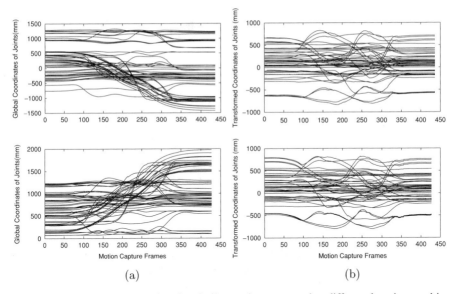

Fig. 7.10. 3D motion capture data for similar motions executed at different locations and in different orientations: (a) before transformation and (b) after transformation.

The transformed local data are positions of different segments relative to a moving coordinate system with the origin at some fixed point of the body, for example, the pelvis. The moving coordinate system is not necessarily aligned with the global system, and it can rotate with the body. So data transformation includes both translation and rotation, and the transformed data would be translation and rotation invariant as shown in Figure 7.10(b). The coordinates of the origin pelvis are not included; thus, the transformed matrices have 54 columns.

Sixty different motions including Taiqi, Indian dances, and western dances were performed for generating motion capture data, and each motion was repeated five times, yielding 60 classes of 300 total human motions. Every repeated motion has a different location and different durations, and can face different orientations.

7.6.3 Performance Evaluation

For hand gesture data, we divide the motions into three data sets. Each data set has data for 110 different motions, and includes data of one of the three similar motions. Sequentially, we use two data sets for training, and the third data set for testing. Three test cases have been run, with one different data set used for testing in each test case. For motion capture data, five data sets are obtained by having each data sets to include 60 different motions, one for each class. All the experiments were performed on a 3.0 GHz Intel processor of a Genuine Intel Linux box, and the code was implemented in C/C++.

The performance has been validated using K-fold cross validation (with $K = 3$ for hand gesture motions and $K = 5$ for the captured motions). Figure 7.11 illustrates

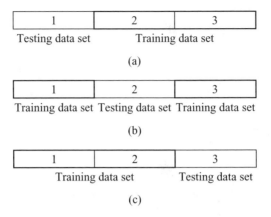

(a)

Fig. 7.11. K-fold cross-validation data sets for hand gesture data, where $K = 3$.

the partitioning of the hand gesture data sets for the K-fold validation (with $K = 3$) and (a), (b), and (c) correspond to the cases with the data sets 1, 2, and 3 being the respective testing data sets. We define the accuracy as the percentage of motions classified or recognized correctly.

Figures 7.12 and 7.13 show that classifiers with decision values outperform classifiers with probability estimates whereas classification of the two different feature

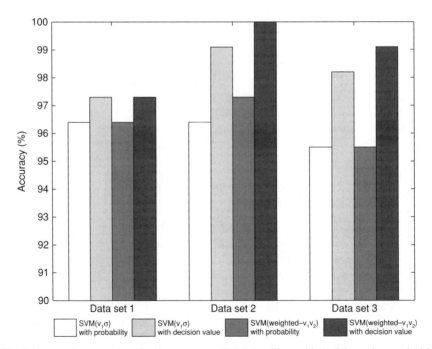

Fig. 7.12. Hand gesture classification accuracy. SVM classifiers with decision values and with probability estimates are compared, and two different feature vectors are also compared.

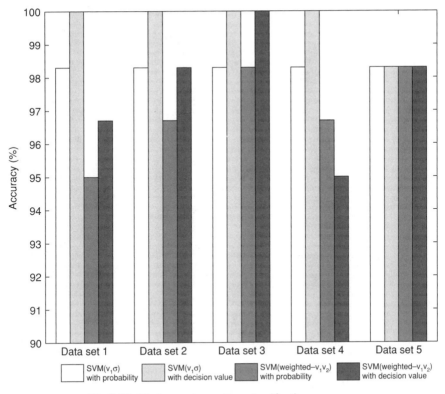

Fig. 7.13. Motion capture pattern classification accuracy.

vectors can give 95–100% accuracy using both classifiers. This observation implies that although classifiers with probability estimates are more suitable than classifiers with decision values for some other applications, such as motion stream segmentation, the accuracy might decrease because of probability estimation. Classifiers with decision values are considered below for further comparison with similarity measures.

Figure 7.14 shows that SVM outperforms all similarity measures except kWAS, which includes more information than the feature vectors extracted for classification. Nevertheless, SVM classifiers still give more than 97% accuracy. In comparison, the two similar motions in each training class are used as patterns for computation of similarity with motions in the testing data set using similarity measures. Motions in the testing data sets were recognized as the corresponding patterns with the highest similarities.

Only one pattern for each different motion is usually assumed for similarity computation using similarity measures, while multiple similar motions are assumed for each class in the training of the SVMs. Figure 7.15 shows the recognition accuracies using similarity measures when only one pattern is used for each different motion. The proposed SVM classification approach obviously outperforms all the similarity

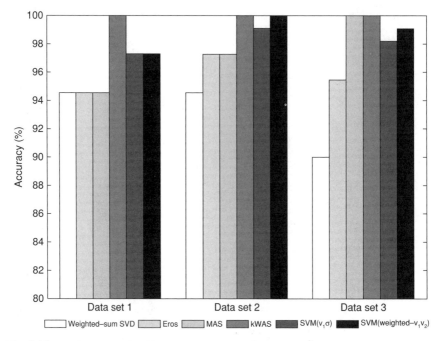

Fig. 7.14. Hand gesture classification accuracy of different approaches when two training patterns in each class are used for similarity testing. k is 5 for kWAS. The first singular vectors v_1 followed by normalized singular value vectors σ are used as the features for SVM ($v_1\sigma$), and the concatenated first two singular vectors v_1 and v_2 weighted by their corresponding singular value portions are used as the features for SVM (weighted-v_1v_2).

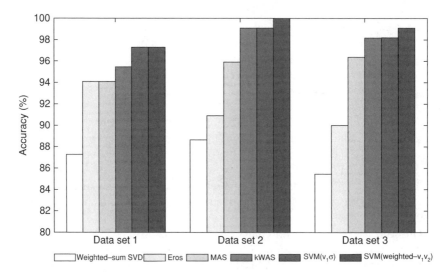

Fig. 7.15. Hand gesture classification accuracy of different approaches when only one training pattern in each class is used for similarity testing.

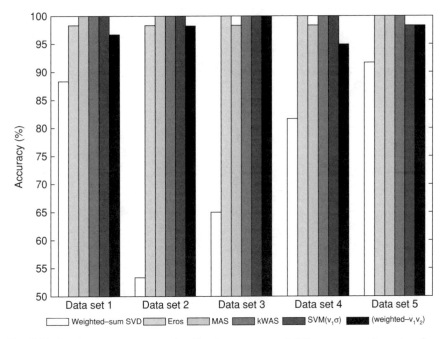

Fig. 7.16. Motion capture pattern classification accuracy of different approaches when four training patterns in each class are used for similarity testing.

measures in finding the most similar patterns or correctly classifying new motion patterns for all testing data sets.

Similar observations can be made for motion capture data as shown in Figures 7.16 and 7.17.

The CPU times taken by SVM classification and similarity measures are shown in Figure 7.18. For motion capture patterns, the proposed SVM classification takes CPU time comparable to that needed by MAS and kWAS, and takes less time than weighted-sum SVD and Eros. For CyberGlove patterns, classification by SVM takes a little more time than all the similarity measure approaches. We observed that after feature vectors have been extracted, classifying a CyberGlove pattern takes about 3.4 ms while classifying a motion capture takes only 1.1 ms. This is true although the feature vectors of CyberGlove patterns have only 44 attributes while the feature vectors of motion capture patterns have 108 attributes.

7.6.4 Discussion

After classification, DTW distance can be used to further determine motion directions if any class has motions following similar trajectories in different directions as discussed in [1]. The motions experimented with in this chapter, including hand gestures and captured human motions, were generated with different durations, and different

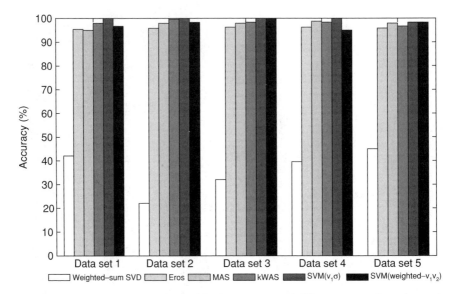

Fig. 7.17. Motion capture pattern classification accuracy of different approaches when only one training pattern in each class is used for similarity testing.

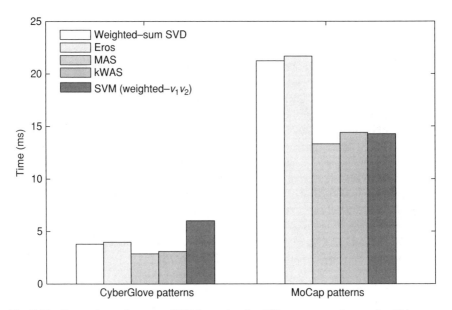

Fig. 7.18. Comparison of average CPU time taken by different approaches to classifying one motion pattern.

motion components can have different generation rates, showing that motions with different lengths and temporal disalignments can be effectively classified.

The weighted-sum SVD similarity measure computes the inner products of all the corresponding singular vectors weighted by their singular values, and takes the minimum of two sums of the inner products as the similarity measure of two matrices. Since the inner products of singular vectors can be both positive and negative, and the weights can be the singular values of either matrix, it is very likely that the weighted sum can drop or jump sharply even if a testing matrix approximately matches some training motion. In contrast, MAS does not consider all singular vectors for the similarity definition. It considers only the dominating first singular vectors and the singular values. By generating a new vector from the normalized singular values, MAS takes into consideration both the dominating direction and the shape of the motion data hyper-ellipsoid, while noises caused by variations of similar motions are reduced by not considering other singular vectors. Eros and kWAS both consider angular similarities of corresponding singular vector pairs, yet they differ in weighting the angular similarities. Eros uses the same weight vector for all patterns, while kWAS uses singular values of corresponding patterns as angular similarity weights, and the weights are different for different patterns. In contrast, the feature vectors we proposed in this chapter consider the dominating singular vectors, and similar to kWAS, the singular vectors are weighted by their associated singular values. The feature vectors do not consider as much information as kWAS; hence, SVM classifiers cannot outperform kWAS if all motion patterns are considered for comparison. More singular vectors have been experimented for feature vector extracted, yet no obvious performance increases can be observed.

7.7 Conclusion

We have shown that by reducing multiattribute motion data into feature vectors by different approaches, SVM classifiers can be used to efficiently classify multiattribute motion data. Feature vectors are close to each other for similar motions, and are different for different motions as shown by the high accuracies of SVM classification we have achieved. RBF function has been used as the kernel function in this chapter, although other kernel functions can also be provided to the SVMs during the training process, which selects a small number of support vectors for the hyperplanes. The high accuracy and low CPU testing time make SVMs a feasible technique to classify and recognize multiattribute data in real time.

Using only a single motion pattern in the database to recognize similar motions allows for less variations in similar motion as shown in Figure 7.15 and Figure 7.17. By reducing multiattribute motion data into feature vectors, and using a group of feature vectors for a class, a new motion has higher expected probability of being recognized by SVMs as optimal hyperplanes are obtained during the training phase.

Two different approaches are explored to extract feature vectors. The first approach considers the first singular vectors and the normalized singular values, while the second approach takes into account the first two dominating singular vectors weighted by their associated singular values. Motions are classified irrespective of their directions at first, and taking into consideration the first left singular vectors by using DTW can further distinguish motions following similar trajectories in different directions [1].

Our experiments with hand gestures and various captured dances further show that SVM classifiers with decision values outperform SVM classifiers with probability estimates. We have addressed the problem of real-time recognition of individual isolated motions accurately and efficiently. Further work needs to be done to explore the feasibilities of the two feature vector extraction approaches for segmenting and recognizing motion streams.

Acknowledgments

We thank Gaurav Pradhan for generating the CyberGlove motion data and thank Punit Kulkarni for assisting with SVM. We also appreciate the reviewers for their insightful comments. The work of Dr. Khan was supported in part by the National Science Foundation grant, NGS-0103709. The work of Dr. B. Prabhakaran was supported in part by the National Science Foundation under grant no. 0237954 for the project CAREER: Animation Databases.

References

1. Li C, Khan L, Prabhakaran B. Real-time Classification of Variable length Multi-attribute Motion Data. *International Journal of Knowledge and Information Systems* (KAIS); 2005.
2. Cristianini N, Shawe-taylor J. *An Introduction to Support Vector Machines and Other Kernel-based Learning Methods*. Cambridge, UK: Cambridge University Press; 2000.
3. Gordan M, Kotropoulos C, Pitas I. Application of support vector machines classifiers to visual speech recognition. In: *Proceedings of the International Conference on Image Processing*, Vol. 3; 2002, pp. 24–28.
4. Vapnik VN. *Statistical Learning theory*. New York: Wiley; 1998.
5. Burian A, Takala J. On signal detection using support vector machines. In: *International Symposium on Signals, Circuits and Systems*, Vol. 2; 2003, pp. 609–612.
6. Shahabi C, Yan D. Real-time pattern isolation and recognition over immersive sensor data streams. In: *Proceedings of The 9th Int'l Conference on Multi-Media Modeling*; 2003, pp. 93–113.
7. Yang K, Shahabi C. A PCA-based similarity measure for multivariate time series. In: *Proceedings of The Second ACM International Workshop on Multimedia Databases*; 2004, pp. 65–74.
8. Li C, Zhai P, Zheng SQ, Prabhakaran B. Segmentation and recognition of multi-attribute motion sequences. In: *Proceedings of The ACM Multimedia Conference 2004*; 2004, pp. 836–843.
9. Li C, Prabhakaran B. A similarity measure for motion stream segmentation and recognition. In: *Proceedings of the Sixth International Workshop on Multimedia Data Mining*; 2005, pp. 89–94.

10. Kahveci T, Singh A, Gurel Ar. Similarity searching for multi-attribute sequences. In: *Proceedings. of 14th Int'l Conference on Scientific and Statistical Database Management*; 2002, pp. 175–184.
11. Lee S, Chun S, Kim D, Lee J, Chung C. Similarity search for multidimensional data sequences. In: *Proceedings. of 16th Int'l Conference on Data Engineering*; 2000, pp. 599–608.
12. Vlachos M, Hadjieleftheriou M, Gunopulos Ds, Keogh E. Indexing multi-dimensional time-series with support for multiple distance measures. In: *SIGMOD*; 2003, pp. 216–225.
13. Huang XD, Ariki Y, Jack MA. *Hidden Markov Models for Speech Recognition*. Edinburgh University Press; 1990.
14. Kundu A, He Y, Bahl P. Recognition of handwritten words: First and second order hidden Markov model based approach. *Pattern Recognition* 1989;22(3):283–297.
15. Starner T, Weaver J, Pentland A. Real-time American sign language recognition using desk and wearable computer based video. *IEEE Transactions on Pattern Analysis and Machine Intelligence* 1998;20(12):1371–1375.
16. Shahabi C, Kaghazian L, Mehta S, Ghoting A, Shanbhag G, McLaughlin M. Analysis of haptic data for sign language recognition. In: *Proceedings of the 9th International Conference on Human Computer Interaction*; 2001, pp. 441–445.
17. Platt JC. Probabilistic outputs for support vector machines and comparison to regularized likelihood methods. In: Smola AJ, Bartlett PL, Scholkopf B, Schuurmans D, editors. *Advances in Large Margin Classifiers*. Cambridge, MA: MIT Press; 2000. Available at: citeseer.nj.nec.com/platt99probabilistic.html.
18. Wu TF, Liu CJ, Weng RC. Probability estimates for multi-class classification by pairwise coupling. *Journal of Machine Learning Research* 2004;(5):975–1005.
19. Chang CC, Lin C. LIBSVM: A library for support vector machines; 2001. Software available at: http://www.csie.ntu.edu.tw/~cjlin/libsvm.
20. Golub GH, Loan CFVan. *Matrix Computations*. Baltimore, MD: The Johns Hopkins University Press; 1996.
21. Schutter BDe, Moor BDe. The singular value decomposition in the extended max algebra. *Linear Algebra and Its Applications* 1997;250:143–176.

Part III
Multimedia Data Indexing and Retrieval

8. FAST: Fast and Semantics-Tailored Image Retrieval

Ruofei Zhang and Zhongfei (Mark) Zhang

Summary. This chapter focuses on developing a Fast And Semantics-Tailored (FAST) image retrieval methodology. Specifically, the contributions of FAST methodology to the CBIR literature include (1) development of a new indexing method based on fuzzy logic to incorporate color, texture, and shape information into a region-based approach to improving the retrieval effectiveness and robustness, (2) development of a new hierarchical indexing structure and the corresponding Hierarchical, Elimination-based A* Retrieval algorithm (HEAR) to significantly improve the retrieval efficiency without sacrificing the retrieval effectiveness; it is shown that HEAR is guaranteed to deliver a logarithm search in the average case and, (3) employment of user relevance feedbacks to tailor the semantic retrieval to each user's individualized query preference through the novel Indexing Tree Pruning (ITP) and Adaptive Region Weight Updating (ARWU) algorithms. Theoretical analysis and experimental evaluations show that FAST methodology holds a great promise in delivering fast and semantics-tailored image retrieval in CBIR.

8.1 Introduction

This work addresses the topic of general purpose content-based image retrieval (CBIR). CBIR has received intensive attention in the literature since this area was started a few years ago, and consequently a broad range of techniques [1] is proposed.

The majority of the early research focuses on global features of imagery. The most fundamental and popularly used feature is the color histogram and its variants, which was used in the classic systems such as IBM QBIC [2] and Berkeley Chabot [3]. Since color histograms do not carry spatial information, which is considered to be related to the semantics of image content, efforts have been reported in the literature to incorporate the spatial information into the histograms. Pass and Zabih [4] proposed the Color Coherence Vector (CCV) to address this issue. Huang et al. [5] went further to use the Color Correlograms to integrate color and spatial information.

Recently region-based approaches have been shown to be more effective. A region-based retrieval system segments images into regions, and retrieves images based on the similarities derived from the regions. Berkeley Blobworld [6] and UCSB NeTra [7] compared images on the basis of individual regions. To query an image, the user was required to select regions and the corresponding features for the similarity computation. Wang et al. [8] proposed an integrated region matching scheme called IRM, which allowed matching a region in one image to several regions in another image. As a result, the similarity between two images was defined as the weighed sum of distances, in a feature space, between all regions from different images. Later, Chen and Wang [9] proposed an improved approach called UFM based on applying coarse fuzzy logic to the different region features to improve the retrieval effectiveness of IRM. Recently Jing et al. [10] presented a region-based, modified inverted file structure analogous to that in text retrieval to index the image database; each entry of the file corresponded to a cluster (called codeword) in the region space. While this method is reported to be effective, the selection of the size of the code book is subjective in nature, and the effectiveness is sensitive to this selection.

To narrow the semantic gap in image retrieval, several recent efforts in CBIR, such as [11] and [12], performed the image retrieval not only based on the content but also based on user preference profiles. Machine learning techniques such as Support Vector Machine (SVM) [13] and Bayesian network [14] were applied to learn the user's query intention through leveraging preference profiles or relevance feedbacks. One drawback of such approaches is that they typically work well only for one specific domain, for example, art image database or medical image database. It has been shown that for a general domain the retrieval accuracy of these approaches is weak [1]. In addition, these approaches are restricted by the availability of user preference profiles and the generalization limitation of machine learning techniques they applied.

While the majority of the literature in CBIR focuses on the indexing and retrieval effectiveness issue, much less attention is paid to the indexing and retrieval efficiency issue. Historically, CBIR research is motivated in the beginning to demonstrate that indexing directly in the image domain can deliver better retrieval effectiveness than indexing through collateral information such as key words, and this perception has been carried on over the years; the retrieval efficiency issue, on the other hand, is not considered to be the focus of the research in the CBIR community, as the general perception is that this issue may be resolved by directly making use of the existing indexing methods developed from the spatial data structure research. Several spatial data structures have been proposed in the literature. Among these data structures, some are based on the ideas of B^+- and B-trees [15], which initially are for organizing 1-D feature vectors or single valued keys of stored items, such as multidimensional B^+-tree [16], while others perform feature searching and updating by "ordering" the multidimensional features either based on feature space partition and filtering, such as k-d tree [17], R-tree [18, 19] and its variants, R^*-tree [20], R^+-tree [21], and TV-tree [22], or by similarity measuring [23]. Another data organization method is the grid file [24], by which an n-dimensional space is divided into equal-sized hypercubes with each hypercube containing zero or more feature vectors. In grid file search, the search scope is reduced from the whole feature space to a hypercube (grid) to facilitate data insertion. However, this classical method is not suitable for very high-dimensional vectors, which are common in multimedia processing.

There are several problems when applying these generic data structures in CBIR directly. First, technically many CBIR algorithms involve complicated distributions in a high-dimensional feature space, and it is difficult and inflexible to directly "order" features in such a high-dimensional space using the existing spatial data structures. Second, while theoretically any CBIR methods can use the existing spatial data structures to address the retrieval efficiency, practically this is not the case because when the dimensionality becomes very high (which is true for almost all the CBIR methods) the overhead for online bookkeeping becomes so demanding [25] that the overall saving in efficiency becomes questionable. Some data structures, such as SS-tree [26] and TV-tree [22], attempt to address this problem, but their overall performances are limited because of the assumptions they are subject to [27]. Third, the existing spatial data structures do not work well for region-based image indexing approaches due to the fact that the mapping between the region space and the image space is typically nonmetric [8–10]. Consequently, a few efforts in the literature have attempted to address the efficiency issue directly in designing specific CBIR algorithms. For example, Berman and Shapiro [28] used a set of keys along with the triangle inequality in image databases for fast search.

Since the evaluation of CBIR retrieval is typically subjective, in recent years methods incorporating user relevance feedbacks start to show promise in resolving this issue. Two directions of research are observed in incorporating user relevance feedback in CBIR: (1) developing a weighting scheme to explicitly "guide" the retrieval [29] and (2) applying machine learning techniques such as Bayesian net and Support Vector Machine to reduce the problem to a standard reasoning and classification problem [30, 31].

On the basis of an extensive literature review, we have identified three problems in the current status of CBIR research: (1) the indexing effectiveness still needs to be improved; (2) the retrieval efficiency needs to be addressed directly in the indexing method; and (3) the retrieval subjectivity issue needs to be further addressed to better deliver a semantic retrieval. This work is motivated to address these three issues simultaneously. The ultimate goal of this project is to design a CBIR methodology that can deliver fast and semantics-tailored image retrieval capability. By fast, we mean that the efficiency issue is well addressed; by semantics-tailored, we mean that the user query preference is inferred online to allow an individualized retrieval to better address the retrieval effectiveness and user preference issues. Consequently, we call the methodology FAST. The contributions of FAST are reflected in these three aspects. An overview of the architecture of FAST is shown in Figure 8.1.

The remainder of this chapter addresses these aspects of FAST methodology in detail. Section 8.2 describes the fuzzified feature representation and indexing scheme. The region matching and similarity computation metrics are also provided in this section. The proposed hierarchical indexing structure and the Hierarchical, Elimination-based A* Retrieval (HEAR) online search algorithm are presented in Section 8.3. Section 8.4 describes the developed Indexing Tree Pruning (ITP) and the Adaptive Region Weight Updating (ARWU) algorithms to capture users' retrieval subjectivity. Section 8.5 presents the empirical evaluations of a FAST prototype. The chapter is concluded in Section 8.6.

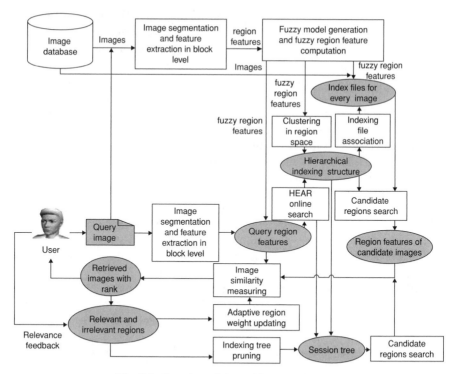

Fig. 8.1. Overview of the architecture of FAST.

8.2 Fuzzified Feature Representation and Indexing Scheme

We propose an efficient, clustering-based, fuzzified feature representation approach to addressing the general-purpose CBIR. In this approach we integrate semantics-intensive, clustering-based segmentation with fuzzy representation of color histogram, texture, and shape to index image databases.

8.2.1 Image Segmentation

In our system, the query image and all images in the database are first segmented into regions. The fuzzy features of color, texture, and shape are extracted to be the signature of each region in one image. The image segmentation is based on the color and spatial variation features using the k-means algorithm [32]. We use this algorithm to perform the image segmentation because it is unsupervised and efficient, which is crucial to segment general-purpose images such as the images in the World Wide Web. To segment an image, the system first partitions the image into blocks with 4×4 pixels to compromise between texture effectiveness and computation time, and then extracts a feature vector consisting of six features from each block. Three of them are average color components in a 4×4 pixel size block. We use the *LAB* color space due to its desired property that the perceptual color difference is proportional to the numerical difference. These features are denoted as $\{C_1, C_2, C_3\}$. The other three features represent energy in the high-frequency bands of the Haar wavelet transform [33], that is, the square root of the second order moment of the wavelet coefficients in the high-frequency bands. To obtain these moments, a Haar wavelet transform is applied to the L component of each pixel. After a one-level wavelet transform, a 4×4 block is decomposed into four frequency bands; each band contains 2×2 coefficients. Without loss of generality, suppose that the coefficients in the HL band are $\{c_{k,l}, c_{k,l+1}, c_{k+1,l}, c_{k+1,l+1}\}$. Then we compute one feature of this block in HL band as

$$f = \sqrt{\frac{1}{4} \sum_{i=0}^{1} \sum_{j=0}^{1} c_{k+i,l+j}} \tag{8.1}$$

The other two features are computed similarly from the LH and HH band. These three features of the block are denoted as $\{T_1, T_2, T_3\}$. They can be used to discern texture by showing L variations in different directions. After we have obtained feature vectors for all blocks, we perform normalization on both color and texture features to whiten them such that the effects of different feature ranges are eliminated. Then the k-means algorithm [32] is used to cluster the feature vectors into several classes with each class corresponding to one region in the segmented image. Since the clustering is performed in the feature space, blocks in each cluster do not necessarily form a connected region in the image. Consequently, we preserve the natural clustering of objects in general-purpose images. The k-means algorithm does not specify how many clusters to choose. We adaptively select the number of clusters C by gradually increasing C until a stop criterion is met. The average number of clusters for all images in the database varies according to the adjusted stop criterion. In the k-means algorithm we use a color-texture weighted $L2$ distance metric

$$\sqrt{w_c \sum_{i=1}^{3} \left(C_i^{(1)} - C_i^{(2)}\right)^2 + w_t \sum_{i=1}^{3} \left(T_i^{(1)} - T_i^{(2)}\right)^2} \tag{8.2}$$

to describe the distance between the features of blocks, where the $C^{(1)}(C^{(2)})$ and $T^{(1)}(T^{(2)})$ are color features and texture features, respectively, of block 1(2). w_c and w_t are the weights specified in specific experiments. After the segmentation, three additional features are determined for each region to describe the shape property. They are normalized inertia [34] of order 1 to 3. For a region H in the two-dimensional Euclidean integer space $\mathbb{Z}^2$ (an image), its normalized inertia of order p is

$$l(H, p) = \frac{\sum_{(x,y):(x,y) \in H} [(x - \hat{x})^2 + (y - \hat{y})^2]^{p/2}}{[V(H)]^{1+p/2}} \tag{8.3}$$

where $V(H)$ is the number of pixels in the region H and $(\hat{x}, \hat{y})$ is the centroid of H. The minimum normalized inertia is achieved by spheres. Denoting the p_{th} order normalized inertia of spheres as L_p, we define the following three features to describe the shape of each region:

$$S_1 = l(H, 1)/L_1, \; S_2 = l(H, 2)/L_2, \; S_3 = l(H, 3)/L_3 \tag{8.4}$$

8.2.2 Fuzzy Color Histogram for Each Region

The color representation would be coarse and imprecise if we simply extract the block color feature to index each region as Wang et al. [8] proposed. Color is one of the most fundamental properties to discriminate images so that we should take advantage of all available information in it. Considering the typical uncertainty stemmed from color quantization and human perception, we develop a modified color histogram, using the fuzzy technique [35, 36] to accommodate the uncertainty.

The fuzzy color histogram is defined as follows. We assume that each color is a fuzzy set while the correlation among colors is modeled as a membership function of different fuzzy sets. A fuzzy set F on the feature space R^n is defined as a mapping $\mu_F : R^n \to [0, 1]$ with μ_F as the membership function. For any feature vector $f \in R^n$, the value of $\mu_F(f)$ is called the degree of membership of f to the fuzzy set F (or, in short, the degree of membership to F). A value closer to 1 for $\mu_F(f)$ means more representative the feature vector f to the fuzzy set F.

An ideal fuzzy color model should have the resemblance inversely proportional to the intercolor distance. Based on this requirement, the most commonly used prototype membership functions include conic, trapezoidal, B-splines, exponential, Cauchy, and paired sigmoid functions [37]. We have tested the conic, trapezoidal, exponential, and Cauchy functions on our system. In general, the performances of the exponential and the Cauchy functions are better than those of the conic and trapezoidal functions. Considering the computational complexity, we use the Cauchy function due to its computational simplicity. The Cauchy function, $C : R^n \to [0, 1]$, is defined as

$$C(\vec{x}) = \frac{1}{1 + \left(\frac{\|\vec{x} - \vec{v}\|}{d}\right)^\alpha} \tag{8.5}$$

where $\vec{v} \in R^n$, d and $\alpha \in R$, $d > 0$, $\alpha \geq 0$, $\vec{v}$ is the center location (point) of the fuzzy set, d represents the width of the function, and α determines the shape (or smoothness) of the function. Collectively, d and α describe the grade of fuzziness of the corresponding fuzzy feature.

Accordingly, the color resemblance in a region is defined as

$$\mu_c(c') = \frac{1}{1 + \left(\frac{d(c,c')}{\sigma}\right)^\alpha} \tag{8.6}$$

where d is the Euclidean distance between color c and c' in the LAB space, and σ is the average distance between colors

$$\sigma = \frac{2}{B(B - 1)} \sum_{i=1}^{B-1} \sum_{k=i+1}^{B} d(c, c') \tag{8.7}$$

where B is the number of bins in the color partition. The average distance between colors is used to approximate the appropriate width of the fuzzy membership function.

The experiments show that the color model performance changes insignificantly when α is in the interval [0.7, 1.5], but degrades rapidly outside the interval. We set $\alpha = 1$ in Eq. (8.6) to simplify the computation.

This fuzzy color model enables us to enlarge the influence of a given color to its neighboring colors according to the uncertainty principle and the perceptual similarity. This means that each time a color c is found in the image, it influences all the quantized colors according to their resemblance to the color c. Numerically, this could be expressed as

$$h_2(c) = \sum_{c' \in \mu} h_1(c')\mu_c(c') \tag{8.8}$$

where μ is the color universe in the image and $h_1(c')$ is the usual normalized color histogram. Finally the normalized fuzzy color histogram is computed as

$$h(c) = \frac{h_2(c)}{\max_{c' \in \mu} h_2(c')} \tag{8.9}$$

which falls in the interval [0,1].

Note that this fuzzy histogram operation is in fact a linear convolution between the "regular" color histogram and the fuzzy color model. This convolution expresses the histogram smoothing, provided that the color model is indeed a smoothing, low-pass filtering kernel. The use of the Cauchy function as the color model produces the smoothed histogram, which is a mean for the reduction of the quantization errors [38].

In the FAST prototype implementation, the *LAB* color space is quantized into 96 bins by using uniform quantization (*L* by 6, *A* by 4, and *B* by 4). To reduce the online computation, for each bin $\mu_c(c')$ is precomputed and implemented as a lookup table.

8.2.3 Fuzzy Representation of Texture and Shape for Each Region

To accommodate the imprecise image segmentation and uncertainty of human perception, we propose to fuzzify each region generated in image segmentation using a parameterized membership function. The parameter for the membership function is determined on the basis of the clustering results of blocks. Similar to the color features, the fuzzification of the texture and shape feature vectors again brings a crucial improvement into the region representation of an image: fuzzy features naturally characterize the gradual transition between regions within an image. In our proposed representation scheme, a fuzzy feature set assigns weights, called degree of membership, to feature vectors of each block in the feature space. As a result, the feature vector of a block belongs to multiple regions with different degrees of membership as opposed to the classical region representation, in which a feature vector belongs to exactly one region. We first discuss the fuzzification of the texture features, and then discuss that of the shape features.

We take each region as a fuzzy set of blocks. In order to propose a unified approach consistent with the fuzzy color histogram representation, we again use Cauchy function to be the fuzzy membership function, that is,

$$\mu_i(f) = \frac{1}{1 + \left(\frac{d(f, \hat{f}_i)}{\sigma}\right)^\alpha} \tag{8.10}$$

where $f \in R^k$ (here $k = 3$) is the texture feature vector of each block, $\hat{f}_i$ is the average texture feature vector of region i, d is the Euclidean distance between $\hat{f}_i$ and any feature f, and σ represents the average distance for texture features among the cluster centers obtained from the k-means algorithm. σ is defined as

$$\sigma = \frac{2}{C(C-1)} \sum_{i=1}^{C-1} \sum_{k=i+1}^{C} \| \hat{f}_i - \hat{f}_k \| \tag{8.11}$$

where C is the number of regions in a segmented image, and $\hat{f}_i$ is the average texture feature vector of region i.

Making use of this block membership function, the fuzzified texture properties of region i is represented as

$$\vec{f}_i^T = \sum_{f \in U^T} f \mu_i(f) \tag{8.12}$$

where U^T is the feature space composed by texture features of all blocks.

On the basis of the fuzzy membership function $\mu_i(f)$ obtained in a similar fashion, we also fuzzify the shape property representation of region i by modifying Eq. (8.3) as

$$l(i, p) = \frac{\sum_{f \in U^S} [(f_x - \hat{x})^2 + (f_y - \hat{y})^2]^{p/2} \mu_i(f)}{[N]^{1+p/2}} \tag{8.13}$$

where f_x and f_y are the x and y coordinates of the block with the shape feature f, respectively; $\hat{x}$ and $\hat{y}$ are the x and y central coordinates of the region i, respectively; and N is the number of blocks in an image and U^S is the block feature space in an image. On the basis of Eqs. (8.4) and Eq. (8.13), we determine the fuzzified shape feature of each region, denoted as $\vec{f}_i^S$.

8.2.4 Region Matching and Similarity Determination

Once we have fuzzified representations for color, texture, and shape features, we apply the normalization on these features before they are written to the index files. For each region, we record the following information as its indexed data: (1) fuzzy color histogram $h(c)$; (2) fuzzy texture feature $\vec{f}^T$; (3) fuzzy shape feature $\vec{f}^S$; (4) the relative size of the region to the whole image w; and (5) the central coordinate of the region area $(\hat{x}, \hat{y})$. Such indexed data of all regions in an image are recorded as the signature of the image.

Based on the fuzzified features for regions in every image, a fuzzy matching scheme is developed to determine the distance between any two regions p and q as well as the overall similarity between images. For fuzzy texture and shape features, we apply the $L2$ distance formula as

$$d_T^{pq} = \| \vec{f_p}^T - \vec{f_q}^T \|$$

and

$$d_S^{pq} = \| \vec{f_p}^S - \vec{f_q}^S \|$$

respectively.

For fuzzy histogram, we use the distance formula

$$d_C^{pq} = \sqrt{\frac{\sum_{i=1}^{B}[h_p(i) - h_q(i)]^2}{B}} \qquad (8.14)$$

where B is the number of bins, and $h_p(i)$ and $h_q(i)$ are fuzzy histogram of region p and q, respectively.

The intercluster distance on color and texture between region p and q is defined as

$$d_{CT}^{pq} = \sqrt{d_C^{pq\,2} + d_T^{pq\,2}} \qquad (8.15)$$

The overall distance between two regions is defined as follows:

$$DIST(p, q) = w d_{CT}^{pq} + (1 - w) d_S^{pq} \qquad (8.16)$$

where w is a weight. In the current FAST prototype, we set $w = 0.7$ to purposively give color and texture more weight than shape, as we have found that the shape features are more vulnerable to the segmentation.

Since image segmentation is usually not perfect, a region in one image could correspond to several regions in another image. Consequently, we construct an image distance measure through the following steps. Suppose that we have M regions in image 1 and N regions in image 2.

Step 1: Determine the distance between one region in image 1 and all regions in image 2. For each region i in image 1, the distance between this region and image 2 is

$$R_{i,\text{Image2}} = \min DIST(i, j) \qquad (8.17)$$

where j is each region in image 2.

Step 2: Similarly, we determine the distance between a region j in image 2 and image 1

$$R_{j,\text{Image1}} = \min DIST(j, i) \qquad (8.18)$$

where i is each region in image 1.

Step 3: After obtaining the $M + N$ distances, we define the distance between the two images (1 and 2) as

$$DistIge(1, 2) = \frac{\sum_{i=1}^{M} w_{1i} R_{i,\text{Image2}} + \sum_{j=1}^{N} w_{2j} R_{j\text{Image1}}}{2} \qquad (8.19)$$

where w_{1i} is the weight for each region in image 1 and w_{2j} is the weight for each region in image 2. We set $w_{1i} = \frac{N_{1i}}{N_1}$, where N_{1i} is the number of blocks in region i and N_1 is the total number of blocks in image 1. w_{2j} is defined similarly. In other words, larger regions are given more significance than smaller regions because we believe that large regions are more semantically related to the content of an image. Clearly, $DistIge(1, 2) = 0$ if image 1 and image 2 are identical, and $DistIge(1, 2)$ becomes larger when image 1 and image 2 differ more substantially. Consequently, for each query q, $DistIge(q, d)$ is determined for each image d in the database and relevant images are retrieved through sorting the similarities $DistIge(q, d)$.

8.3 Hierarchical Indexing Structure and HEAR Online Search

To achieve fast retrieval, we have designed a hierarchical indexing structure in the database and a related online search algorithm to avoid the linear search. An optimal indexing structure is defined in the region space such that a query image needs to be compared only with those in the database that have at least one region that is most similar to a region in the query image, given a specified similarity.

Let S denote the set of all the nodes in the indexing structure, and X be the set of all the regions in the database. Each node $s \in S$ is a set of regions $X_s \subset X$ with a feature vector z_s, the centroid of the region feature set F_s in the node. The children of a node $s \in S$ are denoted as $c(s) \subset S$. The child nodes partition the region space of the parent node such that

$$X_s = \bigcup_{r \in c(s)} X_r \qquad (8.20)$$

Now the question is how to construct such an optimal indexing structure. Recall that we have used a modified k-means algorithm in the image segmentation to form all the regions. After all the images in the database are indexed on the basis of the indexing scheme in Section 8.2, we apply the same k-means algorithm again to all the feature vectors corresponding to all the regions of all the images recursively to form the hierarchy of the indexing structure. All the nodes represent centroid feature vectors of a corresponding set of regions except for the leaf nodes, which, in addition to a set of regions belonging to the corresponding cluster, also record IDs of images that share one region with the feature vectors of the regions in that set. The depth of the indexing structure is determined adaptively on the basis of the size of the image database. The resulting indexing tree is called the Hierarchical Indexing Structure.

Typical search algorithms would traverse the tree top-down, selecting the branch that minimizing distance between a query q and a cluster centroid z_s. However, this search strategy is not optimal since it does not allow backtracking. To achieve an optimal search, we apply A* search algorithm [14] by keeping track of all nodes that have been searched and always selecting the nodes with minimum distance to the query region. The A* search is guaranteed to select the cluster whose centroid has the minimum distance in the set of visited nodes to the query region. Hence, it is optimal.

Note that in general the image set associated with a leaf node is *significantly* smaller than the original image set in the database. We show that this reduced image set may be further filtered in the online query search by exploiting the triangle inequality principle. Recall that the similarity function between two regions defined in Eq. 8.16 is metric, given two regions p and q associated with two images in the image set of a leaf node in the indexing tree. We have

$$DIST(p, q) \geq |DIST(p, z) - DIST(q, z)| \qquad (8.21)$$

where $DIST(p, q)$ is the distance between regions p and q; z denotes a key region feature represented by the centroid of the corresponding leaf node (cluster). Consider a set of I regions $X_h = \{x_{h1}, x_{h2}, \ldots, x_{hI}\}$ at leaf node h and a key region feature z_h. Pre-calculating $DIST(x_{hi}, z_h)$, for $i = 1$ to I, results in a linear table of I entries. To find those regions $x \in X_h$ at node h such that $DIST(r, x) \leq t$ for a query region r and the predefined threshold t, we note that the lower bounds on $DIST(r, x)$ exist by determining $DIST(r, z_h)$, $DIST(x_{hi}, z_h)$ and repeatedly applying Eq. ((8.21)). If $|DIST(r, z_h) - DIST(x_{hi}, z_h)| > t$, x can be safely eliminated from the linear table of I entries, resulting in avoiding search for all the entries in the table. Thus, given a query, we have the retrieval algorithm described in Figure 8.2 called the Hierarchical, Elimination-based A* Retrieval (HEAR), and the theorem stated in Theorem 8.1 guaranteeing the logarithm complexity in average case performance for HEAR.

The symbols used in the HEAR algorithm are introduced as follows.

---

input : q, the query image
output : Ψ, Images retrieved for the query image q
begin
   | **for** *For each region r in the query image q* **do**
   | | $s^* = root$;
   | | $\Omega = \{s^*\}$;
   | | $Nodes Searched = 0$;
   | | **while** *s^* is not a node of desired tree depth* **do**
   | | | $\Omega \leftarrow (\Omega - \{s^*\}) \cup c(s^*)$;
   | | | $Nodes Searched = Nodes Searched + |c(s^*)|$;
   | | | $s^* \leftarrow \arg\min_{s \in \Omega}(DIST(r, z_s))$;
   | | **end**
   | | $\Phi = \{\}$;
   | | **for** *each region p in the node s^** **do**
   | | | **if** $|DIST(p, z_s) - DIST(r, z_s)| \leq t$ **then**
   | | | | $\Phi \leftarrow \Phi \cup \{p\}$;
   | | | **end**
   | | **end**
   | | $\Psi_r = \{$Images having regions in set $\Phi\}$;
   | **end**
   | $\Psi = \bigcup_{r=1}^{m} \Psi_r$;
end

Fig. 8.2. HEAR Algorithm.

m is the number of regions in the query image; s^* is the cluster whose centroid has the minimum distance to the query region r; Ω is the cluster set we have searched; $|c(s^*)|$ is the size of the child set of s^*; z_s is the cluster centroid; *NodesSearched* records the number of nodes we have searched so far; and t is the predefined threshold of the distance between a region and a query region. The resulting Ψ is the final image set to be compared with the query image.

Theorem 8.1. *In average case, FAST algorithm achieves the logarithm retrieval efficiency.*

Proof. Suppose that m is the average branching factor of the Hierarchical Indexing Structure; n is the number of images in the database; l is the average number of regions of an image; and k is the height of the indexing tree. Then nl is the total number of regions. In the average case, it is clear that when $k \geq \log_m nl - \log_m(log_m nl)$, the number of regions in a leaf node $w \leq \log_m nl$. In the selected leaf node s^*, the triangle inequality principle is applied. Without loss of generality, suppose that the distance threshold ratio between a region and the centroid for the region to be selected as a candidate region is $1/\tau$. Consequently, the average number of regions selected to compare with the query region is $q \propto w/\tau^2 = \frac{\log_m nl}{\tau^2}$. We call these regions candidate regions. Each candidate region corresponds to one image in the database. Thus, the total number of images in the database to be compared with the query image is $\lambda lq = \frac{\lambda l \log_m nl}{\tau^2}$, where λ is the ratio that describes the region-to-image correspondence relationship, $\lambda \in [1/l, 1]$. Thus we observe that the average number of images to be compared is bounded in $\left[\frac{\log_m nl}{\tau^2}, \frac{l \log_m nl}{\tau^2} \right]$. l is determined by the resolution of the image segmentation, and typically is small (4 in the FAST prototype). τ is a constant. Hence, the complexity of the online search algorithm HEAR is $O(log_m n)$ for a database of n images.

While any feature-based CBIR methods could apply a clustering algorithm recursively to generate a hierarchy in the (typically high dimensional) feature space, we argue that this does not work in general, and thus show that the contributions reflected in Theorem 1 are unique and significant.

We define that a classification-based clustering in a feature space is *spherically separable* [13] if for any cluster there is always a specific radius R for this cluster such that for any feature vector v, v is in the cluster if and only if $D(v, c) < R$ where c is the centroid vector of the cluster and D is a metric distance measure. Given a CBIR method, if the similarity measure is metric, and if the images are indexed in global features (i.e., each image is indexed by a single feature vector in the image feature space), in order to generate a hierarchy in the feature space by recursively clustering the features of the whole image database, it would require that all the clusters be spherically separable. Clearly this is not true as in a typical image feature space, the distribution of the semantic classes in the feature space is rather complicated (e.g., it is typical that one semantic class is contained by another, or two semantic classes are completely "mixed" together), and thus the spherically separable property is by no means satisfied. This is shown to be a well-known fact even in many special domain image classification or clustering problems such as in face image classification [39], not even speaking for the general domain image retrieval. On the other hand, if the similarity measure is not metric, it would not be possible to generate a hierarchy in a feature space based on the recursive applications of a clustering algorithm as the clustering presumes a metric distance measure. Consequently, the only possibility to generate such an indexing hierarchy is to use a nonglobal feature, that is, to build up this hierarchy in a feature space other than the image feature space. The significance of the development of the Hierarchical Indexing Structure as well as the related HEAR online search algorithm reflected through Theorem 8.1 is that we have explicitly developed an indexing scheme in the *regional feature space* and we have shown that even with this "detour" through the regional feature space, we can still promise a logarithm search complexity in the average case in the image feature space.

We develop the Hierarchical Indexing Structure in the regional feature space based on the following three reasons. First, since the features we have developed to index images are based on the regional feature space, it is natural to build up an indexing hierarchy in the regional feature space. Second, the similarity measure defined in FAST is not metric, and thus it is not possible to directly build up an indexing hierarchy in the image feature space. Third, after segmentations of an image into regions, the features in the regional feature space are essentially "uniform," and consequently they are able to satisfy the spherically separable property in the regional feature space, which is required for the construction of the hierarchy using clustering.

Apart from the above discussions of the Hierarchical Indexing Structure, it is also interesting to compare it with the existing high-dimensional indexing structures, for example, R-tree and its derivative indexing trees. It has been demonstrated that the search efficiency of an R-tree is largely determined by the coverage and overlap [27]. The coverage of a level of an R-tree is the total area of all the rectangles associated with the nodes of that level. The overlap of a level of an R-tree is the total area contained within two or more nodes. Efficient R-tree search demands that both the coverage and overlap be minimized. From the point of view of R-tree-based multidimensional access structures, the proposed Hierarchical Indexing Structure has two advantages. First, the nodes in each level have no overlap since each region feature belongs to only one cluster (node). With this property, multiple-path traversal is avoided, which improves the search efficiency significantly. Second, the search on the Hierarchical Indexing Structure does not depend on the node coverage because no dimension comparisons are required to decide the branch in HEAR. In other words, the minimum bounding region (MBR) of each internal node in the Hierarchical Indexing Structure is determined by the region features per se and can be any possible shape. With the nonoverlapping property between internal nodes of each level and MBR-coverage independent search in HEAR, the efficiency of the Hierarchical Indexing Structure is enhanced as compared with the discussed R-tree as well as its derivative data structures for region-based CBIR.

8.4 Addressing User's Subjectivity Using ITP and ARWU

To achieve semantics-tailored retrieval, we must address the *human perception subjectivity* [40] issue in CBIR. This is resolved through the ITP and ARWU algorithms we have developed with user query preference inferred to deliver individualized retrieval.

Since the relevance subjectivity in FAST resides at the region level as opposed to at the image level, ideally we would like to ask users to indicate the relevant regions in each retrieval, which would add complexity in user interface and users' interaction. As a compromise, FAST assumes that users cast only yes (+) or no (−) vote to each retrieved image as the data collected in the user relevance feedback. Based on this very "qualitative" user relevance feedback, the feedback data is typically sparse and limited. We have developed an algorithm to infer the user preference in order to tailor to the intended retrieval semantics from a sparse distribution of this "qualitative" data. Moreover, we take the advantage of this user relevance feedback information to further expedite the subsequent query search, resulting in achieving the two goals of fast and semantics-tailored retrieval simultaneously.

We note the fact that the similar (common) regions among relevant images are important to characterize relevant images whereas the similar (common) regions among irrelevant images are important to distinguish the retrieved irrelevant images from the relevant images [40]. Assuming that a user personal preference of the intended retrieval semantics is consistent over the whole session of the retrieval, we develop a user relevance feedback algorithm called Indexing Tree Pruning (ITP). The idea of ITP is that we use the k-means algorithm to infer the "typical" regions from the images voted as relevant, and the "typical" regions from the images voted as irrelevant, based on which a standard two-class support vector machine (SVM) [13] is used to generate a separation hyperplane in the region feature space, which in turn "cuts" the space into two halves; the subsequent search may be further constrained to focus on the relevant side of the Hierarchical Indexing Structure using HEAR. Specifically, the ITP algorithm is described in Figure 8.3.

Figure 8.4 illustrates an example of the original indexing tree and one session tree after the pruning using ITP. The actual pruning is done through applying the DBT algorithm [41]. Note that ITP differs from the existing SVM-based user relevance feedback algorithms, such as [42], which typically require a large number of voted samples to obtain a classifier in the feature space. In ITP, the SVM is not used directly to perform image retrieval; instead, it is used to guide a coarse filtering (pruning) such that the Hierarchical Indexing Structure in the database can be tuned in favor of the user's relevancy intention. In Section 5, we shall see that with a relatively small number of leaf nodes (<1000) and reasonable dimensionality of a feature space (9 in the indexing scheme), a relatively small number (15–30) of voted images can boost the performance well, and further expedite the subsequent retrieval at the same time.

While ITP is able to infer the relevancy and irrelevancy from the voted images, we make a further effort in attempting to infer the degree of the relevancy or irrelevancy. Following the "most similar, highest priority (MSHP)" principle [8], we can adaptively update the region weights in Eq. (8.19) based on the feedback data. We implement this idea and call it the Adaptive Region Weight Updating (ARWU) algorithm.

The idea of ARWU is as follows. The cardinality of a cluster to which a query region belongs in the relevant region space is an indicator of the commonality of this region to the relevant image set. With the voted relevant and irrelevant images, for

input   : Images users labeled
output   : Ψ, Images retrieved after learning
begin

  Initialization, set $RegR = \{\}$; $RegI = \{\}$;

  Applying the modified k-means clustering algorithm on the region subspace consisting of relevant images, m cluster are obtained. They are sorted in terms of their number of regions, denoted as $SR = \{R_1, R_2, \ldots, R_m\}$, where $\|R_i\| \geq \|R_j\|$ for $i < j$;

  Applying the modified k-means clustering algorithm on the region subspace consisting of irrelevant images, n cluster are obtained. They are sorted in terms of their number of regions, denoted as $SI = \{I_1, I_2, \ldots, I_n\}$, where $\|I_i\| \geq \|I_j\|$ for $i < j$;

  $RegR \leftarrow RegR \cup R_k, k = 1, \ldots, p$;

  $RegI \leftarrow RegI \cup I_k, k = 1, \ldots, q$;

  A Gaussian RBF based two-class SVM is applied on the relevant and irrelevant region sets $RegR$ and $RegI$ to learn the hyperplane H, which separate the region space into relevancy and irrelevancy parts;

  $Y = \{\}$; $X = \{\}$;

  for *the centroid of each leaf node in the indexing tree, t_i* **do**

    Determine $H(t_i)$;

    if $H(t_i) \geq 0$ **then**
      $Y \leftarrow Y \cup \{t_i\}$;
    else
      $X \leftarrow X \cup \{t_i\}$;
    end

  end

  Pruning the indexing tree, reserving only ancestor nodes of Y to generate a session tree ST;

  Performing online search algorithm HEAR on the session tree ST, return result Ψ;

end

Fig. 8.3. ITP algorithm.

every region in the query image, the weights of the regions that are similar to the regions in the relevant images but dissimilar to the regions in the irrelevant images should increase, and otherwise the weights should decrease. For regions in each target image (i.e., image to be compared with the query image), a high weight is given to regions with a smaller distance to the query image, and in the meantime the weight is adjusted to a higher value if it is the most similar to a query region with a high weight already. Otherwise, the weight of the region is lowered accordingly. Consequently, more importance weights are given to regions on which the user's query intention, learned from the feedback examples by ARWU, focuses. The essence of this weight adjustment algorithm is a discriminant whitening transform learned from both inferred relevant and irrelevant regions. In addition, the weights adjusted still preserve a desired characteristic for the distance metric, that is, *the distance between two identical images equals to 0*. ARWU is used in conjunction with ITP for further improving semantics-tailored retrieval. The ARWU algorithm is shown in Figure 8.5.

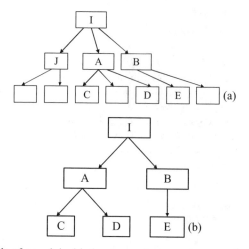

Fig. 8.4. An example of an original index tree and one session tree after pruning using ITP. (a) Original Indexing Tree (lettered leaf nodes are relevant and blank leaf nodes are irrelevant, which are derived from the hyperplane function H); (b) The session tree after pruning.

input   : q, the query image
output   : Updated region weights
begin

    for *each region in the query image, Q_i, i=1,...,M* **do**

        the cluster containing it in the relevant image set is obtained as C_i, $C_i \in SR$, the cluster containing it in the irrelevant image set is obtained as D_i, $D_i \in SI$;

        $WR_i = \frac{\|C_i\|}{\sum_k \|R_k\|}$;

        $WI_i = \frac{\|D_i\|}{\sum_k \|I_k\|}$;

        $W_{1i} = \frac{\eta_i * WR_i}{\sum_{k=1}^{M}(\eta_k * WR_k)}$, where $\eta_i = 1 - WI_i$;

    end

    for *each region in a target image, T_j, j=1,...,N, its most similar region in the query image is denoted as S_j* **do**

        $U_j = \frac{W_{1S_j}}{R_{j,Image1}}$, where $R_{j,Image1}$ is the distance between this region, T_j, and the query image, which is defined in Eq.(8.18);

        The weight for each region is normalized as $W_{2j} = \frac{U_j}{\sum_{k=1}^{N} U_k}$;

    end

    Applying W_{1i} and W_{2j} to Eq.(8.19) to determine the distance between the query image and each target image;

end

Fig. 8.5. ARWU algorithm.

In the algorithm, η_i acts as a penalty, reflecting the effect of negative examples to each region in the query image.

8.5 Experimental Evaluations

We have implemented the FAST methodology in a prototype system. For the discussion and reference purpose, we also call the prototype FAST. The following reported evaluations are performed in a general-purpose color image database containing 10,000 images from the COREL collection of 96 semantic categories, including people, nature scene, building, and vehicles. No prerestriction on camera models, lighting conditions, etc., are specified in the image database for the testing. These images are all in JPEG format. We choose this database to test the FAST methodology because it is available to the public and is used in the evaluations of several state-of-the-art CBIR systems, for example, IRM [43] and UFM [9]. The database is accessible at http://www.fortune. binghamton.edu/download.html. Figure 8.6 shows several samples of the images belonging to a few semantic categories in the database. Each semantic category in this image database has 85–120 associated images. From this database 1500 images are randomly selected from all the categories as the query set. A retrieved image is considered a match if it belongs to the same category of the query image. We note that the category information in the COREL collection is only used to truth the evaluation; we do not make use of this information in the indexing and retrieval.

The FAST prototype is implemented on a Pentium III 800 MHZ computer with 256 M memory. After performing the image segmentation described in Section 8.2.1, the homogenous regions of each image are obtained. The original k-means clustering algorithm [32] is modified to accommodate unknown number of regions in advance in an image for image segmentation. We adaptively select the number of clusters C by gradually increasing C until a stop criterion is met. The average number of regions for all images in the database varies in accordance with the adjustment of the stop criteria. The segmentation results indicate that the regions extracted are related to the objects embodying image semantics. In the evaluation, 56,722 regions are extracted in total for all the 10,000 images in the database, which means in average 5.68 regions are extracted in each image. Image segmentation for the testing database takes 5.5 h to complete, corresponding to about 1.9 s for each image.

For each image, the fuzzy color, texture, and shape features are determined for each region. Based on these features of all regions extracted for the database, the Hierarchical Indexing Structure of four level's is constructed offline. All regions are partitioned into several classes using the modified k-means algorithm. In this evaluation, the total number of classes is determined to be 677 with the maximum number of regions in one class is 194 and the minimum number of regions in one class is 31. For each class, a hash table mapping between the associated regions and the corresponding image names in the database is maintained. The generation of the four-level Hierarchical Indexing Structure takes 70 min. While the entire indexing process is offline, the online query processing is fast. In average, the query time for returning

Fig. 8.6. Sample images in the testing database. The images in each column are assigned to one category. From left to right, the categories are "Africa rural area," "historical building," "waterfalls," "British royal event," and "model portrait," respectively.

the top 30 images is less than 1 s. The retrieval interface of the FAST prototype is shown in Figure 8.7.

FAST is evaluated against one of the state-of-the-art CBIR systems, UFM [9], on the effectiveness comparison. Retrieval effectiveness is measured by the recall and precision metrics [44]. For a given query and a given number of images retrieved, the precision gives the ratio between the number of relevant images retrieved and the number of retrieved images in total. The recall gives the ratio between the number of relevant images retrieved and the total number of relevant images in the collection.

To test the effects of the Hierarchical Indexing Structure and the HEAR algorithm, we have ported FAST into two separate versions: one with the original FAST

Fig. 8.7. A screenshot of the FAST prototype. The query image is in the top left pane and the retrieval results are returned in the right pane.

methodology (which uses the Hierarchical Indexing Structure in the region feature space and the HEAR online search), called WIS, and the other with the Hierarchical Indexing Structure and the HEAR disabled, that is, using the FAST indexing scheme in a linear search, called NIS. Both versions of FAST are compared with UFM in the 10,000 image database. The precision-scope data is recorded in Figure 8.8, which demonstrates that the retrieval effectiveness of FAST is in general superior to that of UFM and the application of the Hierarchical Index Structure and the HEAR algorithm does not degrade the performance perceivably; in fact, the performance of NIS is always about the same as that of WIS.

The Hierarchical Indexing Structure of FAST is generated as a tree with the depth of 4 and the average branching factor as 5. The tree is almost balanced, which verifies that the clustering in the region feature space based on FAST methodology is almost spherically separable [13]. This configuration is a trade-off between the recall and precision. In FAST, each node of the tree is implemented as an object serialized to a physical file on the disk. Thus the parallel searching on the indexing tree is made possible (which is an expected improvement for the future further development of FAST). We set the threshold for the triangle-inequality comparison of the region distance in all the leaf nodes as an adjustable parameter, which can be set by the

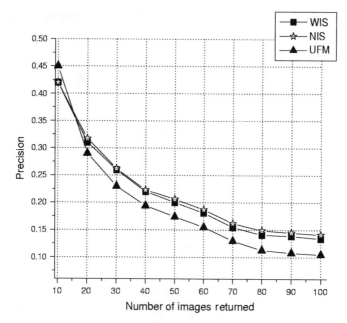

Fig. 8.8. Average precision/scope comparisons between two versions of FAST (WIS and NIS) and UFM.

users. Given the normalized region feature distance in [0, 1], the current value of the threshold in FAST is 0.3.

To study the scalability of FAST, we incrementally sample the original 10,000 image database to generate two smaller databases, one with 3000 images and the other with 6000 images. These two databases contain sampled images form all the 96 categories. Consequently, the depths of the Hierarchical Indexing Structures for the two databases are set to be $\lfloor \log_5 nl - 3 \rfloor$ accordingly based on the same principle used for the original image database, resulting in 2 and 3, respectively. We randomly sample 100 images to form a query set from each of the three databases. For the query images the average number of images compared in each of the three databases, the average indexing structure search overhead (the processing time to traverse the Hierarchical Indexing Structure for searching the pursued leaf node), the average query processing time in FAST, and the average query processing time in linear search are documented in Table 8.1. It shows that the average number of compared images is significantly reduced in comparison with the database size. In addition, as indicated in Table 8.1, although the Hierarchical Indexing Structure search introduces the computation overhead, the average total query processing time is still much less than the average query processing time in the linear search due to the reduced number of images to be compared with. The computation overhead for the Hierarchical Indexing Structure search is small because few additional distance computations are performed and highly efficient hash table searches are applied. With the increase of the database

Table 8.1. Retrieval efficiency results; percentage of images compared in the three databases

Database size	Average # of compared images	Average percentage of images examined	Average search overhead in FAST (second)	Average query processing time in FAST (second)	Average query processing time in linear search (second)
3,000	795	26.5%	0.08	0.55	1.78
6,000	1032	17.2%	0.12	0.79	3.04
10,000	1140	11.4%	0.15	0.98	3.96

size, the percentage of the images examined and the average computation overhead remain relatively stable. The average query processing time is much less than that in the linear search in all three testing databases. The average efficiency improvement on the query processing time to the linear search is 72.7%. This result, combined with the results observed in Figure 8.8, indicates the promise of FAST for efficiently handling large image databases without sacrificing retrieval effectiveness.

Since in FAST the size of the class level (clusters in the region feature space) information is much smaller than that of the index files for images in the database (in our experiments, the size ratio is 1/95–1/120), it is practical and desirable to deposit the class-level information in the main memory. With such design the I/O costs for each query are proportional only to the number of images compared. The reduced I/O costs in the FAST query processing are observed as shown in Table 8.1 as well.

In the indexing scheme we use the Cauchy function to correlate color descriptions and to smooth the regions (equivalent to a convolution in computer vision) so that the color perception uncertainty and segmentation inaccuracy issue are addressed explicitly. To evaluate the effectiveness of the indexing scheme for improving the robustness to color variations and segmentation-related uncertainties, we compare the performances of FAST and UFM for color variations and coarseness of image segmentation. Color variations can be simulated by changing colors to their adjacent values for each image and the segmentation-related uncertainties in an image can be characterized by the entropy. For image i with C segmented regions, its entropy, $E(i)$, is defined as

$$E(i) = - \sum_{j=1}^{C} P\left(R_j^i\right) \log\left[P\left(R_j^i\right)\right] \qquad (8.22)$$

where $P(R_j^i)$ is the percentage of image i covered by region R_j^i. The larger the value of the entropy, the higher the uncertainty level. As we can see, the entropy $E(i)$ increases with the increase of the number of regions C. Thus, we can adjust the uncertainty level by changing the value of C. C is controlled by modifying the stop criteria of the modified k-means algorithm. For a fair comparison between FAST and UFM at different color variation and uncertainty levels, we perform the same evaluations for different degrees of color variations and average values of C (4.31, 6.32, 8.64, 11.62, and 12.25) on the 3000 image database introduced above. To evaluate the robustness in the color variations, we apply color changes to an image (target image) in the database. The modified image is then used as the query image, and the rank

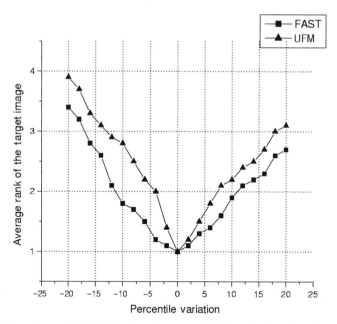

Fig. 8.9. Comparison of FAST indexing scheme and UFM method on the robustness in the color variations. Every image in the 3000 image database is altered and used as query image.

of the retrieved target image is recorded. Repeating the process for all images in the testing database, the average rank for target images are computed for FAST and UFM. The result is shown in Figure 8.9. The average rank of the target image of FAST is lower than that of UFM for each level of color variations (in an acceptable range of color changes that do not affect semantics perception). To evaluate the robustness in the segmentation-related uncertainties, the performance in terms of overall average precision in the top 30 returned images is evaluated for both approaches. The result is given in Figure 8.10. As we have known, the entropy $E(i)$ (uncertainty) level increases when the image is segmented into more regions. At all uncertainty levels, FAST performs better than or as well as the UFM method. Combining these two experiments of robustness, we have observed that the FAST indexing scheme is more robust than that of UFM for color variations and segmentation-related uncertainties. The performance differences between FAST and UFM can be explained as follows. The UFM method uses the representative feature (one feature vector) of each region to model the segmentation uncertainty, which is coarse and artificial. The model generated is not accurate enough to fit the segmented images well. However, FAST indexing scheme leverages all block features in every region to generate fuzzy models for each feature component, and thus describes the segmentation-related uncertainty more precisely and effectively.

In FAST with the user relevance feedback mode, the Gaussian kernel function used in SVM is $K(x, y) = e^{-\|x-y\|^2/2\sigma^2}$ with $\sigma = \sqrt{2}/2$. In order to evaluate the capability of algorithm ITP and ARWU, FAST is run on the 10,000 image database with user

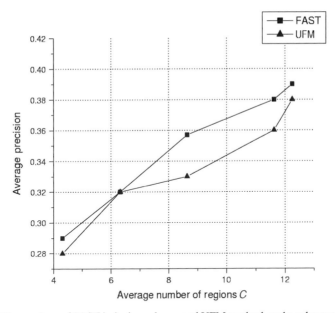

Fig. 8.10. Comparison of FAST indexing scheme and UFM method on the robustness in image segmentation uncertainties.

relevance feedback mode for the 1500 query-image set with a varied number of the top retrieved images. Different users are asked to run FAST initially without relevance feedback interaction, and then to place their relevance feedback. We plot the retrieval curves of the precision versus the number of the top retrieved images. Figure 8.11 shows the average precision on three and five rounds of feedbacks, respectively. The semantics-tailored capability empowered by ITP and ARWU enhances the retrieval effectiveness in all the scenarios.

Another experiment is performed to verify the promise of FAST ITP itself on the basis of the 100 query images. We record the average number of images compared in the first retrieval and after the 3rd and 5th retrieval iterations, respectively, in the three databases. The results are shown in Figure 8.12.

The reduction of the number of images compared in each iteration due to the tree pruning in ITP is observed. The efficiency boost between the third iteration and the initial retrieval is significant because of the relatively large portion of the leaf nodes pruned in the first several iterations. With the progress of iterations, the ratio of nodes classified to the irrelevancy side of the SVM decreases quickly such that the efficiency boost decays accordingly.

To evaluate the effects of ARWU algorithm for further enhancing semantics-tailored retrieval, we compare the average precision for the same 1500 query image set on the 10,000 image database, in the scenarios with and without running ARWU. The experiment is based on the average of the precisions for the top 30 returned images for each query. The results are shown in Figure 8.13. As is shown, the semantics-tailored retrieval effectiveness is improved substantially with ARWU.

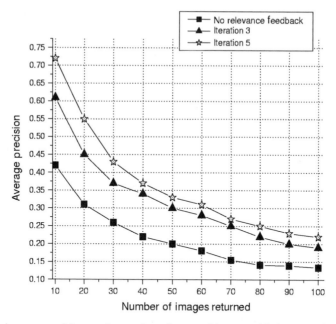

Fig. 8.11. Average precision vs. the number of returned images with three and five rounds of user relevance feedback.

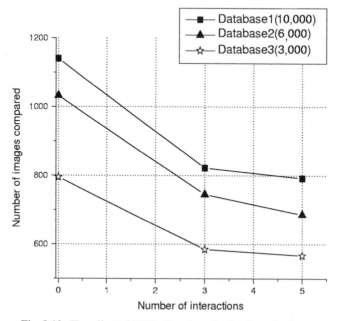

Fig. 8.12. The effect of ITP in iterations for the three databases.

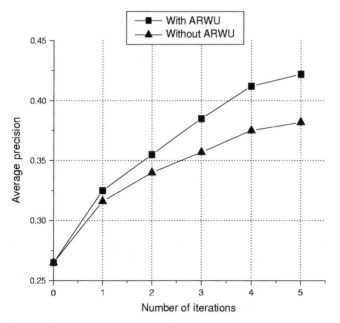

Fig. 8.13. Accuracy comparison when FAST ITP is run with and without ARWU algorithm

8.6 Conclusions

We have developed a new CBIR methodology on the basis of the goal of delivering fast and semantics-tailored retrieval, and thus we call it FAST. FAST incorporates a new indexing scheme, a hierarchical indexing structure with a hierarchical, elimination-based A* online search algorithm called HEAR. We have shown that HEAR promises a logarithm search instead of linear search in an average case. FAST also offers user relevance feedback capability to not only address the individualized retrieval based on user intended semantics, but also take advantage of the Hierarchical Indexing Structure and the HEAR algorithm to achieve more effective and efficient semantics-tailored retrieval through applying the ITP and ARWU algorithms. The promise FAST demonstrates and the benefits FAST offers are sufficiently supported by the extensive experimental evaluations.

References

1. De Marsicoi M, Cinque L, Levialdi S. Indexing pictorial documents by their content: A survey of current techniques. *Image and Vision Computing* 1997;15:119–141.
2. MFlickner, et al. Query by Image and Video Content: The QBIC System. *IEEE Computer* 1995;28(9):23–32.
3. Ogle Virginia, Stonebraker Michael. Chabot: Retrieval from a relational databases of images. *IEEE Computer* 1995;28(9):40–48.

4. Greg P, Ramin Z. Histogram Refinement for Content-based Image Retrieval. In: IEEE *Workshop on Applications of Computer Vision*. Sarasota, FL; 1996.
5. Jing H, Kumar SR et al. Image indexing using color correlograms. In: *IEEE Int'l Conf. Computer Vision and Pattern Recognition Proceedings*, Puerto Rico; 1997.
6. Carson C, Thomas M, Belongie S, et al. Blobworld: A system for region-based image indexing and retrieval. In: *The 3rd Int'l Conf. on Visual Information System Proceedings*. Amsterdam, Netherlands; 1999, pp. 509–516.
7. Ma WY, Manjunath B. NeTra: A toolbox for navigating large image databases. In: *IEEE Int'l Conf. on Image Processing Proceedings*, Santa Barbara, CA, 1997, pp. 568–571.
8. Wang James Z, Li Jia, Gio Wiederhold. SIMPLIcity: Semantics-sensitive integrated matching for picture libraries. *IEEE Trans on PAMI* 2001;23(9).
9. Yixin C, Wang James Z. A region-based fuzzy feature matching approach to content-based image retrieval. *IEEE Trans on PAMI* 2002;24(9):1252–1267.
10. Feng Jing et al. An efficient region-based image retrieval framework. In: *ACM Multimedia Proceedings*, Juan-les-Pins, France; 2002.
11. YuKai et al. Knowing a tree from the forest: Art image retrieval using a society of profiles. In: *ACM MM Multimedia 2003 Proceedings*, Berkeley, CA; 2003.
12. Cox Ingemar J, Miller Matt L, Minka Thomas P, Papathomas Thomas V, Yianilos Peter N. The Bayesian image retrieval system, picHunter: Theory implementation and psychophysical experiments. *IEEE Trans on Image Processing* 2000;9(1):20–37.
13. Vapnik V. *The Nature of Statistical Learning Theory*. New York: Springer; 1995.
14. Russell Stuart, Norvig Peter. *Artificial Intelligence—A Modern Approach*. Prentice-Hall; 1995.
15. Elmasri R, Navathe AB. *Fundamentals of Database Systems*. 2nd ed. Redwood City, CA: Benjamin Cummings; 1994.
16. Dao S, Yang Q, Vellaikal A. MB^+-$tree$: An index structure for content-based retrieval. In: Nwosu KC, Thuraisingham B, Berra PB, eds. *Multimedia Database Systems: Design and Implementation Strategies*. Norwell, MA: Kluwer; 1996. .
17. Bentley L. Multi-dimensional binary search trees in database applications. *IEEE Trans on Software Eng* 1979;4:333–340.
18. Roussopoulos Nick, Kelley Stephen, Vincent Frédéic. Nearest neighbor queries. In: *Proceedings of the 1995 ACM SIGMOD International Conference on Management of Data*, San Jose, CA: 1995, pp. 71–79.
19. Guttman O. R-tree: A dynamic index structure for spatial searching. In: ACM SIGMOD *Proceedings*. Boston, MA; 1984, pp. 47–57.
20. Beckmann et al. The R^*-tree: An efficient and robust access mehtod for points and rectangles. In: *ACM SIGMOD Int'l Conf. on Management of Data Proceedigns*, Atlantic City, NJ; 1990, pp. 322–331.
21. Sellis T, Roussopoulos N, Faloutsos C. The R^+-tree: A dynamic index for multi-dimensional objects. In: *The 13th Conf. on Very Large Databases Proceedings*, Brighton, UK; 1987, pp. 507–518.
22. Lin KI, Jagadish HV, Faloutsos C. The TV-tree: An index structure for high-dimensional data. *VLDB Journal* 1994;3:517–546.
23. Prabhakar S, Agrawal D, Abbadi AE. Data clustering for efficient range and similarity searching. In: *SPIE Conf. on Multimedia Storage and Archiving System III Proceedings*. Vol. 3527, Boston, MA; 1998, pp. 419–430.
24. Nievergelt J, Hinterbergre H, Sevcik KC. The grid file: an adaptive, symmetric multikey file structure. *ACM Trans on Database Systems* 1984;9.

25. Samet H. *Applications of Spatial Data Structures: Computer Graphics, Image Processing, and GIS*. Addison-Wesley; 1989.
26. White DA, Jain R. Similarity Indexing with the SS-tree. In: *12th IEEE Int'l Conf. on Data Engineering Proceedings*; 1999.
27. Lu Guojun. Techniques and data structures for efficient multimedia retrieval based on similarity. *IEEE Trans on Multimedia* 2002;4(3):372–384.
28. Berman A, Shapiro LG. Efficient image retrieval with multiple distance measure. In: *SPIE Proceedings*, Vol. 3022; 1997, pp. 12–21.
29. Porkaew K, Chakrabarti K, Mehrotra S. Query refinement for multimedia similarity retrieval in MARS. In: *ACM Multimedia Proceedings*; 1999.
30. Su Zhong, Li Stan, Zhang Hongjiang. Extraction of feature subspace for content-based retrieval using relevance feedback. In: *ACM Multimedia Proceedings*, Ottawa, Canada; 2001.
31. Tong S, Chan E. Support vector machine active learning for image retrieval. In: *ACM Multimedia 2001 Proceedings*, Ottawa, Canada; 2001.
32. Hartigan JA, Wong MA. Algorithm AS136: A K-means clustering algorithm. *Applied Statistics* 1979;28:100–108.
33. Daubechies I. *Ten Lectures on Wavelets*. Capital City Press; 1992.
34. Gersho A. Asymptotically optimum block quantization. *IEEE Trans on Information Theory* 1979;25(4):373–380.
35. Pal Sankar K, Ghosh Ashish, Kundu Malay K. Soft Computing for Image Processing, Physica-Verlag; 2000.
36. Vertan Constantin, Boujemaa Nozha. Embedding fuzzy logic in content based image retrieval. In: *The 19th Int'l Meeting of the North America Fuzyy Information Processing Society Proceedings*, Atlanta; 2000.
37. Hoppner F, Klawonn F, Kruse R, Runkler T. *Fuzzy Cluster Analysis: Methods for Classification, Data Analysis and Image Recognition*. New York: John Wiley & Sons; 1999.
38. Kautsky J, Nichols NK, Jupp DLB. Smoothed histogram modification for image processing. CVGIP: *Image Understanding* 1984;26(3):271–291.
39. Brunelli R, Poggio T. Face recognition: Features versus templates. *IEEE Trans on PAMI* 1993;15:1042–1053.
40. Rui Y, Huang TS, Ortega M, Mehrotra S. Relevance feedback: A power tool in interactive content-based image retrieval. *IEEE Trans on Circuits and Systems for Video Tech* 1998;8(5):644–655.
41. Kearns Y, Mansour MJ. A Fast, bottom-up decision tree pruning algorithm with near-optimal generalization. In: *The 15th Int'l Conf. on Machine Learning*, Madison, WI; 1998, pp. 269–277.
42. Chapelle Olivier, Haffner Patrick, Vapnik Vladimir N. Support vector machines for histogram-based image classification. *IEEE Trans on Neural Networks* 1999;10(5):1055–1064.
43. Wang JZ, Du YP. Scalable integrated region-based image retrieval using IRM and statistical clustering. In: *Proc. of ACM and IEEE Joint Conf. on Digital Libraries*, Roanoke, VA; 2001.
44. Baeza-Yates R, Ribeiro-Neto B. *Modern Information Retrieval*. Addison-Wesley; 1999.

9. New Image Retrieval Principle: Image Mining and Visual Ontology

Marinette Bouet and Marie-Aude Aufaure

Summary. Image data are omnipresent for various applications. A considerable volume of data is produced, and we need to develop tools to efficiently retrieve relevant information. Image mining is a new and challenging research field that tries to overcome some limitations reached by content-based image retrieval. Image mining deals with making associations between images from large database and presenting a summarized view. After a state of the art in the image retrieval field, this chapter presents some work and ideas about the need to define new descriptors to integrate image semantics. Clustering and characterization rules are combined to reduce the search space and produce a summarized view of an annotated image database. These data mining techniques are performed separately on visual descriptors and textual information (annotations, key words, Web pages). A visual ontology is derived from the textual part, and enriched with representative images associated to each concept of the ontology. Ontology-based navigation can also be seen as a user-friendly and powerful tool to retrieve relevant information. These two approaches should make the exploitation and the exploration of a large image database easier.

9.1 Introduction

These last decades, a considerable volume of multimedia data has been produced. These data are complex data and more and more applications need to efficiently retrieve relevant information. These data can be made of text, image, video, and audio. A spatiotemporal component can also be found for some data. Multimedia databases store huge volume of complex data and are used to efficiently retrieve these data, thanks to indexing capabilities. A data is always carrying information but it is not always easy to interpret it. For example, 107079 is a data but what is the underlying information? Now, imagine that 107079 is the answer to the following query: "what is the identification number of the employee named Durand?" In a relational database, the semantics of the data is contained into the schema. For example, a relation Employee (identification number, name, surname, position, birth date, date of employment) is designed to store data about the employees of a company. Data stored into a relational database are coherent when the data acquisition and entry are correctly done. The same information about the employee named "Durand" can be represented by "Durand identification number:107079" or by <identification number> 107079

<identification number> <name> Durand <name>. In these cases, the semantic is introduced by an annotation, which is a data surcharge. Data giving some information about other data are called metadata. Multimedia data need metadata because these data do not contain information that is directly exploitable.

For this reason, we point out the major importance of metadata in the context of multimedia data. An image data does not directly contain information. Preprocessing is performed to extract a set of metadata that can be classified as follows:

- metadata related to the type of multimedia data,
- descriptive metadata: author's name, date, etc.
- content metadata (semantic, visual, spatial relationships): visual content deals with shape, color, and texture, and semantic content is an image interpretation.

The main problem is to process data from pixel to knowledge. At the pixel level, visual descriptors are extracted from image and query is performed by content. A lot of research works can be found in the field of computer vision that emphasize on visual features. In this case, information retrieval consists in similarity search based on a distance between visual features extracted from image data. This is known as CBIR (Content-Based Image Retrieval) [1]. The next level of abstraction deals with objects or regions extracted from image data. The user can select objects so that his query is more precise. Spatial relationships are taken into account at this level. The semantic level is dedicated to the extraction and generation of semantic metadata, and can be processed using ontologies [2]. Last, the knowledge level uses the semantic level to discover hidden knowledge, relationships between objects and to resume and characterize a large image database.

Image mining is still a recent research field [3, 4] and is not very developed yet because extracting relevant knowledge from image data still remains a difficult task. Classical data mining [5] techniques cannot be directly applied to image data because of the nonstructured nature of such data. Data mining techniques can be achieved in a descriptive or predictive goal. Knowledge discovery in image databases is based on the following phases: (1) collecting images, (2) choosing relevant images for the data mining task, (3) extracting visual and semantic features, (4) discovering patterns at image or image group level, and (5) validating and interpreting the discovered patterns.

In our framework, we want to extract a summarized view of an image database. Clustering is performed to reduce the search space and characterization rules will characterize the clusters. We also want to build a visual ontology to enhance the retrieval process.

This chapter is organized as follows: Section 9.2 describes textual and visual descriptors and image retrieval methods; these systems suffer from a limited expressive power and we need to define new methods to efficiently retrieve relevant information. Section 9.3 deals with image mining and with ontology to add semantic information to multimedia data. Section 9.4 proposes architecture dedicated to improve the exploration of an image database based on classification and visual ontology. Our first experiments are also detailed in this section. Section 9.5 concludes and gives some directions for future work and experimentation.

9.2 Content-Based Retrieval

This section relates the current state of the art in the image retrieval field. The content-based image retrieval requires principally two modules: the logical indexation and the retrieval. The first one extracts the metadata (textual descriptors, visual features) associated to images and stores the extracted metadata in the database. The second one assists final users, even those unfamiliar with the database field, to retrieve efficiently images based on their visual and/or textual descriptions. Figure 9.1 illustrates the classic image media retrieval and access system architecture.

In this context, the scope of queries addressed to multimedia databases is very large and may include objective and subjective content. Three levels of abstraction are distinguished [6]: (1) syntactic level: visual features, spatial localization, and spatial constraints are used to retrieve images. This level is purely algorithmic. For instance, a query may be "Give me all the images containing red circles"; (2) semantic level including only objective content. In this level, objects appearing in images have to be identified. A query example may be "Give me all the images in which my children appear"; (3) semantic level with subjective content. This level involves complex reasoning about objects or scenes using human perception. Such a query may be "Give me all the images representing the notion of liberty" or "Give me all the images in which my friends are happy." This level is also related to scene recognition as for an example, a child birthday: this scene can be characterized by balloons, young faces, candles, cakes, etc.

Both the logical indexation and query modules are briefly presented in the following subsections.

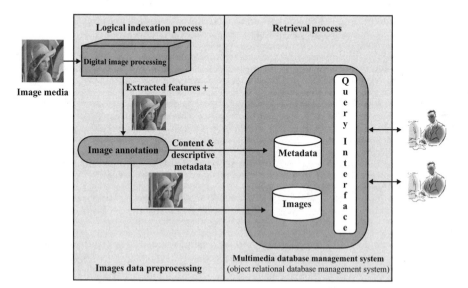

Fig. 9.1. The classic image media retrieval and access system architecture.

9.2.1 Logical Indexation Process

In the image retrieval system domain, the retrieval may be performed from textual descriptions (key words, annotations, etc.) and from visual descriptions (color, shape, texture, spatial localization, spatial constraints). Consequently, these features must be modelled in a well-suited representation to satisfy the need of efficient and relevant retrieval of image media in both heterogeneous (image database with no specific application domain) and homogeneous (faces, finger printings databases) voluminous databases. Moreover, the feature computing is not made during each retrieval process because it is time-consuming task. They are previously represented in an appropriate form (logical indexation) and then stored in the database [7].

On the one hand, the textual descriptors may be divided into content metadata like key words and database modelling. In the systems based on key word search, one or more key words are associated to an image. The system then selects the images related to the key word searched. This process is strongly limited because semantic relationships that exist between key words are not taken into account, like for example, the fact that a horse is an animal. If the query key word is "horse" then the horse's images annotated by the key word "animal" will not be returned. A significant improvement consists in using an ontology to capture the semantic relationships between objects. This point will be discussed in Section 9.3.1.

From a database point of view, many propositions have been developed to model and query image databases. Most systems propose a manual description of image semantics. We can note the DISIMA model [8] on the basis of an object-oriented database and the ICDM model [9, 10] on the basis of a relational object database. In the first prototype, a class hierarchy is defined by the user. An image is composed by an OID, a set of physical representations (raster or vector), a content (spatial relationships, salient objects). The link between an object that is detected in an image and an object of the salient objects class is done manually. In the second prototype, the data model can be divided into four abstraction levels: (1) the image level containing the global properties of an image; (2) the syntactic level capturing local characteristics; syntactic objects are created in this level; (3) the content level in which syntactic objects are grouped; and (4) the semantic level in which semantic hierarchies are defined. The major interest of this model relies to this semantic level that uses relationships like synonymy, hyponymy, etc.

Semistructured models are also well-suited to model image databases. MPEG 7 (Multimedia Content Description Interface) [11] is a standard dedicated to multimedia content description. This description is written using XML and corresponds to the semistructured approach.

On the second hand, the visual descriptor extracting of an image is a major step in content-based image retrieval since these visual features model the visual image content. Moreover, an interesting representation of these descriptors must be compact, reliable, and accurate. Without a real synergy between digital image processing, signal processing, and mathematics, such an objective cannot be reached. One or several representations are associated to each extracted feature.

The most used descriptor for content-based access today is the color feature. Well-known color representations are based on color histograms and their extensions such as weighted color histograms [12], statistical moments [13], the dominant color, the color sets [14]. Colour is considered in a color space like RGB or HSV [15]. A well-suited similarity distance is necessary to each feature representation. To estimate the similarity between two color representations, several distances may be referred like the L1 metric [12], the quadratic distance [16], the Euclidean distance [16], etc. Each distance has its advantages and its limits. For example, the quadratic distance appreciates correctly the color similarity, but it is time-consuming.

While texture is usually represented by a grey-level histogram, statistical moments, and/or co-occurrence matrix, and more recently by Fourier transform, wavelets, Gabor modelling [17–20] the shape representations are classified into two categories: boundary-based (perimeter, curvature, Freeman's code, Fourier descriptors, etc.) and region-based (area, compactness, bounding box, moments, etc.) [15, 17, 18, 21, 22]. As far as texture is concerned, its modelling is hard since it is expressed by qualitative criteria like contrast, directionality, coarseness, etc. As far as shape is concerned, it represents significant regions or relevant objects in images. Ideally, shape segmentation would be automatic and efficient, but it is either impossible or difficult with heterogeneous images. Segmentation algorithms generally compute regions sharing several properties. Nevertheless, each calculated region does not correspond to a relevant entire object. Since obtaining relevant objects, suited representations must be chosen.

Others usual important features are considered in content-based retrieval systems like spatial localization (for a semiautomatically or automatically extracted object) and spatial constraints between two regions called spatial relationships. Spatial constraints are based on extended Allen's relationships [23]. All the previous visual feature representations correspond to psych-visual human criteria. However, some CBIR systems do not use such criteria; they use only one or several entire image signatures. By example, while in [19] these features are calculated by means of Fourier transform, wavelet transform, etc., in [24], the extracted features contain a lot of photometric information.

To conclude this visual descriptor paragraph, it may be noticed: for each visual feature, a lot of representations have been proposed in the last decade. The representation choosing to hold is very sensitive and closely connected to the considered domain application and the wanted aims. Nevertheless, these properties are often stored into a numeric vector called a visual descriptor that summarizes the photometric image information. This vector has a high dimensionnality that raises physical indexing problems in databases since these extracted features are excellent candidates to the physical indexation. Despite their importance, these aspects will not be presented in this chapter. For more details, [23, 25, 26] may be referred.

9.2.2 Retrieval Process

The visual retrieval systems usually include a visual query tool that lets users to form a query by painting, sketching, and selecting colors, shapes, textures, etc. or by selecting an or several interesting image(s) from the database. So, through a user-friendly and intuitive interface, the final users formulate their queries from both textual descriptions and visual descriptions (from features previously extracted and stored in the database during the logical indexation process). These two kinds of metadata are necessary to improve the retrieval effectiveness since the use of text or visual information alone is not enough to fully describe the semantic content of images (each form has limited expressive power on its own). For instance, colors and shapes are good for capturing visual aspects of a region and they are not very accurate to represent high-level concept, while textual annotations are good at describing high-level concept and they are weak to capture visual content. These features tend also to be incomplete and not effective. Moreover, the content-based image retrieval systems must be flexible since images may belong to different fields.

Then, the retrieval process by means of a suited distance for each feature computes the similarity between the user's query and the image database. The best similar images according to their similarity value are then displayed by decreasing similarity.

Because some of the features extracted from images may be imprecise, the retrieval process generally involves probabilistic querying and relevance feedback. It means that the user may get ranked results, if he is not satisfied with the result images of his query, he may refine the query and resubmit it. To refine his query, the user chooses from the returned image set, positive and negative examples. New results are obtained using this information and this process may be iterated. The reader can refer to [27] for a complete review of visual information retrieval.

From a database point of view, queries are expressed using extensions of OQL. New predicates like *contains* and *similar* are introduced. These queries can be qualified as exact queries. Fuzzy predicates can be introduced [28] to allow the specification of imprecise queries.

However, textual and visual feature combinations are sometimes not sufficient, particularly when semantic querying is predominant, that is, when the image and its context are necessary (as for instance the retrieval of audiovisual sequences about unemployment, the retrieval of images in which the sadness feeling is heavy). This limit is known as the semantic gap between the visual appearance of an image and the idea the user has in his mind of what images he wants to retrieve, including semantics. So, the content-based retrieval suffers from a lack of expressive power because they do not integrate enough semantics. This problem prevents end user from making good explorations and exploitations of the image database. This is the reason why many research works are recently performed on image semantics, which is the scope of the following section.

9.3 Ontology and Data Mining Against Semantics Lack in Image Retrieval

Users can automatically assign semantics to an image, using the visual content and their own knowledge. Image retrieval systems suffer from a lack of expressive power because they do not integrate enough semantics. Colour, texture, shape, etc., properties as well as key words are not sufficient to capture all the concepts a user wants to express. Images that are similar from a visual content point of view may be semantically very different. This is the reason why many research works are performed on image semantics. Many approaches intend to propagate annotations starting from partially annotated image databases. Different point of view can be considered: key words annotation propagation, semiautomatic annotation, use of ontology, knowledge discovery.

As far as we are concerned, we are focusing on the two last points. We think that without a real synergy between ontology and data mining, the gap reducing between low-level textual visual descriptors and high-level concepts can not be reached. It is well-known that ontologies help the process of information retrieval. But, the combination of data mining techniques with ontologies to mine, interpret, and (re)organize knowledge is less common. For us, ontology may be seen as a priori knowledge and used to improve the data mining process, and conversely data mining process may be useful for creating ontology. Moreover, these techniques should also improve both navigation and image retrieval. More precisely, our goal is to build a visual ontology dedicated to a specific application and to use it for large image database exploration. Indeed, these techniques should not only allow an efficient access to large image databases by providing a relevant synthetic view, but also play a filter role by reducing the search space that is essential in media retrieval. The contribution of each technique (ontology and data mining) to more ingenious image retrieval is developed in the following sections.

9.3.1 Knowledge Discovery in Large Image Databases

Data mining techniques are part of knowledge discovery methods whose aim is to discover knowledge in large databases without predetermined information about the application field that is well-known as KDD [29]. Data mining methods try to discover knowledge from an exploratory or a decisional point of view.

Today, data mining techniques have been extensively used for traditional data. However, in the context of multimedia data, the databases contain both numeric features as in lots of current databases, and voluminous quantities of non standard data. Image mining (more generally multimedia mining) does not consist to apply alphanumerical mining techniques to image. Classical data mining methods may not be directly applied to image because of their nature. Indeed, image data may be considered as complex data owing their high dimensionality [25]. Some approaches for extracting knowledge from multimedia data have been proposed. However, we think that image (more generally multimedia) mining seems to be a promising issue to overcome the semantics problem in visual retrieval system. This research field is still in its infancy, but image or multimedia generates new challenges by knowledge learning and discovering from large quantities of these nonstructured data. In the image context, among data mining techniques (classification obtained by decision trees or neural networks, clustering, associated rules), the more used methods are clustering, association rules [30], and neural networks.

In recent years, some approaches for extracting knowledge from multimedia data have been proposed. The SKICAT system [31] deals with knowledge discovery in astronomical images and integrates techniques for image processing and classification. Decision trees are used to classify objects obtained by image segmentation.

In [32], authors have proposed methods for mining content-based associations with recurrent items and with spatial relationships from large visual data repositories. A progressive resolution refinement approach has been proposed in which frequent item sets at rough resolutions levels are mined, and progressively, finer resolutions are mined only on candidate frequent item sets derived from mining through rough resolution levels. The proposed algorithm is an extension of the famous A Priori algorithm that takes account of the number of object occurrences in the images.

In [33], an algorithm about discovering association rules in images databases based on image content has been proposed. This algorithm relies on four majors steps: feature extraction, object identification, auxiliary image creation, and object mining. The main advantage of this approach is that it does not use any domain knowledge and does not produce meaningless rules or false rules. However, it suffers from several drawbacks, the most important is the relative slowness of feature extraction step and it does not work well with complex images.

In [34], the author proposes an architecture that integrates knowledge extraction from image databases. Association rules are extracted to characterize images, and they are used to classify new images during insertion.

In [35], a recent experiment has been done to show the dependencies between textual and visual indexation. This experiment is performed on different corpus containing photographs manually indexed by key words. Then, the authors compare text-only classification, visual-only classification, and the fusion of textual and visual classification. They show that the fusion is significantly improving text-only classification.

The following section presents how the ontology concept may be seen as a priori knowledge and used to improve the data mining process.

9.3.2 Ontologies and Metadata

Semantics can be expressed using weak semantics like taxonomies or rich semantics like ontologies [17, 36]. Semantic information may also appear as semantic annotations or metadata. Several formats have been designed to meet this goal, among which the Resource Description Framework [37] from the W3C. RDF aims at describing resources and establishes relationships among them. RDF can be enriched with an RDFS Schema, which expresses class hierarchies and typing constraints, for example, to specify that a given relation type can connect only specific classes. A taxonomy is a hierarchically organised controlled vocabulary. The world has a lot of taxonomies, because human beings naturally classify things. Taxonomies are semantically weak. A thesaurus is a "controlled vocabulary arranged in a known order and structured so that equivalence, homographic, hierarchical, and associative relationships among terms are displayed clearly and identified by standardized relationship indicators" [38]. The purpose of a thesaurus is to facilitate documents retrieval. Wordnet [39] is a thesaurus that organizes English nouns, verbs, adverbs, and adjectives into a set of synonyms and defines relationships between synonyms. According to [40], "an ontology is an explicit specification of a conceptualization." Ontologies consist of a hierarchical description of important concepts of a domain and a description of each concept's properties. They can be defined more or less formally from natural language to description logics [41]. OWL (Web Ontology Language) [42] belongs to this last category. OWL is built upon RDF and RDFS and extends them to express class properties.

Many tools and methodologies exist for the construction of ontologies [43–46]. Their differences are the expressiveness of the knowledge model, the existence of an inference and query engine, the type of storage, the formalism generated and its compatibility with other formalisms, the degree of automation, consistency checking and so on. But building an ontology from scratch is a tedious and time-consuming task. In order to reduce the effort to build ontologies, several approaches for the partial automation of the knowledge acquisition process have been proposed. They use natural language analysis and machine learning techniques [47–49].

Data mining techniques contribution to ontology construction can be seen from two different points of view according to the existence of prior knowledge. In the first case, the ontology construction from text will be done according to semantic matching with an existing ontology or thesaurus. In the other case, the ontology is built from scratch and the quality of the resulting ontology is very difficult to evaluate. Several similarity measures can be used in these two cases. Clustering is then performed using a well-suited distance.

Medianet [50] is an example of a multimedia knowledge database built with the help of Wordnet and including semantic and perceptual relationships. Several representations can be associated with a concept (text, image, video, audio); concepts are linked using semantic relationships (e.g., specialization) and perceptual relationships (e.g., similar shape). The construction is semiautomatic; the user has to specify which interpretation of an annotation given by Wordnet is correct. The knowledge base is built starting from a set of images partially annotated, visual feature extraction tools, and Wordnet.

9.4 Toward Semantic Exploration of Image Databases

To propose a better image database exploration, we want to exploit the complementarity of visual and textual image characterizations. For us, this objective may not be achieved without a strong synergy between image mining and visual ontology.

While Section 9.4.1 is dedicated to a new architecture to support more intelligent image retrieval systems, Section 9.4.2 presents a few first experimentations based on different data types.

9.4.1 The Proposed Architecture

Our architecture presented in Figure 9.2 is based on the two well-known processes: extraction process and retrieval process. In the first process, a summarized view

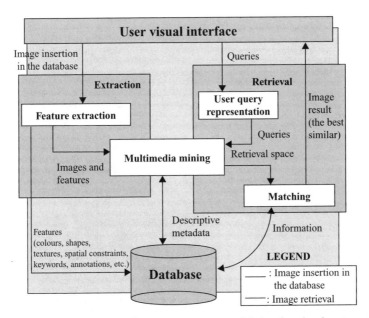

Fig. 9.2. The proposed architecture to more powerful visual retrieval systems.

of the image database is created. After extracting and storing visual and textual features of images, the system summarizes the image database by means of data mining techniques. As we try to extract a set of clusters and rules from visual and textual descriptors, our approach is situated in an exploratory context (descriptive data mining). Indeed, we try to extract a set of clusters and rules from visual and textual descriptors. These descriptors can be seen as metadata associated to our image database. This process called "multimedia mining" and detailed in Figure 9.3 is the heart of our proposition. Extraction and retrieval processes are articulated around this kernel. Multimedia mining is made of several methods such as clustering and extraction of characteristic rules from clusters.

While clustering [34] is performed to reduce the research space, the characterization rules are used to describe each cluster and to classify automatically a new image in the appropriate clusters. This unsupervised learning corresponds to descriptive data mining. Because of their nature difference (numeric versus symbolic), textual descriptions (key words, annotations, etc.) and visual descriptions (color, shape, texture, spatial constraints) are separately dealt with well-suited techniques. Starting from feature sets (such as color set, key word set, texture set, color and shape set, etc.), the system automatically clusters together similar images. The clustering is based on a well-suited method to application domain. Famous methods are Self-Organising Maps [51], k-means, BIRCH, CLIQUE [52], etc. Then, to qualify the previous clusters, a more powerful representation than the cluster centroid has been chosen. These characterization rules may be obtained either from all the points of a cluster (in order to have the most frequent patterns) or from a data aggregation (as for example, a

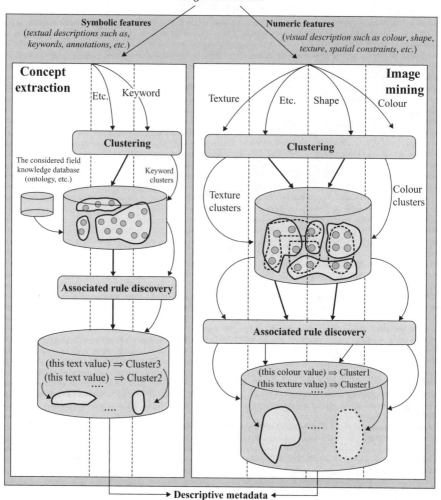

Fig. 9.3. The multimedia mining process.

median histogram is the case of color clusters, which is representative of the cluster content).

In the image context, these rules are in the form of antecedent $\Rightarrow$ consequent with certain confidence and support, where antecedent and consequent correspond respectively to a visual feature value and a cluster. The accuracy is fundamental to estimate the quality of the induced rules. Statistical measures are used to estimate the rule accuracy.

As far as the textual description processing is concerned, it requires a pre-processing phase to reduce the number of key words and to keep only relevant key words. This task is a difficult and time-consuming one, and need an expert to validate the results obtained. Textual descriptions need to find relevant similarity measure. Clustering can be performed by conceptual clustering like Cobweb, or by other techniques such as k-means after transformation of the initial key words into numerical vectors. The extracted concepts are then hierarchically organized, using a priori knowledge, hierarchical classification techniques or the expert's knowledge of the application domain.

If the textual information is reduced to key words, domain ontology is necessary to produce semantic relationships between concepts. If documents (like Web pages for example) are associated with images, relationships between concepts can be automatically extracted, without a priori knowledge.

Indeed, after computing the reduced view of the image database, the system should be able to automatically classify new images in the appropriate cluster, thanks to the characterization rules. The image classification in the appropriate clusters is possible if the metadata extracted previously are globally respected. If not, it raises a crucial problem requiring additional works: several solutions may be envisaged: (1) the "noise" cluster generation, (2) taking the new image and its effects on the clustering and characterization rules account, etc. The image deletion in a database is not presented in this chapter, but it points out the same problem.

Once the search space reduction and the cluster characterization by means of rules performed, descriptive metadata are stored in the database. These metadata represent the characteristics discovered and shared by images appearing in the same cluster. They play an important role because they allow the user to navigate from the textual world toward the visual world, and back. Image database navigation is made through a visual ontology: starting from the extracted concepts, a hierarchy is built, and for each concept, a set of representative images is associated. Each concept is linked to a set of visual classes in which a prototype is extracted as a representative image and associated to the concept.

The architecture presented in Figure 9.3 is well-suited to specific databases like fingerprints databases, face databases, etc. Indeed, image mining results depend on both the chosen clustering method and the estimated similarity quality. Without a real synergy between application field, considered visual features, their modeling and the estimation of their similarity degree, obtained descriptive metadata are not relevant to allow a more interesting image database exploration. This architecture may also be adapted to general databases, and more particularly to the Web. As Web databases contain images of any domain, visual features are not very representative of particular concepts. It is the reason why only the concept extraction phase (Figure 9.3) is made. Visual clusters are deduced from textual clusters since they contain semantics by nature. Obtained visual clusters are then characterized by using the rules. This proposed architecture adaptation may be a new way to navigate Web image databases.

First experimentations based on several databases are described in the next section.

9.4.2 First Experimentations

A first experimentation based on texture images and clustering with self-organized maps was made. The considered database contained 1098 procedural texture images

Fig. 9.4. The protein Q9UV00_BOTCI and its predicted domains or patterns.

(i.e., generated mathematically). Considered image features are characterized by a numeric vector extracted using the Gabor filter technique. The similarity between two feature vectors is computed by using the well-suited weighted mean variance distance. The well-known k-means and self-organizing maps methods [51] were implemented to obtain interesting image clusters. The obtained results were promising and encourage us to continue in this way.

Nevertheless, this database is semantically poor and does not allow us to fully implement the proposed architecture. That is the reason why new experiments based on more complex annotated image databases are being done. It means both a database having several visual features of images and a database with more semantics.

The first one concerns the bioinformatics domain. The main objective is to help biologists find the protein function in cells according to a bioinformatics analysis. A protein is composed of several predicted ordered domains or patterns. Some of these domains explain the protein function. The ordered domain sequence is represented by an image (Figure 9.4). The idea is to determine the minimal domain/pattern sequence expressing the considered function. So, predicted images are exploited to retrieve a matching between functional clusters obtained by the Gene Ontology [53] after a biological analysis and clusters based on predicted domains (obtained by Pfam [54], for example). In this context, the considered data are complex for a large volume of data (thousands of proteins), data protein is modeled by a score of domains/patterns, and lastly each domain/pattern is characterized by several numerical and textual features (prediction source, the domain/pattern beginning, its length, the color associated to its molecular function). Since a protein is a domain/pattern sequence, a clustering method taking account of the data order is required. Moreover, the high-dimensional data and the different characterized vector size must be taken into consideration. To achieve this objective, k-means and self-organizing maps are not well-suited to bioinformatics data: a relevant similarity distance is not easy to define because the notion of sequence does not exist, etc. Clustering methods based on grid or on density are more interesting in the protein context. The CLIQUE method [52] has been studied and used. The first results we obtained are interesting, but CLIQUE is time-consuming owing to the data complexity. A data preprocessing is necessary to reduce the protein complexity. Data analysis is perhaps a way to explore.

This experimentation shows that no clustering method may be advocated. Only the data nature (complexity, volume, sequence, etc.) leads to a particular clustering method category (hierarchical clustering, partitioning clustering, fuzzy clustering, density-based clustering, grid-based clustering). Then, the chosen method must be adapted to the data vector and vice versa.

The second one concerns the art domain. The objective is to help users retrieve pertinent images according to visual or textual features. Annotations from paintings are stored in a database and we extract knowledge from the paintings titles. Images are stored separately. The database contains a large volume of data corresponding to the paintings that belongs to a French museum. Starting from these titles and after a preprocessing that consists in eliminating irrelevant words such as stop-words, we build a co-occurrence matrix. We then apply a hierarchical clustering. A thesaurus of the art domain is also exploited to associate semantic to the obtained clusters. Using a similarity measure like the Resnik measure [55], concepts extracted from texts can be matched with the thesaurus. We are still working on this corpus to exploit the results.

A third experimentation of text clustering and computed ontology was also achieved [56]. This experiment is dedicated to the architecture based on Web databases. In this case, we start from the text contained into the Web pages and then, we explore the image part. Starting from Web pages (in French) in the tourism domain, we have extracted a set of concepts, using unsupervised clustering method. The World Wide Web provides a vast source of information. This information is often semistructured, although you may also find both structured and free text. The information is also dynamic; it contains hyperlinks and is globally shared over multiple sites. For our case, we have a semistructured text that is an intermediate point between unstructured collection of textual documents and fully structured tuples of typed data. Some forms of structure we can find in this information source are HTML tags. In our case, we want to exploit the specific elements of our Web pages in order to give an added value for some words, thanks to the associated specific HTML tags. After a preprocessing step, we applied different clustering methods to group similar words and extract concepts. This preprocessing step is very important to obtain correct results. We use tools like Tree-Tagger in order to obtain the lemmatized form of each word. This experiment was based on 585 Web pages. We first apply a hierarchical clustering method on words that have been tagged as title, subtitle, words appearing in bold or in color, etc. We obtained a fist concept hierarchy that we refine using principal component analysis on the all text.

Another clustering method [57] was applied to images found on the Web. In this case, we have selected a set of Web pages related to a specific domain and extracted words appearing near the images according to a specific distance from the images (from 5 to 10 words before and after each image). An affinity matrix between the words is computed according to the following formula: $affinity = 1/(1 + distance(M1, M2))$, where distance represents the number of words separating the words $M1$ and $M2$ in the Web page. The clustering algorithm defined by Cleuziou & al is then applied upon this matrix. The last step is related to the association between the extracted concepts and the images. In this last experiment, we obtain significant results of associations between words and images. These first results encourage us to go on exploring this research axis.

9.5 Conclusion and Future Work

After a review of existing techniques related to multimedia information retrieval, we point out that these methods are not powerful enough to retrieve efficiently relevant information including semantic concepts.

We propose an architecture that combines multimedia mining and visual ontology. Visual and textual features are separately processed. The clustering process and the characterization rule process are respectively performed on these features and on each previous calculated cluster. While clustering is used to reduce the search space, characterization rules are performed to describe each cluster and to classify a new image in the appropriate database clusters. These techniques improve also the system retrieval time since the system matches the selected features with only the database image features of right clusters. Nevertheless, new image inserting and image deleting raise a crucial problem (consequences on this action on the cluster and characterization rule organization) requiring additional works.

Moreover, a visual ontology, which is a concept hierarchy, is built according to the set of annotations. The retrieval process is based on this visual ontology.

Currently, we continue to develop the proposed framework and to look for the best appropriate algorithms and methods to compute interesting relevant descriptive metadata and suited visual ontology.

References

1. Venters CC, Cooper MD. A review of content-based image retrieval systems. In: *JISC Technology Applications Program*; 2000.
2. Fensel D. *Ontologies: Silver Bullet for Knowledge Management and Electronic Commerce*. Springer-Verlag; 2000.
3. Simoff SJ, Djeraba C, Zaïane OR. MDM/ KDD2002: Multimedia Data Mining between Promises and Problems. In: *ACM SIGKDD Explorations*. vol. 4(2); 2002.
4. Zhang J, Hsu W, Lee ML. Image mining: Issues, frameworks and techniques. In: *Second International Workshop on Multimedia Data Mining (MDM/KDD)*. San Fransisco, USA; 2001.
5. Han J, Kamber M. *Data Mining: Concepts and Techniques*. Morgan Kaufmann; 2001.
6. Eakins JP. Towards intelligent image retrieval. In: *Pattern Recognition*. vol. 35; 2002. p. 3–14.
7. Khoshafian S, et al. *Multimedia and Imaging Databases*. San Francisco, CA: Morgan Kaufmann; 1996.
8. Oria V, Özsu T, Iglinski PJ. Querying images in the DISIMA DBMS. In: *Proceedings of the 7th International Workshop on Multimedia Information Systems*. Capri, Italy; 2001, pp. 89–98.
9. Meharga MT. An integrated approach for querying general-purpose image database. In: *EPFL Thesis*; 2002.
10. Meharga MT, Monties S. An image content data model for image database interrogation. In: *CBMI'01, International Workshop on Content-Based Multimedia Indexing*, Brescia; 2001.
11. Chang SF, Sikora T, Purl A. Overview of the MPEG-7 standard. In: *IEEE Transactions on Circuits and Systems for Video Technology—Special Issue on MPEG-7*; 2001, pp. 688–695.
12. Swain MJ, Ballard DH. Color indexing. *International Journal of Computer Vision*. vol. 7; 1991.
13. Stricker M, et al. *Similarity of Color Images*; 1995.
14. Smith JR, Chang SF. Tools and Techniques for color image retrieval. In: *Storage and Retrieval for Image and Video database IV, SPIE Proceedings*. vol. 2670; 1996.

15. Gonzalez RC, Woods RE. *Digital Image Processing.* 2nd ed. Prentice-Hall; 2002.
16. Niblack W, et al. The QBIC Project: Querying images by content using colour, texture and shape. In: *In Proceedings SPIE Storage and Retrieval for Image and Video Databases*; 1994.
17. Pitas I. *Digital Image Processing Algorithms*; 1993.
18. Jähne B. *Digital Image Processing—Concepts, Algorithms and Scientific Applications.* 4th ed. Springer; 1997.
19. Nastar C, et al. SurfImage: A flexible content-based image retrieval system. In: *The 6th ACM International Multimedia Conference (MM'98).* Bristol, England; 1998.
20. Ma WY. NETRA: A toolbox for navigating large image databases. In A Dissertation submitted in partial satisfaction of the requirements for the degree of Doctor of Philosophy in Electrical and Computer Engineering. University of California at Santa Barbara; 1997.
21. Zahn CT, et al. Fourier descriptors for plane closed curves. In: *IEEE Transactions on Computers.* vol. C-21; 1972.
22. Persoon E, et al. Shape discrimination using Fourier descriptors. In: *IEEE Transactions on Systems, Man, and Cybernetics.* vol. SMC-21; 1977.
23. Subramanian VS. *Principles of Multimedia Database Systems.* San Francisco, CA; 1998.
24. Schmid C, et al. Comparing and evaluating interest points. In: *In Proceedings of the 6th International Conference on Computer Vision.* Bombay, India; 1998.
25. Böhm C, et al. Searching in high-dimensional spaces: Index structures for improving the performance of multimedia databases. In: *ACM Computing surveys.* vol. 33; 2001.
26. Li C, et al. Clustering for approximate similarity search in high-dimensional spaces. In: *TKDE.* vol. 14; 2002. pp. 792–808.
27. Del Bimbo A. *Visual Information Retrieval*; 1999.
28. Dubois D, Prade H, Sedes F. Fuzzy logic techniques in multimedia databases querying: A preliminary investigation of the potentials. In: *IEEE TKDE.* vol. 13; 2001. pp. 383–392.
29. Fayyad UM, et al. *Advanced in Knowledge Discovery and data Mining.* MIT Press; 1996.
30. Agrawal R, et al. Fast algorithms for mining association rules. In: *In Proceedings of International Conference Very Large Data Bases (VLDB'94).* Santiago, Chili; 1994. pp. 487–499.
31. Fayyad U, Haussler D, Stolorz P. Mining scientific data. In: *Communications of the ACM.* vol. 39; 1996, pp. 51–57.
32. Zaïane O R, Han J, Zhu H. Mining recurrent ttems in multimedia with progressive resolution refinement. In: *Proc. 2000 Int. Conf. on Data Engineering (ICDE'00).* San Diego, CA; 2000.
33. Ordonez C, Omiecinski E. Discovering association rules based on image content. In: *IEEE Advances in Digital Libraries (ADL'99)*; 1999.
34. Djeraba C. Association and content-based retrieval. In: *IEEE Transaction on Knowledge and Data Engineering*; 2002.
35. Tollari S, Glotin H, Le Maitre J. Enhancement of textual images classification using segmented visual contents for image search engine. In: Multimedia Tools and Applications. vol. 25; Springer, 2005, pp. 405–417.
36. Guarino N. Formal ontology, conceptual analysis and knowledge representation. *International Journal of Human and Computer Studies.* 1995;43:625–640.
37. W3C (World Wide Web Consortium). Resource Description Framework (RDF) Model and Syntax Specification; 1999.
38. ANSI. ANSI/NISO Z39.19-1993 (R1998);.
39. Miller GA. WordNet: A lexical database for English. *Communications of the ACM.* 1995;38:39–41.

40. Gruber T. Toward principles for the design of ontologies used for knowledge sharing. 1993. Special issue on Formal Ontology in Conceptual Analysis and Knowledge Representation.

41. Baader F, Calvanese D, McGuiness D, Nardi D, Patel-Schneider P. *The Description Logic Handbook.* Cambridge; 2003.

42. Heflin J. OWL Web Ontology Language Use Cases and Requirements. 2004. W3C Recommendation.

43. Uschold M, King M. Towards a methodology for building ontologies. In: Skuce D, ed. *IJCAI'95 Workshop on Basic Ontological Issues in Knowledge Sharing*; 1995, pp. 6.1–6.10.

44. Grüninger M, Fox MS. Methodology for the design and evaluation of ontologies. In: Skuce D, ed. *IJCAI'95 Workshop on Basic Ontological Issues in Knowledge Sharing*, Canada, 1995.

45. Gomez-Perez A, Fernandez-Lopez M, Corcho O. *Ontological Engineering.* Springer; 2003.

46. Staab S, Studer R, Sure Y. Knowledge processes and ontologies. *IEEE Intelligent Systems.* 2001;16(1):26–34.

47. Maedche A. *Ontology Learning for the Semantic Web. Kluwer Academic Publishers*; 2002.

48. Faure D, Nedellec C. A corpus-based conceptual clustering method for verb frames and ontology. In: Verlardi P, ed. *Proceedings of the LREC Workshop on Adapting lexical and corpus resources to sublanguages and applications.* 1998.

49. Bisson G, Nedellec C, Canamero L. Designing clustering methods for ontology building— The Mo'K workbench. In: *Proceedings of the ECAI Ontology Learning Workshop*; 2000.

50. Benitez A, Smith JR, Chang SF. MediaNet: A multimedia information network for knowledge representation. In: *Conference on Internet Multimedia Management Systems*, vol. 4210, IST/SPIE; 2000.

51. Kohonen T. *Self-Organizing Maps.* Berlin: Springer; 1995.

52. Agrawal R, Gehrke J, Gunopulos D, Raghavan P. Automatic subspace clustering of high dimensional data for data mining applications. In: *Proceedings ACM SIGMOD'99*; 1999.

53. http://www.geneontology.org/index.shtml.

54. http://www.sanger.ac.uk/Software/Pfam.

55. Resnik P. Using information content to evaluate semantic similarity in a taxonomy. In: *In Proceedings of the 14th Joint Conference on Artificial Intelligence.* Montreal; 1995.

56. Karoui, L Aufaure MA, Bennacer N. Ontology discovery from Web pages: Application to Tourism. In: *Workshop on Knowledge Discovery and Ontologies (KDO)*, Pisa, Italy; September 2004, pp. 115–120. Colocated with ECML/PKDD.

57. Cleuziou G, Martin L, Vrain C. PoBOC: An Overlapping clustering algorithm. Application to rule-based classification and textual data. In: de Mántaras RLópez, Saitta L, eds. *In Proceedings of the 16th Biennial European Conference on Artificial Intelligence (ECAI'04).* Valencia, Spain: IOS Press; August 2004, pp. 440–444.

10. Visual Alphabets: Video Classification by End Users

Menno Israël, Egon L. van den Broek, Peter van der Putten, and Marten J. den Uyl

Summary. The work presented here introduces a real-time automatic scene classifier within content-based video retrieval. In our envisioned approach end users like documentalists, not image processing experts, build classifiers interactively, by simply indicating positive examples of a scene. Classification consists of a two-stage procedure. First, small image fragments called patches are classified. Second, frequency vectors of these patch classifications are fed into a second classifier for global scene classification (e.g., city, portraits, or countryside). The first stage classifiers can be seen as a set of highly specialized, learned feature detectors, as an alternative to letting an image processing expert determine features a priori. The end user or domain expert thus builds a visual alphabet that can be used to describe the image in features that are relevant for the task at hand. We present results for experiments on a variety of patch and image classes. The scene classifier approach has been successfully applied to other domains of video content analysis, such as content-based video retrieval in television archives, automated sewer inspection, and porn filtering.

10.1 Introduction

This work has been done as part of the EU Vicar project (IST). The aim of this project was to develop a real-time automated video indexing, classification, annotation, and retrieval system. Vicar was developed in close cooperation with leading German, Austrian, Swedish, and Dutch broadcasting companies. These companies generally store millions of hours of video material in their archives. To increase sales and reuse of this material, efficient and effective video search with optimal hit rates is essential. Outside the archive, large amounts of video material are managed as well, such as news feeds and raw footage [1,2].

Generally, only a fraction of the content is annotated manually and these descriptions are typically rather compact. Any system to support video search must be able to index, classify, and annotate the material extensively so that efficient mining and search may be conducted using the index rather than the video itself. Furthermore, these indices, classifications, and annotations must abstract from the pure syntactical appearance of the video pixels to capture the semantics of what the video is about (e.g., a shot of Madonna jogging in a park).

Within Vicar a variety of visual events is recognized, including shots, camera motion, person motion, persons, and faces, specific objects, etc. In this chapter we will focus on the automated classification of visual scenes. For searching and browsing video scenes, classifiers that extract the background setting in which events take place are a key component. Examples of scenes are indoor, outdoor, day, night, countryside, city, demonstration, and so on. The amount of classes to be learned is generally quite large—tens to hundreds—and not known beforehand. So, it is generally not feasible to let an image processing expert build a special purpose classifier for each class.

Using our envisioned approach, an end user like an archive documentalist or a video editor can build classifiers by simply showing positive examples of a specific scene category. In addition, an end user may also construct classifiers for small image fragments to simplify the detection of high-level global scenes, again just by showing examples (e.g., trees, buildings, and road).

We call these image fragments patches. The patch classifiers actually provide the input for the classification of the scene as a whole. The patch classifiers can be seen as automatically trained data preprocessors generating semantically rich features, highly relevant to the global scenes to be classified, as an alternative to an image processing expert selecting the right set of abstract features (e.g., wavelets, Fourier transforms). In addition, the interactive procedure is a way to exploit a priori knowledge, the documentalist may have about the real world, rather than relying on a purely data-driven approach. In essence, the end user builds a visual alphabet that can be used to describe the world in terms that matter to the task at hand.

Note that the scene is classified without relying on explicit object recognition. This is important because a usable indexing system should run at least an order of magnitude faster than real time, whereas object recognition is computationally intensive. More fundamentally, we believe that certain classes of semantically rich information can be perceived directly from the video stream rather than indirectly by building on a large number of lower levels of slowly increasing complexity. This position is inspired by Gibson's ideas on direct perception [3]. Gibson claims that even simple animals may be able to pick up niche specific and complex observations (e.g., prey or predator) directly from the input without going through several indirect stages of abstract processing.

This chapter is expository and meant to give a nontechnical introduction into our methodology. A high-level overview of our approach is given in Section 10.2. Section 10.3 provides more detail on the low-level color and texture features used, and Section 10.4 specifies the classifying algorithms used. Experimental results for patch and scene classification are given in Sections 10.4.1 and 10.4.2. Next, we highlight three applications in which scene classification technology has been embedded (Section 10.6). We finish with a discussion and conclusion (Sections 10.5 and 10.7).

10.2 Overall Approach

In Vicar a separate module is responsible for detecting the breaks between shots. Then for each shot a small number of representative key frames is extracted, thus generating a storyboard of the video. These frames (or a small section of video around these key frames) are input to the scene classifier.

10.2.1 Scene Classification Procedure

The scene classifier essentially follows a two-stage procedure: (i) Small image segments are classified into patch categories (e.g., trees, buildings, and road) and (ii) these classifications are used to classify the scene of the picture as a whole (e.g., interior, street, and forest). The patch classes that are recognized can be seen as an alphabet of basic visual elements to describe the picture as a whole.

In more detail, first a high-level segmentation of the image takes place. This could be some intelligent procedure recognizing arbitrarily shaped segments, but for our purposes we simply divide images up into a regular n by m grid, say 3-by-2 grid segments for instance. Next, from each segment patches (i.e., groups of adjacent pixels within an image, described by a specific local pixel distribution, brightness, and color) are sampled. Again, some intelligent sampling mechanism could be used to recognize arbitrarily sized patches. However, we divided each grid segment by a second grid, into regular size image fragments, ignoring any partial patches sampled from the boundary. These patches are then classified into several patch categories, using color and texture features (see Section 10.3). See Figure 10.1 for a visualization of this approach.

For each segment, a frequency vector of patch classifications is calculated. Then, these patch classification vectors are concatenated to preserve some of the global location information (e.g., sky above and grass below) and fed into the final scene classifier. Various classifiers have been used to classify the patches and the entire picture, including kNN, naive Bayes, and back-propagation neural networks.

10.2.2 Related Work

Literature on scene classification is relatively limited. Early retrieval systems like QBIC [4, 5], VisualSEEk [6], PicHunter [7], PicToSeek [8], and SIMPLIcity [9] as well as recent systems such as MARVEL [10], M4ART [11], and the system proposed by Wu et al. [12], use color, shape, and texture representations for picture search. Minka and Picard [13], Picard [14], and Picard and Minka [15] extended Photobook with capabilities for classifying patches into so-called "stuff" categories (e.g., grass, sky, sand, and stone), using a set of competing classification models (society of models approach).

In Blobworld, Belongie, Carson, Greenspan, and Malik [16, 17] segment pictures into regions with coherent texture and color of arbitrary shape ('blobs') and offer the user the possibility to search on specific blobs rather than the low-level characteristics of the full picture. However, these blobs are not classified into stuff nor scene categories [16, 17]. Campbell, Mackeown, Thomas, and Troscianko [18, 19] also segment pictures into arbitrarily shaped regions and then use a neural network to classify the patches into stuff-like categories like building, road, and vegetation.

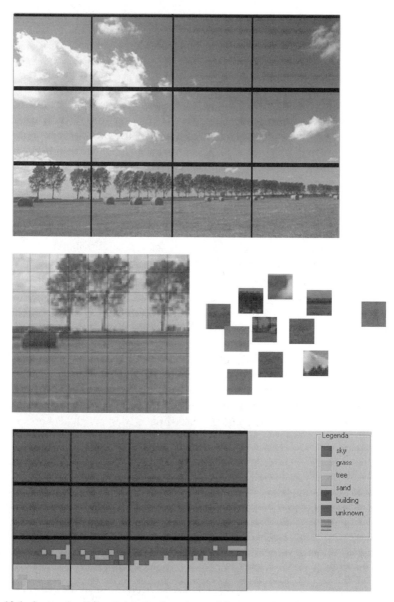

Fig. 10.1. Screenshots visualizing the first phase of the scene classification process. From top to bottom and from left to right: The images with a 4 × 3 grid over it, extraction of the patches from a grid cell, classification of the patches, and the resulting "patch image" with its legend.

Some papers are available on classification of the scene of the picture as a whole. Lipson et al. [20] recognize a limited set of scenes (mountains, mountain lakes, waterfalls, and fields) by deriving the global scene configuration of a picture and matching it to a handcrafted model template. For example, the template for a snowy mountain states that the bottom range of a picture is dark, the middle range very light, and the top range has medium luminance. Ratan and Grimson [21] extend this work by learning the templates automatically. The templates are built using the dominant color-luminance combinations and their spatial relations in images of a specific scene category. They present results for fields and mountains only. Both papers report results only for retrieval tasks, not for classification.

Oliva and Torralba [22] defined global characteristics (or semantic axes) of a scene (e.g., vertical–horizontal, open–closed, and natural–artificial), for discriminating between, for example, city scenes and nature scenes. These characteristics are used to organize and sort pictures rather than classify them. Gorkani and Picard [23] classified city versus nature scenes. The algorithms used to extract the relevant features were specific for these scenes (i.e., global texture orientation). In addition, Szummer and Picard [24] classified indoor and outdoor scenes. They first classified local segments as indoor or outdoor, and then classified the whole image as such. Both classifiers performed well, but it is not known whether these approaches generalize to other scene categories.

10.2.3 Positioning the Visual Alphabet Method

Our method uses the local patch classification as input for the classification of the scene as a whole. To our knowledge, only Fung and Loe [25, 26] reported a similar approach. Note that the final scene classifier has only access to patch class labels. From the point of view of the final classifier, the patch classifiers are feature extractors that supply semantically rich and relevant input rather than generic syntactic color and texture information. Moreover, the patch classifiers are trained rather than being feature extractors a priori selected by an image processing expert.

So, our method differs and improves on the general applicability for a variety of scene categories, without the need to select different and task-specific feature extraction algorithms, for each classification task. Moreover, we used computationally cheap algorithms, enabling real-time scene classification. A more fundamental difference is that we allow end users to add knowledge of the real world to the classification and retrieval engines, which means that it should be possible to outperform any purely data-driven approach, even if it is based on optimal classifiers. This is important given the fact that image processing expertise is scarce and not available to end users, but knowledge of the world is abundant.

10.3 Patch Features

In this section, we discuss the patch features as used for patch classification. They provide the foundation for the scene classifier. In order of appearance, we discuss (i) color quantization, using a new distributed histogram technique, and histogram configurations; (ii) human color categories, color spaces, and the segmentation of the HSI color space; and (iii) an algorithm used to determine the textural features used.

10.3.1 Distributed Color Histograms

At the core of many color matching algorithms lies a technique based on histogram matching. This is no different for the current scene classification system.

Let us, therefore, define a color histogram of size n. Then, each pixel j present in an image has to be assigned to a bin (or bucket) b. Each pixel is assigned to a bin, as follows:

The bin b_i, with $i \in \{0, n - 1\}$, for a pixel j with value x_j, is determined using:

$$\beta_i = \frac{x_j}{s}, \tag{10.1}$$

where x_j is the value of pixel j and s is the size of the intervals, with s determined as follows:

$$s = \frac{\max(x) - \min(x)}{n}, \tag{10.2}$$

where $\max(x)$ and $\min(x)$ are respectively the maximum and minimum value x_j can take.

For convenience, Eq. 10.2 is substituted into Eq. 10.1, which yields:

$$\beta_i = \frac{n \cdot x_j}{\max(x) - \min(x)}. \tag{10.3}$$

Now, b_i is defined as the integer part of the decimal number β_i.

As for each conversion from a originally analog to a digital (discrete) representation, one has to determine the precision of the discretization and with that the position of the boundaries between different elements of the discrete representation. To cope with this problem, we distributed each pixel over three bins, instead of assigning it to one bin.

Let us consider an image with p pixels that has to be distributed over n bins. Furthermore, we define $\min(b_i)$ and $\max(b_i)$ as the borders of bin i (b_i). Then, when considering an image pixel by pixel, the update of the histogram for each of these pixels is done as follows:

$$b_i += 1 \tag{10.4}$$

$$b_{i-1} += 1 - \frac{|x_j - \min(b_i)|}{\max(b_i) - \min(b_i)} \tag{10.5}$$

$$b_{i+1} += 1 - \frac{|x_j - \max(b_i)|}{\max(b_i) - \min(b_i)} \tag{10.6}$$

where $\min(b_i) \leq x_j \leq \max(b_i)$, with $i \in \{0, n - 1\}$ and $j \in \{0, p - 1\}$.

Please note that this approach can be applied on all histograms, but its effect becomes stronger with the decline in the number of bins a histogram consists of.

10.3.2 Histogram Configurations

Several histogram configurations have been presented over the years [27]. For example, the PicHunter [7] image retrieval engine uses a HSV ($4 \times 4 \times 4$) (i.e., 4 Hues,

4 Saturations, and 4 Values) quantization method. In [28], a HSV($18 \times 3 \times 3$) bin quantization scheme is described. The QBIC configuration used 4096 bins [4, 5]: RGB($16 \times 16 \times 16$). For more detailed discussions concerning color quantization, we refer to [27, 29–33].

Histogram matching on a large number of bins has a big advantage: Regardless of the color space used during the quantization process, the histogram matching will have a high precision. Disadvantages of our approach are its high computational complexity and poor generalization.

When a coarse color quantization is performed, these disadvantages can be solved. So, since the system should work real-time and the classifiers have to be able to generalize over images, a coarse color quantization is needed.

However, to ensure an acceptable precision, it is of decisive importance that human color perception is respected during quantization. Hence, the combination of color space and the histogram configuration is crucial for the acceptance of the results by the user.

10.3.3 Human Color Categories

As mentioned by Forsyth and Ponse [34], "It is surprisingly difficult to predict what colors a human will see in a complex scene; this is one of the many difficulties that make it hard to produce really good color reproduction systems."

From literature [30, 35–41] is known that people use a limited set of color categories. Color categories can be defined as a fuzzy notion of some set of colors. People use these categories when thinking of or speaking about colors or when they recall colors from memory. Research from various fields of science emphasizes the importance of focal colors in human color perception. The use of this knowledge may provide the means for bridging the semantic gap that exists in image and video classification.

No exact definition of the number nor the exact content of the color categories is present. However, all research mentions a limited number of color categories: ranging between 11 [29, 30, 35] and 30 [37], where most evidence is found for 11 color categories. We conducted some limited experiments with subjective categories (categories indicated by humans) but these did not give better results to 16 evenly distributed categories, so for simplicity we used this categorization. Now that we have defined a coarse 16 bin color histogram to define color with, we need a color space on which it can be applied.

10.3.4 Color Spaces

No color quantization can be done without a color representation. Color is mostly represented as tuples of (typically three) numbers, conform certain specifications (that we name a color space). One can describe color spaces using two important notions: perceptual uniformity and device dependency. Perceptually uniform means that two colors that are equally distant in the color space are perceptually equally distant.

A color space is device dependent when the actual color displayed depends on the device used.

The RGB color space is the most used color space for computer graphics. It is device-dependent and not perceptually uniform. The conversion from a RGB image to a gray value image simply takes the sum of the R,G, and B values and divides the result by 3.

The HSI/HSV (Hue, Saturation, and Intensity/Value) color spaces are more closely related to human color perception than the RGB color space, but are still not perceptual uniform. In addition, they are device-dependent.

Hue is the color component of the HSI color space. When Saturation is set to 0, Hue is undefined and the Intensity/Value-axis represents the gray-scale image.

Despite the fact that the HSI and HSV color spaces are not perceptually uniform, they are found to perform as good of better than perceptual uniform spaces such as CIE LUV [42]. Therefore, we have chosen to use the HSI color space.

Hereby, we took into account human perceptual limitations. If Saturation was below 0.2, Intensity was below 0.12, or Intensity was above 0.94, then the Hue value has not been taken into account. This, since for these Saturation and Intensity values the Hue is not visible as a color.

Since image and video material is defined in the RGB color space, we needed to convert this color space to the HSI color space. This was done as follows [43]:

$$H = \arctan\left(\frac{\frac{\sqrt{3}}{2}(G - B)}{R - \frac{1}{2}(G + B)}\right) \tag{10.7}$$

$$S = \sqrt{\left(R - \frac{\sqrt{3}}{2}(G - B)\right)^2 + \left(\frac{1}{2}(G + B)\right)^2} \tag{10.8}$$

$$I = \frac{R + G + B}{3}. \tag{10.9}$$

Note that all H, S, and I values were normalized to values between 0 and 1.

10.3.5 Segmentation of the HSI Color Space

Our 16-color categories are defined by an equal division of the Hue axis of the HSI color space, since the Hue represents color. So far, only color was defined and luminance is ignored.

Luminance is represented by the Intensity axis of the HSI color space. Again we have chosen for a coarse quantization: the Intensity-axis is divided into six equal segments (see Figure 10.2).

The original RGB color coordinates were converted to Hue and Intensity coordinates by Eqs. 10.7 and 10.9, as adopted from Gevers and Smeulders [43]. Next, for both the Hue and the Intensity histogram, using Eq. 10.3 each pixel is assigned to a bin. Last, Eqs. 10.4, 10.5, 10.6 are applied on both histograms to update them. Since both histograms were a coarse quantization, this method (i) is computationally

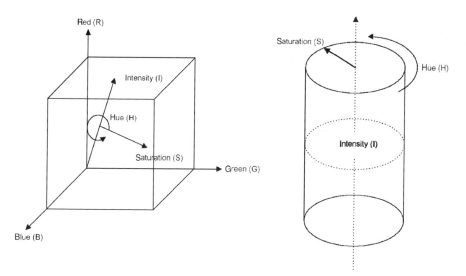

Fig. 10.2. Left: The relation between the RGB and the HSI color space, from the perspective of the RGB color space. Right: The cylinder-shaped representation of the HSI (hue, saturation, and intensity) color space, as used in this research. The figure is adopted from Van den Broek [30].

cheap (making real-time classification possible) and (ii) facilitates in generalization by classifiers.

10.3.6 Texture

Next to color, texture can be analyzed. Jain and Karu [44] state, "Texture [eludes] a formal definition." Let us define texture as follows: A repetitive arrangement of pixels values that either is perceived or can be described as such.

For texture analysis, in most cases the intensity of the pixels is used, hereby ignoring their color [36,45–47]. Several techniques are used to determine the patterns that may be perceived from the image [27,30,36,46–48]. With most texture analyzes, textural features are derived from the image, instead of describing arrangements of the individual pixels. This reduces the computational costs significantly, which is essential for applications working real time.

Therefore, we used a texture algorithm that extracts three textual features for each position of a mask that is run over the image. Here, the size of the mask determines the ratio between local and global texture analysis. The position of the mask is defined by its central pixel. Note that the mask is a square of $n \times n$ pixels, with n being an odd integer.

For each pixel of the mask, the difference between both its horizontal neighbors as well as the difference between its vertical neighbors is determined. (p, q) denotes the elements (i.e., pixels) of the image with (i, j) being the coordinates of the pixels located in a mask, surrounding an image pixel (p, q). Function f determines the normalized value of pixel (i, j) for a chosen color channel (i.e., H, S, or I), using Eqs. 10.7, 10.8, and 10.9.

Using the algorithm below, for each mask M_{11}, M_{12}, and M_{22} are determined, defining the symmetric covariance matrix M. Let ev_1 and ev_2 be the eigenvalues of M. For more details, see, for example, Jähne [49] on structure tensor. Recent work on nonlinear structure tensors has been presented by Brox et al. [50].

$$
\begin{aligned}
&\text{foreach}(p, q) \in \text{Image} \\
&\quad \text{foreach}(i, j) \in \text{Mask}(p, q) \\
&\quad\quad \text{Sum} += f(i, j) \\
&\quad\quad \text{SqSum} += f(i, j)^2 \\
&\quad\quad M_{11} += (f(i+1, j) - f(i-1, j))^2 \\
&\quad\quad M_{12} += (f(i, j+1) - f(i, j-1))^2 \\
&\quad\quad M_{22} += (f(i+1, j) - f(i-1, j)) \cdot (f(i, j+1) - f(i, j-1))
\end{aligned}
$$

Given this algorithm, three textural features can be determined:

$$F_1 = \text{SqSum} - \text{Sum}^2 \tag{10.10}$$

$$F_2 = \frac{\min\{ev_1, ev_2\}}{\max\{ev_1, ev_2\}} \tag{10.11}$$

$$F_3 = \max\{ev_1, ev_2\} \tag{10.12}$$

F_1 (see Eq. 10.10) can be identified as the variance (σ^2), indicating the global amount of texture present in the image. The other two features, F_2 and F_3 (see Eqs. 10.11 and 10.12), indicate the structure of the texture available. If ev_1 and ev_2 differ significantly, stretched structures are present (e.g., lines). When ev_1 and ev_2 have a similar value (i.e., F_2 approximates 1; see Eq. 10.11), texture is isotropic. In the case both ev_1 and ev_2 are large (i.e., both F_2 and F_3 are large; see Eqs. 10.11 and 10.12), clear structure is present, without a clear direction. In the case ev_1 and ev_2 are both small (i.e., F_2 is large and F_3 is small; see Eqs. 10.11 and 10.12), smooth texture is present. Moreover, F_2 and F_3 are rotation-invariant.

Hence, this triplet of textural features provides a good indication for the textural properties of images, both locally and globally. In addition, it is computationally cheap and, therefore, very useful for real-time content-based video retrieval.

10.4 Experiments and Results

In the previous section (Section 10.3), the features used were introduced. These features were used for the first phase of classification: the classification of patches, resulting in a frequency vector of patch classes for each grid cell.

In the second phase of classification, a classifier is used to classify the whole image. The input for the classifier is the concatenation of all frequency vectors of patch classes for each grid cell.

So, two phases exist, each using their own classifier. We have experimented with two types of classifiers: A K-nearest neighbors classifier (kNN) and a neural network.

We will now discuss both the patch classification (Section 10.4.1) and the scene classification (Section 10.4.2).

The advantage of kNN is that it is a lazy method; that is, the models need no retraining. This is an important advantage given that we envisage an interactively learning application. However, given that kNN does not abstract a model from the data, it suffers more from the curse of dimensionality and will need more data to provide accurate and robust results. The neural network needs training, parameter optimization, and performance tuning. However, it can provide good results on smaller data sets providing that the degrees of freedom in the model are properly controlled. The experiments discussed in the next two subsections all used the Corel image database as test bed.

10.4.1 Patch Classification

In this section, we will discuss the patch classification. In the next section, the classification of the image as a whole is discussed.

Each of the patches had to be classified to one of the nine patch categories defined (i.e., building, crowd, grass, road, sand, skin, sky, tree, and water). First, a kNN classifier was used for classification. This is because it is a generic classification method. In addition, it could indicate whether a more complex classification method would be needed. However, the classification performance was poor. Therefore, we have chosen to use a neural network for the classification of the grid cells, with nine output nodes (as much as there were patch classes).

On behalf of the neural network, for each of the nine patch classes both a train and a test set were randomly defined, with a size ranging from 950 to 2500 patches per category. The neural network architecture was as follows: 25 input, 30 hidden, and 9 output nodes. The network ran 5000 training cycles with a learning rate of 0.007.

With a patch size of 16×16, the patch classifier had an overall precision of 87.5%. The patch class crowd was confused with the patch class building in 5.19% of the cases. Sand and skin were also confused. Sand was classified as skin in 8.80% of the cases, and skin was classified as sand in 7.16% of the cases. However, with a precision of 76.13% the patch class road appeared the hardest to classify. In the remaining 23.87% of the cases road was confused with one of the other eight patch classes, with percentages ranging from 1.55 to 5.81. The complete results can be found in Table 10.1.

Table 10.2 shows the results for a 8×8 patch classifier in one of our experiments. The 16×16 patch classifier clearly outperforms the 8×8 patch classifier with an overall precision of 87.5% versus 74.1%. So, the overall precision for the 8×8 patch classifier decreases with 13.4% in comparison with the precision of the 16×16 classifier. The decline in precision for each category is as follows: sand 22.16%, water 21.26%, building 17.81%, skin 17.48%, crowd 17.44%, tree 16.8%, and road 7.16%. Only for the categories grass and sky, the classification was similar for both patch sizes.

Note that Figure 10.1 presents a screenshot of the system, illustrating both the division of an image into grids. The classified patches are resembled by little squares in different colors.

Table 10.1. Confusion matrix of the patch (size: 16 × 16) classification for the test set. The *x*-axis shows the actual category, and the *y*-axis shows the predicted category.

	Building	Crowd	Grass	Road	Sand	Skin	Sky	Tree	Water	Unknown
Building	**89.23**	3.02	0.09	1.11	1.02	0.60	0.38	3.70	0.85	0.00
Crowd	5.19	**87.25**	0.19	1.81	0.44	0.50	0.38	2.94	0.06	1.25
Grass	0.00	0.00	**94.73**	0.73	0.60	0.00	0.00	3.00	0.93	0.00
Road	1.55	5.48	2.84	**76.13**	1.55	1.74	1.81	5.81	3.10	0.00
Sand	1.84	0.88	2.24	1.44	**83.68**	8.80	0.24	0.00	0.64	0.24
Skin	0.32	2.53	0.00	0.63	7.16	**89.37**	0.00	0.00	0.00	0.00
Sky	0.21	0.00	0.00	2.57	0.93	0.00	**91.71**	0.36	3.86	0.36
Tree	1.12	3.44	2.60	0.32	0.16	0.24	0.56	**88.44**	0.84	2.28
Water	0.00	0.00	4.00	4.44	0.52	0.00	3.04	0.44	**87.26**	0.30

So far, we have discussed only patch classification in general. However, it was applied on each grid cell separately: For each grid cell, each patch was classified to a patch category. Next, the frequency of occurrence of each patch class, for each grid cell, was determined. Hence, each grid cell could be represented as a frequency vector of the nine patch classes. This served as input for the next phase of processing: scene classification, as is discussed in the next subsection.

10.4.2 Scene Classification

The system had to be able to distinguish between eight categories of scenes, relevant for the Vicar project: interiors, city/street, forest, agriculture/countryside, desert, sea, portrait, and crowds. In pilot experiments several grid sizes were tested: a 3 × 2 grid gave the best results. The input of the classifiers were the normalized and concatenated grid vectors. The elements of each of these vectors represented the frequency of occurrence of each of the reference patches, as they were determined in the patch classification (see Section 10.4.1).

Again, first a kNN classifier was used for classification. Similarly to the patch classification, the kNN had a low precision. Therefore, we have chosen to use a neural network for the classification of the complete images, with eight output nodes (as much as there were scene classes).

Table 10.2. Confusion matrix of the patch (size: 8 × 8) classification for the test set. The *x*-axis shows the actual category, and the *y*-axis shows the predicted category.

	Building	Crowd	Grass	Road	Sand	Skin	Sky	Tree	Water	Unknown
Building	**71.42**	9.00	0.85	2.69	2.43	2.86	0.26	6.53	0.77	3.20
Crowd	10.38	**69.81**	1.13	1.56	2.13	5.56	0.69	6.44	0.19	2.13
Grass	0.80	0.07	**93.87**	0.73	0.07	0.73	1.20	1.20	0.87	0.47
Road	2.65	5.81	2.45	**68.97**	2.97	1.87	5.48	3.10	4.52	2.19
Sand	3.44	3.12	2.88	1.84	**61.52**	15.20	8.80	0.16	2.80	0.24
Skin	1.16	7.79	0.42	0.11	13.47	**71.89**	4.42	0.11	0.11	0.53
Sky	0.00	0.00	0.00	0.29	1.36	2.57	**91.43**	0.07	4.07	0.21
Tree	4.56	11.08	8.20	1.88	0.52	0.76	0.24	**71.64**	0.56	0.56
Water	0.37	0.52	3.26	9.78	3.85	3.85	11.41	0.52	**66.00**	0.44

Table 10.3. Confusion matrix of the scene classification for the test set. The x-axis shows the actual category, and the y-axis shows the predicted category.

	Interior	City/street	Forest	Country	Desert	Sea	Portraits	Crowds
Interior	**82.0**	8.0	2.0	0.0	0.0	0.0	2.0	6.0
City/street	10.0	**70.0**	4.0	8.0	0.0	0.0	2.0	6.0
Forest	2.0	4.0	**80.0**	2.0	2.0	8.0	0.0	2.0
Country	0.0	6.0	28.0	**54.0**	10.0	0.0	0.0	2.0
Desert	8.0	6.0	2.0	10.0	**64.0**	4.0	4.0	2.0
Sea	4.0	14.0	0.0	2.0	0.0	**80.0**	0.0	0.0
Portraits	8.0	0.0	0.0	4.0	4.0	2.0	**80.0**	2.0
Crowds	4.0	14.0	0.0	0.0	2.0	0.0	0.0	**80.0**

For each of the eight scene classes both a train and a test set were randomly defined. The train sets consisted of 199, 198, or 197 images. For all scene classes, the test sets consisted of 50 images. The neural network architecture was as follows: 63 input, 50 hidden, and 8 output nodes. The network ran 2000 training cycles with a learning rate of 0.01.

The image classifier was able to classify 73.8% of the images correct. Interior (82% precision) was confused with city/street in 8.0% and with crowds in 6.0% of the cases. City/street was correctly classified in 70.0% of the cases and confused with interior (10%), with country (8.0%), and with crowds (6.0%). Forest (80% precision) was confused with sea (8.0%). Country was very often (28.0%) confused with forest and was sometimes confused with either city/street (6.0%) or desert (10%), which resulted in a low precision: 54.0%. In addition, also desert had a low precision of classification (64%); it was confused with interior (8.0%), city/street (6.0%), and with country (10%). Sea, portraits, and crowds had a classification precision of 80.0%. Sea was confused with city/street in 14%, portraits were confused with interior in 8.0% of the cases, and crowds were confused with city/street in 14.0% of the cases. In Table 10.3 the complete results for each category separately are presented.

10.5 Discussion and Future Work

Let us discuss the results of patch and scene classification separate, before providing overall issues. For patch classification, two patch sizes have been applied.

The 16×16 patch classifier gave clearly a much higher precision than the 8×8 patch classifier. Our explanation is that a 16×16 patch can contain more information of a (visual) category than a 8×8 patch. Therefore, some textures cannot be described in a 8×8 patch (e.g., patches of buildings). A category such as grass, on the other hand, performed well with 8×8 patches. This is due to its high frequency of horizontal lines that fit in a 8×8 patch.

Therefore, the final tests were carried out with the 16×16 patch size, resulting in an average result of 87.5% correct. Campbell and Picard [14, 15, 19] reported similar results. However, our method has major advantages in terms of a much lower computational complexity. Moreover, the classified patches themselves are intermediate image representations and can be used for image classification, image segmentation as well as for image matching.

A major challenge is the collection of training material for the patch classes to be recognized. The patches with which the classifiers are trained have to be manually classified. Consequently, the development of an automatic scene classifying system requires substantial effort since for all relevant patch classes, sets of reference patches have to be manually collected. For a given class, the other classes act as counterexamples. We are currently looking into several directions to reduce this burden. One approach would be to generate more counterexamples by combining existing patches. Another direction is the use of one class classification algorithms that require only positive examples [51].

The second phase of the system consists of the classification of the image representation, using the concatenated frequency patch vectors of the grid cells. An average performance of 73.8% was achieved. The least performing class is Country (which includes the categories countryside and agriculture) with 54% correct. What strikes immediately, when looking at the detailed results in Table 10.2, is that this category is confused in 28% of the times with the category forest and in 10% of the times with the category desert.

The latter confusions can be explained by the strong visual resemblance between the three categories, which is reflected in the corresponding image representations from these different categories. To solve such confusions, the number of patch categories could be increased. This would increase the discriminating power of the representations. Note that if a user searches on the index rather than on the class label, the search engine may very well be able to search on images that are a mix of multiple patches and scenes.

To make the system truly interactive, classifiers are needed that offer the flexibility of kNN (no or very simple training) but the accuracy of more complex techniques. We have experimented with learning algorithms such as naive Bayes, but the results have not been promising yet.

Furthermore, one could exploit the interactivity of the system more, for instance by adding any misclassification identified by the user to the training data. Finally, the semantic indices not only are useful for search or classification but may very well be used as input for other mining tasks. An example would be to use index clustering to support navigation through clusters of similar video material.

10.6 Applications

The scene classifier has been embedded into the VICAR system for content-based video retrieval. In addition, the same visual alphabet approach has been used for other video classification applications such as porn filtering, sewage inspection, and skin infection detection. The initial versions of these classifiers were built within very short time frames and with sufficient classification accuracy. This provides further evidence that our approach is a generally applicable method to quickly build robust domain specific classifiers.

One of the reasons for its success in these areas is its user-centered approach: the system can easily learn knowledge of the domain involved, by showing it new patch types and so creating a new visual alphabet, simply by selecting the relevant regions or areas in the image. In this section we will describe a number of these applications in a bit more detail.

10.6.1 Vicar

The scene classifier has been integrated into the Vicar Video Navigator [2]. This system utilizes text-based search, either through manual annotations or through automatically generated classifications like the global scene labels. As a result, Vicar returns the best matching key frames along with information about the associated video. In addition, a user can refine the search by combining a query by image with text-based search.

The query by image either can be carried out on local characteristics (appearance) or may include content-based query by image. In the first case, the index consisting of the concatenated patch classification vectors is included in the search. In the latter case, the resulting index of scores on the global scene classifiers is used (content).

In Figures 10.3 and 10.4, an example search is shown from a custom-made Web application based on the Vicar technology: the first screenshot shows one of the key

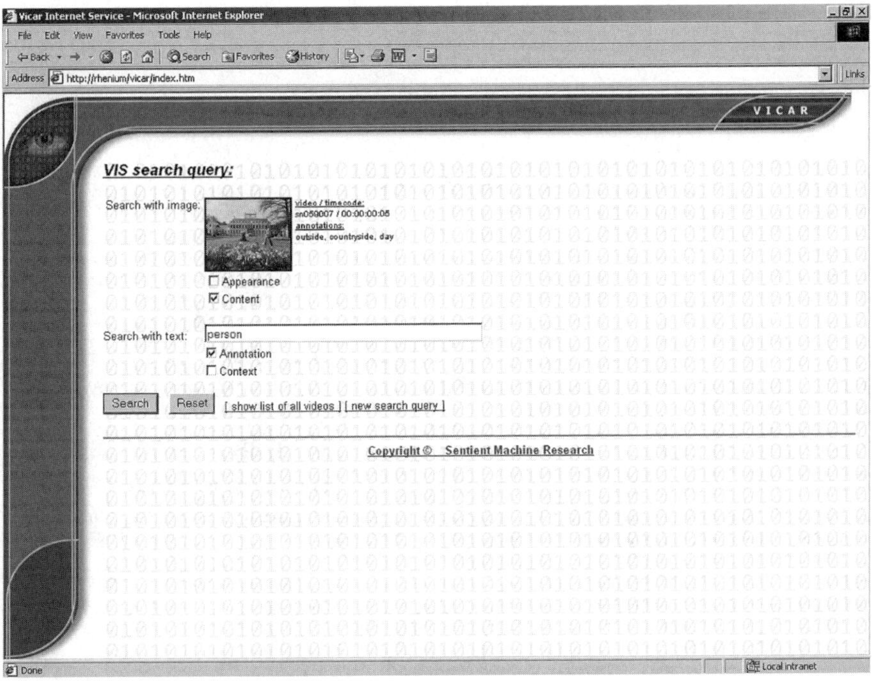

Fig. 10.3. A query for video material.

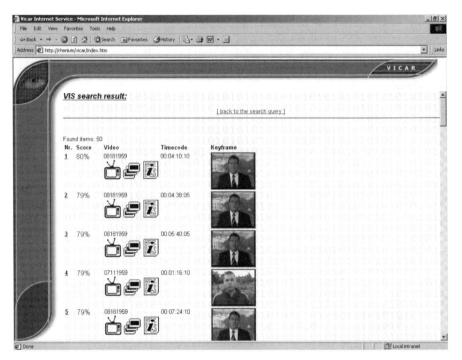

Fig. 10.4. The result of a query for video material.

frames that has been retrieved from the archive using the (automated annotated) key word countryside. An extra key word person (also automated annotated) is added in the search, as well as the content index of the image. In the second screenshot the results of the combined queries are shown: persons with a similar background scene as the query image.

10.6.2 Porn Filtering

To test the general applicability of our approach, we built a new classifier to distinguish pornographic from nonpornographic pictures. Within half a day a classifier was constructed with a precision of over 80%. As a follow-up, a project for porn filtering was started within the EU Safer Internet Action Plan (IAP) program. Within this project, SCOFI, a real-time classification system was built, which is currently running on several schools in Greece, England, Germany, and Iceland. The porn image classifier is combined with a text classifier and integrated with a smart cards enabled authentication server to enable safe Web surfing (see Figure 10.5). The text classifier and the proxy server have been developed by Demokritos, Greece, and are part of the FilterX system [52].

For this application of the system, we first created image representations using the patch classification network as mentioned in Section 10.4.1. With these image

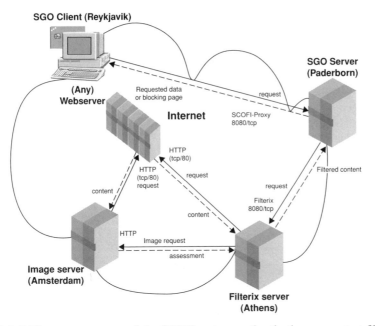

Fig. 10.5. Different components of the SCOFI system: authentication server, text filtering server, and porn image classification server.

representations we trained the second phase classifier, using 8000 positive (pornographic) and 8000 negative (nonpornographic) examples. The results: the system was able to detect 92% of the pornographic images in a diverse image collection of 2000 positive examples and 2000 negative examples (which includes non pornographic pictures of people). There were 8% false positives (images that are not pornographic are identified as pornographic images) and 8% false negatives. Examples of false positives were close-ups of faces and pictures like deserts and fires. For a description of the complete results, we refer to Israël [53]. To improve results, within the SCOFI project a Vicar module was used that detects close-ups of faces.

The integrated SCOFI system that combines text and image classification has a performance of 0% overblocking (i.e., 100% correct on nonpornographic Web pages) and 1% underblocking (i.e., 99% correct on pornographic Web pages). As such it is used as a real-time filter for filtering pornography on the Internet, in several schools throughout Europe.

10.6.3 Sewer Inspection

Our image classification approach is also applied to support the inspection of sewers in the RESEW project (EU GROWTH program for competitive and sustainable growth). Many European cities are spending increasing amounts to improve their sewage systems, so the inspection of deteriorating structures is becoming more and more important.

Currently, robots are used for sewer inspection, but these are completely controlled by operators and the video material that is collected is analyzed manually, which is a costly, time-consuming, and an error-prone process. For instance, a UK-based waste water utility company taking part in the project has 7000 recent tapes of video material available, corresponding to thousands of kilometers of sewers. Real-time monitoring of the entire system would increase the need of automated analysis even further.

Automated and integrated systems for damage identification and structural assessment that are based on video analysis can be used to increase the speed and accuracy of the inspection and evaluation process and lower the cost. To prove the feasibility of the above, the project partners have developed an integrated and automated detection, classification, structural assessment and rehabilitation method selection system for sewers based on the processing of Closed Circuit Television (CCTV) inspection tapes. The research prototype provides the user with an easy, fast, and accurate method of sewer assessment. It consists of an intuitive interface to the sewage network with typical Geographic Information System functionality, a digital archive of indexed CCTV inspection tapes and a classification module to analyze video material for defects.

The RESEW classification method builds on the approach presented in this chapter. The primary goal of the classifier is to detect longitudinal cracks. First the central "tunnel eye" is detected and a spherical rather than rectangular grid is placed around it (see Figure 10.6; separate specialized modules extract the sewer joints and any CCTV text).

Neural networks are used to classify the extracted patches into crack and noncrack classes. For this local patch classification, we achieved an accuracy of 86.9%, with balanced train, validation, and test sets of 40,000, 18,562, and 20,262 instances, respectively. In the next stage, patch class histograms along the vanishing direction

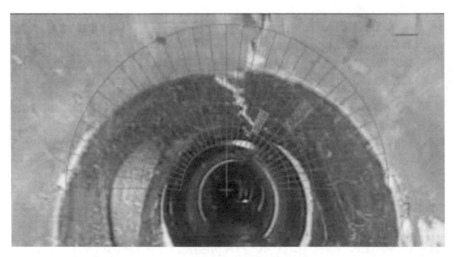

Fig. 10.6. A spherical grid is placed on video footage of a sewer.

are classified to detect global longitudinal cracks. As an alternative method, a region growing approach is used that takes patch class probabilities as input. The latter approach generally produces more favorable results.

The environment is designed to be utilized in several utility contexts (water networks, sewer networks) where different engineering models are developed (e.g. structural reliability models for water pipes, reliability models taking into account seismic risk, safety models based on digital imagery of sewer interior, rehabilitation models for the previous). The system may be adapted to fit the needs of CCTV inspection of boreholes, shafts, gas and oil pipelines, and other construction sectors. Going forward, the methods for analyzing the video material can also be used to build autonomous sewer robots that can explore sewage systems more or less independently.

10.7 Conclusion

In the work presented here, a general scene classifier is introduced that does not rely on computationally expensive object recognition. The features that provide the input for the final scene classification are generated by a set of patch classifiers that are learned rather than predefined, and specific for the scenes to be recognized rather than general.

Although the results on different scene categories can still be improved, the current system can successfully be applied as a generic methodology for creating domain-specific image classifiers for content-based retrieval and filtering. This is demonstrated by its success in various applications such as the Vicar Video Navigator video search engine, the RESEW sewer inspection system, and the SCOFI real-time filter for pornographic image material on the Internet.

Acknowledgments

The work presented in this chapter was partially supported by the EU projects VICAR (IST-24916), SCOFI (IAP-2110; http://www.scofi.net/), and RESEW (GRD1-2000-25579). We thank all project team members involved in these projects. We especially thank Robert Maas for his work on the texture algorithm. Furthermore, we gratefully acknowledge the reviewers, for their valuable comments on the manuscript.

References

1. Israël M, Broek EL van den, Putten P van der, Uyl MJ den. Automating the construction of scene classifiers for Content-Based Video Retrieval. In: Khan L, Petrushin VA, eds. *Proceedings of the Fifth ACM International Workshop on Multimedia Data Mining (MDM/KDD'04)*. Seattle, WA, USA; 2004, pp. 38–47.
2. Putten P van der. *Vicar Video Navigator: Content Based Video Search Engines Become a Reality*. Broadcast Hardware International, IBC edition; 1999.

3. Gibson J. *The Ecological Approach to Visual Perception.* Houghton Mifflin, Boston; 1979.
4. Niblack W, Barber R, Equitz W, Flickner M, Glasman E, Petkovic D, et al. The QBIC project: Querying images by content using color, texture, and shape. *Proceedings of SPIE (Storage and Retrieval for Image and Video Databases)* 1993;1908:173–87.
5. Flickner M, Sawhney H, Niblack W, Ashley J, Huang Q, Dom B, et al. Query by image and video content: The QBIC system. *IEEE Computer* 1995;28(9):23–32.
6. Smith JR, Chang SF. *Querying by Color Regions Using the VisualSEEk Content-Based Visual Query System.* The AAAI Press; 1997, pp. 23–42.
7. Cox IJ, Miller ML, Minka TP, Papathomas TV. The bayesian image retrieval system, PicHunter: Theory, implementation, and psychophysical experiments. *IEEE Transactions on Image Processing* 2000;9(1):20–37.
8. Gevers Th, Smeulders AWM. PicToSeek: Combining color and shape invariant features for image retrieval *IEEE Transactions on Image Processing* 2000;9(1):102–19.
9. Wang JZ. *Integrated Region-Based Image Retrieval.* Boston: Kluwer Academic Publishers; 2001.
10. IBM Research. *MARVEL: Multimedia Analysis and Retrieval System.* Intelligent Information Management Dept., IBM T. J. Watson Research Center; 2005.
11. van den Broek EL, Kok T, Schouten ThE, Hoenkamp E. Multimedia for Art ReTrieval (M4ART). *Proceedings of SPIE (Multimedia Content Analysis, Management, and Retrieval)* 2006;60730Z.
12. Wu S, Rahman MKM, Chow TWS. Content-based image retrieval using growing hierarchical self-organizing quadtree map. *Pattern Recognition* 2005;38(5):707–22.
13. Minka TP, Picard RW. Interactive learning using a "society of models." *MIT Media Laboratory Perceptual Computing Section*; 1996.
14. Picard RW. Light-years from Lena: Video and image libraries of the future. In: *Proceedings of the 1995 International Conference on Image Processing*; 1995, pp. 310–3.
15. Picard RW, Minka TP. Vision Texture for Annotation. *Multimedia Systems* 1995;3(1):3–14.
16. Belongie S, Carson C, Greenspan H, Malik J. *Recognition of Images in Large Databases Using a Learning Framework.* University of California at Berkeley; 1997.
17. Carson C, Belongie S, Greenspan H, Malik J. Blobworld: Image segmentation using expectation-maximization and its application to image querying. *IEEE Transactions on Pattern Analysis and Machine Intelligence* 2002;24(8):1026–38.
18. Campbell NW, Mackeown WPJ, Thomas BT, Troscianko T. The automatic classification of outdoor images. In: *Proceedings of the International Conference on Engineering Applications of Neural Networks.* Systems Engineering Association; 1996, pp. 339–42.
19. Campbell NW, Mackeown WPJ, Thomas BT, Troscianko T. Interpreting Image Databases by Region Classification. *Pattern Recognition* 1997;30(4):555–63.
20. Lipson P, Grimson E, Sinha P. Configuration based scene classification and image indexing. In: *Proceedings of 16th IEEE Conference on Computer Vision and Pattern Recognition.* IEEE Computer Society; 1997, pp. 1007–13.
21. Ratan AL, Grimson WEL. Training templates for scene classication using a few examples. In: *Proceedings of the IEEE Workshop on Content-Based Analysis of Images and Video Libraries*; 1997, pp. 90–7.
22. Oliva A, Torralba A. Modeling the Shape of the Scene: A Holistic Representation of the Spatial Envelope. *International Journal of Computer Vision* 2001;42(3):145–75.
23. Gorkani MM, Picard RW. Texture Orientation for Sorting Photos at a Glance. In: *Proceedings of the International Conference on Pattern Recognition*; 1994, pp. 459–64.

24. Szummer M, Picard RW. Indoor-outdoor image classification. In: *IEEE International Workshop on Content-Based Access of Image and Video Databases (CAIVD)*. Bombay, India: IEEE Computer Society; 1998, pp. 42–51.

25. Fung CY, Loe KF. Learning primitive and scene semantics of images for classification and retrieval. In: *Proceedings of the 7th ACM International Conference on Multimedia '99*. Orlando, Florida, USA: ACM; 1999, pp. 9–12.

26. Fung CY, Loe KF. A new approach for image classification and retrieval. In: *Proceedings of the 22nd Annual International ACM SIGIR Conference on Research and Development in Information Retrieval*. ACM; 1999, pp. 301–2.

27. Broek EL van den, Rikxoort EM van, Schouten ThE. Human-centered object-based image retrieval. *Lecture Notes in Computer Science (Advances in Pattern Recognition)* 2005;3687:492–501.

28. Smith JR, Chang SF. Single color extraction and image query. In: Liu B, editor. *Proceedings of the 2nd IEEE International Conference on Image Processing*. IEEE Signal Processing Society. IEEE Press; 1995, pp. 528–31.

29. Broek EL van den, Kisters PMF, Vuurpijl LG. Content-based image retrieval benchmarking: Utilizing color categories and color distributions. *Journal of Imaging Science and Technology* 2005;49(3):293–301.

30. Broek EL van den. *Human-Centered Content-Based Image Retrieval*. Ph.D. thesis. Nijmegen Institute for Cognition and Information, Radboud University Nijmegen; 2005. Available from: http://eidetic.ai.ru.nl/egon/PhD-Thesis/.

31. Prasad B, Gupta S, Biswas K. Color and shape index for region-based image retrieval. In: Arcelli C, Cordella L, di Baja GSanniti, eds. *Proceedings of 4th International Workshop on Visual Form*. Capri, Italy: Springer Verlag; 2001, pp. 716–25.

32. Redfield S, Nechyba M, Harris JG, Arroyo AA. Efficient object recognition using color. In: Roberts R, ed. *Proceedings of the Florida Conference on Recent Advances in Robotics*. Tallahassee, Florida; 2001.

33. Schettini R, Ciocca G, Zuffi S. A survey of methods for colour image indexing and retrieval in image databases. J. Wiley; 2001.

34. Forsyth DA, Ponse J. *Computer Vision: A Modern Approach*. Pearson Education, Inc., Upper Saddle River, NJ; 2002.

35. Berlin B, Kay P. *Basic Color Terms: Their Universals and Evolution*. Berkeley: University of California Press; 1969.

36. Broek EL van den, Rikxoort EM van. Parallel-Sequential Texture Analysis. *Lecture Notes in Computer Science (Advances in Pattern Recognition)* 2005;3687:532–41.

37. Derefeldt G, Swartling T. Colour concept retrieval by free colour naming: Identification of up to 30 colours without training. *Displays* 1995;16(2):69–77.

38. Derefeldt G, Swartling T, Berggrund U, Bodrogi P. Cognitive color. *Color Research & Application* 2004;29(1):7–19.

39. Goldstone RL. Effects of categorization on color perception. *Psychological Science* 1995;5(6):298–304.

40. Kay P. Color. *Journal of Linguistic Anthropology* 1999;1:29–32.

41. Roberson D, Davies I, Davidoff J. *Colour Categories Are Not Universal: Replications and New Evidence From a Stone-Age Culture*. Lanham, MD: University Press of America Inc.; 2002.

42. Lin T, Zhang HJ. Automatic Video scene extraction by shot grouping. In: *Proceedings of the 15th IEEE International Conference on Pattern Recognition*. vol. 4. Barcelona, Spain; 2000, pp. 39–42.

43. Gevers Th, Smeulders AWM. Color based object recognition. *Pattern Recognition* 1999;32(3):453–64.
44. Jain AK, Karu K. Learning texture discrimination masks. *IEEE Transactions on Pattern Analysis and Machine Intelligence* 1996;18(2):195–205.
45. Palm C. Color texture classification by integrative Co-occurrence matrices. *Pattern Recognition* 2004;37(5):965–76.
46. Rikxoort EM van, Broek EL van den, Schouten ThE. Mimicking human texture classification. *Proceedings of SPIE (Human Vision and Electronic Imaging X)* 2005;5666:215–26.
47. Broek EL van den, Rikxoort EM van, Kok T, Schouten ThE. M-HinTS: Mimicking Humans in Texture Sorting. *Proceedings of SPIE (Human Vision and Electronic Imaging XI)* 2006;60570X.
48. Rosenfeld A. From image analysis to computer vision: An annotated bibliography, 1955–1979. *Computer Vision and Image Understanding* 2001;84(2):298–324.
49. Jähne B. *Practical Handbook on Image Processing for Scientific Applications*. CRC Press; 1997.
50. Brox T, Weickert J, Burgeth B, Mrázek P. Nonlinear structure tensors. *Image and Vision Computing* 2006;24(1):41–55.
51. Tax DMJ. *One-Class Classification; Concept Learning in the Absence of Counter-Examples*. PhD thesis, Delft University of Technology; 2001.
52. Chandrinos KV, Androutsopoulos I, Paliouras G, Spyropoulos CD. Automatic Web Rating: Filtering Obscene Content on the Web. In: Borbinha J, Baker T, eds. *Proceedings of the 4th European Conference on Research and Advanced Technology for Digital Libraries*; 2000, pp. 403–6.
53. Israël M. *ParaBot: Text and Image Classification for the Internet*. Amsterdam, The Netherlands: Sentient Machine Research; 1999.

Part IV

Multimedia Data Modeling and Evaluation

11. Cognitively Motivated Novelty Detection in Video Data Streams

James M. Kang, Muhammad Aurangzeb Ahmad, Ankur Teredesai, and Roger Gaborski

Summary. Automatically detecting novel events in video data streams is an extremely challenging task. In recent years, machine-based parametric learning systems have been quite successful in exhaustively capturing novelty in video if the novelty filters are well-defined in constrained environments. Some important questions however remain: How close are such systems to human perception? Can results derived from comparing human perception with machine novelty help tasks such as storing (indexing) and retrieval of novel events in large video repositories? In this chapter a quantitative experimental evaluation of human-based vs. machine-based novelty systems is canvassed. A machine-based system for detecting novel events in video data streams is first described. The issues of designing an indexing-strategy or "Manga" (comic-book representation is termed as "manga" in Japanese) to effectively determine the "most-representative" novel frames for a video sequence are then discussed. The evaluation of human-based vs. machine-based novelty is quantified by metrics based on location of novel events, number of novel events, etc. Low-level image features were used for machine-based novelty detection and do not include any semantic processing such as object detection to keep the computational load to a minimum.

11.1 Introduction

Extracting novelty from video streams is gaining attention because of the ready availability of large amounts of video being collected and due to insufficient means of automatically extracting important details from such media. Different ways to summarize video based on novel or important aspects of the video are being explored by a wide range of industries [9, 17, 24]. Businesses that use video conferencing are interested in ways to capture important sections of meetings and make an outline of each meeting available for future reference. Likewise, security/surveillance-based industries are looking for ways to detect novel events in huge streams of seemingly unimportant video data.

We explore interesting ways to generate a cluster index of video frames, based on image features within the frames. Human novelty detection is then compared against a machine-based novelty detection technique. An example of such comparison is shown in Figure 11.1. The frames in the figure are the "representative novel frames" of a cluster found for both human and the machine. Differences and similarities between

Fig. 11.1. Human vs. machine novelty. The top image is the original video frame depicting an office scene where an employee is typing things into a computer. The image on the lower left depicts the novelty component found by a human subject in the study using an eye tracker. The image on the lower right is the novelty as determined automatically by a machine vision system we developed (termed VENUS). The two novelty components for the same video frame show that both the human and machine can find similar parts to be novel.

the humans and machines detected novelties are explored with metrics based on region and location. A framework to cluster the results from the two techniques and show a comparison metric between the two will be discussed and analyzed.

We term this particular framework for indexing, retrieval and human comparison of video novelty detection as VENUS (Video Exploitation and Novelty Understanding in Streams). VENUS is a computational learning-based framework for novelty detection. The framework extracts low-level features from scenes, based on the focus of attention theory and combines unsupervised learning with habituation theory for learning these features. VENUS uses a simple habituation technique for "remembering" novelties in order to compensate for recurring events within a scene. The eye-tracking system used in the experiments detects novelty items based on certain aspects of human eye tracks such as fixation duration and saccade velocity. However, it can be extended to incorporate many more features.

In this chapter, we first go over related work in different fields and how this work compares with other novelty detection systems. The VENUS framework is then described, followed by a description of how data for human novelty detection was obtained. We then describe how novel clusters were obtained and indexed. The process of selection of representative frame for creating manga is then described. Lastly we compare the results obtained from novelty detection by humans and the machine system.

11.2 Related Work

11.2.1 Video Streams

In the past, a number of systems have explored novelty in video streams. Video surveillance has been a major concern especially since the September 11 attacks. Diehl and Hampshire [6] examined novelty that occurs within a video and classification of new objects based on previously labeled objects. They initially classified each image with a label, and then classification is done on a sequence of images. There are a number of differences between their system and VENUS. Their system uses a motion detection camera for novelty detection; hence, they assume that all the video consists of motion. In VENUS, on the other hand, still frames can also be considered to be novel. Also it is not apparent what features other than motion were used as a basis for novelty detection in their approach. One can say that the Diehl approach is a comparison of new images with a preclassified set of images to find novel events within a video.

Work by Medioni et al. [19], part of the Video Surveillance and Monitoring System project, is an example of a system for tracking and detecting events in videos collected from an unmanned airborne vehicles. Prior to that work, semantic event detection approach by Haering, et al. [11] successfully tracked and detected events in wild-life hunt videos. Research by Stauffer et al. [25] proposed detecting events in real time by learning the general patterns of activity within a scene. This learnt information is subsequently used for activity classification and event detection in the videos. Recently, Tentler et al. [28] proposed an event detection framework based on the use of low-level features. The proposed VENUS framework also uses the low-level features and then advances the state-of-the-art by combining the focus of attention theory and habituation-based clustering.

The cognitive apparatus of humans and animals is gauged to detect novelór óut of the ordinary changes in their environment. This observation has been applied in robotics by Crook et al. [4] and also by Marsland et al. [18]. The former used images taken by a camera for robot navigation while the later uses such images in conjunction with sonar for the same purpose. There are certain similarities and affinities between these two systems and VENUS. Hence the feature set used by VENUS is quite similar to the feature set used by Crooks et al. [4]. Both the systems use color, intensity, and orientation as features. According to Marsland et al. [18], the base concept for their system design is same as VENUS, namely Habituation. Habituation is the idea that as the frequency of repetition of an event increase, the less novel the event becomes.

Other related work deals with extracting features from a video stream using the background of the video [2]. The assumption made by these approaches is that the background will be the same throughout the video. Consequently any changes to the background causes a novel event. However, if the background changes, then everything would be considered to be novel. Where in the VENUS system the actual content in the video does not affect the novelty found but changes dynamically as described in Section 11.3.1.

11.2.2 Image Novelty

Even though the topic primarily focuses on video streams, image detection is an important step in reaching the goal of analyzing video streams and detecting corresponding novel events. The following applications discussed here use low-level features, similar to VENUS, and also illustrate the utility of this approach.

Consider the case of breast cancer diagnosis. Detecting breast cancer efficiently has always been a problem. According to Tarassenko [27], there are about 26,000 new cases in the United Kingdom each year. On average there needs to be at least two analysts to review an x-ray image to diagnose breast cancer, implying the great need to reduce the time required for diagnosis. Tarassenko [27] describes a tool for analysts to focus on areas with larger mass regions in certain parts of the images, although the process is not fully automated. This allows an expert to look at areas that are most important.

Novelty Detection is done using features of shape, texture, boundary (edges), and contour. These features form the basis of the function that distinguishes between normality and abnormality. A density function based on the feature vector is used to detect novelty. If the density function gives a value that is below a predefined threshold, then the frame is considered to be novel.

11.2.3 Clustering Novelty in Video Streams

Clustering is an effective technique for grouping elements together that are similar to each other. Clustering was an important component in implementing the VENUS framework. Instead of showing every novel event, VENUS shows a summary of novel events that are representative of the whole cluster. Video Manga [30] explains how a video can be summarized and viewed as a comic book or Manga. Manga is a Japanese term that refers to comics. A summary of a video is generated through several steps. Initially, they compressed on all similar regions and then used many hours of office meetings videos for novelty detection. Normally, when a person is talking in a meeting, only the person's mouth and hands are moving. All other body parts remain still. These images are compressed into a single image. This is done for all the events. However, the details of such image comparison were not given.

The algorithm we use is based on low-level features like the pixel count of red, green, and blue, and uses the concept of major colors. If the pixel count of a certain color is greater than a threshold, the image is then considered to have this major color. This is done for all three colors. Once this is completed for all the images, each image will then have a binary representation, where "101" means that they have the Major Colors of Red and Blue. These images are then grouped together with similar binary values. The VENUS clustering method is a modified form of this approach.

11.2.4 Event vs. Novelty Clustering

Novelty clustering should not be confused with Event clustering within a video stream. Any set of frames that are found to be out of normality in a video stream can be considered to be Event clusters since the goal of type of detection is to determine specific periods of time that are different from other time periods. For example, an event could be students walking to a bus or cars on a highway. These can be an event that occurred within a video.

Novelty clustering refers not only to anything that is different from normality, but also to anything that can be deemed unusual. Students walking to a bus or cars driving from left to right are not considered unusual. A car crash can be considered an event and to be novel. The VENUS framework is based on Novel events rather than on any event within a video.

Novelty clustering should also not be confused with temporal event clustering. Even though the novel frames generated from the VENUS system also include the frame number that denotes the time the novel frame occurred, it does not have any effect on the clustering procedure. Similar frames within a video are clustered together. Within temporal event clustering, the time each image is taken is used to determine the event it belongs to [3]. With this said, the novel series cannot be represented as a time series. Lin and Keogh [16] suggest that clustering of time series data is meaningless, but since novelty series is itself a sampling of the raw video consisting of complete description of what was found novel, clustering novelty does produce meaningful results unlike other time series clustering using a sliding window.

11.3 Implementation

11.3.1 Machine-Based Process

11.3.1.1 The VENUS System

Figure 11.2 shows that a block diagram of the VENUS novelty detection model consists of two major components: a focus of attention component that generates the low-level features, and the learning component that handles novelty detection. Since the amount of visual information available within a scene is enormous, we humans "process" only a subset of the entire scene.

Humans tend to focus on the interesting aspects of the scene, ignoring the uninteresting ones. The attention system in our framework is based on a topographically saliency map that represents an object's saliency with respect to its surrounding. VENUS filters out noninteresting events thereby greatly reducing the amount of information to be analyzed. These interesting events are termed as novel or inconsistent events. The event detection model described in this chapter consists of the following two major components:

- A focus of attention component that generates the low-level features.
- The learning component that handles novelty detection. In this section we describe each of these components in detail.

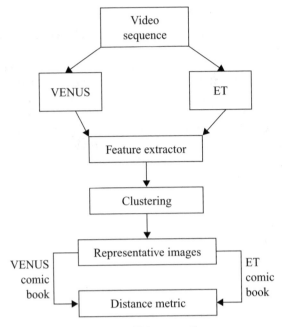

Fig. 11.2. VENOM system diagram.

The first phase of the project focused on detecting novel events. Consider the following example. If a casual observer is positioned on a freeway overpass where the vehicles below are traveling at about the same speed, after a short period of time the observer will generally ignore the individual cars (consistent events), but if a particular vehicle is traveling much slower or faster than the average speed of the other vehicles it is the subject of the observer's attention as a novel or inconsistent event. The VENUS system behaves in a manner similar to a human observer. It will first learn the normal, consistent events in a visual scene, and then detect novel or inconsistent events in the scene. A key point in the system is not programmed to detect fast or slow moving cars, but learns that they are novel in this environment. A common approach in prior work is to first manually define and then to store descriptions of inconsistent events in a database or they are defined using a predefined grammar. Events are then compared to stored events to determine their novelty. The VENUS system thus has the significant advantage of not requiring events to be detected to be predefined, but automatically learns what is normal and detects events that differ from normalcy.[1]

---

[1] The VENUS project is spearheaded at the Center for Advancing the Study of CyberInfrastructure (http://www.lac.rit.edu).

11.3.1.2 The Attention System

The VENUS framework is based on the selective attention theory initially modeled by Itti and Koch [13], where a saliency map topographically represents the objects saliency with respect to its surrounding. Attention allows us to focus on the relevant regions in the scene and thus reduces the amount of information needed for further processing as verified in Gaborski et al. [8]. The 2D spatial filters used in the system are modeled after biological vision principles simulating underlying the functioning of the retina, lateral geniculate nucleus, and the early visual cortical areas. The spatial filters are convolved with the input image to obtain the topographical feature maps. Intensity contrast is extracted using difference of Gaussian filters. The intensity contrast filtering simulates the function of the retinal ganglion cells that possess the center-surround mechanism. The color information is extracted using the color opponent filters. Objects that are highly salient in the scene are further tracked for possible novel events. The video sequences are processed in the still and motion saliency channels.

Motion information in video sequences is extracted using the 3D spatiotemporal filters tuned to respond to moving stimuli [31]. Motion detection in our system is achieved by using a set of difference of offset Gaussian spatiotemporal filters. Hence The still saliency channel processes every frame individually and generates topographical saliency maps. Consider an airport scene where someone leaves an object in a restricted area and walks away. The still saliency channel detects this object as a salient item. Since this object was not part of the original scene, the introduction of the object fires a novel event, which is a feature of the still learning and novelty detection module. The motion saliency channel detects the salient moving objects of the scene, in this case the motion of the person who brought the object.

11.3.1.3 Feature Extraction

The Feature Extraction takes place once the novel frames are generated from VENUS or the eye-tracker shown in Figure 11.2. Low-level features are extracted from a set of images using a color extractor that works on top of the HSV color space. HSV was chosen over RGB because of its similarity with the way in which humans perceive color. Feature sets are created based off of a set of query colors. The extractor scans images or regions of images for each query color and returns a hue score (proximity from the query color) for each pixel within the scanned region. The mean value of all the hue scores for a given query color is calculated and saved as that region's total score. During execution, multiple color features are used in extraction and their results saved as feature sets. These feature sets are used for indexing and clustering the images for later comparison and retrieval.

11.3.1.4 Machine Novelty Detection

Figure 11.3 shows the working of the motion novelty detection module. Novelty detection and learning in this system is region based, where a region is an 8-by-8 pixel

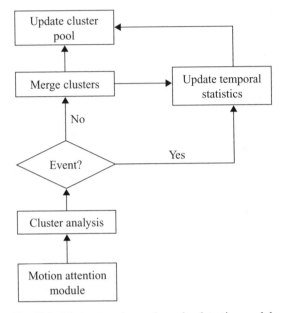

Fig. 11.3. Motion learning and novelty detection module.

area on a frame of the video. A direction map encodes motion values for the direction of motion. The regions of the direction maps that detect motion get excited if there is a change in the direction of motion in successive frames. These direction maps are input to the motion learning and event detection module. Within each region, a Gaussian mixture model represents the values obtained from the directional maps over a period of time. Each distribution in the mixture is represented by a cluster resulting in a pool of clusters representing the entire distribution. Novelty detection is thus reduced to identifying novel clusters in every region.

The following example illustrates how VENUS novelty detects novelty in video streams. Consider a video sequence in which people are walking from right to left at a speed of 5 mph. When a person passes over a region (within a group of contiguous frames), the left directional motion map gets invoked. The excited regions of the map provide motion values that correspond to the speed of the person walking. A single cluster representing a Gaussian distribution is formed from these values in the cluster analysis step in Figure 11.3. This cluster is compared with existing clusters in the pool of cluster. If this cluster is similar (in its distribution) to any cluster in the pool, it is merged with the cluster in the pool. Otherwise, if the cluster cannot be merged with any existing cluster, a new cluster is inserted into the pool. The similarity measure between two clusters is a function of their means and standard deviations. If a similar cluster is already found in the pool, then this implies that a similar event had occurred in the past. Referring back to the example, when multiple people walk at 5 mph over a region, clusters representing their speeds are merged. This indicates that people walking is not a novel event anymore. Now, when a person runs at 15 mph from right to left, a new cluster for 15 mph is formed. This represents occurrence of a novel event. Similarly the above phenomenon will be observed if a person walks from left to right, thereby firing an event in the right directional map. This algorithm is incremental in nature in that the clusters for a region are updated as events occur in the scene. The algorithm does not limit the number of clusters per region since the number of novel event cannot be predicted ahead of time.

New clusters added to the pool are assigned an initial habituation value and an initial decay rate that determine its temporal characteristics. The decay rate symbolizes the forgetting term described by Kohonen [14]. The slower the decay rate the longer is the retention period for the event. The habituation function for a cluster is given by $H(t) = 1 - [1/(1 + e^{-a})]$, where $H(t)$ is the habituation value after t frames the creation of the cluster and a is the current decay rate of the cluster. When clusters are merged we update the decay rate for the older cluster. This indicates that the learnt event was reinforced resulting in increased retention. A cluster with habituation value below the cutoff threshold is considered completely decayed and is discarded from the pool of clusters. Effectively, the system has forgotten the event that the discarded cluster represented. Hence the forgotten event becomes novel once again. This models the concept of forgetting in habituation theory. The initial decay rate is set to zero which can go up to 1. Value of 0 indicates no decay (longer retention) while one indicates maximum decay (shorter retention). The decay rate for a cluster is adjusted as follows: $a_t = 1 - [e/f]$ where a_t is the decay rate t frames after its creation, f is the number of frames passed since the creation of the cluster and e is the number of times the cluster is merged with similar clusters. e/f term indicates the reinforcement (cluster merging) rate. Higher the reinforcement rate, closer the new decay rate to 0. Smaller the reinforcement rate, closer the new decay rate will be to 1.

As per habituation theory, an event is not instantaneously learnt. It takes some number of occurrences before a system gets completely habituated. The recovery in degree of habituation prior to the system reaching complete habituation (also known as stable state) is lesser than the recovery after reaching complete habituation as seen in Figure 11.3. Novelty is inversely related to the degree of habituation the cluster has attained. Higher the habituation value, the lower is its features novelty and vice versa. The novel events gathered from each motion direction map are combined with still novelty map to form a final novelty map.

11.3.2 Human-Based System

11.3.2.1 Capturing the Eye Track

The Eye tracker is a system that captures eye tracks of how humans observe their environment. The Eye tracker is thus representative human system that is compared to the machine system shown in Figure 11.2. Human eye tracks are recorded while the subject watches the video to be processed. The experimental setup for the Eye

Table 11.1. Eye track example format. This is an example of the type of data that is extracted from the eye track images.

HR	MN	Sec	Total Secs	VPOS	HPOS
14	39	35.617	52775.617	−6.270	−1.645
14	39	35.633	52775.633	−6.245	−1.615
14	39	35.650	52775.650	−6.195	−1.545
14	39	35.667	52775.667	−6.205	−1.545
14	39	35.683	52775.683	−6.250	−1.525
14	39	35.700	52775.700	−6.295	−1.515
14	39	35.717	52775.717	−6.325	−1.500
14	39	35.733	52775.733	−6.385	−1.510

Tracker is as follows:

- The Eye Tracker is first calibrated to align the laser to the person's eye.
- It takes from 5 to 10 min of test video to confirm the calibration of the system.
- The actual test video is shown to the user.
- The system then reads the eye movement information as fixations within the video.

The eye track data are then filtered and modified for calibration and readable representation. This results in an easily parsable format for the attention finder algorithm. The format of this data file (Table 11.1) may vary depending on implementation; however, VENUS requires at least X and Y coordinates across a time series.

11.3.2.2 Extract Scan-Path

The data file is read in and the linear scan-path that the users' eye followed during his or her session is cleaned and saved. The path structure is later analyzed to group fixations together into "Attention Areas."

11.3.2.3 Segment Eye-Tracking Data

Due to the temporal nature of eye track data and the fact that there will almost always be at least one fixation per frame of the video, the data are segmented by a user specified amount. What this does is group together multiple fixations for a certain time period that is later analyzed for groups of fixations that may or may not correspond with Attention Areas (Figure 11.4).

11.3.2.4 Cluster Fixations

The clustering technique used in VENUS is simple, though effective. It can be replaced by a more robust method. For each segment, VENUS determines the centroids of groups of nearby fixations. VENUS uses a simple threshold measure to determine if fixations are "nearby" and thus belong to a particular cluster.

Centroids (Figure 11.5) are created to determine the most likely center point of groups of fixations that will later be used to create the mask that will highlight

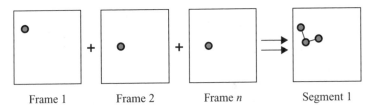

Fig. 11.4. The circle represents single fixation. Each frame has at least one fixation made by the subject. Based on the number of frames that is predefined beforehand, the frames are combined and clustered as Segment 1.

the Attention Areas and ultimately produce the novel image analogous to the Venus output.

11.3.2.5 Novelty Images and Novelty Video

For each centroid in a segment, the Attention Area is determined and a binary mask is created. This binary mask is applied to the corresponding frame from the video and is saved. The effect of combining the binary mask with a frame is to "black out" all areas that are not found as being novel. Novelty frames are then stitched together to create an AVI video of the sequence of novelty frames (Figure 11.6). (This last step is optional but is a good visualization of the progression of detected novelty.)

The novelty images constitute the desired output (Figure 11.5) of this process. The black areas correspond to the mask while the visible regions are the Attention Areas for each of the segments processed. VENUS uses a simple rule (size of area corresponds directly to the number of fixations used to determine the centroid) for determining the actual Attention Area; the rule can be changed should the need arise to use a more sophisticated measure in the future. Presently VENUS uses the first frame of the segment being processed to apply the mask to. It is, however, not known if this is the best way to representation purposes. However, this can easily be modified to use any frame number desired.

11.3.2.6 Experiment Setup and Usability Testing

The eye tracks were captured using the ASL head mounted ES501 system. A magnetic head tracker was not used in the experiments. Subjects were first calibrated and

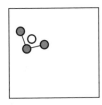

Fig. 11.5. The lighter circle represents a centroid. In a cluster made by the frames in Figure 11.4, a centroid is founded where this is the main fixation made for this set of frames.

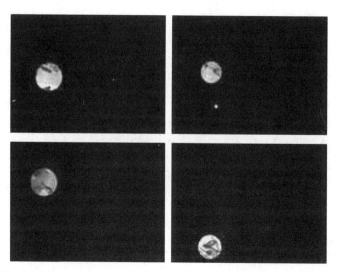

Fig. 11.6. Fixation Example Output. The visible part is the region of attention that is determined by centroids in a manner similar to Figure 11.3. The black areas are the mask that is very similar to how VENUS shown its novel frames.

then were instructed to watch a series of videos and to keep their heads relatively still. Subjects were shown four videos that were mainly from security or office cameras. These videos were chosen for their relatively small amount of motion and consistent viewing angle. After the subject finished watching all four videos, their data were saved and converted to ASCII format for later processing. The subjects who volunteered for our study came from a wide range of ethnic groups which ensured that the results were not skewed because of the person's background.

11.3.3 Indexing and Clustering of Novelty

Video data usually contain a large amount of novel events, although the frequency of novel events varies. For example, surveillance video of a basement warehouse will most likely contain less novel events than say an action movie. When many novel frames are extracted from a video, it is helpful to have an index of novelty frames with which to browse the novelty set. For this reason, VENUS creates this index, using an algorithm described by Mukherjea [20] shown in the system diagram in Figure 11.2.

11.3.3.1 Total Clustering

VENUS creates clusters of similar novelty images based on the feature set. In the current design, only low-level colors are used to generate these clusters. Table 11.2 shows an example of a set of features taken from a video. Here a tuple represents a score for each color in the novel frame. A threshold is created by taking the averages of each color's score. The algorithm (Figure 11.7) is based on the concept that major

Table 11.2. Example of Features. This is an example
of a feature set take from novel frames from either
VENUS or the Eye-tracker.

Red	Green	Blue
85	66	100
25	63	44
10	12	90
85	30	98

colors and pixel counts can be used to determine the most prevalent color of the image. In VENUS's implementation color score was substituted by the pixel count. Instead of using just the average as the threshold, a confidence interval is needed to ensure that features close to the average are included as part of the cluster. Without this confidence interval, very similar frames may be in different clusters. The confidence interval estimation is defined as: $\bar{x} \pm Z * (S/\sqrt{n})$, where $\bar{x}$ is the threshold, Z is the interval coefficient, S is the standard deviation of a feature within the population, and n is the size of the population. A confidence interval of 95% ($z = 1.96$ for normal distribution) was expected for the current implementation. The standard deviation of each feature set is expressed by $s_N = \sqrt{\frac{1}{N}\sum_{i=1}^{N}(x_i - \bar{x})^2}$, where s_N is the standard deviation of N, N is the size of the population, x_i is each feature value, and $\bar{x}$ is the average of the feature population. For each color in Table 11.2, a 1 or a 0 is assigned if that color meets the threshold $\pm$ confidence interval. Hence each frame will then be described by a binary number. Similar combinations are then clustered together. The algorithm for this process is shown in the following figure.

```
1  For each image
2      Calculate the sum of each color
3  end for
4  Find the average of each color and
5      store as threshold
6  For each image
7      For each color
8          If color is greater than threshold
9              Set "1" to color
10         Else
11             Set "0" to color
12     end for
13 end for
14 Group Images based on Binary Values
```

Fig. 11.7. Total clustering algorithm. The word *total* emphasizes that the algorithm does not pay attention to time or the frame number. It clusters the whole set of frames for its similarity.

11.3.3.2 Sequence Clustering

An interesting method of creating clusters is to identify the start and end points of each of the novelty that occurs within a video, instead of comparing all the novel frames within a video to find similar frames. The sequence of the novel frames that are similar is clustered. Figure 11.7 shows the sequence clustering algorithm. For example, suppose that there were five novel frames in a video, each occurring right after the other. If the distance between frames 1 and 2 is under the predefined threshold, then they are put within the same cluster. On the other hand, if the distance between frames 3 and 2 is greater than the threshold, then a new cluster is generated. This will create sections within the video stream of when a new novel event occurs. There are numerous forms of distance metrics that can be used such as Euclidean, Mahalanobis, Minkowski, Block Row, and Chebychev. Euclidean distance was used for clustering in the present case for simplicity. Each image can then be represented as a feature vector consisting of low-level features. Thresholds are created on the basis of the average or median of all the distances.

The total distances are not in a form of a matrix since the distance was based on the previous and following frame. Once a cluster has been created, a representative image of the cluster needs to be found to facilitate presentation in a comic book format.

Although the above algorithm describes the process of clustering together visually similar images, it does not prescribe a particularly good way of representing each cluster. To solve this problem VENUS uses pixel scores to get mean values for each color. Next, a distance is calculated for the features of each image with respect to the mean. The image whose features have the smallest distance with respect to the mean is used as the representative image. Representative images are then arranged on the

```
1  For each image
2      Calculate Euclidean distance between
3          image and the next image
4  end for
5  Find the average of all distances and store
6          as threshold
7  Find Confidence Interval (x̄)
8  For each image and distance
9      If image and next image distance is less than
10         threshold ± x̄
11             Cluster images together
12     Else
13             Create new cluster
14 end for
```

Fig. 11.8. Sequence clustering algorithm. Sequence means that time is a factor within this algorithm. A frame can be clustered only if it is similar enough to the previous frame based on a threshold.

```
1  For each cluster
2      Calculate total amount of color pixels
3      Add into the cluster average of pixels
4      For each image
5          Calculate distance from image to average
6      end for
7      Find shortest distance between image and average
8      Assign image as representative cluster
9  end for
```

Fig. 11.9. Representative image algorithm. Finds the centroid of the novel frame clusters for both the VENUS and Eye-tracker systems.

basis of the time when the respective frame occurs in the video. The images are then laid out in a comic book-like format (Figure 11.10).

11.3.4 Distance Metrics

11.3.4.1 Location Similarity

The first metric used by VENUS is location similarity. Novel frames usually contain only a small amount of novel area. The task here is to extract the actual location on the image where a certain novelty is present and to compare that with the location of novelty from a corresponding frame in order to determine whether or not the novelty detected by both systems captures the same location.

Novel location regions are extracted from the images using a recursive dissection technique. The algorithm recursively breaks up the image into subregions until a specified depth using quad-trees. Not only are novel regions quickly located, but a hierarchy of such regions is also created. This hierarchy can then be used later for further feature comparison, as in the case of the feature similarity metric. Figure 11.11 shows the comparison of similar regions between two novel images and the corresponding scores.

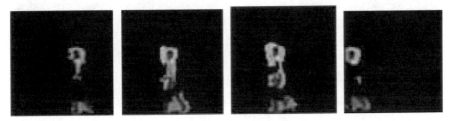

Fig. 11.10. Example of VENUS Manga. This is the represented frames generated by the algorithm in Figure 11.8. The frames are organized by time or frame number that represents a comic book or a summary of novel events within a video.

11.3.4.2 Feature Similarity

The second metric is feature similarity. Feature similarity is an abstract concept and can therefore be used for comparison of any type of comparable feature. In the case of VENUS, pixel color is the comparable feature. Regions of an image are compared to regions of other images on the basis of the mean hue scores generated by the feature extractor. The regions to be compared are identified via the location similarity metric detailed above. The feature similarity metric is able to identify regions across images that are similar to each other by using the hierarchy of similar regions. The user can specify how detailed of a comparison to perform, which facilitates fast comparison across very different images as well as detailed comparison between images that are very similar. Figure 11.11 shows scores for the feature similarity metric.

Figure 11.11 shows a visualization of the metrics VENUS uses. The second image is compared to the first, while the third image shows the novel regions as well as the intersection of those regions. Scores are calculated based off of the two metrics and printed on the middle image. As one can see, although the first image has a 0% location similarity to the second, their features are still 98% similar. Likewise, the features of the second comparison are 99% similar, with a location similarity of 15%.

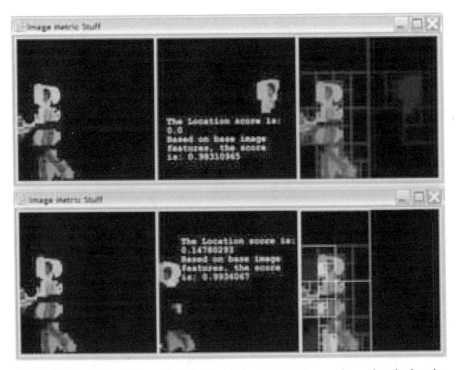

Fig. 11.11. Location and feature similarity metrics. The top image shows that the location feature is large since the two novel images are not within the same region. The image below shows that the distance feature is small since the two novel images overlap eachother.

These image metrics enable VENUS to compare entire sets of novel images across different novelty detection systems shown in Figure 11.2.

11.4 Results

11.4.1 Clustering and Indexing of Novelty

11.4.1.1 Total Clustering Approach

VENUS' motion maps alone can give good visual results, although these results are not sufficient for identifying novelty. Figures 11.12 and 11.13 show a comparison between using motion versus all three measures.

VENUS' and the Eye-Tracking novel images were clustered using the Total Clustering algorithm discussed in Section 11.2.3. The results from this process were good. Images with similar features were grouped together into clusters that were later linked via their representative images. Figure 11.14 shows a graph of clusters obtained for a set of the Venus data. Since low-level features were used to cluster and index, images within clusters are visually very similar. New features can easily be incorporated to improve these results. The human-based novelty frames were also processed in the same manner and are also separated into visually similar groups.

11.4.1.2 Sequence Clustering Approach

Figure 11.14 also shows two types of distance equations within the graph. The first measures the distance from an image within a cluster to the representative frame and can be expressed as $D(C_i, I_j)$, where C_i is the centroid of the cluster and I_j is the image within that cluster. This distance is in terms of the difference in value of features in the base image and the query image (base image being Venus and

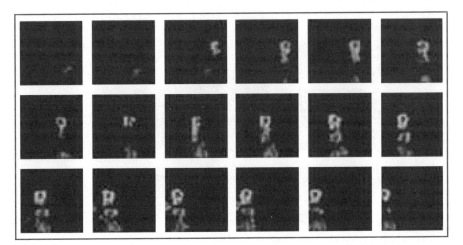

Fig. 11.12. Three measures: motion, still, and color.

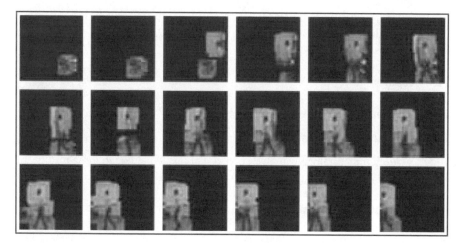

Fig. 11.13. One measure: Motion. VENUS using only the Motion measure. Since the goal of our project is to compare novelties between two different systems, the most visible novel areas should be used. This is why we chose to use just motion instead of all three shown in Figure 11.12.

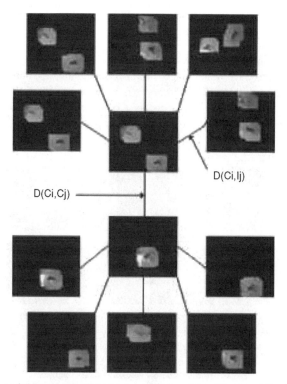

Fig. 11.14. Clustering example. This is an example of two clusters. The links within the cluster show the Euclidean distance between the cluster elements and the centroid. The distance between the two centroids are based on time or frame number.

Table 11.3. Human vs. machine total clustering. This is a comparison to show that the number of clusters generated by the Total Clustering algorithm, for both machines and humans is very similar. The average number of human clusters is based on 11 testers with each having 10 novel frames.

Video	Total number of novel frames	Machine clusters	Average human clusters
1	195	7	3
2	181	6	4
3	227	6	3
4	205	5	3

query image being the E.T. novel image). The second measures the distance between representative images within a video and can be expressed as $D(C_i, C_j)$, where C_i is the centroid of each cluster. Here, distance is expressed in terms of time, or frame number, and is used for the layout of the final comic book strip. After clusters are temporally linked together, each cluster's representative image is displayed and the comic book is formed.

The novel frames generated from Venus and the Eye Tracker were clustered together with this interesting clustering approach. The representing frames were generated in the same manner as the Total Clustering approach. The clusters are very similar to the ones shown in Figure 11.14, but each novel frame within a cluster was found to be within the same sequence. The results from this approach was very different from the results in the Total Clustering approach. The clusters generated by the previously described algorithm exhibited more intracluster similarities as compared to the Sequence Clustering approach. Table 11.3 shows the average number of clusters generated for the human-based and the machine-based approach using the Total Clustering algorithm.

Within the Eye Tracker and the Venus system, there were a total of 4 videos and 10 users for the Eye Tracker that we experimented with. These values are based on the average of those results. Each of these videos had very similar time duration even though the contents of these videos came from different domains.

Figure 11.8 shows the same statistics obtained via the Sequence Clustering algorithm. These results show that there is a significant difference between the human and machine novel approaches. This also shows that we are still far from reaching human-like novelty detection level. The number of clusters differ greatly against the total clustering algorithm shown in Table 11.4. This shows that Machine novelty detection is still significantly different from Human novelty detection.

Table 11.4. Human vs. machine sequence clustering. This is a comparison between machine and human clusters using the sequence algorithm.

Video	Total number of novel frames	Machine clusters	Average human clusters
1	195	69	2.8
2	181	57	3.0
3	227	42	4.2
4	205	60	3.4

11.4.2 Human Novelty Detection

Human novelty detection proved to be much more subjective, which was expected. Many factors came together to influence a subject's tests but all subjects' results were very similar as far as Attention Areas were concerned. First time novelty within the video gained high attention and quickly dropped down as new novelty was introduced. Essentially, humans tend to focus upon novelties "one at a time" and for short periods. On the other hand, a machine-based approach like Venus is capable of detecting all novelties simultaneously within a video.

The comic strip based on human novelty detection that was created was very homogeneous. It was observed that low-level features were not sufficient in creating and using a distance metric for comparison of novel images. This conclusion is a result of the manner in which representative images were produced. Using the similarity average of low-level features and the similarity of shared locations resulted in the selection of the largest Attention Area found within the subject's novel image set as the closest pairing to each of VENUS' representative images. This shows us that higher level features need to be considered in order to get more accurate scores between a subject's novelty and VENUS' novelty.

11.4.3 Human vs. Machine

The most apparent difference that was observed between the human novelty and VENUS' novelty was in the apparent habituation of incoming novel areas (see Table 11.5 and Table 11.6). Venus uses a habituation technique where new novel events are "remembered" for a while and their significance to the current novelty within the video gracefully degrades over time. An example of where this is useful would be a busy airport. Initially, dozens of people walking around the airport would be very novel and Venus will display them as novelty within the scene. Over time, VENUS becomes used to dozens of people walking around and will not register them as being novel any longer. The real use of the habituation is in a situation where a person in the same airport drops a red bag on a chair and walks away. VENUS will pick this red bag up as being very novel and therefore show it in its results.

It has been observed that humans tend to have this same type of habituation [7]. Humans tend to pick up novelty within the video very quickly and, if it was not a major event, return their attention to the previous Attention Area just as quickly. This

Table 11.5. Total clustering: The table shows the raw data of every subject's novelty clusters for each video we tested against the number of clusters generated from VENUS-based novelty detection.

	Total number of novel frames	Machine clusters	Human clusters									
			1	2	3	4	5	6	7	8	9	10
Video 1	195	7	3	4	3	2	3	3	3	3	3	3
Video 2	181	6	7	4	2	2	3	4	2	3	2	3
Video 3	227	6	2	2	3	4	2	4	3	3	2	3
Video 4	205	5	4	2	3	4	2	2	3	2	3	4

Table 11.6. Sequence clustering: This table shows the raw data of every subject's cluster for each video we tested against the number of clusters generated from VENUS based novelty detection.

	Total number of novel frames	Machine clusters	Human clusters									
			1	2	3	4	5	6	7	8	9	10
Video 1	195	69	2	3	4	1	3	2	1	1	4	4
Video 2	181	57	3	3	3	3	3	1	2	1	2	4
Video 3	227	42	4	4	4	4	3	4	3	4	4	2
Video 4	205	60	3	4	2	4	4	2	2	4	2	3

is an important aspect of the comparison between VENUS and a Human's novelty detection mechanisms and will be discussed in the next session.

Human novelty detection using segmented video and low-level feature extraction does not produce the quantity of novel frames for a comprehensive comparison to a machine-based approach. This was shown by the homogeneity of the final comic Human strip as well as the similarity among scores of each human novelty image. There does not seem to be any way in which to increase the number of novel frames without either repeating much of the novelty information in each frame or losing the high-level Attention Areas to many small fixation areas that would not visually show any usable results.

11.5 Discussion

11.5.1 Issues and Ideas

11.5.1.1 Venus

At present, the VENUS system does not gather semantic information about how relevant incoming novelty may be. Consequently it is difficult to model VENUS' habituation algorithm to focus on "important" novelties rather than all novelty, where important novelties are defined as what is considered novel by a human being. It may be however possible to tweak the habituation mechanism to be trainable by a human expert whose job it is to discern between "important" and "unimportant" novelty. A system such as this would have great impacts on security surveillance systems, gambling monitors, highway safety, and many other areas. How this type of system may be implemented is still an open question.

Video indexing has not recieved as much attention in the community as novelty detection. With regards to video indexing, it is important to note the work of Furht and Saksobhavivat on video indexing [7], Sun, Majunath, and Divakarn, on using motion to detect different levels in a video to index [26], and Detyniecki, who uses color features within key frames of a video for indexing [5]. Figure 11.15 gives an example of novelty detected by VENUS over the course of a video.

Another issue for Venus is the preprocessing time to generate novel images. Currently VENUS can take only uncompressed images, which can take up quite a bit of space. For example, consider the case when a 4-min compressed. AVI was

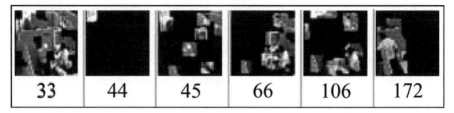

Fig. 11.15. Example of novelty detected in a Video with the respective frame numbers

used. When the file was uncompressed, the size of the decompressed file increased from 50 Mb to about 2 Gb. This .AVI movie had about 8000 frames and it took close to 30 s for each frame to be processed by Venus. This is a scalability issue and is an area of future development. By looking over the results from the Human novelty detection, it can be suggested that within the particular domain we experimented with (surveillance video) Human novelty detection most closely mirrored VENUS' motion images. This could be a way to speed up VENUS' processing time; i.e., by only processing the color and still maps when needed as opposed to every frame.

11.5.1.2 Eye Tracking

The issues concerning the eye-tracking experiments and setup mainly revolved around proper calibration of the subject's gaze. Without the support of a magnetic head tracker, each subject's gazes had some error associated with them. The error was reduced for many subjects by gradual tweaking. However, the error persisted for some subjects even after tweaking. The nature of the experiments however did not call for extremely precise measurements and can therefore receive little alarm.

For any real-time training of VENUS to take place by a Human, a noninvasive eye tracker would be needed. Remote eye trackers such as Tobii 1750 [5] or ASL's 504 HS model [6] would be ideal for this type of scenario. With these newer, noninvasive eye tracking systems many real-time applications of this sort would become possible.

11.5.1.3 Novelty Comparison

One of the goals of this chapter was to compare machine-based novelty and Human-precieved novelty from the eye tracker. It was observed that the number of novel clusters detected by the machine is far greater than the novelty clusters detected by a human. This is to be expected since VENUS exhaustively finds novel events in the video streams and as previously mentioned in Section 11.2.2.

Anything out of the ordinary is considered to be novel by VENUS. In this regard it can be said to perform better than the human. On the other hands, VENUS does not really distinguish between "important" or "unimportant" events that may be context dependent. This situation can be conceptualized as follows: Video novelty is just a subset of what is considered novel by a human being, e.g., if the video is that of a conversation between different people, in addition to visual changes in the video as being considered novel, any sudden change in the topic of discussion would also be considered novel by a human. Such novelty is, however, not currently included in the scope of this project.

11.5.1.4 Future Work

A possible future project may involve using VENUS's framework to create graphs of novelty such as those described in Section 11.3.1. Mining these graphs may give a way to process difficult queries such as "Show me all of the events in videos X, Y and Z where this type of novelty occurred" or "Search for novel events that tend to lead up to a certain type of novel event" and others. To mine digital media in such a way, one needs a traditional structure in which to store these types of events. Future analysis of novelty, novelty clusters, novelty graphs, and representative images could lead to this type of data structure, on which more traditional search strategies can be applied.

11.5.2 Summary

A machine novelty detection system called VENUS was described in this chapter. VENUS successfully employs the theory of habituation for learning novel events over time in a video data stream. The utility of this approach was demonstrated by a series of experiments. VENUS does not use semantic information for novelty detection but rather uses low-level image features. An attempt was made to compare machine-based novelty detection scheme with the human-based novelty scheme gleaned from the eye-tracking system. It was, however, observed that the low level features for human based novelty detection were inadequate for such a comparison.

The data from the machine novelty system VENUS and novelty precieved by a human as recorded by the Eye Tracker were used to analyze different novelty detection strategies, compare them, and lay them out in a manga-like format. Important events in the video were described by the novelty detected in the video. In addition, indexing schemes for clustering and indexing novel frames was also implemented and discussed. A framework for comparison between the machine-based and human-precieved novelty was also implemented and tested. The results of the respectove tests and experiments were listed and reviewed.

11.6 Acknowledgments

We thank the Vision and Data Mining Group for allowing us to use VENUS as the basis for novelty detection comparison. We also thank the Usability Group at RIT for allowing us to use their eye tracker. And lastly, we thank all of the volunteers who participated in the eye-tracking experiments for their time and patience.

References

1. Applied Science Laboratories [homepage on the Internet] Available from: http://www.a-s-l.com

2. Burl MC. Mining patterns of activity from video data. *SIAM Int. Conf. on Data Mining*, April 2004.
3. Cooper M, Foote J, Girgensohn A, Wilcox L. Temporal event clustering for digital photo collections. In: *Proceedings of the 11th ACM International Conference on Multimedia*, Berkeley, CA, 2003, pp. 364–373.
4. Crook P, Marsland S, Hayes G, Nehmzow U. A tale of two filters—On-line Novelty Detection. In: *Proceedings of International Conference on Robotics and Automations (ICRA'02)*, Washington, DC, 2002: 3894–3900.
5. Detyniecki M. Discovering indexing rules for video-news. In: *Proceedings of the European Symposium on Intelligent Technologies*, Hybrid Systems and their implementation on Smart Adaptive Systems—EUNITE'2002, Algarve, Portugal, September, 2002: 44–6.
6. Diehl CP, Hampshire JP II. Real-time object classification and novelty detection for collaborative video surveillance. In: Proceedings of the 2002 International Joint Conference on Neural Networks, 3: 2620–2625.
7. Furht B, Saksobhavivat P. A fast content-based video and image retrieval technique over communication channels. In: Proc. of SPIE Symposium on Multimedia Storage and Archiving Systems, Boston, MA, November 1998.
8. Gaborski R, Vaingankar V, Chaoji V, Teredesai A, Tentler T. VENUS: A system for novelty detection in video streams with learning. In: *Proceedings of the 17th International FLAIRS Conference*, South Beach, FL, 2004.
9. Journal of Net Centric Warfare [homepage on the Internet] Navy SEALs Using New Video Storage and Editing Laptop [cited 2005 February 14] Available from http://www.isrjournal.com/story.php?F=658407
10. Hayashi A, Nakashima R, Kanbara T, Suematsu N. Multi-object motion pattern classification for visual surveillance and sports video retrieval. In: *Proceedings of the 15th International Conference on Vision Interface*, Calgary, Canada, 2002.
11. Haering NC, Qian RJ, Sezan MI. A Semantic Event Detection Approach and Its Application to Detecting Hunts in Wildlife Video. *IEEE Transactions on Circuits and Systems for Video Technology*, 1999;10:857–868.
12. Keim D, Sips M, Ankerst M. Visual data mining. In: *Visualization Handbook*, Eds. Johnson C.R., Hansen C.D., Academic Press, 2004.
13. Itti L, Koch C. Computational modeling of visual attention. *Nature Neuroscience Review*; 2001;2(3):194–203.
14. Kohonen T. *Self-Organization and Associative Memory*. New York: Springer-Verlag; 1988.
15. VirtualDub [homepage on the Internet]. Lee A. Available from: http://www.virtualdub.org
16. Lin J, Keogh E, Truppel W. Clustering of streaming time series is meaningless. In: *Proceedings of the 8th ACM SIGMOD Workshop on Research Issues in Data Mining and Knowledge Discovery*, 2003;56–65.
17. TechTrax [homepage on the Internet]. Holographic Video Storage. TechTrax; c2002-2005 [cited 2005 Dec 9] Available from: http://pubs.logicalexpressions.com/Pub0009/LPMArticle.asp?ID=118
18. Marsland S, Nehmzow U, Shapiro J. Detecting novel features of an environment using habituation. In: *Proceedings of Simulation of Adaptive Behavior*, MIT Press 2000; 189–198.
19. Medioni G, Cohen I, Brmond F, Hongeng S, Nevatia R. Event detection and analysis from video streams. *IEEE Transactions on Pattern Analysis and Machine Intelligence* 2001;23(8):873–889.
20. Mukherjea S, Hirata K, Hara Y. 2000. Using clustering and visualization for refining the results of a WWW image search engine. In: *Proceedings of the CIKM 1998 Workshop on*

New Paradigms in Information Visualization and Manipulation (NPIV 1998), Nov 3-7, 1998 ACM. 1998;29–35.

21. Nairac A, Corbett-Clark T, Ripley R, Townsend N, Tarassenko L. Choosing an appropriate model for novelty detection. In: *Proceedings of the 5th IEEE International Conference on Artificial Neural Networks*, Cambridge, 1997;227–232.

22. Qiu G, Ye L, Feng X. Fast image indexing and visual guided browsing. In: *Third International Workshop on Content-Based Multimedia Indexing*, Sep 22–24, 2003 IRISA, Rennes, France.

23. S. Singh, M. Markou. An approach to novelty detection applied to the classification of image regions. *IEEE Trans. Knowledge Data Eng.* 16(4);Apr, 2004; 396–407.

24. Streamload [homepage on the Internet]. Available from: http://www.streamload.com/

25. Stauffer C, Grimson E. Learning Patterns of Activity Using Real-Time Tracking. *IEEE Transactions on Pattern Analysis and Machine Intelligence*. 2000; 22(8):747–757.

26. Sun X, Manjunath BS, Divakaran A. Representation of motion activity in hierarchical levels for video indexing and filtering. In: *Proceedings of IEEE International Conference on Image Processing (ICIP)*, Rochester, NY, Sep 2002: 149–152.

27. Tarassenko L. Novelty detection for the identification of masses in mammograms. In: *Proceedings of the 4th IEE International Conference on Artificial Neural Networks*, Cambridge, UK, 1995, 4:442–447.

28. Tentler A, Vaingankar V, Gaborski R, Teredesai A. Event Detection in Video Sequences of Natural Scenes. In : *Western New York Image Processing Workshop*, Rochester, New York, 2003.

29. Tobii Technology. [homepage on the Internet]. Available from: http://www.tobii.se.

30. Uchihashi S, Foote J, Girgensohn A, Boreczky J. 1999. Video Manga: Generating Semantically Meaningful Video Summaries. In: *Proceedings ACM Multimedia*, (Orlando, FL) ACM Press, October 30, 1999; 383–392.

31. Young RA, Lesperance RM, Meyer WW, The Gaussian Derivative model for spatialtemporal vision: I. Cortical Model. *Spatial Vision*, 2001;14(3,4);261–319.

32. Zhu X, Fan J, Elmagarmid AK, Wu X. Hierarchical video content description and summarization using unified semantic and visual similarity. *Multimedia Syst.* 2003;9(1):31–53.

33. Zhu L, Rao A, Zhang A. Advanced feature extraction for Keyblock-based image retrieval. In: *Proceedings of the 2000 ACM Workshops on Multimedia*, Los Angeles, CA, 2000, pp. 179–183.

12. Video Event Mining via Multimodal Content Analysis and Classification

Min Chen, Shu-Ching Chen, Mei-Ling Shyu, and Chengcui Zhang

Summary. As digital video data become more and more pervasive, the issue of mining information from video data becomes increasingly important. In this chapter, we present an effective multimedia data mining framework for event mining with its application in the automatic extraction of goal events in soccer videos. The extracted goal events can be used for high-level indexing and selective browsing of soccer videos. The proposed multimedia data mining framework first analyzes the soccer videos by using multimodal features (visual and audio features). Then the data prefiltering step is performed on raw video features with the aid of domain knowledge, and the cleaned data are used as the input data in the data mining process using the Nearest Neighbor with Generalization (NNG) scheme, a generalized Instance-Based Learning (IBL) mechanism. The proposed framework fully exploits the rich semantic information contained in visual and audio features for soccer video data, and incorporates a data mining process for effective detection of soccer goal events. This framework has been tested using soccer videos with different styles as produced by different broadcasters. The results are promising and can provide a good basis for analyzing the high-level structure of video content.

12.1 Introduction

With the increasing amount of digital video data, mining information from video data for efficient searching and content browsing in a time-efficient manner becomes increasingly important. Motivated by the strong interest of automatic annotation of the large amount of live or archived sports videos from broadcasters, research toward the automatic detection and recognition of events in sports video data has attracted a lot of attention in recent years. Soccer video analysis and events/highlights extraction are probably the most popular topics in this research area.

The major challenges in soccer event detection lie in the following four aspects. First, the value of sports video drops significantly after a short period of time [5], which poses the requirement of real-time (or close to real-time) processing. Second, unlike some of the other sports, such as baseball, tennis, etc., where the presence of canonical scenes (e.g., the pitching scene in baseball, the serve scene in tennis, etc.) could greatly simplify the technical challenges, soccer videos possess a relatively loose structure. Third, the important video segments (events or highlights) in a sports video constitute only a minor portion of the whole data set. Consequently, the limited number of training data points increases the difficulties in detecting these so-called *rare events*, especially in the present of noisy data introduced during the production process. Last, but not least, the video data obtained from various sources might be inconsistent due to different production styles and postproduction effects. In other words, although some basic production rules might apply, the overall presentations vary greatly.

In the literature, many researches have been devoted to address these issues from the media content analysis [3, 12, 14, 25, 26, 33–35, 37] to the supervised classification techniques [1, 20, 21, 27, 30, 31]. An overview of the related work will be detailed in Section 12.2. However, few approaches possess the capabilities of tackling all the above-mentioned challenges. In response to these issues, in this paper, an effective multimedia data mining framework is proposed with its application on the soccer goal event detection, which seamlessly integrates the multimodal content analysis and the Nearest Neighbor with Generalization (NNG) scheme which is a generalized Instance-Based Learning (IBL) mechanism. Here, an event is defined in the shot level as the shot is widely regarded as a self-contained unit with an unbroken sequence of frames taken from one camera.

In our proposed framework, multiple cues from different modalities including audio and visual features are fully exploited and used to capture the semantic structure of soccer goal events. Then the NNG scheme is applied for event detection. Currently, most existing classification techniques adopted in the event detection area are called *model-based* approaches as they compute the global approximation (or called *model*) of the target classification function, which is then used to classify the unseen testing data. In contrast, the IBL mechanism is called *lazy* method in the sense that the generalization of the observed (training) data delays until each new query instance is encountered [24]. Therefore, it can use the query instance for selecting a local approximation to the target classification function [13] each time when a query instance is given. The importance of incorporating the query instance lies in the fact that the current production style is one of the key factors in determining the pattern of a targeted event. Therefore, by adopting the IBL mechanism, we direct our focus on the instances themselves rather than on the rules that govern their attribute values. In addition, in response to the requirements of real-time processing and rare event detection, a data prefiltering step is integrated in the IBL mechanism to perform on the raw video features with the aid of the specific domain knowledge. We have evaluated the performance of the proposed framework by using a large amount of soccer video data with different styles and different broadcasters. The experimental results demonstrate the effectiveness and the generality of our proposed framework.

The contributions of the proposed framework are summarized as follows:

- First, an advanced video shot detection method is adopted in this work, which can not only output the shot boundaries, but also generate some important visual features during the process of shot detection. Moreover, since object segmentation is an embedded subcomponent in video shot detection, the higher level semantic information, such as the grass areas, which serves as an important indication in soccer goal detection, can be derived from the object segmentation results. Therefore, just a small amount of work needs to be done in order to extract the visual features for each shot, which distinguishes our framework from most of the other existing approaches.

- Second, when choosing the proper data mining technique, we take into consideration the data inconsistency posed by various production types. In other words, with widely varied production styles and preferences, it is difficult to achieve a global approximation accurately with regard to the event patterns as targeted by the model-based approaches. In contrast, the IBL mechanism defers the decision-making process until the presence of the new query instance, where the local optimization for this particular instance is considered.

- Third, the proposed data prefiltering step is critical to apply the IBL mechanism to this specific application domain when considering the real-time processing requirement, the influence of the noisy data, and the small percentage of the positive samples (goal shots) compared to the huge amount of negative samples (nongoal shots) in soccer video data. To our best knowledge, there is hardly any work addressing this issue.

The chapter is organized as follows. Section 12.2 gives an overview of the related work. In Section 12.3, the proposed multimedia data mining framework is discussed in details. Experimental results are presented and analyzed in Section 12.4. Finally, Section 12.5 concludes our study and presents some future research directions.

12.2 Related Work

Research work has been conducted to study the respective roles of visual [14, 26], auditory [25, 33], and textual [3] modalities in sports video analysis. Recently, the approaches using multimodal analysis have drawn increasing attentions [12, 37] as the content of a video is intrinsically multimodal and its meaning is conveyed via multiple channels. For instance, in [12], a multimodal framework using combined audio/visual/text cues was presented, together with a comparative analysis on the use of different modalities for the same purpose. However, the use of the textual transcript is not always available although it contains rich semantic information for event identification. In addition, to boost robustness against the variations in low-level features and to improve the adaptability of event detection schemes, mid-level representation has also been used in event detection, including the camera view types (global, medium, or close-up) [32], audio key words [15, 33], etc. Therefore, in our framework, multimodal content analysis is carried out in the audio and visual channels, where both low-level and mid-level features are explored.

Despite numerous efforts in video content analysis, it remains a major challenge in terms of effectively integrating the multiple physical features to infer the semantic events due to the well-known semantic gap. In response to this issue, some research efforts have been directed to extend the basic content analysis methods with the facilitation of more supervised approaches, such as heuristic method [21], E-R model [27], and Hidden Markov Model (HMM) [2]. In [21], a set of fixed rules is derived on the basis of the multimodal cues. However, the derivation process becomes infeasible with the increment of the number of multimodal features. In addition, the fixed thresholds adopted in the rules are not general enough for a large number of video samples. In [27], Tovinkere and Qian proposed a hierarchical E-R model on the basis of 3D data of the locations of players and ball, trying to model the semantic meaning and domain knowledge for soccer games. A set of rules is thereafter generated to determine the occurrence of the event. However, the generalization of this work is highly limited as the 3D information is not generally available in the video data. In [2], a method to detect and recognize soccer highlights using Hidden Markov Model (HMM) was proposed, in which each model is trained separately for each type of event. As shown in their preliminary results, this method can detect and recognize free kick and penalty event. However, it has the problem to deal with long video sequences.

More recently, data mining approaches, with their promising capabilities in discovering interesting patterns from large data sets, have been evolved to support fully automated event detection. In our earlier studies, the PRISM classification rule algorithm [4, 8] and decision-tree learning method [10] were applied for event detection. However, the rules induced by the PRISM algorithm may not exclude each other and possess no execution priority order. Such situations are called conflicts and are difficult to cope with in the real application. Alternatively, the decision-tree learning algorithm was applied in our recent work [10], which avoids the conflicts by adopting the divide-and-conquer approach. Meanwhile, in [38], the multilevel sequential association mining is introduced to explore associations among the audio and visual cues, classify the associations by assigning each of them with a class label, and use their appearances in the video to construct video indices. However, the source video clips are required to have all the commercials removed.

To our best knowledge, almost all the classification methods adopted in the video event detection area are model-based approaches, which present some good qualities when the video data are with a high level of consistency. For instance, they are generally with an explicit model representation and computationally efficient for new data classification. However, they inevitably suffer from the data inconsistency problem in the sense that they are targeted to achieve the global approximation. The IBL mechanism, on the other hand, is capable of dealing with this issue at the possible cost of the high computational requirement, implicit rule representation, and noise sensitivity. Therefore, in our framework, the Nearest Neighbor with Generalization (NNG) [29], a generalized IBL mechanism with a nearest neighbor like algorithm using nonnested generalized exemplars, is adopted together with the proposed prefiltering process to overcome these obstacles.

12.3 Goal Shot Detection

12.3.1 Instance-Based Learning

Instance-based learning (IBL) is a conceptually intuitive approach to approximate the real-valued target functions, which in our case are the classification functions. In brief, the learning in IBL starts with the storage of the presented training instances $S = \{<I_i, L_i>, i = 1, 2, \ldots, N\}$. Here, $<I_i, L_i>$ denotes a training instance, where I_i is represented by an attribute set $\{a_{ij}\}$ with the size of T (i.e., $j = 1, 2, \ldots, T\}$ and L_i is the class label, and N indicates the number of instances in the training set. In our case, $L_i \in L$, where $L = \{yes, no\}$ denotes the two class labels of the instances. The class label "*yes*" indicates a goal event and "*no*" indicates it is not a goal event. As opposed to the model-based approach where S is used to construct a (parametric) model and is then discarded, the training instances contribute in a more direct way to the inference result. More specifically, when a new query instance $Q = \{a_{qj}, j = 1, 2, \ldots, T\}$ is encountered, the relationship of the query instance Q with the instances from S is examined to assign a target function value (class label L_q) for Q. As illustrated in Figure 12.1, the simplest way to define the relationship is to apply a certain distance metric (e.g., Euclidean distance, Manhattan or city-block metric, etc.) and the class of Q is set to L_x, where L_x is the label of the closest instance $I_x \in S$ in terms of Q.

However, several key aspects or issues have to be taken into considerations in this simple scheme.

1) How to define the attribute set $\{a_{ij}\}$ for each instance?
2) A basic distance metric, say Euclidean distance, between two instances Q and I_x is defined as follows:

$$|Q, I_x| = \sqrt{\left(a_{q1} - a_{x1}\right)^2 + \left(a_{q2} - a_{x2}\right)^2 + \cdots + \left(a_{qT} - a_{xT}\right)^2} \qquad (12.1)$$

As can be seen from Eq. (12.1), each attribute will have exactly the same influence on the decision making, which is generally not the case for video event detection. Therefore, how to derive suitable attribute weights from the training set becomes an essential problem improve the distance metric.

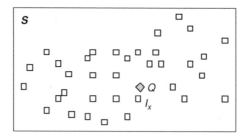

Fig. 12.1. The basic IBL mechanism.

3) The scheme is sensitive to the noisy data. For instance, if instance I_x is corrupted by the noise, instance Q might be misclassified. Therefore, a solution must be sought to dramatically reduce the effect of the noise.

4) In the current scheme, it would be quite time-consuming for a data set with a realistic size because all the training instances $I_i \in S$ need to be scanned in order to classify each test instance Q. The computational cost must be greatly reduced for the sake of real-time processing.

5) Different from the model-based approaches that present the knowledge explicitly by the constructed models, such as the rules in PRISM and the tree structure in the decision tree algorithm, the knowledge is expressed implicitly in IBL, which usually impedes the problem understanding.

In the following sections, all the above-mentioned issues will be detailed. More specifically, we will discuss the video feature extraction in Section 12.3.2 to address the first aspect, i.e., the construction of the attribute set $\{a_{ij}\}$. Then the remaining issues are tackled by the prefiltering process and the generalized IBL scheme in Sections 12.3.3 and 12.3.4, respectively.

12.3.2 Multimodal Analysis of Soccer Video Data

12.3.2.1 Shot-Based Video Event Mining

There are two widely used schemes for modeling and mining videos—shot-based approach and object-based approach. The shot-based approach divides a video sequence into a set of collections of video frames with each collection representing a continuous camera action in time and space, and sharing the similar high-level features (e.g., semantic meaning) as well as similar low-level features like color and texture [16]. In the object-based modeling approach, temporal video segments representing the life-span of the objects as well as some other object-level features are used as the basic units for video mining. Object-based modeling is best suitable where a stationary camera is used to capture a scene (e.g., video surveillance applications). In such a setting, shot-based modeling is not applicable since there is one and only one long shot according to the traditional shot definition [16]. In contrast, a soccer video sequence typically consists of hundreds of shots, with their durations ranging from seconds to minutes. Although an event boundary does not necessarily coincide with a shot boundary in soccer videos, there are several good reasons for using shot-based event detection for soccer videos:

1) First of all, the occurring of certain soccer events is often indicated by the visual/audio clues in a shot with some temporal constraints. For example, a corner kick event typically starts a new shot in which both the player and a corner of the playfield are present followed by a camera pan during the first seconds of that shot. As another example, a goal shot is usually followed by another shot showing the excitement of the commentator and the crowd. A foul event is usually accompanied by a close-up shot of a referee.

2) Shot-based modeling, while it conforms to the hierarchical (i.e., scene/shot hierarchy) semantic modeling of video data for easy browsing and searching, also provides important visual cues critical for event mining during the process of shot detection. In addition, based on our experience with approximately 30 soccer videos with different production styles, audio cues, especially the crowd noise level, tend to be more consistent within a shot.

For the above reasons, in this chapter, we focus on the shot-based approach for event mining in soccer videos. Although shot detection has a long history of research, it is not a completely solved problem [19], especially for sports videos. According to [17], due to the strong color correlation between soccer shots, a shot change may not be detected since the frame-to-frame color histogram difference is not significant. Second, camera motions and object motions are largely present in soccer videos to track the players and the ball, which constitute a major source of false positives in shot detection. Third, the reliable detection of gradual transitions, such as fade in/out, is also needed for sports videos. We also need to take into consideration the requirements of real-time processing as it is essential for building an efficient sports video management system.

In this chapter, the visual feature extraction is based on video shots. Thus, a three-level filtering architecture is used for shot detection, namely *pixel-histogram comparison*, *segmentation map comparison*, and *object tracking*. The pixel-level comparison basically computes the differences in the values of the corresponding pixels between two successive frames. This can, in part, solve the strong color-correlation problem because the spatial layout of colors also contributes to the shot detection. However, though simple as it is, it is very sensitive to object and camera motions. Thus, to address the second concern of camera/object motions, the histogram-based comparison is added to pixel-level comparison to reduce its sensitivity to small rotations and slow variations. However, the histogram-based method also has problems. For instance, two successive frames will probably have the similar histograms but with totally different visual contents. On the other hand, it has difficulty in handling the false positives caused by the changes in luminance and contrast. The reasons of combining the pixel-histogram comparison in the first level filtering are twofolds. (1) Histogram comparison can be used to exclude some false positives due to the sensitivity of pixel comparison, while it would not incur much extra computation because both processes can be done in one pass for each video frame. Note that the percentage of changed pixels (denoted as *pixel_change_percent*) and the histogram difference (denoted as *histo_change*) between consecutive frames, obtained in pixel-level comparison and histogram comparison respectively, are important indications for camera and object motions and can be used to extract higher level semantics for event mining. (2) Both of them are computationally simple. By applying a relatively loose threshold, we can ensure that most of the correct shot boundaries will be included, and in the meanwhile, a much smaller candidate pool of shots is generated at a low cost.

We take the third observation into account by introducing two other filters, namely *segmentation map comparison* and *object tracking*, which are implemented on the

(a)   (b)

Fig. 12.2. An example segmentation mask map. (a) An example soccer video frame; (b) the segmentation mask map for (a).

basis of an unsupervised object segmentation and tracking method proposed in our previous work [6, 7]. A novel feature introduced is the *segmentation mask map* of a video frame, which can be automatically extracted and contains the segmentation result of that frame. In other words, a *segmentation mask map* contains the significant objects or regions of interests extracted from that video frame. Thus, the pixels in each frame have been grouped into different classes (e.g., 2 classes), corresponding to the foreground objects and background areas, respectively. Then two frames can be compared by checking the differences between their segmentation mask maps. An example segmentation mask map is given in Figure 12.2. The segmentation mask map comparison is especially effective in handling the fade in/out effects with drastic luminance changes and flash light effects [9]. In addition, to better handle the situation of camera panning and tilting, the object tracking technique based on the segmentation results is used as an enhancement to the basic matching process. Since the segmentation results are already available, the computation cost for object tracking is almost trivial compared to those manual template-based object tracking methods. It needs to be pointed out that there is no need to do object segmentation for each pair of consecutive frames. Instead, only the shots in the small candidate pool will be fed into the segmentation process. The performance of segmentation and tracking is further improved by using incremental computation together with parallel computation [36]. As a result, the combined speed-up factor can achieve 100–200. The time for segmenting one video frame ranges from 0.03 to 0.12 second depending on the size of the video frames and the computer processing power.

12.3.2.2 Visual Feature Analysis and Extraction

In the proposed framework, multimodal features (visual and audio) are extracted for each shot based on the shot boundary information obtained in the shot detection step. The proposed video shot detection method can not only detect shot boundaries, but also produce a rich set of visual features associated with each video shot. For examples, the pixel-level comparison can produce the percentage of changed pixels between consecutive frames, while the histogram comparison provides us with the histogram differences between frames, both of which

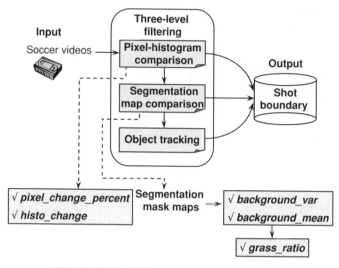

Fig. 12.3. Visual feature analysis and extraction.

are very important indications for camera and object motions. In addition, the object segmentation can further provide us with the higher level semantic information such as the object locations and foreground/background areas. By taking these advantages brought by video shot detection, we include the following five visual features in our multimedia data mining framework for soccer goal detection, namely *pixel_change_percent, histo_change, background_mean, background_var*, and *grass_ratio*. Here, *pixel_change_percent* denotes the average percentage of the changed pixels between the consecutive frames within a shot. Similarly, *histo_change* represents the mean value of the frame-to-frame histogram differences in a shot. Obviously, as illustrated in Figure 12.3, *pixel_change_percent* and *histo_change* can be obtained simultaneously and at a low cost during the video shot detection process. As mentioned earlier, both features are important indications of camera motion and object motion. For example, a close-up shot with a high *pixel-change* value and a low *histo_change* value usually indicates the object motion but a slow camera motion. Usually in global shots, the visual effects of object motion or camera motion are not that significant, and thus, low values for both *pixel_change* and *histo_change* can be observed.

While *pixel_change_percent* and *histo_change* can be easily obtained, the *grass_ratio* feature is derived from the *background_var* and *background_mean* features which can be obtained via object segmentation (see Figure 12.3). *grass_ratio* is an important domain-specific feature for soccer highlights detection [12]. As we can see from Figure 12.4 (a) and (b), a large amount of grass areas are present in global shots (including **goal** shots), while less or hardly any grass areas are present in the mid- or the close-up shots (including the cheering shots following the goal shots). Another observation is that the global shots usually have a much longer duration than the close-up shots. In this study, the mean value of *grass-ratio* within a shot is used to indicate the shot type (global, close-up, etc.). However, it is a challenge to

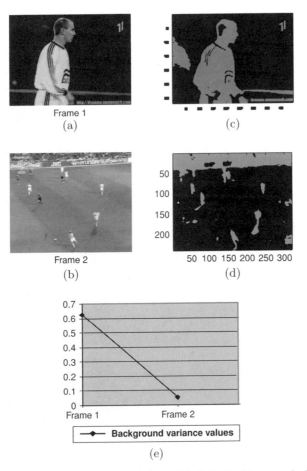

Fig. 12.4. (a) A sample frame from a goal shot (global view); (b) a sample frame a close-up shot; (c) object segmentation result for (a); (d) object segmentation result for (b); and (e) background variance values for frame 1 and frame 2.

distinguish the grass colors from others because the color values may change under different lighting conditions, different play fields, different shooting scales, etc. The method proposed in [18] relies on the assumption that the play field is always green to extract the grass areas, which is not always true for the reasons mentioned above. The methods based on the dominant color for grass area detection are more robust [17]. Our proposed method also does not assume any specific value for the play field color. The proposed grass area detection and feature extraction process is conducted in the following steps.

First, the object segmentation component from the *segmentation map comparison* filter (see Figure 12.3) is used to segment the video frames drawn at the 50-frame interval into the background areas (grass, crowd, etc.) and foreground areas (player, ball, etc.). It is worth noting that the segmentation is conducted in the HSV color space since it is a proven perceptual color space particularly amenable to color image analysis [11]. As shown in Figure 12.4 (c) and (d), the foreground areas are marked with the gray color and the background areas are marked with the black color. It can be observed that the grass field tends to be much smoother in terms of its color and texture distributions. Thus, for each frame, the color variance of each class is captured using the standard deviation of its pixels' values. The class with a smaller color variance is called background, and the mean and variance of background pixels are recorded for each frame. As the segmentation mask maps shown in Figure 12.4, in the global view frames (see Figure 12.4(b)), the grass area tends to be detected as the background with low background variance values (see Figure 12.4(e)). On the other hand, in close-up frames (see Figure 12.4(a)), the background is very complex and may contain crowd, signboard, etc., resulting in higher background variance values, as can be seen from Figures 12.4(c) and 12.4(e). Therefore, the background is considered as a candidate grass area if its *background_var* is less than a small threshold. The *grass_ratio* of that frame is then set temporarily to the ratio of the background area within that frame.

The second step is to select reference frames to learn the field colors. All the frames containing candidate grass areas identified in previous step are considered as the reference frames. The *background_mean* value of a reference frame actually represents the mean color value of a candidate grass area. Thus, their corresponding *background_mean* values are collected, and the color histogram is then calculated over the pool of the possible field colors collected for a single video clip. However, prior to the histogram calculation, a prefiltering step is needed to filter out the outliers in the candidate pool by taking out those shots that are too short and those shots whose *background_mean* values are out of a reasonable scope of the average *background_mean*. Another way to improve this could be to select those reference frames with their *grass_ratio* values greater than a threshold, and such frames are more likely to come from global shots. Based on our observations on a large set of video data, there are two possible situations in the histogram: (1) there is a single peak in the histogram, indicating a good video quality and stable lightning conditions, and (2) there are multiple peaks in the histogram, which correspond to the variations in grass colors caused by camera shooting scale and lightning condition. For example, Figure 12.5 depicts the histogram distribution of *background_mean* values of the reference frames from a 20-minute long soccer video sequence. It can be observed from this figure that most of the *background_mean* values of the reference frames fall into two major histogram bins. By carefully studying the data for this video, we found that the reference frames from the close-up shots form the left peak in Figure 12.5; while the right peak mainly consists of reference frames from the global shots. We can also tell from this figure that the number of close-up reference frames is much smaller than that of the global reference frames. This conforms to the observation that the global shots usually have a much longer duration than the close-up shots. In situation (1), the single peak is selected as the grass pixel detector to calculate the actual *grass_ratio* for each sample frame; while in situation (2), multiple peaks within a reasonable range are all selected as grass detectors. The threshold for selecting the histogram peaks can be adjusted.

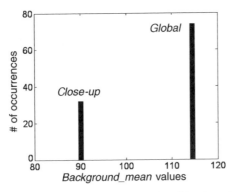

Fig. 12.5. The histogram of the candidate grass values for a 20-minute long soccer video. Two peaks correspond to two major types of shooting scales in the video data—global and close-up.

Figure 12.6 shows the detected grass areas for two sample frames from different types of shots (close-up, global, etc.), and the results are very promising.

Thus, the shot-level features *background_var*, *background_mean*, and *grass_ratio* are computed as the mean values of the corresponding frame-level features within the shot. It is worth noting that the proposed grass area detection method is unsupervised and the grass values are learned through unsupervised learning within each video sequence, which is invariant to different videos.

The major theoretical advantages of our approach are summarized as follows.

1) The proposed method allows the existence of multiple dominant colors, which is flexible enough to accommodate variations in grass colors caused by different camera shooting scales and lightning conditions.

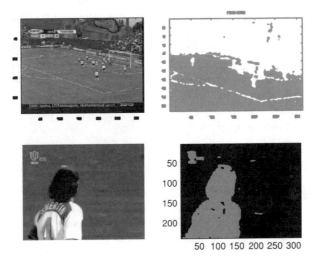

Fig. 12.6. Detected grass areas (black areas on the right column) for two sample video frames.

2) In the learning process, the proposed method adopts an automated and robust approach to choose the appropriate reference frames for the learning process.

While the existing dominant color-based methods tend to ignore the fact that the nongrass areas may have the similar color (e.g., signboards, player clothes, etc.) to that of the filed and thus introduce false positives, the propose method uses an advanced strategy to obtain the *grass_ratio* value at the region level instead of the pixel level to alleviate this problem with minor extra effort. For example, as can be seen from the upper-left sample frame in Figure 12.6, the green area at the top of the frame (the area inside the blue polygon) is correctly identified as nongrass area due to the good localization properties of the segmentation method [7].

12.3.2.3 Audio Feature Analysis and Extraction

Extracting effective audio features is essential in achieving a high distinguishing power in audio content analysis for video data. A variety of audio features have been proposed in the literature for audio track characterization [22, 28]. Generally, they fall into two categories: time domain and frequency domain. With respect to the requirements of specific applications, the audio features may be extracted at different granularities such as frame level and clip level. In this section, we describe several features that are especially useful for classifying audio data.

The proposed framework exploits both time-domain and frequency-domain audio features. To investigate the semantic meaning of an audio track, the high-level features representing the characteristics of a comparable longer period are necessary. In our case, we explore both clip-level features and shot-level features, which are obtained via the analysis of the finer granularity features such as frame-level features. In this framework, the audio signal is sampled at 16,000 Hz, i.e., 16,000 audio samples are generated for a 1-s audio track. The sample rate is the number of samples of a signal that is taken per second to represent the signal digitally. An audio track is then divided into clips with a fixed length of 1 s. Each audio feature is first calculated on the frame level. An audio frame is defined as a set of neighboring samples which last about 10–40 ms. Each frame contains 512 samples shifted by 384 samples from the previous frame as shown in Figure 12.7. A clip thus includes around 41 frames. The audio feature analysis is then conducted on each clip (e.g., an audio feature vector is calculated for each clip).

12.3.2.4 Audio Feature Analysis

The generic audio features utilized in our framework can be divided into three groups, namely, *volume related features*, *energy related features*, and *Spectrum Flux related features*.

- *Feature 1: Volume.* Volume is one the most frequently used and the simplest audio features. As an indication of the loudness of sound, volume is very useful for soccer video analysis. Volume values are calculated for each audio frame. Figure 12.8 depicts samples of two types of sound tracks: speech and music. For speech, there are local minima which are close to zero interspersed between high values. This

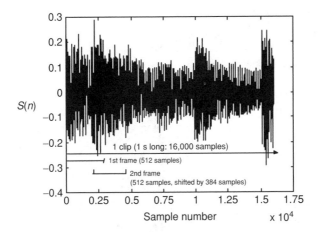

Fig. 12.7. Clip and frames used in feature analysis.

is because when we speak, there are very short pauses in our voice. Consequently, the normalized average volume of speech is usually lower than that of music. Thus, the volume feature will help not only identify exciting points in the game but also distinguish commercial shots from regular soccer video shots. According to these observations, four useful clip-level features related to volume can be extracted: (1) average *volume (volumn_mean)*; (2) *volumn_std*, the standard deviation of the volume, normalized by the maximum volume; (3) *volumn_stdd*, the standard deviation of the frame to frame difference of the volumes, and (4) *volume_range*, the dynamic range of the volume, defined as $(\max(v) - \min(v))/\max(v)$.

- *Feature 2: Energy.* Short-time energy means the average waveform amplitude defined over a specific time window. In general, the energy of an audio clip with music content has a lower dynamic range than that of a speech clip. The energy of a speech

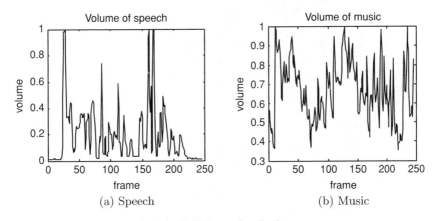

(a) Speech   (b) Music

Fig. 12.8. Volume of audio data.

clip changes frequently from high peaks to low peaks. Since the energy distribution in different frequency bands varies quite significantly, energy characteristics of subbands are explored as well. Four energy subbands are identified, which cover respectively the frequency interval of 1Hz-(fs/16)Hz, (fs/16)Hz-(fs/8)Hz, (fs/8)Hz-(fs/4)Hz, and (fs/4)Hz-(fs/2)Hz, where *fs* is the sample rate. Compared to other subbands, subband1 (1Hz-(fs/16)Hz) and subband3 ((fs/8)Hz-(fs/4)Hz) appear to be most informative. Several clip-level features over subband1 and subband3 are extracted as well. Thus, the following energy-related features are extracted from the audio data: (1) *energy_mean,* the average RMS (Root Mean Square) energy; (2) The average RMS energy of the first and the third subbands, namely *sub1_mean* and *sub3_mean,* respectively; (3) *energy_lowrate,* the percentage of samples with the RMS power less than 0.5 times of the mean RMS power; (4) The energy-lowrates of the first subband and the third band, namely *sub1_lowrate* and *sub3_lowrate,* respectively; and (5) *sub1_std,* the standard deviation of the mean RMS power of the first subband energy.

- *Feature 3: Spectrum Flux.* Spectral Flux is defined as the two norms of the frame-to-frame spectral amplitude difference vector. Spectrum flux is often used in quick classification of speech and nonspeech audio segments. In this study, the following Spectrum Flux related features are explored: (1) *sf_mean,* the mean value of the Spectrum Flux; (2) the clip-level features *sf_std,* the standard deviation of the Spectrum Flux, normalized by the maximum Spectrum Flux; (3) *sf_stdd,* the standard deviation of the difference of the Spectrum Flux, which is also normalized; and (4) *sf_range,* the dynamic range of the Spectrum Flux.

Please note that the audio features are captured at different granularities: frame-level, clip-level, and shot-level, to explore the semantic meanings of the audio track. Totally 15 generic audio features are used (4 volume features, 7 energy features, and 4 Spectrum Flux features) to form the 15 out of 17 components of an audio feature vector for a video shot. Another two audio features are directly derived from the volume related features. For each shot, the feature *sumVol* keeps the summation of the peak volumes of its last 3-s audio track and its following shot's first 3-s track (for short, nextfirst3). Then the mean volume of its nextfirst3 forms another audio feature *vol_nextfirst3*.

Once the proper video features and audio features have been extracted, they are ready to be fed into the prefiltering step which is critical to the performance of the proposed multimedia data mining framework for the reasons as discussed in next subsection.

12.3.3 Prefiltering

As mentioned earlier, the obtained feature set may contain noisy data that were introduced during the video production process. Moreover, the data amount is typically huge and among them the number of goal shots only accounts for less than 1% in our case. For the sake of accuracy and efficiency, it is judicious and essential to reduce the density of exemplars that lie well inside the class boundaries whereas keep the data points near the boundaries [29]. The basic idea is illustrated in Figure 12.9.

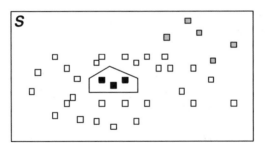

Fig. 12.9. Prefiltering.

In Figure 12.9, let the black cubes be the positive instances whereas the white and gray points represent the negative exemplars which are close to or far away from the class boundary (the black polygon), respectively. It is intuitive that with the removal of the gray points, the classification results for any unseen data remain the same while the computational cost can be reduced.

Therefore, a prefiltering process is proposed to clean the data and to select a small set of training exemplars using domain knowledge. Here, domain knowledge is defined as the empirically verified or proven information specific to the application domain that is served to reduce the problem or search space [29]. In general cases, both positive and negative exemplars can be reduced on the basis of the above-mentioned principle. However, as discussed earlier, the interested events (i.e., goal events in our study) in the soccer video are quite scarce and are of great importance. Consequently, the intention of the proposed prefiltering process is to greatly reduce the irrelevant negative exemplars (nongoal events). Furthermore, as discussed in the Introduction section, although some basic rules exist, the overall presentations of the videos are generally varied from each other. Therefore, it would normally be a major challenge in terms of achieving an effective trade-off between the generality and specialty possessed by the source data, which is in fact one of the key reasons that a global approximation might fail to capture. Fortunately, the ultimate goal of this process is to remove the negative exemplars far away from the class boundaries (for short, they will be called far-negative exemplars from now on). Therefore, in this section, we present this prefiltering process using some computable observation rules with loose thresholds on the soccer videos, which can be classified into two categories, namely audio rules and visual rules.

12.3.3.1 Audio Rules

In the soccer videos, the sound track mainly includes the foreground commentary and the background crowd noise. According to the observation and prior knowledge, the commentator and crowd become excited at the end of a goal shot. In addition, different from other sparse happenings of excited sound or noise, normally this kind of excitement will last to the following shot(s). Thus, the duration and intensity of sound can be used to capture the candidate goal shots and remove the far-negative exemplars as defined in the following rule:

- **Rule 1**: As a candidate goal shot, the audio track of its last 3 (or less) seconds and that of the first 3-s (or less) of its following shot should both contain at least one exciting point.

Here the exciting point is defined as a 1-s period whose volume is larger than 60% of the highest 1-s volume in this video. It is worth mentioning that actually this volume threshold can be assigned to an even higher value for most of the videos. However, based on our experiments, 60% is a reasonable threshold since the number of the candidate goal shots can be reduced to 28% of the whole search space while including all the goal shots. In addition, this rule performs as a data cleaning step to remove some of the noise data because, though normally the noise data has a high volume, it will not last for long.

12.3.3.2 Visual Rules

As mentioned earlier, we have two basic types of shots, close-up shots and global shots, for soccer videos based on the ratio of the green grass area. We observe that the goal shots belong to the global shots with a high grass ratio and are always closely followed by the close-up shots that include cutaways, crowd scenes, and other shots irrelevant to the game without grass pixels, as shown in Figure 12.10. Figure 12.10(a)–(c) capture three consecutive shots starting from the goal shot (Figure 12.10(a)), and Figure 12.10(d)–(f) show another three consecutive shots where Figure 12.10(d) is the goal shot. As can be seen from this figure, within two consecutive shots that follow the goal shot, usually there is a close-up shot (Figures 12.10(b) and (f), respectively).

(a)   (b)   (c)

(d)   (e)   (f)

Fig. 12.10. Goal shots followed by close shots: (a)–(c) are three consecutive shots in a goal event, where (a) is the goal shot and (b) is the close shot that follows the goal shot; (d)–(f) are another goal event and its three consecutive shots, where (d) is the goal shot and (f) is the close shot follows the goal shot.

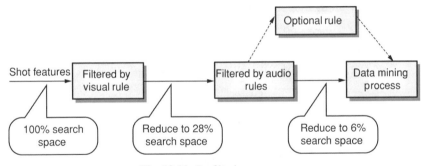

Fig. 12.11. Prefiltering process.

According to these observations, two rules are defined as follows:

- **Rule 2**: A goal shot should have a grass ratio larger than 40%.
- **Rule 3**: Within two succeeding shots that follow the goal shot, at lease one shot should belong to the close-up shots.

Note that the threshold defined in Rule 2 can be altered to a higher value for most of the videos. However, our experiments show that about 80% of the candidate pool obtained after applying Rule 1 can be reduced using Rule 2 and Rule 3, which means that only less than 6% of the whole search space remains as the input for the data mining process. In addition, according to the prior knowledge, a goal shot normally lasts more than 3 s, which can be used as an optional filter called Optional Rule. In our case, since the search space has been dramatically reduced, this rule has small effects. In summary, the workflow as well as the performance of the prefiltering process is illustrated in Figure 12.11.

In summary, the prefiltering process is mainly targeted to solve the fourth problem mentioned above. In other words, by reducing the number of far-negative exemplars for the data mining process, the computational cost can be dramatically decreased. In addition, some noisy data can also be filtered out by the audio rule.

12.3.4 Nearest Neighbor with Generalization (NNG)

As mentioned earlier, the basic IBL mechanism is sensitive to the noisy data. Although the prefiltering process is capable of removing part of the noisy data, a generalized IBL, called Nearest Neighbor with Generalization (NNG) [23], is adopted in our framework to overcome this limitation.

Let T be the number of attributes in the attribute set, the basic idea for the NNG algorithm is to create a group of T-dimensional rectangles or so-called hyper-rectangles, where each of them covers a portion of examples without overlap. To simplify the idea, Figure 12.12 shows a two-dimensional instance space with two classes of instances (represented by the black and white cubes, respectively), and the possible rectangular regions are created as the results of the generalization process. For more detailed information about the generalization process, the interested readers can refer to [23].

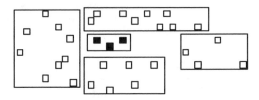

Fig. 12.12. The basic idea of the NGG algorithm.

In brief, NNG represents a trade-off between the specificity of the basic IBL scheme and the generality of the model-based approach. More specifically, the hyper-rectangles can be considered as rules, which, when extracted, can facilitate knowledge understanding. Given an unknown instance Q, it will be assigned the corresponding class label if it falls within one of these rectangles, which is similar to the general rule induction approaches. Otherwise, the usual nearest neighbor rule applies except that the distances are calculated between Q and each of the rectangles (instead of the instances). Formally, the difference between the instance Q and a rectangle R with regard to its ith attribute (denoted as a_{qi} and R_i, respectively) is defined as follows:

$$\left| a_{qi} - R_i \right| = \begin{cases} a_{qi} - R_i^{\max} & \text{if } a_{qi} > R_i^{\max} \\ R_i^{\min} - a_{qi} & \text{if } a_{qi} < R_i^{\min} \\ 0 & \text{otherwise} \end{cases} \tag{12.2}$$

Here, $R_i^{\max}$ and $R_i^{\min}$ denote the boundaries of the hyperrectangle R with regard to the ith feature. As the distance is measured to a group of data points instead of one single instance, it will greatly reduce the adverse effect of the noisy data, as long as the noisy data accounts for a reasonable small portion of the instance set.

As far as the distance metric is concerned, as mentioned earlier, the basic Euclidean function considers all the attributes with an equal relevance in decision making. However, it is generally the case in event detection (and many of the other domains) that the significance of the attributes with regard to the outcome varies from each other. Therefore, an intuitive improvement toward the Euclidean function is to introduce the attribute weights as $w_1, w_2, \ldots,$ and w_T, and Eq. (12.1) can be redefined to calculate the distance between instance Q and the hyperrectangle R as follows:

$$|Q, R| = \sqrt{w_1^2 \left| a_{q1} - R_1 \right|^2 + w_2^2 \left| a_{q2} - R_2 \right|^2 + \cdots + w_T^2 \left| a_{qT} - R_T \right|^2} \tag{12.3}$$

In our work, the dynamic feature weighting scheme proposed in [1] is adopted to define the weights.

12.4 Experimental Results and Discussions

12.4.1 Video Data Source

Soccer game video files used in our experiments were collected from a wide range of sources via the Internet. After excluding those video files that either have poor digital quality or do not contain any goal scene, there are 25 video files left, with different styles and produced by different broadcasters. Those video files last from several minutes to more than half an hour. The corresponding sound tracks have been extracted from the original video files.

12.4.2 Video Data Statistics and Feature Extraction

12.4.2.1 Information Collecting

Information such as the total number of video frames and the durations is necessary and can be obtained by using video editing software. The average duration and number of frames are about 22 min and 35,000 frames, respectively.

To facilitate the extraction of audio and visual features that represent the media contents, shot boundaries need to be located, which is achieved by parsing the video files using the proposed shot detection algorithm. Because of the good performance of the shot detection algorithm (with >92% precision and >98% recall value), only little effort is needed to correct the shot boundaries. On an average, those soccer video files contain about 184 shots. The detailed statistics of all the video files are listed in Table 12.1.

Table 12.1. Detailed statistics of all the video data files

Files	Frame #	Shot #	Duration ([hours:] minutes: seconds)	Goal #
File 1	30,893	148	20:36	2
File 2	20,509	83	13:40	1
File 3	23,958	93	15:58	4
File 4	42,083	194	23:24	2
File 5	48,153	346	32:6	2
File 6	14,612	96	9:44	1
File 7	13,122	106	8:45	1
File 8	51,977	418	34:21	1
File 9	49,959	238	33:18	1
File 10	41,817	212	27:53	1
File 11	46,472	230	30:59	3
File 12	27,624	149	18:25	2
File 13	35,283	150	23:31	2
File 14	22,230	95	14:49	1
File 15	15,198	129	10:8	1
File 16	40,973	322	27:19	3
File 17	19,149	119	12:46	1
File 18	33,943	137	18:53	1
File 19	43,320	173	24:5	2
File 20	65,677	294	36:31	2
File 21	32,788	125	18:14	1
File 22	17,288	81	9:37	1
File 23	21,518	95	11:58	1
File 24	73,138	371	40:40	1
File 25	42,335	197	23:33	1
Total	**874,019**	**4601**	**9:1:13**	**39**

12.4.2.2 Feature Extraction and Instances Filtering

Both visual and audio features are computed for each video shot via the multimodal content analysis process presented in Section 12.3.2 and are contained in each feature vector. Prefiltering techniques are applied to reduce the noise and outliers in the original data set, which generates the candidate shots pool for the data mining stage. The resulting pool size after prefiltering is 258.

12.4.3 Video Data Mining for Goal Shot Detection

These 258 candidate shots are randomly selected to serve as either the training data or the testing data. In our experiments, two experiments are designed and the rigorous fivefold cross-validation scheme is adopted to test the effectiveness of the proposed framework. In other words, the whole data set is randomly divided into a training data set and a testing data set in five times. Consequently, five different models are constructed and tested by the corresponding testing data set.

The first experiment is designed to testify the effects of the proposed prefiltering process in term of the accuracy and efficiency of the whole framework. Therefore, the classifications are conducted with and without the prefiltering step and the performance is summarized in Table 12.2. It is worth noting that the classification program [39] we adopted was written in Java and is running on a 3.06 GHz Pentium 4 personal computer with 1 GB RAM. As can be seen from this table, the classification results achieved with the integration of both NNG and the prefiltering process is quite promising, where by average the recall and precision values reach around 90% and 84%, respectively. In addition, the prefiltering step plays an important role in improving the overall classification performance. More specifically, the accuracy rates are more than double and the running time is reduced more than 95% by comparing to the ones without the prefiltering process.

The intention of the second experiment is to compare the performance of this proposed framework with our earlier approach where the C4.5 decision tree algorithm

Table 12.2. Classification performance of NNG on the testing data sets with and without the prefiltering step

Model	# of goals	Prefiltering	Identified	Missed	Misidentified	Recall (%)	Precision (%)	Running time (s)
1	15	Without	1	14	2	6.7	33.3	1.0
		With	12	3	2	80.0	85.7	0.05
2	15	Without	6	9	7	40.0	46.2	1.84
		With	14	1	3	93.3	82.4	0.05
3	13	Without	4	9	7	30.8	36.4	1.03
		With	12	1	3	92.3	80.0	0.06
4	13	Without	4	9	6	30.8	40.0	1.26
		With	12	1	2	92.3	85.7	0.05
5	12	Without	3	9	7	25.0	30.0	1.14
		With	11	1	2	91.7	84.6	0.06
Average		Without				26.7	37.2	1.25
		With				89.9	83.7	0.05

Table 12.3. Classification performance of C4.5 decision tree on the testing data sets with and without the prefiltering step

Model	# of goals	Prefiltering	Identified	Missed	Misidentified	Recall (%)	Precision (%)
1	15	Without	4	11	3	26.7	57.1
		With	12	3	3	80.0	80.0
2	15	Without	6	9	4	40.0	60.0
		With	14	1	3	93.3	82.4
3	13	Without	3	10	8	23.1	27.3
		With	12	1	3	92.3	80.0
4	13	Without	3	10	3	23.1	50.0
		With	12	1	3	89.9	80.2
5	12	Without	4	8	4	33.3	50.0
		With	11	1	3	91.7	78.6
Average		Without				29.2	48.9
		With				89.9	80.2

is adopted [10]. Here, the comparison with the PRISM scheme [8] is not performed because of its possible conflict problem discussed earlier. As an example, the PRISM approach induces 31 and 19 rules for *No* and *Yes* classes, respectively, in one training model, where 6 of them are conflicting rules. Therefore, the PRISM approach is excluded in our comparative experiment as many extra efforts are required to refine the classification results. For the purpose of comparison, the same attribute set is extracted and the same fivefold cross-validation scheme is adopted to test the decision tree based classification framework. In addition, the results are recorded by applying the classification algorithms with and without the prefiltering scheme, which has exactly the same criteria as the ones used in the first experiment. Table 12.3 shows the classification results, from which we have the following observations. First, the prefiltering process is critical for both NNG and decision tree classification algorithms in the sense that it greatly reduces the outliers and the noisy data. Second, without the facilitation of the prefiltering process, both the recall and precision rates achieved by the NNG algorithm are much lower than the ones obtained by the decision tree algorithm, which indicates that NNG is more sensitive to noise. However, after the prefiltering process, the accuracy of NNG is higher than that of the decision tree, which shows that NNG is more capable of dealing with the data inconsistency problem. It is worth mentioning that since the C4.5 program we use was coded in C language, the running time is not listed for comparison. Third, with the facilitation of the proposed multimodal analysis and the prefiltering process, we are able to achieve quite encouraging results by adopting various classification algorithms such as NNG and C4.5 decision tree, which fully demonstrates the effectiveness and generality of the proposed framework.

12.5 Conclusions

In this chapter, we have presented an effective multimedia data mining framework for the detection of soccer goal shots by using combined multimodal content analysis, data prefiltering process, and generalized Instance-Based Learning (IBL) scheme. The proposed framework has many implications in video indexing and summarization, video database retrieval, semantic video browsing, etc. The proposed method allows effective and efficient mining of soccer goals by using a selective mixture of low-level features, middle-level features, and object-level features. By using the object-segmentation results (segmentation mask maps) produced during shot detection, some high-level features such as the grass ratio can be derived at a low cost, which are further used in the detection of the goal events. The proposed framework takes into account the various production styles of soccer videos by adopting an Instance-Based Learning scheme known for its focus on the local optimization for a particular query instance. In particular, a data prefiltering step is performed on the raw video features with the aid of domain knowledge, in order to alleviate the problem of noise sensitivity of IBL. The basic IBL is further generalized by using the so-called Nearest Neighbor with Generalization (NNG) for two main purposes, that is, to further reduce the adverse effect of noise data, and to expedite the classification process. Experiments have been conducted to examine the effect of the prefiltering process and the performance of the proposed multimedia data mining framework when compared with other popular model-based methods like decision trees. Our experiments over diverse video data from different sources have demonstrated that the proposed framework is highly effective in classifying the goal shots for soccer videos. Our future work will be conducted in the following three directions: (1) to extend the proposed framework to detect other soccer events (e.g., fouls, free kicks, etc.), (2) to identify more high-level semantic features that can be directly or indirectly derived from the existing object-level features, and (3) to investigate more effective methods for temporal data modeling and mining.

Acknowledgments

For Shu-Ching Chen, this research was supported in part by NSF EIA-0220562 and NSF HRD-0317692. For Mei-Ling Shyu, this research was supported in part by NSF ITR (Medium) IIS-0325260. For Chengcui Zhang, this research was supported in part by SBE-0245090 and the UAB ADVANCE program of the Office for the Advancement of Women in Science and Engineering.

References

1. Aha D. Tolerating noisy, irrelevant, and novel attributes in instance-based learning algorithms. *International Journal of Man-Machine Studies* 1992;36(2):267–287.
2. Assfalg J, Bertini M, Bimbo AD, Nunziati W, Pala P. Soccer highlights detection and recognition using HMMs. In: *Proceedings of IEEE International Conference on Multimedia and Expo*; 2002, pp. 825–828.
3. Babaguchi N, Kawai Y, Kitahashi T. Event based indexing of broadcasted sports video by intermodal collaboration. *IEEE Transactions on Multimedia* 2002;4(1):68–75.

4. Cendrowska J. PRISM: An algorithm for inducing modular rules. *International Journal of Man-Machine Studies* 1987;27(4):349–370.
5. Chang SF. The holy grail of content-based media analysis. *IEEE Multimedia* 2002; 9:6–10.
6. Chen S-C, Shyu M-L, Zhang C, Kashyap RL. Video scene change detection method using unsupervised segmentation and object tracking. In: *Proceedings of IEEE International Conference on Multimedia and Expo*; 2001. pp. 57–60.
7. Chen S-C, Shyu M-L, Zhang C, Kashyap RL. Identifying overlapped objects for video indexing and modeling in multimedia database systems. *International Journal on Artificial Intelligence Tools* 2001;10(4):715–734.
8. Chen S-C, Shyu M-L, Zhang C, Luo L, Chen M. Detection of soccer goal shots using joint multimedia features and classification rules. In: *Proceedings of the Fourth International Workshop on Multimedia Data Mining (MDM/KDD2003)*, in conjunction with the ACM SIGKDD International Conference on Knowledge Discovery & Data Mining; 2003, pp. 36–44.
9. Chen S-C, Shyu M-L, Zhang C. Innovative shot boundary detection for video indexing. In: Sagarmay Deb, editor. *Video Data Management and Information Retrieval*. Idea Group Publishing, ISBN: 1-59140546-7; 2005, pp. 217–236.
10. Chen S-C, Shyu M-L, Zhang C, Chen M. A multimodal data mining framework for soccer goal detection based on decision tree logic. *International Journal of Computer Applications in Technology*, Special Issue on Data Mining Applications. In press.
11. Cheng HD, Jiang XH, Sun Y, Wang J. Color image segmentation: advances and prospects. *Pattern Recognition* 2001;34(12):2259–2281.
12. Dagtas S, Abdel-Mottaleb M. Extraction of TV highlights using multimedia features. In: *Proceedings of IEEE International Workshop on Multimedia Signal Processing*; 2001, pp. 91–96.
13. Deshpande U, Gupta A, Basu A. Performance enhancement of a contract net protocol based system through instance-based learning. *IEEE Transactions on System, Man, and Cybernetics, Part B* 2005;35(2):345–358.
14. Duan LY, Xu M, Yu XD, Tian Q. A unified framework for semantic shot classification in sports videos. In: *Proceedings of ACM Multimedia*; 2002, pp. 419–420.
15. Duan LY, Xu M, Chua TS, Tian Q, Xu CS. A mid-level representation framework for semantic sports video analysis. In: *Proceedings of ACM Multimedia*; 2003, pp. 33–44.
16. Ekin A. Sports video processing for description, summarization, and search [dissertation]. Department of Electrical and Computer Engineering, School of Engineering and Applied Sciences, University of Rochester; 2003.
17. Ekin A, Tekalp AM, Mehrotra R. Automatic soccer video analysis and summarization. *IEEE Transactions on Image Processing* 2003;12(7):796–807.
18. Gong Y, Sin LT, Chuan CH, Zhang H, Sakauchi M. Automatic parsing of TV soccer programs. In: *Proceeding of IEEE Multimedia Computing and Systems*; 1995, pp. 167–174.
19. Hanjalic A. Shot-boundary detection: unraveled and resolved. *IEEE Transactions on Circuits and Systems for Video Technology* 2002;12:90–105.
20. Leonardi R, Migliorati P, Prandini M. Semantic indexing of soccer audio-visual sequences: a multimodal approach based on controlled Markov chains. *IEEE Transactions on Circuits and Systems for Video Technology* 2004;14(5):634–643.
21. Li B, Pan H, Sezan I. A general framework for sports video summarization with its application to soccer. In: *Proceedings of IEEE International Conference on Acoustics, Speech, and Signal Processing*; 2003, pp. 169–172.

22. Liu Z, Wang Y, Chen T. Audio feature extraction and analysis for scene segmentation and classification. *Journal of VLSI Signal Processing Systems for Signal, Image, and Video Technology* 1998;20(1/2):61–80.

23. Martin B. Instance-based learning: nearest neighbor with generalization [thesis]. Department of Computer Science, University of Waikato, New Zealand; 1995.

24. Mitchell T. *Machine Learning*. New York: McGraw-Hill; 1997.

25. Rui Y, Gupta A, Acero A. Automatically extracting highlights for TV baseball programs. In: *Proceedings of ACM Multimedia*; 2000, pp. 105–115.

26. Tan YP, Saur DD, Kulkarni SR, Ramadge PJ. Rapid estimation of camera motion from compressed video with application to video annotation. *IEEE Transactions on Circuits and Systems for Video Technology* 2000;10(1):133–146.

27. Tovinkere V, Qian RJ. Detecting semantic events in soccer games: towards a complete solution. In: *Proceedings of IEEE International Conference on Multimedia and Expo*; 2001, pp. 1040–1043.

28. Wang Y, Liu Z, Huang J. Multimedia content analysis using both audio and visual clues. *Signal Processing Magazine* 2000;17:12 – 36.

29. Witten IH, Frank E. *Data Mining-Practical Machine Learning Tools and Techniques with Java Implementations*. San Francisco: Morgan Kaufmann Publishers; 1999.

30. Xie L, Chang SF, Divakaran A, Sun H. Structure analysis of soccer video with Hidden Markov Models. In: *Proceedings of the IEEE International Conference on Acoustics, Speech and Signal Processing*; 2002, pp. 13–17.

31. Xie L, Chang SF, Divakaran A, Sun H. Unsupervised discovery of multilevel statistical video structures using Hierarchical Hidden Markov Models. In: *Proceedings of the IEEE International Conference on Multimedia and Expo*; 2003, pp. 29–32.

32. Xie L, Xu P, Chang SF, Divakaran A, Sun H. Structure analysis of soccer video with domain knowledge and Hidden Markov Models. *Pattern Recognition Letters* 2003;24(15):767–775.

33. Xu M, Maddage NC, Xu CS, Kankanhalli M, Tian Q. Creating audio keywords for event detection in soccer video. In: *Proceedings of IEEE International Conference on Multimedia and Expo*; 2003, pp. 281–284.

34. Xu P, Xie L, Chang SF, Divakaran A, Vetro A, Sun H. Algorithms and system for segmentation and structure analysis in soccer video. In: *Proceedings of IEEE International Conference on Multimedia and Expo*; 2001, pp. 928–931.

35. Yow D, Yeo BL, Yeung M, Liu B. Analysis and presentation of soccer highlights from digital video. In: *Proceedings of 2nd Asian Conference on Computer Vision*; 1995, pp. 499–503.

36. Zhang C, Chen S-C, Shyu M-L. PixSO: A system for video shot detection. In: *Proceedings of the Fourth IEEE Pacific-Rim Conference on Multimedia*; 2003, pp. 1–5.

37. Zhu W, Toklu C, Liou SP. Automatic news video segmentation and categorization based on closed-captioned text. In: *Proceedings of IEEE International Conference on Multimedia and Expo*; 2001, pp. 1036–1039.

38. Zhu X, Wu X, Elmagarmid AK, Feng Z, Wu L. Video data mining: Semantic indexing and event detection from the association perspective. *IEEE Transactions on Knowledge and Data Engineering* 2005;17(5):665–677.

39. Weka 3: data mining software in Java. Available from: http://www.cs.waikato.ac.nz/ml/weka/.

13. Exploiting Spatial Transformations for Identifying Mappings in Hierarchical Media Data

K. Selçuk Candan, Jong Wook Kim, Huan Liu, Reshma Suvarna, and Nitin Agarwal

Summary. The functioning of a multimodal integration system requires metadata, such as ontologies, that describe media resources and media components. Such metadata are generally application and domain dependent, which causes difficulties when media need to be shared across domains. Thus, there is a need for a mechanism that can relate the key terms and/or media components in data from different sources. In this chapter, we present an approach for mining and automatically discovering mappings in hierarchical media data, metadata, and ontologies, using the structural information inherent in hierarchical data. This approach is applicable even when the mappings are imperfect, fuzzy, and many-to-many. We show that structure-based mining of relationships provides high degrees of precision.

13.1 Introduction

Semantic networks of media, wherein different applications can exchange information and integrate multimodal data, require information about each medium to be represented in a detailed and structured manner. To enable such information exchanges, various hierarchical metadata frameworks have been proposed. Furthermore, many multimedia standards define objects as structured or hierarchical collections of media data components. Examples include virtual reality modeling languages (e.g., X3D) and media content description frameworks (e.g., MPEG7 [9]). For example, X3D [10], a file format and related access services for describing interactive 3D objects and worlds, uses a hierarchical structure to describe a scenegraph. When integrating data from different sources, a mechanism to mine and relate semantically similar but syntactically different data and metadata is needed. In this chapter, we present algorithms to automatically mine mappings in hierarchical media data, metadata, and ontologies.

13.1.1 Integration of RDF-Described Media Resources

If application and media content experts could easily associate metadata with each resource they create, then this metadata could be used by integration engines to increase efficiency and precision. In order to enable this, the metadata format used by different applications must be compatible. Ontologies, formalisms that define

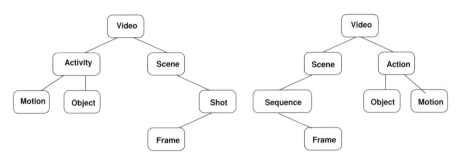

Fig. 13.1. Two similar hierarchical namespaces.

the relationships among terms in a given application, describe the context in which metadata are applied. They are used to link, compare, and differentiate information provided by various application resources.

RDF, for instance, provides a rich data model where entities and relationships can be described. RDF uniquely identifies property names by using the Namespace mechanism [8]. A namespace can be thought of as a context or an ontology that gives a specific meaning to what might otherwise be a general term. It provides a method for unambiguously identifying the semantics and conventions governing the particular use of property names by uniquely identifying the governing authority of the vocabulary. Although with the help of namespaces, we can uniquely identify and relate the metadata to a particular governing authority or a community, there is no straightforward way to map and relate terms or properties among different communities. Consider the two hierarchical namespaces provided in Figure 13.1 (the hierarchy usually corresponds to the concept/class structure) of the underlying domains. As it is implied by the similar structures of these namespace hierarchies, the terms *shot* and *sequence* are semantically related. Therefore, if the user integrates two data domains each using one of these two namespaces, whenever a query is issued using the property name *shot*, the content having the property name *sequence* should also be retrieved.

Automatic mapping of the semantically similar but syntactically different terms from the different namespaces necessitates the integration of content from independently created data sources. An automated mechanism that relates the common and uncommon terms (components) of various metadata communities is needed.

13.1.2 Matching Hierarchical Media Objects

Figure 13.2 shows an example hierarchical scenegraph which can be represented in X3D [10]. X3D nodes are expressed as XML [11] elements, that is, tagged names. The hierarchical structure and the nodes in this hierarchy give information about the relationships between the tags: the document structure corresponds to the structure of the scenegraph of the 3D world. Consequently, given two similar multimedia object hierarchies (i.e., two similar worlds), it should be possible to identify associations between these nodes using an analysis of the hierarchical document structures themselves.

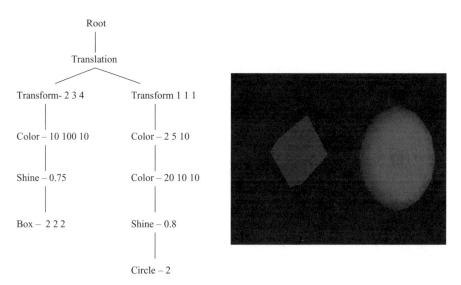

Fig. 13.2. An example X3D document and the corresponding 3D world.

13.1.3 Problem Statement

The problem we address in this chapter is to mine mappings between the nodes of hierarchical media data, metadata, and ontologies. The main observation is that the structural similarity between two given trees (such as hierarchical media objects, XML documents, or name spaces) can provide clues about the semantic relationships between their nodes.

In general, the nodes in the two trees can be divided into common and uncommon nodes. The common nodes are those shared by both trees and can either have the same labels or (in the case of multimedia data) they may have application dependent features that provide nonzero or greater-than-a threshold degrees of similarities [12]. In other words, common nodes are those nodes in the two trees that are known to be related, whereas the uncommon nodes are those nodes in the two trees that are not known whether (and how) they relate to the nodes in the other tree. In many works [13–15], it is assumed that the mapping between the two input trees relates each one node of one schema to only one node of the other; thus, the initial partial mapping is 1-to-1. Furthermore, these works assume that the input mapping is nonfuzzy (i.e., a given node perfectly maps to the other one or does not map to that node at all). We also used these assumptions in our earlier work [16,17]. These assumptions might be valid when the two tree structures represent metadata, such as schemas, where the mapping is naturally 1-to-1 and binary. However, when the two input trees being compared are media trees (such as MPEG7 [9] or X3D [10]), two complications arise:

- First, the known mappings between the nodes may be 1-to-many or many-to-many; that is, a given node may correspond to multiple nodes in the other tree.
- Second, the correspondence between the object nodes may be imperfect, that is, fuzzy or similarity-based.

Therefore, the *many-to-many* and *fuzzy* nature of the known correspondences need to be considered while matching the nodes of the input trees.

In this chapter, we do not focus on how common nodes are discovered, as this is a domain specific task. Our aim is to relate the uncommon nodes of two given hierarchical structures, based on the information provided by the structural relationships between the common nodes. Therefore, formally, we can state the problem as follows:

Given

- two trees, $T1(V1, E1)$ and $T2(V2, E2)$, where V denotes the set of nodes in a tree and E denotes the set of edges between the nodes, and
- a *partially known* mapping (or correspondence) function, $\mu : V1 \times V2 \rightarrow [0, 1] \cup \{\perp\}$, between the nodes in $V1$ and $V2$
  (If $\mu(v_i, v_j) = \perp$, it is not known whether v_i is related to v_j; i.e., v_i and v_j are unmapped)

estimate the degree of mapping for v_i and v_j, where $\mu(v_i, v_j) = \perp$, using the structural information embedded in $T1$ and $T2$.

13.1.4 Our Approach

We introduce a multistage algorithm that mines mappings in hierarchical media data, metadata, and ontologies using the inherently available structural information. This algorithm uses Multidimensional Scaling [2–5] to map the nodes of two different but similar structures (multimedia hierarchies, ontologies, or namespaces) into their private *spaces* and then exploits the weighted Procrustes [6, 7] technique to align the two private spaces and their nodes within such that the syntactically different but semantically similar components are mapped to each other.

13.2 Related Work

Matching has been recognized as an important problem in diverse application domains. For instance, automated schema or model matching, which takes two schemas as input and produces a mapping between elements of the two schemas that correspond semantically to each other, has been investigated in various data management contexts, including scientific, business, and Web data integration [13, 18–20]. A survey of the techniques, for the automated schema matching problem, presented in [21], classifies these based on various dimensions, including whether data instances are used for schema matching, whether linguistic information, key constraints, or other auxiliary information are used for matching, and whether the match is performed for individual elements (such as attributes) or for complex structures. Using the approach we presented in this chapter, both data instances and hierarchical schemas can be matched. The approach does not need additional linguistic information or key constraints, although these can certainly help improving the overall precision. The proposed approach uses not only the individual elements but the entire structures to produce the required mappings between the elements of the two schemas.

Clio [22] accepts XML and RDF documents, a name matcher provides initial element-level mapping, and a structural matcher provides the final mapping. LSD [13] uses machine-learning techniques to match a new data source against a previously determined global schema; thus, it needs a user-supplied mapping as well as a training process to discover characteristic instance patterns and matching rules. SKAT [20,23] uses first-order logic rules to express match and mismatch relationships between two ontologies. Name and structural matching is performed on the basis of the is-a relationships between the intersection (or articulation) ontology and source ontologies. The work in [14] uses structures (schema graphs) for matching; matching is performed node by node starting at the top; thus, this approach presumes a high degree of similarity (i.e., low structural difference) between the schemas. Furthermore, unlike our approach, if no match is found for a given node, user intervention is required to select a match candidate. After performing linguistic matching of the nodes, Cupid [24] transforms the original schema into a tree and then performs bottom-up structure matching, based on the similarity of the leaf sets of pairs of elements. As in our work, the DIKE system [15] uses the distance of the nodes in the schemas to compute the mappings; while computing the similarity of a given pair of objects, other objects that are closely related to both count more heavily than those that are reachable only via long paths of relationships. Similar approaches, where closer entities in a given graph add more to the overall similarity than farther entities, have also been used while mining Web document associations [25–27] as well as for finding similarities between terms in a natural language [28–31].

Recently there has been a large body of relevant work for efficient indexing and retrieval of tree-structured data [32–39]. Most of these works focus on indexing and exact matching of paths and path-expressions on trees. The problem of *inexact* matches of trees and graphs, on the other hand, is significantly harder. Structural matching techniques between two labeled trees with potential "rename" mismatches and other differences are used in [40–42]. These works use the tree edit-distance concept [43–46] to measure how similar two trees are. A good survey of approaches to tree edit- and alignment-distance problems can be found in [47]. Unfortunately, the general unordered edit-distance problem has been shown to be NP-complete [40]. Certain special cases can be solved efficiently if appropriate local edit costs are available. In [40,43], for instance, postorder traversal-based algorithms are provided for calculating the editing distance between ordered, node-labeled trees. Zhang and Shasha [42] extend the work to connected, undirected, acyclic, graphs where only edges are labeled. They first show that the problem is, as expected, NP-hard and then they provide an algorithm for computing the edit distance between graphs where each node has at most two neighbors. Chawhate et al. [48,49] provide alternative, and more flexible, algorithms to calculate the edit distance between ordered node-labeled trees. Schlieder [50, 51] introduces a query language, approXQL, for retrieval of approximate matches in hierarchical data. ApproXQL relies on an edit-distance-based approach, where the cost of a sequence of transformations provides the similarity between a query and a result. In order to deal with the NP-complete nature of the edit-distance-based approaches and render similarity-based search applicable in large databases, Kailing et al. [52] introduce a set of filter methods (e.g., filtering based on heights and degrees of the nodes) for structural and content-based information in tree-structured data. Papadopoulos and Manolopoulos [53] introduce the concept of *graph histograms*, where given a graph, a histogram representing the entire graph is obtained by calculating the degree of each vertex of the graph. Each vertex corresponds to a different histogram bin, and the bins are sorted in the decreasing order. The difference between two graphs, then, is computed as the L_1 distance between their corresponding histogram vectors. The concept of *graph probes*, which are essentially filters invariant across graph or subgraph isomorphisms, are introduced in [54, 55]. Other research in tree and graph similarity can be found in [56–61]. Unlike our approach where the structural match between the nodes is captured holistically in the multidimensional space obtained through the MDS transformation, the edit-distance-based approaches associate explicit costs to each one of the local tree edit operations of deleting, inserting, and relabeling of the nodes and aim finding a minimum-cost sequence of such edit operations that would transform one of the input trees into the other. Thus, in addition to being costly in terms of execution time, these approaches need appropriate local edit costs to function. Furthermore, unlike our approach that evaluates *similarities* between individual nodes, these approaches generally evaluate similarities between entire trees and graphs.

13.3 Structural Matching

The use of structural information for mining of semantic relationships is an established technique. We used structural information available on the Web for mining Web document associations, summarizing Web sites, and answering Web queries [25–27]. The language taxonomies and IS-A hierarchies [28–31] are used to define the similarity

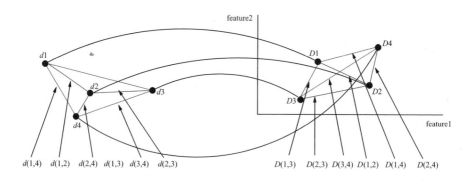

Fig. 13.3. MDS mapping of four data points onto a two-dimensional space.

and distance between terms in natural language. Other techniques are discussed in the related work section (Section 13.2). These mainly rely on the observation that given a tree, $T(V, E)$ and two nodes, a and b, in the tree, we can compute a distance, $d(a, b)$, between the nodes by considering the structure of the tree, for instance by counting the number of edges between them. *The main challenge we address in this chapter is to find the degree of mapping (or similarity) between two nodes in two* **different** *trees, where there may be no common structure to compare these two nodes.* This is because the two trees may have arbitrarily different structures, finding a mapping between the nodes is not trivial.

In order to match two nodes in two different trees, we need to find a mapping such that the distance values in two trees between the common nodes are preserved as much as possible. In this chapter, we present an approach which addresses this challenge by mapping the two trees into a shared space using the matched common nodes and comparing the unmapped nodes in this shared space. The proposed solution can be broken down into four steps:

1. Map the nodes of $T1$ and $T2$ into their private multidimensional spaces, $S1$ and $S2$, both with the same number (k) of dimensions.
2. Identify transformations required to align the space $S1$ with the space $S2$ such that the *common nodes* of the two trees are mapped as close to each other as possible in the resulting aligned space.
3. Use the same transformations to map the *uncommon nodes* in $S1$ onto $S2$.
4. Now that the nodes of the two trees are mapped into the same space, compute their similarity or distance in this space and/or use clustering and nearest-neighbor algorithms to find the related in the two trees.

In this section, we will describe each step in detail.

13.3.1 Step I: Map Both Trees Into Multidimensional Spaces

Multi-Dimensional Scaling (MDS) is a family of data analysis methods, all of which portray the structure of the data in a spatial fashion [2–5]. MDS is used to discover the underlying spatial structure of a set of data items from the distance information among them. We employ MDS to map two trees $T1$ and $T2$ into two private k-dimensional spaces $S1$ and $S2$, respectively.

MDS works as follows: given as inputs (1) a set of N objects, (2) a matrix of size $N \times N$ containing pairwise distance values, and (3) the desired dimensionality k, MDS tries to map each object into a point in the k-dimensional space Figure 13.3. The criterion for the mapping is to minimize a stress value defined as

$$\text{stress} = \sqrt{\sum_{i,j} \frac{(d'_{i,j} - d_{i,j})^2}{\sum_{i,j} d^2_{i,j}}}$$

where d_{ij} is the actual distance between two nodes v_i and v_j and d'_{ij} is the distance between the corresponding points p_i and p_j in the k-dimensional space. If for all such pairs, d_{ij} is equal to d'_{ij}, then the overall stress would be 0, that is, minimum. MDS starts with some, possibly random, initial configuration of points in the desired space. It then applies some steepest descent algorithm, which modifies the locations of the points in the space iteratively, to minimize the stress. Steepest descent algorithms, at each iteration, identify a point location modification that will give the largest reduction in stress, and move the point in space accordingly.

In general, the more dimensions (i.e., larger k) is used, the better is the final fit that can be achieved. Since multidimensional index structures do not work well at high number of dimensions, it is important to keep the dimensionality as low as possible. One method to select the appropriate value of k is known as the *scree* test where stress is plotted against the dimensionality, and the point in the plot where the stress stops substantially reducing is selected.

MDS places objects in the space based on their distances: objects that are closer in the original distance measure are mapped closer to each other in the k-dimensional space; those that have large distance values are mapped away from each other. Therefore, in order to be able to use MDS to map a given tree into a k-dimensional space, we need a *distance* function between the nodes of the tree. The distance function should capture the *structural* relationships of the nodes in the tree. One way to achieve this is to define the distance of a pair of nodes in a given tree as the number of edges between them. In tree-structured data, for example, in a namespace, similar or related nodes are closer to each other and have a fewer number of edges between them than the dissimilar nodes. Other methods [28–31], which consider the depth of the nodes in the tree or the density of the tree neighborhoods from which the pair of nodes are taken, can also be applied to define a distance measure.

13.3.2 Step II: Compute Transformations to Align the Common Nodes of the Two Trees in a Shared Space

In the previous step, the two trees are mapped to their own private k-dimensional spaces. In this step, we align these spaces such that related nodes are colocated in the new shared space. The information available to us for the alignment process is the common nodes, known to denote similar concepts.

Once both trees are mapped onto their private k-dimensional spaces, we need to relate the common nodes of the two trees. To achieve this, we need to identify transformations required to map the common nodes from both trees to each other as close as possible in the shared space. In order to match the common nodes, we use the Procrustes alignment algorithm [62–64].

13.3.2.1 Using Procrustes for 1-to-1, Nonfuzzy Correspondences

Given two sets of points, the Procrustes algorithm uses linear transformations to map one set of points onto the other set of points. Procrustes has been applied in various diverse domains including psychology [63] and photogrammetry [6], where alignment of related but different data sets are required. The orthogonal Procrustes problem [62] aims finding an orthogonal transformation of a given matrix into another one in a way to minimize the sum of squares of the residual matrix. Given matrices A

and B, both of which are $n \times k$, the solution to the orthogonal Procrustes problem is an orthogonal transformation T, such that the sum of squares of the residual matrix $E = AT - B$ is minimized. In other words, given the $k \times k$ square matrix $S = E^T E$ (note that M^T denotes the transpose of matrix M)

$$\text{trace}(S) = \sum_{i=1}^{k} s_{ii} = \sum_{i=1}^{n} \sum_{j=1}^{k} e_{ij}^2 \quad \text{is minimized.}$$

The extended Procrustes algorithm builds on this by flexibly redefining the residual matrix as $E = cAT + [11 \ldots 1]^T t^T - B$, where c is a scale factor, T is a $k \times k$ orthogonal transformation matrix, and t is a $k \times 1$ translation vector [65]. The general Procrustes problem [63] further extends these by aiming to finding a least-squares correspondence (with translation, orthogonal transformation, and scaling) between more than two matrices.

Note that the orthogonal or the extended Procrustes algorithms above can be used for aligning two k-dimensional spaces given a set of *common* points in each space. In our case, the inputs to the algorithm are the common of nodes of two trees, $T1$ and $T2$, mapped to their private k-dimensional spaces. Therefore, orthogonal or the extended Procrustes algorithms may be applicable when $T1$ and $T2$ are tree structures represent metadata, such as schemas, where the mapping of the common nodes is naturally 1-to-1 and binary. However, when the two input trees being compared are media trees (such as MPEG7 [9] or X3D [10]), two complications arise. First, the mapping between the nodes may be many-to-many; that is, a given node may correspond to multiple nodes in the other tree. Second, the correspondence between the object nodes may be fuzzy. Therefore, in this second step of the algorithm, where we identify transformations required to align the two input spaces such that the *common nodes* of the two trees are as close to each other, we need to consider the *many-to-many* and *fuzzy* nature of the common nodes.

One intuitive solution to this problem is to eliminate the *many-to-many* and *fuzzy* nature of the mappings by (1) not considering the mappings below a certain quality of matchs; (2) for each node in one of the trees, selecting the best mapping node as the corresponding peer; and (3) eliminating the rest of the low ranking mappings from further consideration. Although simple, this approach would result in loss of information and errors in mapping. An alternative approach is to use, instead of orthogonal or the extended Procrustes, an alignment algorithm that takes the *many-to-many* and *fuzzy* nature of the mappings while identifying the appropriate transformations to map one set of points on the other set of points. In this chapter, we focus on this second approach.

13.3.2.2 Weighted Procrustes for Dealing with Fuzzy Correspondences

Weighted Extended Orthogonal Procrustes [7] is similar to Extended Orthogonal Procrustes in that it uses an orthogonal transformation, scaling, and translation to map points in one space onto the points in the other. However, unless the original algorithm, it introduces *weights* between the points in the two space. Given two $n \times k$ matrices A and B, while the Extended Orthogonal Procrustes minimizes the *trace* of the term $E^T E$, where $E = cAT + [11 \ldots 1]^T t^T - B$, the Weighted Extended

Orthogonal Procrustes minimizes the trace of the term $S_w = E^T W E$, where W is an $n \times n$ weight matrix: i.e.,

$$\text{trace}(S_w) = \sum_{i=1}^{k} s w_{ii} = \sum_{i=1}^{n} \sum_{h=1}^{n} \sum_{j=1}^{k} w_{ih} e_{ij} e_{hj}$$

is minimum. Note that if the weight matrix, W, is such that $\forall i \; w_{ii} = 1$ and $\forall h \forall i \neq h \; w_{ih} = 0$ (i.e., if the mapping is one-to-one and nonfuzzy); then, this is equivalent to the nonweighted Extended Orthogonal Procrustes mapping. On the other hand, when $\forall i \; w_{ii} \in [0, 1]$ and $\forall h \forall i \neq h \; w_{ih} = 0$, then we get

$$\text{trace}(S_w) = \sum_{i=1}^{k} s w_{ii} = \sum_{i=1}^{n} \sum_{j=1}^{k} w_{ii} e_{ij}^2$$

In other words, the mapping errors are weighted in the process. Consequently, those points which have large weights (close to 1.0) will likely to have smaller mapping errors than those points which have lower weights (close to 0.0).

Let us assume that we are given the mapping function, μ, between the nodes of the two input trees, $T1$ and $T2$; let us further assume $\mu(v_i, v_j) \in [0, 1]$ and μ is 1-to-1. Then, μ can be used to construct a weight matrix, W, such that $\forall i \; w_{ii} \in [0, 1]$ and $\forall h \forall i \neq h \; w_{ih} = 0$. This weight matrix can then be used to align the matrices A and B, corresponding to the trees $T1$ and $T2$, using the weighted Extended Orthogonal Procrustes technique.

13.3.2.3 Weighted Procrustes for Dealing with Many-to-Many Correspondences

Procrustes assumes that there is a 1-to-1 correspondence between the points in the two k-dimensional spaces. Therefore, when the known correspondence between the nodes of the two trees, $T1$ and $T2$, is also 1-to-1, the application of Procrustes for alignment of the two trees is natural.

However, when the known correspondence between the nodes of the two trees is not 1-to-1 but many-to-many, we cannot directly apply Procrustes; we need a different approach to alignment. In the section, we discuss two possible alternative approaches, depicted in Figure 13.4:

• *Evaluate each possible 1-to-1 combination independently and choose the best mapping:* Let us assume that m points in the first space correspond to m points in the second space. This, for instance, would occur if m objects in one tree are similar to m objects in the other. One way to find a suitable mapping in this case is to
1. enumerate all possible 1-to-1 mappings,
2. compute the trace for each Procrustes trace for each combination, and
3. pick the overall smallest one as the best transformation (Figure 13.4(b)).
Note that there would be $m!$ different 1-to-1 mapping combinations to consider. Therefore, this approach can have a significantly large cost, especially if the number, m, of related points (or nodes in the tree) is large.

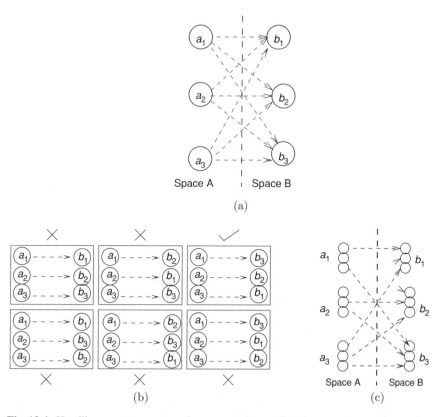

Fig. 13.4. Handling many-to-many node correspondences: (a) Many-to-many correspondence between the nodes in two spaces; (b) evaluating each alternative 1-to-1 mapping to choose the one with the best match; and (c) virtual point-based transformation from many-to-many to 1-to-1 correspondence.

- *Create virtual points, each corresponding to a single alignment alternative:* Let us assume that a single point, a_g, in the first space, A, is known to correspond to m points in the second space, B. To accommodate the multiple alternative mappings of a_g, we generate m virtual points, $a_g[1], \ldots, a_g[m]$, in the first space (in lieu of a_g) and m corresponding virtual points, $b_g[1], \ldots, b_g[m]$, in the second space for each $a_g[i]$. After this transformation, there is a 1-to-1 mapping between the virtual points created. Thus, the W matrix becomes larger, but it is still diagonal and we can minimize

$$\text{trace}(S_w) = \sum_{i \in \{1, \ldots, k\} - \{g\}} \sum_{j=1}^{k} w_{ii} e_{ij}^2 + \frac{1}{m} \sum_{i=1}^{m} w_{gg}[i] e_{gg}[i]^2$$

where $w_{gg}[i]$ is the degree similarity between a_g and its ith alternative mapping and $e_{gg}[i]$ is the alignment error between them.

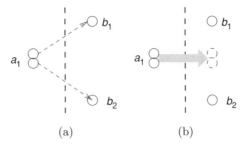

(a)   (b)

Fig. 13.5. A possible alignment error due to the virtual point-based handling of many-to-many node correspondence: instead of being aligned to one of the two possible candidates, $a1$ may be mapped to a space between the two candidate nodes to minimize the total error; consequently, $a1$ may be far from both of the candidate nodes.

It is easy to expand this to the cases where there are more points in the first space mapped to multiple points in the second space. Figure 13.4(c), where all three points in the first space are mapped to all three points in the second space (through virtual points), illustrates this. The virtual point-based approach requires extending the matrices such that there exists one row for each alternative mapping. Consequently, if there are many-to-many mappings, the cost of this approach is a quadratic increase in the number of points that need to be considered.

The virtual point-based approach is significantly cheaper than the enumeration approach. However, since each 1-to-1 mapping is not explicitly considered, the final transformation does not provide a discreet mapping, but a weighted mapping which can introduce errors as shown in Figure 13.5: If, in this figure, $a1$ was mapped to b_1 (or $b2$), the total error would be $|b1 - b2|^2$; however, mapping to a point in the middle of b_1 and $b2$ gives a total error of $(\frac{|b1-b2|}{2})^2 + (\frac{|b2-b1|}{2})^2 = \frac{|b1-b2|^2}{2}$, which is less than $|b1 - b2|^2$.

In fact, this problem exists even when there are more than one points in the many-to-many correspondence cluster. Figure 13.6(a) shows a scenario where there is a 2-to-2 correspondence and Figure 13.6(b) shows a desirable, distance preserving, alignment. Note that the total error for this desirable solution is $2 \times |b1 - b2|^2$, as two correspondences are not satisfied (shown in dotted arrows in Figure 13.6(b)). On the other hand, since Procrustes allows scaling during the alignment, it can instead lead to the configuration in Figure 13.6(c), where the distance between the two nodes, $a1$ and $a2$, is scaled down to almost zero and both $a1$ and $a2$ are mapped to a region in the middle of $b1$ and $b2$. The total error in this configuration is $2 \times (\frac{|b1-b2|}{2})^2 + (\frac{|b2-b1|}{2})^2 = |b1 - b2|$, which is less than the error in the desired alignment of Figure 13.6(b). Thus, Procrustes will choose this *undesirable* mapping. We call this *overeager scaling*.

Note that this misalignment problem is likely to be less sever when there are multiple clusters of many-to-many correspondence of nodes. In general, it is not likely that the same erroneous *center* point will be suitable for all clusters (Figure 13.7). Since a single scaling and transformation cannot map all of the many-to-many correspondence

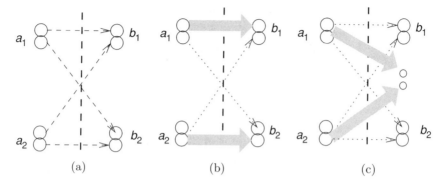

Fig. 13.6. Alignments errors are possible even when there are multiple candidate nodes in each space: (a) there is a 2-to-2 alignment problem; (b) the desired alignment, where one node from each space is mapped to one node from the other, while maintaining the distance relationships in the original space; (c) a potential misalignment due to overeager scaling, in this arrangement, the total mean square error may be smaller than (b).

clusters to their erroneous, but trace-minimizing, centers, overeager scaling is not as likely to occur. When they occur, however, it is possible to recognize such errors by studying the scaling factor chosen by Procrustes. If the scaling factor is smaller than expected, then it is likely that the Procrustes algorithm minimized the overall error

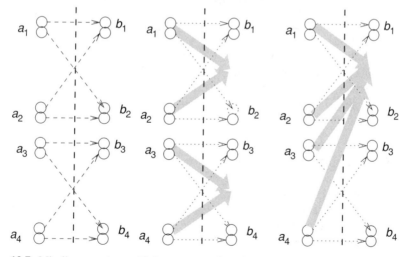

Fig. 13.7. Misalignment is not likely to occur when there are multiple clusters of many-to-many correspondences: (a) a scenario where there are two such clusters, (b) misalignment configuration (each cluster is mapped to its own center after scaling), and (c) such overeager scaling-based misalignment is not likely to occur when there are multiple clusters; after scaling (unless the cluster centers overlap), it is not possible that the nodes of both clusters will be mapped to their own cluster centers.

rate by mapping clusters to their centers. If that is the case, we can correct the error, by *fixing* the scaling factor c in the Procrustes algorithm. Procrustes will need to find a transformation and translation using the scaling factor fixed in advance. In general, the scale of the data can be compared by computing the spread of the data points in the two spaces (especially those that are known to map to each other) and picking a scaling factor that will equalize the spreads of the points in their spaces. This is not a loss of generalization as the initial MDS algorithm that maps the tree nodes to the k-dimensional spaces will try to protect the original distances between the nodes and those will not introduce any scaling variances in the different dimensions of these spaces.

13.3.3 Step III: Use the Identified Transformations to Position the Uncommon Nodes in the Shared Space

The previous step returns the transformations (rotation, scaling, and translation) required to modify the given spaces such that the common nodes of both trees are aligned with each other as much as possible. Using the transformations identified in the previous step, the uncommon nodes in two trees are mapped into the space in terms of their distances from the common nodes in respective trees. The uncommon nodes of both trees that are approximately at the same distance or at the same distance range from the common nodes in their respective trees are likely to be similar and will be mapped close to each other in the shared k-dimensional space.

13.3.4 Step IV: Relate the Nodes from the Two Trees in the Shared Space

At this point we have two trees whose nodes are mapped onto a shared k-dimensional space such that the common nodes are close to each other in the space. Furthermore, more similar nodes are more likely to be mapped closer to each other, whenever there are trade-offs. In other words, the point distances in the common space correspond to the *distance* between the objects. Thus, we can compute the *similarity* between the objects using the distances in this space or use clustering and nearest-neighbor approaches to identify related uncommon nodes.

13.4 Experimental Evaluation

In this section, we provide an experimental evaluation of the proposed approach for mining mappings between the nodes of hierarchical data. In order to properly evaluate the proposed approach and to observe the effects of various data parameters (like the number of nodes in the two trees and their degrees or fanouts), we need a large number of trees. Furthermore, we need to be able to vary these parameters in a controlled manner to observe the performance under different conditions. Therefore, we systematically generated a large number of tree-structured data (i.e., the ground truth) with varying parameters and use these trees in our initial experimental evaluation. After observing the effectiveness of our algorithm using this approach, we also used real collections of data to verify our results.

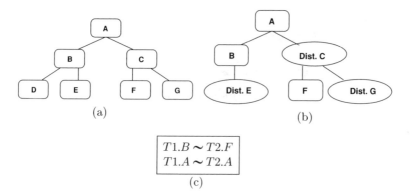

Fig. 13.8. Tree differentiation process for ground truth generation (the ellipses marked as "*Dist.*" stand for the distorted regions of the differentiated tree): (a) An original tree ($T1$); (b) a differentiated tree ($T2$); and (c) similarity annotations.

13.4.1 Synthetic and Real Data

The challenge addressed in this chapter is to relate nodes of two trees based on the information inherent in their structures. In general, trees can structurally differ from each other in terms of the number and density of nodes, node labels, and the degrees of similarity of the nodes in the trees. Therefore, to systematically generate two related but different trees, we

1. first randomly generate an original tree (Figure 13.8 (a)); and
2. then distort (i.e., differentiated from the original) a copy of this tree by
   - relabeling existing nodes,
   - deleting nodes from,
   - adding new nodes to the original tree, and
   - varying the degrees of matches between the nodes
   to generate a different tree (Figure 13.8 (b)).

The original and the differentiated trees act as two similar, but not identical trees for our evaluations.

13.4.1.1 Synthetic Tree Generation for Controlled Experiments

The trees for the controlled experiments are created on the basis of two parameters: the number of nodes and the maximum fanout (degree). For the experiments reported in this chapter, we generated original trees with the configuration shown in Table 13.1. Each node of a given synthetic tree has a different label as shown in Figure 13.8(a). For

Table 13.1. Parameters for tree generation

Number of nodes in the tree	25 and 200
Fanout (degree)	2 and 8

the experiments we are reporting here, we created multiple trees for each combination of tree parameters and we are reporting the average results.

13.4.1.2 Tree Differentiation Process

Given a synthetic tree, we applied various differentiation strategies to observe the behavior of the algorithm under different matching scenarios:

- *Exp. Synth1:* The first set of experiments involved structurally identical trees with mismatching labels. For these experiments, for each original synthetic tree, we generated two classes of differentiated trees, with 5% and 65% renaming, respectively.
- *Exp. Synth2:* To observe the impact of structural differences, we used combinations of addition, deletion, and rename operations to structurally differentiate trees. To each input tree, we applied two different levels of structural distortion:
  −15% (5% addition + 5% deletion + 5% rename),
  −45% (15% addition + 15% deletion + 15% rename).
- To observe the impact of imperfect matching of nodes, we modified the degrees of matching between the nodes in the original tree and the differentiated tree (Figure 13.8 (c)):
  - *Exp. Synth3:* To observe the impact of imperfect matching between the corresponding nodes, we downgraded the matching degree between these nodes as follows:
    - 40% have $1.0 \geq$ match ≥ 0.8,
    - 30% have $0.8 >$ match ≥ 0.6,
    - 15% have $0.6 >$ match ≥ 0.4,
    - 8% have $0.4 >$ match ≥ 0.2, and
    - 7% have $0.2 >$ match ≥ 0.0.
  - *Exp. Synth4:* To observe the impact of many-to-many, but fuzzy, correspondences between the nodes of the two trees, we introduced fuzzy matches between the noncorresponding nodes. We experimented with two different distributions:
    Synth4-low:
    - 90% of the nodes do not match any other nodes except the one they correspond to,
    - the remaining 10% of the nodes match
      - 25% of the others with $0 <$ match ≤ 0.2,
      - 15% with $0.2 <$ match ≤ 0.4,
      - 10% with $0.4 <$ match ≤ 0.6,
      - 6% with $0.6 <$ match ≤ 0.8, and
      - 4% with $0.9 <$ match ≤ 1.0.
    Synth4-high:
    - 10% of the nodes do not match any other nodes except the one they correspond to,
    - the remaining 90% of the nodes match other nodes with the same distribution as above.

13.4.1.3 Experiments with Real Trees

In addition to synthetic trees, we also ran our experiments with two sets of real data:

- *Exp. Real1:* For experiments with nonfuzzy and 1-to-1 matching, we used the Treebank data set [66], which has a deep recursive structure (whereas our synthetic trees were mostly balanced). The data nodes themselves are encrypted; therefore, content-based similarity information is not available.
- *Exp. Real2:* For experiments with fuzzy and many-to-many matching, we used data collected from the CNN Web site [67]. For this purpose, we took two snapshots of the cnn.com site, 12 hours apart. Two news categories (and their subcategories) are selected from each snapshot. Top-two news stories are stored for each subcategory to obtain a total of 32 news entries for each snapshot. The news items are first compared in terms of their key word similarities. The highly similar node pairs are then used as *common* nodes for mapping the rest of them using the structural information inherent in the Web site.

13.4.2 Evaluation Strategy

In our implementation, we use MDS and Procrustes transformations to map the input tree nodes (from original and differentiated trees) into a shared multidimensional space. Then, at the final phase of the algorithm, we used a *k-means* [68] based clustering technique to retrieve the related nodes from the two trees. We used the nodes of the original tree as the centroid for the *k*-means clustering and we used the distance in the Euclidean space to perform clustering. As a result, returned clusters contain a node from the original tree as the centroid and one or more nodes from the differentiated tree as the potential matches.

In the reported experiment results, the term **number of nodes** denotes the number of nodes in the original tree. The total number of points in the space is the number of nodes in the original tree plus the number of nodes in the differentiated tree.

When a given query node of a given tree does not map to the corresponding node of the other tree, then the mapping is said to be an erroneous mapping. The types of erroneous mappings include

- mapping to a sibling of the correct node,
- mapping to the parent node of the correct node (when the correct node does not have a sibling),
- mapping to the parent node of the correct node (when the correct node has at least one sibling),
- mapping to the sibling of the parent,
- mapping to a distant node, and
- no mapping (this is also an erroneous mapping case).

Each such erroneous mapping corresponds to a different degree of structural error. To account for the different degrees of structural errors, we defined a **structurally**

weighted precision as

$$\frac{m_1 + m_2 + \cdots + m_k}{k}$$

where k is the number of nodes returned and m_i is the degree of matching of node v_i in the result:

$$m_i = \frac{1}{1 + \text{strerr}_i}.$$

Note that a node with a lower degree of structural error (strerr) contributes more to the precision. The degree of error is defined as follows for different types of erroneous mappings:

- mapping to a sibling of v_j [strerr $= 1$]
- mapping to the parent node of v_j (v_j does not have a sibling) [strerr $= 1$]
- mapping to the parent node of v_j (the v_j has at least one sibling) [strerr $= 2$]
- mapping to the sibling of the parent [strerr $= 3$], and
- mapping to a distant node from v_j [strerr $= 4$].

If the algorithm does not return any matches, the corresponding structurally weighted precision is defined as 0.

In the following subsections, we present two groups of experiments. In Subsections 4.3–4.6, we discuss experiment results of 1-to-1, nonfuzzy mappings; and in Subsection 4.7–4.10, we report results of fuzzy and/or many-to-many mappings.

13.4.3 Experiment Synth1–Label Differences

First set of experiments shows the performance of the proposed algorithm when the structures of the trees that are being compared are identical, but some of the nodes are labeled differently. This data set assumes that there are no known similarity matches between the elements. Figure 13.9 provides the following observations that are further discussed in subsections below.

- As the differentiation rate increases the error rate also increases. The error pattern observed is similar in case of trees with a total number of nodes 25 and 200.
- As the fanout increases, the error also increases. For trees with fanout $= 2$, no errors are observed.
- The structurally weighted precision is close to perfect (1.0) for low label differences. For heavy (65%) levels of label differentiation, the weighted precision can drop slightly for trees with large fanouts.

13.4.3.1 The Effect of the Amount of Label Mismatches

The higher the number of common nodes between the two trees, the easier is to discover structural similarities between the two trees. An increase in the rate of differentiation reduces the number of common nodes between the two trees; as a result, the error rate increases.

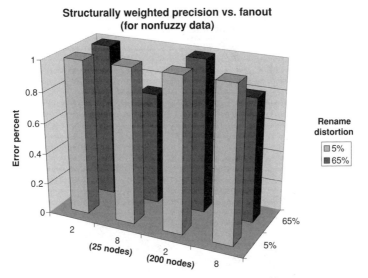

Fig. 13.9. Structurally weighted precision for *label* differentiated trees.

13.4.3.2 The Effect of Fanout

For trees with maximum fanout $= 2$, when only one of the two siblings is relabeled, there is still a high probability of correct mapping of the mislabeled node. However, when the fanout is higher, the probability that siblings (especially those leaf siblings that are structurally identical to each other) will be erroneously mapped to each other increases. Hence, as the fanout increases, the rate of correct mapping decreases. We observed that, in most erroneous cases, the label-differentiated nodes are simply mapped to a sibling of the correct node.

13.4.3.3 Structurally Weighted Precision

The structurally weighted precision is close to perfect (1.0) for low degrees of renaming. In the case of heavy renaming (65%), on the other hand, the weighted precision drops as the fanout increases. However, the degree of drop (around 15%) in the precision is less significant than the degree of difference (65%) between the trees, which means that even when the algorithm cannot find a perfect match, it returns a node close to what was expected. More importantly, the results show that as the number of nodes in the tree increases, the weighted precision significantly improves. This shows that, as the number of available nodes increases, distance-based mapping of nodes into the search space becomes more robust and this leads into better matches.

13.4.4 Experiment Synth2-Structural Differences

Figure 13.10 provides the following observations. They are further elaborated in subsections below.

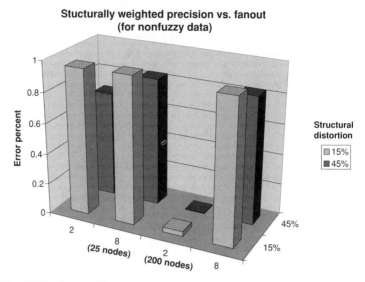

Fig. 13.10. Structurally weighted precision in structurally differentiated trees.

- As the rate of structural differentiation increases, the error also increases.
- *Unlike* the experiments with only label-differentiated trees, when the fanout low, the error percentage is the highest. The error percent drops sharply for higher fanouts.

13.4.4.1 The Effect of Structural Difference

In this experiment, we used a combination of addition, deletion, and rename operations to generate structural differentiation between trees. As expected, the higher the rate of differentiation, the lower the number of common nodes between the two trees; hence, the greater the probability of unsuccessful mappings.

13.4.4.2 The Effect of Fanout

In trees with lower fanouts, each node is close to only a few nodes. Therefore, each of these nearby nodes is highly important in achieving a correct mapping. If any of these nodes is deleted, then we lose important distance information. Hence, it becomes difficult to achieve good mappings.

If the tree has a high fanout, each node has a large number of siblings and nearby nodes. Even if one of these nodes is deleted, there are many other nearby nodes to help with the mapping. Although there is an increased probability with which the given node wrongly maps to a sibling, there is still a relatively high probability of correct mapping.

13.4.4.3 Structurally Weighted Precision

Figure 13.10 shows the structurally weighted precision obtained by the proposed algorithm when trees are structurally differentiated. From this figure, it is clear that the result precision is high for large fanouts. An increase in the number of nodes in the tree, on the other hand, has different effects, depending on the fanout of the nodes. If the fanout is low (say 2), a larger tree actually means a bigger drop in precision:

- In label-differentiated trees, a smaller fanout means smaller chance of mapping a node to the sibling of the correct node. Hence, a smaller fanout translates into a smaller error rate.
- In structurally differentiated trees, on the other hand, when the fanout is very low, the overall tree structure could be drastically changed by a small amount of node deletions and additions. Since the proposed algorithm is based on the structure of the tree, the resulting error rate is considerably high in cases with a small fanout. For large fanouts, however, too many renamings can still be highly detrimental.

13.4.5 Experiment Real1: Treebank Collection

In addition to the synthetic trees we used in the first two sets of experiments, we also run experiments with the Treebank data set available at [66]. The deep recursive structure of this data set (maximum depth 36, average depth, 7.87), in contrast to the mostly balanced structures we used in experiments with synthetic trees provides opportunities for additional observations. For the experiments with real-world data, in order to observe the effects of differentiation, we clustered the trees in the collection based on their numbers of nodes. Therefore, for instance, if we wanted to observe the precision for trees with 100 nodes, from the collection we selected trees that have around 100 nodes. Then, we applied various types of differentiations on these trees.

13.4.5.1 Effects of Label Differences on Treebank Data

Figure 13.11(a) shows the weighted precisions obtained by the proposed algorithm in experiments with Treebank data (with only node relabelings). The results show that the proposed algorithm is very robust with respect to labeling differences in real data. Even when 65% of the nodes are relabeled, the approach is able to identify the correct node with up to 90% precision. When we compare the results presented in this figure with the results obtained using synthetic trees (Figure 13.9), we see that for large fanouts, the precision the algorithm provides on real data is significantly higher (up to 90% precision even with 65% relabelings) than the precision obtained on synthetic tree sets (60% precision with 65% relabelings).

We observed that for trees with 200 nodes around 70% of the errors were due to the nodes that did not match any other node. This is in contrast with the results with synthetic data where the *no-mapping* errors were close to 0. Nevertheless, the overall precision for the Treebank data is higher than the case for synthetic data; i.e., when there were nodes that are returned in the result set, the structural errors for these nodes were closer to 0.

13.4.5.2 Effects of Structural Differences on Treebank Data

Figure 13.11(b) shows the weighted precisions obtained by the proposed algorithm in experiments with Treebank data (all types of differentiations, including additions and

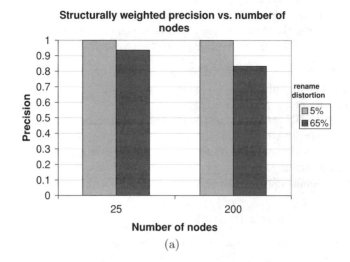

(a)

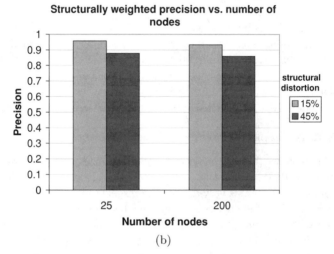

(b)

Fig. 13.11. Structurally weighted precision in experiments with Treebank data; (a) label- and (b) structural-differentiations.

deletions of nodes, are allowed). From this figure, it is clear that the precision pattern of the proposed algorithm using real data matches the precision pattern using the synthetic tree sets in the previous experiments (Figures 13.9 and 13.10). As expected, because of structural differentiations, the weighted precisions are lower than the case for only relabelings, but they are above 80% even with 45% structural differences.

13.4.6 Execution Time

Here we report the execution times required by the proposed algorithm under different matching scenarios for the Treebank data. Results are presented in Tables 13.2

Table 13.2. Execution time for matching under label differentiation

Rate of differentiation	25 nodes	200 nodes
25%	0.079 s	2.57 s
65%	0.080 s	3.10 s

through 13.5. Experiments were performed on a PC with Pentium M CPU 1400 MHz and 512 MB main memory running Windows XP. The transformations were implemented using MatLab 6.5. Each value presented is computed as the average of results from twenty runs.

Table 13.2 presents the case where the structures of the trees that are being matched are similar, but a certain portion of the nodes are relabeled. As shown in the table, the execution time increases with both the number of nodes in the trees that are being matched and the amount of difference that has to be accounted for. Nevertheless, the algorithm scales well against the amount of label differentiations, while the required time is quadratic in the number of nodes in the trees that are being compared. Thus, the number of nodes is a more important factor in total execution time than the amount of difference. Table 13.3 presents the time needed for matching when the trees are also structurally differentiated. Again, the execution time needed is similar to (only very slightly higher than) the case with only label differences.

Table 13.6 shows how the execution time is split among the four individual steps (mapping trees onto a space using MDS, finding transformations using Procrustes, mapping uncommon nodes using these transformations, and finding the appropriate matchings using k-means clustering) of the algorithm. As shown in this table, 80%–85% of the time is spent on the final (clustering) step of the algorithm, while the first (MDS) step of the algorithm takes 10%–20% of the total time. As seen prominently for the 200 nodes case, when the amount of differences increases, the major contributor to the corresponding increase in the execution time is the clustering step of the algorithm. This is expected as, because of differences between the trees, the precision drops; this causes more matches to be found and returned, slightly increasing the execution time. On the other hand, when we compare the two tables for 25 nodes and 200 nodes, respectively, we see that while the execution times for both first and last steps of the algorithm increase in absolute terms, the major contributor to the large increase in the overall execution time is the first step where MDS is used for mapping trees onto multidimensional spaces.

Finally, Table 13.5 shows the effect of the tree fanout change on the execution time of the algorithm. Here we are reporting the results for the set of experiments with trees of 200 nodes and an overall 30% structural differentiation rate. Results for other scenarios are similar. The fanout affects the execution time, especially of the clustering phase, significantly. Given a fixed number of nodes, when the fanout

Table 13.3. Execution time for matching under structural differentiation

Rate of differentiation	25 nodes	200 nodes
(5+5+5) 15%	0.078 s	2.66 s
(15+15+15) 45%	0.083 s	3.26 s

Table 13.4. Distribution of the execution time among the individual steps

Diff.	Total time	MDS	Proc.	Trans.	Cluster
25 nodes					
15%	0.078 s	10.9%	2.6%	0.6%	85.9%
45%	0.083 s	10.8%	2.4%	0.6%	86.2%
200 nodes					
15%	2.04 s	22.2%	1.1%	0.1%	76.6%
45%	2.63 s	18.3%	1.2%	0.0%	80.5%

is large, the distance between the nodes is smaller (more nodes are siblings or close relatives of each other); this leads to more work in the clustering and cluster-based retrieval phase of the algorithm, thus increasing the total execution time significantly.

13.4.7 Synth3: When the Corresponding Nodes in the Two Trees Match Imperfectly

Figure 13.12 shows the results for the experiments where the degree of matches between the corresponding nodes in the input trees is less than perfect. If we compare the label- and structure-differentiated experiment results in Figure 13.12 to Figures 13.9 and 13.10 respectively, we see that the performance of the proposed algorithm is largely unaffected by the loss of precision in the matching of corresponding nodes. In other words, weighted Procrustes is capable of aligning the corresponding nodes as long as the correspondence between the nodes in the input trees is one-to-one.

13.4.8 Synth4: Many-to-Many Correspondences Between Nodes

Figures 13.13 and 13.14 show results for the experiments where nodes of input trees have many-to-many correspondences.

The first observation is that, when Weighted Procrustes is applied without taking care of the scale of the distances, the precision drops significantly (Figure 13.13(a)). As discussed in Section 13.3.2, when no constraints are imposed on the scaling transformations, weighted Procrustes can *overeagerly* scale down the data to bring them closer to the cluster centers in the new space. In fact, even though the distances of the nodes in the input trees in our experiments are not of different scale, when the amount of many-to-many mappings is high, we observed that Procrustes can return scaling factors as low as 0.2. Once again, as expected, this problem is especially prominent when the fanout (i.e., the number of nearby nodes, such as siblings) is low.

When the scale of the data is properly fixed in advance, however, the problem does not occur. Figure 13.13(b) shows the precision for label-differentiated data with 10%

Table 13.5. The effect of the fanout on the execution time of the algorithm

Fanout	MDS	Proc.	Trans.	Cluster	Total
2	0.62 s	0.01 s	0.001 s	0.61 s	1.24 s
8	0.59 s	0.09 s	0.003 s	3.79 s	4.47 s

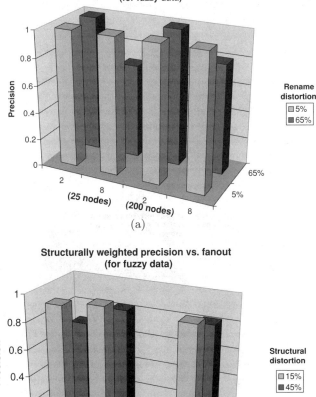

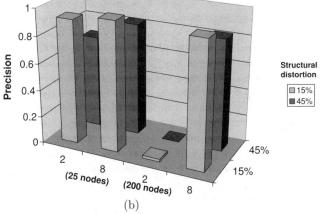

Fig. 13.12. Structurally weighted precision in experiments with fuzzy matches between given nodes: (a) label differentiation and (b) structural differentiation.

of the nodes having many-to-many mappings. In this figure, Procrustes is constrained such that data scaling is fixed at 1.0 (i.e., data are not scaled). When we compare this with Figure 13.9, we see that the matching performance is similar to the case with nonfuzzy, one-to-one trees. In fact, even when the ratio of the nodes with many-to-many mappings is heavily increased to 90%, the overall performance degrades only slightly (Figure 13.13(c)).

Finally, Figure 13.14 shows the result when the input trees are structurally different, as well as nodes have fuzzy and many-to-many matches. When we compare

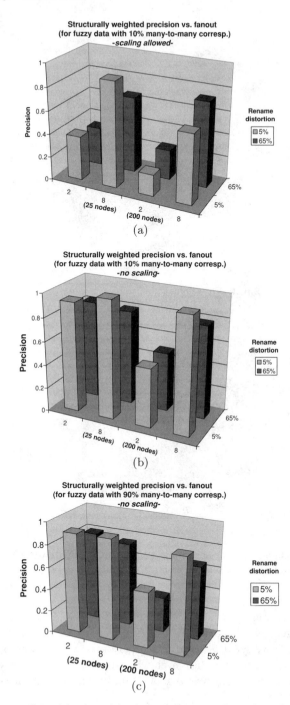

Fig. 13.13. Structurally weighted precision in experiments on fuzzy data with labeling differentiation: (a) 10% many-to-many corresp., Procrustes scaling; (b) 10% many-to-many corresp., scaling fixed at 1.0; and (c) 90% many-to-many corresp., scaling fixed at 1.0.

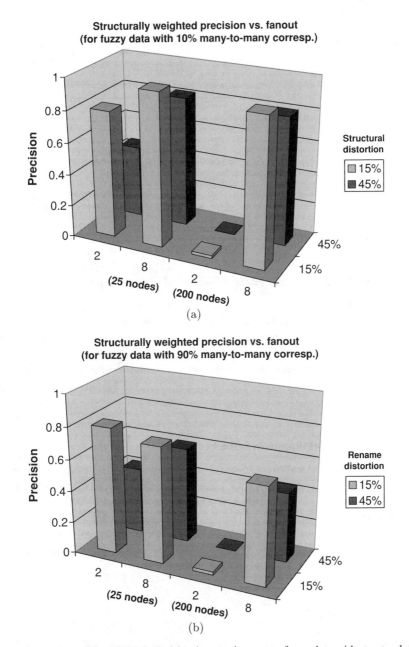

Fig. 13.14. Structurally weighted precision in experiments on fuzzy data with structural differentiations: 10% many-to-many corresp., no scaling and (b) 90% many-to-many corresp., no scaling.

Table 13.6. Distribution of the execution time among the individual steps of the algorithm, when 10% of the nodes in the trees have many-to-many mappings

Diff.	Total time	MDS	Proc.	Trans.	Cluster
		25 Nodes			
45%	0.13 s	5.33%	59.40%	0.08%	35.19%
		200 Nodes			
45%	6.74 s	6.16%	76.41%	0.01%	17.42%

Figure 13.14(a) with Figure 13.10, we see that the matching performance is similar to nonfuzzy, one-to-one trees, when the ratio of nodes with many-to-many mappings is low. On the other hand, when both the rate (65%) of structural difference and the ratio (90%) of nodes with many-to-many mappings are high, the matching performance is expectedly low as there is little structural information to help choose among various alternative mappings (Figure 13.14(c)).

13.4.9 Execution Time with Fuzzy, Many-to-Many Mappings

Table 13.6 shows the execution times when 10% of the nodes have many-to-many mappings. As discussed in Section 13.3.3, the complexity of the Procrustes mapping stage of the algorithm is quadratic in the number of nodes with many-to-many mappings. Indeed, as the number of nodes increase, the total execution time and the share of the Procrustes algorithms' execution time both increase. An 8- (= $\frac{200}{25}$) fold increase in the number of nodes results in a 67-(= $\frac{76.41 \times 6.74}{59.40 \times 0.13}$) fold increase in the execution of the Procrustes phase; that is, very close to $8^2 = 64$, as we expect.

13.4.10 Real2: Experiments with the CNN Data

Finally, we ran experiments to observe the performance for a real CNN data set (with many-to-many and fuzzy mappings). Here two snapshots from CNN Web site are compared using two different ratios of known common nodes. When the ratio of already known mappings is high (95%), the algorithm provides very high precision (~1.0). When only a small set (35%) of common nodes are available to support the mapping, the precision obtained by the algorithm presented in this chapter was still above 70%.

13.5 Conclusions

An automated multimodal media integration system requires mappings across data and metadata. Therefore, a mapping mechanism is needed to mine and relate the common and uncommon data and metadata components. In this chapter, we introduced algorithms to automatically discover mappings in hierarchical media data, metadata, and ontologies. The proposed algorithm uses the inherent structural information to map semantically similar but syntactically different terms and components.

We extensively evaluated the performance of the algorithm for various parameters and showed that the algorithm is very effective in achieving high degrees of correct matches.

Acknowledgments

This work is supported by NSF-ITR #0326544 and an ASU/CEINT grant.

References

1. Resource Description Framework (RDF) schema specification. http://www.w3.org/TR/RDF-schema.
2. Dublin Core Initiative And Metadata Element Set, 1995, http://dublincore.org
3. Kruskal, J.B.: Nonmetric Multidimensional scaling: A numerical method. *Psychometrika*, 29(2):115–129, 1964.
4. Torgerson, W.S.: Multidimensional Scaling: I. Theory and Method, *Psycometrika*, 17:401–419, 1952.
5. Kruskal, J.B., Myron, W.: Multidimensional Scaling, SAGE publications, Beverly Hills, 1978.
6. Akca, D.: Generalized Procrustes Analysis and its Applications in Photogrammetry Internal Colloquium at Photogrammetry and Remote Sensing Group of IGP - ETH Zurich, Zurich, Switzerland, 1 July 2003.
7. Goodall, C.: Procrustes methods in the statistical analysis of shape. *Journal Royal Statistical Society Series B-Methodological*, 53(2), pp. 285–339, 1991.
8. Namespaces in XML, 1999, http://www.w3.org/TR/REC-xml-names.
9. The Moving Picture Experts Group (MPEG) 2001 http://www.chiariglione.org/mpeg/
10. Extensible 3D (X3D) Graphics, 2000, http://www.web3d.org/x3d.html
11. Extensible Markup Language (XML), 2004, http://www.w3.org/TR/REC-xml
12. Candan, K.S., Li, W.S.: On similarity measures for multimedia database applications. *Knowledge and Information Systems* 3(1): 30–51, 2001.
13. Doan, A., Domingos, P., Levy, A.: Learning source descriptions for data integration. *Proc. WebDB Workshop*, pp. 81–92, 2000.
14. Milo, T., Zohar, S.: Using schema matching to simplify heterogeneous data translation. *Conf. On Very Large Data Bases*, pp. 122–133, 1998.
15. Palopoli, L., Sacca, D., Ursino, D.: An automatic technique for detecting type conflicts in database schemas. *Proc 7th Int Conf On Information and Knowledge Management (CIKM)*, pp. 306–313, 1998.
16. Candan, K.S., Kim, J.W., Liu, H., Suvarna, R.: Structure-based Mining of Hierarchical Media Data, Meta-data, and Ontologies. Multimedia Data Mining workshop in conjunction with the ACM KDD, 2004.
17. Candan, K.S., Kim, J.W., Liu, H., Suvarna, R.: Discovering mappings in hierarchical data from multiple sources using the inherent structure. *KAIS Journal*, in press.
18. Li, W., Clifton, C.: Semantic integration in heterogeneous databases using neural networks. *Proc 20th Int Conf On Very Large Data Bases*, pp. 1–12, 1994.
19. Miller, R., Ioannidis, Y., Ramakrishnan, R.: Schema equivalence in heterogeneous systems: Bridging theory and practice. *Inf Syst* 19(1):3–31, 1994.

20. Mitra, P., Wiederhold, G., Jannink, J.: Semiautomatic integration of knowledge sources. *Proc. of Fusion '99*, Sunnyvale, USA, 1999.
21. Rahm, E., Bernstein, P.A.: A survey of approaches to automatic schema matching, *VLDB Journal* 10, pp. 334–350, 2001.
22. Miller, R.J., Haas, L., Hernandez, M.A.: Schema mapping as query discovery. *Proc 26th Int Conf OnVery Large Data Bases*, pp. 77–88, 2000.
23. Mitra, P., Wiederhold, G., Kersten, M.: A graph oriented model for articulation of ontology interdependencies. *Proc Extending DataBase Technologies, LNCS*, Vol. 1777, pp. 86–100, 2000.
24. Madhavan, J., Bernstein, P.A., Rahm, E.: Generic Schema Matching with Cupid. *Proc 27th Int Conf On Very Large Data Bases*, pp. 49–58, 2001.
25. Li, W.S., Candan, K.S., Vu, Q., Agrawal, D.: Query relaxation by structure and semantics for retrieval of logical web documents. *TKDE* 14(4): 768–791, 2002.
26. Candan, K.S., Li, W.S.: Discovering web document associations for Web site summarization. *DaWaK* 152–161, 2001.
27. Candan, K.S., Li, W.S.: Using random walks for mining Web document associations. *PAKDD*, pp. 294–305, 2000.
28. Resnik, P.: Using information content to evaluate semantic similarity in a taxanomy. *IJCAI*, pp. 448–45, 1995.
29. Resnik, P.: Sematic similarity in a taxanomy: An information-based measure and its application to problems of ambiguity in natural language. *Journal of Artificial Intelligence Research*, 11, 95–130, 1999.
30. Rada, R., Mili, H., Bicknell, E., Blettner, M.: Development and application of a metric on semantic nets. *IEEE Transactions on Systems, Management, and Cybernetics*, 19(1): 17–30, 1989.
31. Lee, J., Kim, M., Lee, Y.: Information retrieval based on conceptual distance in IS-A hierarchies. *Journal of Documentation*, 49(2): 188–207, 1993.
32. Zhang, C., Naughton, J.F., DeWitt, D.J., Luo, Q., Lohman, G.M.: On supporting containment queries in relational database management, 2001.
33. Goldman, R., Widom, J.: Enabling Query Formulation and Optimization in Semistructured Databases, pp. 436–445. *VLDB*, 1997.
34. Bremer, J., Gertz, M.: An efficient XML node identification and indexing scheme. *VLDB*, 2003.
35. Li, Q., Moon, B.: Indexing and querying XML data for regular path expressions. *VLDB*, 2001.
36. Wang, H., Park, S., Fan, W., Yu, P.: ViST: A dynamic index method for querying XML data by TreeStructures. *SIGMOD*, 2003.
37. Rao, P., Moon, B.: PRIX: Indexing and Querying XML using prufer sequences. *ICDE*, 2004.
38. Milo, T., Suciu, D.: Index structures for path expressions. ICDT'99, pp. 277–295. ICDT, 1999.
39. Cooper, B.F., Sample, N., Franklin, M.J., Hjaltason, G.R., Shadmon, M.: A Fast Index for Semistructured Data. pp. 341–350. VLDB, 2001.
40. Zhang, K.: The editing distance between trees: Algorithms and applications. PhD thesis, Courant Institute, Departement of Computer Science, 1989.
41. Wang, J., Zhang, K. Jeong, K., Shasha, D.: A System for Approximate Tree Matching. IEEE TKDE. 559–571, 1994.
42. Zhang, K., Shasha, D.: Simple fast algorithms for the editing distance between trees and related problems. *SIAM J Comput* 18:1245–1262, 1989.

43. Tai, K.C.: The tree-to-tree correction problem. *J. ACM*, 36, 422–433, 1979.
44. Zhang, K., Shasha, D.: Approximate Tree Pattern Matching. In Pattern Matching in Strings, Trees, and Arrays. A. Apostolico and Z.Galil (eds.), Oxford University, Oxford, pp. 341–371, 1997.
45. Zhang, K., Wang, J.T.L., Shasha, D.: On the editing distance between undirected acyclic graphs. *International Journal of Computer Science*, 7(1), pp. 43–57, 1996.
46. Lu, S.Y.: A tree-to-tree distance and its application to cluster analysis. *IEEE Trans. PAMI*, 1, 219–224, 1979.
47. Bille, P.: A Tree Edit Distance, Alignment Distance and Inclusion. IT University of Copenhagen Technical Report Series, TR-2003-23, 2003.
48. Chawathe, S.: Comparing hierarchical data in external memory. In: *Proceedings of the Twenty-fifth International Conference on Very Large Data Bases*, Edinburgh, Scotland, UK, 1999.
49. Chawathe, S., Garcia-Molina, H.: Meaningful change detection in structured data. In: *Proceedings of the ACM SIGMOD International Conference on Management of Data*, pp. 26–37, Tucson, Arizona, 1997.
50. Schlieder, T.: ApproXQL: Design and implementation of an approximate pattern matching language for XML. Technical Report B 01-02, Freie Universitat Berlin, May 2001.
51. Schlieder, T.: Schema-driven evaluation of approximate tree-pattern queries. In: *Proc. EDBT*, pp. 514–532, Prague, Czech Republic, 2002.
52. Kailing, K., Kriegel, H.P., Schonauer, S., Seidl, T.: Efficient similarity search for hierarchical data in large databases. In: *Proc. 9th Int. Conf. on Extending Database Technology*, pp. 676–693, Heraklion, Greece, 2004.
53. Papadopoulos, A.N., Manolopoulos, Y.: Structure-based Similarity Search With Graph Histograms. In: *Proceedings of the DEXA/IWOSS International Workshop on Similarity Search*, pages 174–178. IEEE Computer Society, 1999.
54. Lopresti, D., Wilfong, G.: Comparing Semi-structured documents via graph probing. In: *Proceedings of the Workshop on Multimedia Information Systems*, pp. 41–50, November 2001.
55. Lopresti, D., Wilfong, G.: Applications of graph probing to Web document analysis. In: *Proceedings of the International Workshop on Web Document Analysis*, Seattle, US, September 2001.
56. Kriegel, H.P., Schonauer, S.: Similarity search in structured data. *DAWAK* 2003.
57. Fu, J.J.: Approximate pattern matching in directed graphs. Combinatorial Pattern Matching (CPM'96), pp.373–383, 1996.
58. Selkow, S.: The Tree-to-Tree editing problem. *Information Processing Letters*, 6(6), pp. 184–186, 1977.
59. Luccio, F., Pagli, L.: Approximate matching for two families of trees. *Information and Computation*, 123(1), 111–120, 1995.
60. Farach, M., Thorup, M.: Sparse dynamic programming for evolutionary tree comparison. *SIAM Journal on Computing*, 26(1):210–23, 1997.
61. Myers, E.: An O(ND) difference algorithms and its variations. *Algorithmica*, 1(2), pp. 251–266, 1986.
62. Schoenemann, P.H.: A generalized solution of the orthogonal procrustes problem. *Psychometrika*, 31(1), pp. 1–10, 1966.
63. Gower, J.: Generalized procrustes analysis. *Psychometrika*, 40:33–51, 1975.
64. Kendall, D.G.: Shape manifolds: Procrustean metrics and complex projective spaces. *Bulletin of the London Mathematical Society*, 16:81–121, 1984.

65. Schoenemann, P.H., Carroll, R.: Fitting one matrix to another under choice of a central dilation and a rigid motion. *Psychometrika*, 35(2), 245–255, 1970.
66. University of Pennsylvania Treebank Project collection at http://www.cs.washington.edu/research/xmldatasets/www/repository.html
67. CNN.com, http://www.cnn.com
68. MacQueen, J.: Some methods for classification and analysis of multivariate observations. In: *5th Berkeley Symp. Math. Statist. Prob.*, Vol. 1, pp. 281–297, 1967.

14. A Novel Framework for Semantic Image Classification and Benchmark Via Salient Objects

Yuli Gao, Hangzai Luo, and Jianping Fan

Summary. Interpreting semantic image concepts via their dominant compounds is a promising approach to achieve effective image retrieval via key words. In this chapter, a novel framework is proposed by using the salient objects as the semantic building blocks for image concept interpretation. This novel framework includes (a) using Support Vector Machine to achieve automatic detection of the salient objects as our basic visual vocabulary; (b) using Gaussian Mixture Model for semantic image concept interpretation by exploring the quantitative relationship between the semantic image concepts and their dominant compounds, i.e., salient objects. Our broad experiments on **natural images** have obtained significant improvements on semantic image classification.

14.1 Introduction

As high-resolution digital camera becomes affordable and popular, high-quality digital images have exploded the Internet. With this exponential growth in online publishing of digital images, it is becoming more and more important to develop effective image database indexing and retrieval at the semantic level [1].

There have been many published works on exploiting semantic meaning from digital images. In general, the success of these existing content-based image retrieval (CBIR) systems depends on two interrelated issues: (1) The effectiveness of the underlying image patterns that are selected for image content representation and feature extraction; (2) the accuracy of the underlying image classification algorithms.

Three approaches have been widely used for image content representation:

(a) *Scene-based* approaches treat an entire image as the underlying image patterns for feature extraction; thus, only the global visual properties are used for image content representation [8–12]. A well-known example is the system developed by Torralba and Oliva, which uses *discriminant structural templates* to represent the global visual properties of natural scene images [10]. The major advantage of the scene-based approach is that it avoids the generally hard problems of image segmentation and object detection, and it captures the overall structure of major elements in an image. However, these approaches may not work well for images composed of individual objects [2–4] that are identified by human users to interpret the semantics of images.

(b) *Region-based* approaches take homogeneous image regions or connected image regions with consistent color or texture (i.e., image blobs) as the underlying image patterns for feature extraction [5–8]. For example, Carson et al. proposed a blob-based framework [5], and the similarity between images are calculated by the similarity of the blobs. Wang, Li, and Wiederhold have also developed an integrated region matching technique for binary image classification [6]. One common weakness of these region-based image classification techniques is that homogeneous image regions may have little correspondence with the semantic concepts—a big semantic gap for effective semantic image classification. In addition, these region-based approaches may suffer from overdetection of semantic concepts [2, 14].

(c) *Object-based* approaches take semantic objects as the representative image patterns for feature extraction [13–15]. The major problem for such approaches is that automatic semantic object extraction is generally difficult because homogeneous image regions in color or texture do not correspond to the semantic objects directly [2–4].

From these different approaches of image representation, we can see that image semantics can be described and modeled at multiple levels—both at the content level and at the concept level. Content-level description can be used to characterize images with distinctive objects and concept-level description can be used to characterize events revealed by the global structure of an image. Thus a good image classification system should enable automatic annotation of both the dominant image components and the relevant semantic concepts. However, few existing work has achieved such multilevel annotation of images.

On the basis of this understanding, we propose a novel framework to achieve automatic interpretation of semantic image concepts by using *salient objects*, the basic unit of our visual representation vocabulary. And then we interpret the high-level semantic concepts of an image via the joint distribution of its relevant salient objects.

This chapter is organized as follows: Section 2 presents our image content representation framework by using salient objects; Section 3 introduces automatic detection of salient objects via *Support Vector Machine*; Section 4 introduces a semantic image concept interpretation framework using *Gaussian Mixture Model*; Section 5 shows our broad experiments on natural images; and we conclude in Section 6.

14.2 Image Content Representation Via Salient Objects

As mentioned above, the quality of low-level visual features largely depends on the underlying image patterns that are selected for image content representation and feature extraction. As shown in Figure 14.1, semantics of natural images can be identified by human users in two different ways: (a) through objects of interest such as animals, sky, and water together with their background visual properties, one

Fig. 14.1. Examples of natural images. Human beings interpret the semantics of images based on different salient objects: (a) object of interest; (b) the global configuration of the scene.

recognizes certain activities being performed by the object; (b) through scenes with no particular objects of focus, it unfolds a global configuration such as openness, naturalness that is often related to certain events like sailing, skiing, and hiking.

The low-level visual features that are extracted by using entire images or homogeneous image regions do not have the ability to capture the objects of interest like those in (a), because of the lack of correspondence between regions and semantic objects. On the other hand, extracting the semantic object for global scenes like those in (b) is not only very difficult but also ineffective because the entire image should be appreciated as a whole. Therefore, there has been great interest in developing more effective image content representation framework using middle-level understanding of image contents, through which a higher level understanding of the image concept can be achieved.

In order to obtain a middle-level understanding about image contents, we propose a novel semantic-sensitive image content representation framework by using the salient objects. The salient objects are defined as the visually distinguishable image compounds [14] or the global visual properties of whole images that can be identified by using the spectrum templates in the frequency domain [10]. For example, the salient object "sky" is defined as the connected image regions with large sizes (i.e., dominant image regions) that are related to the human semantics "sky." The salient objects that are related to the global visual properties in the frequency domain can be obtained easily by using wavelet transformation [10]. In the following discussion, we will focus on modeling and detecting the salient objects that are related to the visually distinguishable image compounds. The *basic vocabulary structure* of such salient objects is modeled by using the taxonomy of image compounds of *natural scenes* as shown in Figure 14.2.

Since the concept-sensitive salient objects are semantic to human beings, they can act as a middle-level representation of image content and break the semantic gap into two smaller but bridgeable gaps as follows: (a) Gap 1: the gap between low-level digital image signals and the concept-sensitive salient objects; (b) Gap 2: the gap between the salient objects and the relevant semantic image concepts. In our implementation, we use Support Vector Machine to bridge gap 1, and Gaussian Mixture Model to bridge gap 2.

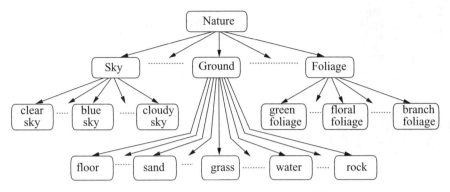

Fig. 14.2. Examples of the taxonomy of natural images.

14.3 Salient Object Detection

In our image content representation framework, salient objects serve as the basic units of representation. Thus, the objective of this step is to parse the natural images into salient objects in the vocabulary designed for certain vision purposes. Each type of the salient objects can be taken as an abstraction of some visual properties that are meaningful to certain vision purposes. On the basis of the basic vocabulary as shown in Figure 14.2, we have designed a set of detection functions and each function is able to detect one certain type of these salient objects in the basic vocabulary.

We use our detection function for the salient object "grass" as an example to show how we can design our salient object detection functions. As shown in Figure 14.3, image regions with homogeneous color or texture are first obtained by using mean shift segmentation techniques [23]. It can be observed that oversegmentation is common in the segmented image, which fractures an object into multiple small regions that have little semantic meaning to human beings. This problem of oversegmentation will be remedied at a later stage by merging to form the concept-sensitive salient objects.

Since the visual characteristics of a certain type of salient objects will look differently at different lighting and capturing conditions [2–4], using only one image is very difficult to represent its characteristics and thus this automatic image segmentation procedure is performed on a set of training images with the salient object "grass." The homogeneous regions obtained from the training images that are related to the salient object "grass" are selected and labeled by human interaction.

Region-based low-level visual features are then extracted for characterizing the visual properties of these labeled image regions that are explicitly related to the salient object "grass." These include one-dimensional coverage ratio (i.e., density ratio between the pixels of real object region and the pixels of its rectangular bounding box) for approximate shape representation, six-dimensional region locations (i.e., 2 dimensions for region center and 4 dimensions to indicate the rectangular bounding box), 7-dimensional LUV dominant colors and color variances (i.e., 3-dimensional average colors and 3-dimensional variance along every dimensions and 1-dimensional variance in joint color space), 14-dimensional Tamura texture, and 28-dimensional

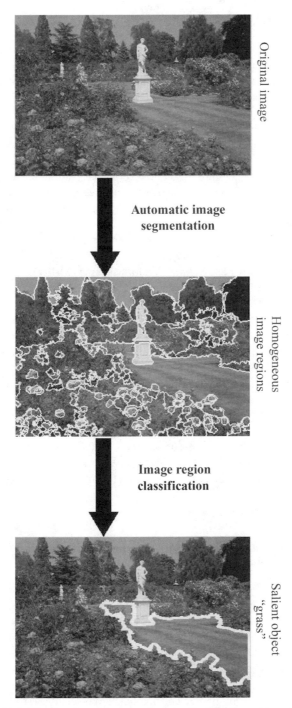

Fig. 14.3. The flowchart for automatic detection of salient object: Grass.

wavelet texture features. The 6-dimensional region locations will be used to determine the contextual relationships among different types of salient objects. The contextual relationships among different types of salient objects (i.e., coherence among different types of salient objects) can be used to distinguish different salient objects with similar visual properties such as "grass" versus "tree," where the salient object "tree" has strong coexistence with the salient object "sky," and the salient object "grass" has strong coexistence with the salient object "flower."

We use *one-against-all* rule to label the training samples $\Omega_{g_j} = \{X_l, G_j(X_l) \mid l = 1, \ldots, N\}$, where $G_j(X_l) \in \{+1, -1\}$: positive for a specific visual salient object and negative for all other samples. Each labeled training sample is a pair $(X_l, G_j(X_l))$ that consists of a set of region-based low-level visual features X_l and the semantic label $G_j(X_l)$ for the corresponding labeled homogeneous image region. Based on the available visual features and labels, an image region classifier is learned from these labeled homogeneous image regions.

As described before, in addition to the image representation framework, the choice of a good classifier is a very important factor in building good semantic image classification systems. Thus we use Support Vector Machine (SVM) [24, 25] for learning the binary image region classifier because of its recent success in a large variety of applications.

Formally, consider a binary classification problem with sample set $\Omega_{g_j} = \{X_l, G_j(X_l) \mid l = 1, \ldots, N\}$, where the semantic label $G_j(X_l)$ for the labeled homogeneous image region with the visual feature X_l is either $+1$ or -1. For the positive samples X_l with $G_j(X_l) = +1$, there exists a hyperplane with parameters ω and b in the kernel-induced feature space such that $\omega \cdot \Phi(X_l) + b \geq +1$. Similarly, for negative samples X_l with $G_j(X_l) = -1$, we have $\omega \cdot \Phi(X_l) + b \leq -1$, where $\Phi(X)$ is the kernel-induced mapping from the input space to the higher dimensional feature space. The margin between these two supporting planes is $2/||\omega||^2$. SVM is designed to maximize the margin with the constraints $\omega \cdot \Phi(X_l) + b \geq +1$ for the positive samples and $\omega \cdot \Phi(X_l) + b \leq -1$ for the negative samples.

The margin maximization procedure is then transformed into a convex optimization problem:

$$\min_{\omega, b, \xi} \quad \frac{1}{2}\omega \cdot \omega + C \sum_{l=1}^{N} \xi_l$$
$$\text{subject to} \quad G_j(X_l) \cdot (\omega \cdot \Phi(X_l) + b) \geq 1 - \xi_l,$$
$$\xi_l \geq 0, l = 1, \ldots, N.$$

where $\xi_l \geq 0$ is the error slack variable and $C > 0$ is the penalty parameter for the training error. Using kernel, we can implicitly map the original input space X_l into a much higher dimensional feature space $\Phi(X_l)$ and the kernel function is defined as $\kappa(X_i, X_j) = < \Phi(X_i) \cdot \Phi(X_j) >$. In our current implementation, we select Gaussian radial basis function (RBF) as the kernel function with $\kappa(X_i, X_j) = \exp(-\gamma||X_i - X_j||^2)$, $\gamma > 0$, where γ and C are automatically determined by 10-fold cross-validation on the training set. The optimal parameters (C, γ) for some detection functions are given in Table 14.1.

Table 14.1. The optimal parameters (C, γ) of some detection functions

Salient	Brown horse	Grass	Purple flower	Red flower	Rock
C	8	10	6	32	32
γ	0.5	1.0	.05	0.125	2
Salient	Water	Human skin	Sky	Snow	Sunset/sunrise
C	2	2	8192	512	8
γ	0.5	0.125	0.03125	0.03125	0.5
Salient	Yellow flower	Forest	Sail cloth	Sand field	Waterfall
C	8	32	64	8	32
γ	0.5	0.125	0.125	2	0.0078125

At the testing phase, a new image will be first segmented with the same parameters using mean shift technique, and then low-level features $\hat{X}$ will be extracted for all the homogeneous regions. Finally the existence of certain salient objects will be predicted by $sgn(\omega \cdot \Phi(\hat{X}) + b)$.

After automatic segmentation and classification is done, we perform region merging for neighboring regions of the same class to obtain salient objects. This is shown as the second step in Figure 14.3. Although mean shift segmentation partitions single object into multiple homogeneous image regions with none of them being representative for the object, salient objects have the capacity to characterize the principal visual properties of the corresponding image object, and be visually distinguishable and meaningful to human beings. This can be found from examples of salient objects

Fig. 14.4. The detection results of salient objects: Grass.

Fig. 14.5. The detection results of salient objects: Sand Field.

in Figures 14.4 and 14.5. In addition, the key words for interpreting the salient objects can be used to achieve image annotation at the content level.

After the detection of salient objects, a set of visual features are calculated in preparation for the higher level conceptual modeling. They are 1-dimensional coverage ratio (i.e., density ratio) for a coarse shape representation, 6-dimensional object locations (i.e., 2 dimensions for region center and 4 dimensions to indicate the rectangular box for coarse shape representation of salient object), 7-dimensional LUV dominant colors and color variances, 14-dimensional Tamura texture, and 28-dimensional wavelet texture features.

14.4 Interpretation of Semantic Image Concepts

To interpret the semantic image concept quantitatively using the contextual relationship among salient objects, we use Gaussian mixture model (GMM) to approximate the class distribution for different types of the relevant salient objects:

$$P(X, C_j, \kappa, \omega_{c_j}, \Theta_{c_j}) = \sum_{i=1}^{\kappa} P(X|S_i, \theta_{s_i})\omega_{s_i} \qquad (14.2)$$

where $P(X|S_i, \theta_{s_i})$ is the ith multivariate Gaussian mixture components with n independent means and a common $n \times n$ covariance matrix, κ indicates the optimal number of mixture Gaussian components, $\Theta_{c_j} = \{\theta_{s_i}, i = 1, \ldots, \kappa\}$ is the set of the parameters for these mixture Gaussian components, $\omega_{c_j} = \{\omega_{s_i}, i = 1, \ldots, \kappa\}$ is the set of the relative weights among these mixture Gaussian components, $X = (x_1, \ldots, x_n)$ is the n-dimensional visual features that are used for representing the relevant salient objects. For example, the semantic concept, "beach scene," is related to at least three types (classes) of the salient objects such as "sea water," "sky pattern," "beach sand," and other hidden image patterns.

The visual characteristics of a certain type of these salient objects will look differently at different lighting and capturing conditions. For example, the salient object "sky pattern," it consists of various appearances, such as "blue sky pattern," "white(clear) sky pattern," "cloudy sky pattern," and "sunset/sunrise sky pattern," which have very different properties on color and texture under different viewing conditions. Thus, the data distribution for each type of these salient objects is approximated by using multiple mixture Gaussian components to accommodate the variability within the same class.

For a certain semantic image concept, the optimal number of mixture Gaussian components and their relative weights are acquired automatically through a machine learning process by using our adaptive EM algorithm [22]. It has the following advantages in comparison with the traditional EM algorithm [26]: (a) It does not require a careful initialization of the model structure by starting with a reasonably large number of mixture components, and the model parameters are initialized directly by using the labeled samples. (b) It is able to take advantage of negative samples to achieve discriminative classifier training. (c) It is able to escape the local extrema and enable a global solution by reorganizing the distribution of mixture components and modifying the optimal number of mixture components.

Once the GMM model for the N_c predefined semantic are obtained, our system takes the following steps to class a new image into semantic categories as shown in Figure 14.6: (1) Given a test image I_i, its salient objects are detected using our detection function from the SVM model obtained previously. Since it is common that one test image contain multiple salient objects S_j, we denote $I_i = \{S_1, S_2, \ldots, S_n\}$. (2) We calculate the class conditional probability for the salient object feature distributions, given each semantic image class: $P(X|C_j, \kappa, \omega_{c_j}, \Theta_{c_j})$. (3) The test image is finally classified into semantic image class C_j, that yields the maximum posterior probability:

$$P(C_j|X, I_i, \Theta) = \frac{P(X|C_j, \kappa, \omega_{c_j}, \Theta_{c_j})P(C_j)}{\sum_{j=1}^{N_c} P(X|C_j, \kappa, \omega_{c_j}, \Theta_{c_j})P(C_j)}$$

where $\Theta = \{\kappa, \omega_{c_j}, \Theta_{c_j}, j = 1, \ldots, N_c\}$ is the set of mixture parameters and relative weights, and $P(C_j)$ is the prior probability of the semantic image concepts C_j in the database. Thus this approach takes into account multiple salient objects detected within an image and model its class-conditional distribution of the relevant semantic image concept from the features of these salient objects. Some results of semantic image classification are shown in Figures 14.7, 14.8, and 14.9.

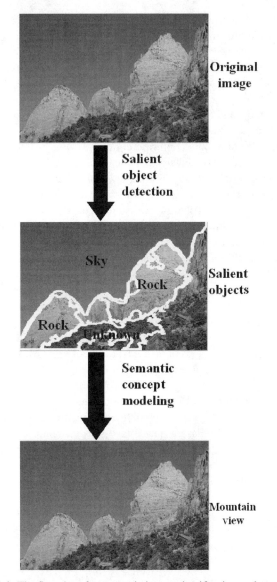

Fig. 14.6. The flowchart for semantic image classification and annotation.

Note that once we detect salient objects from a test image and obtain its image semantic class, we can use the text for keyword-based image retrieval. The salient object provides a natural image annotation at the content level, while the semantic category gives an annotation at the concept level. This multilevel annotation enables more power and expressiveness in semantic image retrieval and offers a common user more flexibility to specify their query concepts via various key words at different semantic levels.

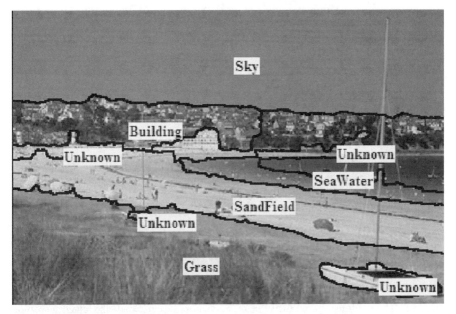

Fig. 14.7. The semantic image classification and annotation results for the semantic concepts "beach" with the most relevant salient objects.

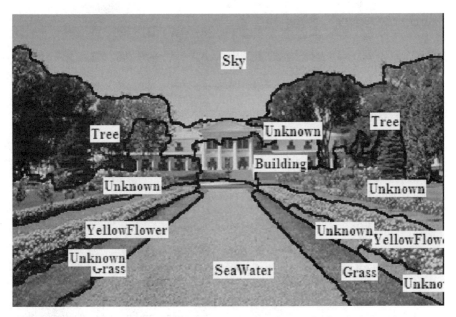

Fig. 14.8. The semantic image classification and annotation results for the semantic concepts "garden" with the most relevant salient objects.

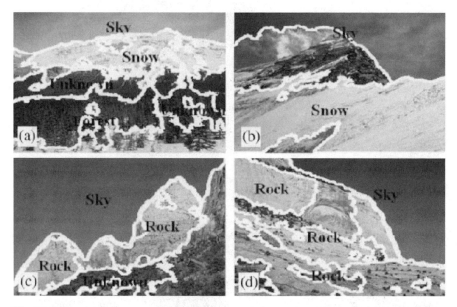

Fig. 14.9. The result for our multilevel image annotation system, where the image annotation includes the key word for the concept-sensitive salient objects "sky," "rock," "snow," "forest," and the semantic concept "mountain view."

14.5 Performance Evaluation

Our experiments are conducted on two image databases: photography database that is obtained from Google search engine and Corel image database. The photography database consists of 35,000 digital pictures, which are semantically labeled by the search key. The Corel image database includes more than 125,000 pictures with different image concepts. These images' semantics are labeled by their original categories maintained by Corel. All the unrepresentative image categories are manually removed for a better control experiment. Salient objects are labeled interactively within each image.

Precision ρ and recall ϱ are used to measure the average performance of our salient object detection functions:

$$\rho = \frac{\eta}{\eta + \varepsilon}, \qquad \varrho = \frac{\eta}{\eta + \vartheta} \tag{14.3}$$

where η is the set of true positive samples that are related to the corresponding type of salient object and detected correctly, ε is the set of false positive samples that are irrelevant to the corresponding type of salient object and detected incorrectly, ϑ is the set of false negative samples that are related to the corresponding type of salient object but misdetected. The average performance for some detection functions is given in Table 14.2.

Table 14.2. The average performance of some salient object detection functions.

Salient	Brown horse	Grass	Purple flower
ρ	95.6%	92.9%	96.1%
ϱ	100%	94.8%	95.2%
	Red flower	Rock	Sand field
ρ	87.8%	98.7%	98.8%
ϱ	86.4%	100%	96.6%
	Water	Human skin	Sky
ρ	86.7%	86.2%	87.6%
ϱ	89.5%	85.4%	94.5%
	Snow	Sunset/sunrise	Waterfall
ρ	86.7%	92.5%	88.5%
ϱ	87.5%	95.2%	87.1%
	Yellow flower	Forest	Sail cloth
ρ	87.4%	85.4%	96.3%
ϱ	89.3%	84.8%	94.9%
	Elephant	Cat	Zebra
ρ	85.3%	90.5%	87.2%
ϱ	88.7%	87.5%	85.4%

The *benchmark metric* for classifier evaluation includes *classification precision* α and *classification recall* β. They are defined as:

$$\alpha = \frac{\pi}{\pi + \tau}, \qquad \beta = \frac{\pi}{\pi + \mu} \qquad (14.4)$$

where π is the set of true positive samples that are related to the corresponding semantic concept and classified correctly, τ is the set of false positive samples that are irrelevant to the corresponding semantic concept and classified incorrectly, μ is the set of false negative samples that are related to the corresponding semantic concept but misclassified.

As mentioned above, two key issues may affect the performance of the classifiers: (a) the performance of our detection functions of salient objects; (b) the performance of the semantic classifier training techniques. Thus the real impacts for semantic image classification come from these two key issues, the *average precision* $\bar{\rho}$ and *average recall* $\bar{\varrho}$ are then defined as

$$\bar{\rho} = \rho \times \alpha, \qquad \bar{\varrho} = \varrho \times \beta \qquad (14.5)$$

where ρ and ϱ are the precision and recall for our detection functions of the relevant salient objects, α and β are the classification precision and recall for the semantic classifiers.

The average performance for our semantic image classification technique is obtained by averaging classification accuracy and misclassification ratio over the Corel images and the Google photographies. In order to identify the real impact of salient objects on semantic–sensitive image content characterization, we compared the performance differences for two image content characterization frameworks: one using image blobs and the other using salient objects. As shown in Table 14.3, one can

Table 14.3. The semantic image classification performance (i.e., average precision versus average recall) comparison using Gaussian Mixture Model—salient object vs. blob-based

Concept		Mountain view	Beach	Garden
Salient	$\bar{\rho}$	81.7%	80.5%	80.6%
Objects	$\bar{\varrho}$	84.3%	84.7%	90.6%
Image	$\bar{\rho}$	73.5%	73.6%	71.3%
Blobs	$\bar{\varrho}$	75.5%	75.9%	78.2%
		Sailing	Skiing	Desert
Salient	$\bar{\rho}$	87.6%	85.4%	89.6%
Objects	$\bar{\varrho}$	85.5%	83.7%	82.8%
Image	$\bar{\rho}$	79.5%	79.3%	76.6%
Blobs	$\bar{\varrho}$	77.3%	78.2%	78.5%

find that our image content characterization framework by using the salient objects outperform the semantic image classifier using image blobs.

In order to compare the performance of semantic image classification using different classifiers, we perform SVM training for image semantic interpretation at the conceptual level in comparison with the result of GMM model. The SVM training process starts with unification of the salient object feature spaces into a joint image feature space. Then the same SVM training process is preformed as described in Section 3, using RBF kernel. The resulting optimal parameters for these SVM classifiers are obtained from 10-fold cross-validation and shown in Table 14.4. The performance comparison for semantic image classification using GMM vs. SVM is shown in Table 14.5 in comparison with Table 14.3. By determining the optimal model structure and reorganizing the distributions of mixture components in our adaptive EM algorithm, our proposed classifiers are very competitive with the SVM classifiers.

14.6 Conclusions

This chapter has proposed a novel framework to achieve a multilevel semantic image annotation and classification. First, salient objects are detected using Support Vector Machine for a natural middle-level image content representation. Then, Gaussian Mixture Model is trained on top of the features of salient objects to accommodate the visual variability within each semantic image category.

Table 14.4. The optimal parameters (C, γ) of the SVM classifiers for semantic concepts

Semantic concept	Mountain view	Beach	Garden
C	512	32	312
γ	0.0078	0.125	0.03125
	Sailing	Skiing	Desert
C	56	128	8
γ	0.625	4	2

Table 14.5. The semantic image classification performance comparison using Support Vector Machine—salient object vs. blob-based.

Concept		Mountain view	Beach	Garden
Salient	$\bar{\rho}$	81.2%	81.1%	79.3%
Objects	$\bar{\varrho}$	80.5%	82.3%	84.2%
Image	$\bar{\rho}$	80.1%	75.4%	74.7%
Blobs	$\bar{\varrho}$	76.6%	76.3%	79.4%
		Sailing	Skiing	Desert
Salient	$\bar{\rho}$	85.5%	84.6%	85.8%
Objects	$\bar{\varrho}$	86.3%	87.3%	88.8%
Image	$\bar{\rho}$	72.5%	76.3%	73.6%
Blobs	$\bar{\varrho}$	75.6%	79.4%	81.7%

Based on this novel semantic-sensitive image content representation and semantic image concept interpretation framework, our semantic image classification system has achieved very good performance in our large-scale experimentation with natural images. More importantly, it provides a flexible way for novice users to query images by key words.

References

1. Smeulders A, Worring M, Santini S, Gupta A, Jain R. Content-based image retrieval at the end of the early years. *IEEE Trans. on PAMI* 2000;22:1349–1380.
2. Chang S, Chen W, Sundaram H. Semantic visual templates: linking visual features to semantics. *Proc. ICIP* 1998.
3. Mojsilovic A, Kovacevic J, Hu J, Safranek R, Ganapathy S. Matching and retrieval based on the vocabulary and grammar of color patterns, *IEEE Trans. on Image Processing* 2000;9:38–54.
4. Forsyth D, Fleck M. Body plan. *Proc. of CVPR* 1997: 678–683.
5. Carson C, Belongie S, Greenspan H, Malik J, Blobworld: Image segmentation using expectation–maximization and its application to image querying. *IEEE Trans.* PAMI 2002;24(8).
6. Wang J, Li J, Wiederhold G. SIMPLIcity: Semantic-sensitive integrated matching for picture libraries. *IEEE Trans. on PAMI* 2001.
7. Wang W, Song Y, Zhang A., Semantic-based image retrieval by region saliency. *Proc. CIVR* 2002.
8. Smith J, Li C. Image classification and querying using composite region templates. *Computer Vision and Image Understanding* 1999;75.
9. Lipson P, Grimson E, Sinha P, Configuration based scene and image indexing, *Proc. CVPR* 1997.
10. Torralba A, Oliva A. Semantic organization of scenes using discriminant structural templates. *Proc. ICCV* 1999.
11. Vailaya A, Figueiredo M, Jain A, Zhang H. Image classification for content-based indexing. *IEEE Trans. on Image Processing* 2001;10:117–130.
12. Chang E, Goh K, Sychay G, Wu G. CBSA: Content-based annotation for multimodal image retrieval using Bayes point machines. *IEEE Trans. CSVT* 2002.

13. Weber M, Welling M, Perona P. Towards automatic discovery of object categories. *Proc. CVPR* 2000.
14. Luo J, Etz S. A physical model-based approach to detecting sky in photographic images. *IEEE Trans. on Image Processing* 2002;11.
15. Li S, Lv X, Zhang H, View-based clustering of object appearances based on independent subspace analysis. *Proc. IEEE ICCV* 2001: 295–300.
16. Benitez A, Chang S. Semantic knowledge construction from annotated image collections. *Proc. ICME* 2002.
17. Aslandogan A, Their C, Yu C, Zon J, Rishe N, Image retrieval using WordNet. *ACM SIGIR* 1997.
18. Zhu X, Huang T. Unifying keywords and visual contents in image retrieval. *IEEE Multimedia* 2002:23–33.
19. Blei D, Jordan M. Modeling annotated data. *ACM SIGIR* 2003:127–134.
20. Branard K, Duygulu P, Freitas N de, Forsyth D, Blei D, Jordan MI. Matching words and pictures. *Journal of Machine Learning Research* 2003;3:1107–1135.
21. Wu Y, Tian Q, Huang TS. Discriminant-EM algorithm with application to image retrieval. *Proc. CVPR* 2000:222–227.
22. Fan J, Luo H, Elmagarmid AK. Concept-oriented indexing of video database: towards more effective retrieval and browsing. *IEEE Trans. on Image Processing* 2004;13(5).
23. Comanicu D, Meer P. Mean shift: A robust approach toward feature space analysis. *IEEE Trans. PAMI* 2002;24.
24. Tong S, Chang E. Support Vector Machine active learning for image retrieval. *ACM Multimedia* 2001.
25. Joachims T. Transductive inference for text classification using support vector machine. *Proceedings of ICML* 1999.
26. McLachlan G, Krishnan T. *The EM Algorithm and Extensions*, Wiley, New York, 2000.

15. Extracting Semantics Through Dynamic Context

Xin Li, William Grosky, Nilesh Patel, and Farshad Fotouhi

Summary. In this chapter, we introduce an MPEG-7 friendly system to extract semantics of aerial image regions semiautomatically, through the mediation of user feedback. Geographic information applications are unique in that their domain is highly dynamic. Such data sets are a singularly appropriate environment in which to illustrate our approach to emergent semantics extraction.

15.1 Introduction

Recently, many methods have been proposed to segment images and label image regions for content-based image region retrieval and annotation [1, 2]. In this chapter, we introduce a new MPEG-7 friendly system that integrates a feedback process with image segmentation and region recognition, supporting users in the extraction of image region semantics in highly dynamic environments.

Extracting semantics from image regions refers to labeling their semantic content with a set of semantic descriptors. This can be performed either manually, automatically, or, as in some experimental systems where user-friendly interfaces are provided, semiautomatically. Given an image collection as input, such a system does the following: segments the images and clusters the resulting regions according to their properties; provides the ability to efficiently index and query by image regions; and uses specific standards to describe the semantic content of these regions. This topic is attracting increasing interest as information technology proliferates throughout our society, and it is especially being encouraged by the development of the World Wide Web as a digital communications infrastructure.

The topics discussed in the remainder of this chapter is as follows. In Section 15.2, we touch on some existing work in the area of feedback-based semantic extraction for image data. Section 15.3 presents our overall system architecture, whereas Sections 15.4 and 15.5 discuss our approaches to segmentation and semantics extraction, respectively. Section 15.6 presents an experimental justification for the power of our system, whereas Section 15.7 covers our system's MPEG-7 compatibility. Finally, in Section 15.8, we present our conclusions and possible improvements to our system.

15.2 Related Work

Despite the large amount of research in this field, there are few matured systems folded into applications, because of several difficulties, the most important of which is the problem of the semantic gap [3], the mismatch between users' high-level semantic concepts and the way that systems try to describe these concepts using low-level image features. Experience has shown that it is extremely difficult to find a general approach to accurately describe abstract semantic concepts by simply using low-level image features in a straightforward manner.

To overcome the semantic gap, and because of the fact that users often do not have the necessary domain knowledge for content-based image retrieval (CBIR) applications, many user feedback methods have been proposed. Their goal is to learn interactively the semantic queries that users have in mind, overcoming the semantic gap through user interaction [4]. In [5], it is proposed to start this user interaction process from a coarse query, allowing the users to refine their queries as much as necessary. Most of the time, user information consists of annotations (labels) indicating whether or not an image belongs to a desired category. In such a strategy, the system would use these labels to refine the computation of new relevant images.

Semantic labels comprise potential domain knowledge that can be reused in future interaction processes [6, 7]. The accumulation of labels during many retrieval sessions constitutes knowledge about the database content. Semantic learning, which exploits this information, enables the system to enhance the representation of the images, and thus, to increase its overall performance.

In [8], these feedback methods are defined as a continuous refining process over CBIR query space:

$$Q = \{I_Q, S_Q, F_Q, Z_Q\} \tag{15.1}$$

where I_Q is the selected image set from the whole image archive, S_Q is the selected image feature set, F_Q is the selected similarity function, and Z_Q is the set of labels to capture the semantics. Notice that all the four elements are goal dependent, and therefore, depend on specific applications and users.

In most CBIR systems that support feedback processes, the query and labeling processes are iterated. These systems try to learn a user's goals, and update the query space automatically or semiautomatically. This iterative process will continue until the user feels satisfied with the query results. Therefore, such an interactive session can be described as a series of state changes over the query space:

$$\{Q^1, Q^2, \ldots, Q^n\} \tag{15.2}$$

where Q^n captures the user's goals. In most of these approaches, however, it is assumed that the users know the image set, features, and similarity function. Unfortunately, this assumption may not be true in many applications. For example, geographic information systems often need to handle incremental data. Also, different users may choose different similarity functions for different applications. However, most users cannot specify these at the start, as they need to see the query results to decide whether the current query space fulfills their semantic concepts. Therefore, the learning process is the key issue for CBIR systems that support feedback processes.

Normally, as data sets grow large and the available processing power matches that growth, the opportunity arises to learn from experience [8]. Taking advantage of this, in [9], learning semantics from examples for CBIR applications is considered as a traditional classification problem. Different techniques are discussed and compared concerning this issue.

Although the above systems discuss user feedback, most of them do not address extracting region semantics. Also, geographic information applications often show properties of increasing data and emergent domain knowledge. It is often the case that user semantics evolve on the basis of interaction with a particular geographic data management system. These systems need to learn from example queries in order to decide the segments and corresponding semantics in the feedback process. On the other hand, users also need to see query results to decide whether the next step should be resegmentation or labeling. Therefore, when we extend the feedback process to the finer granularity of image regions, the situation will become more complex, as systems needs to learn from examples to label existing regions, as well as to perform frequent resegmentation in order to generate new regions.

15.3 System Architecture

In most cases, it is very hard to generate a proper segmentation without proper domain knowledge. For example, users normally do not know the number of clusters when they try to utilize a clustering-based segmentation method. Also, they do not know the criterion for merging regions when they try to perform a region growing method for image segmentation. Thus, we cannot expect accurate image segmentation in the initial segmentation stage. Instead, we update the segments on the basis of user interaction. Therefore, by extending user interaction to the finer granularity of image regions, the system can learn to label regions, as well as to generate new ones.

Our system supports extracting an emergent segmentation and semantics through dynamic context. Figure 15.1 shows the data flowchart of our system. In our approach, there are two kernel data structures. The first one is an image region database that stores each image region's property data, such as various histograms, position, and a pixel list. The second kernel data structure is a decision tree that is rebuilt each time

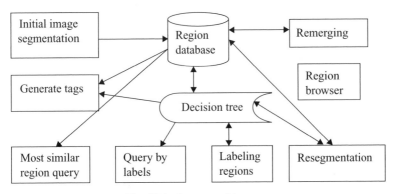

Fig. 15.1. System architecture.

a user labels a region. Our system supports performing initial segmentation, labeling regions, resegmenting regions, browsing regions, querying regions, and generating MPEG-7 tags for regions. In our approach, the system automatically selects the next proper region for the user to label through our interface.

15.4 Segmentation

We have developed two approaches for the initial segmentation stage as well as for any subsequent resegmentation: a chi-square–based approach and a kruskal-Wallis–based approach. The former is a supervised method, whereas the latter is unsupervised. These methods are integrated into a unified framework to support further labeling and resegmentation, as users may want to refine or update their labeling and image segmentation.

Even though users may not have enough domain knowledge in advance, they can still avoid the tedious process of selecting proper template regions for training, as the semantics of these image regions will be extracted gradually through effective user interaction. Therefore, initial segmentation is not a crucial stage in our method, although we do discuss its details in this chapter, as it generates image regions for further analysis.

Most of the existing image segmentation methods fit into two categories: boundary detecting-based approaches, which partition an image by discovering closed boundary contours, and clustering-based approaches, which group similar neighboring pixels into clusters [10]. These methods try to explore two basic properties of pixels in relation to their local neighborhood: discontinuity and similarity, respectively. Unfortunately, they both suffer some weaknesses due to local noise.

In boundary detecting approaches, conventional border detection techniques are widely used to detect discontinuities in pixel properties. However, in many cases, it is hard to detect the real border, because of noise inside regions that do not have uniform properties. Most of the conventional border detection techniques assume that edges in images are areas with strong intensity contrasts—a jump in local features from one pixel to the next (or from one sliding window to the next).

Thus, these approaches suffer the problem of overdetecting false borders, where local features vary dramatically. We show an example of how the texture changes in a region of the sea in an aerial image in Figure 15.2. In this example, we notice that the texture property of the sea area that is near the shore changes dramatically, which may cause a false border using conventional edge detection algorithms.

15.4.1 Chi-Square Method

In our chi-square–based approach, our method has the following steps:

1. Generate all possible regions with an existing clustering method.
2. Merge very small regions to larger regions.
3. Decide real borders from all possible borders and perform a region-growing algorithm.

Fig. 15.2. Example aerial image.

In the first stage of our initial approach, we perform a two-dimensional Haar wavelet transform over the original image to extract corresponding wavelet coefficients and then use linear interpolation to extend the size of the wavelet coefficients matrix to that of the original image. We compute the feature for each pixel with coordinates (x, y) below:

$$F_m = \frac{1}{n \times n} \sum_{i=1}^{n \times n} W(x_i, y_i) \tag{15.3}$$

$$F_d = W(x, y) - F_m \tag{15.4}$$

where $n \times n$ is the size of sliding window whose center is (x, y); features F_m and F_d are the local mean and deviation for each pixel over its neighborhood (sliding window). We then choose some sample regions on the basis of their texture, manually label them with key words for future classification, and compute the feature vector (F_m, F_d) of pixels from these sample regions. Considering the domain of our application, the textures of aerial image regions with the same semantic meaning are quite stable. We assume that such feature vectors of pixels follow certain normal distributions. Therefore, we can estimate the corresponding parameters $N(\mu_i, \sigma_i)$ through sample regions that belong to particular clusters.

Our last step is to compute the chi-square intensity for each sliding window whose center is (x, y). Assuming that all pixel feature vectors are independent, and that they follow the normal distribution of the ith semantic class with parameters, the chi-square intensity is

$$\sum_{k=1}^{m} (x_k - \mu_i)^T \times \sigma_i^{-1} \times (x_k - \mu_i) \tag{15.5}$$

where $n \times n$ is the number of pixels in each sliding window, x_k is the two-dimensional feature vector of pixel k in the given sliding window, μ_i is the two-dimensional mean vector of the ith semantic class, and σ_i is the 2×2 covariance matrix of the ith semantic class.

According to our assumption, this chi-square value follows the centered chi-square distribution with free degree of $n \times n \times d$, where $d = 2$ is the dimensionality of the pixel feature vector. Therefore, on the basis of Bayes rule, we derive that pixel (x, y) belongs to the ith semantic class as long as its chi-square value is smallest.

In the second stage, we diminish those very small patches in the result of the first stage for the convenience of the third stage. We order regions from the first stage by their area and merge any region whose area is smaller than a given threshold. For each pixel in the region to be merged, we compute its adjacent pixels. If the given pixel is adjacent to some other regions, we assign this pixel to the region with the most pixels adjacent to the given pixel. With this method, we gradually grow all the regions that are adjacent to the region to be merged, until this region is diminished.

We cannot detect complete real borders by directly computing the chi-square intensity from the original image, because this intensity changes dramatically along the border. We have to generate all border candidates through a clustering method in the split stage and detect the real border by computing mean chi-square intensities along these possible borders.

Figure 15.3 shows the comparison of the segmentation result: the left segmentation result is generated from clustering Haar wavelet coefficients by the fuzzy c-mean clustering method, while the right segmentation result is generated from the chi-square method. Notice that, compared to the fuzzy c-mean clustering method, the chi-square method alleviates the problem of oversegmentation, as the chi-square method diminishes small patches and has merged adjacent regions without dramatic change of chi-square intensity along the possible borders.

We then use a decision tree to recognize the regions. First, we compute the percentile of each pixel for each semantic cluster based on Bayes rule:

$$P(C_i | (F_m, F_d)) = \frac{P((F_m, F_d)|C_i)P(C_i)}{\sum_{j=1}^{m} P((F_m, F_d)|C_j)P(C_j)} \tag{15.6}$$

where $P(C_i)$ refers to the probability of an image containing pixels belonging to semantic group i, $P((F_m, F_d)|C_i)$ refers to the probability of a pixel having feature

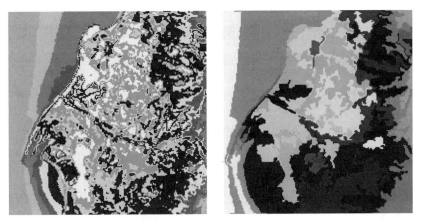

Fig. 15.3. Comparison of segmentation results.

value (F_m, F_d), given that it is in semantic cluster i, $P(C_i|(F_m, F_d))$ refers to the probability of a pixel belong to semantic cluster i, given its feature value as (F_m, F_d), and m is the number of semantic clusters (key words).

As a simplification, assuming that $P(C_1) = P(C_2) = .. = P(C_m)$, we can compute the percentile as

$$P(C_i|(F_m, F_d)) = \frac{P((F_m, F_d)|C_i)}{\sum\limits_{j=1}^{m} P((F_m, F_d)|C_j)} \tag{15.7}$$

and compute the feature vector $(P_1, P_2, \ldots, P_m)$ for each region as

$$P_i = \frac{\sum\limits_{k=1}^{l} P(C_i|(F_{m_k}, F_{d_k}))}{l} \tag{15.8}$$

where l is the number of pixels in the merged regions. Finally, we build a decision tree for regions, on the basis of the feature vector $(P_1, P_2, \ldots, P_m)$. We train this decision tree by feature vectors of sample regions and label regions, using this decision tree.

Our work shows that classification methods can be utilized for region recognition, but we also realize that there is more work to be done for improvement. First, users have to select enough sample regions to train the decision tree properly. Not only does this increase the workload of users, however, but it also makes the quality of the end result very sensitive to individual user selections. If a user does not select proper sample regions or simply does not include a given semantic class, the recognition power will be reduced. Second, the centroids of the different semantic classes of image regions can be close, creating noise that affects the recognition quality. This problem limits the number of semantic classes that we can recognize. We also have assumed that the probabilities of pixels belonging to each semantic class are equal. Experience shows, however, that this assumption may not apply to different image collections. Finally, we notice that we need to describe a similarity distance of sliding windows more related to human perception. Therefore, our work has focused on the following aspects.

1. Reduce users' interaction loads and instrumentally-based subjective factors that negatively affect the system's power.
2. Extend our work to a complete database environment.

Generally, we notice that many problems are due to the fact that users initially lack domain knowledge. For example, users do not know in advance how many image region classes there are, nor do they know in advance the proper label set. Unfortunately, our initial method depends on knowing this domain knowledge, as it is used to derive various parameters. Therefore, this prompts us to turn to unsupervised methods to reduce the workload for the users and the requirements for applying our method.

15.4.2 Kruskal–Wallis Method

Our Kruskal–Wallis–based image segmentation approach has the following steps.

1. Generate all possible regions with an existing clustering method and store the wavelet decomposition data in MPEG-7 format.
2. Diminish small patches.
3. Merge the possible regions based on the nonparametric statistical method of the Kruskal–Wallis test.

In the third stage, we detect real borders and merge those possible regions. Our first step is to extract the borders along all those possible regions. As we have segmented the image, it is easy to use existing edge detection methods to detect the possible borders. There are many false borders in the image due to oversegmentation, however, and it is natural that users may want to incorporate some global information to merge these regions. The key idea here is to detect the change of features along each border, rather than globally. In Figure 15.2, notice that even the regions with the same semantic meaning have largely varying texture, such as sea areas. This problem causes oversegmentation, as similarity-based methods only cluster the pixels or sliding windows based on local features, without considering changes in their neighborhoods. Unfortunately, it is very hard to define the scope of a proper neighborhood, as this depends on the context of images and the application domain. In our case, we can define the scope of neighborhoods as pixels or sliding windows along the possible borders within a certain distance.

The Kruskal–Wallis test is a nonparametric test for comparing three or more independent groups of sampled data independent of their distributions. It is utilized as an alternative to the independent group ANOVA when the assumption of normality or equality of variance is not met. This method is similar to many other nonparametric tests, and is based on an analysis of variances using the ranks of the data values instead of the data values themselves to calculate the statistics. The hypotheses for the comparison of two independent groups are:

- H_0: The samples come from identical populations.
- H_1: The samples come from different populations.

In our method, we perform a Kruskal–Wallis test with three groups of data to decide whether the border is false and that we should merge two adjacent regions A and B: the neighborhood pixels in regions A and B along the border, as well as the pixels on the border itself. Our assumption is that if the border is false, the texture change across the border should be moderate and gradual. A Kruskal–Wallis test will show that these groups of pixels come from an identical population. On the other hand, if the border is real, the change across the border will be dramatic, and the Kruskal–Wallis test will show that the groups of pixels come from different populations.

$$P = \text{Kruskal–Wallis}(G_{\text{regionA}}, G_{\text{border}}, G_{\text{regionB}}) \tag{15.9}$$

where G_{regionA}, G_{border}, and G_{regionB} are feature values from the appropriate groups of pixels. If P is more than the threshold, we will merge the two regions; otherwise, we will leave the border as a real border. Figure 15.4 shows an example of segmentation after we have merged some regions. Notice that oversegmentation is reduced, both on the sea and on land areas.

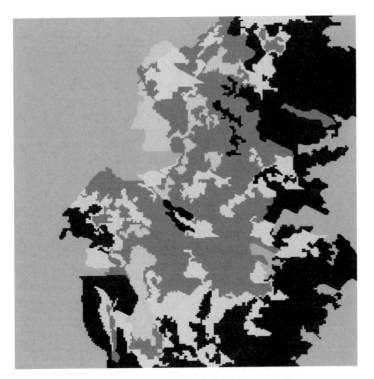

Fig. 15.4. Results of Kruskal–Wallis method.

To recognize the regions using the Kruskal–Wallis method, we predefine a given number of nodes for this approach, each one corresponding to a possible semantic category for the region descriptors. After the clustering, we choose a number of random, so-called template, regions that cluster around each node, and annotate them manually, choosing a semantic category in which all of these regions participate. Notice that we label each cluster according to template regions that are generated automatically (the system will generate the template regions whose features are closest to the centroids of the clusters). Once a particular cluster is labeled, all the regions in that cluster will be labeled with same key word.

15.5 Extracting Semantics

As we previously discussed, to reduce the workload and inherent instrumental subjectivity of the users, we tried the unsupervised Kruskal–Wallis method. However, it turns out that an unsupervised method also has its weaknesses. It is hard to know certain domain knowledge in advance, such as the appropriate number of clusters and the threshold of merging two adjacent image regions. Therefore, it is a natural extension to build a system that supports a feedback process. By implementing such a system with a convenient interface that can learn from patterns given by the users during interaction, we reduce the workload of the users, as well as the risk inherent in subjectively selecting the template image regions, as the users always can resegment and reclassify the image regions according to the latest domain knowledge that they have. In this section, we will introduce the functionality of our system and show its effectiveness.

In our system, even though we inherit the image segmentation result of Kruskal–Wallis method, we provide a convenient interface to label the image regions, as well as to resegment the images based on knowledge gained by the users. For example, if two adjacent regions have the same label according to either user interaction or the system's classification, these two adjacent regions need to be merged into one new region. Therefore, each time a user labels a region, the decision tree may be changed, with a resultant change in the segmentation of every image.

To improve performance, the system only performs remerging over the image being browsed. The remainder of the images will not be remerged according to the updated decision tree until the users actually view them. Each image has a dirty bit. Once the decision tree is updated, all the dirty bits will be set to 1. If an image is remerged, the corresponding dirty bit will be reset to 0.

Each region that the users label is considered as ground truth. Thus, the label for these regions will be considered correct and never changed. These cases will also be added to the decision tree as training data. If the decision tree has been updated, all dirty bits will be set for the remerging process.

The nonground truth regions will be reevaluated according to the decision tree each time a user labels a region as ground truth, but only some of these regions will be assigned labels. We have built a system that supports a feedback process. The domain knowledge will continue to grow as long as the users continue to label the regions.

Thus, the decision tree will also keep growing until the users are satisfied. Initially, there are few ground truth cases, and the decision tree often can overfit the training data. Labels generated under these conditions may not be very accurate. When users continuously input new ground truth cases, however, the decision tree will become more stable. In our algorithm, after reevaluating the regions' labels according to the updated decision tree, only the regions whose features have distances less than a given threshold to those of the nearest ground truth cases with the same labels will be assigned semantic labels, the rest of the regions remaining as unknown. Note that it is possible that labels for these regions can be changed in the next round of labeling, as the decision tree keeps growing and being updated.

Finally, the system will request that users label uncertain cases. These cases are defined as the unknown regions that are nearest to the current ground truth case in the feature space. Labeling them will expand the known area of semantic classes in the space of features. Therefore, each time a user labels a region, both the number of ground truth cases and the number of uncertain cases increase. This functionality can help the users label the regions more efficiently, as they need not label those regions of which the system is quite sure (the regions that are very close to the ground truth cases in the feature space). Therefore, the feedback process affects not only the system by providing training data on the one hand, but also a user's next labeling action on the other hand.

The interface also allows the user to ask the system to identify the region that should be labeled next. This is an important strategy, as the system will decide which region is worth labeling for the purpose of efficient learning.

15.5.1 Image Resegmentation

We merge two adjacent regions only if they have the same semantic label. Even though the segmentation of an image can be changed over time, the unknown regions in this image will remain the same, as they do not have any semantic labels assigned to them. Therefore, all the remaining uncertain regions will never change because of remerging, as they are also unknown regions. They can only be affected by two factors: an unknown region can be assigned an uncertain semantic label when the decision tree is rebuilt or a ground truth semantic label when a user directly labels it; on the other hand, new uncertain regions can be generated when a user labels an uncertain region as a ground truth region. By implementing this schema, we avoid remerging regions from all images each time a user labels a region. The system only remerges regions from a particular image when necessary. The effect of this is the same as remerging regions from all images immediately after reclassification, as the ground truth cases, uncertain cases, and the images presented to the users are always updated according to the latest knowledge.

The size of the image regions will increase if remerging is performed, and decrease if resegmentation is performed. Remerging is automatically triggered when users browse image regions, while resegmentation is triggered manually by the users. Figures 15.5 and 15.6 show an example of remerging and resegmentation. Initially, this region is segmented incorrectly, as it contains both sea and urban areas. The user

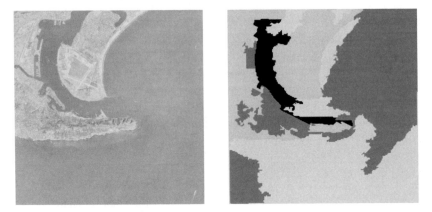

Fig. 15.5. Initial segmentation results.

resegments the current region in the first step. In the second step, the user labels other regions and accumulates ground truth cases. When domain knowledge accumulates to a certain point, the two adjacent sea regions are merged together as they have the same semantic label. Finally, when the user is satisfied, this image is completely labeled and the corresponding MPEG-7 tags are generated.

In Figure 15.5, we show an image with its initial segmentation result. Figure 15.6 shows an example of how a recognized region in an image grows when a user continuously labels other sea regions. Compared with the initial segmentation method, there are two advantages. First, segmentation can be changed according to domain knowledge. For example, a mixed region can be split because of resegmentation. Second, users need not predefine many parameters such as the number of clusters, and need not provide a predefined training set. Thus, the system avoids some potential problems due to the lack of domain knowledge, such as an error in labeling, due to

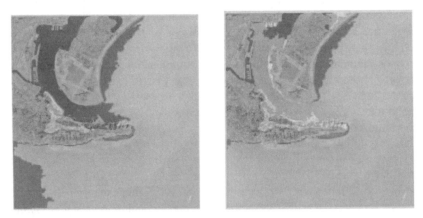

Fig. 15.6. Recognition results.

an improper training set. Instead, users can adjust the training sets during interactive sessions.

Relabeling a region either with an existing label or with a new label will update the decision tree, automatically affecting the labels of other regions. This is particularly convenient for users who do not have enough domain knowledge in advance. For example, a user may only know at first that there are two categories of regions: *sea* and *land*. After a series of interactive labeling, he realizes that there should be more subcategories for land. Therefore, he relabels some regions previously labeled as *land*, by the labels *urban area* or *trees*. Therefore, users can extract an emergent semantics through a dynamic context. They need not know the number of clusters and proper label sets in advance. Instead, they can label regions incrementally. This is a particular advantage of our system, especially for applications that need to handle incremental data and fulfill the requirements of different users, as it is very hard to give a unified predefined training data set and a corresponding label set in the initial segmentation stage.

Because users often do not have enough domain knowledge in advance, they often do not have a proper predefined set of key words at the very beginning of the labeling process, nor know the proper granularity of the region clusters. Therefore, users initially can set the number of classes too small, causing a very scattered distribution of the features from the same class. This suggests that there can be more semantic subclasses of the features with different semantic meaning, and that we need to reclassify the features with a finer granularity. For example, a user can find that it is too general to describe the content of image regions with the label *land*, as the texture properties and semantic meanings of regions with this label are very different. Therefore, this user needs to refine the semantic class of *land* with more detailed semantic classes, such as *urban area* and *farm*.

To control this reclustering process, we need a parameter, called a *reclustering index* in our system, to evaluate the scatter degree of the distribution of the features in a particular semantic cluster. The average distance of each data element from the centroid of the same class serves as its definition. If this parameter is larger than a given threshold, the system will prompt the users to perform a reclustering process.

$$\text{Reclustering Index}_j = \frac{1}{n} \sum_{i=1}^{n} \text{Distance}(x_i^j, \text{centroid}_j) \qquad (15.10)$$

$$\text{centroid}_j = \frac{1}{n} \sum_{i=1}^{n} x_i^j \qquad (15.11)$$

The reclustering index for each semantic class is shown on our interface. For example, suppose that the reclustering index for the *land* class is much larger than that for the *sea* class. This suggests that the *land* semantic class may need refining. To refine our labeling, the user can retrieve all regions with the *land* label by a label query. This process can continue until the users are satisfied. The reclustering index provides the users with a measurement for the goodness of the existing semantic classes. However, the users will make the final decisions, as to whether to generate

Fig. 15.7. An image segmentation and label example (recognized manually).

new semantic classes. As long as this process continues, new labels will be generated continuously by the users to extract an emergent semantics in a dynamic context.

Figure 15.7 shows an example of an image that is labeled manually by the user. We use this ground truth example and a series of snapshots, shown in Figure 15.8, to show some subsequent image segmentation and labeling. In these snapshots, the blue area represents sea; the cyan area represents an urban area; the red area represents a trees area; and the white area represents an unknown area. Each snapshot was taken after six labeling actions. Notice that some white area still remains, which suggests that the process will continue.

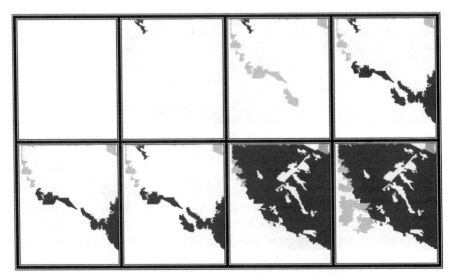

Fig. 15.8. Snapshots of image segmentation and the labels of the regions.

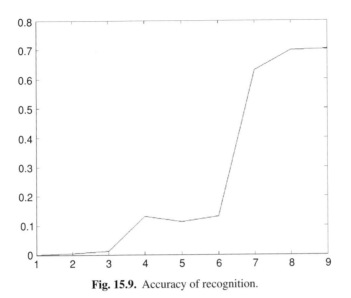

Fig. 15.9. Accuracy of recognition.

15.6 Experimental Results

In our approach, we use the aerial images from the USC-SIPI image database for our new approach. This image database (http://sipi.usc.edu/database/Database.html) is maintained by the Electrical Engineering Department at University of Southern California. We used only the images of resolution 1024×1024, and transformed them into gray scale images, as we are concerned with employing texture-based features for CBIR applications. In our experiment, we generated 1168 regions in the initial segmentation stage.

To evaluate the performance of recognition accuracy, we computed this measure as follows:

$$\text{accuracy} = \frac{\text{Number of Correctly Labeled Pixels}}{\text{Total Number of Pixels}} \quad (15.12)$$

Figure 15.9 shows the recognition accuracy of nine snapshots, the first of eight of which are taken from Figure 15.8. Each snapshot was taken after six labeling actions. Notice that the recognition accuracy increases smoothly at first, then increases dramatically when the number of ground truth cases reaches a certain amount, after which it increases smoothly again. This shows that when the domain knowledge accumulates to a certain amount, the recognition accuracy can be greatly affected.

We also compare our feedback approach with that of the chi-square and decision tree method that we mentioned before, using the same training sets.

This result shows that our feedback system is promising (see Table 15.1), not only because of the current recognition result, but its potential to further improve by

Table 15.1. Comparison of recognition accuracy.

Chi-square and decision tree method	0.6707
Feedback system	0.7025

more interactions. For example, we can improve our resegmentation method for more accurate region set or improve the learning strategies to reduce users' workload.

15.7 Supporting MPEG-7

In our system, we integrate several MPEG-7 descriptors to describe the semantic content of image regions. These descriptors are extended to a database environment (eXist). We also discuss the access strategy of the database system for these descriptors and the schema that manages the incremental database. As our system utilizes the accumulated training set during interactive sessions, users can extract emergent semantics to a deeper level. With this user interaction, users can more accurately extract the structure of the high-level concepts in their mind, carry out the relabeling processes with more convenience, reduce the reclustering load of the system, avoid the potential problems due to the lack of domain knowledge, and manage the increased data more efficiently.

In our approach, aerial images are stored in an aerial image database while various MPEG-7 image descriptors are stored in the eXist database system. Image insertion and querying are multistage processes that overlap somewhat, producing various types of MPEG-7 descriptors that are stored in an integrated fashion in eXist.

We used MATLAB and eXist software to implement our system. eXist is an Open Source native XML database featuring efficient, index-based XQuery processing, automatic indexing, extensions for full-text search, XUpdate support, and tight integration with existing XML development tools. The database implements the current XQuery 1.0 working draft as of November 2003, with the exception of the XML schema related features. The database is lightweight, completely written in Java, and may be easily deployed in a number of ways, running either as a stand-alone server process, inside a servlet-engine, or directly embedded into an application.

After we label clusters of image regions with key words, we generate the corresponding MPEG-7 files to describe their semantics. These files will be loaded in eXist to support further XQuery and XUpdate.

15.8 Conclusion

We have investigated several different methods to negotiate the semantic gap in different stages of the image segmentation and annotation process, and have the following summary.

1. Clustering-based image segmentation methods often tend to generate an oversegmented result. Because of the lack of domain knowledge, these methods often fail to integrate global image information and generate scattered image regions

according to dramatic changes of the neighborhood features. Therefore, it is a natural extension for us to utilize a split-and-merge process to reduce the over-segmentation. The crucial idea is to merge adjacent regions that do not have a dramatic change of texture property along their borders. Notice that our methods merge the adjacent regions based on the changes of texture properties along the entire border between them. Thus, we utilize global image information to reduce the oversegmentation. We implemented both supervised (chi-square–based) and unsupervised (Kruskal–Wallis–based) methods. These methods have been integrated into our system. However, we notice the split-and-merge process can only achieve limited success for image segmentation and annotation due to the lack of domain knowledge. For example, in the chi-square–based method, users need to decide the number of semantic classes and provide proper training examples for each semantic class, while in the Kruskal–Wallis method, users need to decide the merge threshold of adjacent image regions. These parameters and training sets need to be predefined by the users in advance. However, as we mentioned previously, in most CBIR applications, the users do not have such domain knowledge at the start. Instead, they need to accumulate this knowledge through a dynamic context. Thus, lacking domain knowledge comprises the main difficulty of our methods utilizing split-and-merge processes.

2. We have integrated image segmentation and classification into a feedback process. As we emphasized previously, when we extend CBIR applications from images to image regions, the data object set still needs to be automatically updated, even though the users do not add new images. This is an obvious difference from those feedback systems concerning only with global images, as initial image segmentation normally cannot be accurate due to the lack of domain knowledge. Instead, image segmentations need to be updated as the system continues to learn patterns from the user's interactions in order to perform classification and resegmentation.

3. We direct the users to label specific uncertain regions to extract semantics efficiently. As the system needs to learn the domain knowledge through a dynamic context, efficient learning is important for user interaction. Normally, the system expects to know the label of the unknown regions whose features are far enough from the already-known ones (ground truth cases). We expect that the ground truth cases (regions that the users label) are evenly distributed in the feature space spanned by all the region features.

4. We have integrated different MPEG-7 descriptors in a dynamic context to extract emerging semantics. MPEG-7 has shown its potential in some projects. However, current work focuses on describing the semantics of the entire image, rather than individual image regions. Besides, most of the works test only a single MPEG-7 tag in CBIR applications; few of them integrate and test multiple MPEG-7 tags. Our experience shows that it is important to integrate multiple MPEG-7 tags in a unified framework and extend it to a database environment such as the eXist database system.

Our system also shows potential of further improvements. These possible improvements include the following aspects:

- Extend the current system to integrate more MPEG-7 descriptors under a unified platform.
- Our system needs to be extended to support multiple views.
- We need to develop efficient learning strategies.
- We need to extend region labeling from key words to arbitrary ontologies.

References

1. Anderson HL, Bajcsy R, Mintz M. *A Modular Feedback System for Image Segmentation.* GRASP Laboratory. Philadelphia, Pennsylvania, USA; 1987.
2. Stehling Renato O, Nascimento Mario A, Falco Alexandre X. An adaptive and efficient clustering-based approach for content-based image retrieval. In: *Proceedings of the International Database Engineering and Applications Symposium,* Grenoble, France; 2001, pp. 356–365.
3. Gudivada V, Raghavan V. Design and evaluation of algorithms for image retrieval by spatial similarity. *ACM Transactions on Information Systems,* 1995;13(1):115–144.
4. Gosselin P, Cord M. Semantic kernel updating for content-based image retrieval. In: *Proceedings of the IEEE Sixth International Symposium on Multimedia Software Engineering,* Miami, FL, 2004, pp. 537–544.
5. Chang E, Li B, GWu, Goh K. Statistical learning for effective visual information retrieval. In: *Proceedings of the IEEE International Conference on Image Processing,* Barcelona, Spain; 2003, pp. 609–612.
6. Fournier J, Cord M. A flexible search-by-similarity algorithm for content-based image retrieval. In: *Proceedings of the International Conference on Computer Vision, Pattern Recognition and Image Processing,* Duram, North CA, 2002, pp. 672–675.
7. Han J, Li M, Zhang H, Guo L. A memorization learning model for image retrieval. In: *Proceedings of the IEEE International Conference on Image Processing,* Barcelona, Spain; 2003, pp. 605–608.
8. Smeulders A, Worring M, Santini S, Gupta A, Jain R. Content-based image retrieval at the end of the early years. *Proceedings of the IEEE Transactions on Pattern Analysis and Machine Intelligence,* 2000;22(12):1349–1380.
9. Vasconcelos N, Lippman A. A probabilistic architecture for content-based image retrieval. In: *Proceedings of the IEEE Conference on Computer Vision and Pattern Recognition,* Hilton Head Island, SC;2000, pp. 1216–1221.
10. Xu Y, Olman V, Uberbacher E. A segmentation algorithm for noisy images. In: *Proceedings of the IEEE International Joint Symposia on Intelligence and Systems,* Rockville, MD, 1996, pp. 220–226.

16. Mining Image Content by Aligning Entropies with an Exemplar

Clark F. Olson

Summary. To efficiently answer queries on image databases at run time, content must be mined from the images offline. We describe a technique for locating objects in the library for which we have an exemplar to compare against. We match the images against the exemplar by comparing the local entropies in the images at corresponding positions. This representation is invariant to many imaging phenomena that can cause appearance-based techniques to fail. It can succeed even when the images are captured with different sensors (e.g., CCD vs. FLIR). We employ a search strategy that combines sampling in the space of exemplar positions, the Fast Fourier Transform (FFT) for efficiently evaluating object translations, and iterative optimization for pose refinement. Experiments indicate that the sampling can be somewhat coarse. The techniques are applied to matching exemplars with real images. We describe strategies for scaling this approach to multimedia databases and conclude with a discussion of future work that would be beneficial for mining content from images and video data.

16.1 Introduction

Many current image and video databases are databases in name only. They are unmanaged collections of data, rather than being managed by a database management system (DBMS) that provides a facility for forming and processing complex queries on the data. For these to become true databases, they require not only integration with a DBMS, but the DBMS must also have tools to perform content-based queries on the images. Considerable work on content-based image retrieval has studied methods to extract general information from images in order to support some queries at run time [1]. However, the generality of these methods precludes them from supporting specific, complex queries, such as "In which video sequences does Tiger Woods appear after Annika Sorenstam?" or "Which patients have MRI images that contain both benign and malignant tumors?" To create true databases from collections of multimedia data (specifically images and video sequences) content must be mined from the data offline in order to efficiently support complex queries at run time.

One solution is to retrieve images based on shapes present in the images. However, shape-based image retrieval is a difficult problem. The reason for this is the intractability of the segmentation problem to extract shape information from complex image data. Extending such retrieval to video data gains the benefit (and the curse) of orders

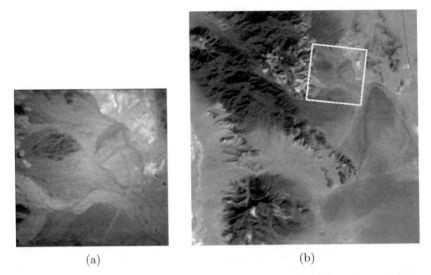

(a)   (b)

Fig. 16.1. Motivating example. (a) Aerial image captured in the the Mojave Desert, California. (b) Orbital image of the Avawatz Mountains and Silurian Valley in the Mojave Desert, California. The box shows the location of the aerial image in the orbital image.

of magnitude more data to examine. For this reason, we believe it is likely that the most common method for extracting content from image and video databases will be through matching against appearance-based exemplars. Appearance-based matching has achieved good results in many areas of computer vision, including face recognition [2] and object classification [3]. However, appearance-based techniques face difficulties when objects vary from the expected appearance due to differences in sensor, lighting, and configuration.

We build upon previous work for robust image matching [4–6] to extract matches in the database using image exemplars. Figure 16.1 shows an example of appearance-based recognition using an exemplar. In this example, a location in an orbital image is detected using an aerial image of the same location even though the images were captured with different sensors, at different resolutions, and somewhat different viewing direction.

The goal of this work is to develop a matching measure that is robust to changing sensors, lighting conditions, and image motion together with an efficient search strategy for locating good matches according to the measure. This would allow the technique to be used, for example, to detect all instances of a particular location in a database of geographical images using an exemplar.

Maximization of mutual information [7,8] has been successful in robust matching. However, this technique has limitations that prevent it from being successful in some cases. One drawback is that there is no efficient strategy for large search spaces. It is common to use an iterative technique, but these require a good starting location for refinement. In addition, the robustness of maximization of mutual information makes it susceptible to false positives. In the example in Figure 16.1, this strategy fails to find the correct location, even when searching over just translations of the exemplar at the correct rotation and scale. A final problem with this technique is that it is not able to find matches between images when there are smooth shading changes (e.g., owing to curved surfaces) unless more than one exemplar is used.

The correct match in Figure 16.1 was found by transforming both the exemplar and the search image into new images, replacing each pixel with a local entropy measurement. The scoring function for each position of the exemplar examines how well the local entropies are correlated between the exemplar and the corresponding locations in the search image. The optimal match was detected over affine transformations of the exemplar image.

To find matches for an exemplar, we use a search strategy that samples positions from the space of rotations and scales (also shears, when using affine transformations). The Fast Fourier Transform (FFT) is used to perform fast search over the translations of the exemplar at each sampled rotation and scale. The candidates found in this search are refined using an iterative optimization to locate the best position(s). This strategy has been effective on small collections of images. For large databases, further advances are likely to be necessary. We discuss strategies that have potential for efficient performance in these cases.

Our search strategy can be applied to any method that maximizes the correlation or normalized correlation of statistics between an exemplar and database images over a space of transformations. For example, we could apply this strategy to image matching using gradients, as is done in [9]. We use local entropies, rather than gradients, since they appear to retain more of the information content in the original image and have produced fewer false positives in our experiments. In the search, we can include translations, similarity transformations, affine transformations, and, potentially, more complex transformations. This strategy can also be extended to handle multiple statistics and vector-valued images, such as the entropies computed at multiple scales.

16.2 Related Work

A large body of previous work exists on retrieving images satisfying various characteristics from an image collection [1]. Influential early systems include QBIC [10], Photobook [11], and the Virage engine [12]. The QBIC (Query By Image Content) system uses image frames and objects that have been segmented (manually or automatically) from an image. Images and objects segmented from them are represented by sets of features representing color, texture, shape, location, and sketch. Queries can be performed on entire images or individual objects using these features. Photobook similarly allows searches to be performed using extracted image features. Three types of image properties are used: appearance (e.g., segmented faces), two-dimensional shape (tools, fish, etc.), and texture (wood, honeycomb, grass). Each of the image properties is represented in the database using a small set of coefficients (30 to 100) from which the original image can be reconstructed with little error. The image properties can also be combined to form searches that are more complex. Virage provides an image search engine has three functional parts: image analysis, image comparison, and management. Preprocessing operations and primitive extraction are performed during image analysis. During image comparison, similarity measures are applied to pairs of primitive vectors that have been extracted from images and combined using weights. The management function performs initialization, and manages the weights and primitive vector data.

Recent systems include NeTra [13], which first performs segmentation of the image into distinct regions. Queries are performed through indexing using color, texture, shape, and spatial location. PicHunter [14] uses relevance feedback to predict the image desired by the user given their actions. The overall approach is Bayesian, with an explicit model of the user's actions. PicHunter uses annotated images; however, the annotations are hidden from the user to reduce confusion on the user's part. PicToSeek [15] uses color and shape invariants to retrieve images from a database. New color models are used to gain invariance to viewpoint, geometry, and illumination. Shape is extracted through color invariant edge detection. The shape and color invariants are combined into a single high-dimensional feature set for discriminating between objects. Blobworld [16] segments images into regions that have uniform color and texture through clustering. Images are retrieved by examining the similarity between user-selected example regions and those extracted from the image collection. Users are given access to the internal representation to develop improved queries.

Aside from these systems, many interesting techniques have been described. Color histograms [17] were an early method to index an image collection based on color information in the image. While this technique is able to find images with a similar color distribution, the precision of this technique is not always high owing to false positives. Joint histograms [18] improve color image histograms by adding additional information, such as edge density, texturedness, gradient magnitude, and intensity rank. Additional improvement can be gained by adding spatial information, such as in color correlograms [19]. These are essentially a form of histogram, where each bin records the number of pairs of pixels with specified colors and distance between them.

Most previous systems compute global image descriptors for the example image and the images in the database in order to compare them. This approach inherently limits the method to cases where the example image and the matches encompass roughly the same structure, without occlusion or additional clutter in either image. An alternative is to index images using invariants or quasi-invariants of local image features [20, 21]. This allows images to be indexed even if only a small portion of the exemplar is present in image.

Note that most content-based image retrieval systems require a user in the loop in order to refine queries and locate the desired images in the database. The techniques described here extract content from multimedia databases automatically. User involvement is required only for queries on the database, after the relevant information has been extracted from the multimedia data.

16.3 Matching with Entropy

The basic technique that we use for detecting matches is to compare local entropies in an exemplar image against reference images from a database over some space of

relative positions between the images [4]. Let us say that a discrete random variable
A has marginal probability distribution $p_A(a)$. The entropy of A is defined as

$$H(A) = -\sum_a p_A(a) \log p_A(a). \tag{16.1}$$

Note that

$$\lim_{x \to 0} x \log x = 0. \tag{16.2}$$

The (undefined) value of $0 \cdot \log 0$ is, thus, taken to be zero.

We transform both the exemplar and each database image by replacing each pixel
with an estimate of the local entropy in the image. Here we are treating the pixels in
a small neighborhood around each location as samples from a random variable and
estimating the entropy of this random variable. For the pixel at location (r, c), the
sample set consists of the neighboring pixels in a $k \times k$ image patch centered at (r, c).
The pixel intensities are placed in a histogram and the entropy of the distribution
is computing using Eq. (16.1). Our implementation uses a histogram with 64 bins
and we smooth the histogram with a Gaussian ($\sigma = 1.0$ bins) prior to computing the
entropy to improve the estimate.

Figure 16.2 shows the entropy images generated for several neighborhood sizes.
The entropy transformation captures the degree of local variation near each pixel

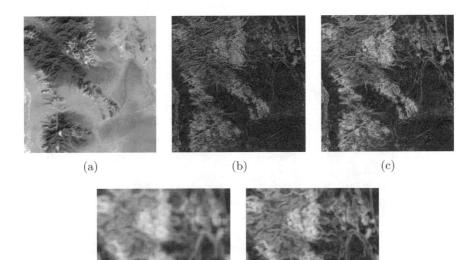

Fig. 16.2. Entropy images computed using different neighborhood sizes. (a) Original image.
(b) Entropy image for 3×3 window. (c) Entropy image for 5×5 window. (d) Entropy image
for 11×11 window. (e) Entropy image for 21×21 window.

in the image. Larger neighborhoods yield smoother entropy images, while smaller neighborhoods yield sharper images. We expect this to be a useful property in order to create a multiresolution search strategy, using entropy images. The generated images are invariant to a constant additive change (bias) to the images. While the images are not invariant to multiplicative change (gain), the correlation peaks are invariant to such changes (modulo smoothing and binning effects). The entropy images are insensitive to other image effects, such as illumination change and even changes in sensor modality.

To find matching positions of the exemplar in a collection of images, we can find positions of the exemplar that maximize the normalized correlation between the entropies in the exemplar and a reference image from the collection. To find the best positions, we have to take into account rotation and scaling of the exemplar (and sometimes shearing) with respect to the reference image. This implies that the shape and scale of the exemplar will vary over the search space and we must account for this in the normalization. When transforming the exemplar, we generate a second image that stores the shape of the transformed exemplar. Pixels covering the position of the transformed exemplar will have a value of 1, except for the borders pixels, which will have smaller weights according to bilinear interpolation. Now, when we perform correlation with the transformed exemplar, we perform the same correlation with the shape image. This yields the normalization value for the reference image.

16.4 Toward Efficient Search

Since multimedia databases can store terabytes of information, it is necessary to use highly efficient strategies for processing the data. In some cases it will be unacceptable for the mining to require days to operate, but it may be acceptable in large databases to mine the data over the course of hours (or overnight), since this step can be performed offline. Current strategies for robust appearance-based matching are computationally intensive. Matching using mutual information [7, 8] is a leading technique for such matching. However, there is currently no search strategy that is both general and efficient for this technique.

Our current approach combines fast two-dimensional matching using the FFT, coarse sampling of the remaining pose parameters, and iterative refinement to detect the optimal position(s) [4]. Search over the two degrees-of-freedom corresponding to translation in the image can be performed very quickly in the frequency domain using the FFT, since this allows cross-correlation to be performed in $O(n \log n)$ time, where n is the size on the image. In more complex search spaces, including similarity and affine transformations, we sample the remaining parameters on a grid to ensure that a sample point is close to every point in the search space. For each sample point, the translation parameters are searched with the FFT and strong candidates are further refined using Powell's iterative optimization method [22].

Since our search strategy relies on sampling the space of rotations, scales, and shears of the exemplar, we must determine how finely these parameters must be sampled to find instances of the exemplar. A sparse sampling facilitates efficient

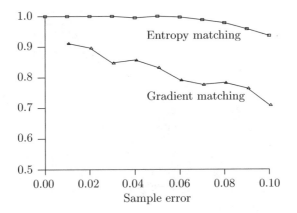

Fig. 16.3. Experiment to determine the capture range. The detection rate is plotted versus the maximum sample error for both entropy matching and gradient matching.

matching, but may miss instances that are desired. We, thus, need to know how far a sample point can be from the correct positions and still find a match for the exemplar after the iterative step in our search strategy. This implies that the initial correlation step must find a large enough peak to trigger the refinement step and the iterative refinement must also converge to the correct location. Experiments indicate that a somewhat coarse sampling is sufficient.

We tested the sampling resolution necessary using several sample problems. Examples can be seen in Figures 16.1, 16.2, 16.5–16.8. Two of the problems (Figures 16.1 and 16.3) used affine transformations (6 degrees-of-freedom):

$$\begin{bmatrix} x' \\ y' \end{bmatrix} = \begin{bmatrix} a & b \\ c & d \end{bmatrix} \begin{bmatrix} x \\ y \end{bmatrix} + \begin{bmatrix} t_x \\ t_y \end{bmatrix}. \tag{16.4}$$

The other problems used similarity transformations (with 4 degrees-of-freedom). In these problems the following constraints were enforced:

$$a = d. \tag{16.5}$$

and

$$b = -c. \tag{16.6}$$

Our tests considered samples from the search space that were in error by a bounded amount for each of the parameters a, b, c, and d. The search strategy described above was then applied for finding translations with sufficiently large scores for further evaluation and iterative optimization of those locations. Figure 16.4 shows a plot of the detection rate versus the maximum sample error for our technique. Results are also shown for this search strategy applied to gradient images instead of entropy images. The data points in each plot were determined using 100 trials for each of the sample problems. For small errors, the techniques using entropy work extremely well. Up to an error of 0.05 in the parameters, very few errors occur. The error of 0.05

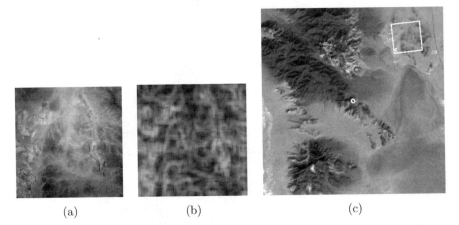

(a)   (b)   (c)

Fig. 16.4. Location matching using aerial and orbital images. (a) Aerial image of California desert. (b) Entropy image computed from (a). (c) Detected location in an orbital image. Entropy can be seen in Figure 16.2.

represents a 5% scale change or a (roughly) 3 degree rotation of the exemplar. This implies that we can sample the parameters at intervals of 0.10 (10% scale change or 6 degree rotation), since this will result in a sample point within 0.05 of each point in the search space.

When applied to gradient images, this sampling performs less well. While the gradients are like the entropies, robust to many changes in the image, including a change in sensor modality, the gradient images do not appear to retain as much information as the entropy images. The entropy-based method had a better detection rate on each of the test images examined.

16.5 Results

Figures 16.3 and 16.5–16.8 show the result of applying these techniques to real images. Figure 16.3 shows an experiment where the exemplar is an image captured from a helicopter at an elevation of 800 m. The reference image is an orbital image that encompasses the same location. While the correct location is not obvious to the human eye, the entropy matching techniques were able to find it using an affine transformation of the exemplar. Figure 16.1 showed a similar example.

Figures 16.5 and 16.6 show cases where military vehicles were imaged with both a CCD camera and an FLIR (infrared) camera. In both cases, the exemplar used is the infrared image and a regular image is the reference image. In both cases, the correct position of the exemplar was found, despite the considerable change in appearance between the images. These examples illustrate that successful extraction can be performed even when the exemplar has a very different appearance from the image to which it is matched. The entropy matching technique succeeds despite camouflage that is not apparent in the infrared image.

Fig. 16.5. Exemplar matching using images with different sensor modality. (a) Tank exemplar in FLIR image. (b) Extracted tank location in a CCD image. (c) Entropy image computed from (a). (d) Entropy image computed from (b).

The final examples are images from Mars (Figures 16.7 and 16.8). Both templates and reference images were captured with the Imager for Mars Pathfinder (IMP) cameras. The images were captured at different times during the day, so the illumination and the shadowing of the terrain are different between the images. In Figure 16.7, the reference image has undergone a nonlinear warping operation to remove lens distortion, while the template has not. The matching algorithm found the correct match in both cases, despite the differing appearance of the object in the reference image.

16.6 Large Image Databases

Our methodology yields good results for matching in a small collection of images, but it is likely to be prohibitively expensive when matching against a very large database

(a)

(b)

(c)

(d)

Fig. 16.6. Exemplar matching using FLIR and CCD camera images. (a) FLIR image of military vehicles. (b) Registered location in a CCD image. (c) Entropy image computed from (a). (d) Entropy image computed from (b).

of images and video. A promising technique for this case is guaranteed search for image matching [5, 23]. This method is able to prune large sections of the search space using little computation. These techniques have not, yet, been applied to image matching using statistical measures, such as mutual information or entropy matching. However, previous work on entropy matching [4] can be framed as a multiresolution search problem, making such techniques feasible.

Video databases with both spatial and temporal properties are even more complicated. One approach that has been suggested is the use of 3D strings in the x, y, and time dimensions [24]. Liu and Chen [25] use three-dimensional pattern matching techniques for this purpose. Their approach scales linearly with the number of video

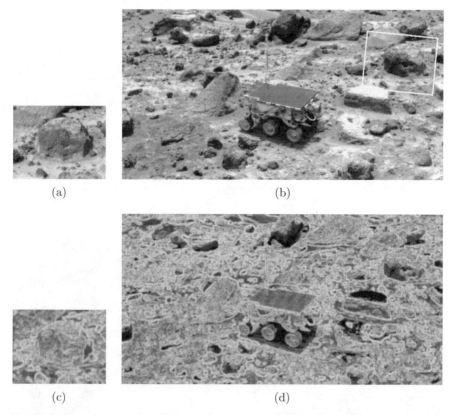

(a)   (b)

(c)   (d)

Fig. 16.7. Exemplar matching of Martian images under differing illumination. (a) Image of a Martian rock. (b) Detected location of the rock in another image. (c) Entropy image computed from (a). (d) Entropy image computed from (b).

objects. To achieve efficient operations on very large databases, it will be necessary to obtain a sublinear relationship with the number of video objects. This may be achieved using a hierarchy of video objects. The top of the hierarchy would be coarse, but would allow many video objects to be removed from consideration. Lower levels of the hierarchy would add detail and remove more video objects, until the remaining video objects could be examined explicitly.

This hierarchical methodology is similar to work in object recognition that uses a hierarchy of positions in the space of object positions (i.e., the pose space) [26–28]. At the upper levels of the hierarchy, the method tries to prove that each cell of the pose space cannot contain a position meeting the search criteria. If successful for some cell, the entire cell can be removed from the search. Otherwise, the cell is subdivided into smaller cells (lower in the hierarchy) and the process is applied recursively. This technique succeeds since it never prunes a cell that could contain a position meeting the search criteria. Application of similar ideas to video databases has the potential to yield gains in efficiency when dealing with large databases.

(a)   (b)

(c)   (d)

Fig. 16.8. Exemplar matching of Martian images under differing illumination. (a) Image of a Martian rock. (b) Detected location of rock in another image. (c) Entropy image computed from (a). (d) Entropy image computed from (b).

16.7 Future Work

In addition to research to find highly efficient search strategies for matching against exemplars, we have identified two other important areas for future work: highly robust tracking in video images and grouping of extracted objects.

16.7.1 Tracking

Tracking objects in video is easier than detecting them. However, highly robust methods are necessary to maintain query integrity. It is unacceptable for the tracking procedure to be fooled into locking onto a background object or drift off the correct target. Since the tracked object will change appearance over the course of the video sequence, the template used to track the object must be periodically (or continually) updated. However, each time the template is updated, the target on which the template is centered drifts slightly from the desired position.

For the tracking to be successful over a long sequence, localization must be performed with high precision each time the template is updated. One approach is to compute the motion not just relative to the previous frame, but to use a set of previous frames [29]. This approach might be strengthened using a robust template matching framework and high-precision subpixel estimation techniques [5]. Another modification would be to update the target template only when necessary, to reduce the opportunities for drift. The decision of when to update the target template can be determined using a quality of match measure between the current template and video frame. For example, we may decide that the template must be updated when an estimate of the standard deviation in the localization or the probability of failure has risen above a predetermined value.

16.7.2 Grouping

If objects are mined from video using exemplars, then the identity of the objects is known and they are easily grouped according to the exemplar that generated them. Alternatively, techniques can be integrated into this framework that do not use exemplars. In addition, techniques for applications such as face recognition may use general face exemplars, without distinguishing between faces belonging to different people. For cases where there is no obvious partitioning of the detected objects, we wish to classify the objects according to meaningful characteristics. In addition, in a video containing people, we should be able to detect cases where a particular face leaves the image sequence and subsequently returns. This requires grouping the detected face instances according to the appearance of each face, rather than classifying them as different objects.

An initial approach to matching separate face images, while allowing differences in lighting and affine transformation, could use techniques similar to the problem of extraction using exemplars [4, 5]. With this methodology, the extracted objects (such as faces) are treated as exemplars for matching against other extracted objects. For highly nonplanar objects, this approach can be extended to use shape information inferred from the object class and image. For example, the three-dimensional structure of a face can be well approximated using a small number of parameters extracted from an image of the face. This shape information can be used to improve the robustness of matching between two images of a face observed from different viewpoints, since a nonlinear image warping making use of the shape information brings the images into better alignment.

16.8 Summary

Our goal in this work is to demonstrate that the data can be mined from image and video databases by performing matching against exemplars. The technique that we use for matching is based on comparing the local entropies in the images at some relative position that can encompass translation, rotation, scaling, and skew. This allows matches to be detected even when the images are taken by different sensors and from different viewpoints. Search strategies for performing matching are currently efficient for small collections of images. We have suggested techniques for future work that may lead to efficient search in large databases.

Acknowledgments

This work expands upon work previous published in the IEEE Computer Society Conference on Computer Vision and Pattern Recognition [4] and in the Fourth International Workshop on Multimedia Data Mining [6]. Portions of the research described in this chapter were carried out at the Jet Propulsion Laboratory, California Institute of Technology, under a contract with the National Aeronautics and Space Administration.

References

1. Veltkamp RC, Tanase M. Content-based image retrieval systems: A survey. http://www.aa-lab.cs.uu.nl/cbirsurvey/index.html, revised from technical report UU-CS-2000-34, Dept. of Computing Science, 2001.
2. Turk MA, Pentland AP. Face recognition using eigenfaces. In: *Proceedings of the IEEE Conference on Computer Vision and Pattern Recognition* 1991;586–91.
3. Murase H, Nayar SK. Visual learning and recognition of 3-d objects from appearance. *International Journal of Computer Vision* 1995;14:5–24.
4. Olson CF. Image registration by aligning entropies. In: *Proceedings of the IEEE Computer Society Conference on Computer Vision and Pattern Recognition* 2001;2:331–6.
5. Olson CF. Maximum-likelihood image matching. *IEEE Transactions on Pattern Analysis and Machine Intelligence* 2002;24(6):853–7.
6. Olson CF. Image mining by matching exemplars using entropy. In: *Proceedings of the Fourth International Workshop on Multimedia Data Mining* 2003;87–92.
7. Maes F, Collignon A, Vandermeulen D, Marchal G, Suetens P. Multimodality image registration by maximization of mutual information. *IEEE Transactions on Medical Imaging* 1997;16(2):187–98.
8. Viola P, Wells WM. Alignment by maximization of mutual information. *International Journal of Computer Vision* 1997;24(2):137–54.
9. Brown LMG, Boult TE. Registration of planar film radiographs with computed tomography. In: *Proceedings of the Workshop on Mathematical Methods in Biomedical Image Analysis* 1996;42–51.
10. Flickner M, Sawhney H, Niblack W, Ashley J, Huang Q, Dom B, et al. The QBIC system. *IEEE Computer* 1995;28(9):23–32.
11. Pentland A, Picard RW, Sclaroff S. Photobook: Content-based manipulation of image databases. *International Journal of Computer Vision* 1996;18(3):233–54.
12. Bach JR, Fuller C, Gupta A, Hampapur A, Horowitz B, Humphry R, et al. Virage image search engine: An open framework for image management. In: *Storage and Retrieval for Image and Video Databases, Proc. SPIE 1996;*2670: 76–87.

13. Ma WY, Manjunath BS. NeTra: A toolbox for navigating large image databases. *Multimedia Systems* 1999;7(3):184–98.
14. Cox IJ, Miller ML, Minka TP, Papathomas TV, Yianilos PN. The Bayesian image retrieval system, PicHunter: Theory, implementation and psychophysical experiments. *IEEE Transactions on Image Processing* 2000;9(1):20–37.
15. Gevers T, Smeulders AWM. PicToSeek: Combining color and shape invariant features for image retrieval. *IEEE Transactions on Image Processing* 2000;9(1):102–19.
16. Carson C, Belongie S, Greenspan B, Malik J. Blobworld: Image segmentation using expectation–maximization and its application to image querying. *IEEE Transactions on Pattern Analysis and Machine Intelligence* 2002;24(8):1026–38.
17. Swain MJ, Ballard DH. Color indexing. *International Journal of Computer Vision* 1991;7(1):11–32.
18. Pass G, Zabih R. Comparing images using joint histograms. *Journal of Multimedia Systems* 1999;7(3):234–40.
19. Huang J, Kuma SR, Mitra M, Zhu WJ, Zabih R. Spatial color indexing and applications. *International Journal of Computer Vision* 1999;35(3):245–68.
20. Lowe DG. Distinctive image features from scale-invariant keypoints. *International Journal of Computer Vision* 2004;60(2):91–110.
21. Schmid C, Mohr R. Local grayvalue invariants for image retrieval. *IEEE Transactions on Pattern Analysis and Machine Intelligence* 1997;19(5):530–34.
22. Press WH, Teukolsky SA, Vetterling WT, Plannery BP. *Numerical Recipes in C.* Cambridge University Press, 1988.
23. Rucklidge WJ. Efficient guaranteed search for gray-level patterns. In: *Proceedings of the IEEE Conference on Computer Vision and Pattern Recognition* 1997;717–23.
24. Chang SF, Chen W, Meng HJ, Sundaram H, Zhong D. VideoQ: An automated content based video search system using visual cues. In: *Proceedings of the ACM Multimedia Conference* 1997;313–24.
25. Liu CC, Chen ALP. 3d-List: A data structure for efficient video query processing. *IEEE Transactions on Knowledge and Data Engineering* 2002;14(1):106–22.
26. Breuel TM. Fast recognition using adaptive subdivisions of transformation space. In: *Proceedings of the IEEE Conference on Computer Vision and Pattern Recognition* 1992;445–51.
27. Huttenlocher DP, Rucklidge WJ. A multi-resolution technique for comparing images using the Hausdorff distance. In: *Proceedings of the IEEE Conference on Computer Vision and Pattern Recognition* 1993;705–6.
28. Olson CF. A probabilistic formulation for Hausdorff matching. In: *Proceedings of the IEEE Computer Society Conference on Computer Vision and Pattern Recognition* 1998;150–6.
29. Rahimi A, Morency LP, Darrell T. Reducing drift in parametric motion tracking. In: *Proceedings of the International Conference on Computer Vision* 2001;1:315–22.

17. More Efficient Mining Over Heterogeneous Data Using Neural Expert Networks

Sergio A. Alvarez, Carolina Ruiz, and Takeshi Kawato

Summary. Artificial neural networks (ANN) have proven to be successful in uncovering patterns in multidimensional data sets, and are therefore natural candidates for data mining tasks over domains such as multimedia in which heterogeneous data sources occur. However, training of a standard fully connected ANN is slow. We present a neural experts ANN architecture that enables faster ANN training for data sets that can be decomposed into loosely interacting sets of attributes. We precisely describe the expressiveness of this architecture in terms of functional composition. Our experimental results show that our neural experts architecture can achieve classification performance that is statistically identical to that of a fully connected feedforward ANN while significantly improving training efficiency.

17.1 Introduction

Artificial neural networks (ANN) are a machine learning paradigm that has been used to successfully tackle difficult data mining tasks involving complex data. For example, in [1], an ANN classifier is applied to the problem of detecting tumors in digital mammography images; in [2], ANN are used for text mining, in order to extract "typical messages" from e-mail discussions in a computer–supported collaborative work environment; in [3], a hybrid technique that combines ANN with rule-based inference is used to detect genes in DNA sequences; in [4], neural networks are used to automatically detect faces in images. Several industrial applications of ANN are described in [5]. A recent collection of papers on ANN techniques for multimedia data processing is available in [6]. The success of ANN across such a wide variety of tasks is explained at least in part by theoretical universal approximation results that show that ANN can approximate arbitrary nonlinear mappings from inputs to outputs as closely as desired, see e.g. [7–9]; see also [10] for a survey of related universal approximation results.

17.1.1 Scope of the Chapter

The present chapter explores the use of ANN as a data mining technique for data that originate from heterogeneous sources, as occurs naturally in many contexts, including multimedia data mining [11, 12].We are concerned, in particular, with reducing the complexity of training ANN for use in classification and regression tasks in such situations. Toward this end, we employ a modular ANN architecture that is adapted to multisource data. In this architecture, which we call a *mixture of attribute experts*, the set of input attributes (or a set of features extracted from the input attributes) is partitioned into disjoint subsets corresponding to data sources. Each of these subsets is fed into a dedicated *expert* consisting of a single layer of processing units, and the outputs of the different experts are then combined in a separate output layer. As we will show, this reduces the number of network connections and the time required for network training. On the other hand, the reduced complexity of mixture of attribute experts networks leads to a potential reduction in expressiveness for some data sets, depending on how the set of input attributes is partitioned into subsets corresponding to sources/experts. The main requirement on the partition in order to allow good performance is that only "loose" interactions be needed across sources to predict the target attribute. The input data sources need not be selected to correspond with distinct data types (e.g., images, speech, video) that might be present in a multimedia context. Our technique may be applied profitably to iterative supervised ANN learning algorithms such as, but not limited to, the classical error backpropagation algorithm.

Our experimental results for the Internet Advertisements and Spambase data sets from the UCI Machine Learning Repository [13] show that the mixture of attribute experts architecture can achieve classification performance comparable to that of a standard fully connected feedforward ANN while allowing significantly faster training.

17.1.2 Related Work

Modular ANN architectures have been considered previously by several authors. For example, a collection of papers dealing with modular ANN appeared in [14]. One of the most important and best known modular ANN paradigms is that of *hierarchical mixtures of experts* (HME) of Jacobs et al. [15]. In HME as presented in [15], the experts are feedforward ANN. Each expert operates on the full set of input attributes. Separate gating networks, also feedforward ANN that receive all of the attributes as inputs, are used to implement a "soft partition" of the input space into regions corresponding to experts; the outputs of a layer of experts are weighted as dictated by the gating networks, and the combined output is fed into the next layer. Jacobs et al. [15] evaluated HME for a vowel recognition task, with good results. An HME approach based on [15] has been applied to text categorization [16]. In contrast with HME, in the approach of the present chapter it is the set of data attributes that is partitioned, not the input space that has the set of all attributes as coordinates. In our approach no two experts share any input attributes. This results in a significant reduction in the total number of network connections that emanate from the input layer. This reduction has a beneficial effect on training time but may lead to a loss of representational power if the target task requires strong interactions among attributes in different cells of the input partition.

An interesting application using modular ANN is considered in [17]. There are two key differences between [17] and the approach of the present chapter. Each expert in [17] is trained to recognize a specific value of the target (class) attribute, while in the present chapter we associate experts with partitions of the set of input attributes. Moreover, Petrushin [17] is concerned mainly with the classification performance of various approaches in the target domain of emotion recognition in speech and, in terms of the architecture described, focuses on classification accuracy. In contrast, we will, in the present chapter explicitly address also issues of efficiency and representational limitations associated with the system architecture.

It has long been recognized that reducing network complexity in ANN is desirable to reduce training time and improve generalization performance. One technique for reducing network complexity is that of "optimal brain damage" (OBD) proposed by LeCun et al. [18], in which some measure of "saliency" is used to delete selected network connections during training. Saliency of a given connection is measured simply by the magnitude of the corresponding weight, or, as proposed in [18], by using estimates of the second derivatives of the error function with respect to the connection weights. A key difference between the approach of the present chapter and OBD as proposed in [18] is that OBD reduces network complexity iteratively: training commences with a fully connected topology and weights are considered for deletion only after sufficiently many training iterations have been completed. OBD has the possible advantage of producing a simplified network structure that is adapted to the target task. On the other hand, OBD will also require greater training time than the mixture of attribute experts approach of the present paper because the complexity of the intermediate networks during OBD training is greater than that of the final network that results from the iterative deletion process.

17.1.3 Outline of the Chapter

Our chapter begins with a description of ANN in general and of the mixture of attribute experts topology in particular. We discuss representational and complexity issues for this topology and contrast it with the standard fully connected feedforward topology. We describe the representational power of mixture of attribute experts networks in terms of functional composition, and prove that these networks do not satisfy the universal approximation property of fully connected feedforward networks. Instead, representability of a target mapping by a mixture of attribute experts network depends on whether the mapping can be expressed as a composition in a special factored form that reflects the structure of the network. This leaves open the issue of whether such a factorization is feasible in practical situations. To investigate this issue, we compare the performance of mixture of attribute experts ANN and fully connected feedforward ANN architectures in the context of detecting advertisements in images embedded in web documents and of detecting unsolicited commercial e-mail, using the Internet Advertisements and Spambase data sets from the UCI Machine Learning Repository [13]. We present our experimental results over these data sets, which show that mixture of attribute experts networks can achieve the same classification performance as fully connected networks while training in less time. We close with conclusions and suggestions for future work.

17.2 Artificial Neural Networks

Artificial neural networks (ANN) are models of distributed computing by a network of very simple processing units. The concept of an ANN is inspired by the view of the brain as a system of interconnected neurons. Among several alternative ANN models, we will focus on *multilayer perceptrons*. Formally, a typical feedforward multilayer perceptron can be defined by a weighted directed acyclic graph (G, E, w). The nodes of G are the *processing units*. The state of each processing unit i is described by its *activation value*, usually assumed to be a real-valued function of time. The weights $w_{i,j}$ attached to the edges $E(j, i)$ (from unit j to unit i) measure the relative importance of the activations of various units j in determining the activation of unit i.

We will assume a memoryless model in which the activation y_i of node i at a given time is an instantaneous function of the activation values y_j at the same time of all nodes j for which the weight $w_{i,j}$ is nonzero. Specifically, we assume the activation y_i to be the result of applying a nonlinear *activation function* f to a linear combination of the activations y_j:

$$y_i = f\left(\sum_j w_{i,j} y_j\right) \tag{17.1}$$

The activation function f is assumed to be a logistic, or sigmoid function:

$$f(x) = \frac{1}{1 + e^{-\sigma x}}, \tag{17.2}$$

where σ is a "steepness" parameter. Models with activation memory could also be considered, by allowing the evolution of the activation values to be described instead by integrodifferential equations. It is important to note that the memoryless activation assumption most certainly does *not* preclude learning in the system. Rather, learning is associated with changes in the weights between processing units, as described below in Section 17.2.2.

17.2.1 Network Topologies

The pattern of interconnections among processing units in an ANN is known as the *topology* of the network. Together with the numerical values of the connection weights, the topology plays a key role in determining the behavior of the network. We will consider two different network topologies, each corresponding to a feedforward ANN structure with two layers of processing units. In both of the topologies considered, there are distinct sets of special input and output units. The network inputs feed directly into the units of the first, or *hidden* layer, and the hidden units feed into the units of the second, or *output* layer.

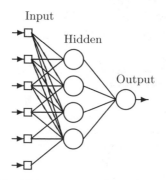

Fig. 17.1. Fully connected network.

Such an ANN may be viewed as computing a mapping from inputs to outputs. The precise mapping computed by an ANN depends also on the values of the connection weights, which are determined through supervised learning as discussed in Section 17.2.2.

17.2.1.1 Fully Connected Topology

Figure 17.1 shows the standard network topology in this context, the *fully connected* (FC) topology. In an FC network, every input is connected to every hidden unit, and every hidden unit is connected to every output unit.

17.2.1.2 Mixture of Attribute Experts Topology

We introduce a second network topology which we call a *mixture of attribute experts* (MAE). In this topology, the set of inputs and the units of the hidden layer are partitioned into k disjoint groups. The groups in the hidden layer are called *experts*. Each of the experts will process data from a different source. Each expert is fully connected to its corresponding set of inputs, but is disconnected from the remaining inputs. The hidden layer is fully connected to the output layer. Figure 17.2 shows a

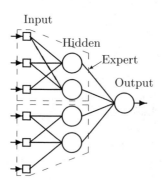

Fig. 17.2. Mixture of experts network.

mixture of attribute experts network with two experts. As discussed in the Introduction, our mixture of attribute experts architecture differs from the hierarchical mixture of experts architecture described in [15]; in the latter, all inputs are fed into each expert, and separate gating networks are used to effect the mixture of the experts' outputs.

17.2.2 Network Training

The purpose of ANN training (supervised learning) is to adjust the values of the connection weights between processing units so as to approximate a given target mapping that is implicit in a set of training data. Supervised learning algorithms require that a set of training pairs $(I_k, \hat{O}_k)$ be presented to the network to be trained, where I_k is an input vector and $\hat{O}_k$ is the desired output vector corresponding to I_k. The network weights are adjusted during training so as to reduce the output error, that is, some measure of dissimilarity between the desired outputs $\hat{O}_k$ and the actual outputs O_k produced by the network on input I_k. This training process is often performed in an iterative fashion: training instances are examined sequentially and the values of the connection weights are updated after each instance is processed. Multiple passes over the entire set of training data are typically needed.

The best known iterative ANN supervised learning algorithm is the method of error backpropagation (see e.g. [19]), which is described in pseudocode below. The manner in which error backpropagation adjusts the network weights corresponds to a gradient search in weight space relative to the mean square error between actual and desired outputs. The term error back–propagation is derived from the recursive form of the δ equations in the pseudocode; the errors e_k at the output layer are "propagated back" through previous layers by Eq. 17.3. Many alternative ANN supervised learning algorithms are available, including RPROP [20] and QuickProp [21]. The experimental results presented in Section 17.5 were obtained using error backpropagation. Nonetheless, the analysis in Section 17.3 suggests that the efficiency advantage of the mixture of experts architecture presented here may extend to other iterative ANN training algorithms.

17.2.2.1 Error Backpropagation Pseudocode

1. Pseudo–randomly initialize the network weights.
2. Repeat steps (a)–(d) below until the termination condition is satisfied:
   (a) Present the next training instance pair $(I_k, \hat{O}_k)$ consisting of inputs I_k and target outputs $\hat{O}_k$ to the network.
   (b) Propagate the inputs I_k forward toward the output layer by repeatedly applying Eq. 17.1.
   (c) Compute δ values for all output nodes and hidden nodes, as follows. For each output node k and each hidden node h:

$$e_k = \hat{O}_k - O_k$$
$$\delta_k = O_k(1 - O_k)e_k \qquad (17.3)$$
$$\delta_h = y_h(1 - y_h) \sum_{\text{outputs } k} w_{k \leftarrow h} \delta_k$$

Here, y_h is the activation level of node h, and $w_{k \leftarrow h}$ is the current value of the connection weight from node h to node k.

(d) Update the weights for all pairs of nodes using the δ values as follows (η is the learning rate):

$$\text{new } w_{j \leftarrow i} = \text{old } w_{j \leftarrow i} + \eta \delta_j y_i \qquad (17.4)$$

Termination Criteria

Various termination conditions may be used. For example, training can be terminated when the error over some reserved validation set of instances has not decreased for a certain number of iterations. If the initial weights happen to be chosen sufficiently close to a particular local minimum of the output error, and if the learning rate η is sufficiently small, then error backpropagation is guaranteed to produce a sequence of weights that converges to this local minimum. Nonglobal optimality may be addressed by comparing the results of error backpropagation for different pseudorandom choices of the initial weights. For example, an automatic random restarting mechanism may be considered [21–23].

17.3 Efficiency and Expressiveness

In this section we discuss how MAE and FC networks compare in terms of the time required for training and of the generality with which they can accurately represent functional relationships among the input and target attributes. The reduced network complexity of MAE networks can be expected to allow faster training. On the other hand, we show that MAE networks do not satisfy the universal approximation property of FC networks and that a loosely interacting partition of the input attributes is needed in order for an MAE network to accurately represent a given target function.

17.3.1 Time Complexity of Training

Neural network learning may be viewed concretely as a search for suitable vectors in the space of connection weights. Since an MAE network has fewer connections than an FC network with the same number of hidden nodes, the MAE network will usually train faster. Indeed, the total training time in an iterative supervised learning algorithm such as error back–propagation (see Section 17.2.2.1) or QuickProp [21] is proportional to the number of weight updates; the number of weight updates in turn equals the product of the number of network connections and the number of training iterations required for convergence.

17.3.1.1 Network Complexity

It is straightforward to calculate the number of network connections in each of the two architectures. The number of inputs is generally much larger than the number of hidden and output nodes of the network, so connections between the input and hidden layers dominate the overall count. Since in the FC architecture there is one weight for each pair consisting of an input attribute and a hidden node, the total number of weights between the input and hidden layers in the FC architecture is the product nh of the number of input attributes n and the number of hidden nodes h. For the MAE architecture with k experts of roughly equal sizes, each input is connected to about h/k hidden nodes, so the number of weights from the input layer to the hidden layer is roughly nh/k. Therefore, *the MAE architecture can reduce the number of network connections by a factor roughly equal to the number of experts.* If the experts are of different sizes, efficiency will improve by a smaller factor.

17.3.1.2 Number of Training Iterations

It is difficult to provide precise *a priori* estimates of the number of iterations required for convergence of the training algorithm. This is because of the complex nature of the error surface, that is, the surface described by the function that maps a vector of connection weight values to the mean square error attained by the corresponding network with respect to a given set of training data. Indeed, the very space of weights over which the error surface is defined is different for FC and MAE. Evidence that such differences in the error surfaces can be significant is provided by some of the experimental results in Section 17.5. However, our results do not point to any penalty in the training time required for MAE as compared with FC. Some of our experiments in a different domain, that of combined collaborative and content-based information for personalized item recommendations [22] have shown a distribution of training times for the mixture of attribute experts architecture that has a heavier tail than that of the fully connected architecture. This has led us to propose a random restarting technique in [22] that brings the average number of training iterations closer for the two architectures in such situations, thereby allowing the reduction in the number of network connections associated with the mixture of attribute experts architecture to be reflected in a similar reduction in the overall time complexity of training.

17.3.2 Expressive Power

There is a difference in the intrinsic complexities of the learning tasks for FC and MAE which may be understood in terms of the relative dimensions of the spaces in which learning takes place. For either architecture, the target of learning is a function from the n–dimensional Euclidean space $\mathbb{R}^n$ to the y–dimensional Euclidean space $\mathbb{R}^y$, where n is the number of inputs and y is the number of outputs. However, each of the two architectures explores a different portion of this function space as we point out below. As a result, MAE networks achieve improved time efficiency as discussed above. However, the set of functions that they can represent is constrained.

We will now describe the representational power of MAE networks in terms of functional composition. We show that not all input–output mappings can be represented in the special factored MAE form. Furthermore, we will show that this behavior persists in the limit, in the sense that any function that can merely be approximated by MAE input–output mappings must also be expressible in the factored MAE form. We then briefly discuss the practical implications of this expressive limitation.

17.3.2.1 MAE Networks and Factorization

Consider an MAE architecture with k experts, in which the i-th expert has n_i inputs and h_i hidden nodes, and a FC architecture with the same total number of inputs $n = \sum_{i=1}^{k} n_i$ and the same total number of hidden nodes $h = \sum_{i=1}^{k} h_i$. The FC network targets a general function from $\mathbb{R}^n$ to $\mathbb{R}^y$ expressed as a composition

$$f(g(x_1, \ldots, x_n))$$

of a function $g : \mathbb{R}^n \to \mathbb{R}^h$ and a function $f : \mathbb{R}^h \to \mathbb{R}^y$. This claim is substantiated by the universality results for multilayer ANN (e.g. [7–10]) which in this context essentially state that any nonlinear function from $\mathbb{R}^n$ to $\mathbb{R}^y$ may be approximated arbitrarily closely by a FC network with the given structure.

On the other hand, because of the grouping of inputs and hidden nodes into k mutually noninteracting experts, the input–output mapping of the MAE network will necessarily have the following more restricted factored form

$$f\left(g_1(x_1^{(1)} \ldots x_{n_1}^{(1)}), \ldots, g_k(x_1^{(h)} \ldots x_{n_h}^{(h)})\right) \tag{17.5}$$

Here, g_i represents the i-th expert, and hence is a function $g_i : \mathbb{R}^{n_i} \to \mathbb{R}^{h_i}$, where n_i is the number of inputs assigned to expert i and h_i is the number of hidden nodes in expert i. The "outer" function $f : \mathbb{R}^h \to \mathbb{R}^y$ maps the hidden unit activations to the network outputs.

Notice that the space of the outer functions $f : \mathbb{R}^h \to \mathbb{R}^y$ is the same for both the FC and MAE networks, since the total number of hidden nodes h and the total number of outputs y is the same in both cases. However, while training of the FC network amounts to a search for a single g in the nh-dimensional space of all functions from $\mathbb{R}^n$ to $\mathbb{R}^h$, training of the MAE network will instead perform k searches for g_1 through g_k, with the i-th search taking place in the $n_i h_i$-dimensional space of functions from $\mathbb{R}^{n_i}$ to $\mathbb{R}^{h_i}$. Since the former (FC) space has higher dimensionality, the FC architecture, and indeed any method that will potentially consider the full function space, has a more complex task to consider than does MAE or any other factorization method. One consequence of this is that MAE trains more quickly than FC. Another consequence, however, is a reduction in the expressive power of MAE, as we now show.

17.3.2.2 A Function That Cannot be Factored in MAE Form

Intuitively, the fact that there are groups of inputs that feed into different experts makes it difficult for an MAE network to model relationships across such input groups exactly. We will show that this is indeed true, by showing that there are functions of $m + n$ variables that cannot be expressed in the MAE form of Eq. 17.5 corresponding to two experts that have, respectively, m and n inputs.

We consider the specific case $m = 2, n = 2$, and assume that the partition of the input attributes into experts is predetermined, with (x_1, x_2) and (x_1', x_2') as the two halves. We focus on functions of the form $\phi(x_1 x_1', x_2 x_2')$, where ϕ is a nonconstant function and the arguments are products of one variable from each of two "halves" of the input vector. Specifically, take the example in which ϕ is the sum operator, so that the target function is $(x_1, x_2, x_1', x_2') \mapsto x_1 x_1' + x_2 x_2'$.

In order for this particular target function to equal the MAE composition $f(g(x_1, x_2), g'(x_1', x_2'))$, the following four conditions must hold:

$$x_1 = f(g(x_1, x_2), g'(1, 0)) \Rightarrow g(x_1, x_2) \text{ is independent of } x_2$$
$$x_2 = f(g(x_1, x_2), g'(0, 1)) \Rightarrow g(x_1, x_2) \text{ is independent of } x_1$$
$$x_1' = f(g(1, 0), g'(x_1', x_2')) \Rightarrow g'(x_1', x_2') \text{ is independent of } x_2'$$
$$x_2' = f(g(0, 1), g'(x_1', x_2')) \Rightarrow g'(x_1', x_2') \text{ is independent of } x_1'$$

Taken together, the above conditions imply that the selected target function $x_1 x_1' + x_2 x_2'$ must be constant, but of course it is not. This contradiction shows that the target function in question is not expressible by an MAE network.

17.3.2.3 Non–Universality: Limits of MAE Mappings

We now show that the requirement imposed by the factored MAE form of Eq. 17.5 persists in the limit, that is, mappings that can be approximated by input-to-output mappings of MAE networks must also have the form of Eq. 17.5. In particular, since there are functions that cannot be expressed in this form as shown above in Section 17.3.2, this establishes that the universal approximation property of FC networks does not carry over to MAE networks. We will assume that network processing units have activation functions with uniformly bounded slope. The crucial consequence of this assumption is that the associated input–output transfer functions form an equicontinuous family.

Theorem 17.1. *Let ϕ be any function defined on a domain D consisting of a product of finitely many compact real intervals. Assume that ϕ can be uniformly approximated arbitrarily closely by the input–output mappings of MAE networks with a given (shared) topology as in Eq. 17.5. Then ϕ may itself be expressed as a composition of continuous functions on D in the form of Eq. 17.5.*

Proof. Given an approximating sequence ϕ^m, $m = 1, \ldots, \infty$ of composite functions of the form

$$\phi^m(x) = f^m \left(g^m_1(x_1^{(1)} \ldots x_{n_1}^{(1)}), \ldots, g^m_k(x_1^{(k)} \ldots x_{n_k}^{(k)}) \right),$$

by the assumption that the nodal activation functions of all networks considered have a slope that is bounded by some finite shared constant, the family of functions (g_i^m) is equicontinuous. This means that if some target oscillation bound $\epsilon > 0$ is specified, then a radius $\delta > 0$ exists such that *all* of the functions g_i^m oscillate by less than ϵ when their arguments oscillate by less than δ. The same statement is true about the outer functions f^m. Equicontinuity (see [24]) yields a subsequence of indices m for which the corresponding functions g_i^m (for fixed i) and f^m converge uniformly on their respective compact domains as m goes to infinity, and the limit functions g_i

(fixed i) and f are continuous. Also, the limit of the composite functions, which equals ϕ by our initial assumption, is expressible as the composition

$$\phi(x) = f\left(g_1(x_1^{(1)}\ldots x_{n_1}^{(1)}), \ldots, g_k(x_1^{(k)}\ldots x_{n_k}^{(k)})\right)$$

of the limiting functions f and g_i. This completes the proof.

17.3.2.4 Loose Interactions: Factored Universality

Because of the non-universality of MAE networks as demonstrated above, the success of an MAE approach in a particular context will depend on the possibility of partitioning the set of input attributes in a way that allows the target function to be well approximated by factored MAE functions relative to the selected input partition. We informally say that the target function involves only *loose interactions* among attributes in different groups of such a partition. The meaning of "loose" may be made more precise by noting that the space of attainable target functions should be as described by Eq. 17.5. Thus, if the terms in Eq. 17.5 are standard sigmoids operating on linear combinations as in Eqs. 17.1 and 17.2, then we see that the mappings that can be represented through loose interactions will include those that can be approximated by linear combinations of sigmoids over the input attributes in different cells of the partition. If the experts are themselves allowed to be multilayer perceptrons, then it is possible to prove that the resulting MAE networks have the *factored universal approximation* property of approximating *any* mapping that can be expressed in a factored form similar to that of Eq. 17.5 (without restricting the terms to linear combinations of sigmoids) arbitrarily closely [25]. Our chapter [25] describes more general versions of the factored universality property for arbitrary modular networks.

The issue of what data set properties guarantee that the target function may be expressed in terms of some loosely interacting partition of the set of input attributes is an important one. The experimental results described in the present chapter, in which MAE networks achieved the same classification performance as FC networks, suggest that the loose interactions requirement may occur in some multimedia data mining applications. Another domain in which such a data partition appears to occur naturally is that of information filtering or recommendation based on a combination of social (collaborative) and content information; we have obtained promising results in this domain using the approach of the present chapter [22].

17.4 Experimental Evaluation

In this section we describe the experimental setup that we used to compare the fully connected (FC) and mixture of attribute experts (MAE) network architectures. Most of the experiments were performed over the Internet Advertisements data set [26]. This section describes details of this data set, the FC and MAE network configurations that were used (including the partition of the input attributes into experts in the case of MAE), performance metrics, and the experimental protocol. Results for the Internet Advertisements data set appear in Section 17.5. Additional experiments using the

Spambase spam e-mail data set [13] were also performed. The experimental setup and results for this second data set are reported in Section 17.5.4.

17.4.1 Web Images Data

We used the Internet Advertisements data set [26], available through the UCI Machine Learning Repository [13]. The 3279 instances of this data set represent images embedded in Web pages; roughly 14% of these images contain advertisements and the rest do not. There are missing values in approximately 28% of the instances. The proposed task is to determine which instances contain advertisements based on 1557 other attributes related to image dimensions, phrases in the URL of the document or the image, and text occurring in or near the image's anchor tag in the document.

17.4.1.1 Attributes

A description of the attributes for the Internet Advertisements data set appears below as presented in the data set's summary page at the UCI Machine Learning Repository [13]. The first three attributes encode the image's geometry; *aratio* refers to the aspect ratio (ratio of width to height). The binary *local* feature indicates whether the image URL points to a server in the same Internet domain as the document URL. The remaining features are based on phrases in various parts of the document; the terms origurl, ancurl, alt refer respectively to the document URL, anchor (image) URL, and alt text in the anchor tag for the image. Finally, the class attribute determines whether a given instance is an ad or not. See [26].

1. height: continuous. } possibly missing
2. width: continuous. } possibly missing
3. aratio: continuous. } possibly missing
4. local: 0,1.
5. 457 features from url terms,
   each of the form "url*term1+term2...";
   for example: url*images+buttons: 0,1.
6. 495 features from origurl terms, in same form;
   for example: origurl*labyrinth: 0,1.
7. 472 features from ancurl terms, in same form;
   for example: ancurl*search+direct: 0,1.
8. 111 features from alt terms, in same form;
   for example: alt*your: 0,1.
9. 19 features from caption terms, in same form;
   for example: caption*and: 0,1.
10. class attribute: ad/nonad

17.4.1.2 Input Partition

Applying a mixture of attribute experts network to the above data requires that the set of non-class attributes be split into disjoint subsets to be used as inputs for the respective experts. We will adopt the simplest possible approach to this task here by using a natural grouping present in the list above. The first four attributes in the enumeration will constitute the first group. Each of the other items in the enumeration except for the target attribute will be a group also. Thus, we will have six experts in all, corresponding to the following groups of input attributes:

1. Image geometry
2. Phrases in image's URL
3. Phrases in base URL
4. Phrases in anchor URL
5. Phrases in alt text
6. Phrases in caption

17.4.1.3 Feature Extraction

We preprocess the input attribute vectors, using the singular value decomposition (SVD). The SVD reduces the dimensionality of the data and provides a good set of features for supervised learning. This allows training to be completed more quickly and enhances classification performance of both the fully connected and mixture of attribute experts networks. We apply the SVD to each expert's group of input attributes separately so that both the fully connected and the mixture of attribute experts architectures operate on the same input data. Only groups 2–5 in the list above were processed using SVD. We are able to halve the number of attributes by keeping only the largest singular values after applying the SVD, discarding those that contain a total of 1% or less of the "energy." That is, if the singular values are $\sigma_1 \geq \sigma_2 \geq \cdots \sigma_N$, then we keep $\sigma_1 \cdots \sigma_n$, where n is the smallest integer such that

$$\frac{\sum_{j=n+1}^{N} \sigma_j^2}{\sum_{j=1}^{N} \sigma_j^2} < 0.01$$

The effect of SVD on the size of the input attribute groups is summarized in Table 17.1.

17.4.2 Networks

17.4.2.1 Mixture of Attribute Experts Module

We used the implementation of error backpropagation for feedforward neural networks provided in the Weka 3 system [27]. We implemented the mixture of attribute experts architecture as a new module, ExpertNetwork, which we added to the Weka neural network module. The new module was included in the weka.classifiers.neural directory together with the standard Weka modules and may be accessed through

Table 17.1. Attribute count before and after SVD

	Geom	URL	OrURL	AncURL	Alt	Capt
Before	4	457	495	472	111	19
After	4	265	196	279	107	19

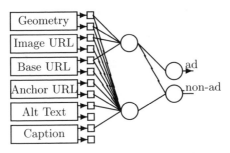

Fig. 17.3. Fully connected network.

the Weka GUI. The new module allows one to set the structure of the network by assigning only specific inputs to the hidden neurons. As an example, one can assign the first 2000 inputs to one neuron and the following 3000 inputs to two other neurons by typing [2000,1][3000,2] in the expertString field.[1] We also added the capability of tracking the precision and the accuracy of a network output every certain number of iterations as specified by the user. One can specify the file to write this information to in the precAccFile field, and the number of iterations between writings in the precAc-cPerIter field.[2] Finally, we added the capability of writing the final network outputs for each test instance to a file. The module uses the first input as an ID so that one can track whether there are any trends in the network outputs. One trick for giving a reasonable ID to the module is to embed the ID into the data as the first attribute, and then assign 0 hidden neurons ([1,0]...) to the first input so that it does not affect network training.

17.4.2.2 Network Configurations

We consider two basic architectures: a standard fully connected feedforward network as depicted in Figure 17.3, and a mixture of attribute experts network as shown in Figure 17.4. Note that the precise numbers of attributes within input groups appear in the second row of Table 17.1.

In both architectures, two output nodes are used, each corresponding to one of the possible values of the class attribute (ad, nonad); the classification decision for a given input instance is determined by selecting the output with the greatest numerical value for that instance. We consider fully connected networks with 2, 3, and 6 hidden nodes, and mixture of attribute experts networks with either 1 or 2 nodes per expert.[3] The number of experts is fixed at 6. Network inputs are obtained directly as the output of SVD preprocessing of the data attributes as explained in Section 17.4.1 above.

---

[1] The number of hidden neurons specified in the expertString field must be lower than or equal to the number of hidden neurons specified in hiddenLayers field.

[2] One must note that specifying this field will affect the training time considerably, and that one should use the default value to obtain a reliable training time.

[3] The "two nodes per expert" MAE architecture has 10 hidden nodes: one for each of the image geometry and caption terms experts, and two for each of the others.

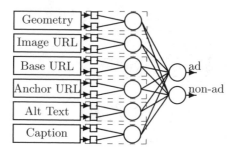

Fig. 17.4. Mixture of experts network.

17.4.3 Performance Metrics

Several different metrics were used to evaluate the classification performance and time efficiency of the various networks, including classification accuracy (fraction of labeled test instances for which the system's predicted classification matches the class label), the F-measure, defined in terms of the information retrieval metrics of precision (specificity, fraction of true positives among true and false positives) and recall (coverage, fraction of true positives among true positives and false negatives) by the formula:

$$F = \frac{2 * \text{precision} * \text{recall}}{\text{precision} + \text{recall}},$$

and the total training time needed for convergence of the error backpropagation algorithm.

17.4.4 Evaluation Protocol

We employed n-fold cross-validation throughout. The number of folds, n, was either 4 or 10, depending on the experiment. For each experiment, we randomly partitioned the data into n parts and proceeded to carry out n training and testing trials. For each of these trials, one of the n parts of the data set was reserved for testing and the union of the other $n - 1$ parts was randomly split into a 70% portion used for training and a 30% portion used as a validation set to determine when to stop training. The networks were trained using the error backpropagation algorithm with a learning rate of 0.3 and a momentum coefficient of 0.2. Training continued until 20 consecutive iterations resulted in no increase in the accuracy as measured over the validation set, or until a maximum of 2000 training iterations had been carried out. After training was completed, performance measures were evaluated on the basis of the networks' performance on the reserved testing part of the data for that trial. The values of the performance measures were then averaged over the n trials; these averages are the values that we report here. Statistical significance information was computed using a large sample normal approximation t test.

Table 17.2. Classification accuracy

Architecture	Mean	Median
Fully connected (2 hidden nodes)	0.94	0.96
Fully connected (4 hidden nodes)	0.96	0.96
Fully connected (6 hidden nodes)	0.94	0.96
Experts (1 node per expert)	0.96	0.96
Experts (2 nodes per expert)	0.96	0.96

17.5 Results

This section describes the results of our comparison of the FC and MAE network architectures using the experimental setup described in the preceding section of the chapter. The Internet Advertisements data set described in Section 17.4 was used unless otherwise stated. Results for the Spambase data set appear at the end in Section 17.5.4.2.

17.5.1 Classification Performance

Table 17.2 shows the classification accuracy obtained for the different system architectures. The evaluation protocol used in this experiment was fourfold cross-validation. As the figure shows, the accuracy values are very close for all architectures tested. In fact, the different values are statistically indistinguishable from one another ($P < 0.05$).

The similarity in the accuracy values hides a noteworthy difference in the classification performance of the different networks. This difference becomes apparent when we examine the observed values of the F-measure in Table 17.3 (computed using fourfold cross-validation). Although Table 17.3 shows little difference across architectures in the median values, an appreciable drop is observed in the mean value of the F-measure for the fully connected architecture with 2 or 6 hidden nodes. The difference in the mean values of the F-measure across architectures is borderline in the sense of statistical significance, being not quite large enough to be significant at the level $P < 0.05$. Nonetheless, it is interesting to understand the origin of this phenomenon. It is associated with convergence of the error backpropagation training algorithm for the fully connected networks to nonglobal minima of the output error landscape in some of the runs; the resulting classifiers predict the same class (e.g., nonad) for all test instances. It is possible that a random restarting version of error backpropagation [22] would reduce this phenomenon.

Table 17.3. F-measure

Architecture	Mean	.Median
Fully connected (2 hidden nodes)	0.65	0.85
Fully connected (4 hidden nodes)	0.87	0.86
Fully connected (6 hidden nodes)	0.65	0.86
Experts (1 node per expert)	0.85	0.87
Experts (2 nodes per expert)	0.85	0.84

Table 17.4. Training times (seconds)

Architecture	Mean	Median
Fully connected (2 hidden nodes)	1532.5	925.3
Fully connected (4 hidden nodes)	2578.8	2167.6
Fully connected (6 hidden nodes)	4243.7	4631.3
Experts (1 node per expert)	1977.2	2324.7
Experts (2 nodes per expert)	890.4	830.5

17.5.2 Time Efficiency

The total time required to train each network over 75% of the set of 3279 instances is reported in Table 17.4 (fourfold cross-validation). This experiment was performed in the Weka 3 system with our neural experts module, using JVM version 1.4.1 on a Pentium–based system with 2.0 GHz clock rate and 256 MB RAM.

Table 17.4 shows that the mixture of attribute experts architecture with two nodes per expert trained faster than the fully connected architectures. Qualitatively, this phenomenon appears to be stable. However, we note that the precise training times depend significantly on the stopping criteria used for training. See the discussion below for additional comments.

17.5.3 Discussion

The results in Table 17.4 show that the fully connected architecture with four and six hidden nodes took much longer to train than either of the mixture of attribute experts architectures, each of which has at least six hidden nodes. Thus, the mixture of attribute experts architecture provides a more efficient way of making use of the available computational resources. As Tables 17.2 and 17.3 above show, this time advantage is achieved without sacrificing classification performance. This supports the implicit assumption that the chosen assignment of input attributes to experts yields a "loosely interacting" partition as described in Section 17.3.2.

The only version of the fully connected architecture that trained in a time comparable to the slower of the two mixture of attribute experts networks is that with two hidden nodes. However, Table 17.3 shows that this particular fully connected network displayed inferior classification performance in the sense of the F-measure on some of the runs. The fastest training was achieved by the mixture of attribute experts architecture with two nodes per expert. Remarkably, this architecture trained even faster than the mixture of attribute experts architecture with only one node per expert. This may point to differences in the output error landscape that make it more difficult to find the minimum points in weight space when the experts contain only one hidden node.

17.5.4 Additional Experimental Results

17.5.4.1 Internet Advertisements Data set

We carried out an additional cross-validation experiment over the Internet Advertisements data set, increasing the number of folds from 4 to 10 in order to better assess the

Table 17.5. F–measure (10-fold cross-validation)

Architecture	Mean	Median
Fully connected (3 hidden nodes)	0.79	0.87
Experts (1 node per expert)	0.85	0.86
Experts (2 nodes per expert)	0.87	0.87

statistical stability of the above results. We increased the number of hidden nodes from 10 to 12 in the larger of the MAE architectures[4] and compared the results with those for a fully connected network with 3 hidden nodes. Again, error backpropagation for the fully connected architecture fails to converge on some runs. This is reflected in a significantly lower mean value of the F-measure for the fully connected architecture with 3 hidden nodes in Table 17.5, just as previously observed for the fully connected architecture with 2 or 6 nodes in Table 17.3. These results provide further support for the finding that the mixture of attribute experts architecture has better classification performance in this context.

Table 17.6 shows an increase in the mixture of attribute experts training time relative to the results in Table 17.4, which is consistent with the increased number of hidden nodes in the larger of the MAE networks. Nonetheless, the computational superiority of the mixture of attribute experts architecture with two nodes per expert is still evident in Table 17.6.

17.5.4.2 Spambase Data Set

Data Set Characteristics

Our final set of experiments used a subset of the Spambase spam e-mail data set from the UCI Machine Learning Repository [13]. This data set contains 4601 instances (e-mails), of which 1813 (39.4%) are labeled as spam and the remaining 2788 (60.6%) are labeled as not spam. Each instance is described by 57 continuous attributes, plus the spam/no-spam class attribute. There are no missing attribute values. For our experiments, we extracted a random stratified subsample consisting of 460 instances of the Spambase data set.

Attributes

The original 57 attributes were used directly. No additional feature extraction or dimensionality reduction steps were carried out. The attributes are described below (from the Spambase documentation at the UCI Machine Learning Repository [13]). The terms WORD and CHAR refer to specific selected words (e.g., "money," "free," "650," "credit," "edu") and characters (';', '(', '[', '!', '$', '#') that may occur within an e-mail message.

---

[4] By using 2 hidden nodes instead of 1 for the image geometry and caption terms experts as well as for the other experts.

Table 17.6. Training times (second), 10-fold cross-validation

Architecture	Mean	Median
Fully connected (3 hidden nodes)	2760.8	2086.9
Experts (1 node per expert)	2676.8	2779.0
Experts (2 nodes per expert)	1568.8	1131.8

1. 48 continuous real [0,100] attributes, word_freq_WORD = percentage of words in the e-mail that match WORD, i.e., 100 * (number of times the WORD appears in the e-mail)/total number of words in e-mail. A "word" in this case is any string of alphanumeric characters bounded by nonalphanumeric characters or end-of-string.
2. 6 continuous real [0,100] attributes, char_freq_CHAR = percentage of characters in the e-mail that match CHAR, i.e., 100 * (number of CHAR occurences)/total characters in e-mail.
3. 1 continuous real attribute, capital_run_length_average = average length of uninterrupted sequences of capital letters.
4. 1 continuous int attribute, capital_run_length_longest = length of longest uninterrupted sequence of capital letters.
5. 1 continuous int attribute, capital_run_length_total = sum of length of uninterrupted sequences of capital letters = total number of capital letters in the e-mail.
6. 1 nominal 0,1 class attribute, spam = denotes whether the e-mail was considered spam (1) or not (0), i.e., unsolicited commercial e-mail.

Network Configurations: MAE Input Partition

We considered fully connected (FC) and mixture of attribute experts (MAE) neural networks, in configurations similar to those described for the Internet Advertisements data set in Section 17.4. MAE networks were implemented in Weka 3 [27] as described in Section 17.4. Two experts were used for the MAE networks. The first 48 attributes of the Spambase data set (which comprise item number 1 in the above listing) were grouped together and assigned to the first expert; the remaining 9 nonclass attributes were assigned to the second expert. The number of hidden units in the first expert was either 1 or 3. One hidden unit was used for the second expert in all cases.

Experimental Protocol

Networks were trained using the error backpropagation algorithm with a learning rate of 0.3 and a momentum of 0.2 until the error over a reserved 30% validation portion of the data set did not decrease for 20 consecutive training iterations, or until a maximum of 500 iterations had been carried out. A 10-fold cross-validation protocol was used. Furthermore, F–measure and training time results were averaged over 10 separate repetitions of 10-fold cross-validation (a total of 100 runs for each experiment). This reduces the variance and enables us to more readily gauge statistical significance of the results using a t test.

Table 17.7. Spambase F–measure, 10-fold c-v

Architecture	Mean	Median
Fully connected (2 hidden nodes)	0.84	0.85
Fully connected (4 hidden nodes)	0.84	0.85
Experts (1 node experts)	0.84	0.84
Experts (3 and 1 node experts)	0.83	0.85

Results

Classification quality as gauged by the F-measure is reported in Table 17.7. Training times appear in Table 17.8. These results for the Spambase data set confirm our previous findings for the Internet Advertisements data set. First, the MAE and FC networks achieve essentially the same classification quality (the observed differences in the F-measure are all statistically insignificant at the level $P < 0.05$). Convergence of the error back-propagation learning algorithm to nonglobal local minima, which was observed for the FC architecture in the case of the Internet Advertisements data set (see Section 17.5.1) did not occur in the case of the Spambase data set. The second finding concerns the greater efficiency of the MAE architecture. For both data sets, the MAE networks train in significantly less time than the FC networks ($P < 0.05$).

17.6 Conclusions and Future Work

We have presented a mixture of attribute experts neural network architecture that provides reduced network complexity and improved training efficiency when using iterative supervised learning techniques for classification tasks involving multiple loosely coupled data sources. We have provided a description of the representational power of mixture of attribute experts networks in terms of functional composition, showing in particular that mixture of attribute experts do not satisfy the universal approximation property of fully connected networks. Rather, a given target function can be represented accurately by a mixture of experts network only if the function can be expressed in terms of functional composition in a way that reflects the partition of the set of input attributes into groups associated with experts. We have applied the mixture of attribute experts approach to the task of detecting advertisements in images embedded in Web pages. In this context, we found that a mixture of attributes network trained in less time while maintaining the same level of classification performance as a fully connected network operating on the same input data. Thus, the

Table 17.8. Spambase training times (second), 10-fold c-v

Architecture	Mean	Median
Fully connected (2 hidden nodes)	26.6	29.6
Fully connected (4 hidden nodes)	43.9	49.4
Experts (1 node experts)	17.5	18.3
Experts (3 and 1 node experts)	19.6	12.6

potential representational limitation of mixture of attribute experts networks does not manifest itself in this task. Convergence of the error backpropagation algorithm to nonglobal local minima of the error function was observed in the case of the fully connected network architecture in some of our experiments. The mixture of attribute experts architecture did not exhibit this problem. This phenomenon points to qualitative differences between the error landscapes for the two architectures. It would be desirable to understand in detail how the error landscape depends on whether a mixture of attribute experts is used. For example, does the mixture of attribute experts architecture reduce the number or depth of local minima on the error surface? Changes in the error surface will affect all supervised learning algorithms that are driven by the same error function. This fact, together with the reduced number of connections in a mixture of attribute experts network as compared with a fully connected network with the same number of processing units, implies that the mixture of attribute experts architecture should yield efficiency improvements for all such algorithms. An experimental evaluation of the relative efficiency gain and classification performance of mixture of attribute experts networks for ANN learning techniques other than error back-propagation would be of interest. As we pointed out, the success of the mixture of attribute experts approach in a given context depends on whether a set of input attributes can be found that can be partitioned into subsets with relatively limited mutual interaction in determining the value of the target attribute. It would be beneficial to identify domains in which such partitions occur naturally, as well as feature selection techniques that contribute to this goal in situations in which a suitable partition cannot easily be identified. The degree to which the advantages of the mixture of attribute experts approach can be realized may depend on the intrinsic complexity of the target task. Exploring this issue would be a worthwhile goal for future work.

References

1. Antonie ML, Zaïane OR, Coman A. Application of Data Mining Techniques for Medical Image Classification. In: *Proc. of Second Intl. Workshop on Multimedia Data Mining (MDM/KDD'2001)*. San Francisco, CA; 2001, pp. 94–101.
2. Berthold MR, Sudweeks F, Newton S, Coyne R. Clustering on the Net: Applying an autoassociative neural network to computer mediated discussions. *J Computer Mediated Communication* 1997;2(4).
3. Noordewier MO, Towell GG, Shavlik JB. Training knowledge-based neural networks to recognize genes. In: Lippmann RP, Moody JE, Touretzky DS, editors. *Advances in Neural Information Processing Systems*. Vol. 3. Morgan Kaufmann Publishers, Inc.; 1991, pp. 530–536.
4. Rowley HA, Baluja S, Kanade T. Neural network-based face detection. *IEEE Transactions on Pattern Analysis and Machine Intelligence* 1998;20(1):23–38.
5. Widrow B, Rumelhart DE, Lehr MA. Neural networks: Applications in industry, business, and science. *Communications of the ACM* 1996;37(3):93–105.
6. Guan L, Adali T, Katagiri S, Larsen J, Principe J. Guest editorial, special issue on intelligent multimedia processing. *IEEE Transactions on Neural Networks* 2002;13(4):789–792.

7. Cybenko G. Approximations by superpositions of a sigmoidal function. *Mathematics of Control, Signals, and Systems* 1989;2:303–314.

8. Funahashi KI. On the approximate realization of continuous mappings by neural networks. *Neural Networks* 1989;2:183–192.

9. Hornick K, Stinchcombe M, White H. Multilayer feedforward networks are universal approximators. *Neural Networks* 1989;2:359–366.

10. Tikk D, Kóczy LT, Gedeon TD. A survey on universal approximation and its limits in soft computing techniques. *Int J Approx Reasoning* 2003;33(2):185–202.

11. Simoff SJ, Djeraba C, Zaïane OR. MDM/KDD2002: Multimedia data mining between promises and problems. *SIGKDD Explorations* 2003;4(2):118–121.

12. Zaiane O, Simoff S, Djeraba C. Mining multimedia and complex data. vol. 2797 of Lecture Notes in Artificial Intelligence. Springer; 2003.

13. Blake CL, Merz CJ. UCI Repository of machine learning databases. [http://www.ics.uci.edu/~mlearn/MLRepository.html]; 1999. Dept. of Information and Computer Science, University of California, Irvine.

14. Sharkey AJC. Special Issues on Combining Artificial Neural Nets: Ensemble and Modular Approaches. *Connection Science* 1996 and 1997;8(3/4) and 9(1).

15. Jacobs RA, Jordan MI, Nowlan SJ, Hinton GE. Adaptive mixtures of local experts. *Neural Computation* 1991;3:79–87.

16. Ruiz ME, Srinivasan P. Hierarchical text categorization using neural networks. *Information Retrieval* 2002;5(1):87–118.

17. Petrushin V. Emotion recognition agents in the real world. In: Socially Intelligent Agents: the Human in the Loop, Papers from the 2000 AAAI Fall Symposium (K. Dautenhahn, Chair). Technical Report FS-00-04, AAAI Press; 2000. pp. 136–138.

18. LeCun Y, Denker J, Solla S, Howard RE, Jackel LD. Optimal brain damage. In: Touretzky DS, editor. *Advances in Neural Information Processing Systems II.* Morgan Kauffman; San Mateo, CA, 1990. pp. 598–605.

19. Rumelhart DE, Hinton GE, Williams RJ. Learning internal representations by error propagation. In: Rumelhart DE, McClelland JL, editors. *Parallel Distributed Processing,* Vol. 1. Cambridge, MA: MIT Press; 1986, pp. 318–362.

20. Riedmiller M, Braun H. A direct adaptive method for faster backpropagation learning: the RPROP algorithm. In: *Proc. of the IEEE Intl. Conf. on Neural Networks*; San Francisco, CA, 1993. pp. 586–591.

21. Fahlman S. An empirical study of learning speed in back-propagation networks; 1988. CMU Technical Report CMU-CS-88-162, Carnegie Mellon University.

22. Alvarez SA, Ruiz C, Kawato T, Kogel W. Faster neural networks for combined collaborative and content-based recommendation. *Journal of Computational Methods in Sciences and Engineering* In: press.

23. Magdon-Ismail M, Atiya AF. The early restart algorithm. *Neural Computation* 2000;12(6):1303–1313.

24. Rudin WE. *Principles of Mathematical Analysis.* 3rd ed. McGraw–Hill; 1976.

25. Alvarez SA. Modularity and universal approximation; 2005. Preprint.

26. Kushmerick N. Learning to remove Internet advertisements. In: *Proc. of the Third Annual Conference on Autonomous Agents (AGENTS99).* Seattle, WA: ACM; 1999. pp. 175–181.

27. Witten IH, Frank E. *Data Mining: Practical Machine Learning Tools and Techniques.* 2nd ed. Morgan Kaufmann Publishers; 2005.

18. A Data Mining Approach to Expressive Music Performance Modeling

Rafael Ramirez, Amaury Hazan, Esteban Maestre, and Xavier Serra

Summary. In this chapter we present a data mining approach to one of the most challenging aspects of computer music: modeling the knowledge applied by a musician when performing a score in order to produce an expressive performance of a piece. We apply data mining techniques to real performance data (i.e., audio recordings) in order to induce an expressive performance model. This leads to an expressive performance system consisting of three components: (1) a melodic transcription component that extracts a set of acoustic features from the audio recordings, (2) a data mining component that induces an expressive transformation model from the set of extracted acoustic features, and (3) a melody synthesis component that generates expressive monophonic output (MIDI or audio) from inexpressive melody descriptions using the induced expressive transformation model. We describe, explore, and compare different data mining techniques for inducing the expressive transformation model.

18.1 Introduction

Modeling expressive music performance is one of the most challenging aspects of computer music that in the past has been studied from different perspectives (e.g. [2,7,24]). The main approaches to empirically studying expressive performance have been based on statistical analysis (e.g. [23]), mathematical modelling (e.g. [29]), and analysis-by-synthesis (e.g. [5]). In all these approaches, it is a person who is responsible for devising a theory or mathematical model that captures different aspects of musical expressive performance. The theory or model is later tested on real performance data to determine its accuracy.

This chapter describes a data mining approach to investigate how skilled musicians (saxophone Jazz players in particular) express and communicate their view of the musical and emotional content of musical pieces by introducing deviations and changes of various parameters such as timing and dynamics. The deviations and changes we consider here are on note duration, note onset, and note energy. The study of these variations is the basis of an inductive content-based transformation system for performing expressive transformations on musical phrases. The system consists of three components: (a) a melodic transcription component that extracts a symbolic representation of the expressive aspects of a set of audio recordings, (b) a data mining component that induces an expressive transformation model from the symbolic representation, and (c) a melody synthesis component that generates expressive monophonic output (MIDI or audio) from inexpressive melody descriptions using the induced expressive transformation model. We describe and compare different classification and regression data mining techniques for inducing the expressive transformation model.

The rest of the chapter is organized as follows: Section 18.2 describes the melodic description component of the system. Section 18.3 describes the different approaches we have considered for the inductive part of the system and presents a comparison among them. Section 18.4 briefly describes how the system generates both MIDI and audio output. Section 18.5 reports on some related work, and finally Section 18.6 presents some conclusions and indicates some areas of future research.

18.2 Melodic Description

In this section, we summarize how we extract a symbolic description from the monophonic recordings of performances of Jazz standards. We need this symbolic representation to apply data mining techniques to the data. In this chapter, our interest is to model note-level transformations such as onset deviations, duration transformations, and energy variations. Thus, descriptors providing note-level information are of particular interest.

18.2.1 Algorithms for Feature Extraction

Figure 18.1 represents the steps that are performed to obtain a melodic description from audio. First of all, we perform a spectral analysis of a portion of sound, called analysis frame, whose size is a parameter of the algorithm. This spectral analysis lies in multiplying the audio frame with an appropriate analysis window and performing a Discrete Fourier Transform (DFT) to obtain its spectrum. In this case, we use a frame width of 46 ms, an overlap factor of 50%, and a Keiser–Bessel 25 dB window. Then, we perform a note segmentation using low-level descriptor values. Once the note boundaries are known, the note descriptors are computed from the low-level and the fundamental frequency values.

18.2.2 Low-Level Descriptors Computation

The main low-level descriptors used to characterize expressive performance are instantaneous energy and fundamental frequency.

18.2.2.1 Energy Computation

The energy descriptor is computed on the spectral domain, using the values of the amplitude spectrum at each analysis frame. In addition, energy is computed in different

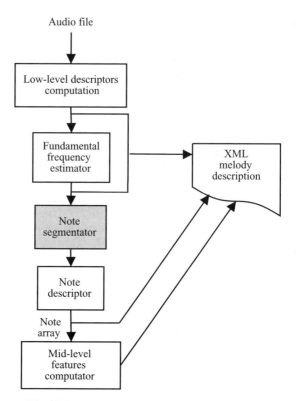

Fig. 18.1. Block diagram of the melody descriptor.

frequency bands as defined in [11], and these values are used by the algorithm for note segmentation.

18.2.2.2 Fundamental Frequency Estimation

For the estimation of the instantaneous fundamental frequency, we use a harmonic matching model derived from the Two-Way Mismatch procedure (TWM) [13]. For each fundamental frequency candidate, mismatches between the harmonics generated and the measured partials frequencies are averaged over a fixed subset of the available partials. A weighting scheme is used to make the procedure robust to the presence of noise or absence of certain partials in the spectral data. The solution presented in [13] employs two mismatch error calculations The first one is based on the frequency difference between each partial in the measured sequence and its nearest neighbor in the predicted sequence. The second is based on the mismatch between each harmonic in the predicted sequence and its nearest partial neighbor in the measured sequence. This two-way mismatch helps avoid octave errors by applying a penalty for partials that are present in the measured data but are not predicted, and also for partials whose presence is predicted but which do not actually appear in the measured sequence.

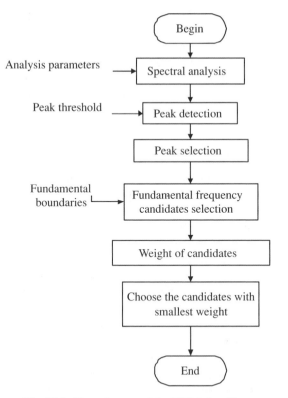

Fig. 18.2. Flow diagram of the TWM algorithm.

The TWM mismatch procedure has also the benefit that the effect of any spurious components or partial missing from the measurement can be counteracted by the presence of uncorrupted partials in the same frame.

Figure 18.2 shows the block diagram for the fundamental frequency estimator following a harmonic-matching approach.

First, we perform a spectral analysis of all the windowed frames, as explained above. Second, the prominent spectral peaks of the spectrum are detected from the spectrum magnitude. These spectral peaks of the spectrum are defined as the local maxima of the spectrum whose magnitude is greater than a threshold. The spectral peaks are compared to a harmonic series and a two-way mismatch (TWM) error is computed for each fundamental frequency candidates. The candidate with the minimum error is chosen to be the fundamental frequency estimate.

After a first test of this implementation, some improvements to the original algorithm where implemented to deal with some errors of the algorithm:

- *Peak selection*: A peak selection routine has been added to eliminate spectral peaks corresponding to noise. The peak selection is done according to a masking threshold around each of the maximum magnitude peaks. The form of the masking threshold

depends on the peak amplitude, and uses three different slopes depending on the frequency distance to the peak frequency.
- *Context awareness*: We take into account previous values of the fundamental frequency estimation and instrument dependencies to obtain a more adapted result.
- *Noise gate*: A noise gate based on some low-level signal descriptor is applied to detect silences so that the estimation is performed only in nonsilent segments of the sound.

18.2.3 Note Segmentation

Note segmentation is performed using a set of frame descriptors, which are energy computation in different frequency bands and fundamental frequency. Energy onsets are first detected following a band-wise algorithm that uses some psycho-acoustical knowledge [11]. In a second step, fundamental frequency transitions are also detected. Finally, both results are merged to find the note boundaries (onset and offset information).

18.2.4 Note Descriptor Computation

We compute note descriptors, using the note boundaries and the low-level descriptors values. The low-level descriptors associated to a note segment are computed by averaging the frame values within this note segment. Pitch histograms have been used to compute the pitch note and the fundamental frequency that represents each note segment, as found in [14]. This is done to avoid taking into account mistaken frames in the fundamental frequency mean computation.

First, frequency values are converted into cents by the following formula:

$$c = 1200 \cdot \frac{\log\left(\frac{f}{f_{\text{ref}}}\right)}{log2} \tag{18.1}$$

where $f_{\text{ref}} = 8.176$. Then, we define histograms with bins of 100 *cents* and hop size of 5 *cents* and we compute the maximum of the histogram to identify the note pitch. Finally, we compute the frequency mean for all the points that belong to the histogram. The MIDI pitch is computed by quantization of this fundamental frequency mean over the frames within the note limits.

18.3 Expressive Performance Knowledge Induction

In this section, we describe different inductive approaches to learning an expressive performance model from the symbolic representation extracted from a set of monophonic recordings by a skilled saxophone Jazz player. Our aim is to explore different data mining techniques in order to be able to predict accurately how a particular note in a particular context should be played (e.g., longer or shorter than its nominal duration and by how much).

18.3.1 Training Data

The training data used in our experimental investigations are monophonic recordings of four Jazz standards (*Body and Soul, Once I loved, Like Someone in Love*, and *Up Jumped Spring*) performed by a professional musician at 11 different tempos around the nominal tempo. For each piece, the nominal tempo was determined by the musician as the most natural and comfortable tempo to interpret the piece. Also for each piece, the musician identified the fastest and slowest tempos at which a piece could be reasonably interpreted. Interpretations were recorded at regular intervals around the nominal tempo (five faster and five slower) within the fastest-slowest tempo limits. The resulting data set is composed of 4360 performed notes. Each note in the training data is annotated with its corresponding deviations (i.e., duration, onset, and energy deviations) and a number of attributes representing both properties of the note itself and some aspects of the musical context in which the note appears. Information about intrinsic properties of the note includes the note duration and the note metrical position, while information about its context includes duration of previous and following notes, extension and direction of the intervals between the note and the previous and following notes, and the note Narmour structure(s) [16]. The computation of the Narmour structures of a note is motivated by the fact that musicians perform music considering a number of abstract structures (e.g., musical phrases). In this context, we have initially based our musical analysis on the *implication/realization model* proposed by Narmour [16, 17].

18.3.2 Musical Analysis

The Implication/Realization model is a theory of perception and cognition of melodies. The theory states that a melodic musical line continuously causes listeners to generate expectations of how the melody should continue. The nature of these expectations in an individual are motivated by two types of sources: innate and learned. According to Narmour, on the one hand, we are all born with innate information that suggests to us how a particular melody should continue. On the other hand, learned factors are due to exposure to music throughout our lives and familiarity with musical styles and particular melodies. According to Narmour, any two consecutively perceived notes constitute a melodic interval, and if this interval is not conceived as complete, it is an *implicative interval*, that is, an interval that implies a subsequent interval with certain characteristics. That is to say, some notes are more likely than others to follow the implicative interval. Two main principles recognized by Narmour concern *registral direction* and *intervallic difference*. The principle of registral direction states that small intervals imply an interval in the same registral direction (a small upward interval implies another upward interval and analogously for downward intervals), and large intervals imply a change in registral direction (a large upward interval implies a downward interval and analogously for downward intervals). The principle of intervallic difference states that a small (five semitones or less) interval implies a similarly sized interval (plus or minus two semitones), and a large interval (seven semitones or more) implies a smaller interval. Based on these

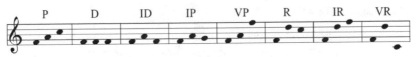

Fig. 18.3. Prototypical Narmour structures.

two principles, melodic patterns or groups can be identified that either satisfy or violate the implication as predicted by the principles. Such patterns are called structures and are labeled to denote characteristics in terms of registral direction and intervallic difference. Figure 18.3 shows prototypical Narmour structures. A note in a melody often belongs to more than one structure. Thus, a description of a melody as a sequence of Narmour structures consists of a list of overlapping structures. We parse each melody in the training data to automatically generate an implication/realization analysis of the pieces. Figure 18.4 shows the analysis for a melody fragment.

18.3.3 Data Mining Techniques

In order to induce predictive models for duration ratio, onset deviation, and energy variation, we have applied two types of data mining techniques, namely numerical techniques and rule-based classification techniques. On one hand, numerical methods induce expressive performance models capable of *endowing* a computer generated music performance with the expressiveness that characterizes human generated music, i.e., transforming an inexpressive description of a musical piece into an expressive performance of the piece. On the other hand, rule-based classification methods are good at *explaining* the predictions they provide but are restricted to a set of discrete classes as prediction space. Our problem at hand is one that requires the prediction precision of numerical methods for generating accurate solutions (i.e., expressive performances) but at the same time it is highly desirable to be able to explain the system predictions. Having this in mind, we have explored both approaches applying a sample of both numerical and rule-based classification methods (we have also applied non–rule-based classification methods for comparison purposes).

18.3.3.1 Numerical Methods

We have explored different numerical methods to induce predictive models for duration ratio, onset deviation, and energy variation. The methods we have included in our research are as follows:

Fig. 18.4. Narmour analysis of *All of Me* (from [8]).

- **Linear regression** is the simplest scheme for numeric prediction that has been widely used in statistical applications. The idea is to express the predicted value as a linear combination of the attributes, with predetermined weights that are calculated from the training data, in order to minimize the overall deviation between the training values and the model. Linear regression is not the best choice to approximate nonlinear functions. As confirmed by the results (Section 18.4), expressive performance does not seem to be a linear function on the attributes. However, we have decided to include linear regression in our experiments as a baseline reference for the other methods.

- **Model trees** build an induction tree which has a different linear model on each leaf. Model trees behave well as each of the leaves' linear models approximates a set of more specific cases than with a global linear model; that is, model trees approximate continuous functions by linear "patches," a more sophisticated representation than simple linear regression.

- **Support Vector Machines** take great advantage of using a nonlinear attribute mapping that leads them to be able to predict nonlinear models (though they remain linear in a higher dimensional space). Thus, they provide a more flexible prediction, but with a higher computational cost necessary to perform all the computations in the higher dimensional space. Training a Support Vector Machine requires the solution of a very large quadratic programming optimization problem. The quadratic programming resolution has been optimized in terms of speed and memory usage with the sequential minimal optimization algorithm [31]. They have been applied to numerical prediction [32] and the results largely depend on the tuning of the algorithm, for example, the choice of the kernel evaluation function and the parameters that control the amount up to which deviations are tolerated (denoted by epsilon). The kernel function defines implicitly the higher dimensional mapping applied to the training vector. With an appropriate tuning, it is possible to control the number of support vectors that define a boundary between two classes. We were interested in obtaining a model with a relatively reduced number of support vectors (i.e., less than a third of the training instances) in order to avoid overfitting and thus have tuned empirically four support vector machines with the following parameters: (1) Linear kernel, C = 1, epsilon = 0.05; (2) 2nd order polynomial kernel, C = 1, epsilon = 0.05; (3) 3rd order polynomial kernel, C = 1, epsilon = 0.05; and (4) Radial Basis Function kernel, gamma exponent = 0.95, C = 10, epsilon = 0.05.

18.3.3.2 Classification Methods

We have also explored different classification methods. We discretized the input values into classes, and used classification techniques to induce predictive models for duration ratio, onset deviation, and energy variation. The number of classes was determined by the distribution of the input values. We applied a fix-width discretization for duration ratio and onset deviation with nine and seven classes, respectively. The case of energy variation is quite different as there is no information about note energy in the score and we have to characterize each note energy in relation to the note average energy in the recordings. Thus we performed a frequency discretization; that is, each target class contains the same number of cases, and characterize soft, normal, and loud notes. Consequently, the classification results presented in Section 18.3.4 are to be compared with the accuracy of a random classification, i.e., 11.11% for duration ratio, 14.28% for onset deviation, and 33.33% for energy variation. The methods we have included in our research are:

- The **naive Bayes classifier** is based on Bayes rule on conditional probability propagation. It is called "naive" because this rule assumes that the attributes of an instance are independent from each other. This can lead to weak results when attributes have a strong correlation. The algorithm implements redundant attributes filtering as preprocess [30]. Despite being one of the simplest algorithms, it has outperformed more complex techniques in a significant number of cases.

- **Lazy Methods** are based on the notion of lazy learning that subsumes a family of algorithms that store the complete set of given (classified) examples of an underlying example language and delay all further calculations until requests for classifying yet unseen instances are received. The K-Nearest Neighbor algorithm is one of the most popular instanced-based algorithm, which handles well noisy data if the training set has an acceptable size. The main idea of this algorithm is to compare a test set with its nearest neighbors (the number is determined by the user and the computational cost largely depends on it). A major problem of the simple approach of K-Nearest Neighbor is that the vector distance will not necessarily be suited for finding intuitively similar examples, especially if irrelevant attributes are present. We empirically found the best number of neighbors: 5 for the duration ratio model, 11 for the onset deviation model, and 1 for the energy variation model. KStar algorithms proceed in an similar fashion as K-NN, but use an entropy similarity measure distance to find the neighbors of a test vector.

- **Tree induction algorithms** build a tree model by selecting at each node the most relevant attribute. We compare the results of C4.5 [18, 20], C4.5 with boosting, and the random forest algorithm. Boosting refers to a meta-algorithm that may improve the results of any classification algorithm by giving to each instance of the training set a particular weight proportional with the difficulty to classify such instance. That is, a first classification model is proposed giving the same weight to all the training instances. Misclassified instances with the model are then given a greater weight, and so on. After a user defined number of iterations (in our case 10 iterations) the resulting model is able to deal with "difficult" training instances. This boosting method can drastically improve the results of an inaccurate model, thought overfitting can occur. The random forest algorithm uses a bagging technique: it combines the decision of different models amalgamating the various outputs in a single prediction. The decision can be seen as a vote between the models. Each tree is built using random features selection. We used 20 random trees in our test with the random forest algorithm.

- **Inductive logic programming.** Conditions in rules obtained by the C4.5 algorithm (and by most of the rule learning algorithms) involve testing an attribute value against a constant. Such rules are called *propositional* because they have the same expressive power as *propositional logic*. In many cases, propositional rules are sufficiently expressive to describe a concept accurately. However, there are cases where more expressive rules; for example, first-order logic rules would provide a more intuitive concept description. These are cases where the knowledge to be learned is best expressed by allowing variables in attributes. One important special case involving learning sets of rules containing variables is called *inductive logic programming* [19,25]. Inductive logic programming has proved to be an extremely well-suited technique for learning expressive performance rules. This is mainly due to (1) the possibility of considering an arbitrary-size note context (not necessarily the context given by the previous and following note) without explicitly defining extra attributes and (2) the possibility of introducing *background knowledge* (i.e., music theory knowledge) directly into the learning task. The background knowledge is useful to guide the rule construction or to simply make rules more readable. Using the training data, we applied a standard inductive logic programming sequential covering algorithm that incrementally constructs a theory as a set of first-order rules (Horn clauses) by learning new rules one at a time, removing the positive examples covered by the latest rule before attempting to learn the next rule. Note that the algorithm considers two-class classification problems whereas our classification task involves three classes, for example, in the case of duration the classes are *shorten, lengthen,* and *same.* We have reduced our problem to a two-class classification problem by taking the examples of one class as positive examples and the examples of the other two classes as negative examples. We applied the learning algorithm with the following target predicates: duration/2, onset/2, and energy/2. (where /n at the end of the predicate name refers to the predicate arity, i.e., the number of arguments the predicate takes). Each target predicate corresponds to a particular type of transformation: duration/2 refers to duration transformation, onset/2 to onset deviation, and energy/2 to energy transformation. For each target predicate we use as example set the complete training data specialized for the particular type of transformation; for example, for duration/2 we used the complete data set information on duration transformation (i.e., the performed duration transformation for each note in the data set). The arguments are the note in the piece and performed transformation. We use (background) predicates to specify both note musical context and background information. The predicates we consider include context/6, narmour/2, succ/2, and member/3. Predicate context/8 specifies the local context of a note. We used the Aleph inductive logic programming system [27].

The induced rules are of different types. Some focus on features of the note itself and depend on the performance tempo while others focus on the Narmour analysis and are independent of the performance tempo. Rules referring to the local context of a note, i.e., rules classifying a note solely in terms of the timing, pitch and metrical strength of the note and its neighbors, as well as compound rules that refer to both the local context and the Narmour structure were discovered. To exemplify the discovered rules, we present some of them below (':-' is read 'if', i.e., ':-' represents the logical implication connective ←).

```
D-1: [Pos cover  =  21 Neg cover  =  1]
duration(C, shorten) :-
succ(C, D), succ(D, E),
context(E, [nargroup(p, 1)|F]),
context(C, [nargroup(p, 2)|F]).
```

"Shorten a note n if it belongs to a P Narmour group in second position and if note n + 2 belongs to a P Narmour group in first position"

```
D-2: [Pos cover  =  41 Neg cover  =  1]
duration(C, same) :-
succ(C, D), succ(D, E),
context(E, [nargroup(vr, 3)|F]),
member(nargroup(p, 1), F).
```

"Do not stretch a note n if note n + 2 belongs to both VR Narmour group in third position and P Narmour group in first position"

```
O-1: [Pos cover  =  41 Neg cover  =  2]
onset(C, same) :-
succ(C, D),
context(D, [nargroup(vr, 3)|E]),
member(nargroup(d, 1), E).
```

"Play a note at the right time if its successor belongs to a VR Narmour group in third position and to a D Narmour group in first position"

```
O-2: [Pos cover  =  17 Neg cover  =  1]
onset(C, advance) :-
succ(C,D), succ(D,E),
context(E,[nargroup(ip,1)|F]),
context(D,[nargroup(p,3)|F]).
```

"Play a note n in advance if n+1 belongs to a P Narmour group in third position and if n+2 belongs to an IP Narmour group in first position"

```
E-1: [Pos cover  =  26 Neg cover  =  0]
energy(C, loud) :-
succ(D, C),
context(D, [nargroup(d, 2)|E]),
context(C, [nargroup(id, 1)|E]).
```

"Play loudly a note if it belongs to an ID Narmour group in first position and if its predecessor belongs to a D Narmour group in second position"

```
E-2: [Pos cover  =  34 Neg cover  =  1]
energy(C, soft) :-
succ(C, D),
context(D, [nargroup(p, 4)|E]),
context(C, [nargroup(p, 3)|E]).
```

Table 18.1. Cross-validation results for duration ratio.

Algorithm	C.C.I (%)	C.C	R.A.E (%)	R.R.S.E (%)
C4.5	74.59	—	68.07	86.84
C4.5 with boosting	72.99	—	72.87	87.35
Random forest	70.51	—	62.74	89.85
KStar	73.71	—	63.04	86.65
KNN	67.15	—	72.77	95.57
Naive bayes	59.97	—	98.18	103.07
ILP	80.37	—	45.25	76.96
Linear regression	—	0.33	98.69	94.39
Least med square regression	—	0.29	95.22	96.60
Model tree regression	—	0.72	74.89	69.14
SVM regression (1)	—	0.29	95.30	96.15
SVM regression (2)	—	0.48	89.01	88.24
SVM regression (3)	—	0.66	76.65	75.47
SVM regression (4)	—	0.70	81.11	71.23

"Play soft two successive notes if they belong to a P Narmour group respectively in third and forth position"

18.3.4 Results

We present a comparative table for each of the expressive transformation aspects we are dealing with, namely note duration (Table 18.1), onset (Table 18.2), and energy (Table 18.3). We performed a 10-fold cross validation for all the algorithms. In Tables 18.1, 18.2, and 18.3, C.C.I refers to the correctly classified instances rate, C.C to the correlation coefficient, and R.A.E to the relative absolute error and R.R.S.E the root relative squared error which are calculated as follows. Note that the formulas we present are used to compute statistics for each cross-validation run. Consequently the values presented in Tables 18.1, 18.2, and 18.3 are averaged over the 10 cross-validation runs.

$$C.C.I = \frac{N_{C.C}}{N_{C.C} + N_{I.C}} \tag{18.2}$$

where $N_{C.C}$ (respectively $N_{I.C}$) stands for the total number of correctly (respectively incorrectly) classified instances.

$$C.C = \frac{\sum_{i=1}^{N}(O_i - \bar{O})(T_i - \bar{T})}{\sqrt{\sum_{i=1}^{N}(O_i - \bar{O})^2 \sum_{i=1}^{N}(T_i - \bar{T})^2}} \tag{18.3}$$

$$R.A.E = \frac{\sum_{i=1}^{N}|O_i - T_i|}{\sum_{i=1}^{N}|T_i - \bar{T}|} \tag{18.4}$$

$$R.R.S.E = \sqrt{\frac{\sum_{i=1}^{N}(O_i - T_i)^2}{\sum_{i=1}^{N}(T_i - \bar{T})^2}} \tag{18.5}$$

Table 18.2. Cross-validation results for onset deviation.

Algorithm	C.C.I (%)	C.C	R.A.E (%)	R.R.S.E (%)
C4.5	78.61	—	68.47	88.12
C4.5 with boosting	78.56	—	57.72	87.72
Random forest	78.09	—	59.22	85.73
KStar	76.49	—	66.34	88.63
KNN	74.27	—	82.46	94.87
Naive bayes	68.85	—	104.87	104.03
ILP	90.02	—	70.12	87.45
Linear regression	—	0.17	101.12	98.41
Least med square regression	—	0.01	92.50	101.32
Model tree regression	—	0.43	91.51	90.16
SVM regression (1)	—	0.14	99.92	98.88
SVM regression (2)	—	0.24	89.34	98.18
SVM regression (3)	—	0.38	95.41	92.50
SVM regression (4)	—	0.44	94.56	90.34

Table 18.3. Cross-validation results for energy variation.

Algorithm	C.C.I (%)	C.C	R.A.E (%)	R.R.S.E (%)
C4.5	72.83	—	55.38	76.25
C4.5 with boosting	73.3	—	44.56	74.1
Random forest	70.3	—	51.7	78.04
KStar	70.92	—	52.42	75.5
KNN	58.01	—	61.91	102.67
Naive bayes	54.8	—	80.17	91.16
ILP	79.8	—	36.61	71.52
Linear regression	—	0.27	95.69	96.13
Least med square regression	—	0.22	87.92	108.01
Model tree regression	—	0.67	66.31	74.31
SVM regression (1)	—	0.25	89.28	98.57
SVM regression (2)	—	0.47	82.53	89.4
SVM regression (3)	—	0.56	75.47	82.95
SVM regression (4)	—	0.64	69.28	77.23

In Equations 18.3, 18.4, and 18.5, N is number of instances considered in a given cross-validation run, O_i is the output value of the model for the example indexed by i, T_i is the target value for the example indexed by i, $\bar{O}$ (respectively $\bar{T}$) is the mean of the output (respectively target) for all the instances considered in the run.

The main indicators for the numerical algorithms and classification algorithms are the correlation coefficient and the correctly classified instances, respectively. The correlation coefficient measures the statistical correlation between the predicted and actual values. Note that here a higher number means a better model, with a 1 meaning perfect statical correlation and a 0 meaning there is no correlation at all. This performance measure is used only for numerical input and output. The correctly classified instances rate is self-explanatory. Relative absolute error is the total absolute error made relative to what the error would have been if the prediction simply had been the average of the actual values. Root relative squared error is the total squared error made relative to what the error would have been if the prediction had been the average of the absolute value. This error exaggerates the cases in which the prediction error was significantly greater than the mean error.

Among the regression methods we explored, model tree regression is consistently the most accurate method, and thus, it is the model it produces the one we have implemented in our expressive performance system. Among the classification methods we explored, inductive logic programming is the most accurate classification method. This can be explained by the fact that inductive logic programming uses background knowledge for inducing the model. Thus, the algorithm allows to consider wider temporal windows (via the succ predicate), as opposed to the fixed width window containing only a note and its immediate neighbors. A positive result is that the requirement of inducing an understandable model does not involve any penalty in terms of accuracy (compared to the other classification methods).

Most of the misclassified instances by inductive logic programming are classified into neighbor classes to the correct class. As mentioned before, linear regression performs poorly since, as expected, expressive performance is a complex and multilevel phenomenon which cannot be handled accurately by a linear model. Also as expected, support vector machines perform well only with a radial function kernel, or a 3rd-order polynomial kernel or higher.

18.4 Expressive Melody Generation

On the basis of the expressive music performance model induced by model tree regression (Section 18.3), we have implemented an expressive performance system capable of generating expressive performances of melodies. The system is able to generate either an expressive MIDI performance from an inexpressive MIDI description of a melody or an expressive audio file from an inexpressive audio file. Recently, and more interestingly from the music synthesis point of view, we have extended the system so it is capable of generating an expressive audio file from an inexpressive MIDI description of a melody [21,22]. Figures 18.5 and 18.6 show snapshots of the system generating a MIDI expressive performance (from a MIDI inexpressive description) and the system generating an audio file (from an inexpressive audio), respectively.

In the case of the generation of an expressive MIDI performance from an inexpressive description of the melody (i.e., the score description), we compute the expressive duration of a note by multiplying the predicted duration ratio and the inexpressive note duration. The expressive note onset is obtained adding the predicted onset deviation and the inexpressive onset value. The case of the energy is different as the relation between note energy and corresponding MIDI velocity (an integer between 0 and 127) is quite arbitrary. We defined the audio energy to MIDI velocity mapping as $velocity = 63 * log_{10}(energy) + 64$ where the audio energy is normalized to $1 \leq energy \leq 10$.

In the case of expressive audio generation from an inexpressive audio source, the input is an audio file (which can either be generated by a synthesizer or be given as an audio recording). The system transforms the input audio file according to the induced

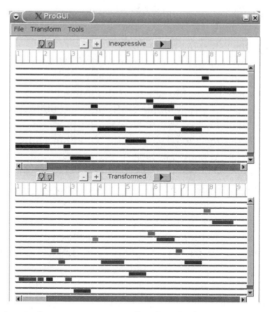

Fig. 18.5. Expressive performance generator showing the inexpressive MIDI description of *Like Someone in Love* (top) and the transformed expressive MIDI description (bottom).

model using SMSTools [26] into an expressive audio file without affecting any other perceptual feature, such as pitch or spectral shape.

18.5 Related Work

Previous research addressing expressive music performance using data mining techniques has included a broad spectrum of music domains. The most related work to

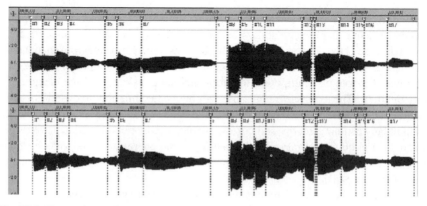

Fig. 18.6. Expressive performance generator tool showing the inexpressive audio file of *Body and Soul* and the transformed expressive audio file.

the research presented here is the work by Lopez de Mantaras et al. [12]. Lopez de Mantaras et al. report on SaxEx, a performance system capable of generating expressive solo performances in jazz. Their system is based on case-based reasoning, a type of analogical reasoning where problems are solved by reusing the solutions of similar, previously solved problems. To generate expressive solo performances, the case-based reasoning system retrieve, from a memory containing expressive interpretations, those notes that are *similar* to the input inexpressive notes. The case memory contains information about metrical strength, note duration, and so on, and uses this information to retrieve the appropriate notes. However, their system is incapable of explaining the predictions it makes.

With the exception of the work by Lopez de Mantaras et al., most of the research in expressive performance using data mining techniques has focused on classical piano music where the tempo of the performed pieces is not constant. Thus, these works focus on global tempo and energy transformations while we are interested in note-level tempo and energy transformations (i.e., note onset and duration).

Widmer [33] reported on the task of discovering general rules of expressive classical piano performance from real performance data via inductive machine learning. The performance data used for the study are MIDI recordings of 13 piano sonatas by W.A. Mozart performed by a skilled pianist. In addition to these data, the music score was also coded. The resulting substantial data consist of information about the nominal note onsets, duration, metrical information, and annotations. When trained on the data, an inductive rule learning algorithm discovered a small set of quite simple classification rules [33] that predict a large number of the note-level choices of the pianist.

Tobudic et al. [28] describe a relational instance-based approach to the problem of learning to apply expressive tempo and dynamics variations to a piece of classical music, at different levels of the phrase hierarchy. The different phrases of a piece and the relations among them are represented in first-order logic. The description of the musical scores through predicates (e.g., *contains(ph1,ph2)*) provides the background knowledge. The training examples are encoded by another predicate whose arguments encode information about the way the phrase was played by the musician. Their learning algorithm recognizes similar phrases from the training set and applies their expressive patterns to a new piece.

Other inductive approaches to rule learning in music and musical analysis include [1,4,9,15]. In [4], Dovey analyzes piano performances of Rachmaniloff pieces using inductive logic programming and extracts rules underlying them. In [1], Van Baelen extended Dovey's work and attempted to discover regularities that could be used to generate MIDI information derived from the musical analysis of the piece. In [15], Morales reports research on learning counterpoint rules. The goal of the reported system is to obtain standard counterpoint rules from examples of counterpoint music pieces and basic musical knowledge from traditional music. In [9], Igarashi et al. describe the analysis of respiration during musical performance by inductive logic programming. Using a respiration sensor, respiration during cello performances was measured and rules were extracted from the data together with musical/performance knowledge such as harmonic progression and bowing direction.

There are a number of approaches that address expressive performance without using data mining techniques. One of the first attempts to provide a computer system with musical expressiveness is that of Johnson [10]. Johnson developed a rule-based expert system to determine expressive tempo and articulation for Bach's fugues from the *well-tempered clavier*. The rules were obtained from two expert performers.

A long-term effort in expressive performance modeling is the work of the KTH group [2,5,6]. Their *Director Musices* system incorporates rules for tempo, dynamics, and articulation transformations. The rules are obtained from both theoretical musical knowledge, and experimentally from training using an analysis-by-synthesis approach. The rules are divided into *differentiation rules* that enhance the differences between scale tones, *grouping rules* which specify what tones belong together, and *ensemble rules* which synchronize the voices in an ensemble.

Canazza et al. [3] developed a system to analyze the relationship between the musician's expressive intentions and her performance. The analysis reveals two expressive dimensions, one related to energy (dynamics) and another one related to kinetics (rubato).

18.6 Conclusion

We have described an approach to perform expressive transformation in monophonic Jazz melodies (the deviations and changes we consider are on note duration, note onset, and note energy). Our approach consists of (1) a melodic transcription component that extracts a set of acoustic features from monophonic audio recordings, (2) a data mining component that induces expressive transformation models from the set of extracted acoustic features, and (3) a melody synthesis component that generates expressive monophonic phrases from inexpressive phrases using the induced expressive transformation model. For the data mining component, we explored and compared both classification and numerical data mining techniques. Of particular interest are the models obtained using inductive logic programming and model trees that proved to be the most accurate techniques. As future work, we plan to increase the amount of training data, the amount of descriptors to be extracted from it (e.g. vibrato), and combine this two with global structure-level information. This will certainly generate a more complete model of expressive performance. We are also working on an expressive model for the transitions among notes in a melody. With this aim we have developed a model that characterizes the different note transitions, for example, sttacato, legato. We are planning to apply the methodology presented in this chapter to other wind instruments.

Acknowledgments

This work is supported by the Spanish TIC project ProMusic (TIC 2003-07776-C02-01). We thank Emilia Gomez, Maarten Grachten, and Ismael Mosquera for their invaluable help in processing the data.

References

1. Van Baelen E, De Raedt L. Analysis and prediction of piano performances using inductive logic programming. In: *International Conference in Inductive Logic Programming*; 1996, pp. 55–71.
2. Bresin R. *Virtual Visrtuosity: Studies in Automatic Music Performance*. PhD Thesis, KTH, Sweden; 2000.
3. Canazza S, De Poli G, Roda A, Vidolin A. Analysis and synthesis of expressive intention in a clarinet performance. In: *Proceedings of the 1997 International Computer Music Conference*. San Francisco, International Computer Music Association; 1997, pp. 113–120.
4. Dovey MJ. Analysis of Rachmaninoff's piano performances using inductive logic programming. In: *European Conference on Machine Learning*, Springer-Verlag; 1995.
5. Friberg A, Bresin R, Fryden L, Sunberg J. Musical punctuation on the microlevel: Automatic identification and performance of small melodic units. *Journal of New Music Research*; 1995, 27(3):217–292.
6. Friberg A, Bresin R, Fryden L. Music from motion: Sound level envelopes of tones expressing human locomotion. *Journal of New Music Research*; 2000, 29(3):199–210.
7. Gabrielsson A. The performance of music. In: D.Deutsch (ed.), *The Psychology of Music* (2nd ed.) Academic Press; 1999.
8. Grachten M, Arcos J, Lopez de Mantaras R. Melodic similarity: Looking for a good abstraction level. In: *Proceedings of International Symposium on Music Information Retrieval*, Barcelona, Spain; 2004.
9. Igarashi S, Ozaki T, Furukawa K. Respiration reflecting musical expression: Analysis of respiration during musical performance by inductive logic programming. In: *Proceedings of Second International Conference on Music and Artificial Intelligence*, Springer-Verlag; 2002.
10. Johnson ML. An expert system for the articulation of Bach fugue melodies. In: D.L. Baggi (ed.), *Readings in Computer-Generated Music*. IEEE Computer Society; 1992, pp. 41–51,
11. Klapuri A. Sound onset detection by applying psychoacoustic knowledge. In: *Proceedings of the IEEE International Conference on Acoustics, Speech and Signal Processing*, 1999, ICASSP.
12. Lopez de Mantaras R, Arcos JL. AI and music, from composition to expressive performance. *AI Magazine*; 2002,23–3.
13. Maher RC, Beauchamp JW. Fundamental frequency estimation of musical signals using a two-way mismatch procedure. *Journal of the Acoustic Society of America*; 1994, 95:2254–2263.
14. McNab RJ, Smith Ll. A, Witten IH. *Signal Processing for Melody Transcription*, SIG working paper, 1996, Vol. 95–22.
15. Morales E. PAL: A pattern-based first-order inductive system. *Machine Learning*, 1997;26:227–252.
16. Narmour E. *The Analysis and Cognition of Basic Melodic Structures: The Implication Realization Model*. University of Chicago Press; 1990.
17. Narmour E. *The Analysis and Cognition of Melodic Complexity: The Implication Realization Model*. University of Chicago Press; 1991.
18. Quinlan JR. Induction of decision trees. *Machine Learning*, 1986; 1(1):81–106.
19. Quinlan JR. Learning logical definitions from relations. *Machine Learning*, 1990; 5:239–266.

20. Quinlan, JR. *C4.5: Programs for Machine Learning*. San Francisco, Morgan Kaufmann. 1993.

21. Ramirez R, Hazan A. Modeling expressive music performance in Jazz. In: *Proceedings International Florida Artificial Intelligence Research Society Conference*, AAAI Press; 2005.

22. Ramirez R, Hazan A. A learning scheme for generating expressive music performances of Jazz standards. In: *International Joint Conference on Artificial Intelligence (IJCAI05)*; 2005.

23. Repp BH. Diversity and commonality in music performance: An analysis of timing microstructure in schumann's 'Traumerei'. *Journal of the Acoustical Society of America*. 1992;104.

24. Seashore, CE (ed.). *Objective Analysis of Music Performance*. University of Iowa Press; 1936.

25. Shapiro, E. *Algorithmic Program Debugging*. Cambridge MA, MIT Press; 1983.

26. SMS Tools: http://www.iua.upf.es/sms

27. Srinivasan A. *The Aleph Manual*. 2001.

28. Tobudic A, Widmer G. Relational IBL in music with a new structural similarity measure. In: *Proceedings of the International Conference on Inductive Logic Programming*, Springer Verlag; 2003.

29. Todd N. The dynamics of dynamics: A model of musical expression. *Journal of the Acoustical Society of America*. 1992; 91.

30. Langley P, Sage S. Induction of selective Bayesian classifiers. In: *Proceedings of the Tenth Conference on Uncertainty in Artificial Intelligence* Seattle, WA: Morgan Kaufmann; 1994, pp. 388–406.

31. Platt J. *Fast Training of Support Vector Machines Using Sequential Minimal Optimization*. 1998.

32. Smola AJ, Schölkpof B. *A Tutorial on Support Vector Regression*. NeuroCOLT2 Technical report series; 1998.

33. Widmer G. Machine discoveries: A few simple, robust local expression principles. *Journal of New Music Research*. 2002; 31(1): 37–50.

Part V
Applications and Case Studies

19. Supporting Virtual Workspace Design Through Media Mining and Reverse Engineering

Simeon J. Simoff and Robert P. Biuk-Aghai

Summary. Supporting virtual collaboration can be a complex and time-consuming exercise. One of the key components in setting up virtual collaboration is the design of the virtual workspace as a coherent medium to support the activities involved in collaborative project development. The availability of information about virtual collaboration in virtual workspaces, in the form of action patterns, offers the opportunity for utilization of such information and its future reuse. This chapter presents a new approach for supporting design and redesign of virtual workspaces, based on combining integrated data mining techniques for refining the lower level models with a reverse engineering cycle to create upper level models. The methodology is based on the combination of a new model of vertical information integration related to virtual collaboration (the Information Pyramid of Virtual Collaboration), which encompasses information about objects and actions that make up action patterns at different levels of granularity. The approach allows comparison at all levels of the initial model of a process built based on the top-down requirements engineering approach with the model built from the actual workspaces by the proposed reverse engineering cycle.

19.1 Introduction

Virtual collaboration, understood to mean the collaboration of teams across boundaries of space and time and aided by information and communication technology, has become increasingly common in recent years [1]. The environment that supports virtual collaboration is referred to as a virtual workspace (VW). Many organizations are relying on the ability to bring together people for joint work in a virtual space, without having to bring the people involved together in a traditional face-to-face setting. There are several motivations for doing so, the most obvious being budgetary (saving travel and lodging expenses), and safety-related (avoiding the risks inherent in air travel).

Supporting virtual collaboration can be a complex and time-consuming exercise. One of the key components in setting up virtual collaboration is the design of the virtual workspace as a coherent medium to support the activities involved in collaborative project development. In the early days, to develop such collaborative environments, the developer had to be proficient in conceptual modelling, network programming, object management, graphics programming, device handling, and user interface design. During the recent years, an alternative approach has been to design VWs, using and integrating existing underlying workflow and groupware technologies [2]. The design of virtual workplaces is focused on the "arrangement" of the workplace in a way that will support virtual collaboration between geographically dispersed participants. The goal of the design of a VW is to meet some needs, or requirements, of the collaborators, whether this be an educational, research, or business collaboration. Such requirements are usually expressed in terms of activities (see [3, 4] for examples of how the notion of activities is used in design, and how a design ontology can be refined, respectively) and their attributes (e.g., people who are executing those activities, objects (artefacts) involved in the activities, etc.). Thus, the design of a VW can be viewed as an *arrangement*, or ordering, of the VW in such a way that it supports the collaborative processes that constitute the virtual collaboration.

Virtual architecture [5] (the "spatial view") and requirements engineering (the "process view") are the two most common approaches to systematic design of virtual workspaces. Relevant to our work is the "process view" approach, which assumes that sufficient a priori knowledge about the virtual collaboration process is available to make it possible to model it. Processes can be classified as either deterministic or nondeterministic. In deterministic processes, the steps within the process are well defined; thus, the process can be modelled with the workflow methodologies, and is referred to as a workflow process. In nondeterministic processes, not all steps can be planned ahead. While workflow processes have received much attention in the literature [2], and are supported by a number of modelling methods, few techniques exist for modelling partially planned or emergent collaboration processes. Such processes are common in knowledge-intensive activities such as product innovation or collaborative design, and usually follow only general process structures, with details of the process emerging during execution. Processes of this type are not well supported by workflow technology, which requires entire processes to be defined in advance, and then enacted according to this definition. Instead, such collaboration processes need a greater degree of flexibility. Environments that are based on the notion of collaboration spaces (a set of virtual workspaces), incorporating features of document management, interpersonal and group communication, notification, and a configurable governance structure provide a more adequate form of support [6].

Another aspect of VW design is the human factor. One approach is to base the modelling in this case on the soft systems methodology [7]. An instance of such a modelling methodology that addresses the requirements of collaboration processes, and that is tailored to the use of collaboration spaces, has been proposed in [8]. The methodology consists of four consecutive modelling steps (see Figure 19.1):

1. *System analysis*: develop an understanding of the current system, which is documented in an analysis model using a modified form of rich pictures, accompanied by so-called transition diagrams.
2. *Requirements analysis*: develop a requirements model, which describes required changes to the existing system.

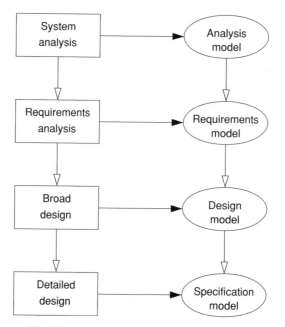

Fig. 19.1. Requirements engineering approach.

3. *Broad design*: prepare a design model, which describes the modified collaboration process, incorporating the requirements identified in the previous step, and which is again represented by a modified rich picture notation and transition diagrams.
4. *Detailed design*: produce a specification model that shows the detailed setup of collaboration spaces needed to support the new design, using a notation called MOO diagrams.

As an overall approach of conceptual modelling, this is an activity-centred approach. We illustrate the main modelling steps and notations by applying them to the formalization of a manuscript preparation process. Figure 19.2 shows a rich picture that conveys high-level properties of the process. The figure reveals the main activities (shown as clouds), the roles, or main actors (shown as stick figures) that are engaged in these activities, and the main artefacts (shown as boxes) that are used and produced by these activities. This amounts to the main features that may be known in advance about a partially planned process.

The transition diagram in Figure 19.3 shows the sequence in which the activities of this process are carried out. It can be seen that two of the activities, "Chapter acquisition" and "Reviewing," may be performed iteratively.

For each activity in the rich picture, a separate MOO diagram shows details of required support from a collaboration space. This is illustrated in Figure 19.4, the MOO diagram for the Reviewing activity. It shows which roles (ovals) have which kind of access (directionality of arrows) to which artefacts (boxes with rounded corners), and which discussion forums (hexagons) they are assigned to. The example

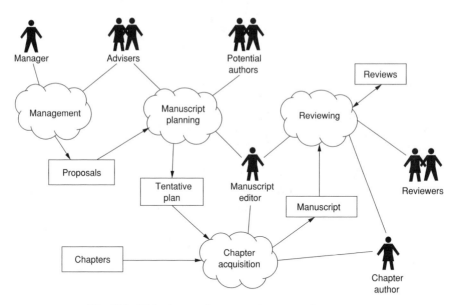

Fig. 19.2. Rich picture of a manuscript preparation process.

Fig. 19.3. Transition diagram of a manuscript preparation process.

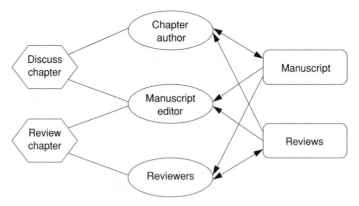

Fig. 19.4. MOO diagram of the reviewing activity.

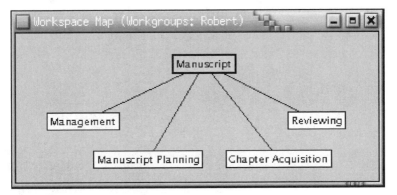

Fig. 19.5. The VW at the end of the top-down requirements engineering cycle.

illustrates the double-blind review process where communications between authors and reviewers are mediated through a separate entity.

As a result of the design of the VW, a workspace with the corresponding features is created for each MOO diagram. This is where the requirements engineering top-down approach ends. The example in Figure 19.5 illustrates this idea—the formalized process is the actual design. *This initial configuration is built on the premise that processes in virtual collaboration will be organized and conducted in a way similar to the conventional (face-to-face) collaboration.* However, during the collaborative process, the initial configuration evolves according to the emerging needs of the particular process and its branching. Hence the design of the VW will gain significantly if we are able to know what is, and has been, "going on" during the virtual collaboration, relate that to the changes in the VW and restore a more accurate high-level picture of the process.

The example in Figure 19.6 shows the result of the evolution of the original design of the VW as a result of emergent processes during the project's execution—it contains more workspaces than were initially identified and created.

Can we predict some elements of the evolution of a new collaborative process, on the basis of similarities and analogies with processes formalized and supported before? Can we capture and utilize in the virtual workspace design process the evolutionary component so that we can provide better support to the developers of collaborative workspaces?

This chapter addresses these questions. The rest of the chapter presents a new approach for supporting design and redesign of virtual workspaces, based on combining integrated data mining techniques for refining the lower level models with a reverse engineering cycle to create upper level models. The approach allows comparison at all levels of the initial model of a process built based on the top-down requirements engineering approach with the model built from the actual workspaces by the proposed reverse engineering approach. The approach proposed in this chapter is applied to data collected in virtual workspaces in an educational setting. The underlying philosophy of this approach differs from the approach taken by the Process

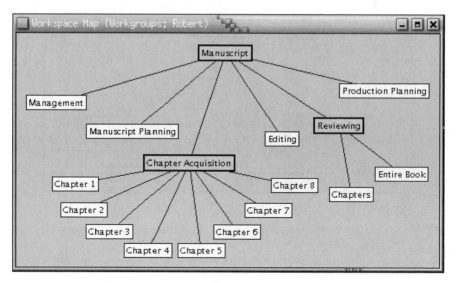

Fig. 19.6. The VW as a result of the evolution of the process.

Mining Research Group at the Technical University of Eindhoven in their work on workflow/process mining [9, 10], who based their process modelling technique on Petri nets.

19.2 Principles of the Approach Toward Reverse Engineering of Processes Using Data Mining

The approach presented in this chapter is based on the following principles:

- The *information pyramid of virtual collaboration* (referred to hereafter as the *information pyramid*) is an information model capturing essential aspects of virtual collaboration. This is a prerequisite for the development of effective reverse engineering methods in VW.
- *Integrated collaboration data*, collected during the evolution of the virtual workplace, is the source for the reverse engineering discoveries.
- *Data mining methods* applied to this integrated collaboration data need to take into account the information pyramid.

The following section presents the information pyramid in detail, which is central to this approach.

19.2.1 The Information Pyramid Formalism

Virtual collaboration is usually described in terms of the performance of *actions* in virtual workspaces that involves manipulations of *objects*. To distinguish virtual workspaces from the actual underlying groupware technology, we refer to the latter as *collaboration systems*. An example is posting a discussion statement to an electronic discussion forum. The act of posting constitutes the action, whereas both the discussion statement and the discussion forum constitute objects. An object is defined as a static entity provided and maintained by a collaboration system. Examples of objects include people, documents, and communication channels. An action is defined as a function or operation that can be performed in a collaboration system. Examples of actions include "creating a collaboration space," "entering a collaboration space," "creating a document," "reading a document," and "sending a message to another user."

Actions as defined here are independent of objects. However, almost every action involves objects. To fully describe an action therefore requires inclusion of *context information*. Action context is the set of information identifying the subject, referent, and location of an action. Here, subject refers to the action performer (a human user of the collaboration system, or a computational entity); referent is that which is being acted upon (such as a discussion forum); and location is the virtual place where the action occurs. A given action may occur in many different action contexts. For example, the action of posting a discussion statement to a bulletin board could be performed by different subjects (users); have different referents (discussion forums); and be performed in different locations (collaboration spaces). Collections of similar actions can be generalized into *action patterns*, describing an action together with a particular action context.

The information pyramid formalism consists of information about objects and actions, and their combination into specific action patterns, related to virtual collaboration. It consists of six levels, as depicted in Figure 19.7.

At the bottom of the information pyramid is the most small scale, detailed information, whereas at the top is the most large-scale, abstract information. This is

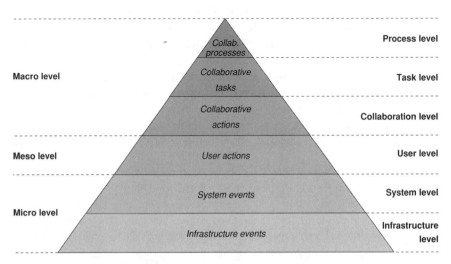

Fig. 19.7. The information pyramid formalism.

expressed in the shape and level of shading in Figure 19.7. The shape of the figure suggests that the amount of information at higher levels is smaller, as it constitutes a higher level of abstraction. The different levels of shading suggest that information at higher levels is denser than that at lower levels, in the sense that each unit of higher level information corresponds to several units of lower level information. From bottom up, the different levels contain the following information.

Infrastructure level: This is the level of the underlying software infrastructure running "below" the collaboration system itself. In the case of a Web-based collaboration system, for instance, the underlying infrastructure is a Web server. At this level, objects are recorded in the files under the control of the underlying system. Actions are typically recorded as events occurring in the software infrastructure, such as Web server access requests recorded in a Web server log. Records in the transaction log maintained by a database management system, in the case where a collaboration system operates on top of such a system, are another such example. Action patterns at this level correspond to events in the software infrastructure.

System level: This is the level of the collaboration system itself, through which collaboration is carried out. Records of objects at this level are contained in the application data of the collaboration system, typically residing in files or database tables. Actions are the commands issued to the collaboration system. Collaboration systems are typically structured as client-server systems, where multiple clients are served by one server. In this case, clients send service requests to a server, which then performs the requested actions. Records of such service requests, such as in a server log, constitute records of actions at this level. This information is of a larger scale than the corresponding information on the infrastructure level, so a single object or action on the system level usually corresponds to multiple objects or actions on the infrastructure level. Action patterns at this level correspond to operations performed by the collaboration system.

User level: This is the level on which individual users operate. These users perform actions on objects residing in collaboration spaces. Objects at this level are the collaboration spaces and other objects contained in them, whereas actions at this level are the operations performed by users, such as for instance opening a document for reading. Objects at this level are often abstractions of corresponding objects at the system level. Likewise, actions at this level often correspond to multiple actions on the system level; that is, a single action performed by the user may require the collaboration system to perform several system-level actions. Action patterns at this level correspond to operations performed by a single user.

Collaboration level: At this level, multiple users work in collaboration with each other. Objects at this level, as on the user level, are the collaboration spaces and other objects contained in them, whereas actions at this level are the operations performed by multiple users. Objects at this level mostly correspond closely to those at the user level. However, actions at this level are abstractions of multiple user-level actions. Action patterns at this level correspond to operations performed by groups of users.

Task level: At this level, larger-scale activity involving several lower level actions takes place. Objects at this level are groupings of multiple lower level objects, whereas actions at this level are the tasks performed by multiple users. These tasks consist of certain combinations of actions and objects from lower levels. Action patterns at this level correspond to tasks performed by groups of users.

Process level: At this, the highest level of the Information Pyramid, collections of tasks are performed by groups of users. These constitute work processes, that is, collections of related tasks. Objects at this level are combinations of multiple lower-level objects involved in the process. Actions at this level are collections of task-level actions. Action patterns at this level correspond to processes performed by groups of users.

A broad categorization of levels in the information pyramid formalism is shown by the labels on the left hand side in Figure 19.7: *micro* level, *meso* level, and *macro* level. This categorization is centred on the user level, for it is here that the actual actions performed by users of the collaboration system take place. This level is designated as the meso level in this categorization. At levels below the meso level, multiple smaller scale operations corresponding to each user action occur, thus the designation micro level. On the other hand, at levels above the meso level are aggregations of individual user actions into multiuser actions, tasks, and processes, thus the designation macro level.

19.2.2 Integrated Collaboration Data and Data Mining Framework

The information pyramid provides most of the semantic information needed for understanding and designing the data collection. A framework that embeds knowledge discovery in the design and use of collaborative virtual environments, known as the "Space-Data-Memory" framework, has been presented in detail in [11], and is shown in Figure 19.8.

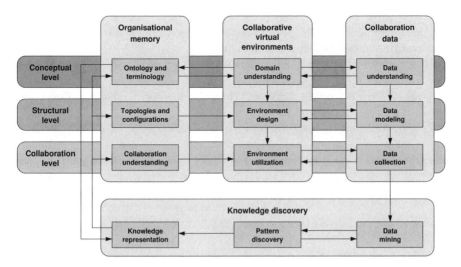

Fig. 19.8. The integrated data mining framework used in the reverse-engineering approach (adapted from [11]).

This framework suggests (1) how to obtain process knowledge from VWs, and (2) how to "recover" discovered process knowledge back into the design of the VWs. The framework consists of four interwoven components: collaborative virtual environments (or virtual workspaces), collaboration data, knowledge discovery, and organizational memory (equivalent in terms of computing to a case-based reasoning system). Combined with the information pyramid formalism, this framework provides the background for the reverse engineering approach described in this chapter.

Reverse engineering of processes from VW is possible through the analysis of collaboration data. Generally, such data are of two kinds: structural and behavioral data. Structural data capture static aspects of collaboration, such as the setup of a collaboration space. For example, structural data can capture the variety of roles and artefacts in each workspace, and the links between the workspaces. Behavioral data captures dynamic aspects of collaboration, such as the actions performed by a virtual team in a collaboration space, and the dynamics of discussion threads and discussion content. The assumption is that such data reflects the types of activities supported in the environment, the corresponding topology of the collaboration space, and the corresponding underlying technological representation.

19.3 Method for Reverse Engineering of Processes

The reverse engineering method employs the "Space-Data-Memory" framework and the information pyramid, aiming to recover, or discover, the design of a collaborative process, and express it using the modelling notations introduced in the introduction, that is, rich pictures, transition diagrams, and MOO diagrams. Rich pictures are used for representing entire processes, transition diagrams for showing task sequences, and MOO diagrams for showing individual task detail. The method proceeds in the reverse order of the methodology presented in [8]: first individual task models are obtained, then these are combined to a process model, and finally a model of task sequences is obtained, as illustrated in Figure 19.9.

Task analysis: Individual collaboration spaces are seen as being equivalent to individual tasks (or activities in the terminology adopted in [8]). Analyzing a task aims to produce a task model, represented in the form of a MOO diagram. Depending on the collaborative system in which the collaboration was carried out, this may be a straightforward mapping through the information pyramid that can be fully automated, or it may require a manual process of identifying and mapping modelling elements. MOO diagrams contain mainly three modelling elements, namely roles, artefacts, and discussion forums, which may be related through certain defined types of relationships.

Process analysis: Once task models have been produced, relationships between tasks need to be analyzed in order to discover which tasks belong to the same process. A number of methods are available to aid in this analysis. One method is to analyze shared task elements, such as artefacts, discussion forums, roles, users, etc. The higher the proportion of shared elements between a pair of collaboration spaces, the greater the likelihood that the tasks in the two spaces are related and are part of

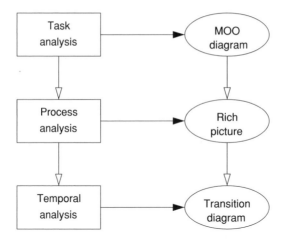

Fig. 19.9. Method for reverse engineering of processes.

the same process. Another method of analysis is to mine traversal patterns between collaboration spaces. This can reveal a network of spaces among which their users traverse back and forth. Such networks are a good indication of related tasks that are part of the same process. A further method is to look for so-called "handover points," where objects are passed from one collaboration space to another. Such handovers occur when an object, such as an artefact, is produced by one task as its output, and is received by another task as its input. A handover point usually is a good indicator that two tasks are part of the same process. To produce the final set of tasks belonging to the same process, each of the above methods is applied to every pair of collaboration spaces, producing an *individual process predictor* value. Next, all of these values are summed together, to yield the *total process predictor* value. The tasks are considered to belong to the same process if their total process predictor value exceeds a given threshold, which is empirically defined. Pairs of tasks are linked together into a task network in such a way that each pair of connected nodes in the network is represented in the set of pairs of tasks remaining from the previous elimination step. The final output of this step is a process model, expressed as a rich picture.

Temporal analysis: Once a process model has been obtained, further analysis can be performed to derive a task sequence model. This analysis takes the temporal relationship of actions in different collaboration spaces into account. Actions that occur in different spaces can be related to each other in time in different ways. Looking at all the actions occurring in a collaboration space in their entirety, fundamentally there are only two temporal relationship types: either actions in one space precede actions in another space, or actions in two spaces occur in parallel. Usually a combination of these relationship types exists in a given pair of collaboration spaces, for example, partially overlapping actions, interleaved actions, etc. To determine task sequences, an analysis of temporal action relationships is performed on a pair of tasks taken from the process model. This analysis is based on action levels, which refers to the temporal clustering of actions in a given task, that is, task intensity. For each collaboration space, action levels over the entire recorded history of the space are obtained, broken down per unit of time (e.g., day, week). Next, based on the observed distribution of action levels, a threshold is established above which activity in the collaboration space is considered to represent task activity. Using this threshold, a temporal sequencing of actions in collaboration spaces, and thus of corresponding tasks, is now possible. It also makes it possible to identify parallel or interleaved tasks, where after the handover from one task to another, the previous task resumes activity. When this is followed by a switch back to the successor task, an iteration, or loop, is identified. Once all task sequences have been identified, a task sequence model can be produced, represented in the form of a transition diagram.

The information pyramid assists with the above-described analyses by providing specifications of transformations of information to higher levels. Information on the levels above the base level of the information pyramid can be derived from those at lower levels through transformations such as aggregations. This is achieved through initial specification of a model of each level of the information pyramid, in terms of its constituent information items (objects, actions, action patterns), in the form of an ontology of the given collaboration system. This is followed by the specification of the transformations that produce an information item from one or more information items on the level below it. All these specifications become part of an ontology that covers all levels of the information pyramid from the base level up, and the transformations between them. This is shown in Figure 19.10, which also depicts the information flows from one level's model through a set of transformations to the next-higher level's model.

These transformations link consistently the action patterns between levels, as action patterns on a given level (with the exception of the lowest level) are aggregations of action patterns on the level below, as illustrated in the example in Figure 19.11. Thus an instance of a higher-level action pattern corresponds to multiple instances of lower-level action patterns. In this way there is a chain of correspondences of action patterns from the lowest level to the highest level of the information pyramid.

At the end of the reverse engineering cycle, a set of models is available which reflect certain essential process features, expressed in terms of the information pyramid of the virtual workspace from which they were obtained. These can be deposited in an organizational memory as expressions of how collaboration has occurred, that is, as procedural memory, complementing other information on the outcomes of the collaboration. Such process models thus become available for future retrieval and reuse, supporting the design of new virtual workspaces.

19.4 Example of Reverse Engineering of Knowledge-Intensive Processes from Integrated Virtual Workspace Data

In this section we present an example of the application of our methodology for reverse engineering of processes from integrated data, collected from virtual workspaces. The presented reverse engineering method for process extraction was applied to data collected from a set of virtual workspaces implemented in the LiveNet collaboration

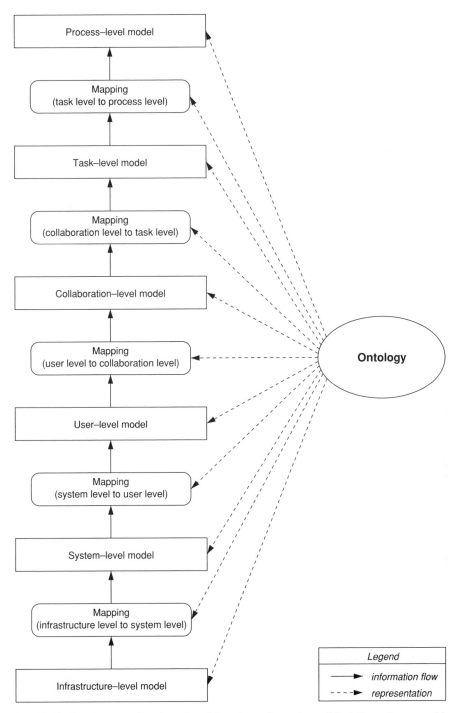

Fig. 19.10. Ontology specification of models and transformations of the information pyramid.

Level	Action pattern

Process   Product–concept–development

Task   Product–brainstorming Concept–development Final–report–preparation Market–study Financial–analysis

Collaboration   Document–preparation Group–discussion Document–sharing

User   Post–discussion–statement Opendiscussion–statement

System   add_statement get_block_tree

Fig. 19.11. Chain of correspondences of action patterns provided by the information pyramid to the reverse engineering method.

system. LiveNet is a collaboration system developed at the University of Technology, Sydney [12]. It supports mainly asynchronous collaboration of distributed groups of people, that is, different-time, different-place interactions, which influences the patterns that can be discovered. A central server is accessed across the network through one of several client interfaces, most commonly through a Web interface (an example of which is shown in Figure 19.12).

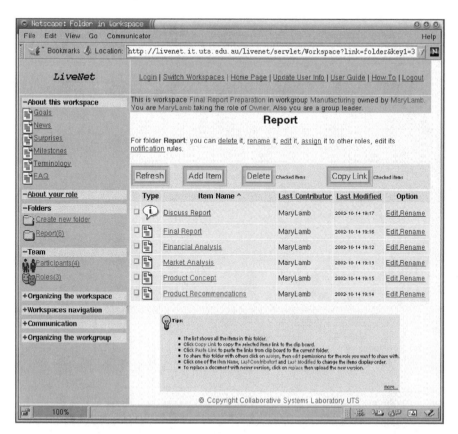

Fig. 19.12. A view of LiveNet user interface (Web version).

The data originated from 513 student and staff users at the University of Technology, Sydney, who used LiveNet for a number of purposes. The collaboration data span a 3-month period, during which time a total of 721 workspaces were created. Reverse engineering focused on a set of workspaces that were set up by students learning to use collaboration technology, in this case to support a construction management task.

19.4.1 Task Analysis

Initially, visual data exploration aided the identification of potential candidates for reverse engineering. A specialized tool, the workspace visualiser, developed by us for the visualization of instances of workspaces, was used for this purpose. An example of a so-called *inter-workspace map*, displaying relationships between workspaces, is shown in Figure 19.13.

This map reveals a number of clusters of workspaces that appear to be closely related and could be part of the same work process. Later, process analysis will show whether this assumption can be supported. First, task analysis is performed for all workspaces. To illustrate this, Figure 19.14 shows an *intra-workspace map* (also produced by our visualization tool), displaying the relationships among the elements internal to a workspace, such as roles, documents, and discussion forums. Figure 19.15 shows the MOO diagram that has been derived from this intra-workspace map.

Both figures show that almost all assignments of documents and discussion forums to roles in the workspace are identical. The only differences exist in the

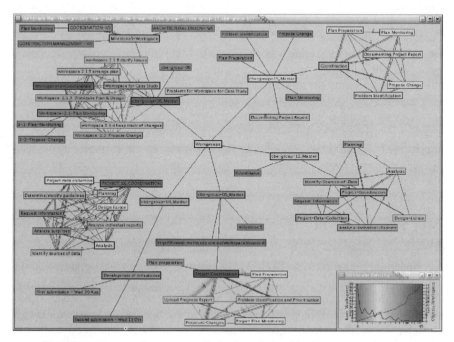

Fig. 19.13. Inter-workspace map displaying relationships between workspaces.

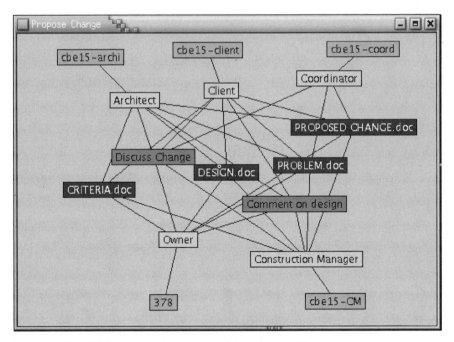

Fig. 19.14. Intra-workspace map of the "Propose Change" workspace.

creation/modification of the Problem and Proposed Change documents (arrow pointing from the role to the document), which may be performed only by the Client and Coordinator roles, respectively. Coupled with the presence of the discussion forums for commenting on the design and discussing changes, this indicates a participatory work process: all roles may read all documents and join in the discussions, while changes to documents are coordinated by having only one role in charge of making such changes.

Given an ontology of the collaboration system and a set of rules, the task analysis and derivation of a MOO diagram can be performed automatically. The task analysis is performed for all workspaces under consideration. In the example of the inter-workspace map shown in Figure 19.13, this is done for 65 workspaces (out of the total of 721).

19.4.2 Process Analysis

Following task analysis, process analysis attempts to discover which tasks (i.e., their corresponding workspaces) are likely part of the same process. This begins by examining shared task elements, traversal patterns, and handover points, as discussed earlier. Table 19.1 shows an extract from the top of the list of all candidate pairs of workspaces under consideration, together with their individual and total process predictor values. The table shows, for example, that the two workspaces "Plan Preparation" and "Propose Change," listed at the top, have 10 items in common, were involved in traversals

Table 19.1. Process predictor values for candidate workspace pairs (extract).

Workspace 1	Workspace 2	Shared elements	Traversals	Handover points	Total Process Predictor Value
Plan preparation	Propose Change	10	3	1	14
Coordination	Plan preparation	9	1	2	12
Plan monitoring	Plan preparation	5	7	0	12
Plan monitoring	Problem identification	7	4	1	12
⋮	⋮	⋮	⋮	⋮	⋮

from one to the other workspace 3 times, and have 1 item that serves as a handover point, that is, constitutes the outcome of one task and the input of the next, yielding a total process predictor value of 14.

Following the derivation of these process predictor values, those pairs of workspaces for which the value is below the defined threshold are eliminated from further consideration. In this case the threshold was set at 3, below which predictors were insignificant in predicting process membership. This left 13 pairs of workspaces, which next were linked together into a task network according to the established relationship. By adding shared roles and artefacts, this network was augmented to produce a process rich picture. The cluster of workspaces is shown in the inter-workspace map of Figure 19.16, and the corresponding rich picture is shown in Figure 19.17.

Both of these figures reveal the greatly interconnected nature of the tasks in this process: most of the tasks (i.e., their corresponding workspaces) share a majority of both artefacts and roles, and every task has some relationship to every other task. This is typical of collaborative and knowledge-intensive work processes, which have been

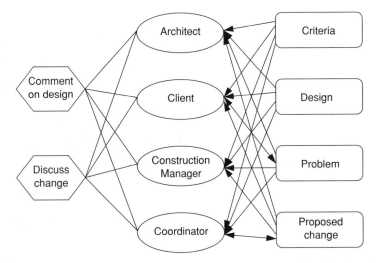

Fig. 19.15. Corresponding MOO diagram capturing essential aspects of the "Propose Change" workspace.

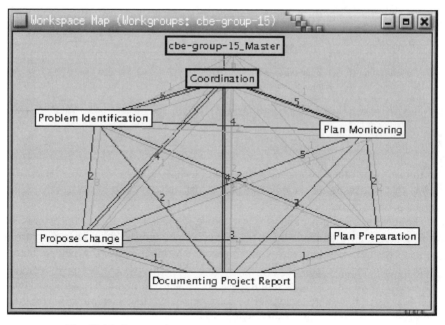

Fig. 19.16. Inter-workspace map showing a cluster of workspaces.

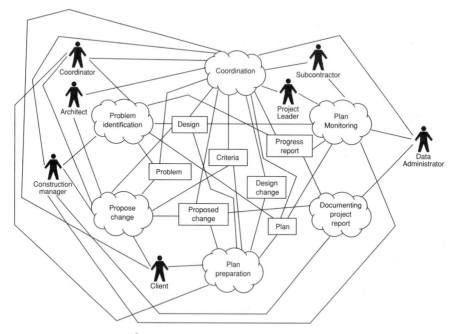

Fig. 19.17. Rich picture of the corresponding tasks of the workspace cluster.

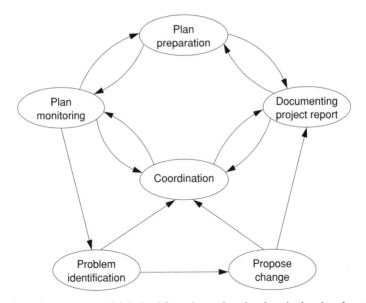

Fig. 19.18. Task sequence model derived from the analyzed actions in the virtual workspace.

described in the literature as resulting in "disconnected and parallel work that must nevertheless be guided to a common goal" [12].

19.4.3 Temporal Analysis

The final step of reverse engineering consists of performing temporal analysis on the actions in the workspaces of the derived process model in order to obtain a task sequence model. First, the history of actions in the workspaces is broken down into chunks, in this case at the level of days. Based on the distribution of action levels per day, which ranged from a minimum of 1 to a maximum of 120, with the majority of workspaces having action levels in the 10–20 range on most days, a threshold of 5 was set to distinguish tasks. Below this value, an excessive number of task switches resulted, often incurred only for such "tasks" as entering another workspace to look up a document or discussion item.

Temporal analysis then obtained sequences of task switches, which were consolidated into the task sequence model shown in Figure 19.18. The temporal analysis revealed that tasks in this process were tightly integrated: not only was work interleaved, with frequent switching between tasks, but also was it often parallel. Nonetheless, the transition diagram in Figure 19.18 does reveal definite patterns of task switching.

For example, there is only unidirectional switching in five cases (such as from Plan monitoring to Problem identification), and bidirectional switching in four cases (such as between Plan monitoring and Coordination). Certain potential paths do not exist at all (e.g., there is no switch between Plan preparation and Problem identification). This indicates to us that even in such relatively poorly structured processes—as compared to workflow processes—certain patterns of work emerge, which are reflected in the collected collaboration data and subsequently the derived process models.

19.5 Conclusions and Future Work

The availability of information about virtual collaboration in virtual workspaces, in the form of action patterns, offers opportunity for utilization of such information and its future reuse. This chapter has presented a novel methodology for reverse engineering of virtual collaboration (expressed as work processes performed through virtual workspaces). It produces design models at micro (task) and macro (process) levels of these processes using notations from a (forward engineering) design methodology intended for virtual collaboration. Through the presented methodology, it not only becomes possible to trace the evolution of processes from an initial design, in the case where such a design has been performed, but also allows the discovery of ad hoc and emergent processes for which no such initial design was prepared. In both cases, processes obtained through reverse engineering can be retained in a library (case-base) of reusable process templates.

The methodology is based on the combination of a new model of vertical information integration related to virtual collaboration (the Information Pyramid of Virtual Collaboration), which encompasses information about objects and actions that make up action patterns at different levels of granularity. Information at these levels ranges from fine-grained system events to entire work processes, integrated through defined transformations that specify how an information item on one level can be derived from information items on a lower level. Definitions of information at different levels, and of transformations, are specified in an ontology of a given collaboration system. The complete information model makes it possible to abstract from fine-grained events to large-scale work activities and to drill down from larger scale activities to their constituent smaller scale activities.

The integration of the information pyramid and the "Space-Data-Memory" framework provides the basis of a process reverse-engineering methodology for discovering knowledge about collaboration processes in virtual workspaces. The presented methodology is independent of the underlying collaboration system employed, and requires only knowledge of its ontology. Only the concrete implementation of the data mining methods used needs to be adapted to the given collaboration system so as to capture different elements needed in the calculation of process predictors. Likewise, the interpretation of discovered patterns will need to be framed in the context of the collaboration system utilized.

Our proposed approach has also the potential to influence the way collaboration systems are designed or redesigned. Insights obtained through the analysis of collaboration processes can, for example, reveal deficiencies in the levels of support provided by a particular collaboration system implementation, leading to a redesign of a future version of the system. In this way, the approach can become the backbone of a new design methodology—design of collaboration systems by adaptation.

Finally, the illustrated combination of data mining techniques and reverse engineering, and the availability of a rich source of data on actual collaborative practices, can lead to a better understanding of the influence of computer mediation on collaborative processes. Future work will be focused on the analysis of the artefacts and their content involved in the collaboration process.

Acknowledgments

This research work was supported by the Australian Research Council, the University of Technology, Sydney, and the University of Macau.

References

1. Lipnack J, Stamps J. *Virtual Teams: Reaching Across Space, Time, and Organizations with Technology.* New York: Wiley; 1997.
2. Bolcer GA, Taylor RN. *Advanced Workflow Management Technologies.* University of California. Irvine; 1998.
3. Richards D, Simoff S. Design ontology in context—A situated cognition approach to conceptual modelling. *AI in Engineering* 2001;15(3):121–136.
4. Simoff S, Maher ML. Designing with the activity/space ontology. In: Gero JS, Sudweeks F, editors. *Artificial Intelligence in Design 98.* Dordrecht: Kluwer Academic; 1998, pp. 23–44.
5. Maher ML, Simoff SJ, Gu N, Lau KH. Two approaches to a virtual design office. *International Journal of Design Computing* 1999;2.
6. Biuk-Aghai RP. Virtual workspaces for web-based emergent processes. In: *Fourth Pacific Asia Conference on Information Systems: Electronic Commerce and Web-Based Information Systems.* Hong Kong, China; 2000, pp. 864–880.
7. Patching DC. *Practical Soft Systems Analysis.* London: Pitman; 1990.
8. Hawryszkiewycz IT. Analysis for cooperative business processes. In: Zowghi D, editor. *Proceedings of the Fifth Australian Workshop on Requirements Engineering.* Brisbane, Australia; 2000, pp. 3–11.
9. van der Aalst WMP, van Dongen BF, Herbst J, Maruster L, Schimm G, Weijters AJMM. Workflow mining: A survey of issues and approaches. *Data and Knowledge Engineering* 2003;47(2):237–267.
10. van der Aalst WMP, Weijters AJMM. Process mining. In: Dumas M, van der Aalst WMP, ter Hofstede AHM, editors. *Process-Aware Information Systems: Bridging People and Software through Process Technology.* Wiley; 2005, pp. 235–255.
11. Simoff SJ, Biuk-Aghai RP. Multimedia mining of collaborative virtual workspaces: An integrative framework for extracting and integrating collaborative process knowledge. In: Zaïane OR, Simoff SJ, Djeraba C, editors. *Mining Multimedia and Complex Data.* Heidelberg: Springer; 2003, pp. 164–182.
12. Hawryszkiewycz IT. Workspace networks for knowledge sharing. In: Debrency R, Ellis A, editors. *Proceedings of AusWeb99, the Fifth Australian World Wide Web Conference.* Ballina, Australia; 1999, pp. 219–227.

20. A Time-Constrained Sequential Pattern Mining for Extracting Semantic Events in Videos

Kimiaki Shirahama, Koichi Ideno, and Kuniaki Uehara

Summary. In this chapter, we present a time-constrained sequential pattern mining method for extracting *semantic patterns* associated with semantically relevant events (*semantic events*) in videos. Since a video itself is just a raw material, we transform the video into a multistream of raw level metadata. This multistream not only characterizes the semantic events in the video but also can be operated by data mining technique. Then, we extract semantic patterns as sequential patterns, each of which is a temporally ordered set of raw level metadata. At this time, regarding the temporal characteristics of the video, we introduce two types of time constraints: *semantic event boundaries* and *temporal localities* to eliminate sequential patterns which are unlikely to be semantic patterns. Furthermore, by taking the high computational cost of our mining method into account, we also present a method for parallelizing the pattern mining process. Finally, we evaluate the effectivenesses of raw level metadata, our mining method, and extracted semantic patterns.

20.1 Introduction

Data mining is a technique to discover previously unknown and interesting patterns from a large amount of data. These patterns are high-level descriptions of underlying low-level data. Discovering patterns such as customer's purchase for marketing or network access for intrusion detection benefits the users in various fields. In this context, our data mining is dealing with video data called *video data mining*. Our task is to discover *semantic patterns* that are associated with semantically relevant events (*semantic events*) in the video, to support the user's content-based access to the *unstructured* video, where there is no clear structure to describe its rich and complicated semantic contents [1].

There exists a crucial difference between the traditional alpha-numeric data and video data. Data mining conventionally deals with data whose alpha-numeric representation directly describes the semantic contents of the data and relationship operators (e.g., equal, not equal, etc.) are well-defined [1]. On the other hand, the digitized representation of video data cannot directly describe the semantic contents of the video and relationship operators are ill-defined. Thus, a video itself is just a raw material that is computationally intractable. To extract semantic patterns from the video, we should first derive *raw level metadata*. This is one of the most important tasks

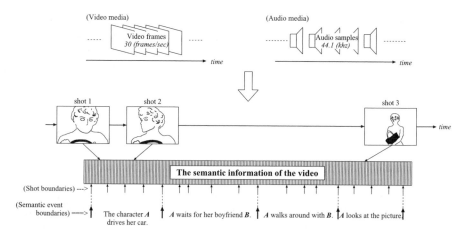

Fig. 20.1. An example of the semantic information of a video, conveyed through video and audio media.

since the derivation of raw level metadata constructs the building blocks for video data mining [2]. Then, video data mining can be achieved by applying data mining techniques to the raw level metadata.

In general, a video involves two types of media: video and audio media. They are known as *continuous media* [3]. As shown in Figure 20.1, video and audio media are sequences of media quanta (i.e., video frames and audio samples) that convey their semantic contents only when media quanta are continuously played in terms of time. Therefore, the semantic information of the video is time-dependent.

To efficiently handle such a time-dependent semantic information, it is useful to define two types of aspects of the semantic information: *spatial* and *temporal* aspects. A spatial aspect means a semantic content presented by a video frame, such as the location, characters, and objects shown in the video frame. A temporal aspect means a semantic content presented by a sequence of video frames in terms of temporal order, like a change of locations, character's action, and object's movement presented in the sequence.

A *shot* is a segment of video frames recorded continuously by a single camera. The shot is a basic physical unit to successfully capture the spatial and temporal aspects in a video [4]. But, as shown in Figure 20.1, the shot cannot convey a semantic event by itself. Figure 20.1 describes that adjacent shots form a continuous semantic event. For example, the leftmost semantic event consists of four separate shots. From this point of view, we define a semantic pattern as a sequential pattern that sequentially relates the adjacent shots.

To extract the above semantic patterns from a video, we first construct a multistream of raw level metadata derived from each shot sequentially. After that, we extract sequential patterns from the multistream. In this process, we should consider the following two types of temporal characteristics of the video: *semantic event boundaries* and *temporal localities*. A semantic event boundary is namely a boundary between two consecutive semantic events, where the viewer can recognize an important change on semantic contents, such as change of character's action and change of the location. For instance, in Figure 20.1, the character A drives her car in the leftmost event, while A waits for her boyfriend outside her car in the next event. Hence, a semantic event boundary can be found between the forth and fifth shots from the left in Figure 20.1.

A temporal locality means that the shots in the same semantic event have to be temporally close to each other [5–7]. For example, in Figure 20.1, the same character A appears in the three shots, *shot 1*, *shot 2*, and *shot 3*. *shot 1* is temporally very close to *shot 2*, while *shot 3* is far from both *shot 1* and *shot 2*. At this time, *shot 1* and *shot 2* are more likely to be included in the same semantic event. On the other hand, the semantic event of *shot 3* should be different from that of *shot 1* and *shot 2* because several different semantic events may be appeared between *shot 2* and *shot 3*. We utilize semantic event boundaries and temporal localities as time constraints to eliminate sequential patterns that are unlikely to be associated with semantic events.

20.2 Related Works

In this section, we review previous works in the research fields of video data mining and sequential pattern mining. We also describe our contributions of this chapter to both research fields.

20.2.1 Video Data Mining

For efficient video data management, such as content-based video indexing, retrieval and browsing, many video data mining approaches have been proposed in recent years [2, 6–11]. Pan et al. extracted some patterns of news and commercial video clips for content-based video retrieval and browsing [8]. Specifically, they extracted essential characteristics of news and commercial video clips by applying Independent Component Analysis (ICA) to a n-by-n-by-n cube which can represent both spatial and temporal video (or audio) information in a video clip.

Pan et al. also extracted some patterns of plot evolutions of news and commercial video clips [9]. Given a video clip, they group similar shots into shot-groups based on DCT coefficients of I-frames in a shot. It leads to detect basic shot-groups that contain shots that often appear in the video clip. The graph of these basic shot-groups reveals the plot structure of the video clip. They reported that such graphes for news and commercial video clips are quite different from each other.

Oh et al. extracted some patterns of object's appearance and disappearance in a surveillance video [2]. They group incoming frames obtained from a fixed camera into segments of different categories. Furthermore, each segment is indexed by its motion feature that is defined as an accumulated difference of two consecutive frames in the segment. Finally, segments are clustered again into groups of similar segments based on segment's category and motion.

Zhu et al. extracted sequential patterns of shots for addressing video semantic units (e.g., events, scenes, and scenario information) in news, medical and basketball videos [6, 7]. To begin with, they cluster shots into groups of visually similar shots and construct a sequence consisting of the group names. Then, sequential patterns of shots with strong temporal correlations are extracted from the sequence.

All of the above video data mining approaches extract semantic patterns only from *rule-dependent* videos, where there are apparent rules associated with semantic events. For example, in the interview events of news videos, a shot where an interviewer appears, followed by that of an interviewee, is repeated one after the other [8]. Similarly, in goal events on ball game videos, the score in the telop changes after audience's cheers and applause occur [7]. Also, in surveillance videos recorded with fixed cameras, if an object actively moves, the difference between two consecutive frames is clearly large [2]. Like this, these apparent rules tell what kind of raw level metadata should be used to extract semantic patterns in *rule-dependent* videos. Thus, the extracted semantic patterns are not previously unknown but previously known.

Compared with the above *rule-dependent* videos, we extract semantic patterns from *rule-independent* videos (e.g., movies), where there is no apparent rule that characterizes any kind of semantic events. For example, battle events in movies are presented in various ways, depending on semantically arbitrary factors, such as characters, weapons, location, time, and weather. Hence, neither what kind of raw level metadata should be used nor what kind of semantic patterns are extracted can be determined in advance. With respect to this point, we use several types of raw level metadata accepted as useful in the fields of image, video and audio processing researches. By using these raw level metadata, we can extract previously unknown semantic patterns from *rule-independent* videos.

There are some studies for video data mining on *rule-independent* movies [10–12]. Wijesekera et al. proposed a video data mining framework on movies by using existing audio and video analysis techniques [10]. They also examined the suitability of applying existing both data mining concepts and algorithms to multimedia data, although no experimental result was reported. In [11], we extracted two types of editing patterns from movies: *cinematic rules* and *frequent events*. Cinematic rules are not semantic patterns because they do not characterize any kind of semantic events but are editing patterns for successfully conveying the editor's idea to the viewers. Frequent events are semantic patterns, but they are previously known. The reason is that metadata used to extract these patterns (e.g., *Character's name*, *Direction of character's gaze*, *Character's motion*, and *Sound type*) represent considerably high semantic contents by themselves.

In [12], we extracted character's appearance and disappearance patterns for characterizing topics, each of which corresponds to a semantic event where the character plays a particular action and role in the movie. For instance, the character talks to someone or makes love with a partner in a topic. This kind of topic can be detected as an interval where durations of character's appearance and disappearance are roughly constant. But, semantic contents in the topic, such as what action the character performs and what kind of situation the topic involves, cannot be identified by only using character's appearance and disappearance.

20.2.2 Sequential Pattern Mining

Extracting sequential patterns from categorical streams is a research area of great interest in data mining. A categorical stream is defined as a sequence on a set of finite kinds of symbols. This task is challenging, because a search space of possible sequential patterns is extremely large. As described in [13], even in the case of a one-dimensional stream defined on a set of n kinds of symbols, there are $O(n^k)$ possible sequential patterns of time length k. In order to efficiently extract sequential patterns from categorical streams, many methods have been proposed [6, 7, 11, 13–23]. As shown in Table 20.1, these methods are classified into six categories, in terms of the number of dimensions of a categorical stream and a search technique for reducing the extremely large search space.

The number of dimensions of a categorical stream greatly affects the efficiency of the sequential pattern extraction. As a simple example, suppose m-dimensional multistream, where each component stream contains n kinds of symbols. In this multistream, there are $O(n^{mk})$ possible sequential patterns of time length k. Like this, extracting sequential patterns from a multistream requires much more expensive search than that of a one-dimensional stream. With respect to this problem, Tanaka et al. transformed an original multistream into a one-dimensional stream by using Principle Component Analysis (PCA) [23]. This kind of transformation approach was also proposed by Zhu et al., where they used a re-arrangement mechanism to maintain the original temporal order [7].

Search techniques can be classified into the following three types: *window-based*, *apriori–based*, and *two-step* approaches. A window-based approach scans a given stream by sliding the window of a user-specified time length [24]. Sequential patterns are extracted as sets of symbols within the window, which are validated by the sliding window scan. The window-based approach limits a search space of possible sequential patterns since the time length of any extracted sequential pattern is up to window's length. The user needs to specify the maximum time length of extracted sequential patterns in advance.

Chudova et al. extracted fixed-length sequential patterns by using a Hidden Markov Model (HMM) [21]. The HMM has k states for modeling symbols included in a pattern of time length k and one state for modeling symbols which are not in the pattern. By learning the parameters of the HMM, the symbol that is the most likely symbol to appear in the i-th position in the pattern is determined. Eventually, this approach and the window-based approach heavily rely on a priori knowledge of

Table 20.1. The classification of sequential pattern mining methods in terms of the number of dimensions of a categorical stream and a search technique.

	One-dimension	Multi-dimensions
Window–based	[19] [20] [21]	[16] [17] [13]
Apriori–based	[6] [7]	[14] [15] [18] [11]
Two–steps	[22] [23]	

extracted sequential patterns, so both of them may be more generally called *model-based* approaches.

An apriori–based approach iteratively extracts longer sequential patterns from shorter ones. Each iteration starts with the generation of *candidate patterns*, each of which is generated by concatenating a symbol (or a set of symbols) to a pattern extracted in the previous iteration. It follows that candidate patterns that are unlikely to be patterns are eliminated. Finally, the remaining candidate patterns are examined whether they are actually sequential patterns or not. This iteration terminates when no more sequential pattern is extracted. Like this, the apriori–based approach efficiently and dynamically reduces the search space of possible sequential patterns in the given stream.

A two-step approach namely follows two steps for the extraction of sequential patterns. In the first step, some criteria are used to obtain the optimum time length of sequential patterns to be extracted. For example, Tanaka et al. computed such an optimum time length by using Minimum Description Length (MDL) principle [23]. Also, Berberids et al. computed the optimum time length by using the autocorrelation function [22]. The optimum time length obtained in the first step is used to reduce the search space of possible time lengths of sequential patterns in the second step. Like this, the two-step approach can be considered as an extended window-based approach. Specifically, the time length of extracted sequential patterns is automatically obtained in the two-step approach while it is user-specified in a window-based approach. Finally, in Table 20.1, we could not find any two-step approach for extracting sequential patterns from a multi-dimensional categorical stream.

Our method extracts sequential patterns from a multi-dimensional categorical stream using an apriori–based approach. So, our method is classified into the same category to [11, 14, 15, 18] in Table 20.1. To eliminate sequential patterns that are unlikely to be semantic patterns, we incorporate two types of a priori information specific to video data: *semantic event boundaries* and *temporal localities*. In addition, there are many possibilities to locate a sequential pattern in the stream. Thus, how to locate the sequential pattern in the stream is a very important issue. But, it has never been discussed in the previous works listed in Table 20.1. We propose a method for finding the location of the sequential pattern in the stream. Finally, we also propose a method for parallelizing the process of our mining method, since it requires multiple scans over the stream to locate each candidate pattern.

20.3 Raw Level Metadata

In this section, we give a detail explanation about raw level metadata used to characterize the spatial and temporal aspects in a shot. Note that each type of raw level metadata is a categorical value. Consequently, deriving several types of raw level metadata from the shot can be considered as a discretization of the spatially and temporally continuous semantic content into a set of categorical values. By sequentially aggregating raw level metadata, we can obtain a multistream of raw level metadata shown in Figure 20.2.

Shot No.	1	2	3	4	5	6	7	8	9	10	11	12	13	14
stream 1 CH:	CH4	CH7	CH3	CH2	CH7	CH6	CH6	CH6	CH6	CH6	CH6	CH6	CH2	CH2
stream 2 CS:	CS4	CS4	CS4	CS4	CS4	CS4	CS4	CS4	CS4	CS4	CS4	CS4	CS4	CS0
stream 3 CV:	CV2	CV2	CV3	CV0	CV1	CV0	CV0	CV0	CV0	CV0	CV0	CV0	CV0	CV1
stream 4 LN:	LN3	LN3	LN2	LN1	LN1	LN2	LN3	LN1	LN3	LN3	LN1	LN2	LN1	LN1
stream 5 LL:	LL0	LL3	LL1	LL0	LL1	LL1	LL3	LL0	LL0	LL1	LL0	LL0	LL0	LL0
stream 6 LB:	LB2	LB0	LB3	LB2	LB2	LB0	LB1	LB0	LB1	LB1	LB1	LB3	LB0	LB2
stream 7 SA:	SA2	SA2	SA1	SA1	SA2	SA2	SA2	SA2	SA2	SA2	SA2	SA2	SA1	SA2
stream 8 LA:	LA0	LA2	LA1	LA0	LA0	LA0	LA1	LA0	LA0	LA0	LA0	LA0	LA0	LA1
stream 9 SL:	SL4	SL4	SL3	SL4	SL4	SL1	SL1	SL1	SL1	SL2	SL1	SL0	SL0	SL0
stream 10 MS:	MS3	MS3	MS2	MS4	MS5	MS4	MS4	MS4	MS4	MS4	MS3	MS3	MS0	MS0
stream 11 MV:	MV1	MV4	MV0	MV1	MV0	MV0	MV1	MV1	MV0	MV0	MV0	MV0	MV3	MV2
stream 12 SM:	SM1	SM1	SM1	SM1	SM1	SM1	SM1	SM1	SM1	SM1	SM1	SM2	SM0	SM0
stream 13 AM:	AM1	AM3	AM2	AM3	AM3	AM2	AM3	AM3	AM2	AM2	AM2	AM2	AM2	AM2

Time

Fig. 20.2. An example of a multistream of raw level metadata, where several types of raw level metadata are derived from each shot in a video.

Since the spatial aspects presented by the video frames are continuous, we assume that the salient spatial aspect is represented by the middle video frame in a shot, called *keyframe*. One can change the definition of a keyframe [5, 6, 8]. Anyway, we derive the following types of raw level metadata from the keyframe:

CH: *CH* reflects the semantic content about the background or dominant object in a keyframe, such as water, sky/clouds, snow, fire, and human face [25]. *CH* represents the color composition in the keyframe on H(ue) axis of HSV color space. We first compute the intensity histogram on H axis for each keyframe. Then, we cluster keyframes into groups with similar histograms, where we use k-means algorithm as a clustering algorithm [26] and histogram intersection as a distance measure [27]. Finally, we assign the categorical value of *CH* to each keyframe by analyzing the cluster including the keyframe.

CS: Similar to *CH*, *CS* reflects the semantic content about the background or dominant object in a keyframe. But, *CS* characterizes a keyframe that contains objects with saturated colors, such as fruits, flowers, and man-made objects. *CS* represents the color composition in the keyframe on S(aturation) axis of HSV color space. We assign the categorical value of *CS* to each keyframe by using the k-means clustering method.

CV: Unlike *CH* and *CS*, *CV* reflects the semantic content about the brightness in a keyframe, such as bright and dark. *CV* represents the color composition in the keyframe on V(alue) axis of HSV color space. Categorical values of *CV* are also assigned by the k-means clustering method.

LN: *LN* basically reflects the number of objects displayed in a keyframe. This means that the more objects are displayed in the keyframe, the more straight lines tend to be derived from the keyframe. On the other hand, objects' boundaries are obscure in a keyframe in a night or foggy situation, and few straight lines are derived. *LN* represents the number of straight lines contained in the keyframe. We assign the categorical value of *LN* to each keyframe by comparing the number of straight lines in the keyframe with some threshold values.

LL: *LL* reflects the shape feature of man-made objects in a keyframe, for instance, buildings and windows have long straight lines that define these objects' boundaries. To be exact, *LL* represents the distribution of straight line lengths in the keyframe. In order to assign such a categorical value of *LL* to each keyframe, we compute the intensity histogram of the lengths of straight lines. This histogram is then normalized so that it is independent of the number of straight lines. Finally, we assign the categorical value of *LL* to each keyframe by using the *k*-means clustering method.

LB: *LB* reflects the dominant direction of most straight lines contained in a keyframe. For example, buildings and windows have vertical straight lines, while a natural scene has different directions of straight lines [25]. Thus, *LB* represents the distribution of straight line directions in the keyframe. As with *LL*, we compute the normalized histogram of straight line directions. Then, we assign the categorical value of *LB* to the keyframe by using the *k*-means clustering method.

SA: *SA* reflects the size of the main character displayed in a keyframe. *SA* represents the area of the largest skin colored region in the keyframe. We assign the categorical value of *SA* to each keyframe by comparing the area of the largest skin colored region with some threshold values.

LA: *LA* reflects the presence of weapons in a keyframe. Note that keyframes where laser-beams from weapons are presented have some large light colored regions. On the other hand, keyframes where sunshines (or lighting effects) are presented, not only have some large light colored regions, but also have many small light colored blobs due to the light dispersions. Based on the above observation, *LA* represents the area of the largest light colored region, divided by the total number of light colored regions in a keyframe. By comparing this value with some threshold values, we assign the categorical value of *LA* to the keyframe.

The above types of raw level metadata are derived by using functions prepared in OpenCV library [28]. Besides these types of raw level metadata for characterizing the spatial aspect, we derive the following types of raw level metadata for characterizing the temporal aspect.

SL: *SL* represents the duration of a shot. In other words, *SL* represents the speed of the camera switching from a shot to the next shot. Generally, thrilling events, such as battles and chases, are presented by shots with short durations, while romantic events, such as hugging and kissing, are presented by shots with long durations. We assign the categorical value of *SL* to each shot by comparing its duration with some threshold values.

MS: *MS* represents the movement of some objects or background in a shot. For example, in a shot where characters actively move or the background significantly changes, the movement is large, whereas the movement is small when characters are still and the background hardly changes. To extract the movement, we select MPEG as the video format. Because MPEG compresses a video by predicting the color change between two consecutive video frames. The size and direction of the predicted color change are represented as a *motion vector*. Every motion vector is defined in a *macro block* which is a unit block consisting of 16×16 pixels. On the basis of this definition of motion vector, the movement is defined as a sum of motion vector sizes in all macro blocks. We assign the categorical value of *MS* by comparing the movement with some threshold values.

MV: *MV* represents the direction of movement of objects or the background in a shot. For example, in a shot where characters move to a certain direction, the direction of the movement is constant, whereas the movement has no direction in a shot where characters are still. The direction of movement is defined as follows: we prepare four direction counters: up, down, left, and right. These counters are used to count the directions of motion vectors in all macro blocks. If the count in every direction is smaller than the threshold value, no direction is assigned to the shot. Otherwise, the direction with the largest count is assigned to the shot.

SM: *SM* represents the sound type that frequently appears in a shot, such as *speech*, *music*, and *no-sound*. For example, *speech* frequently appears in a shot where characters are talking. On the other hand, *music* frequently appears in a shot where BGM with large sound volume is used. We assign the categorical value of *SM* to each shot in the following way: we convert the sound stream into Mel-Frequency Cepstrum Coefficients (MFCCs). The MFCCs are compared with a human voice model and music model constructed by using Gaussian Mixture Model (GMM) [29]. As a result, we can assign a categorical value of *SM* to the shot.

AM: *AM* represents the largest sound volume in a shot. For example, a shot that involves a scream, explosion, or gunshot has a large sound volume, while a shot with a chat or infiltration has a small sound volume. We assign the categorical value of *AM* to each shot by comparing the maximum amplitude of the sound stream with some threshold values.

Finally, by deriving raw level metadata from each shot, the video is transformed from a computationally intractable raw material into a 13-dimensional categorical stream. An example of this categorical stream is presented in Figure 20.2. In Figure 20.2, each component stream is constructed for one type of raw level metadata. A symbol in the stream consists of two capital letters representing the type of raw level metadata and the number representing the categorical value. For example, stream 1 is constructed for *CH* and the symbol *CH*4 in *shot 1* represents that the categorical value 4 is assigned to *shot 1*.

20.4 Time-Constrained Sequential Pattern Mining

In this section, we present our time-constrained sequential pattern mining method to extract sequential patterns from a multi-dimensional categorical stream. First of all, we formally define sequential patterns together with time constraints. Then, we present our mining algorithm with time constraints. Finally, we extend our algorithm for parallelizing the mining process.

20.4.1 Formulation

We assume a multi-dimensional categorical stream S, where none of the same symbol occurs in different component streams of S. A symbol v that occurs in a component

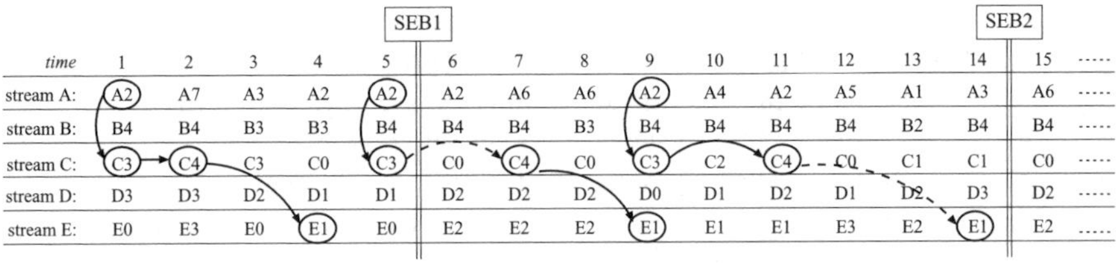

time	1	2	3	4	5	6	7	8	9	10	11	12	13	14	15	
					SEB1									SEB2		
stream A:	A2	A7	A3	A2	A2	A2	A6	A6	A2	A4	A2	A5	A1	A3	A6	.....
stream B:	B4	B4	B3	B4	B4	B4	B4	B3	B4	B4	B4	B4	B2	B4	B4	.....
stream C:	C3	C4	C3	C0	C3	C0	C4	C0	C3	C2	C4	C0	C1	C1	C0	.....
stream D:	D3	D3	D2	D1	D1	D2	D2	D2	D0	D1	D2	D1	D2	D3	D2	.....
stream E:	E0	E3	E0	E1	E0	E2	E2	E2	E1	E1	E1	E3	E2	E1	E2	.....

Fig. 20.3. An example of a multi-dimensional categorical stream S where only the occurrence of a 4-pattern $p_4 = (A2, nil), (C3, parallel), (C4, serial), (E1, serial)$ from the time point $t = 1$ to $t = 4$ satisfies both SEB and TDT time constraints.

stream s at a time point t can be represented as (v, t) because v does not occur in the other component streams. An example of such a multi-dimensional categorical stream is shown in Figure 20.3, where the capital letter in the left side indicates the component stream name and the number in the right side indicates the categorical value. Thus, the symbol $A2$ occurring in *stream A* at the time point 1 is represented as $(A2, 1)$.

For any pair of two symbols in S, the relative temporal relationship is either *serial* or *parallel*.[1] For example, the relationship between $(A2, 1)$ and $(C3, 1)$ is parallel; that is, these symbols occur at the same time point. On the other hand, the relationship between $(C3, 1)$ and $(C4, 2)$ is serial; that is, these symbols occur at different time points. Note that a serial relationship does not require that two symbols belong to the same component stream, so the relationship between $(C4, 2)$ and $(E1, 4)$ is also serial. For two symbols (v_1, t_1) and (v_2, t_2), the serial and parallel relationships are formulated as follows:

$$t_1 \neq t_2 \longrightarrow serial,$$
$$t_1 = t_2 \longrightarrow parallel. \tag{20.1}$$

Now we define a sequential pattern p_l as a temporally ordered set of l symbols and call p_l as *l-pattern*. In Figure 20.3, 4-pattern p_4 is presented by the temporally ordered set of 4 symbols surrounded by the circles. For p_l, we represent the temporal order of l symbols as a sequence of serial and parallel relationships between two consecutive symbols. Therefore, p_l is formulated as follows:

$$p_l = (v_1, nil), (v_2, tr_2), (v_3, tr_3), \ldots, (v_l, tr_l), \tag{20.2}$$

where for all $i = 2, \ldots, l$, (v_i, tr_i) represents a symbol v_i whose relationship with (v_{i-1}, tr_{i-1}) is tr_i (i.e., $tr_i = serial$ or $tr_i = parallel$). In Figure 20.3, p_4 is denoted as $p_4 = (A2, nil), (C3, parallel), (C4, serial), (E1, serial)$. In the above equation (20.2), if $tr_i = serial$, the serial relationship between $(v_i, tr_i = serial)$ and (v_{i-1}, tr_{i-1}) is restricted by the following two types of time constraints:

---

[1] Our usage of a serial and parallel relationships is different from those of [16].

Semantic event boundaries: A multi-dimensional categorical stream S can be divided into some semantic events. For example, a stream of highway traffic sensor data can be divided into semantic events of different traffic conditions. An e-mail stream can be divided into semantic events where certain topics appear [30]. By restricting an occurrence of p_l in one semantic event, p_l can become a useful sequential pattern associated with a certain semantic content in S. Thus, the serial relationship between (v_{i-1}, tr_{i-1}) and (v_i, tr_i) must not cross over any *Semantic Event Boundaries (SEBs)*. In Figure 20.3, where two *SEBs* (*SEB1* and *SEB2*) are shown, it is not acceptable that p_4 occurs between the time point $t = 5$ and $t = 9$, because the serial relationship between $(C3, 5)$ and $(C4, 7)$ crosses over *SEB1*.

Temporal localities: Using only *SEB* time constraint falls into extracting many sequential patterns that are not relevant to semantic patterns. Thus, we further use the time constraint proposed in [6, 7]. Considering temporal localities that two shots in the same semantic event have to be temporally close to each other, two consecutive symbols in p_l have to be temporally close to each other.[2] Hence, in order for p_l to be a semantic pattern, the relative temporal distance between (v_{i-1}, tr_{i-1}) and (v_i, tr_i) must be less than *Temporal Distance Threshold (TDT)*. In Figure 20.3, where *TDT* is set to 2, it is not acceptable that p_4 occurs between the time point $t = 9$ and $t = 14$ because the temporal distance between $(C4, 11)$ and $(E1, 14)$ is 3.

By using *SEB* and *TDT* time constraints, we do not count occurrences of p_l, which are irrelevant to a semantic pattern. As a result, we can avoid extracting unnecessary sequential patterns that are unlikely to be semantic patterns. In Figure 20.3, only the occurrence of p_4 between $t = 1$ and $t = 4$ satisfies both *SEB* and *TDT* time constraints. It should be noted that p_l is just a template that specifies the temporal order of l symbols where each symbol is denoted as (v_i, tr_i). In contrast, an occurrence of p_l is an actual instance of p_l where each symbol is detected by using (v_i, t_i) in S.

20.4.2 Mining Algorithm

As described in Section 20.2.2, our mining algorithm extracts sequential patterns from a multi-dimensional categorical stream S by using an apriori–based approach. It is outlined below:

Process 1: Initialize $l = 1$. l is a number of symbols included in a pattern. Subsequently, extract every 1-pattern p_1 from S, which satisfies an interestingness measure f. Here, f is used to measure the usefulness of each candidate pattern in order to determine whether it is regarded as a pattern or not.

Process 2: Increment l, and generate a set of *candidate l-patterns* from the set of $(l - 1)$-patterns.

---

[2] Apart from video data, this time constraint has been applied to various kinds of data such as transactional data [15] and biological data [31].

Process 3: Locate each candidate l-pattern cp_l in S by taking *SEB* and *TDT* time constraints into account, and count the number of cp_l's occurrences in S. Then, regard cp_l as a l-pattern p_l only if cp_l satisfies f.

Process 4: If no p_l is extracted, terminates the mining process. Otherwise, go to process 2.

In order to complete our mining algorithm, we need to discuss the following three issues in more detail: how to generate candidate patterns at process 2, how to locate cp_l in S at process 3, and how to define f at process 1 and 3.

20.4.2.1 Generating Candidate Patterns

Although the definition of a sequential pattern in [14] is different from our definition, an efficient algorithm of candidate pattern generation is presented in [14]. So, we revise this algorithm to generate a set of candidate l-patterns from the set of $(l-1)$-patterns extracted in the previous iteration. Figure 20.4 illustrates the generation of a candidate l-pattern cp_l from two $(l-1)$-patterns p_{l-1} and p'_{l-1}. In Figure 20.4, we select the following p_{l-1} and p'_{l-1}: the temporally ordered set of $l-2$ symbols generated by removing the first symbol (v_1, nil) from p_{l-1}, is exactly the same as the one generated by removing the last symbol (v'_{l-1}, tr'_{l-1}) from p'_{l-1}. Note that the symbol (v_2, tr_2) is replaced with (v_2, nil), because it is now the starting symbol in the temporally ordered set of $l-2$ symbols. Then, cp_l is generated by concatenating (v'_{l-1}, tr'_{l-1}) and p_{l-1}.

Locating all candidate l-patterns in S needs much more expensive computational cost. Hence, we should delete candidate l-patterns which are unlikely to become l-patterns without searching them in S. For cp_l, we remove any $(v_i, parallel)$ from cp_l to form a temporally ordered set of $l-1$ symbols. Note that even if we delete $(v_i, parallel)$ from cp_l, the original temporal order of cp_l is preserved. Therefore, all of the above temporally ordered sets of $l-1$ symbols have to be already extracted as $(l-1)$-patterns. Otherwise, it is impossible for cp_l to be p_l and thus delete cp_l from the set of candidate l-patterns.

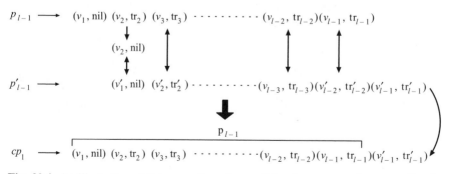

Fig. 20.4. An illustration of the generation of a candidate l-pattern cp_l from two $(l-1)$-patterns, p_{l-1} and p'_{l-1}.

20.4.2.2 Locating a Candidate Pattern in the Stream

The outline of our approach for locating p_l in S is illustrated in Figure 20.5. In the stream A, a symbol $(A1, t)$ $(t = 1, 2, 3, 5, 6, 8)$ represents "the woman appears at a time point t (i.e. in a shot t)," and a symbol $(A2, t)$ $(t = 4, 7)$ represents "the woman does not appear at t." In this condition, we discuss locating 2-pattern $p_2 = (A1, \text{nil}), (A1, \text{serial})$ by focusing on the three occurrences: Occ_1, Occ_2, and Occ_3. The semantic contents represented by these occurrences are as follows:

- $Occ_1 \cdots$ The woman meets the man, and she talks to him.
- $Occ_2 \cdots$ The woman meets the man, and she walks with him.
- $Occ_3 \cdots$ The woman meets the man, and she drives her car.

Occ_3 is clearly meaningless because it spans two different semantic events. Such an occurrence can be prevented by SEB time constraint. Occ_1 is assumed to be more meaningful than Occ_2. It is because, based on the discussion of temporal localities in Section 20.1, a serial relationship occurring in a short temporal distance between two symbols is assumed to represent a coherent semantic content. Thus, if there are some possible occurrences of the serial relationship within the temporal distance specified by TDT time constraint, the serial relationship is located by using the shortest temporal distance like Occ_1 in Figure 20.5.

Figure 20.6 illustrates our approach for locating 3-pattern p_3 in S. In Figure 20.6, where TDT is set to 3, by tracing along the solid arrows, we can find three occurrences of p_3. In addition to SEB and TDT time constraints, we further introduce the search constraint represented by three dashed arrows. That is, if (v, t) is used to find an occurrence of p_l, (v, t) cannot be used to find any later occurrences of p_l. For example, the leftmost dashed arrow represents that $(B1, 3)$ is used to find p_3's occurrence starting from $t = 1$; thus, it cannot be used again and $(B1, 4)$ is used to find p_3's occurrence starting from $t = 2$. We call a symbol (v, t), which has not yet been used to find any p_l's occurrence *unused*.

We describe the reason why we search p_l's occurrences by using only *unused* symbols. Suppose that, in Figure 20.6, $(B1, 3)$ is used by $(A3, 1)$ and $(A3, 2)$ to find p_3's occurrences. Consequently, at the time point $t = 5$, two p_3's occurrences are counted, which is contradictory to that two different occurrences end at different time points. Hence, we use only *unused* symbols to detect p_3's occurrences.

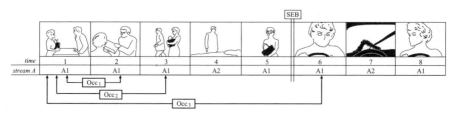

Fig. 20.5. An example of occurrences of 2-pattern $p_2 = (A1, \text{nil}), (A1, \text{serial})$, where Occ_1 represents the most coherent semantic content among three occurrences.

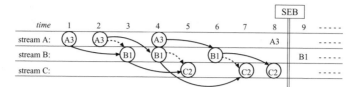

Fig. 20.6. An example of our approach for locating $p_3 = (A3, \text{nil}), (B1, \text{serial}), (C2, \text{serial})$ in S, where $TDT = 3$ and three occurrences of p_3 are located.

Now, we describe our algorithm for locating p_l in S. Our algorithm finds p_l's occurrences one by one according to the temporal order. For example, in Figure 20.6, the occurrence of p_3 starting from $t = 1$ is firstly detected, the occurrence from $t = 2$ is secondly detected, and the occurrence from $t = 4$ is thirdly detected. In each detection of p_l's occurrence, our algorithm switches *Forward* and *Backward* phases introduced in [15]. But, in order to deal with *SEB* and *TDT* time constraints and the above search constraint, we extend *Forward* and *Backward* phases. Suppose that we are now searching an occurrence of p_l where the first i symbols are already detected as $(v_1, t_1), \ldots, (v_i, t_i)$.

Forward phase: On the basis of the already detected symbols, we select a symbol (v_{i+1}, t_{i+1}) for the $(i + 1)$-th symbol.

> If the $(i + 1)$-th temporal relationship is **serial**, select the unused symbol (v_{i+1}, t_{i+1}) where t_{i+1} is larger than t_i. If the serial relationship between (v_i, t_i) and (v_{i+1}, t_{i+1}) satisfies both *SEB* and *TDT* time constraints, recursively perform *Forward* phase for selecting (v_{i+2}, t_{i+2}). Otherwise, switch to *Backward* phase for backtracking.

> If the $(i + 1)$-th temporal relationship is **parallel**, select the unused symbol (v_{i+1}, t_{i+1}) where t_{i+1} is equal or larger than t_i. If $t_i = t_{i+1}$, recursively perform *Forward* phase. Otherwise (i.e. $t_i \neq t_{i+1}$), switch to *Backward* phase for backtracking.

> In the case of $i + 1 = l$, if (v_i, t_i) and (v_{i+1}, t_{i+1}) satisfy the serial (or parallel) relationship, one occurrence of p_l is detected.

Backward phase: Suppose that two already selected symbols (v_i, t_i) and (v_{i+1}, t_{i+1}) do not satisfy the $(i + 1)$-th temporal relationship. So, we select (v_i, t_i') as an alternative of (v_i, t_i).

> If the $(i + 1)$-th temporal relationship is **serial**, select the unused symbol (v_i, t_i') where t_i' is not only larger than the nearest *SEB* before t_{i+1}, but also larger than $t_{i+1} - TDT$.

> If the $(i + 1)$-th temporal relationship is **parallel**, select the unused symbol (v_i, t_i') where t_i' is equal or larger than t_{i+1}.

> After modifying (v_i, t_i) into (v_i, t_i'), check whether (v_i, t_i') and (v_{i-1}, t_{i-1}) still satisfy the i-th temporal relationship in p_l. If so, switch to *Forward* phase in order to select a new (v_{i+1}, t_{i+1}) for the modified (v_i, t_i'). Otherwise, recursively starts *Backward* phase for further backtracking. In the case of $i = 1$, where (v_1, t_1) is modified into (v_1, t_1'), immediately switch to *Forward* phase.

In both *Forward* and *Backward* phases, if no symbol can be selected, there is no more occurrence of p_l in S and our algorithm terminates. Finally, the number of p_l's occurrences is defined as the frequency of p_l, and denoted as $freq(p_l)$.

20.4.2.3 Using an Interestingness Measure

On the basis of the frequency of cp_l $freq(cp_l)$, we determine whether cp_l is actually a l-pattern p_l. At this point, many interestingness measures have been proposed to measure the usefulness of cp_l [32]. In this chapter, we use the *support* and *confidence* of cp_l as an interestingness measure f. Note that $cp_l = (v_1, nil), \ldots, (v_{l-1}, tr_{l-1}), (v_l, tr_l)$ is generated by adding (v_l, tr_l) to $(l-1)$-pattern $p_{l-1} = (v_1, nil), \ldots, (v_{l-1}, tr_{l-1})$. This means that the first $(l-1)$ symbols in cp_l denoted by $pre(cp_l) = (v_1, nil), \ldots, (v_{l-1}, tr_{l-1})$ are already validated as p_{l-1}. Therefore, on the basis of the usefulness of connecting $pre(cp_l)$ and (v_l, tr_l) measured by f, we determine whether cp_l can be p_l or not.

We denote the support and confidence of cp_l by $sup(cp_l)$ and $conf(cp_l)$, respectively. They are defined as follows:

$$
\begin{aligned}
\text{for } cp_l \ (l \geq 1), \quad & sup(cp_l) = freq(cp_l), \\
\text{for } cp_l \ (l \geq 2), \quad & conf(cp_l) = P(cp_l \mid pre(cp_l)).
\end{aligned}
\tag{20.3}
$$

In the above Equation (20.3), $sup(cp_l)$ is the frequency of cp_l in S, and represents the statistical significance of cp_l in S. $conf(cp_l)$ is the conditional probability of cp_l given that $pre(cp_l)$ occurs, and represents the strength of the association between $pre(cp_l)$ and (v_l, tr_l). cp_l is regarded as a l-pattern p_l only when both $sup(cp_l)$ and $conf(cp_l)$ are larger than the minimum support and confidence thresholds.

20.4.3 Parallel Algorithm

To reduce the computational cost of our mining algorithm, we present a parallel algorithm for parallelizing the mining process. Our parallel algorithm assumes a shared-nothing architecture where each of p processors has a private memory and a private disk. These p processors are connected to a communication network and can communicate only by passing messages. The communication primitives are prepared by using MPI (Message Passing Interface) communication library [33].

The outline of our parallel algorithm is as follows: our parallel algorithm starts with the extraction of 1-patterns by using a single processor. Suppose that the total number of 1-patterns is k. These k 1-patterns are evenly distributed to p processors; that is, k/p 1-patterns are distributed to each processor. Then, by using our mining algorithm described in the previous section, each processor performs the extraction of sequential patterns where distributed k/p 1-patterns are used as the starting symbols of these sequential patterns. After all of p processors finish extracting sequential patterns, all of extracted sequential patterns are gathered in one processor, and output as the final mining result.

The above algorithm cannot be considered as an efficient parallel algorithm. The reason is that when the number of sequential patterns extracted at one processor is fewer than those of the other processors, the processor has a long *idle time* in which it waits for the other processors to finish their mining tasks. Thus, we need to reduce such idle times on p processors used in our parallel algorithm.

Our parallel algorithm is improved by using a *load balancing* technique where mining tasks of p processors are dynamically re-distributed. Specifically, when a processor PE_i has an idle time, PE_i sends *task requests* to the other processors. If a processor receives the task request from PE_i, the processor reports the current progress of its mining task to PE_i. Thereby, PE_i can select a *donor processor* that requires the longest time to finish its mining task. After that, a part of the mining task of the donor processor is re-distributed to PE_i. Finally, PE_i receives the re-distributed task from the donor processor, and starts to run this task.

Suppose that a processor $PE_j(j = 1, 2, \ldots, p \mid j \neq i)$ receives a task request from PE_i after extracting l_j-patterns. In addition, the number of different starting symbols in l_j-patterns is m_j, and the total number of sequential patterns extracted at PE_j is n_j. After PE_i receives l_j, m_j and n_j from another processor PE_j, PE_i determines a donor processor in the following way: first of all, PE_j with $m_j = 1$ cannot be a donor processor because it has no distributable task. Among the remaining processors, PE_i selects PE_j with the smallest l_j as a donor processor. This is based on the assumption that since l_j represents the number of iterations which PE_j has finished, the smaller l_j indicates a slower progress of PE_j's mining task. Nonetheless, if some processors have the same smallest l_j, PE_j with the largest n_j is selected as a donor processor. We assume that the more sequential patterns PE_j extracts (i.e., the larger n_j PE_j has), the more candidate patterns are generated. After determining a donor processor $PE_{j'}$ where $l_{j'}$-patterns are classified into $m_{j'}$ groups of different starting symbols, $PE_{j'}$ sends $(m_{j'}/2)$ groups to PE_i. Afterward, PE_i extracts sequential patterns whose first $l_{j'}$ symbols are $l_{j'}$-patterns in the groups sent from $PE_{j'}$.

20.5 Experimental Results

We selected three movies, Star Wars Episode 2 (*SWE2*), Star Wars Episode 4 (*SWE4*) and Men In Black (*MIB*). For our experiment, our video data mining approach was tested on the six fragments with about 30 minutes in the above three movies. These six fragments are listed below:

- *video 1* is a fragment in *SWE2* and contains 444 shots.
- *video 2* is a fragment in *SWE2* and contains 725 shots.
- *video 3* is a fragment in *SWE4* and contains 578 shots.
- *video 4* is a fragment in *SWE4* and contains 439 shots.
- *video 5* is a fragment in *MIB* and contains 444 shots.
- *video 6* is a fragment in *MIB* and contains 453 shots.

All of the above videos are compressed in MPEG-1 format with a frame rate of 29.97 *frames/second*. Shot boundaries are detected by using MP-Factory (MPEG Software Development Kit) library [34]. Note that *video 2* contains a larger number of shots

Table 20.2. The performance evaluations of assigning categorical values of SM.

	video 1	video 2	video 3	video 4	video 5	video 6
Precision (speech)	52.9 (%)	57.29	72.11	74.94	97.2	96.2
Precision (music)	37.53	82.67	49.72	50.0	21.5	29.5
Recall (speech)	72.34	31.14	41.28	64.6	49.6	25.4
Recall (music)	20.68	92.8	78.44	61.2	90.5	96.8

than the other videos because almost all semantic events are battle events presented by fast transitions of shots with short durations.

20.5.1 Evaluations of Assigning Categorical Values of SM

For the experimental videos, we evaluate the performances of our method for assigning categorical values of SM to shots. These performances are presented in Table 20.2. The precision and recall of each video are computed by comparing our method with the human observer. If a shot contains both *speech* and *music*, the lauder one is selected as the ground truth for the shot. As shown in Table 20.2, none of the performances in the experimental videos are good because these videos contain various kinds of sounds (e.g., sound effects and sounds of machine engines) apart from *speech* and *music*. In regard to these low performances, in order to extract reliable semantic patterns from the experimental videos, we manually assign a categorical value of SM, such as *speech*, *music*, *others*, or *no-sound* to each shot.

20.5.2 Evaluation of Semantic Event Boundary Detections

In order to detect semantic event boundaries in a video, we use the method introduced in [5] that intelligently merges semantically related shots into a semantic event. In this method, semantic event boundaries are dynamically updated on the basis of time-adaptive shot grouping where the spatial and temporal information and temporal localities are used. But, since temporal localities rely on the average of shot durations in the whole video, the method in [5] does not work well when some segments have significantly different averages of shot durations. For example, shot durations are relatively long in one segment where romantic events are presented, while shot durations are relatively short in another segment where thrilling events are presented. The overall average of shot durations in these two segments is not suitable for capturing temporal localities in any of two segments. So, the method in [5] should not be applied to the whole video but be applied to segments separately. In each segment, shot durations are almost similar, thus the average of these shot durations is suitable for capturing temporal localities in the segment.

In order to divide a video into segments, we use the method introduced in [30]. It models shot durations in the video by using an infinite-state automaton, where each state is associated with a probabilistic density function having an expected value of shot duration. Furthermore, to make this modeling robust to many insignificant changes of shot durations, costs are assigned to state transitions. As a result, the video

Table 20.3. The performance evaluations of our semantic event boundary detection method.

	video 1	video 2	video 3	video 4	video 5	video 6
# of segments	4	3	4	3	3	3
Precision	64.9 (%)	55.8	63.2	54.3	25.0	62.1
Recall	77.4	71.7	85.7	73.1	42.0	75.0

is divided into some segments, in each of which shot durations are modeled by a single state in the infinite-state automaton. That is, shot durations in the segment are relatively constant toward the expected value of the state. Finally, by applying the method in [5] to each segment separately, the detection of semantic event boundaries can be much more accurate than the detection by simply applying it to the whole video.

Table 20.3 shows the performance evaluation of our semantic event boundary detection method. The row of *# of segments* shows that each experimental video is divided into three or four segments. The precision and recall in each video are computed by comparing our method with the human observer. The reasonably high recall values indicate that most of true semantic event boundaries are detected by our method although the relatively low precision values indicate that our method over-detects semantic event boundaries. The main reason is that the spatial and temporal information in a shot cannot be successfully obtained only from the color information. For example, semantically related shots where a character performs similar actions in different background locations cannot belong to the same semantic event. Since we cannot extract reliable semantic patterns by using erroneous semantic event boundaries detected by our method, we manually correct these semantic event boundaries.

20.5.3 Evaluations of Extracted Semantic Patterns

By using our time-constrained sequential pattern mining method, we extracted semantic patterns from the experimental videos. Examples of extracted semantic patterns are shown in Table 20.4, where the three columns from the left represent the properties of extracted semantic patterns and the rest of four columns represent the results of retrieving semantic events by using these patterns. In the third column, a serial relationship between two consecutive symbols X and Y is represented as $X - Y$ and a parallel relationship is represented as XY. Extracted semantic patterns can be classified into the following three groups. The first group is called *action* group, which includes the semantic events where characters perform specific actions (i.e., talk, move and violence). The second one is called *situation* group which includes the specific situations (i.e., dark, close-up, and thrilling). The third one is called *combination* group including the semantic events where characters perform specific actions in specific situations (i.e., talk in thrilling situation, talk in dark situation, and so on).

For each semantic pattern in Table 20.4, the precision (P) and recall (R) are computed on the basis of semantic events retrieved by using the semantic pattern. In addition, a video annotated with * means that the semantic pattern cannot be

Table 20.4. Examples of extracted semantic patterns

Group	Event	Pattern	video 1	video 2	video 3	video 4	video 5	video 6
Action	talk	SM1 – SM1	P:56.0 R:100	P:66.7 R:88.9	P:84.2 R:100	P:85.0 R:73.9	P:100 R:91.7	P:75.0 R:93.8
		SM1MV0	P:65.0 R:92.9	P:66.7 R:100	P:72.3 R:100	P:90.5 R:89.5	P:100 R:100	P:65.2 R:93.8
		MV0 – MV0	P:78.6 R:78.6	*	P:70.4 R:100	P:77.3 R:85.0	P:100 R:100	P:65.2 R:93.8
	move	MV4SM2	P:73.3 R:91.7	*	*	*	*	*
		MS5SM2	P:87.5 R:93.8	P:88.9 R:80.0	*	*	*	*
	violence	SM2 – SM2	P:84.2 R:100	P:76.7 R:62.2	P:53.3 R:88.9	P:43.8 R:100	*	*
		SL0 – SL0	*	P:81.8 R:90.0	P:60.0 R:100	P:46.7 R:100	*	P:40.0 R:100
Situation	dark	CV2	P:87.5 R:100	*	P:35.5 R:100	P:47.1 R:100	*	P:35.3 R:100
	close-up	LN1	P:52.2 R:85.7	P:42.2 R:86.4	*	*	P:46.2 R:100	P:89.5 R:85.0
		SA3	P:48.1 R:92.9	P:41.2 R:95.5	P:100 R:61.1	P:66.7 R:82.4	*	P:94.7 R:90.0
	thrilling	CS4	P:56.2 R:100	P:60.0 R:84.0	P:71.4 R:100	P:71.4 R:83.3	*	*
	talk + thrilling	CS4SM1	P:30.0 R:100	*	*	*	*	*
		CV2SM2	P:61.1 R:84.6	*	*	*	*	P:14.3 R:66.7
	talk + dark	CV2 – CV2LN1SA4	P:66.7 R:72.7	*	*	*	*	*
Combination	talk + close-up	SA3SM1MV0	P:53.3 R:100	*	P:100 R:47.4	P:90.9 R:62.5	*	P:50.0 R:80.0
		LN1SM1MV0	*	*	P:92.6 R:65.0	P:75.0 R:100	P:72.7 R:80.0	P:40.0 R:50.0
	talk + indoor	LN2SM1MV0	P:78.6 R:84.6	*	*	*	*	P:73.3 R:100
	dark + close-up	CV2LN1SA3	P:71.4 R:83.3	*	*	*	*	*
	dark + close-up + violence	CV2LN1	P:55.6 R:55.6	*	*	*	*	*
		SA3SL0						

extracted from the video. In accordance with these notations, we briefly explain extracted semantic patterns while evaluating the retrieval results of these patterns.

First of all, the semantic patterns associated with talk events $SM1 - SM1$, $SM1MV0$, and $MV0 - MV0$ are characterized by "two continuous shots with human voice," "a shot with human voice and no direction of movement," and "two continuous shots with no direction of movement" respectively. The considerably high recall values for these patterns indicate that characters talk to each other and hardly move in most of talk events. The semantic pattern associated with move event $MV4SM2$ is characterized by "a shot with a constant movement direction and music." This pattern indicates that background music is frequently used when some vehicles or characters move. The semantic patterns associated with violence events $MS5SM2$, $SM2 - SM2$, and $SL0 - SL0$ are characterized by "a shot with a large amount of movement and music," "two continuous shots with music," and "two continuous shots with short durations" respectively. Especially, $MS5SM2$ and $SM2 - SM2$ reveal an interesting nature of violence events, where background music is generally more emphasized than character's voice. But, we could not extract them from MIB where background music is hardly used. So, $SL0 - SL0$ is only the semantic pattern for characterizing violence events in MIB and this pattern is also applicable to $SWE2$ and $SWE4$. Finally, all of the above semantic patterns in the action group consist of raw level metadata for temporal aspects.

Apart from the action group, the situation group includes semantic patterns consisting of raw level metadata for spatial aspects. The semantic pattern associated with dark situation $CV2$ is characterized by "a shot where brightnesses of most pixels are of low value." Although all recall values are $100(\%)$, the low precision values of *video 3*, *video 4*, and *video 6* represent that semantic events retrieved by using $CV2$ include many semantic events where black-costumed characters play important roles. Examples of such black-costumed characters are Darth Vader in *SWE4* and characters wearing black suits and sunglasses in *MIB*. Two semantic patterns associated with character's close-up $LN1$ and $SA3$ are characterized by "a shot containing few straight lines" and "a shot containing a large skin colored region" respectively. $LN1$ is confirmed by the fact that a human face is generally rounded, so few straight lines can be derived from its boundary. $SA3$ agrees with our intuition that SA reflects the size of the main character in a keyframe. But, the low precision values in *video 1* and *video 2* indicate that $SA3$ does not work well for videos where there are many skin colored objects (e.g., rock and desert). The semantic pattern associated with thrilling situation $CS4$ is characterized by "a shot where saturations of most pixels are of low value." This kind of shot generally displays a blurred situation where an explosion or chase with high speed takes place. But, $CS4$ is not extracted from MIB because the dominant color in most of shots is black.

For the semantic patterns in the combination group, $CS4SM1$, $CV2SM2$, $CV2 - CV2LN1SA4$, $SA3SM1MV0$, $LN1SM1MV0$, $LN2SM1MV0$, $CV2LN1SA3$, and $CV2LN1SA3SL0$ are the combinations of the action and situation groups. For example, $LN1SM1MV0$ is associated with talk events of character's close-up. This pattern is the combination of $LN1$ for character's close-up and $SM1MV0$ for talk events. Also, $CV2LN1SA3SL0$, which is associated with violence events of dark and character's close-up, is the combination of three types of semantic patterns $CV2$ for dark situation, $LN1$ and $SA3$ for character's close-up and $SL0$ for violence events. Like this, the combination group specifies more complex semantic events than those of the action and situation groups.

20.6 Conclusion and Future Works

Currently we are facing with the problem that transforming a raw material video into a multistream of raw level metadata inevitably involves *semantic noises*. A semantic noise means that the same categorical value of raw level metadata is assigned to semantically different shots. For example, the same categorical value of SA can be assigned to two types of shots, one is a shot where a character appears close to the camera, the other is a shot where a skin colored background is shown. Such semantic noises may prevent us from extracting some interesting semantic patterns. With respect to this, we plan to develop a video data mining approach which extracts semantic patterns without deriving raw level metadata from a raw material video. To achieve this goal, a *data squashing* technique [35] seems to be useful because it scales down a large original video data into a smaller *pseudo data*, while preserving nearly the same structure to the original data. Since each *pseudo data* element has a weight for reflecting the distribution of the original data, we must introduce a new data mining technique that accepts weights to extract semantic patterns.

Acknowledgments

First of all, we thank Toshiya Hirata for proposing our parallel mining framework. We also greatly thank Kuangyi Zhu for his contribution to this chapter. Finally, we much appreciate Akihiko Izutani for implementing our mining algorithm.

References

1. Hampapur A. *Designing Video Data Management Systems*. University of Michigan: Ph.D dissertation; 1995.
2. Oh J, Bandi B. Multimedia data mining framework for raw video sequences. In: *Proc. of 3rd International Workshop on Multimedia Data Mining (MDM/KDD 2002)*; 2002, pp. 1–10.
3. Gemmell D, Vin H, Kandlur D, Rangan P, Rowe L. Multimedia storage servers: A tutorial. *IEEE Computer* 1995;28(5):40–49.
4. Davenport G, Smith T, Pincever N. Cinematic primitives for multimedia. *IEEE Computer Graphics and Applications* 1991;11(4):67–74.
5. Rui Y, Huang T, Mehrotra S. Constructing table-of-content for videos. *ACM Multimedia Systems Journal* 1999;7(5):359–368.
6. Zhu X, Wu X. Mining video associations for efficient database management. In: *Proc. of 8th International Joint Conference on Artificial Intelligence (IJCAI 2003)*; 2003, pp. 1422–1424.

7. Zhu X, Wu X, Elmagarmid A, Feng Z, Wu L. Video data mining: Semantic indexing and event detection from the association perspective. *IEEE Transactions on Knowledge and Data Engineering* 2005;17(5):665–677.

8. Pan J, Faloutsos C. VideoCube: A novel tool for video mining and classification. In: *Proc. of 5th International Conference on Asian Digital Libraries (ICADL 2002)*; 2002. p. 194–205.

9. Pan J, Faloutsos C. *VideoGraph: A new tool for video mining and classification.* In: *Proc. of the ACM/IEEE-CS Joint Conference on Digital Libraries (JCDL 2001)*; 2001, pp. 116–117.

10. Wijesekera D, Barbara D. Mining cinematic knowledge: Work in progress. In: *Proc. of the International Workshop on Multimedia Data Mining (MDM/KDD 2000)*; 2000, pp. 98–103.

11. Matsuo Y, Shirahama K, Uehara K. Video data mining: Extracting cinematic rules from movie. In: *Proc. of 4th International Workshop on Multimedia Data Mining (MDM/KDD 2003)*; 2003, pp. 18–27.

12. Shirahama K, Matsuo Y, Uehara K. Mining semantic structures in movies. *Lecture Notes in Computer Science* 2005;3392:116–133.

13. Zaki M. SPADE: An efficient algorithm for mining frequent sequences. *Machine Learning* 2001;42(1/2):31–60.

14. Agrawal R, Srikant R. Mining sequential patterns. In: *Proc. of 11th International Conference on Data Engineering (ICDE 1995)*; 1995, pp. 3–14.

15. Srikant R, Agrawal R. Mining sequential patterns: Generalizations and performance improvements. In: *Proc. of 5th International Conference on Extending Database Technology (EDBT 1996)*; 1996, pp. 3–17.

16. Mannila H, Toivonen H, Verkamo A. Discovering frequent episodes in sequences. In: *Proc. of the International Conference on Knowledge Discovery and Data Mining (KDD 1995)*; 1995, pp. 210–215.

17. Oates T, Cohen P. Searching for structure in multiple streams. In: *Proc. of 13th International Conference on Machine Learning (ICML 1996)*; 1996, pp. 346–354.

18. Das G, Lin K, Mannila H, Renganathan G, Smyth P. Rule discovery from time series. In: *Proc. of 4th International Conference on Knowledge Discovery and Data Mining (KDD 1998)*; 1998, pp. 16–22.

19. Han J, Dong G, Yin Y. Efficient mining of partial periodic patterns in time series database. In: *Proc. of 15th International Conference on Data Engineering (ICDE 1999)*; 1999, pp. 106–115.

20. Yang J, Wang W, Yu P. Mining asynchronous periodic patterns in time series data. In: *Proc. of 6th International Conference on Knowledge Discovery and Data Mining (KDD 2000)*; 2000, pp. 275–279.

21. Chudova D, Smyth P. Pattern discovery in sequences under a markov assumption. In: *Proc. of 8th International Conference on Knowledge Discovery and Data Mining (KDD 2002)*; 2002, pp. 153–162.

22. Berberidis C, Vlahavas I, Aref W, Atallah M, Elmagarmid A. On the discovery of weak periodicities in large time series. In: *Proc. of 6th European Conference on Principles of Data Mining and Knowledge Discovery (PKDD 2002)*; 2002, pp. 51–61.

23. Tanaka Y, Iwamoto K, Uehara K. Discovery of time-series motif from multi-dimensional data based on MDL principle. *Machine Learning* 2005;58(2/3):269–300.

24. Dietterich T. Machine learning for sequential data: A review. *Lecture Notes in Computer Science* 2002;2396:15–30.

25. Mojsilovic A, Rogowitz B. Capturing image semantics with low-level descriptors. In:

Proc. of the 2001 IEEE International Conference in Image Processing (ICIP 2001); 2001, pp. 18–21.

26. Jain A, Murty M, Flynn P. Data clustering: A review. *ACM Computing Surveys* 1999;31(3):264–323.

27. Smith J, Chang S. Tools and techniques for color image retrieval. In: *Proc. of SPIE Storage and Retrieval for Image and Video Databases*; 1996, pp. 426–437.

28. OpenCV: Open Source Computer Vision Library. Intel; http://www.intel.com/research/mrl/research/opencv/.

29. Lamel L, Gauvain J. Speaker recognition with the switchboard corpus. In: *Proc. of International Conference on Acoustics, Speech and Signal Processing (ICASSP 1997)*; 1997, pp. 1067–1070.

30. Kleinberg J. Bursty and hierarchical structure in streams. In: *Proc. of 8th International Conference on Knowledge Discovery and Data Mining (KDD 2002)*; 2002, pp. 91–101.

31. Ferreira P, Azevedo P. Protein sequence pattern mining with constraints. *Lecture Notes in Artificial Intelligence* 2005;3721:96–107.

32. Hilderman R, Hamilton H. Knowledge discovery and measures of interest. Kluwer Academic Publishers; 2001.

33. MPI: A Message-Passing Interface Standard. Message Passing Interface Forum; http://www.mpi-forum.org.

34. MPFactory: MPEG Software Development Kit. KDDI; http://w3-mcgav.kddilabs.jp/mpeg/mpfs40/indexe.html.

35. DuMouchel W, Volinsky C, Johnson T, Cortes C, Pregibon D. Squashing flat files flatter. In: *Proc. of 5th International Conference on Knowledge Discovery and Data Mining (KDD 1999)*; 1999, pp. 6–15.

21. Multiple-Sensor People Localization in an Office Environment

Gang Wei, Valery A. Petrushin, and Anatole V. Gershman

Summary. This chapter describes an approach for people localization and tracking in an office environment using a sensor network that consists of video cameras, infrared tag readers, a fingerprint reader, and a PTZ camera. The approach is based on a Bayesian framework that uses noisy, but redundant data from multiple sensor streams and incorporates it with the contextual and domain knowledge that is provided by both the physical constraints imposed by the local environment where the sensors are located and by the people who are involved in the surveillance tasks. The experimental results are presented and discussed.

21.1 Introduction

The proliferation of a wide variety of sensors (video cameras, microphones, infrared badges, RFID tags, etc.) in public places such as airports, train stations, streets, parking lots, hospitals, governmental buildings, shopping malls, and homes has created the infrastructure that allows the development of security and business applications. Surveillance for threat detection, monitoring sensitive areas to detect unusual events, tracking customers in retail stores, controlling and monitoring movements of assets, and monitoring elderly and sick people at home are just some of the applications that require the ability to automatically detect, recognize, and track people and other objects by analyzing multiple streams of often unreliable and poorly synchronized sensory data. A scalable and robust system built for this class of tasks should also be able to integrate this sensory data with contextual information and domain knowledge provided by both the humans and the physical environment to maintain a coherent and logical picture of the world over time. While video surveillance has been in use for decades, systems that can automatically detect and track people (or objects) in multiple locations using multiple streams of heterogeneous and noisy sensory data is still a great challenge and an active research area. Since the performance of these automatic systems is not at the level at which they can work autonomously, there are human experts who are still part of the loop. It is important to develop techniques that can help human experts in this task by organizing and presenting the video surveillance data in a summarized manner, and highlighting unusual or rare events for further research by the experts. Many approaches have been proposed for object tracking in recent years.

They differ in various aspects such as number of cameras used, type of cameras and their speed and resolution, type of environment (indoors or outdoors), area covered (a room or a hall, a hallway, several connected rooms, a parking lot, a highway, etc.), and location of cameras (with or without overlapping fields of view). Some of the approaches are reviewed below. However, the performance of most systems is still far from what is required for real-world applications.

The objective of our research is to bridge the gap between the needs of practical applications and the performance of current surveillance algorithms. We seek solutions in the following directions:

- Developing a framework for logical integration of noisy sensory data from multiple heterogeneous sensory sources that combines probabilistic and knowledge-based approaches. The probabilistic part is used for object identification and tracking, and the knowledge-based part is used for maintaining overall coherence of reasoning.
- Exploiting local semantics from the environment of each sensor. For example, if a camera is pointed at a location where people usually tend to stand, the local semantics enable the system to use the "standing people" statistical models, as opposed to a camera pointing at an office space where people are usually sitting.
- Taking advantage of data and sensor redundancy to improve accuracy and robustness while avoiding the combinatorial explosion.
- Taking advantage of human guidance when it is available.
- Developing approaches and tools for efficient event clustering, classification, and visualization.
- Developing robust and scalable systems that work in real environments.

21.2 Environment

This research is a part of Multiple Sensor Indoor Surveillance (MSIS) project, which pursues the above-mentioned objectives. The backbone of the MSIS environment consists of 32 AXIS-2100 webcams, a pan-tilt-zoom (PTZ) camera, a fingerprint reader, and an infrared badge ID system (91 readers that are installed on the ceiling) that are sensing an office floor for Accenture Technology Labs in Chicago (Figure 21.1). The webcams and infrared badge system cover two entrances, seven laboratories and demonstration rooms, two meeting rooms, four major hallways, four open-space cube areas, two discussion areas, and an elevator area. Some areas are covered by multiple cameras, the maximum overlap being with up to four cameras. The total area covered is about 18,000 ft^2 (1,670 m^2). The fingerprint reader is installed at the entrance and used for matching an employee with his or her visual representation. The PTZ camera is watching the main entrance and northwestern cube area, and is used for face recognition.

Figure 21.2 presents the architecture of the system. It consists of three layers. The bottom layer deals with real-time image acquisition and feature extraction. It consists of several networked computers, with each computer running an agent that receives signals from 3 to 4 webcams, detecting "events," storing images for that

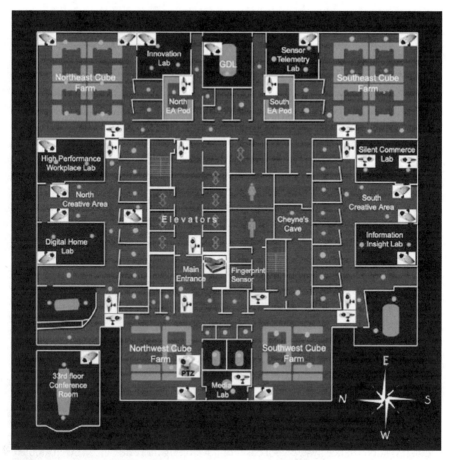

Fig. 21.1. Locations of Web cameras and infrared badge readers. Here IR badge readers are represented as dots, cameras are represented by small images that show their orientation, the PTZ camera has the label "PTZ" on the image, and the fingerprint reader is represented by a corresponding image near the main entrance.

event in the image repository in JPEG format, extracting features and saving them in the database. The event is defined as any movement in the camera's field of view. The average signal sampling frequency is about 3 frames per second. Three more agents acquire and save in the corresponding databases information about events detected by the infrared badge ID system, and the results of fingerprint and face recognition. The event databases serve as a common resource for applications of higher levels.

The middle layer consists of a set of application agents that use the features extracted at the bottom layer. The results of these agents go to the databases. Depending on the objective of the application it may use one, several, or all cameras and some other sensors.

The top layer consists of a set of meta-applications that use the results of the middle layer applications, integrate them, derive behavioral patters of the objects, and

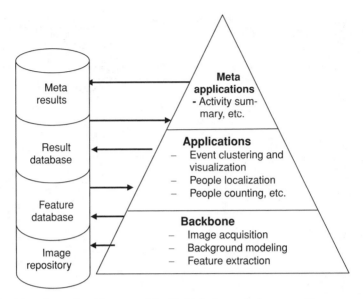

Fig. 21.2. General architecture of the Multiple Sensor Indoor surveillance system.

maintain the consistency of results. The applications of this layer are also responsible for maintaining the databases of the system and creating reports on its performance.

The MSIS project has the following objectives.

- Create a realistic multisensor indoor surveillance environment.
- Create an around-the-clock working surveillance system that accumulates data in a database for three consequent days and has a GUI for search and browsing.
- Use this surveillance system as a base for developing more advanced event analysis algorithms, such as people recognition and tracking, using collaborating agents and domain knowledge.

The following agents or applications have been considered.

- Creating a real-time image acquisition and feature extraction agent.
- Creating an event classification and clustering system.
- Search and browsing of the Event Repository database using a Web browser.
- Counting how many people are on the floor.
- Creating a people localization system that is based on evidence from multiple sensors and domain knowledge.
- Creating a real-time people tracking system that gives an optimal view of a person based on multiple cameras and prediction of person's behavior.
- Creating a system that recognizes a person at a particular location and interacts with him or her, for example, the system can send a voice message to the person and get his or her response.
- Creating a system that recognizes the behavior patterns of people.

- Creating a system that maintains the consistency of dynamic information about the events that was collected or derived by the other agents.

The above-mentioned applications are currently at different stages of completeness (see Chapter 5 in this book for a description of an application for event classification and clustering). This chapter describes the people localization system that is based on evidence from multiple sensors and domain knowledge.

21.3 Related Works

There are many papers devoted to video surveillance using single and multiple cameras. They differ in many aspects such as indoor/outdoor surveillance, people or/and vehicle tracking, using overlapping or nonoverlapping cameras, using mono or stereo, color or grayscale cameras, etc. Below we shall focus on some research that deals with indoor people identification and tracking.

A system described in work [1], which is a single camera system that was created for tracking people in subway stations, used the luminance contrast in YUV color space to separate people blobs from the background. The coordinates and geometric features of the blobs are estimated and two-way matching matrices algorithm has been used to track (overlapping) blobs.

In [2] one color static camera has been used to track people in indoor environment. It used several interacting modules to increase tracking robustness. The modules are a motion tracker that detects moving regions in each frame, a region tracker that tracks selected regions over time, a head detector that detects heads in the tracked regions, and an active shape tracker that uses models of people shape to detect and track them over time. The interaction among modules allows them dynamically incorporating and removing static objects into/from the background model, making prediction about a person's position and moving direction, and recovering after occlusions.

In the Microsoft's EasyLiving project [3] two color stereo cameras have been used for real-time identification and tracking up to three people in a rather small room (5 m by 5 m). The system evaluates 3D models of blobs and clusters them to fit a people-shaped blob model. Then the centroids of the blobs are projected into the room ground plan. The quantized RGB color histogram and histogram intersection are used for person's identity maintenance. A histogram is estimated for each person viewed by each camera in each visited cell of 10×10 grid of the floor plan. The person tracker module keeps the history of the person's past locations and uses it to predict current location. If the predicted location contains several candidates, then color histograms are used to disambiguate them. If no candidates found the system keeps unsupported person tracks active until new data arrive. For supported track their histories are updated and new predictions are calculated. In spite of low image processing rate (about 3.5 Hz) the system works well with up to three people, who are not moving too fast and not wearing similarly colored outfits.

The M2Tracker system [4] uses from 4 to 16 synchronized cameras to track up to six people walking in a restricted area (3.5 m by 3.5 m). The system identifies people using the following models for segmenting images in each camera view: color models at different heights, presence probabilities along the horizontal direction at different heights, and ground plane positions tracked using a Kalman filter. Then the results of one camera segmentation are matched for pairs of cameras to estimate 3D models for each person and estimate the object location on the ground plane using Gaussian kernels to create location likelihood map. The system merges results from several pairs of cameras until the ground plane positions are stable. Then the current positions of people are updated, and new predictions are calculated. Because of high computational complexity, the system cannot work in real time, but the authors hope that code optimization efforts and advances in computing will make it possible in the future.

The system presented in [5] uses several nonoverlapping cameras and knowledge about topology of paths between cameras. It probabilistically models the chain of observation intervals for each tracked person using Bayesian formalization of the problem. To estimate the optimal chain of observation, the authors transform the maximum a posteriori estimation problem into a linear program optimization.

The approach proposed in [6, 7] uses multiple synchronized grayscale overlapping cameras for tracking people and selecting a camera that gives the best view. The system consists of three modules: single view tracking, multiple view transition tracking, and automatic camera switching. The system uses the following features for each person: locations of selected feature points, intensity of the selected feature points, and geometric information related to a coarse 2D human body model. The multivariate Gaussian models and Mahalonobis distances are used for people modeling and tracking. The class-conditional distribution for spatial and spatial–temporal matching is used for the multiple view transition tracking for matching predicted location and body model size. The automatic camera switching is necessary if the person is moving out of the current camera's field of view, or the person moves too far away, or the person is occluded by another person. The system selects a camera that will contain the person over the largest time accordingly the current prediction of the person's movement. The experiments with three cameras in various indoor environments showed high robustness of people tracking (96–98%).

The KNIGHTM system [8, 9] is a surveillance system that uses several overlapping and/or nonoverlapping uncalibrated color cameras for people tracking. The system uses spatial and color Gaussian probability distributions for each person to identify and track people in one camera view. The person identification is based on voting of foreground pixels. If two or more people receive essential percentage of votes from the same region, then the systems assume that partial occlusion of people happens. In case of complete occlusion a linear velocity predictor is used for disambiguation. To track people across multiple cameras, the system during the training period learns the field of view lines of each camera as viewed in the other cameras. This information and knowledge of cameras' location are used for identification of moving people. The experiments with three cameras and three different camera setups gave promising results.

The authors of the paper [10] suggest system architecture and scenarios of multiple camera systems that take advantage of recent achievements in video camera technology, such as omnidirectional and PTZ cameras. Using the combination of such cameras allows creating an intelligent surveillance system that can automatically select an optimal camera view to track and recognize people and their behavior.

21.4 Feature Extraction

In this section we describe camera specification and our approach to extracting visual features that are used by all applications.

21.4.1 Camera Specification

We shall consider using for the surveillance task multiple static cameras with low frame sampling rate (3–5 Hz) which is typical for Web cameras. The advantages of indoor environments comparing to the outdoor ones are the following: there are no sharp shadows, illumination changes rather slow, speed of the objects is low, because the objects of interest are people. Besides, we can use our knowledge for specifying important areas (e.g., working places in cubicles) and unimportant areas (such as reflecting surfaces) in a camera's view. The disadvantages are that many places in an indoor environment are unobservable; people can easily change the direction of movement and the people can be often occluded by furniture or the other people.

Each camera has a specification that includes the following data.

- *Operating zone* is an area that is used for feature extraction. For some cameras, only part of their view area is worth to use. Having smaller operating zone expedites processing.
- *Background modeling type* sets the type of background modeling for the camera. The following background models are currently supported: single frame and median filtering. More information on background modeling can be found below.
- *Indicators* are some small areas and associated with them recognizers that allow detecting some local events such as light in an office is on/off, a door is open/closed, etc. The indicators play a double role—they can be used to improve the background modeling, and they are additional pieces of evidence about the state of the environment.
- *Important areas* are areas that the surveillance system pays special attentions, such as doorways, working places in cubicles, armchairs in a hall, etc.
- *Unimportant areas* are areas that must be ignored because they are sources of noise. Such areas are reflective surfaces, TV screens, computer monitors, etc.
- *Camera calibration data* is location of markers that allow estimating distances to objects in cameras' views. This data is used for estimating objects' location, their geometrical features and speed.

Figure 21.3 gives an example of camera specification. Here there are two indicators that detect such events as lights are on/off (in a meeting room on the left) and the door to the meeting room is open/closed. Areas of indicators are represented as black

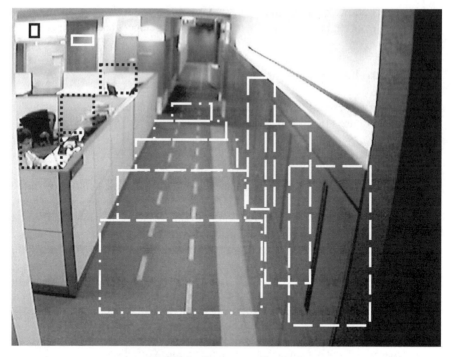

Fig. 21.3. Camera specification.

and white solid rectangles. The light indicator uses average intensity and a threshold as a recognizer, and the door indicator checks for a horizontal edge as a recognition that the door is open. Three black dotted rectangles on the left represent important areas—the working places in cubicles. Three white dashed rectangles on the right mark unimportant areas, which are surfaces that get shadow when a person is passing by. White markers on the floor are used for camera calibration. Five white dash-dotted rectangles split the walkway into zones. Ranges of eligible values for objects' height and width are associated with each zone and are used for blob extraction. A tool with a GUI has been designed to facilitate camera specification.

21.4.2 Background Modeling

The objective of background modeling techniques is to estimate value of pixels of the background frame, that is, the frame without any moving objects. Then this frame is subtracted pixel by pixel from a current frame to detect the pixels that belong to moving objects (foreground pixels). Many approaches for background modeling have been developed [11, 12].

The simplest approach is to use a single frame that is acquired when no motion or changes within a sequence of frames are detected. The single frame method works well when a camera watches a scene that has periods of time without moving objects, for example, for a camera that is watching a hallway. To take into account the change of luminosity over time, the system has to periodically update the single frame model. The advantage of the single frame method is that it does not require any resources for maintaining the model. The disadvantage is that it does not work for scenes with intensive motion.

Another approach is to accumulate and maintain a pool of N frames, where N is an odd number. The value of each pixel of the background model is estimated as medians of the corresponding pixels of frames from the pool. This model is called the median filter background model. An alternative approach is to use mean instead of median; however, such model is sensitive to outliers and requires the large pool size N to be stable. The median filter model works well when each pixel of the scene is covered by moving objects less than 50% of time. The advantage of the median filter model is that it can be used for scenes with high motion, for example, for a camera that is watching cubicles. The disadvantage is that it requires additional memory for storing pool of frames and computations for maintaining the model [11].

The above models assume that each background pixel has only one value, but sometimes it is not true, for example, when a camera watches a bush or a branch of a tree that is shaken by wind; or a billboard that shows sequentially two advertisements. To model such backgrounds more advanced techniques are required. One of the approaches is to use Gaussian mixture models (GMM). In this approach each background pixel is modeled as a mixture of 3–5 Gaussians. Each Gaussian has a weight that is proportional to the frequency of pixels to have the value represented by the Gaussian. It is assumed that Gaussians that represent background values have higher weights and the sum of their weights reaches 0.6–0.8. Instead of subtracting background image from the current frame, each pixel of the current frame is checked for belonging to the background Gaussians if the probability is high it is marked as background, otherwise as foreground. Creating GMM for each background pixel requires intensive training, and changes in luminosity require dynamic adaptation of models. The advantage of the background modeling using GMM is that it works for periodically or stochastically changing environments. The disadvantages are that its success depends on training and parameter tuning, and it has high computational complexity and memory requirements [13, 14].

Real-time processing puts additional restrictions on background modeling. The real-time system cannot wait to accumulate training data, train the models, and then catch up by processing all postponed frames. It does not have enough processing power to implement such scenario. That is why we adopted an approach that uses two background modeling techniques and switches between them when it is needed. The system loops through the basic cycle that consists of the following steps: image acquisition, motion detection, if motion is not detected then the system is idle till the next cycle otherwise it processes the image, which includes extracting foreground pixels, extracting and storing features, and maintaining the background model. A sequence of cycles that have motion forms a *dynamic event*. The dynamic events are separated by events with no motion or *static events*.

If the camera uses the single frame model then the system starts by acquiring a single frame background during a static event and updates it not less than in T

Table 21.1. Using the single frame and adaptive models for real-time processing.

Model type	Initialization	Flicker	Local change of illumination	Global change of illumination
Single frame (SF)	Start a new SF		Patch the effected area	Start a new SF
Adaptive model (AM)	Start a new SF	Skip frame	Generate a SF from AM Patch the effected area	Start a new SF
	Accumulate data Generate and switch to AM		Accumulate data Generate and switch to AM	Accumulate data Generate and switch to AM

seconds by picking up a frame from a static event that lasts not less than D seconds. The parameters T and D can be specified for each camera (the default values are $T = 120$ and $D = 60$). There are three kinds of events that require attention for robust background modeling. The first one is a flicker that is a short abrupt change in illumination due to camera noise. The second kind of events is a local luminosity change; for example, lights get on or off in an office, which is a part of the scene. And the third kind of events is global luminosity change when more then 60% of pixels are changed; for example, when lights get on/off in the room, which is observed by the camera. The system reacts differently for each kind of events. When a flicker occurs, the system skips the frame. When a local luminosity change occurs, the system recognizes this case, using an indicator and patches the effected area with values extracted from the new frame. If the system uses an adaptive background model it first generates a single frame model and then patches the effected area. In case of global change the system acquires a new single frame. If the camera uses an adaptive background model, then the system acquires a single frame model and start accumulate data for creating a new adaptive model. It picks up frames from static events using parameters T and D. When the desired number of frames is reached the systems generates and switches to the adaptive model and begins to maintain it. Table 21.1 summarizes the system's behavior in different modes.

As an adaptive model we used the median filter model with a pool of size $N = 51$. Maintaining the model requires discarding the oldest frame, adding a new one and sorting the values for each pixel. The system using a version of a dynamic deletion–insertion algorithm to avoid sorting and improve the speed of model maintenance.

For dynamic events the background model is subtracted from current frame for detecting foreground pixels. Then some morphological operations are applied to remove noise and shadows. After this, the foreground pixels are separated into blobs using the calibration information for each camera. Finally a set of candidate blobs is selected for feature extraction.

21.4.3 Visual Feature Extraction

A person's most distinguishable visual identity is his or her face. However, in many practical applications the size and image quality of the face do not allow traditional face recognition algorithms to work reliably, and sometimes the human face is not visible at all. Therefore, our people localization system uses face recognition as an auxiliary means that is applied for only some areas of some cameras. The other salient characteristic of a person are sizes of the body, color of the hair, and color of the clothes that is on the person. At any given day, a person usually wears the same clothes, and thus the color of person's clothes is consistent and good discriminator (unless everybody wears a uniform). We use color histograms in different color spaces as major features for distinguishing people on the basis of their clothes.

The blob is processing in the following manner. The top 15% of the blob, which represents the head, and bottom 20%, which represents the feet and also often includes shadow, are discarded and the rest of the region is used for feature extraction. We used the color histograms in RGB, normalized RGB (see Equations (21.1)–(21.2)), and HSV color spaces with the number of bins 8, 16, and 32.

$$r = \frac{R}{R+G+B}, \quad g = \frac{G}{R+G+B}, \quad b = \frac{B}{R+G+B} \tag{21.1}$$

$$l = \frac{R+G+B}{3} \tag{21.2}$$

where r, g, and b are red, green, blue components, and l is the luminance in the normalized RGB space, and R, G, and B are red, green, and blue components in the RGB space.

After some experiments we chose the 8-bin color histogram in the normalized RGB space for the r, g, and l components, which gave a good balance between computation efficiency and accuracy.

21.4.4 People Modeling

For modeling a person on the basis of his or her appearance, we use several approaches. The simplest one is to use all pixels of the blob for training a color histogram. Another approach is to fit a Gaussian or a Gaussian Mixture Model to the training data. A more elaborate person modeling includes two models—one for top and another for the bottom part of the body.

Let us assume that we built a model M_H for a human H. To estimate how well the data D extracted from a new blob R fits the model, we can consider the model as a probability density function and estimate the likelihood of the data set using Equation (21.3), which assumes that pixels' values are independent. The data set D can include all pixels of the blob or a randomly selected subset of particular length (usually 50–100 pixels are enough for reliable classification). In case when two (top and bottom) models are used for modeling, Equation (21.3) should be extended to include products of likelihoods for each model over corresponding data points. In practice, a log-likelihood function is used instead of likelihood one.

$$L(D \mid M_H) = \prod_{i=1}^{N} p(x_i \mid M_H) \tag{21.3}$$

where $x_i \in D$ are points of the data set D, $p(\cdot \mid M_H)$ is the probability distribution function for the model M_H, N is the number of points in the data set D.

The type of probability distribution function depends on the type of the model used. For example, in case of color histogram it can be approximated as a product of corresponding values for pixel's components. Below we shall use H instead of M_H if it does not cause any confusion.

21.5 People Localization

This section presents a Bayesian framework for people localization that allows the integration of evidence of multiple sensor sources. Our task is to localize and track N objects in a space of known geometry with stationary sensors of different kinds. The number of objects may change dynamically over time when an object arrives or leaves. The sensing zones for some sensors can overlap. We assume that there are two types of objects: known objects (employees) and unknown objects (guests or customers). The space is divided into "locations." Time is sampled into ticks. The tick duration is selected depending on the sampling frequencies of the sensors. It should be large enough to serve as a synchronization unit and small enough so that objects can either stay in the same location or move only to an adjacent one within a tick.

21.5.1 Sensor Streams

Each object is represented by a set of features extracted from sensor streams. We are currently using four sources of evidence.

21.5.1.1 Video Cameras

This is very rich data source, but requires a lot of sophisticated processing to extract useful information. Processing this source requires solving problems such as background modeling, object tracking, occlusion resolution, and object recognition. Our system is mostly based on this source. We are using two approaches for people localization—people appearance modeling and face recognition. People appearance modeling is based on color features. An object can have several color models—one or more for each location or even for the time of the day. Object models can be defined (through training) prior to the surveillance task or accumulated incrementally during the task. Appearance modeling works for all cameras, whereas face recognition is efficient only for some cameras where size and orientation of faces are appropriate. We use a dedicated PTZ camera that watches the main entrance to the floor for face recognition. The face recognition system uses the OpenCV algorithm [15] and tries to recognize people from a restricted list.

21.5.1.2 Infrared Badge ID System

The second source of evidence is the infrared (IR) badge system. The system collects data from 91 readers and merges them into a database that indicates where a particular badge was sensed the last time. This source of information is not very reliable because of the following reasons.

1. The badge has to be in the line of sight of a reader on the ceiling. If a person puts his or her badge into a pocket, it cannot be detected.
2. The orientation of the badge affects the detection. A person may be standing under an IR-reader but his badge could trigger another reader nearby depending on the orientation of the badge.
3. A person can leave his or her badge in the office or give it to another person.
4. Detection records are written to the database with a delay creating a discrepancy among different sources of evidence for fast moving objects.

Before processing IR badge sensor signals, the system must determine and maintain the list of active sensors, which are sensors that both transmit signals and move in space.

21.5.1.3 Finger Print Reader

The third source of evidence is the fingerprint reader. This is a very reliable source, but located only at the main entrance, has a restricted number of registered users, and a person only uses it 1–2 times per day for check-in. We mostly use it for acquisition or updating of person appearance models as a person checks-in when entering the office.

21.5.1.4 Human Intervention

The fourth source of evidence is human intervention. People who participate in a surveillance task can interactively influence the system. They can mark an object in a camera view and associate it with a particular person, which causes the system to set the probability of the person being at this location to 1 and recalculate the previous decisions by tracking the person back in time. This is a very reliable, but costly information source. We use it mostly for initializing and updating person appearance models.

21.5.2 Identification and Tracking of Objects

The current state of the world is specified by a probability distribution of objects being at particular locations at each time tick. Let us assume that $P(H_i \mid L_j), i = 1, N, j = 1, K$ are probabilities to find the object H_i at location L_j. The initial (prior) distribution can be learned from data or assumed to be uniform. Each object has a set of models that are location and sensor specific.

21.5.2.1 One Sensor, One Location

Suppose we have only one sensor (camera or IR badge reader). It senses one location, captures events, and saves them in the event database. For the camera, an event is a time-ordered sequence of frames with motion. For an IR reader, an event is a sequence of sets of people IDs detected at this location. Taking into account that the IR badge system gives the list of people IDs directly, we concentrate first on processing data from a camera, and then consider how to merge the decisions from both sensors when they are available.

The task is to identify people whom the camera sees. We assume that we have models for each of N people. We also assume that we have prior probabilities $P(H_i)$ $i = 1, N$ for the person i being in front of the camera. The prior probabilities can be estimated from data or assumed to be equal if no data are available.

The processing agent performs the following algorithm for each event.

Step 1. For the current frame extract regions that correspond to people (objects). The result is a set of regions (blobs) $R = \{R_j\}j = 1, M$.

Step 2. For each region R_j do the following.

    2.1 Estimate likelihoods $P(R_j \mid H_i)$ $i = 1, N$ of the region to belong to the model of person H_i.

    2.2 If all likelihoods are below a threshold Th, then the blob represents an unknown person. In case when the system tracks all people, it creates a new ID and a model for this person, otherwise it marks the blob as "unknown."

    2.3 If one or more likelihood is above the threshold, calculate posterior probabilities using Bayes formula,

$$P\left(H_i \mid R_j\right) = \frac{P\left(R_j \mid H_i\right) \cdot P\left(H_i\right)}{P\left(R_j\right)} \tag{21.4}$$

    where $P\left(R_j\right) = \sum_{i=1}^{N} P\left(R_j \mid H_i\right) \cdot P\left(H_i\right)$ is the complete probability of the region R_j.

    2.4 Assign to the blob a person that maximizes the posterior probability. Exclude this person from the list for the other regions (a person cannot be represented by more than one blob). Pick up another blob, go to Step 2.1.

Step 3. Do steps 1–2 for each frame of the event. There are several ways of how to process the next frame. One of them is to use the same initial prior probability distribution for each frame. In this case we consider each frame independently (a "bag" of frames approach), and the final result does not depend on the sequence of frames. This approach can be more robust when occlusions occur. If an occlusion happens, the system just loses a blob for the current frame. But this gap can be restored at the postprocessing step using median filtering on the probability sequence for the occluded person. Another approach is using current probabilities as the prior probabilities. In this case the frames are processing consequently in forward or backward direction. This approach requires some heuristics in case of occlusions, such as keeping the probability for disappeared blob unchanged.

Step 4. Do postprocessing. It includes applying smoothing procedures, such as median filtering of the probability sequences of detected people and summarizing result for the whole event.

When merging evidence from camera and IR badge sensors, the system takes into account the peculiarities of IR badge sensor mentioned above. First, it shifts data to compensate for 3-s delay of the IR badge signal. Second, it uses signals only from active sensors. Third, in spite of binary evidence the system uses a likelihood function that gives the probability of 0.95 for the people on the evidence list and low probability for all other people (see below for more elaborated likelihood function for multisensor and multilocation case), which is used in Equation (21.4). If no evidence came in the next tick, the likelihood function degrades exponentially.

21.5.2.2 Multiple Sensors and Multiple Locations

In this case we have to deal with new challenges such as synchronization of multiple sensors in time and space.

On one hand, some sensors such as video cameras can have large fields of view that can be divided into nonoverlapping locations. On the other hand, the sensing zones of different sensors can intersect. These intersections can be considered as natural locations. Sometimes the borders of locations are fuzzy.

The concept of location allows making more precise localization, and having person models for each location to improve person identification. On the other hand, we have to create person models for each person and for each location that often is not possible because the person cannot visit all locations during the day. That is why we assume that a person may have models only for some locations. If a person does not have a model for the location under consideration, then the model for the closest location is used.

Each person also has a transition matrix $T(H_k) = \{t_{ij}(H_k)\}k = 1, N, i, j = 1, K$, that specifies the probability of person transition from i-th to j-th location.

The major concern for a multisensor environment is accuracy of data synchronization. Different sensors may have different sampling rates and can acquire signals in nonregular intervals. In general, surveillance cameras are not synchronized. However, computers' clocks can be synchronized and time stamps can be assigned to frames. This means that we cannot synchronize frames, but we can select frames that belong to time interval of some duration (time tick). The time tick should be big enough to contain at least one frame from each camera, but be small enough to allow people moving only inside the current location or to the one of adjacent locations. In our experiments time tick is equal to 1 s.

Another issue is that sensors of the same or different type can have overlapping sensing zones. It poses some restrictions on locations form and size. For example, Figure 21.4 shows two cameras with overlapping field of views. The area has six locations. Locations around the overlap (L_2, L_3, L_4) have more sophisticated geometry. The graph on the right represents transitions among locations. (Here locations HL_1–HL_3 correspond to hidden areas.)

The process of identification and tracking of objects consists of the following steps.

Step 1. Data Collection and Feature Extraction: Collect data from all sensors related to the same time tick. Select data that contain information about a new "event" and extract features.

Step 2. Object Unification From Multiple Sensors: Each sensor detects signals of one or more objects in its sensory field. The signals that come from the same object are merged on the basis of their location and sensory attributes. This gives us a

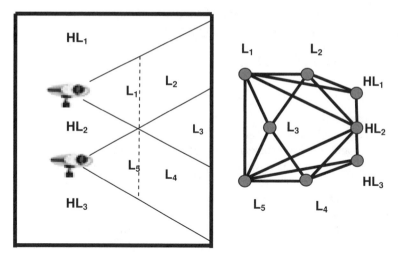

Fig. 21.4. Observed and hidden locations for two cameras.

unified model of how different sensors "see" the same entity. For video cameras, the blobs are first mapped into locations based on their coordinates and calibration data from the cameras. Then the blobs from different cameras that belong to the same location are assigned to the same entity based on their color features. For IR badge data, which consist of binary indicators of a badge being detected at a particular location, the system first spreads the probability to the adjacent IR locations taking into account the space geometry, and then maps IR locations into camera-based locations and associates evidence with entities. The result is a set of entities $O = \{O_r\}$ and a matrix $W = \{w_{kr}\}k = 1, K, r = 1, M_0$, where M_0 is the number of entities. Each w_{kr} is the membership value of r-th entity to belong to the k-th location.

Step 3. Motion Estimation: The locations are selected in a way that an object can either stay in the same location or move to an adjacent location during any single time tick. The specific transition probabilities among locations for a known object or generalized transition probabilities for the other objects are estimated from historical data or provided as prior knowledge by the people involved in the task. These probabilities are taken into account for re-estimating prior probabilities using Equation (21.5).

$$\tilde{P}(H_i \mid L_j) = \frac{\left[\sum_{k=1}^{L} P(H_i \mid L_k) \cdot t_{kj}(H_i)\right] \cdot P(H_i \mid L_j)}{\sum_{l=1}^{L} \left[\sum_{k=1}^{L} P(H_i \mid L_k) \cdot t_{kj}(H_i)\right] \cdot P(H_i \mid L_l)} \tag{21.5}$$

This is a kind of motion prediction in case when we do not know anything about the person's movement except that he or she was previously in a particular location. Adding more information to a person's state, such as direction of movement, velocity, acceleration, etc., makes possible applying more advanced tracking techniques, such as Kalman filtering [16], particle filtering [17], or Bayesian filtering [18].

Step 4. Posterior Probability Estimation: Using the features that belong to the same entity and the person models, the conditional probability that the entity represents a person at a given location is estimated for all entities, objects, and locations. The result is a sequence of probabilities $S_r = \{P(R_j, L_k, C_q \mid H_i,)\}$ associated with the entity $O_r.r = 1, M_0$. Here $R_j, j = 1, M_r$ are the feature data extracted from representations of entity O_r, and $C_q, q = 1, Q$, are sensors. For video cameras, the probabilities that a blob represents an object (person) for given cameras and locations are calculated using blob's features and persons' models (see Equation (21.3)). For IR badge data the probabilities distributed to adjacent locations are used as the conditional probabilities. The output of face recognition system is also used as conditional probabilities. The fingerprint and human intervention evidence sets up the prior probabilities directly. The difference between video sensors and the other sensors is that the data from video cameras are used for every tick, but the data from the other sensors are used only when they are available.

For each entity the estimates of likelihood that the entity represents a particular person at a given location are calculated. If all estimates are less than a threshold, then the entity is marked as "unknown," and a new ID and a new model are generated. Otherwise, the conditional probabilities of signals that are views of the same entity from different sensors are used for estimating posterior probabilities of a person being represented by the entity at the location using Bayes rule (21.6) and the person's ID that maximizes the conditional probability is assigned to the entity. Then the model of the just assigned person is excluded from the model list for processing the other entities.

$$P(H_i \mid O_r, L_k) = \frac{\tilde{P}(H_i \mid L_k) \cdot w_{kr} \cdot \prod_{P(R_j, L_k, C_q) \in S_r} P(R_j, L_k, C_q \mid H_i)}{P(O_r)}$$

(21.6)

where $P(O_r) = \sum_{i=1}^{N} \tilde{P}(H_i \mid L_k) \cdot w_{kr} \cdot \prod_{P(R_j, L_k, C_q) \in S_r} P(R_j, L_k, C_q \mid H_i)$.

Then the probabilities for the entity are normalized over locations using (21.7).

$$P(H_i \mid L_k) = \frac{P(H_i \mid O_r, L_k)}{\sum_{k=1}^{L} P(H_i \mid O_r, L_k)}$$

(21.7)

Step 5. Reestimation: Steps 1–4 are repeated for each time tick.

Step 6. Postprocessing: This step includes some smoothing procedures for whole events and truth maintenance procedures, which use problem domain knowledge to maintain probabilities when no data are available. In case when an object is temporarily invisible, the truth maintenance procedures mark it as "idle" and keep its probability high to be in "hidden" locations that are near the location where the object has been identified last time. For example, Figure 21.4 shows two cameras that watch a room. There are five observed locations (L_1–L_5) and three hidden locations (HL_1–HL_3). The graph on the right shows transitions among locations. If an object has been seen last time at location L_2 then there is high probability for the object to be in the location HL_1, but if no additional evidence is available the probabilities to be in locations HL_2 and HL_3 are also growing over time until all three became equal.

The classical Bayesian approach assumes that (1) there are a constant number of mutually exclusive hypotheses, and (2) the hypotheses cover the whole decision space. In our case the situation is more dynamic—people may enter and leave the floor, and people may be "invisible" to the sensors, for example, a person has his IR badge covered and is standing in a "dead zone," which is not observed by any camera. We extended the framework to cover these problems. The system uses two cameras that watch the elevator area and detects people who are entering or leaving the floor. If a person leaves the floor, his or her model are marked as "inactive." If a person enters the floor, a new object and its appearance model are created and are marked as "new." The system tracks a new object and creates models for it for other locations when it is possible (high probability of identifying the person, no occlusion, etc.). The process continues until enough data is collected.

21.6 Experimental Results

For evaluation we used 15 cameras and 44 IR badge readers that are located in the northern half of the floor. In the first experiment we evaluated the system's performance in the closed set case. It means that the system had models for all 15 people, who participated in the experiment. The second experiment was designed for evaluating the system's performance for the open set problem. Besides 15 "known" people it included 10 "unknown" people, that is, people whose models were not available at the beginning and created during the process. Each experiment lasted for 4 h from 10 AM till 2 PM. In both experiments two evaluations have been done. The first evaluation estimated the accuracy of people localization for each camera separately, and then calculated the average for each person. The second evaluation merged the results from all cameras and IR badge readers. It is worth to mention that only 7 of 15 "known" people (marked by stars in the Table 21.2) and none of "unknown" had active IR badges. The results have been compared to the ground truth data created manually for each tick.

Table 21.2 presents results for both experiments. From the table and Figure 21.5 we can see that in case of closed set problem the average recognition accuracy is about 11% higher than for the open set problem for both single camera and integrated evaluations. For the closed set problem the accuracy of localization for individual person is in range from 44% to 99%. The low accuracy for some people can be explained by the following:

- Poor blob extraction for people who are sitting still for a long time.
- Poor blob extraction when a person is (partially) occluded (e.g., a person was sitting in his office partially visible through the door).

Table 21.2. Accuracy of people localization for open and closed set problems.

| PersonID | Closed set accuracy | | | Open set accuracy | | |
	Single Camera	Cameras and IR badge	Diffe-rence	Single Camera	Cameras and IR badge	Difference
1000	82.14%	87.56%	5.42%	71.39%	77.31%	5.92%
1002	99.27%	99.51%	0.24%	94.54%	95.81%	1.27%
*1003	86.88%	91.07%	4.19%	81.91%	86.10%	4.19%
1005	74.32%	81.69%	7.37%	62.73%	70.59%	7.86%
*1006	45.98%	69.68%	23.70%	43.78%	58.58%	14.80%
*1015	44.08%	41.12%	−2.96%	26.32%	26.58%	0.26%
1020	67.03%	76.71%	9.68%	60.75%	69.24%	8.49%
*1023	64.43%	60.77%	−3.66%	59.82%	58.49%	−1.33%
1024	41.26%	50.72%	9.46%	25.08%	32.78%	7.70%
*1025	69.26%	78.29%	9.03%	57.88%	66.81%	8.93%
1026	71.06%	73.66%	2.60%	41.34%	46.19%	4.85%
*1027	62.04%	73.41%	11.37%	58.13%	67.08%	8.95%
*1029	51.21%	57.88%	6.67%	51.50%	57.21%	5.71%
1064	77.81%	83.42%	5.61%	44.69%	51.69%	7.00%
1072	66.07%	74.49%	8.42%	52.53%	59.67%	7.14%
Average	66.86%	73.33%	6.47%	55.49%	61.61%	6.12%

- Poor blob separation in the hallways.
- Several people have similar models.

Merging evidence from several cameras and IR sensors improves the performance for both cases for about 6%. For the closed set problem the largest improvement (23.7%) was mostly due to IR badge data. In this case, a person ID1006 stayed in the same location for a long time with his badge active. But sometimes merging IR badge

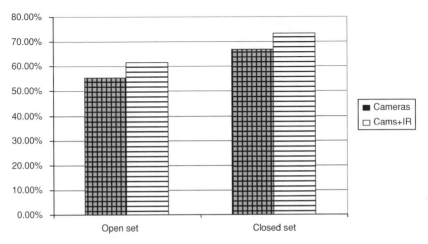

Fig. 21.5. Average accuracy of people localization.

data causes a decrease of localization accuracy. It happens for transient events in the hallways because of poor alignment of visual and IR data (see results for ID1015 and ID1023). The increase from merging visual evidence from several cameras can reach up to 9%.

For the open set problem the localization accuracy for individual person lies in the range from 25% to 94%. Low accuracy for some people can be mostly attributed (besides the above-mentioned reasons) to confusion with people who have similar models. Merging additional evidence can improve performance up to 15%. Merging only visual evidence from several cameras improves performance by 7–8%.

21.7 Summary

In this chapter we described a Bayesian framework that enables us to robustly reason from data collected from a network of various kinds of sensors. In most practical situations, sensors are producing streams of redundant, but noisy data. We proved experimentally that the probabilistic framework presented here gives us the ability to reason from this data by also incorporating the local semantics of the sensors as well as any domain knowledge that can be provided by people involved in these tasks. We believe that this framework is applicable in the larger context of creating robust and scalable systems that can reason and make inferences from different kinds of sensors that are present in the world today.

As to future work, we see that the system could be improved on many levels. On the low level it needs more robust background modeling, blob extraction and blob separation techniques, search for better features, and reliable dynamic modeling of people and other objects' appearance. On the middle level it needs using more advanced tracking approaches such as nonlinear filtering [17, 18] and sensorial data fusion approaches [19]. On the high level the system needs more efficient decision merging approach, which can use domain-specific knowledge and can produce a consistent "big picture" of events in the area under surveillance. We also plan to spend time for developing more attractive visualization techniques and a useable user interface.

References

1. Fuentes, LM, Velastin, SA. People tracking in surveillance applications. In: *Proc. 2nd IEEE International Workshop on PETS*, Kauai, Hawaii, USA, December 2001.
2. Siebel, NT, Maybank, S. Fusion of Multiple Tracking Algorithms for Robust People Tracking. Proc. 7th European Conference on Computer Vision (ECCV 2002), Copenhagen, Denmark, May 2002; IV:373–387.
3. Krumm, J, Harris, S Meyers, B Brumitt, B Hale, M Shafer, S. Multi-camera multi-person tracking for easy living. In: *Proc. 3rd IEEE International Workshop on Visual Surveillance*, July 1, 2000, Dublin, Ireland.

4. Mittal, A, Davis, LS. M2Tracker: A multi-view approach to segmenting and tracking people in a cluttered scene. *International Journal of Computer Vision*, 2003; 51(3):189–203.
5. Kettnaker, V, Zabih, R. Bayesian multi-camera surveillance. In: *Proc. IEEE Conference on Computer Vision and Pattern Recognition*, Fort Collins, Colorado, June 23–25,1999;2253–2259.
6. Cai, Q, Aggarwal, JK. Tracking human Motion using multiple cameras. In: *Proc. International Conference on Pattern Recognition*, Vienna, Austria, August 1996:68–72.
7. Cai, Q, Aggarwal, JK. Tracking human motion in structured environments using a distributed-camera system. *IEEE Transactions on Pattern Analysis and Machine Intelligence*, (1999) 2(11):1241–1247.
8. Khan S, Javed O, Rasheed Z, Shah M. Human tracking in multiple cameras. In: *Proc. 8th IEEE International Conference on Computer Vision*, Vancouver, Canada, July 9–12, 2001;1:331–336.
9. Javed O, Rasheed Z, Atalas O, Shah, M. KnightM: A real time surveillance system for multiple overlapping and non-overlapping cameras. In: *The fourth IEEE International Conference on Multimedia and Expo (ICME 2003)*, Baltimore, MD, July 6–9, 2003.
10. Huang KS, Trivedi MM. Distributed video arrays for tracking, human identification, and activity analysis. In: *The fourth IEEE International Conference on Multimedia and Expo (ICME 2003)*, Baltimore, MD, July 6–9, 2003;2:9–12.
11. Cheung S-CS, Kamath Ch. Robust techniques for background subtraction in urban traffic video. In: *Proc. of SPIE, Visual Communications and Image Processing 2004*, S. Panchanathan, B. Vasudev (Eds), January 2004;5308:881–892
12. Toyama K, Krumm J, Brumitt B, Mayers B. Wallflower: Principles and practice of background maintenance. In: *Intl Conference on Computer Vision (ICCV)*, 1999;255–261.
13. Stauffer C, Grimson WEL. Adaptive background mixture models for real-time tracking. In: *Proc. of IEEE Conference on Computer Vision and Pattern Recognition (CVPR)*, 1999; 246–252.
14. Power PW, Schoonees JA. Understanding background mixture modeling for foreground segmentation. In: *Proc. Image and Vision Computing*, New Zealand, 2002;267–271.
15. Nefian AV, Hayes III. M.H. Maximum likelihood training of the embedded HMM for face detection and recognition. *IEEE International Conference on Image Processing*, September 2000;1:33–36.
16. Grewal MS, Andrews AP. *Kalman Filtering. Theory and Practice Using Matlab*. John Wiley & Sons, 2001.
17. Ristic B, Arulampalam S, Gordon N. *Beyond the Kalman Filter. Particle Filters for Tracking Applications*. Artech House: Boston, London, 2004.
18. Stone LD, Barlow CA, Corwin TL. *Bayesian Multiple Target Tracking*. Artech House: Boston, London, 1999.
19. Hall DL, McMullen SAH. *Mathematical Techniques in Multisensor Data Fusion*. Artech House: Boston, London, 2004.

22. Multimedia Data Mining Framework for Banner Images

Qin Ding and Charles Daniel

Summary. Because of the increasing volume of image data available, it is of importance to develop new applications and techniques to perform multimedia data mining on images. This chapter presents a framework for a novel data mining application on a special type of images, that is, banner images. A banner image is an image file that is displayed on a Web site and used for an advertisement of some product. A banner image is designed in such a way so that it will attract Web users into clicking this image and possibly further completing the sale of the advertised product. By analyzing the relationship between the click-thru rates, measured by the ratio of user clicks and views, and the features of banner images, can help improve the effectiveness of those systems using banner images. In this chapter, we propose a framework called Bayesian Banner Profiler in which we apply Bayesian classification to predict the click-thru rates based on a set of attributes extracted from the banner images. Experimental results show that the proposed framework is promising for data mining on banner images.

22.1 Introduction

In the fast-paced world of Internet Web Advertising, the look and feel of an advertisement can make or break the run of an advertising campaign. Web Advertisements
can take on many forms, one of which is the banner image. A banner image in its
simplest form is an image file displayed on a Web site and used for an advertisement
of some product to attract Web users into clicking this image. Once a Web user clicks
the image, he or she is transported to the advertiser's Web page (also called "the
Landing Page") in order to collect the users' information and to complete the sale of
the advertised product. The point of entry (or initial advertisement placement) is usually on a Web site owned by an individual or a company (called "a Web Publisher")
with no particular relationship to the advertiser of the product they are helping to
advertise. There can be many different points of entry (Web sites) for the placement
of the banner image but they all eventually lead to an advertiser's landing page. The
advertiser's landing page usually consists of a Web page containing a form with fields
asking for particular information about the user (typically name, address, phone, etc.)
that is needed to complete the sale of the product.

Advertisers, contrary to the name given to them by the industry, do not generally handle the advertisement distribution aspects themselves. Rather they leave the
complications of distribution and tracking of advertising media to a third party called

a Network. A Network is basically the middle man between the Advertiser and the Web Publisher (known as an "Affiliate" to the Network). An Affiliate simply places a small piece of HTML on their Web site, which causes a user's Web browser to contact the Network's servers to download a banner image. This download request triggers a "view" hit for the downloaded banner image on the Network's servers. In addition to the HTML banner image reference, the Affiliate also places a hyperlink around the banner image which causes browsers to send a request for a Web page to the Network's server whenever the Web user clicks on the banner image. When the user does click on the banner image and their Web browser sends a page request to the Network's server, it triggers a "click" hit for the banner image and a subsequent HTTP redirect to the Advertiser's landing page. The Network charges the Advertiser for distributing banner images depicting their products to the Web surfing public on Affiliate Web sites. The Network then, after taking a percentage for its commission, pays the Affiliate for the placement of the advertisement on their Web site. To fairly distribute funds to the appropriate Affiliates and charge the Advertiser for the appropriate amount, the Network has to keep track of every single view and click of every single banner image on every one of their Affiliates' Web sites. Needless to say there are millions upon millions of views and clicks tracked every day and all the tracking data are kept in a database table by the Network.

The goal of this chapter is to analyze the statistical information of the ratio of clicks to views, that is, the click-thru rate, and map them out to a classification of banner image attributes, thereby giving us a tool for predicting (with a certain probability) the statistical (click-thru) outcome of a new banner image. The classification method used currently is the Naive Bayesian Classification. The end result is a Web-based program capable of taking in a GIF image as input, calculating the probable classifications (click-thru) based on the attributes chosen for consideration by the user, and outputting the results in a sorted manner.

This banner image profiling tool will be useful for many parties in the Web advertising industry. Advertisers can test new banner images to determine their probable profit (via the click-thru statistics of already run banner images) and choose or design banners such as to maximize their profit. Affiliates can do the same within the scope of their site so that they can determine the types of banner images that do well within their site; they may even go so far as to determine the optimum position for the banner image on their Web site based on the results of the classification. The Network, being the middle man, is capable of using this probability knowledge in classifying new banner images such as to dynamically send statistically probable profit-maximizing banner images to the users' Web browser as they visit an Affiliate's Web site.

Although many works have been done on mining image data [2–5, 7, 8], to the best of our knowledge, our Bayesian Banner Profiler system is a novel application of data mining on banner images. Our system is implemented in Perl, and currently it supports classification on GIF banner images.

The rest of the chapter is organized as follows. Section 2 briefly reviews the naïve Bayesian Classification. Section 3 details the Bayesian Banner Profiler framework. Section 4 presents some implementation details. Finally we conclude the chapter and discuss some future work.

22.2 Naïve Bayesian Classification

A Bayesian Classifier is a statistical method that can predict class membership of an otherwise unclassified object. The classifier is based on Bayes' theorem for calculating "posterior probabilities" [6, 9, 10]. A posterior probability $P(C|A)$ is one in which the probability that the unclassified object belongs to class C, given the known background information A.

Bayes' Theorem provides a way of calculating $P(C|A)$ using the knowledge of $P(C)$, $P(A)$, and $P(A|C)$, where $P(C)$ is the probability of class C occurring in the entire data set, $P(A)$ is the probability of the attributes occurring in the entire dataset (which is a constant across the classes), and $P(A|C)$ is the probability of the attributes A occurring in the class C. Bayes' Theorem can be formalized as follows:

$$P(C|A) = \frac{P(A|C) * P(C)}{P(A)} \tag{22.1}$$

Using this equation, it is possible to compute the probability that an unclassified object having attributes A belongs to each of the classes C. To find the actual class that the unclassified object belongs to, we simply try to maximize on the probability (the highest probability wins). That is:

$$\max(P(C_i|A)) \text{ for all classes } i$$

or,

$$\max(P(A|C_i) * P(C)) \text{ for all classes } i \tag{22.2}$$

Since $P(A)$ is constant across the classes, it can be dropped as it is not worth maximizing.

The Naive Bayesian Classification is named so because of its naive assumption of "class conditional independence," that is, it assumes that there are no dependent relationships between the attributes. However the Naive Bayesian Classification has been shown to have some good results even when the presumption proves false [1].

For the purpose of this chapter, we defined our classes C as click-thru rates (clicks/views) and our attributes A as the various banner image attributes. By doing so it gives us the ability to predict the probabilities that an unknown object (banner image) having the attributes (image attributes) A will belong to a class C (a click-thru value). This means we can extract the image attributes from a new unclassified banner image and figure out the most probable click-thru rate that the banner image will achieve once we actually put it into the real Web world.

22.3 The Bayesian Banner Profiler Framework

The Bayesian Banner Profiler framework consists of four major parts:

- Web-CGI interface server script
- GIF image attribute extraction program

- Attribute quantization algorithm
- Bayesian probability computation algorithm

The current implementation also affords users the ability to choose from different profiler configurations. Each profiler consists of:

- A quantizationSchema, which describes the methods of converting the raw image attribute value into a quantized (or discrete) value that is easier to work with.
- A bayesianCounts, which is a Perl hash table containing the pre-calculated classes (click-thru categories) and counts of the image attributes from our data sets. These counts are used later by the Bayesian classification algorithm.

22.3.1 GIF Image Attribute Extraction

The GIF image attribute extraction program takes in as input a GIF file path. After it has read the GIF file and extracted the image attributes, it is capable of outputting either a plain text output of the image attributes, or a valid Perl hash syntax structure of the image attributes (Perl hash is an associate array that provides fast retrieval of key/value pairs). In the current implementation, the following attributes are extracted from each GIF image:

- Screen Dimensional Data
  - Height: The overall height of the image in screen real-estate pixels
  - Width: The overall width of the image in screen real-estate pixels
- Meta Data
  - num_colors: The number of colors in the color table index of the GIF file
  - has_transparency: A boolean representing the presence (or lack) of transparency portions
  - num_frames: The total number of frames in the entire GIF file
  - total_opaque_pixels: Calculated by counting all nontransparent pixels in all
- Histogram Color Data: The number of occurrences of each color in the entire image
  - histofreq_1 ... histofreq_5: The top five colors in the image (in hex notation)
  - histogram_num_colors: The total number of unique colors in all frames
- Frame Data
  - frame_time:min: The minimum delay from one frame to another between all frames in the entire GIF
  - frame_time:max: The maximum delay from one frame to another between all frames in the entire GIF
  - frame_time:avg: The average delay from one frame to another between all frames in the entire GIF
- Intensity Data (from Hue/Saturation/Intensity color model): The grayscale intensity value obtained by averaging the red, green, and blue channel values together
  - intensity:min: The minimum intensity in the entire GIF
  - intensity:max: The maximum intensity in the entire GIF
  - intensity:avg: The average intensity in the entire GIF (using total_opaque_pixels)

- Primaries Channel Data: Separates a pixel into its primaries parts: red, green, and blue
  - ○ primaries:red_avg: The average red contribution to the entire GIF
  - ○ primaries:green_avg: The average green contribution to the entire GIF
  - ○ primaries:blue_avg: The average blue contribution to the entire GIF
  - ○ primaries:red_percent: Percentage of the GIF contributed to by red
  - ○ primaries:green_percent: Percentage of the GIF contributed to by green
  - ○ primaries:blue_percent: Percentage of the GIF contributed to by blue

Through the Web interface the user is able to choose any combination of attributes to consider when running the Naive Bayesian Classification algorithm on the unclassified object.

22.3.2 Attribute Quantization Algorithm

The attribute quantization algorithm, that is, the quantizer, runs through the image attributes that were extracted and quantizes each to discrete values. For example, the intensity average attribute, which usually has a value ranging from 0 to 255, is split and mapped into eight discrete value ranges. This quantization step helps define the closeness of an attribute between two images.

The quantizer engine takes in as input the raw image attributes hash and a quantizationSchema. It then iterates through the attributes applying the translations that the schema defines for each. It modifies the attributes hash in place with the new quantized values and returns. The quantizationSchema is in reality a Perl hash that mirrors the structure of the attribute hash. For each attribute in the schema:

- If the value is a scalar (i.e., string), it will use the scalar as the new quantized value. This is useful for essentially canceling the effect of an attribute by mapping all values into one value.
- If the value is a subhash, it tries to map the value from the attribute hash as a key in this subhash and uses the value it gets as the new quantized value.
- If the value is a subarray (containing arrays of value ranges), it iterates through the subarray looking for a range that the attribute value falls within and uses that index in the subarray as the new quantized value.
- If the value is a reference to a Perl code (anonymous subroutine), it will call the subroutine passing it the reference to the parent attribute hash and the actual attribute value. It is that subroutine's responsibility to modify the attribute value into a new quantized value.

Currently the system makes use of the subarray of value ranges to map out several of the attributes that deal with pixel values. The anonymous perl code method is also used when we map the histogram subarray (after sorting) into histofreq_1, histofreq_2 . . . histofreq_5; as well as a quick way to mutate and round up the click-thru values (considered the "class" attribute). We believe that this design of the quantizationSchema provides maximum flexibility in translating any arbitrary attribute value into a quantized value.

Since the quantizerSchema is associated with a profiler, we can essentially change the entire inner working of how image attributes are dealt with by simply choosing a different profiler from the user interface.

22.3.3 Bayesian Probability Computation Algorithm

The Bayesian probability computation algorithm uses the Naive Bayesian classification method to compute the probability that the input image falls within a certain class of images based on the image attributes.

The Bayesian algorithm takes in as input the quantized image attributes hash, the bayesianCounts hash, and an array of attributes (input by the user) that it should use in the probability consideration. It then computes for each class (i.e., classification category) the probability, using the quantized image attributes hash that the image belongs to it.

The classes in the current implementation are set up to represent the click-thru rate of the banner images. The click thru rate, as previously mentioned, is a kind of normalizing method on the statistical data (i.e., views and clicks) of all the banner images. The click-thru measurement is an immensely popular way of rating banners and advertising campaigns. It is calculated by dividing the sum of the unique clicks of the banner image to the sum of the unique views of the banner image. If the unique views are less than or equal to 0, we assume that the unique clicks and the click-thru are also 0 since a user cannot possibly click on a banner image that is not displayed to them. Formally the click-thru can be defined as follows:

For a given banner image i,

$$
if \left(\sum_i unique\_view(i) > 0 \right)
$$

$$
click-thru(i) = \frac{\sum_i unique\_click(i)}{\sum_i unique\_view(i)} \tag{22.3}
$$

$$
else
$$

$$
click-thru(i) = 0
$$

Click-thru rates, by nature of the division, can range from values 0.0 to 1.0 (but in the industry they usually top out around 0.20). To deal with these miniscule values, the current implementation actually explodes the value by a factor of 1000 to bring more distinction between the click-thrus and thereby giving us more classes to classify into. In our model, click-thru rates are treated as continuous data.

Rather than tediously recalculating the click-thrus and Bayesian counts for the entire data set each time the user queries the system, the current implementation uses a precomputed hash of counts and classes called the bayesianCounts hash. This hash file is combined with the quantizationSchema to represent a Bayesian Profiler configuration.

Tweaking the quantizationSchema and the building of the bayesianCounts file gives the system an unprecedented flexibility. Since the bayesianCounts file is also governed by a profiler, the user can easily switch to a different set of data (bayesian-Counts) by simply selecting a different profiler in the user interface.

22.4 Implementation

The Bayesian Banner Profiler system is implemented in Perl. Figure 22.1 shows the initial user interface of the Bayesian Banner Profiler tool.

This user interface consists of five important panels:

- The Image Source Panel: This panel contains user interface elements concerned with specifying the sample source image (the test case).
- The Image Upload Panel: When the user chooses "New ... " from the Source pull-down, he or she is prompted to either upload an image file through the browser or specify the URL of an image on the Web.
- The Image Preview Panel: When an image is chosen from the pulldown, a preview (dimension restricted) version of the image is displayed in this panel.

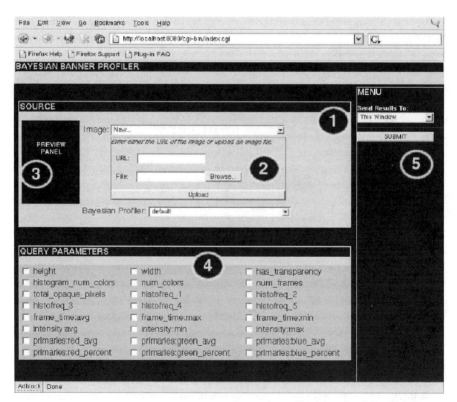

Fig. 22.1. Bayesian banner profiler.

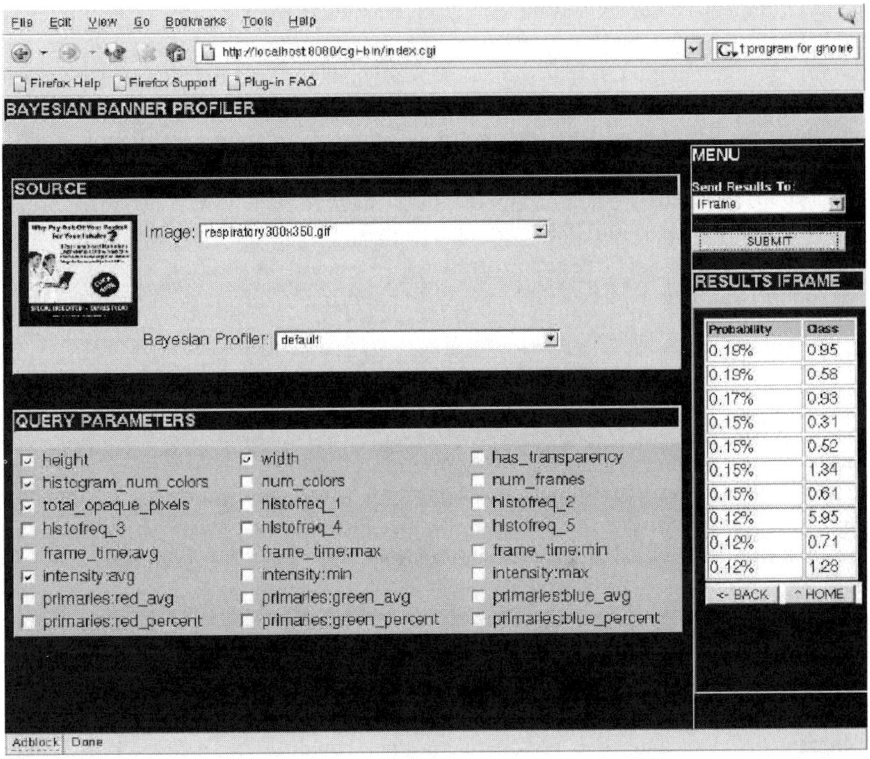

Fig. 22.2. A sample result of classification.

- The Attributes Panel: The user can choose from any combination of image attributes to consider when doing the Bayesian probability computation. At least one attribute is required for the calculation to be useful.
- The Menu Panel: This panel contains the submit button and the hidden results panel. In the future as more general query-specific elements are added they will be placed here.

Figure 22.2 shows the results of a successful classification performed by the profiler. Note how the preview image panel has changed to display the currently selected test case source image and the attributes the user has chosen to consider for the Bayesian classification algorithm.

Figure 22.2 also shows the resulting table of probabilities (sorted in descending order from most probable) and classes displayed below the SUBMIT button. The resulting table of probabilities is currently implemented to list the top 10, but it can easily be changed to any arbitrary splice of the results array. Also note that the range of the click-thru is within 0 to 1 while in the result panel the click-thru (shown in class column) is multiplied by 100 to show the difference.

The system was primarily developed on GNU/Linux. A custom-built limited protocol supporting HTTP server (with Perl-CGI capabilities) was created. The interface between the HTTP server and the Bayesian Banner Profiler program is completely CGI. This means that the Bayesian Banner Profiler program can be taken out and used within Apache (via mod_cgi) or some other CGI standards conforming Web server at no change.

Since the Web advertising industry does most of its banner advertising in GIF formats to support the majority of antique Web browsers, we support GIF format in our system. Currently we do not support PNG image format even though GIF format can be easily translated into PNG format. The reason is that the translated PNG image attributes are not staying true to the original GIF version. In addition, since PNGs do not support animations, we would lose all the interframe information such as frame delay.

22.5 Conclusions and Future Work

In this chapter we have presented a framework for a novel application of classification on banner images, that is, the Bayesian Banner Profiling framework. By classifying the click-thru rates based on the attributes extracted from the banner images can help improve the effectiveness of advertisement.

Currently we support some low-level image attributes. Our test results of banner images vary in accuracy and we feel that adding high-level attributes can aide in improving the accuracy and stability of the system. After all, human beings usually do not click on banner images based on such low-level details as the number of colors; rather they click on banners based on their aesthetic qualities and content. Fortunately the framework of our system is flexible enough to include more attributes, including high-level image attributes.

One of the improvements to this system would come from extracting better image attributes from the GIFs in which to classify on. The current implementation has a limited number of low-level attributes to choose from. There is, however, a largely untapped realm of higher abstraction image analysis awaiting the future of this system, for example, using motion and blink detection, using OCR to detect text in the image, and using object detection to parse individual objects from the image (banners usually clip-art images from image CDs). By doing this, many other attributes can be added to the classification. In addition, we would like to support more banner formats than just GIF images; particularly we would like to add support for JPEG and PNG image as well as Macromedia Shockwave Flash SWF files.

References

1. Han J, Kamber M. *Data Mining concepts and Techniques*. Morgan Kaufmann, 2001.
2. Zaiane OR, Han J, Zhu H. Mining recurrent items in multimedia with progressive resolution refinement. In: *Proceedings of the IEEE International Conference on Data Engineering*, San Diego, CA, March 2000, pp. 461–470.

3. Zaiane OR, Han J, Li ZN, Chee SH, Chiang JY. MultiMediaMiner: A system prototype for multiMedia data mining. In: *Proceedings of the ACM SIGMOD International Conference on Management of Data*, Seattle, WA, June 1998, pp. 581–583.
4. Zhang J, Hsu W, Lee ML. Image mining: Issues, frameworks and techniques. In: *Proceedings of the Second International Workshop on Multimedia Data Mining (MDM/KDD'2001)*, San Francisco, CA, August 2001, pp. 13–20.
5. Ding Q, Perrizo W, Ding Q, Roy A. On mining satellite and other remotely sensed images. In: *Proceedings of the SIGMOD Workshop on Research Issues in Data Mining and Knowledge Discovery*, Santa Barbara, CA, May 2001, pp. 33–40.
6. Denison DGT. *Bayesian Methods for Nonlinear Classification and Regression*. John Wiley & Sons Inc., 2002.
7. Zaiane OR, Simoff S, Djeraba C (Eds). *Mining Multimedia and Complex Data*. Lecture Notes in Artificial Intelligence, Vol. 2797. Springer, 2003.
8. Djeraba C. *Multimedia Mining—A highway to Intelligent Multimedia Documents*. Kluwer Academic Publishers, 2003.
9. Duda R, Hart P. *Pattern Classification and Scene Analysis*. New York: John Wiley & Sons, 1973.
10. Mitchell TM. *Machine Learning*. New York: McGraw-Hill, 1997.

23. Analyzing User's Behavior on a Video Database

Sylvain Mongy, Fatma Bouali, and Chabane Djeraba

Summary. The analysis of user behaviors in large video databases is an emergent problem. The growing importance of video in every day life (e.g., movie production) is linked to the importance of video usage. To cope with the abundance of available videos, users of these videos need intelligent software systems that fully utilize the rich source information hidden in user behaviors on large video databases to retrieve and navigate through videos. In this chapter, we present a framework for video usage mining to generate user profiles on a video search engine in the context of movie production. We suggest a two-level model-based approach for modeling user behaviors on a video search engine. The first level aims at modeling and clustering user behavior on a single video sequence (intravideo behavior), the second one aims at modeling and clustering user behavior on a set of video sequences (intervideo behavior). On the basis of this representation, we have developed a two-phase clustering algorithm that fits these data.

23.1 Introduction

With the fast development in video capture, storage and distribution technologies, digital videos are more accessible than ever. The number and volume of these archives are soaring. To deal with it, video usage mining, which aims at analyzing user behaviors on a set of video data, is one of the key technologies to create suitable tools to help people browsing and searching the large amount of video data. Indeed, as in Web mining field the extracted information will enable to improve video access.

Particularly, the professional users of the audiovisual sector actually need suitable video search engine. They are dealing daily with large video warehouses that require appropriate tools. Classical approaches are based on indexing techniques. Each video is manually or semiautomatically indexed on the basis of the definition of several attributes (place, actors, director, main color ...). The limit of this kind of technique is the inability to deal with a complete well-indexed database. Either automatical or manual indexing leads to indexation errors.

We propose here to analyze the behavior of the users of the video search engine to improve the quality of the retrieved data. Our goal is to understand which, how, and why each video has been viewed by users. On the basis of clustering technique,

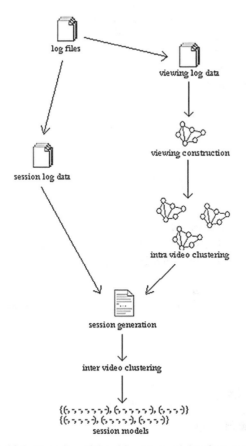

log files

viewing log data

session log data

viewing construction

intra video clustering

session generation

inter video clustering

{(↳↳↳↳↳↳), (↳↳↳↳↳), (↳↳↳)}
{(↳↳↳), (↳↳↳↳), (↳↳↳)}
session models

Fig. 23.1. Overview of the video usage mining framework.

we retrieve the archetype of visitors. Further work will use these results to improve indexing technique and searching algorithms.

In this chapter, we present a framework (Fig. 23.1) that combines intravideo usage mining and intervideo usage mining to generate user profiles on a video search engine in the context of movie production. Specifically, we have borrowed the idea of navigation history from Web browsers used in Web usage mining, and suggest a new approach that defines two types of log from the log data gathered on a video search engine. The first one concerns the way a user views a video sequence (play, pause, forward . . .) and can be called intravideo usage mining. At this level we define the "video sequence viewing" as a behavior unit. The second type of log tracks the transitions between each video sequence viewing. This part gathers requests, results, and successive viewed sequences. At this higher level, as in Web mining we introduce a "session" as a behavior unit.

An intravideo user behavior is modeled by a first-order and nonhidden Markovian model. This model is constructed using the different actions proposed to the user while he is viewing a video sequence (play, pause, forward, rewind, jump, stop). We propose an effective clustering method of these behaviors (K-models). This technique is an adaptation of the well-known k-means [1] to the use of models instead of means. This enables us to characterize several behavior types (complete viewing, overview, open–close, precise scene viewing). Based on these behaviors, viewing will be precisely defined and then we will be able to know which was the use of a video in a session (whether if it is the most important or if it is just the result of a bad search).

An intervideo user behavior is modeled by a session that is a time-ordered sequence of the viewed video sequences. Each video sequence is represented by the intravideo models carried out in the precedent stage. To cluster the sessions, we adapt a classical hierarchical clustering technique to deal with the particularity of these data.

This chapter is organized as follows. In Section 2, we present the related work in Web usage mining field and in video usage mining field and we draw up the differences between these two fields. Section 3 begins by describing the context of our approach that is movie production and the log gathering process, then it presents our two-level model-based approach for modeling users' behaviors on a video search engine. The first level aims at modeling and clustering users' behavior on a single video (intravideo behavior), the second one aims at modeling and clustering users' behavior on a set of video sequences (intervideo behavior). Finally, section 4 describes the evaluation of the technique on some test data sets, and Section 5 gives the conclusion and some future directions.

23.2 Related Work

23.2.1 Web Usage Mining

Web Usage Mining is defined as the use of different data mining techniques to analyze the information collected by Web servers in large log files by modeling Web's user navigational behavior. Several Web usage mining systems have been developed and applied successfully in various fields such as Web analytics and e-commerce, data analysis [2], Web personalization [3], Web site evaluation or reorganization [4], and link prediction and analysis [5].

There are three consecutive steps in the process of data mining from Web access logs: the first step is to gather and preprocess data of the log files, the second one consists of pattern discovering, and the last one consists of analyzing the discovered patterns. To discover relevant patterns a variety of algorithms such as association rule mining, sequential pattern analysis, clustering, classification, and Markovian models can be used on the transformed data.

In paper [6] the authors propose a methodology for the visualization of navigation patterns. A model-based clustering approach is used in which users presenting similar navigation patterns are grouped into the same cluster. The behavior of the users within each cluster is represented by a Markovian model. In [5], the authors proposed a system which is used to demonstrate the utility of Markovian models in link prediction and path analysis on the Web. Experimental results are reported which show that a

Markovian model can be useful both in the prediction of http requests and in the prediction of the next link to be requested.

In paper [7] the authors propose an algorithm based on sequence alignment to measure similarities between Web sessions where sessions are chronologically ordered sequences of visited pages. This measure takes into account the sequence of event in a click-stream visitation. To cluster sessions, after identifying the sessions in a preprocessing phase, they use known clustering algorithms [8]. Their experiments in a context of e-learning show that discovered clusters are more meaningful than those one discovered when the similarity measure used to compare sessions is basically calculated on intersections between these sets, such as the cosine measure or the Jaccard coefficient used for example in [9].

In paper [10] the authors develop a unified framework for the discovery and analysis of Web navigational patterns based on probabilistic latent semantic analysis (PLSA). This technique can automatically characterize the users' underlying navigational objectives and discover the hidden semantic relationships among users as well as between users and Web objects. These relationships are measured in terms of probabilities. Using probabilistic inference, they are able to discover a variety of usage patterns like: the characterization of a task by a group of most related pages; the identification of prototypical users who perform a certain task; the identification of underlying tasks present in a specific user's activity; and the characterization of user groups (or segments) that perform a similar set of tasks.

23.2.2 Video Usage Mining

In the absence of any prior survey of video usage mining, the closest related work can be classified into roughly two types.

The first type of work concerns the analysis of user behaviors without considering the video content. These works report on statistics of user behavior and frequency counts of video access. For example, Reuther and Meyer [11] analyze the student usage of an educational multimedia system. This analysis is based on the student personality types. Indeed, the learning needs and expectations depend on the characteristics of the student personality type. To achieve this, the authors have developed a program that extracts the student's actions on the multimedia system and profiles what each user did each time he has used the system. These user profiles include the following statistics: number of video viewing sessions, total seconds spent viewing videos, number of video viewing sessions that lasted more than 20 min, average duration of a video viewing session, average number commands per minute during video viewing sessions, forward transitions, backward transitions, forward jumps, and jump ratio. While being based on the statistics collected on each type of students, they analyze how the learning multimedia system can be improved to remedy its shortcomings.

In [12] the authors present an analysis of trace data obtained from user access on videos on the Web. The authors examine properties such as how user requests vary on a day-to-day basis, and whether video accesses exhibit any temporal properties. They propose to benefit from these properties to design the multimedia systems such as Web video proxy caches, and video servers. For example the analysis revealed that users preview the initial portion of a video to find out whether they are interested. If they like it, they continue watching, otherwise they stop it. This pattern suggests that caching the first several minutes of video data should improve access performance.

The second type of work relates to the behavior analysis on a single video.

In paper [13] the authors present a framework that combines video content analysis and user log mining to generate a video summary. They develop a video browsing and summarization system that is based on previous viewers browsing log to facilitate future viewers. They adopt the link analysis technique used in Web mining and propose a concept of ShotRank that measures the importance of each video shot. User behavior is simulated with an Interest-guided Walk model, and the probability of a shot being visited is taken as an indication of the importance of that shot. The resulting ShotRank is used to organize the presentation of video shots and generate video skims.

The lack in the previous work is to correlate general behavior of the users with their behavior on each of the videos. They do not take into account actions done during a video viewing while considering navigation between video sequences. In short, these works are rather distant from our context. The navigation and research concepts in a large video data base are missing. Moreover, there are neither standards nor benchmarks on video log data.

Two important points differentiate our approach of these works. First, there are no tools working on usage of complete video database exploration. The only works we have referenced for the field of video analysis consider only a video at once. The closest technique is the one concerning Web Usage Mining. However, here the log data are more complete and we will be able to fully exploit them.

Second, we have developed a clustering technique that fits our data. Indeed, many Web Usage Mining techniques are based on distance-based clustering algorithms and neighborhood comparison. This leads to results that are hard to analyze. In such approaches, two sessions are associated to the same cluster if they are connected by a chain of very close neighbors, even if they are completely different. We introduce here a model to represent cluster that gathered information given by every element, each of these elements corresponding to this model.

23.3 Proposed Approach

23.3.1 Context

One of the needs of the professional users of the audiovisual sector is to be able to find existing video sequences in order to reuse them in the creation of new films. Our approach is based on the use of a well-suited video search engine (Fig. 23.2). Our tool is a classical browser for finding video in large databases. Searches are executed on content-based indexing. Much hidden information can be extracted from the usage and used to improve the closeness between requests and videos returned by the search engine.

To achieve this task, we first need to define what a usage of a video search engine is. Such a behavior can be divided into three parts. (1) Request creation: the user defines its search attributes and values. (2) Result set exploitation: found sequences

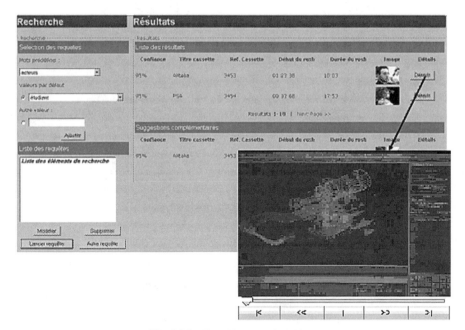

Fig. 23.2. The video search engine.

are presented to the user. They are ordered by an attribute-based confidence value.
(3) Selected sequences viewing: the user is viewing sequences he is interested in.
This viewing is achieved with a video browser offering usual functions (play, pause,
forward, rewind, stop, jump).

Groups of viewed sequences form sessions. They correspond to a visit of a user.
They are a compund of several searches and video sequences viewing episodes.

23.3.2 Gathering Data

All of these data are collected and written into log files. To create these files, we define
an XML-based language. A session is gathered as follows. The first part contains the
request executed and the list of video sequences returned. The second one logs the
viewing of sequences.

The grammar of a session is as follows. A first part contains the request executed
and the list of video sequences returned (Fig. 23.3). A second one logs the viewing
of sequences (Fig. 23.3).

These two XML codes are easily understandable. The first one corresponds to a
request (request tag). It is composed of a list (keywordset tag) of pair keyword–value.
Selectable keywords are the one on which data are indexed. For each pair, we keep
its place in the request (i.e., the order that the user has entered values). In addition to
this list of keywords, we keep trace of the returned sequences (resultset tag). These
sequences are characterized by their identifier and the confidence value given by the

```
<log>                                        <log>
    <request idsession="12">                     <action scene="Scenel" session="Session2">
        <keywordset>                                 <type>play</type>
            <keyword>                                <time>1108948520</time>
                <type>producer</type>                <length>5</length>
                <value>OAV</value>                   <start>0</start>
                <rank>1</rank>                       <end>5</end>
            </keyword>                           </action>
            <keyword>                            <action scene="Scenel" session="Session2">
                <type>weather</type>                 <type>rewind</type>
                <value>sunny</value>                 <time>1108948525</time>
                <rank>2</rank>                       <length>3</length>
            </keyword>                               <start>5</start>
        </keywordset>                                <end>0</end>
        <resultset>                              </action>
            <result>                             <action scene="Scenel" session="Session2">
                <idsequence>1234</idsequence>        <type>play</type>
                <confidence>0.8</confidence>         <time>1108948528</time>
                <rank>2</rank>                       <length>9</length>
            </result>                                <start>0</start>
            <result>                                 <end>9</end>
                <idsequence>8634</idsequence>    </action>
                <confidence>0.82</confidence> </log>
                <rank>1</rank>
            </result>
        </resultset>
    </request>
</log>
```

Fig. 23.3. XML representation of a request (left) and of a video sequence viewing (right).

search algorithm. For example, the request presented in Figure 23.2 corresponds to a search of video sequence with landscape containing a sunny weather and produced by OAV. The second fragment of code shows how the viewing of a sequence is realized. Each basic action (play, pause, forward) is logged with its start time and its duration to respect to the video sequence.

Like Web logfile, our video logfile traces the actions of users. To extract sessions, we have developed a converter that extracts and regroups sessions from this logfile in XML format. The following part of the chapter explains how we propose to model a video session.

23.3.3 Modeling User's Behavior: A Two-Level Based Model

From the log data gathered previously, we generate two models to represent the user's behavior. The first one concerns the way a user views a video sequence (play, pause, forward . . .). At this level we define the "video sequence viewing" as a behavior unit. The second one tracks the transitions between each video sequence viewing. This part gathers requests, results, and successive viewed sequences. At this higher level, we introduce a "session" as a behavior unit.

Presently our work is based only on sequences. We do not take into account the information given by the requests. This will be further investigated.

A session is a list of viewed video sequences. The particularity and the interest of the video log data will be the ability to define the importance of each sequence in each session. More than a simple weight, comparable to time comparison in Web mining [7], we will characterize here several behavior types (complete viewing, overview, open–close, precise scene viewing). On the basis of these behaviors, viewing will be precisely defined and then we will be able to know which has been the use of a video in a session (whether if it is the most important or if it is just the result of a bad search).

23.3.3.1 Modeling and Clustering Intravideo User's Behavior

An intravideo user's behavior is modeled by a first-order nonhidden Markovian model (Fig. 23.4). This model represents the probability to execute an action each second of the viewing of a video. Each vertex represents one of the actions proposed to the user while viewing. These actions are play, pause, forward, rewind, jump, and stop. For example, the edge from play to pause means that when a user is playing a video, there is a probability of 8% that he executes a pause the next second.

This model is fully determined by the following parameters:

V_i the vertices. N is set of the actions proposed to the user during a viewing. We have
   set $N = play, pause, forward, rewind, jump, stop$.
π_i the probability of starting in state i.
$A_i j$ the transition probability from a state V_i to V_j during the next second. This discretization of time (taking the second for unit) introduced by [15] is interesting because it considers time without any additional parameter.

Its limited complexity will allow us to propose an effective clustering method of these behaviors.

We will here introduce the K-models clustering algorithm. This technique is almost an adaptation of the well-known k-means to the use of models instead of means. We try to find K clusters in a set of viewing actions (list of the actions performed by user while viewing a video sequence) by partitioning space. Each

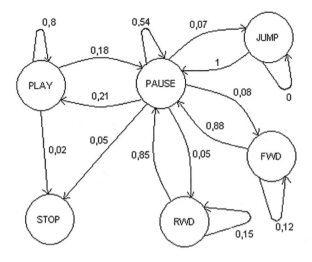

Fig. 23.4. Video sequence viewing behavior.

cluster is represented by one of the models described below. The difference resides in use of probability instead of distance to associate viewings to clusters. We calculate the probability that a viewing has been generated by models. We then associate the viewing to the cluster with the highest probability.

Such algorithm can be split in three phases: initialization, expectation, maximization.

Initialization phase: The initialization phase, like for k-means, appears hard. Indeed it is important to define appropriate models to start the clustering. Here, we have some knowledge about the looked for clusters. First, V_i and π_i are already defined. The remaining problem is to determine the A_{ij}. Even if data are varied, the ways of watching a video is quite limited and constant regarding the type of video type. After some tests on real data sets, we are able to well define the initial models of the clusters, different enough from one to another and approximately corresponding to the resulted models. They are four and correspond to the following profiles: (1) complete viewing; (2) viewing of a precise scene; (3) overview; (4) quick closure.

Expectation phase: For each sequence $e = (e_1 \ldots e_l)$ e_i belonging to N, of length l, for each cluster determined by a model k, we calculate the probability that k has generated e. e is associated to the cluster with the highest probability.

Maximization phase: Each model k representing a cluster c of size m is updated with respect to the data belonging to c. This update corresponds to count each transition in each element e_i and attributes these counts to the transition probability of the model. For each cluster c, probabilities are updated this way.

On the basis of these discovered models, we create a vector of behavior for each viewing. This vector corresponds to the probabilities that the viewing has been generated by each model (Fig. 23.1).

$$v_e = [\ \overset{i=1}{\underset{i=K}{v_i}}\ ], \forall i, v_i = p(e|k_i) \tag{23.1}$$

23.3.3.2 Modeling and Clustering Intervideo User's Behavior

From the initial data set and the vector created with the intravideo clustering, we construct a sequential representation of the sessions. A session is a time-ordered sequence of the viewed video. Each viewing is characterized by a pair of the unique identifier of the video and the vector of behavior connected to it. On the basis of this representation of sessions, we have developed a clustering algorithm that satisfies the following requirements: any element belonging to a cluster has a common part with any other element of the cluster. The generality level of produced clusters relies on the definition of some parameters given by the user.

These requirements lead us to define the representation of a cluster this way: a cluster c is represented by a set of S sessions s_c of minimal length l. A session s is attributed to a cluster if it matches at least p of the S sessions. The session s matches

s_c if s_c is a subsequence extracted from s (23.2).

$$is\ Subsequence((s_1 \ldots s_n), (s'_1 \ldots s'_m))$$
$$= \exists i \leq n \mid \{ \begin{array}{l} s'_1 = s_i \\ is\ Subsequence((s_i \ldots s_n), (s'_2 \ldots s'_m)) \end{array}$$ (23.2)

This way, we ensure the homogeneity of clusters and the fact that there is a common factor between any elements of a cluster. Hence, we avoid obtaining clusters composed of fully different elements, connected by a chain of next neighbors generally produced by distance-based clustering techniques [8]. The minimum length of a representative sequence and the number of sequences needed to model a cluster are given by the analyst to allow him to retrieve clusters of the required homogeneity.

The clustering algorithm itself is based on classical hierarchical clustering algorithm. It starts with considering little groups of sessions as clusters and iteratively merge the two nearest clusters. The algorithm ends when the required level of homogeneity has been reached. Its originality is linked to the representation of clusters. Classical sequence clustering techniques deal with a unique sequence to represent a cluster. Here we have developed tools to be able to compare and merge clusters represented by a set of sequences instead.

Compare Clusters: Let $C_1 = (s_{11} \ldots s_{1S})$ and $C_2 = (s_{21} \ldots s_{2S})$ be two clusters to compare.

$$d(C_1, C_2) = \sum_{i=1}^{S} \min_{j=1}^{j=S} (d(s_{1i}, s_{2j}))$$ (23.3)

This distance function (23.3) is based on a comparison of sessions. This one is based on the longest common subsequence extraction. Given $I = [(i_1, i_2)]$ the list of length l of indices of selected element of the two compared sessions s_1 and s_2, the distance between them is given by (23.4) where v_{xy} is the behavior vector of the yth element of the session x. (23.5) is the distance function between two behavior vector.

$$d(s_1, s_2) = \frac{\sum_{i_1, i_2} d(v_{1i1}, v_{2i2})}{l}$$ (23.4)

$$d(v_1, v_2) = \frac{\sum_{i=1}^{K} |v_{1i} - v_{2i}|}{K}$$ (23.5)

Merge Clusters: The merging function is based on longest subsequence extraction too. It extracts the longest subsequences comparing video identifiers from pairs of sequences, each issued of a different cluster. Merging sequences by two ensures that the proportion p is conserved until the end of the algorithm. Let $c_1 = (s_{11} \ldots s_{1S})$ and $c_2 = (s_{21} \ldots s_{2S})$ be two clusters to merge (23.6).

$$merge(c_1, c_2) = [\ \underset{i=1, j=1}{\overset{i=S, j=S}{merge}} (s_{1i}, s_{2j})]$$ (23.6)

i and j are selected to maximize the length of the merged sequences. To merge two sequences, we extract the longest common subsequence without taking into account the behavior vector. When this subsequence is created, we merge the corresponding behaviors of the two initial sequences calculating the mean on each element. Let $v_1 = (v_{11} \ldots v_{1K})$ and $v_2 = (v_{21} \ldots v_{2K})$ be two behaviors to merge, the result of merging two behaviors is given by (23.7).

$$merge(v_1, v_2) = [\overset{i=K, j=K}{\underset{i=1, j=1}{\frac{(v_{1i}+v_{2j})}{2}}}] \qquad (23.7)$$

23.4 Experimental Results

This part will point out the following two abilities of our technique compared to usual approaches. First, we will see how the analysis of the intravideo behavior allows a division of groups of sessions that are composed of the same video but viewed in a different manner. Then, we will demonstrate the advantage of describing a cluster by a group of sessions compared to a simple subsequence extraction.

23.4.1 Creation of the Test Data Sets

Because of the lack of accurate data concerning video extraction, we have conducted our tests on generated data sets.

The creation of the test data sets is divided into two phases. First, we have created intravideo behavior models. We have defined four typical behaviors (complete play, quick overview, partial play of a part, quick closure). Future experiments on real data will allow us to fully determine these ones based on the use of the search engine. On the basis of these models, we have randomly generated behavior vectors for each viewing of the video sessions. Second, to create the video sessions, we have defined source of clusters with a set of video identifiers sequences. For each cluster, we have created session by randomly merging these sequences. Then, we have added in each generated session about 5–20% of noise by adding into sequences viewing identifiers that have no link with the content of the clusters.

Finally, we have generated different test data sets composed of 2000 sessions. Each session is composed of 5–20 viewings that are linked to behaviors of 10–20 basic actions (play, pause . . .). The test files are then composed of around 100,000–800,000 basic actions.

23.4.2 Exploiting the Intravideo Behavior

This first scenario is based on the following assumption. We have a video database of natural videos containing videos of mountains and volcanoes that is not correctly indexed and many videos dealing with volcanoes are indexed like mountain videos.

We have generated two clusters. The first one corresponds to a search on volcanoes and gives only a unique video completely viewed. The second one is the result of

Table 23.1. Clusters description of the first data set.

Base model	With intra behavior	Basic approach
(1, 2, 3, 4, 5, 6, **10**)	(1, 2, 3, 4, 5, 6, **10**)	(1, 2, 3, 4, 5, 6, **10**)
(**1, 2, 3, 4, 5, 6**)	(**1, 2, 3, 4, 5, 6**)	

a search on mountains and every video are viewed completely (Table 23.1). With a classical approach, that does not take into account intravideo behavior, the two clusters are not discovered and the result is a unique cluster ((1, 2, 3, 4, 5)).

With our double-level approach, the technique is able to discover that the use of videos has been different and the two clusters corresponding to the two searches are discovered. For any value less than 6 of the minimum length of the representative sequence, clusters ((1, 2, 3, 4, 5, 6)) and ((1, 2, 3, 4, 5, 10)) are returned.

23.4.3 Multiple Subsequence Cluster Modeling

The following experiment points out the advantage of modeling clusters with a set of sequences instead of a unique sequence. We have generated data corresponding to four clusters. Three of them are about ski place and are composed of 1 specific sequence and 3 others shared: Mountain, corresponding to the subsequence (18, 73, 29, 41); Snowboard (17, 25, 12, 19, 87); Ski (129, 2, 73, 32, 91). The last cluster is composed of a search on mountain too (18, 73, 29, 41) and an other one on trekking (2, 3, 4, 8). For this set, every video has been completely viewed (Table 23.2).

Setting the minimum quantity of representative sequences to 2 or 3, sessions corresponding to any of the three first clusters are merged to form a cluster corresponding to "sessions dealing with ski places." With a value of 4, this cluster is split and each source cluster is discovered. For this value, the cluster corresponding to mountain and trekking is correctly analyzed and not merged with the other data. But if we use the

Table 23.2. Clustering of the second data set.

Freq. viewed videos	Results		
	minSize = 2 or 3	minSize = 4	minsize = 1
(18, 73, 29, 41) (17, 25, 12, 19, 87) (129, 2, 73, 32, 91) (301, 302, 303, 304)		{(18, 73, 29, 41) (17, 25, 12, 19, 87) (129, 2, 73, 32, 91) (301, 302, 303, 304)}	
(18, 73, 29, 41) (17, 25, 12, 19, 87) (129, 2, 73, 32, 91) (401, 402, 403, 404)	{(18, 73, 29, 41) (17, 25, 12, 19, 87) (129, 2, 73, 32, 91)}	{(18, 73, 29, 41) (17, 25, 12, 19, 87) (129, 2, 73, 32, 91) (401, 402, 403, 404)}	{(18,73,29,41)}
(18, 73, 29, 41) (17, 25, 12, 19, 87) (129, 2, 73, 32, 91) (501, 502, 503, 504)		{(18, 73, 29, 41) (17, 25, 12, 19, 87) (129, 2, 73, 32, 91) (501, 502, 503, 504)}	
(18, 73, 29, 41) (2, 3, 4, 8)	{(18, 73, 29, 41) (2, 3, 4, 8)}	{(18, 73, 29, 41) (2, 3, 4, 8)}	

value of 1, leading to a classical subsequence extraction, all of these data are merged in a unique cluster and the difference between ski places and mountain hiking is not detected by the clustering.

23.5 Future work

We propose a two-level model-based approach for modeling user behaviors on a video search engine. The first level aims at modeling and clustering user behavior on a single video sequence (intravideo behavior), the second one aims at modeling and clustering user behavior on a set of video sequences (intervideo behavior). On the basis of this representation, we have developed a two-phase clustering algorithm that fits these data. We have showed that our approach is able to differentiate sessions dealing with the same videos but in different manners and to discover clusters that are not detected by basic subsequence approaches.

The main remaining work is to validate our technique on real data sets in a context of movie production. We have to ensure that results are still interesting on large video database.

The future objective is to use the extracted profiles to perform better searches. Indeed, these results will allow us to point out the badly indexed data, to change it, and to be able to propose video sequences to the users related to the history of their session.

References

1. MacQueen J. Some methods for classification and analysis of multivariate observations. In: *Proc Fifth Berkeley Symp*, University of California Press, Vol. 1, 1966.
2. Kohavi R, Mason L, Parekh R, Zheng Z. Lessons and challenges from mining retail e-commerce data. *Machine Learning* 2004.
3. Pierrakos D, Paliouras G, Papatheodorou C, Spyropoulos C. Web usage mining as a tool for personalization: A survey. *User Modeling and User-Adapted Interaction* 2003;13:311–372.
4. Srikant R, Yang Y. Mining Web logs to improve website organization. In: *Proceedings of the 10th International World Wide Web Conference* 2001.
5. Sarukkai R. Link prediction and path analysis using markov chains. In: *Proceedings of the 9th International World Wide Web Conference* 2000.
6. Cadez I, Heckerman D, Meek C, Smyth P, White S. Visualization of navigation patterns on a Web site using model based clustering. In: *Proceedings 6th ACM SIGKDD International Conference on Knowledge Discovery and Data Mining*.
7. Wang W, Zaiane OR. Clustering web sessions by sequence alignment. In: *13th International Workshop on Database and Expert Systems Applications (DEXA'02)* 2002.
8. Guha S, Rastogi R, Shim K. An efficient clustering algorithm for large databases. *SIGMOD* 1998.
9. Mobasher B, Dai H, Luo T, Nakagawa M, Sun Y, Wiltshire J. Discovery of aggregate usage profiles for Web personalization. *WEBKDD* 2000.

10. Jin X, Zhou Y, Mobasher B. Web usage mining based on probabilistic latent semantic analysis. *KDD* 2004.
11. Reuther AI, Meyer DG. The effect of personality type on the usage of a multimedia engineering education system. *Frontiers in Education* FIE'02 2002; 1.
12. Acharya S, Smith B, Parnes P. Characterizing user access to videos on the World Wide Web. In: *Proc of Multimedia Computing and Networking* 2000.
13. Yu B, Ma W, Nahrstedt K, Zhang H. Video summarization based on user log enhanced link analysis. MM'03 2003.
14. Branch P, Egan G, Tonkin B. Modeling interactive behaviour of a video based multimedia system. *IEEE International Conference on Communications* 1999;2:978–982.

24. On SVD-Free Latent Semantic Indexing for Iris Recognition of Large Databases

Pavel Praks, Libor Machala, and Václav Snášel

Summary. This chapter presents a method for an automatic identification of persons by iris recognition. A raster image of a human iris is represented as a sequence of color pixels. Information retrieval is conducted by the Latent Semantic Indexing (LSI) method. The pattern recognition algorithm is powered very effectively when the time-consuming Singular Value Decomposition (SVD) of LSI is replaced by the partial symmetric eigenproblem. Numerical experiments on a real 488 MB biometric data collection indicates feasibility of the presented approach as a tool for automated image recognition without special preprocessing.

24.1 Introduction

Methods of human identification using biometric features like fingerprint, hand geometry, face, voice, and iris are widely studied. A human eye iris has its unique structure given by pigmentation spots, furrows, and other tiny features that are stable throughout life (see [1, 2]). It is possible to scan an iris without physical contact in spite of wearing eyeglasses or contact lens. The iris can be hardly forged, for example, replaced or copied. This makes the iris a suitable object for the identification of persons. Iris recognition seems to be more reliable than other biometric techniques like face recognition [3]. Iris biometrics systems for public and personal use have been designed and deployed commercially by British Telecom, US Sandia Labs, UK National Physical Laboratory, NCR, Oki, IriScan, and others. Applications of these systems are expected in personal identification, access control, computer and Internet security, etc. Studies about iris recognition were published in [1–7].

The method proposed by Daugman [1, 2] is based on the transformation of elementary regions of the iris image into polar coordinates. Then, using two-dimensional optimal Gabor functions, a binary iris code is generated. The iris identification consists of comparisons of the generated codes using Hamming distance. In [6] the field of interest is transformed into standardized polar coordinates similarly as in [2]. The characteristic iris vector is computed from the mean brightness levels of elementary ring sectors of the iris image.

Liam et al. [5] use a trained Self-Organizing Map Neural Network to recognize iris patterns. The iris of doughnut shape is converted into a rectangular form and fed to the neural network. Roche et al. [7] propose an iris recognition method where the features of the iris are represented by fine-to-coarse approximations at different resolution levels. In this technique the discrete dyadic wavelet transform was used.

In this article, we present an alternative approach to the recognition of human iris images. The aim is to show that the Latent Semantic Indexing [8, 9] is as a good way for recognizing images as other above-mentioned methods [10]. Moreover, the pattern recognition can be powered very effectively when the time-consuming Singular Value Decomposition, of LSI is replaced by the partial symmetric eigenproblem, which can be solved by using fast iterative solvers [11].

24.2 Image Retrieval Using Latent Semantic Indexing

The numerical linear algebra, especially Singular Value Decomposition, is used as a basis for information retrieval in the retrieval strategy called Latent Semantic Indexing (see [8, 9]). Originally, LSI was used as an efficient tool for semantic analysis of large amount of text documents. The main reason is that more conventional retrieval strategies (such as vector space, probabilistic and extended Boolean) are not very efficient for real data, because they retrieve information solely on the basis of keywords and polysemy (words having multiple meanings) and synonymy (multiple words having the same meaning) are not correctly detected. LSI can be viewed as a variant of the vector space model with a low-rank approximation of the original data matrix via the SVD or the other numerical methods [8].

The "classical" LSI application in information retrieval algorithm has the following basic steps:

i) The Singular Value Decomposition of the term matrix using numerical linear algebra. SVD is used to identify and remove redundant noise information from data.

ii) The computation of the similarity coefficients between the transformed vectors of data and thus reveal some hidden (latent) structures of data.

Numerical experiments pointed out that some kind of dimension reduction, which is applied to the original data, brings to the information retrieval following two main advantages: (i) automatic noise filtering and (ii) natural clustering of data with "similar" semantic (see Figures 24.1 and 24.2).

24.2.1 Image Coding

Recently, the methods of numerical linear algebra, especially SVD, are also successfully used for the face recognition and reconstruction [12], image retrieval [10, 11], and as a tool for information extraction from HTML product catalogues [13]. In this chapter, the Latent Semantic Indexing is used as the tool for solving iris recognition problem.

In our approach [10, 11], a raster image is coded as a sequence of pixels (see Figure 24.3). Then the coded image can be understood as a vector of an m-dimensional

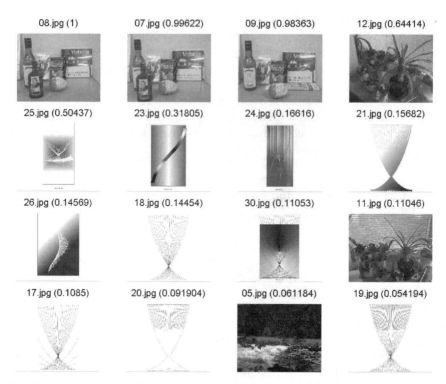

08.jpg (1)   07.jpg (0.99622)   09.jpg (0.98363)   12.jpg (0.64414)

25.jpg (0.50437)   23.jpg (0.31805)   24.jpg (0.16616)   21.jpg (0.15682)

26.jpg (0.14569)   18.jpg (0.14454)   30.jpg (0.11053)   11.jpg (0.11046)

17.jpg (0.1085)   20.jpg (0.091904)   05.jpg (0.061184)   19.jpg (0.054194)

Fig. 24.1. An example of LSI image retrieval results. Images are automatically sorted by their content using the partial eigenproblem.

space, where m denotes the number of pixels (attributes). Let the symbol A denote a $m \times n$ term-document matrix related to m keywords (pixels) in n documents (images). Let us remind that the (i, j)-element of the term-document matrix A represents the color of i-th position in the j-th image document (see Figure 24.4).

24.2.2 Document Matrix Scaling

Our numerical results pointed out that there is a possibility to increase the ability of the LSI method to extract details from images by scaling of the document matrix. This feature of the method was also exploited to iris recognition. Let the symbol $A(:, i)$ denote the i-th column of the document matrix A. We implemented the following scaling[1]:

```
for i = 1:n            % Loop over all images
    A(:,i) = A(:,i)/norm(A(:,i))
end;
```

---

[1] For the description of matrix-oriented algorithms we used the well-known Matlab-like notations [14]. For instance, the symbol $A(:, i)$ denotes the i-th column of the matrix A.

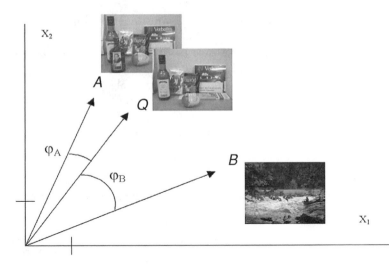

Fig. 24.2. An example of a similarity measure is the cosine similarity. Here A, Q, B represents the vectors. Symbols φ_A and φ_B denote the angle between the vectors A, Q and B, Q, respectively. The vector A is more similar to Q than vector B, because $\varphi_A < \varphi_B$. A small angle is equivalent to a large similarity.

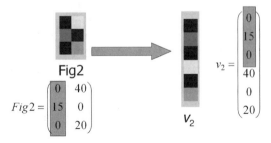

$$Fig2 = \begin{pmatrix} 0 & 40 \\ 15 & 0 \\ 0 & 20 \end{pmatrix}$$

$$v_2 = \begin{pmatrix} 0 \\ 15 \\ 0 \\ 40 \\ 0 \\ 20 \end{pmatrix}$$

Fig. 24.3. Image coding of an 3×2 pixels image example and the corresponding six-dimensional vector.

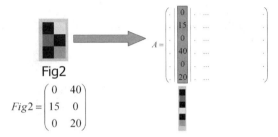

$$Fig2 = \begin{pmatrix} 0 & 40 \\ 15 & 0 \\ 0 & 20 \end{pmatrix}$$

$$A = \begin{pmatrix} \cdot & 0 & \cdot & \cdots \\ \cdot & 15 & \cdot & \cdots \\ \cdot & 0 & \cdot & \cdots \\ \cdot & 40 & \cdot & \cdots \\ \cdot & 0 & \cdot & \cdots \\ \cdot & 20 & \cdot & \cdots \end{pmatrix}$$

Fig. 24.4. An example of document matrix coding. The document matrix A is represented as a sequence of coded images.

24.3 Implementation Details of Latent Semantic Indexing

In this section we will derive the SVD-free Latent Semantic Indexing and we will present the implementation of the LSI algorithms.

We will show two modifications of the original LSI algorithm presented in [9]. Here presented the SVD-free modifications of the original LSI algorithm replaced the time-expensive SVD decomposition of a general document matrix by the approximate solution of a partial symmetric eigenproblem of a square matrix.

24.3.1 LSI and Singular Value Decomposition

Let the symbol A denotes the $m \times n$ document matrix related to m pixels in n images. The aim of SVD is to compute decomposition

$$A = USV^T, \tag{24.1}$$

where $S \in R^{m \times n}$ is a diagonal matrix with nonnegative diagonal elements called the singular values, $U \in R^{m \times m}$ and $V \in R^{n \times n}$ are orthogonal matrices.[2] The columns of matrices U and V are called the left singular vectors and the right singular vectors, respectively. The decomposition can be computed so that the singular values are sorted in decreasing order.

The full SVD decomposition (24.1) is memory and time-consuming operation, especially for large problems. Although the document matrix A is often sparse, the matrices U and V have a dense structure. Because of these facts, only a few k-largest singular values of A and the corresponding left and right singular vectors are computed and stored in memory. The number of singular values and vectors that are computed and kept in memory can be chosen experimentally as a compromise between the speed/precision ratio of the LSI procedure.

We implemented and tested LSI procedure in the Matlab system by Mathworks. The document matrix A was decomposed by the Matlab command `svds`. Using the `svds` command brings following advantages:

- The document matrix A can be effectively stored in memory by using the Matlab storage format for sparse matrices.
- The number of singular values and vectors computed by the partial SVD decomposition can be easily set by the user.

Following [9] the Latent Semantic Indexing procedure can be written in Matlab by the following way.

Procedure Original LSI [Latent Semantic Indexing]
```
function sim = lsi(A,q,k)
% Input:
% A ...    the m × n matrix
% q ...    the query vector
```

---

[2] A matrix $Q \in R^{n \times n}$ is said to be *orthogonal* if the condition $Q^{-1} = Q^T$ holds.

```
% k ...       Compute k largest singular values
and vectors; k ≤ n
% Output:
% sim ...     the vector of similarity coefficients
```

```
[m,n] = size(A);
```

1. **Compute the co-ordinates of all images in the k-dimensional space by the partial SVD of a document matrix A.**
   ```
   [U,S,V] = svds(A,k);
   ```
   % Compute the k largest singular values of A; The rows of V contain the co-ordinates of images.
2. **Compute the co-ordinate of a query vector q**
   ```
   qc = q' * U * pinv(S);
   ```
   % The vector qc includes the co-ordinate of the query vector q; The matrix $pinv(S)$ contains reciprocals of nonzeros singular values (an pseudoinverse); The symbol ' denotes the transpose superscript.
3. **Compute the similarity coefficients between the co-ordinates of the query vector and images.**
   ```
   for i = 1:n      % Loop over all images
   sim(i)=(qc*V(i,:)')/(norm(qc)*norm(V(i,:)));
   end;
   ```
   % Compute the similarity coefficient for i-th image; $V(i,:)$ denotes the i-th row of V.

The procedure lsi returns to a user the vector of similarity coefficients sim. The i-th element of the vector sim contains a value which indicate a "measure" of a semantic similarity between the i-th document and the query document. The increasing value of the similarity coefficient indicates the increasing semantic similarity.

24.3.2 LSI1—The First Enhancement of the LSI Implementation

In this chapter, we will remind the well-known fact how to express matrices S and V without the SVD. Of course, there is an efficient SVD iterative algorithm based on Lanczos algorithm [14], but the SVD of a large document matrix remains still time-expensive.

Let us assume the well-known relationship between the singular value decomposition of the matrix A and the symmetric eigenproblem of the symmetric square matrices $A^T A$:

$$A = USV^T \tag{24.2}$$

$$A^T = (USV^T)^T = VS^T U^T \tag{24.3}$$

$$A^T A = VS^T (U^T U)SV^T = VS^T SV^T \tag{24.4}$$

Furthermore, let us assume the SVD decomposition (24.1) again. Because of the fact that the matrix V is orthogonal, the following matrix identity holds:

$$AV = US. \tag{24.5}$$

Finally, we can express the matrix U in the following way:

$$AVS^+ \approx U \tag{24.6}$$

Here the symbol S^+ denotes the Moore–Penrose pseudoinverse (pinv). Let us accept that the diagonal matrix S contains only strictly positive singular values for real cases; The singular values less than $tol \approx 0$ are cut off by the Matlab eigs(A'*A, k) command, since the number of computed singular values $k \ll n$ for real problems.

Following these observations, the SVD-free Latent Semantic Indexing procedure can be written by the following way.

LSI1 [The SVD-free LSI, Version 1]
```
function sim = lsi1(A,q,k)
% Input:
% A ...    the m × n matrix
% q ...    the query vector
% k ...    Compute k largest singular values and
vectors; k ≤ n
% Output:
% sim ...    the vector of similarity coefficients

[m,n] = size(A);
```

1. **Compute the co-ordinates of all images in the k-dimensional space by the SVD-free approach.**
   ```
   [V,S2] = eigs(A'*A,k);
   ```
   % Compute the k largest eigenvalues and eigenvectors of $A^T A$ to obtain V and S^2 without SVD.
   ```
   S = sqrt(S2);
   U = A * V * pinv(S);
   ```
   % Compute S and U without SVD.
2. **Compute the co-ordinate of the query vector q.**
   ```
   qc = q' * U * pinv(S);
   ```

3. **Compute the similarity coefficients between the co-ordinates of the query vector and images.**
   ```
   for i = 1:n       % Loop over all images
   sim(i)=(qc*V(i,:)')/(norm(qc)*norm(V(i,:)));
   end;
   ```

Compared to the previous version of the LSI, we can see modifications in the first step of the algorithm. The second and the third steps of the algorithm remain the same.

24.3.3 LSI2—The Second Enhancement of LSI

Analyzing the LSI1 procedure deeply, we can see that the matrix U does not have to be explicitly computed and stored in memory during the second step of the LSI. The exploitation of this observation brings us the additional accelerating of the speed and decreasing the memory requirements of the LSI:

LSI2 [The SVD-free LSI, Version 2]

```
function sim = lsi2(A,q,k)
% Input:
% A ...    the m × n matrix
% q ...    the query vector
% k ...    Compute k largest singular values and
vectors; k ≤ n
% Output:
% sim ...    the vector of similarity coefficients

[m,n] = size(A);
```

1. **Compute the co-ordinates of all images in the k-dimensional space by the SVD-free approach.**
   ```
   [V,S2] = eigs(A'*A,k);
   S = sqrt(S2);
   % Compute S and V without SVD.
   ```
2. **Compute the co-ordinate of the query vector q without using the matrix U.**
   ```
   qc = (((q' * A) * V) * pinv(S)) * pinv(S);
   ```

3. **Compute the similarity coefficients between the co-ordinates of the query vector and images.**
   ```
   for i = 1:n      % Loop over all images
   sim(i)=(qc*V(i,:)')/(norm(qc)*norm(V(i,:)));
   end;
   ```

Compared to the LSI1, we can see modifications in the first step and in the second step of the algorithm. The presented choice of parenthesis in the second step of LSI2 is the key implementation detail that extremely influences the efficiency of the LSI speed.

24.4 Iris Recognition Experiments

The iris is scanned by TOPCON optical device connected to the CCD Sony camera. The acquired digitized image is RGB of size 576×768 pixels [15]. Only the red (R) component of the RGB image participates in our experiments. The reason is that the recognition based on the red component appears to be more reliable than recognition based on green (G) or blue (B) components or grayscale images. It is in accord with the study of Daugman [4], where near-infrared wavelengths are used.

Table 24.1. Iris recognition using the SVD-free Latent Semantic Indexing method; Properties of the document matrix (up) and LSI processing parameters (down) for Query1 and Query2.

Properties of the document matrix A	
Number of keywords:	$576 \times 768 = 442,368$
Number of documents:	24
Size in memory:	81 MB
The SVD-Free LSI processing parameters	
Dim. of the original space	24
Dim. of the reduced space (k)	10
Time for $A^T A$ operation	3.38 secs.
Results of the eigensolver	0.26 secs.
The total time	3.64 secs.

24.4.1 The Small-Size Database Query

The testing database contains 24 images: 3 images of the left eye and 3 images of the right eye from 4 persons. The collection of images required 81 MB of RAM. The images were opened using the Matlab (tm) command *imread*. The queries were represented as images from the collection. We used the LSI2 algorithm for image retrieval in all cases.

For example, the name "001L$_3$.tif" implies that the left iris of Person No.1, the series 3 is assumed. The most time consuming part of LSI was multiplying of matrices $A^T \times A$. It takes 3.38 s on a Pentium Celeron 2.4 GHz with 256 MB RAM running MS Windows XP. The computation of the partial eigenproblem by the Matlab command *eigs()* takes only 0.26 s (see Table 24.1).

In the current computer implementation of the Latent Semantic Indexing method, no preprocessing of images and/or a priori information is assumed. However, the numerical experiments presented here indicate quite optimistic availability of the proposed algorithm for automated iris recognition.

24.4.1.1 Query1

All results are sorted out by the similarity coefficient. To achieve lucid results, only 16 of the most significant images are presented. In all cases, the remaining eight images with the negligible similarity coefficient were removed from the presentation.

When the left iris of Person No.2, the series 1, is assumed as the query image (002L$_1$.tif), the most similar image is of course the query image itself with the similarity coefficient 1 (see Fig. 24.5). The subsequent image is 002L$_2$.tif with the similarity coefficient 0.8472. The images 002P$_3$.tif, 002L$_3$.tif and 002P$_2$.tif follow. Analyzing results, we can see that these four most similar images are connected with Person No. 2.

24.4.1.2 Query2

When the right iris of Person No.2, the series 1, is assumed as the query image (002P$_1$.tif), the two most similar images are related to Person No.2, 002P$_2$.tif and

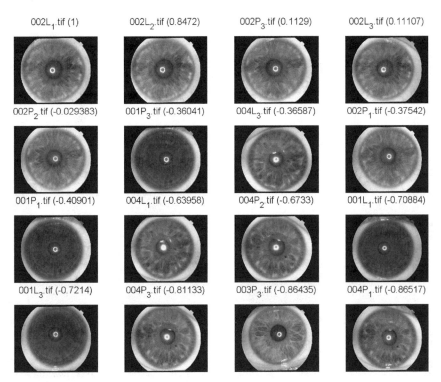

002L$_1$.tif (1)   002L$_2$.tif (0.8472)   002P$_3$.tif (0.1129)   002L$_3$.tif (0.11107)

002P$_2$.tif (-0.029383)   001P$_3$.tif (-0.36041)   004L$_3$.tif (-0.36587)   002P$_1$.tif (-0.37542)

001P$_1$.tif (-0.40901)   004L$_1$.tif (-0.63958)   004P$_2$.tif (-0.6733)   001L$_1$.tif (-0.70884)

001L$_3$.tif (-0.7214)   004P$_3$.tif (-0.81133)   003P$_3$.tif (-0.86435)   004P$_1$.tif (-0.86517)

Fig. 24.5. Image retrieval results related to the query image 002L$_1$.tif (Query1).

002P$_3$.tif (see Fig. 24.6). The image 001L$_3$.tif, which is connected to Person No.1, follow. But two subsequent images 002L$_3$.tif and 002L$_2$.tif are again relative to Person No.2.

24.4.2 The Large-Scale Database Query

Statistically significant numbers of the similarity coefficients for compared "the same" and "different" irides calculated for a database enable to quantify the probability of incorrect iris recognition for the method. For this purpose, a database containing 384 images (3 images of the left eye and 3 images of the right eye taken at different times from 64 persons) was used [15].

The large database query on the same irides was performed by 3×128 comparisons (the maximum possible number of combination of the same irides). Similarly, the test of different irides was made as 72,576 comparisons of irides from different persons.

Figure 24.7 shows the order of steps of the recognition process schematically. The image is acquired and digitized. The positions of the iris boundaries are localized in the image and approximated by concentric circles. The inner circle encircles a pupil and forms the inner boundary, and the outer circle encircles the iris and represents the

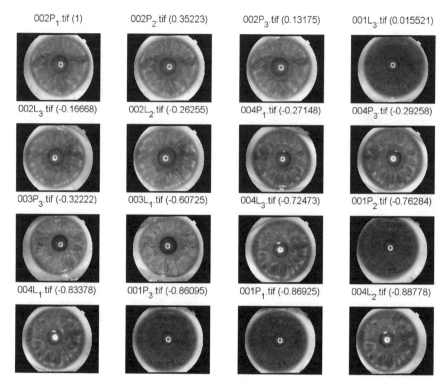

002P$_1$.tif (1)   002P$_2$.tif (0.35223)   002P$_3$.tif (0.13175)   001L$_3$.tif (0.015521)

002L$_3$.tif (-0.16668)   002L$_2$.tif (-0.26255)   004P$_1$.tif (-0.27148)   004P$_3$.tif (-0.29258)

003P$_3$.tif (-0.32222)   003L$_1$.tif (-0.60725)   004L$_3$.tif (-0.72473)   001P$_2$.tif (-0.76284)

004L$_1$.tif (-0.83378)   001P$_3$.tif (-0.86095)   001P$_1$.tif (-0.86925)   004L$_2$.tif (-0.88778)

Fig. 24.6. Image retrieval results related to the query image 002P$_1$.tif (Query2).

outer boundary. The region of interest (in Figure 24.7 marked as several rectangles) that participates in the recognition is chosen within the iris boundaries to avoid the influence of eyelashes and the reflectance of the camera flash. Then the region of interest of the template image of the iris is stored in the database together with the

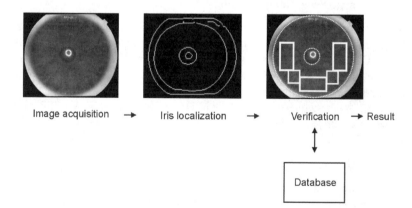

Image acquisition → Iris localization → Verification → Result

Database

Fig. 24.7. The process of the iris recognition for the large-scale iris recognition example.

Table 24.2. The large-scale iris recognition example
using the SVD-free Latent Semantic Indexing method;
Properties of the document matrix (up) and LSI
processing parameters (down).

Properties of the document matrix A	
Number of keywords:	52,488
Number of documents:	384
Size in memory:	157,464 Kbytes
The SVD-Free LSI processing parameters	
Dim. of the original space	384
Dim. of the reduced space (k)	10
Time for $A^T A$ operation	13.906 s
Results of the eigensolver	4.843 s
The total time	18.749 s

information describing the iris geometrical properties (the diameter and the center). Of course, the positions of the iris are usually different on the scanning device and the images are mutually rotated and shifted. These differences are not treated in the current simple implementation of the image preprocessing. The properties of the document matrix and LSI processing parameters are summarized in Table 24.2.

24.4.3 Results of the Large-Scale Database Query

The quality of the recognition is usually quantified by two types of errors: *The False Reject Rate* (FRR) and *The False Accept Rate* (FAR). The FRR represents the percentage of the authentic objects that were rejected. FAR represents the percentage of the impostors that were accepted. FRR and FAR generally depend on the given similarity coefficient threshold of ρ. The lower the threshold ρ the higher is the probability of accepting the impostor.

Similarly, the higher the threshold ρ the higher is the probability of rejecting the authentic object. The intersection of the "impostor" and the "authentic" distributions gives the value of the threshold $\rho = \rho_0$, where the sum $\text{FAR}(\rho_0) + \text{FRR}(\rho_0)$ is minimal. Such distributions obtained from the similarity coefficients through the database are presented in the form of histograms in Figures 24.8 and 24.9. Analyses of the intersection of the distributions gave the value of threshold $\rho_0 = 0.766$ and the errors FAR $= 1.12\%$, FRR $= 2.34\%$ (see Figure 24.10).

Of course, the probability of incorrect iris recognition can be significantly reduced by a preprocessing step including a proper geometrical alignment of any two compared irides before the similarity coefficient is computed.

24.5 Conclusions

This article presents the SVD-free Latent Semantic Indexing method for an automatic verification of persons by iris recognition. Although no special pre-processing of

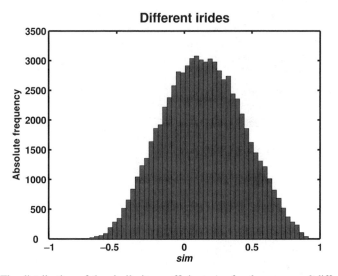

Fig. 24.8. The distribution of the similarity coefficient *sim* for the compared different irides through the database. The big majority of comparing has the similarity coefficient close to 0. This feature indicates the ability of the algorithm to properly recognize irides belonging to a different person.

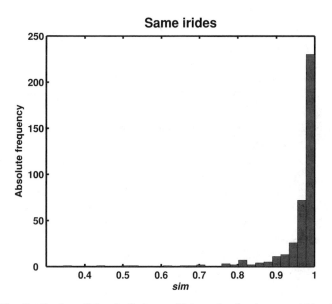

Fig. 24.9. The distribution of the similarity coefficient *sim* for the same irides through the database. The big majority of comparing has the similarity coefficient close to 1. This feature indicates the ability of the algorithm to properly recognize irides belonging to the same person.

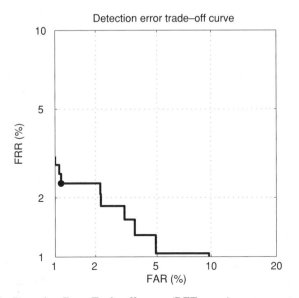

Fig. 24.10. The Detection Error Trade-off curve (DET curve) was computed by using the DET-Curve Plotting software [16].

images and/or a priori information is assumed, our numerical experiments indicate ability of the proposed algorithm to solve the large-scale iris recognition problems.

Of course, the quality of irides images and proper localization influence the resulting errors. We have found that in our case the errors were caused by an inaccurate localization of images. The proper localization is a subject for future work.

Acknowledgments

We thank very much SIAM Linear Algebra 2003 community for valuable comments, especially Zlatko Drmač (Croatia) and William Ferng (U.S.A.) for proposing the scaling of the document matrix.

The research has been partially supported by the program "Information Society" of the Academy of Sciences of the Czech Republic, project No. T401940412 "Dynamic Reliability Quantification and Modelling." The work leading to this chapter and future developments have been and will be partially supported by the EU under the IST 6th FP, Network of Excellence K-Space.

References

1. Daugman JG. Biometric Personal Identification System Based on Iris Analysis. US Patent No 5,291,560 US Government 1993.
2. Daugman JG. High confidence visual recognition of persons by a test of statistical independence. *IEEE Trans Pattern Analysis and Machine Intelligence* 1993;15(11):1148–1161.

3. Daugman JG. Statistical richness of visual phase information: Update on recognizing persons by iris patterns. *International Journal of Computer Vision* 2001;45(1):25–38.
4. Daugman JG. The importance of being random: Statistical principles of iris recognition. *Pattern Recognition* 2003;36(2):279–291.
5. Liam LW, Chekima A, Fan LCh, Dargham JA. Iris recognition using self-organizing neural network. In: *Student Conference on Research and Development*, Shah Alam, Malaysia; 2001, pp. 169–172.
6. Machala L, Pospíšil J. Proposal and verification of two methods for evaluation of the human iris video-camera images. *Optik* 2001;112(8):335–340.
7. Roche DM, Sanchez-Avila C, Sanchez-Reillo R. *Iris Recognition for Biometric Identification Using Dyadic Wavelet Transform Zero-Crossing.* IEEE Press, 2001, pp. 272–277.
8. Berry WM, Drmač Z, Jessup JR. Matrices, vector spaces, and information retrieval. *SIAM Review* 1999;41(2):336–362.
9. Grossman DA, OFrieder. *Information Retrieval: Algorithms and Heuristics.* 2nd ed. Kluwer Academic Publishers; 2000.
10. Praks P, Dvorský J, Snášel V. Latent semantic indexing for image retrieval systems. In: *SIAM Conference on Applied Linear Algebra.* The College of William and Mary, Williamsburg, USA, http://www.siam.org/meetings/la03/proceedings; 2003.
11. Praks P, Dvorský J, Snášel V, Černohorský J. On SVD-free latent semantic indexing for image retrieval for application in a hard industrial environment. In: *IEEE International Conference on Industrial Technology ICIT 2003.* IEEE Press, Maribor, Slovenia; 2003. p. 466–471.
12. Muller N, Magaia L, Herbst BM. Singular Value Decomposition, Eigenfaces, and 3D Reconstructions. *SIAM Review* 2004;46(3):518–545.
13. Svátek V, Labský M, Šváb O, Praks P. Information extraction from HTML product catalogues: Coupling quantitative and knowledge-based approaches. In: *Dagstuhl Seminar on Machine Learning for the Semantic Web.* Ed. N. Kushmerick, F. Ciravegna, A. Doan, C. Knoblock and S. Staab. Research Center for Computer Science, Wadern, Germany, http://www.smi.ucd.ie/Dagstuhl-MLSW/proceedings/labsky-svatek-praks-svab.pdf; 2005.
14. Golub GH, Loan CFVan. *Matrix Computations.* 3rd ed. The Johns Hopkins University Press; 1996.
15. Dobeš M, Machala L. The database of Iris Images. http://phoenix.inf.upol.cz/iris: Palacký University, Olomouc, Czech Republic; 2004.
16. DET-Curve Plotting software for use with MATLAB. http://www.nist.gov/speech/tools: National Institute of Standards and Technology; 2000–2005.

25. Mining Knowledge in Computer Tomography Image Databases

Daniela Stan Raicu

Summary. This chapter presents our research results obtained for texture extraction, classification, segmentation, and retrieval of normal soft tissues in Computed Tomography (CT) studies of the chest and abdomen. The texture extraction step consists of various texture methods applied to the collection of tissue data in order to derive a set of features characterizing the best the visual perception of texture. The classification step involves different data mining learning models used to automatically map similar texture features to the same type of tissues, and produce a set of rules that can be used for automatic classification and annotation of unlabelled image data. When the classification approach is applied at the local (pixel) level, it can be used for automatic segmentation. Each pixel will receive a label through the classification rules and connected pixels having the same labels will form a region or segment in the corresponding image. This type of segmentation will have a significant impact on the current research efforts for providing *automatic context* (i.e., that the cursor is hovering over "liver" in CT images). The image retrieval step consists of the selection of the best similarity metric and the best texture feature representation in order to retrieve the most similar images with the organ query image. Since there is no similarity measure known to perform the best for the CT modality, we compare eight metrics and three different feature representations, and show how the selection of a similarity metric affects the texture-based retrieval. Furthermore, since our work deals with normal tissues, the system proposed here can be considered as *a first step for supporting the clinical decision-making process.*

25.1 Introduction

The human body is an extremely complex system. Images are by far the most efficient way to obtain, interpret, and manage information about complex systems. Physicians increasingly rely on images to understand the human body and to intervene in the processes of human illness and injury. The use of images to manage information about biologic and medical processes is certain to grow, not only in clinical medicine but also in the biomedical imaging research efforts that support it [1].

Advances in biomedical imaging over the years have been driven principally by the continuous evolution of imaging technologies. The ever-present radiographic film that has been the basis of image management for almost 100 years is being displaced by new digital imaging modalities such as:

1. Computed tomography (CT)
2. Magnetic resonance (MR)
3. Nuclear medicine (NM)
   (a) Emission computed tomography (ECT) with compounds releasing positrons (positron emission tomography [PET])
   (b) single photons (single photon emission computed tomography [SPECT])
4. Ultrasound (US)
5. Digital radiography (DF)
6. Computed radiography (CR) using storage phosphor imaging plates or film digitizers
7. Digital angiography (DA)
8. MR spectroscopy (MRS)
9. Electron emission radiography (EMR).

The explosion of the medical imaging technologies has generated mountains of data; depending on the size of the institution, a radiology department can perform between 100 and 5000 examinations daily, generating a myriad of images, patient data, report text, findings, and recommendations [2]. Digital image management systems are under development now to handle these images in digital form. These systems are termed Picture Archiving and Communication Systems (PACS), and they are based on the integration of different technologies that form a system for image acquisition, storage, transmission, processing, and display of images for their analysis and further diagnosis. Availability of digital data within the PACS raises a possibility of health care and research enhancements associated with manipulation, processing, and handling of data by computers, that is a basis for computer-assisted radiology development.

In general, radiology data are well organized but poorly structured, and structuring these data prior to knowledge extraction is an essential first step in the successful mining of radiological data [2]. Furthermore, when compared to text, radiology images are enormous in size and highly variable over time. Another challenge is that the image data itself is contained within PACS systems that are in constant use and quite difficult to mine for image data while in use as clinical systems. Therefore, image processing and data mining techniques are necessary for structuring, classification, and retrieval of image data. For instance, the development of Content-based Image Retrieval (CBIR) systems and their integration into the PACs systems will have many potential applications in three large domains: education, research, and diagnosis. In the domain of education, a teacher could query for images with specific anatomical regions in order to provide visual similar examples to students. Research can benefit from the CBIR systems: by including visual features directly in medical studies, new correlations between the visual nature of a case and its diagnosis or textual description can be found. Finally, the diagnostics will be the hardest but most important application for image retrieval. For domains such as evidenced-based medicine or case-based reasoning it is essential to supply relevant, similar cases for comparison based on special visual image features that model the visual detection of a medical doctor.

Besides the technology push, the recent advances in the medical imaging have also been driven by the concept of biologic/clinical pull [1]. For instance, in our days, CT imaging is used extensively in radiation oncology as a feedback mechanism to shape and guide external beams of radiation so that cancer treatments are optimized in real time during delivery of the radiation. This is an exceptional development in clinical medicine for designing plans for cancer and guiding the delivery of radiation.

The continuous evolution of imaging techniques, the accelerating advances in computer technology, and the innovations in information networking set the stage for major advances in medical image data mining and its contributions to health care. This chapter presents the potential contributions of data mining and image processing to the field of radiology; in particular, we discuss how computer-aided diagnosis (CAD) systems can play a major and important role in early detection, diagnosis, and computerized treatment planning in cancer radiation therapy.

25.2 Mining CT Data: Classification, Segmentation, and Retrieval

In this section, we present an overview of our research work and contributions to the process of classification [3], segmentation [4], and retrieval [5] of normal tissues in CT studies of the chest and of the abdomen.

25.2.1 Image Classification: Related Work

Tissue classification has been largely limited to specific pathologies, typically within a single organ or tissue. Karkanis et al. [6] proposed a scheme that uses textural descriptors based on second-order gray-level statistics and employs a multilayer feed forward neural network to discriminate among normal and cancer regions in colonoscopic images. Chabat et al. [7] proposed an automated technique for differentiation between obstructive lung diseases using a supervised Bayesian classifier on the basis of statistical textural descriptors of thin-section CT images. Sluimer et al. [8] also looked at the automatic differentiation of normal from abnormal lung tissue in HRCT of the lungs and found the best classifier to be k-nearest neighbors when using multiscale filter bank for texture analysis. Fortson et al. [9] applied several Gaussian Maximum Likelihood classifiers to capture the large variety of tissues types inherent to Scleroderma in HRCT of the lung as well. Cios et al. [10] proposed a semiautomatic procedure based on decision trees for analyzing SPECT images of a human heart and classifying the images into several categories. Albrecht et al. presented in [11] a pattern classification method that combines the classical perceptron algorithm with simulated annealing in order to recognize focal liver tumors in CT images. Wolf et al. [12] studied the hierarchical classification of brain tumors by CT-image Walsh spectra.

Our work will provide texture extraction and classification of normal tissue across a wide range of organs and tissues in CT scans. The texture extraction step will consist of various texture methods applied to the collection of tissue data in order to derive a set of features (numerical descriptors) characterizing the best the visual perception of texture. The classification step will involve different learning models that will automatically map similar texture descriptors to the same type of tissues and thus produce a dictionary of texture values for normal tissues in CT scans.

The automatic classification of normal tissues will contribute to the development of new approaches for computerized treatment planning in cancer radiation therapy. Before radiation therapy begins, it is important to precisely locate the cancer, but also accurately determine normal areas of the body through which radiation will pass such that the dose of radiation the cancer and nearby normal tissues will be exposed to will be accurately identified. This will enable radiation oncologists to significantly reduce side effects while improving the ability to deliver a curative radiation dose to cancer-containing areas and minimizing the radiation dose to normal tissue.

25.2.2 Image Segmentation: Related Work

The previous approach for normal tissue classification when applied at the local (pixel) level can be used for automatic segmentation. Each pixel will receive a label through the classification rules and connected pixels having the same labels will form a region or segment in the corresponding image. This type of segmentation will have a significant impact on the current research efforts for providing *automatic context* (i.e., that the cursor is hovering over "liver" in CT images). Accurate tissue segmentation and classification of normal CT structures will allow the radiologist to invoke specific tools named *context sensitive tools* during the interpretation process. These tools may represent further image processing and decision support tools or may invoke tissue specific reporting and annotation tools that should speed radiologic reporting while at the same time promote the acquisition of structured information about the images. In the absence of automatic tissue segmentation and classification, the navigation of structured reporting hierarchies presents too much of a delay to be practicably implemented.

There are a large number of texture-based segmentation algorithms in the literature. Texture segmentation usually involves the combination of texture feature extraction techniques with a suitable segmentation algorithm. Among the most popular feature extraction techniques used for texture segmentation are Gabor filters and wavelets transforms [13–15]. Among the most commonly used segmentation algorithms based on these features are clustering techniques [16, 17], region growing, and split-and-merge [18, 19].

Segmentation using the traditional techniques previously mentioned requires considerable amounts of expert interactive guidance. In the medical imaging field, deformable models are commonly applied because of their capability to capture the irregular shapes and shape deformations found in anatomical structures. The deformable model that has attracted the most attention to date is popularly known as "snakes" [20], and it has been used for different applications such as the segmentation of the heart from cardiac imagery, of neural tissue textures, and of the bone and cartilage in clinical knee magnetic resonance imaging (MRI). However, the application of snakes and other similar deformable contour models to extract regions of interest is not without limitations. One of the limitations is that snakes were designed as interactive (semiautomatic) models. To increase the speed, accuracy, and consistency of the segmentation, automatic segmentation is a desirable, albeit very difficult, long-term goal.

Our proposed approach for segmentation does not require any selection of initial points in order to perform the organ segmentation; moreover, it can be used as an automated first-pass segmentation that can be followed by the snake algorithm.

25.2.3 Image Retrieval: Related Work

In medicine to date, virtually all Picture Archiving and Communications Systems (PACS) retrieve images simply by *textual* indices based on patient name, technique, or some-observer-coded text of diagnostic findings [21]. Fields of text tags, such as patient demographics, diagnostic codes (e.g., ICD-9, American College of Radiology diagnostic codes), image view-plane (e.g., saggital, coronal, etc.) and so on usually are the first handles on this process. This textual approach, however, may suffer from considerable observer variability, high cost of manual classification and manipulation of images by medical experts, and failure to fully account for *quantitative relationships of medically relevant structures within an image* that are visible to a trained observer but not codable in conventional database terms.

In the radiology domain, a study [22] was performed to measure the level of inter- and intraobserver agreement and to evaluate the causes of variability in radiologists' descriptions and assessments of sonograms of solid breast masses. The findings of the study showed the lack of uniformity among observers' use of descriptive terms that produced inconsistent diagnoses even though the appearance of masses was described accordingly to a lexicon that was proposed in an earlier benchmark study. Since radiologists themselves rely on visual texture to detect and describe breast lesions on ultrasound images, a Content-Based Image Retrieval (CBIR) system using automatically extracted *quantitative texture features* could have been used to address this established clinical weakness of the diagnostic process and also complement the radiologists' perceptive abilities.

According to Muller et al. [23], only six research projects currently aim at creating CBIR for general medical applications, namely: I^2C [24], COBRA [25], IRMA [26, 27], KMeD [28], MedGIFT [29], and Image Engine [30]. Most applications for CBIR focus on the analysis of a specific anatomical structure from images produced in radiology, pathology, and cardiology departments. Glatard et al. [31] introduced a CBIR system that uses Gabor filters [32] extracted from segmented cardiac MRI to perform clinically relevant queries on large image databases that do not require user supervision. Mueller et al. [23] compares changes in texture analysis with Gabor filters and the performance of variations in feature space in relation to color (grey level) quantization. Brodley et al. [33] introduced a CBIR system for the retrieval of CT lung images; their proposed system, ASSERT, uses several features (such as co-occurrence texture features, Fourier descriptors, and moments), and relies on expert interaction with the system in addition to various machine learning and computer vision techniques. Zheng et al. [34] designed and analyzed a CBIR system for pathology, using four types of image features and the dot product as a similarity metric.

Wei et al. [35] proposed a CBIR system for the mammography imaging modality using the co-occurrence texture signatures as global features.

In our proposed approach, we use both global-level [36] and local-level co-occurrence texture features to retrieve normal anatomical regions produced by CT as the imaging modality. Since there is no similarity measure known to perform the best for the CT modality, we compare eight metrics and three different feature representations, and show how the selection of a similarity metric affects the texture-based retrieval. Furthermore, since our work deals with normal tissues, the system proposed here can be considered as *a first step for supporting the clinical decision-making process*. Same as the normal workflow in medicine, in order to find out if a new case is normal (nonpathological) or not, the new case will be compared with the existing normal cases from a database doing dissimilarity retrieval as opposed to similarity retrieval. The *distance to normality* of the new case along with the knowledge of the medical specialist will determine the placement of the case either in the normal database or in a pathological database; for the later situation, more specialized computer-aided diagnosis tools or image retrieval systems focusing on the specific pathology can be applied further for evaluation and clinical decision making.

25.3 Materials and Methods

25.3.1 Image Database

25.3.1.1 Data Acquisition

Our preliminary results are based on data extracted from two normal CT studies from Northwestern Memorial Hospital (NMH) PACS. The data consist of multiple, serial, axial CT images derived from helical, multidetector CT abdominal, and chest acquisitions using a HiSpeed CT/i scanner (GE Medical Systems, Milwaukee, WI); the imaging protocol parameters are: 120 kVp, 60-120 mA (depending on body size), 480 mm for the field-of-view (FOV) and 0.9375 for the voxel size. The images were taken at the same time for each of the patients, leading two time points in the data; the patient positioning in the images was FFS (Feet–First–Supine), one of the patient-space coordinate system conventions used in DICOM (Digital Imaging and Communications in Medicine) standard format. The images were transferred via Ethernet to a nearby computer workstation in DICOM format of size 512 by 512 and having 12-bit gray level resolution. An automated software agent (DICOM Valet, ETIAM, Rennes, France) attached to the DICOM Storage Service Class Provider (WinSCP, ETIAM, Rennes, France) performed de-identification according to DICOM Supplement 55.

25.3.1.2 Image Segmentation for the Global Tissue Classification and Retrieval Tasks

Using the Active Contour Models (ACM) algorithm [37], we segmented five organs from 344 2-D axial slices: heart and great vessels, liver, renal and splenic parenchyma, and backbone. We used the ACM segmentation algorithm because it allowed us segment regions with complex shapes, and once several initial points were selected on the boundary, the algorithm calculated automatically the boundary of each of the region of interest.

The main steps involved in our proposed approaches for classification, segmentation, and retrieval are:

1. For each segmented region of interest from the image database, we calculate a set of 10 Haralick texture features at both global and pixel-level; therefore, each organ or pixel is represented as a vector with 10 elements that will be further used for comparing the similarity among the images/organs.

2. Once the features are calculated, they can be represented as either a mean-based vector, binned histogram, or texture signature depending on the level of granularity considered. Furthermore, a preprocessing step is applied: the features are normalized such that the differences in their scales do not influence the similarity results or the classification results. Then, the normalized texture features are used for the three proposed tasks.

3. In the case of the classification task, a decision tree classification model is used to derive a set of classification rules at both the pixel and the global levels. The classification results are evaluated with respect to four performance metrics: sensitivity, specificity, precision, and accuracy. The global rules can be used further for organ tissue classification and annotation while the pixel (local) rules can be used for the CT image segmentation task. Pixels with the same classification labels and being adjacent will form connected components and thus, the regions of interest within the corresponding CT images. In the case of retrieval, eight measures are calculated between the query and all the other images from the database. As a response to a specific query, the system will display the most similar images with the query image. The retrieval performance is evaluated using the precision and recall metrics and each image is considered a query image; therefore, a total of 344 queries are performed and evaluated using the two performance metrics.

25.3.2 Texture Features

In medical image processing, texture is especially important, because it is difficult to classify human body organ tissues using shape or gray-level information. This is because of the uncertainty introduced by the unlimited variability in organ shape distortion and the potential absolute gray-level variability due to the imaging device. While gray levels purely describe pointwise properties of images, texture uses these gray levels to derive some notion of spatial distribution of tonal variations, surface orientation, and scenic depth. Furthermore, contrary to the discrimination of morphologic information (shape, size), there is evidence that the human visual system has difficulties in the discrimination of textural information that is related to higher order statistics or spectral properties in an image. Consequently, texture analysis can potentially augment the visual skills of the radiologist by extracting features that may be relevant to the diagnostic problem but they are not necessary visually extractable [38].

Several approaches have been applied toward the analysis and characterization of texture within medical images including fractal dimension, run-length encoding, discrete wavelet transform, and co-occurrence matrices. While there has not been any conclusive study to prove the superiority of one method over the other methods of capturing texture, we choose to use the Haralick co-occurrence [36] method because it is a well-known, established method that has been proven to correlate well with what experts generally look for in texture features. Also, it has been used successfully to produce good results in classification studies of normal tissues in CT images of chest and abdomen [4].

The Haralick co-occurrence texture model and its texture descriptors capture the spatial dependence of gray-level values and texture structures within an image [36]. There are many statistics that can be used; however, because of the redundancy and the high correlation in these statistics, only 10 statistics are advocated for feature representation in this application. We are using the following 10 descriptors (given by Equations (25.1) through (25.10), where P is the normalized co-occurrence matrix, (i, j) is the pair of gray level intensities i and j, and M by N is the size of the co-occurrence matrix):

$$\text{Entropy} = -\sum_{i}^{M}\sum_{j}^{N} P[i, j] \log P[i, j] \tag{25.1}$$

$$\text{Energy} = \sum_{i}^{M}\sum_{j}^{N} P^2[i, j] \tag{25.2}$$

$$\text{Contrast} = \sum_{i}^{M}\sum_{j}^{N} (i - j)^2 P[i, j] \tag{25.3}$$

$$\text{Homogeneity} = \sum_{i}^{M}\sum_{j}^{N} \frac{P[i, j]}{1 + |i - j|} \tag{25.4}$$

$$\text{SumMean} = \frac{1}{2}\sum_{i}^{M}\sum_{j}^{N} (i * P[i, j] + j * P[i, j]) \tag{25.5}$$

$$\text{Variance} = \frac{1}{2}\sum_{i}^{M}\sum_{j}^{N} ((i - \mu)^2 P[i, j] + (j - \mu)^2 P[i, j]) \tag{25.6}$$

$$\text{Maximum\_Probability} = \underset{i,j}{\overset{M,N}{Max}}\, P[i, j] \tag{25.7}$$

$$\text{Inverse\_Difference\_Moment} = \sum_{i}^{M}\sum_{j}^{N} \frac{P[i.j]}{|i - j|^k} \tag{25.8}$$

$$\text{Cluster\_Tendency} = \sum_{i}^{M}\sum_{j}^{N} (i + j - 2\mu)^k P[i, j] \tag{25.9}$$

$$\text{Correlation} = \sum_{i}^{M}\sum_{j}^{N} \frac{(i - \mu)(j - \mu)P[i.j]}{\sigma^2} \tag{25.10}$$

These descriptors are calculated at both local (pixel) and global (organ) levels, depending on the tasks to be used for and the fundamental structures present in the images. Pixel-level properties are calculated to be able to isolate regional properties within an image, while global-level features summarize the whole image and represent it as one entity.

25.3.2.1 Global-Level Feature Representation

To compute global-level features, the normalized co-occurrence matrices are calculated in four directions ($0°, 45°, 90°$, and $135°$) and five displacements ($d = 1, 2, 3, 4, 5$) generating 20 matrices per segmented image. These rotations and displacements are only in-plane since the images being considered are only 2-dimensional axial slices. The 10 Haralick features are calculated for each of the 20 matrices and then, the 20 values are averaged and recorded as a *mean-based feature vector* for the corresponding segmented image [39].

25.3.2.2 Pixel-Level Feature Representation

To compute pixel-level features, a small neighborhood is considered for each pixel within the segmented region. The size of the neighborhood has to be large enough in order to get enough samples to produce statistically significant texture features at the pixel level and small enough in order to capture the local property of the texture and not to introduce multiple textures within the pixel neighborhood. Therefore, we choose a neighborhood of size 5 by 5 as a trade-off between the level of locality and the statistical significance of the results; the choice of this size is also partially motivated by the good classification accuracy obtained for the classification of pixels and regions of soft tissues when using texture features calculated within a 5×5 neighborhood [4].

Once the neighborhood size is determined, a co-occurrence matrix is calculated for each neighborhood within the corresponding region. While co-occurrence matrices are normally defined for a fixed distance and direction when calculated at the global level, for the pixel-level approach, we do not calculate the co-occurrence along fixed directions and displacements. Instead we consider all pixel pairs within that neighborhood such that there will be enough samples (pairs) for calculating the co-occurrence matrix in order to produce statistically significant results. Thus, our implementation produces a single co-occurrence matrix for each pixel rather than for each choice of distance and direction. Then, for each co-occurrence matrix (each pixel), we calculate 10 Haralick features which can be related to specific characteristics in the image. Figure 25.1(b)–(d) illustrates the image representations of different pixel-level texture features for the original CT image from Figure 25.1(a).

From the pixel-level data, we derive different representations for the texture co-occurrence features: *(1) mean vector-based data, (2) binned histogram data, and (3) texture signatures.* These vectors are the possible representations of the texture features at the pixel-level and they will be evaluated to study the effect of the feature space on the choice of the similarity metric and thus, on the retrieval results.

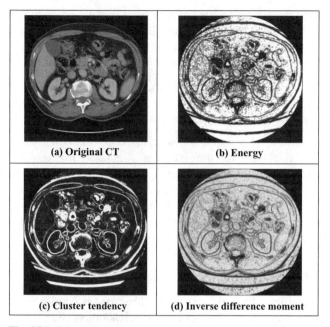

| (a) Original CT | (b) Energy |
| (c) Cluster tendency | (d) Inverse difference moment |

Fig. 25.1. Image representation for the pixel-level texture features.

The *mean vector-based data representation* consists of the average of the normalized pixel-level data for each region such that the texture representation of that corresponding region is a vector instead of a set of vectors given by the pixels' vector representations within that region.

The binned histogram data representation consists of texture values grouped within equal-width bins. The number of bins and their placement are important parameters as they determine how crudely, or how well, the underlying probability distribution (obtained by quantizing the responses into bins and normalizing such that the sum over all bins is unity) is: too many number of bins will overfit the data and introduce noise while less number of bins will make the binning crude. In our experimental results, a number of 256 equal-size bins produced the best results for this representation.

The *texture signature representation* is the clustered representation of the normalized local level data obtained using a k–d tree clustering algorithm [40]. The k–d tree clustering algorithm is chosen because (1) it does not require any assumptions about the data set; (2) it is computational efficient; and (3) it allows clusters of unequal size and thus, it will eliminate the limitation of the binned histogram representation. The k–d tree algorithm iteratively divides the data space using predefined stopping criteria. In our approach, we implement two stopping criteria: the first criterion was to establish a minimum variance within the subset to be divided to prevent creating redundant clusters and oversplitting; the second stopping criterion is used to enforce a minimum cluster size as a percentage of the original data set and to maintain a significant size within the clusters and to prevent outliers from uncontrollably growing the tree. By varying both the variance and minimum cluster size, different texture signatures are obtained. In our experimental results obtained using the directed Hausdorff distance, a variance equal to 10% and a cluster size equal to 20% of the parent cluster's variance and size, respectively, produced the best retrieval results for this representation.

25.3.3 Classification Model

25.3.3.1 Decision Tree Classifier

There are many classifiers that can be used to discriminate among the organ tissue classes in the feature space. In our preliminary work, we evaluated a decision tree classifier because (1) it does not make any assumptions of the distribution of the data; (2) it has a relatively faster learning speed than other classification methods, while still producing classification accuracy comparable with those methods; and (3) it has a good ability to generate decision rules that can be easily understood, interpreted, and used to annotate different tissues in future CT scans. The implementation of our decision tree was based on the Classification and Regression Trees (C&RT) approach and used the SPSS Answer Tree 3.0 software. From the decision tree, a set of the most important decision rules was generated to be used for classification of the regions, and to derive the most relevant texture descriptors for specific organs. To evaluate the performance of the classifier, we calculated four metrics on the regions of interest in the testing set: sensitivity, specificity, precision, and accuracy.

The C&RT tree is constructed by splitting subsets of the data set using all descriptors as predictors to create two child nodes repeatedly, beginning with the entire data set. The best predictor is chosen using the Gini impurity index, which works by choosing a split at each node such that each child node is more pure than its parent node:

$$\text{Gini}(S) = 1 - \sum_{i=1}^{c} p_i^2,$$

where S is the data set to be split, c is the number of classes and p_i is the probability of class i within the data set S. A total pure node is a node for which the Gini index is equal to zero. The goal is to produce subsets of the data that are as homogeneous as possible (producing pure nodes in the tree) with respect to the class label. For each split, each predictive descriptor is evaluated to find the best cut point (our descriptors being continuous predictors) based on improvement score or reduction in impurity. Then, the predictors are compared, and the predictor with the best improvement is selected for the split. The process repeats recursively until one of the stopping rules is triggered: (1) the maximum tree depth, d, has been reached; (2) there is no significant predictive descriptor left to split the node; (3) the number of cases in the terminal node is less than the minimum number, np, of cases for parent nodes; (4) if the terminal node were to split, the number of cases in one or more child nodes would be less than the minimum number, nc, of cases for child nodes; and (5) minimum change in impurity, imp, is reached. Depending on the values set for the parameters (d, np, nc, *imp*), a different tree will be obtained; the "best" tree will be chosen to be the one with the highest classification accuracy.

25.3.3.2 Evaluation Metrics

In order to select the "best" parent and "best" child, and thus the "best" decision tree for our data, the following four performance metrics have to be maximized: (1) sensitivity (the ratio between true positives and total positives), (2) specificity (the ratio between true negatives and total negatives), (3) precision (the ratio between true positives, and the summation of true positives and false positives), and (4) accuracy (the ratio between the summation of the true positives and negatives and the total number of samples). For example, if we are interested in measuring the classification performance for "heart and great vessels" class, a true positive is a tissue region classified as "heart and great vessels" when the original class label (the label given by a human expert) is "heart and great vessels"; a true negative is a tissue region correctly classified as "non-heart and great vessels," a false positive is a tissue region classified as "heart and great vessels" when it is actually a "non-heart and great vessels," total positives is the total number of "heart and great vessels," and total negatives is the total number of "non-heart and great vessels." The same definitions apply for the other tissue types.

25.3.3.3 Decision Rules

The decision tree can be generated at both local and global feature levels. At the local level, its decision rules can be used to classify each pixel within the CT images. Pixels with the same classification labels and being adjacent will form connected components and thus, produce the segmentation of the regions of interest within the corresponding CT images.

Once the optimal decision tree has been constructed, it is a simple matter to convert it into an equivalent set of decision rules. Converting a decision tree to rules has two main advantages: (1) converting to rules removes the distinction between texture features that occur near the root of the tree and those that occur near the leaves and (2) converting to rules improves readability since rules are often easier for people to understand.

25.3.4 Similarity Measures and Performance Evaluation

25.3.4.1 Similarity Metrics Definitions

Similarity metrics describe how similar two images (organs in our case) are. There are many similarity measures proposed in the context of CBIR and the choice of a similarity metric is dependent on both the feature space representation and its property to capture the visual human perception of similarity. Rubner et al. define four categories of similarity measures to calculate the similarity for histogram-based data [41].

Heuristic Distance Metrics: (1) Minkowski 1-distance, d_{Lr} (city block distance or L_1 norm) (Equation (25.11)), (2) weighted-mean-variance, d_{wmv} (uses the means and standard deviations for each of the considered features) (Equation (25.12)):

$$d_{L_r}(H, K) = \left(\sum_i |h_i - k_i|^r \right)^{\frac{1}{r}} \tag{25.11}$$

$$d_{wmv}(H, K) = \sum_i \frac{|\mu_i(H) - \mu_i(K)|}{|\sigma(\mu_i)|} + \frac{|\sigma_i(H) - \sigma_i(K)|}{|\sigma(\sigma_i)|} \tag{25.12}$$

Nonparametric Test Statistics: (1) Cramer-von Mises, d_{CvM} (similar to the squared Euclidean distance but calculated between the distributions and as the maximal discrepancy between the cumulative distributions) (Equation (25.13)); (2) Kolmogorov–Smirnov distance, d_{KS} (used for unbinned data distributions and it is invariant to arbitrary monotonic transformations) (Equation (25.14)), and (3) Chi-square statistics, $d\chi^2$ (used to distinguish whether distributions of the descriptors differ from each other) (Equation (25.15)):

$$d_{CvM}(H, K) = \sum_i \sum_j (F^i(j; H) - F^i(j; K))^2 \tag{25.13}$$

$$d_{KS}(H, K) = \sum_i \max_j (|F^i(j; H) - F^i(j; K)|) \tag{25.14}$$

$$d_{\chi^2}(H, K) = \sum_i \frac{(h_i - m_i)^2}{m_i}, \, m_i = \frac{h_i + k_i}{2} \tag{25.15}$$

Information Theory Divergences: (1) Jeffrey–Divergence, d_{JD} (used to compute the distance between class distributions of two values of the same feature) (Equation (25.16)); and 2) Kullback-Leibler (KL) divergence, d_{KL} (Equation (25.17)):

$$d_{JD}(H, K) = \sum_i \sum_j \left(f(j; H) \log \frac{f(j; H)}{m_j} + f(j; K) \log \frac{f(j; K)}{m_j} \right) \tag{25.16}$$

where $m_j = \frac{f(j;H) + f(j;K)}{2}$

$$d_{KL}(H, K) = \sum_i f(j; H) \log \frac{f(j; H)}{f(j; K)} \tag{25.17}$$

Ground distances: (1) Quadratic Form (QF), d_{QF}, *(Equation (25.18)), and (2) Earth Mover's Distance (EMD),* d_{EMD} : *(Equation (25.19))*

$$d_{QF}(H, K) = \sqrt{(f_H - f_K)^T A (f_H - f_K)} \tag{25.18}$$

$$d_{EMD}(H, K) = \frac{\sum_{i,j} g_{ij} d_{ij}}{\sum_{i,j} g_{ij}} \tag{25.19}$$

H represents the query image that can be thought as of a point in a 10-dimensional space, where the value along each dimension (each of the 10 Haralick texture features) is given by h_i; similarly, K represents a given image from the database and

k_i represents its feature value corresponding to the ith dimension in the feature space. Furthermore, f_H and f_K are vectors that list all entries in $f(i; H)$ and $f(i; K)$, A denotes the similarity matrix, g_{ij} is the optimal flow between two distributions and d_{ij} is the similarity between bin i and j.

We evaluate all similarity measures from the first and second categories and the Jeffrey–Divergence from the third category within the context of both feature representation requirements for each of the metrics and their retrieval performance. Jeffrey–Divergence (d_{JD}) is an information theoretically motivated similarity measure just like Kullback–Leibler [41] and Mutual Information [42]. The latter two are not implemented in this work, but the former is implemented and will serve to represent the performance of similarity measures of this class. Since the two ground distances have high computational complexity and we are interested in evaluating CBIR systems for the medical domain where the retrieval of similar images should be performed very fast and on-the-fly, we do not consider them in the current implementation. In addition to the above metrics, two others are implemented as required by the different texture feature representations: Euclidean distance d_A (Equation (25.20)) and Hausdorff distance, d_{HD} (used for texture signature representation) (Equation (25.21)):

$$d_A(H, K) = \sum_i \sqrt{(h_i - k_i)^2} \tag{25.20}$$

$$d_{HD}(H, K) = \max_{h \in H} (\min_{k \in K}(||h - k||)) \tag{25.21}$$

For more details on the properties of these similarity metrics, we refer the reader to the work of Rubner et al. [41].

25.3.4.2 Performance Metrics

For medical image retrieval systems, the evaluation issue is almost nonexistent in most of the papers and those systems that do perform evaluation often use only screenshots of example results to queries. A single example result does not reveal a great deal about the real performance of the system and is not objective as the best possible query can be chosen arbitrarily by the authors.

We evaluate the system's retrieval results using precision and recall as performance metrics, as defined by Equations (25.22) and (25.23):

$$\text{Precision} = \frac{\#of\_relevant\_retrieved\_images}{total\#of\_retrieved\_images} \tag{25.22}$$

$$\text{Recall} = \frac{\#of\_relevant\_retrieved\_images}{total\_\#of\_relevant\_images} \tag{25.23}$$

Each image is considered a query image; therefore, a total of 344 queries are performed and evaluated using the two performance metrics. The k number of images that are the most similar with the query image is another parameter to be considered in evaluating the two metrics with respect to retrieval.

As a note, the current retrieval system is not required to rank the retrieved organs based on the variability that exists within organs of the same anatomical regions.

Table 25.1. Classification performance on individual tissues of the training set
(number of parents = 28, number of children = 5, cross-validation fold = 10)

Organ	Sensitivity	Specificity	Precision	Accuracy
Backbone	99.7%	99.5%	99.2%	99.6%
Liver	80.0%	96.9%	83.8%	94.1%
Heart	84.6%	98.5%	90.6%	96.5%
Renal	92.7%	97.9%	89.7%	97.1%
Splenic parenchyma	79.5%	96.1%	73.6%	94.1%

Therefore, a retrieved image is "relevant" if belongs to the same anatomical region as the query. However, for the application of this type of system in a more specific discriminatory manner (e.g., to track disease progression, organ distortion, size), it would be useful to rank retrieved images from the same anatomical region.

25.4 Experimental Results and Their Interpretation

25.4.1 Tissue Classification Results

To produce and validate the best decision tree, the 344 segmented images were divided into 4 quadrants producing 1360 images (some quadrants did not contain any tissue so they were ignored) that were used for the training set (66% of the data) and the testing set (34%). The training set was used to create the decision trees based on a 10-fold cross-validation technique. Each of the produced decision trees was then validated on the testing data and the decision tree for which the four performance metrics were maximum was chosen as the optimal tree. The optimal tree resulted in a tree with 41 nodes, 8 levels of depth, and 21 leaves producing 21 decision rules for the classification process.

For the training set, the overall performance (calculated as the weighted average per organ) for all four metrics was better than 89%. For the testing set, the overall performance for sensitivity and precision was above 80% and the performance for specificity and accuracy was above 90%.

Tables 25.1 and 25.2 show the four performance metrics for the training and testing data per organ, respectively; Figure 25.2 shows how the rules are applied to annotate unlabelled tissues in CT images.

The lowest sensitivity and precision values were recorded for spleen that was misclassified as liver most of the time; this indicates that either the used texture

Table 25.2. Classification performance on individual tissues of the testing set
(number of parents = 28, number of children = 5, cross-validation fold = 10)

Organ	Sensitivity	Specificity	Precision	Accuracy
Backbone	100%	97.6%	96.8%	98.6%
Liver	73.8%	95.9%	76.2%	92.5%
Heart	73.6%	97.2%	84.1%	93.2%
Renal	86.2%	97.8%	87.5%	96.0%
Splenic parenchyma	70.5%	95.1%	62.0%	92.5%

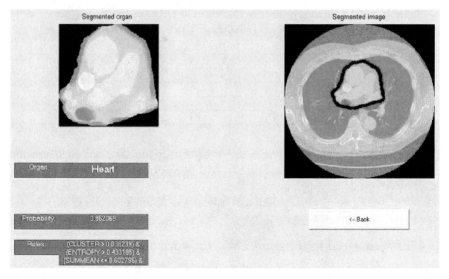

Fig. 25.2. An example of heart classification in our proposed approach with a probability of 0.862.

descriptors did not have enough discrimination power or the decision tree classifier was not able to produce the optimal tree with respect to these two types of tissues. Another possible explanation for the misclassification of the liver and spleen comes from the similarity of the gray levels of these tissues introduced by the linear binning. It is worth mentioning here that low results for the classification of liver and spleen were obtained by Koss et al. [45] when they applied a neural network to segment a CT image into seven and eight classes (tissues) of interest using a pixel-based co-occurrence texture model. Therefore, as future work, we plan to investigate other binning strategies, incorporate additional texture models into our texture analysis, and apply other classification techniques in addition to the decision tree one.

The classifier model obtained using decision tree approach generated a set of 21 rules: 3 rules for the heart, 3 rules for the kidneys, 5 rules for the spleen, 8 rules for the liver, and 2 rules for the backbone. The fact that there are multiple rules to describe a single organ suggests that single classes (organs) may have multiple subclasses (tissues).

25.4.2 Tissue Segmentation Results

To generate the decision tree for the pixel data, we manually selected patches of pure organ tissues from three consecutive slices. The number of patches and their sizes were chosen such that we have an equal number of pixels for each organ of interest. The pixels received the class label of the patch to which they belonged to. Since we want to use the decision tree for the segmentation of entire CT images, additional patches (not containing the organs of interest) were selected and their pixels were labeled as "unknown." We ended up selecting around 1500 pixels for each of the four organs and the "unknown" class. Furthermore, the training set was used to build the classifier, while the second set was used to estimate the accuracy of the classifier when used for tissue/organ annotation of previously unseen pixels.

To select the optimal decision tree (DT) for our data sample, we varied the number of observations (pixels) per node from 25 (number of pixels in a neighborhood) to 1000 and each time we estimated the overall accuracy of the classifier (number of pixels correctly classified divided by the total number of pixels); on the basis of the accuracy of the testing set, the optimal tree was selected. The empirically found optimal parameter for the "observations per parent" was in the range from 274 to 289; any of those values would result in the combined accuracy of the testing set of over 85%. We decided to use a tree with the "observations per parent" of 289 since it resulted in the smallest and most efficient tree.

After we generated and tested the decision tree on the sample data, we applied the tree on several consecutive entire slices to segment the organs of interest. We noticed that the unknown class, the kidneys, and the bones were accurately classified while spleen and liver were very often misclassified (liver pixels were classified as spleen and vice versa). To improve the segmentation, either a median filter or spatial information (such as liver is always in the anatomical left-hand side of the abdomen, and the backbone can be used as a point of reference to find the orientation of the CT scan) can be used as a postprocessing step. For visualization purposes, Figure 25.3 (c)

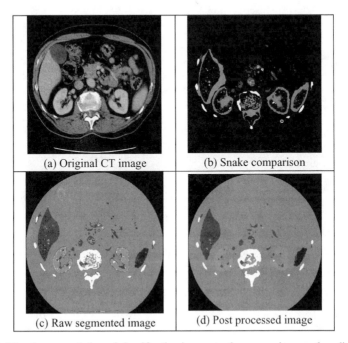

(a) Original CT image	(b) Snake comparison
(c) Raw segmented image	(d) Post processed image

Fig. 25.3. Visual representation of classification image, snake comparison, and median filtered image (5-by-5 filter)

and (d) shows the pixel-level classification image before and after postprocessing with a median filter; different colors represent the organs of interest (red—liver, green—kidney, white—backbone, blue—spleen), gray represents the unknown class (organs that were not of interest for this study) and black is the region outside the body that has not been included in the analysis.

25.4.3 Tissue Retrieval Results

Since several similarity measures and different feature sets are proposed at both pixel-level and global-level data, we will determine and evaluate *the best combination of the texture feature representation and corresponding similarity measure for retrieval of medical images containing specific anatomical regions.* The best result for pixel-level data approaches would also be compared with the best result from global-level data.

To evaluate the significance of the retrieval results, all the 344 images were used as query images. All 11 combinations of feature sets and similarity measures at both levels gave an overall precision over 80% for the number (k) of most similar images retrieved equal to 6 (Table 25.3).

At the global level, there was not much difference in the overall accuracy among the three similarity metrics considered, but the Minkowski and Euclidean distance performed better for liver and spleen than the chi-square statistics metric. At the pixel level, the retrieval precision was, in general, higher for the systems that used binned-histogram data together with the Cramer–von Mises, Jeffrey–Divergence, and the Kolmogorov–Smirnov metrics. The combination of the binned-histogram feature set and the Jeffrey-divergence metric reached a value of 91.57%, making this approach to

Table 25.3. Precision at the global and local levels for the entire image database; the overall performance is the weighted average of the retrieval performance by organ (each image was a query image).

Global-level vector-based precision						
	Backbone	Heart	Kidney	Liver	Spleen	OVERALL
Euclid distance	100.0%	90.4%	93.8%	67.8%	62.1%	87.7%
Chi-square statistics	100.0%	90.7%	93.8%	62.9%	57.5%	86.4%
Minkowski 1 distance	100.0%	90.1%	92.9%	69.0%	62.5%	87.8%
Pixel-level vector-based precision						
Euclid distance	100.0%	76.0%	85.8%	59.8%	46.7%	81.2%
Chi-square statistics	100.0%	81.1%	87.7%	60.1%	47.5%	82.4%
Minkowski 1 distance	100.0%	74.4%	85.2%	59.5%	48.8%	81.0%
Weighted mean variance	100.0%	87.2%	91.7%	58.9%	53.8%	84.5%
Pixel-level binned histogram-based precision						
Cramer/von Mises	100.0%	88.8%	83.6%	64.1%	51.3%	84.0%
Jeffrey-Divergence	100.0%	91.7%	96.0%	77.9%	75.8%	91.6%
Kolmogorov-Smirnov Distance	100.0%	89.1%	89.8%	69.8%	60.0%	87.0%
Pixel-level signature-based precision						
Hausdorff 10% vs. 20% cs	100.0%	81.1%	86.4%	57.8%	42.1%	81.2%

outperform all the other approaches. Pure comparison of the similarity metrics with respect to the granularity of the feature data can be made only between the metrics that were applied to the data represented in the same feature space. Comparing the Euclidean, chi-square, and the Minkowski metrics in [5], the global features overall perform better by about 6%. Even though the overall performance is better when using global-level descriptors for these three metrics, one of the systems considered in the pixel-level approaches outperforms the global-level approaches by up to as much as 10% to 20% for liver and spleen.

Furthermore, comparing the best feature set and similarity metric combination per organ at the pixel level, we notice that the binned-histogram feature set with Jeffrey divergence performs the best with respect to each individual organ: backbone (100%), heart (89.7%), kidneys (96%), liver (77.87%), and spleen (75.83%).

Since the best retrieval results were obtained at the pixel level and for the binned histogram feature set and the Jeffrey–Divergence metric, we evaluated further the performance of this system when more than six similar retrieved images were retrieved for this combination of feature representation and similarity metric. By increasing k, the number of the most similar images retrieved, from 6 to 156 (increments of 10) and calculating the values for precision and recall, we noticed that even for more than six similar images (up to 26 most similar images) the retrieval precision continues to be above 87.79% (the best value obtained for global retrieval and $k = 6$). Evaluating the overall recall, its value increased from 8% for $k = 6$ to above 80% for $k = 156$.

25.5 Conclusions

In conclusion, this chapter presents the potential contributions of data mining and image processing to the field of radiology; in particular, we discussed how computer-aided diagnosis (CAD) systems can play a major and important role in early detection, diagnosis, and treatment planning.

While there has been considerable work done for classification of abnormal tissues within different organs (such as liver, lung, heart, and brain), to our best knowledge, there is little research in regards to interorgan classification. Our preliminary results for classification and segmentation show that using only 10 texture descriptors calculated from Hounsfield unit data, it is possible to automatically segment and classify regions of interest representing different organs or tissues in CT images. Furthermore, the results lead us to the conclusion that the incorporation of some other texture models into our proposed approach will increase the performance of the classifier, and will also extend the classification and segmentation functionality to other organs.

The research work on retrieval presents an extensive evaluation of different co-occurrence texture feature representations and similarity metrics for content-based medical image retrieval. Our experimental results show that the presented approaches are promising to offer new possibilities for content-based access to medical images; new intelligent systems could be created that will be able to choose image features relevant to a specific clinical task, analyze the data, and automatically choose the best similarity metric for corresponding data representation.

Even though there are many challenges that need to be addressed before the approaches presented in this chapter will become a true partner to the diagnostic radiologists, the proposed approaches can be considered as an initial step along these efforts and can open other avenues of exploration for other researchers in the field.

References

1. Hendee WR, Ritonour ER. *Medical Imaging Physics*. Elsevier Academic Press, 2004.
2. Dreyer KJ. The alchemy of data mining. *Imaging Economics*, 2005
3. Xu D, Lee J, Raicu DS, Furst JD, Channin DS. Texture classification of normal tissues in computed tomography. In: *The 2005 Annual Meeting of the Society for Computer Applications in Radiology*, 2005.
4. Kalinin M, Raicu DS, Furst JD, Channin DS. A classification approach for anatomical regions segmentation. In: *The IEEE International Conference on Image Processing (ICIP)*, 2005.
5. Corboy A, Tsang W, Raicu DS, Furst J. Texture-based image retrieval for computerized tomography databases. In: *The 18th IEEE International Symposium on Computer-Based Medical Systems(CBMS'05)*, 2005.
6. Karkanis SA, Magoulas GD, Grigoriadou M, Schurr M. Detecting abnormalities in colonoscopic images by textural descriptors and neural networks. In: *Proceedings of the Workshop Machine Learning in Medical Applications,* 1999;59–62.
7. Chabat F, Yang GZ, Hansell DM. *Obstructive Lung Diseases: Texture Classification for Differentiation at CT, RSNA 2003.*
8. Sluimer IC, van Waes PF, Viergever MA, van Ginneken B. Computer-aided diagnosis in high resolution CT of the lungs. *Medical Physics*, 2003;30(12).
9. Fortson R, Lynch D, Newell J. Automated segmentation of scleroderma in HR CT imagery. *Report LA-UR-95-2401*, 1995.
10. Cios KJ, Goodenday LS, Shah KK, Serpen G. Novel algorithm for classification of SPECT images of a human heart. *IEEE Content-Based Medical Systems*, 1996.
11. Albrecht A, Loomes MJ, Steinhöfel K, Taupitz M. Adaptive simulated annealing for CT image classification. In: *Proceedings of IJPRAI*, 2002;16(5).
12. Wolf M, Ziegengeist S, Michalik M, Bornholdt F, Michalik S, Meffert B. Classification of brain tumors by CT-image Walsh spectra. *Neuroradiology*, 1990;32(6).
13. Jain AK, Farrokhia F. Unsupervised texture segmentation using Gabor filters. *Pattern Recognition*, 1991;24:1167–1186.
14. Chang T, Kuo CC. Texture segmentation with tree-structured wavelet transform. In: *Proceedings of the IEEE-SP International Symposium on Time-Frequency and Time-Scale Analysis*, 1992;543–546.
15. Unser M. Texture classifification and segmentation using wavelet frames. *IEEE Trans. on Im. Proc.*, 1995;4(11):1549–1560.
16. Chang KI, Bowyer KW, Sivagurunath M. Evaluation of texture segmentation algorithms. *IEEE Conference on Computer Vision and Pattern Recognition*, 1999;294–299.
17. Porter R, Canagarajah N. A robust automatic clustering scheme for image segmentation using wavelets. *IEEE Transactions on Image Processing*, 1996;5(4):662–665.
18. Beveridge JR, Gri J, Kohler RR, Hanson AR, Riseman EM. Segmenting images using localized histograms and region merging. *International Journal Computer Vision*, 1989;2:311–347.

19. Adams R, Bischof L. Seeded region growing. *IEEE Transactions Pattern Analysis and Machine Intelligence*, 1994;16(6):641–647.
20. Kass M, Witkin A, Terzopoulos D. Snakes: Active contour models. *International Journal of Computer Vision*, 1988;1:321–331.
21. Tagare DH, Jaffe CC, Duncan J. Medical image databases: A content-based retrieval approach. *Journal of American Medical Informatics Association*, 1997;4(3):184–198.
22. Baker JA, Kornguth PJ, Soo MS, Walsh R, Mengoni P. Sonography of solid breast lesions: Observer variability of lesion description and assessment. *AJR* 1999;172:1621–1625.
23. Müller H, Rosset A, Vallée JP, Geissbuhler A. Comparing feature sets for content-based medical information retrieval. *SPIE Medical Imaging*, 2004.
24. Orphanoudakis SC, Chronaki CE, Kostomanolakis S. I2Cnet: A system for the indexing, storage and retrieval of medical images by content. *Medical Informatics*, 1994;4(3):109–122.
25. El-Kwae EA, Xu H, Kabuka MR. Content-based retrieval in picture archiving and communication systems. *Journal of Digital Imaging*, 2000;13(2):70–81.
26. Guld MO, Wein BB, Keysers D, Thies C, Kohnen M, Schubert H, Lehmann TM. A distributed architecture for content-based image retrieval in medical applications. In: *Proceedings of the International Conference on Enterprise Information Systems (ICEIS2001)*, 2001;299–314.
27. Lehmann T, Wein B, Dahmen J, Bredno J, Vogelsang F, Kohnen M. Content-based image retrieval in medical applications: A novel multi-step approach. In: *Procs. Int. Society for Optical Engineering (SPIE)*, 2000;3972(32):312–331.
28. Chu WW, Cardenas AF, Taira RK. KMED: A knowledge-based multimedia distributed database system. *Information Systems*, 1994;19(4):33–54.
29. Müller H, Fabry P, Geissbuhler A. MedGIFT—Retrieving medical images by there visual content. World Summit of the Information Society, Forum Science and Society, 2003.
30. Image Engine: http://www.bristol.ac.uk/radiology/IntLink/ImageEngine.html
31. Glatard T, Montagnat J, Magnin IE. Texture based medical image indexing and retrieval: application to cardiac imaging. ACM SIGMM international workshop on Multimedia Information Retrieval (MIR'04). In: *Proceedings of ACM Multimedia* 2004.
32. Rubner Y, Tomasi C. Texture metrics. In: *Proceedings of the IEEE International Conference on Systems, Man, and Cybernetics*, 1998;4601–4607.
33. Brodley C, Kak A, Shyu C, Dy J, Broderick L, Aisen AM. Content-based retrieval from medical image databases: A synergy of human interaction, machine learning and computer vision. In: *Proc. of the Sixteenth National Conference on Artificial Intelligence (AAAI'99)*, 1999.
34. Zheng L, Wetzel AW, Gilbertson J, Becich MJ. Design and analysis of content-based pathology image retrieval system. *IEEE Transactions on Information Technology in Biomedicine*, 2003;7(4).
35. Wei CH, Li CT, Wilson R. A general framework for content-based medical image retrieval with its application to mammograms. In: *Proc. SPIE Int'l Symposium on Medical Imaging*, 2005.
36. Haralick RM, Shanmugam K, Dinstein I. Textural features for image classification. *IEEE Transactions on Systems, Man, and Cybernetics*, 1973;Smc-3(6):610–621.
37. Kass M, Witkin A, Terzopoulos D. Snakes: Active contour models. *International Journal of Computer Vision*, 1988;1(4).
38. Tourassi GD. Journey toward computer-aided diagnosis role of image texture analysis. *Radiology*, 1999;213:317–320.

39. Raicu DS, Furst JD, Channin DS, Xu DH, Kurani A. A texture dictionary for human organs tissues' classification. In: *Proc. of the 8th World Multiconf. on Syst., Cyber. and Inform.*, 2004.

40. Bentley JL. Multidimensional binary search trees used for associative searching. *Communications of the ACM*, 1975;18:509–517.

41. Rubner Y, Puzicha J, Tomasi C, Buhmann JM. Empirical evaluation of dissimilarity measures for color and texture. *International Conference on Computer Vision*, 1999; 2: 1165.

42. Pluim JPW, Maintz JBA, Viergever MA. Mutual-information-based registration of medical images: A survey. *IEEE Transactions on Medical Imaging*, 2003;22(8):986–1004

43. Rubner Y, Tomasi C, Guibas L. The Earth Mover's Distance as a metric for image retrieval. Technical Report STAN-CS-TN-98-86, Computer Science Department, Stanford University, 1998.

44. Wei G, Li D, Sethi IK. Detection of side-view faces in color images. In: *Proceedings of Fifth IEEE Workshop on Applications of Computer Vision*, 2000; pp. 79–84.

45. Koss JE, Newman FD, Johnson TK, Kirch DL. Abdominal organ segmentation using texture transforms and a Hopfield neural network. *IEEE Transactions on Medical Imaging*, 1999; 18.

Author Index

Subject Index